W9-CZY-019

Edited by Gerd Hatje

Introduction by Wolfgang Pehnt

Contributors

Kyösti Alander, Helsinki
Reyner Banham, London
Maurice Besset, Paris
Peter Blake, New York
Max Cetto, Mexico City
G. F. Chadwick, Hale Barns, Cheshire
Alexandre Cirici-Pellicer, Barcelona
Robert L. Delevoy, Brussels
Tobias Faber, Copenhagen
Giuseppe Giordanino, Turin
Vittorio Gregotti, Novara
Henry-Russell Hitchcock, Northampton, Mass.
Hubert Hoffmann, Graz
John M. Jacobus Jr., Berkeley, Calif.
Jürgen Joedicke, Stuttgart
William H. Jordy, Providence, R.I.
Shinji Koike, Tokio
Björn Linn, Bromma
Harold Meek, Belfast
Henrique E. Mindlin, Rio de Janeiro
Leonardo Mosso, Turin
Herbert Ohl, Ulm
Arthur Sprague, New York
Margit Staber, Zurich
Klaus-Jakob Thiele, Berlin
Mark Hartland Thomas, Sittingbourne, Kent
Giuseppe Varaldo, Turin
Giulia Veronesi, Milan
J. J. Vriend, Amsterdam
Arnold Whittick, Crawley, Sussex
Gian Pio Zuccotti, Turin

Edited by Gerd Hatje

Introduction by Wolfgang Pehnt

Contributors

Kyösti Alander, Helsinki
Reyner Banham, London
Maurice Besset, Paris
Peter Blake, New York
Max Cetto, Mexico City
G. F. Chadwick, Hale Barns, Cheshire
Alexandre Cirici-Pellicer, Barcelona
Robert L. Delevoy, Brussels
Tobias Faber, Copenhagen
Giuseppe Giordanino, Turin
Vittorio Gregotti, Novara
Henry-Russell Hitchcock, Northampton, Mass.
Hubert Hoffmann, Graz
John M. Jacobus Jr., Berkeley, Calif.
Jürgen Joedicke, Stuttgart
William H. Jordy, Providence, R.I.
Shinji Koike, Tokio
Björn Linn, Bromma
Harold Meek, Belfast
Henrique E. Mindlin, Rio de Janeiro
Leonardo Mosso, Turin
Herbert Ohl, Ulm
Arthur Sprague, New York
Margit Staber, Zurich
Klaus-Jakob Thiele, Berlin
Mark Hartland Thomas, Sittingbourne, Kent
Giuseppe Varaldo, Turin
Giulia Veronesi, Milan
J. J. Vriend, Amsterdam
Arnold Whittick, Crawley, Sussex
Gian Pio Zuccotti, Turin

Edited by Gerd Hatje

Introduction by Wolfgang Pehnt

Contributors

Kyösti Alander, Helsinki
Reyner Banham, London
Maurice Besset, Paris
Peter Blake, New York
Max Cetto, Mexico City
G. F. Chadwick, Hale Barns, Cheshire
Alexandre Cirici-Pellicer, Barcelona
Robert L. Delevoy, Brussels
Tobias Faber, Copenhagen
Giuseppe Giordanino, Turin
Vittorio Gregotti, Novara
Henry-Russell Hitchcock, Northampton, Mass.
Hubert Hoffmann, Graz
John M. Jacobus Jr., Berkeley, Calif.
Jürgen Joedicke, Stuttgart
William H. Jordy, Providence, R.I.
Shinji Koike, Tokio
Björn Linn, Bromma
Harold Meek, Belfast
Henrique E. Mindlin, Rio de Janeiro
Leonardo Mosso, Turin
Herbert Ohl, Ulm
Arthur Sprague, New York
Margit Staber, Zurich
Klaus-Jakob Thiele, Berlin
Mark Hartland Thomas, Sittingbourne, Kent
Giuseppe Varaldo, Turin
Giulia Veronesi, Milan
J. J. Vriend, Amsterdam
Arnold Whittick, Crawley, Sussex
Gian Pio Zuccotti, Turin

Encyclopedia of modern architecture

442 illustrations

Harry N. Abrams, Inc., Publishers, New York

Translations from the German
by Irene and Harold Meek
from the French, Spanish and Italian
by Harold Meek
from the Danish by G. D. Liversage
from the Dutch by E. van Daalen

Asterisks in the text indicate that relevant entries or illustrations are to be found elsewhere in the book.

Library of Congress Catalog Card Number: 63-14758
Published in the United States of America, 1964,
by Harry N. Abrams, Incorporated, New York

Printed in Japan

Joseph Paxton. Crystal Palace. London, 1851

Introduction

In the year 1850, Prince Albert delivered a remarkable speech at a banquet for the chief magistrates of the City of London. His Royal Highness attempted to secure the support of the representatives of this thriving metropolis for his pet scheme for a Great International Exhibition; and the plan he unfolded testified to no mean optimism: 'Nobody who has paid any attention to the peculiar features of our present era will doubt for a moment that we are living at a period of most wonderful transition, which tends rapidly to accomplish that great end, to which indeed, all history points—the realization of the unity of mankind. . . .' Distances between continents were vanishing, scholarship and knowledge were becoming common property, and the products of all nations were available to the citizens to choose from. Gratitude to the Almighty would overwhelm the viewer of this vast exhibition, concluded the Prince.

As amazing as the exhibition itself, the first ever of such proportions, was the building in which it was housed: Joseph *Paxton's Crystal Palace. This huge building, erected in the breathtakingly short period of nine months, seized on the imagination of its contemporaries as did few structures of the 19th century before the Eiffel Tower. The delicate filigree of the metalwork, filled in by glass panes, the immensity of the boundless interior, and the transparency and weightlessness of the walls seemed to the public of the day to herald the arrival of a new style—unless, like Ruskin, they were of the opinion that the Crystal Palace was a greenhouse like others, only larger. Glass and iron were the building materials which made a new aesthetic conception of architecture possible. It was not these materials that were new. The tradition of iron construction went back to the 18th century and had already produced some excellent schemes in the first half of the century. After all, the prize-winning competition design for the Crystal Palace by Hector Horeau, which was not actually used, also envisaged a light iron structure. But the conquest of this vast space by a seemingly insubstantial and unreal tracery of walls and the apparent merging of interior and exterior were new. Contemporary prints prefer to show an interior partly suffused by sunlight and yet shaded in turn by clouds, a hazy light that seems to abolish the limitations of space. New, too, was the impression of a labyrinth without narrowness and weight, similar to the three-dimensional openwork effect of the Eiffel Tower's steel frame three decades later.

The Crystal Palace was no bolt from the blue. As early as 1832, the French social reformer and sectarian Barthélemy Prosper Enfantin unfolded the vision of a new architecture which assigns a principal rôle

Thomas Telford. Design for a bridge over the Thames. London, 1801

to iron, compares parts of the structure with the molecular composition of the body, and speaks of the 'open form' of such an architecture of the future. The 'metallurgical architecture' demanded by an only recently rediscovered architectural theorist, William Vose Pickett, in a book published in 1845 seems to have anticipated modern architecture with its framed and suspended structures and its *brise-soleil*. Paxton's Crystal Palace was not such an unqualified success because it surprised and amazed its generation but because it had fulfilled their secret hopes and ambitions.

William Le Baron Jenney. Home Insurance Building. Chicago, 1883–5

Architectural historians have investigated the 19th century for its pioneer works such as the Crystal Palace, and have long seen in these undoubtedly bold achievements the first steps towards modern architecture. They have pointed to early examples of bridge-building, cast- and wrought-iron vaulting and suspension and girder type bridges, which were already achieving astonishing spans in England and North America. In high structures there were buildings that combined load-bearing masonry and iron frames. The aesthetic charm that emanates from such factory and warehouse buildings with their heavy, solid outer walls and light, internal columns of iron may not have been obvious to contemporaries, but buildings to which the public had access such as Henri *Labrouste's Sainte-Geneviève Library in Paris (1843–50) already display it. American firms were experimenting with façades made up of prefabricated cast-iron units as early as the middle of the century, and these permitted extensive penetration of the outer walls too.

But materials alone do not create a new style. A new style is born only when an individual genius such as Paxton or *Eiffel or an ambitious group such as the architects of the so-called *Chicago School after 1880, adopt the new building materials. *Burnham, *Root and *Sullivan arrived at their imposing, clear and withal lively designs for multi-storey buildings, not, in the first place, thanks to the new system of framed structures, but mainly due to their notions of style derived from the great *Richardson. William Le Baron *Jenney did not know himself that he had created the first steel-frame structure with his Home Insurance Building (1883–5)—that was only discovered when it was later pulled down; and one of the main examples of this school, the Monadnock Building (1889–91) is structurally a traditional solid masonry building. The Chicago School was a special case; it did not found a tradition. Until the advent of the department stores around 1900, the new steel structures were hardly noticeable in the townscape; the façades of the city stations only rarely betrayed the bold lines of the halls hidden beyond the entrance lobbies. Reinforced concrete structures became aesthetically attractive only in the new century, although the effective patents were taken out in the sixties of the 19th century. Despite the Crystal Palace, despite the Machinery Hall and the Eiffel Tower of the World Exhibition of 1889, the type of architecture in which the taste of the age was expressed did not make use of the new opportunities. The Paris Opera by Charles Garnier (1861–74) was more a symptom of its times than the elliptical exhibition galleries (1867) of Frédéric Le Play.

If Prince Albert in his speech before the city fathers praised the availability of all the world's merchandise, his generation exercised this sovereignty with regard to history. The 19th century was the century of stylistic imitations. The boundless availability of forms, which history had taken several thousand years to develop, was at the ready disposal of this well-informed century. The reversion to a distant past had in the first instance a concrete significance. The memory of Greek forms was a memory of classicism, Greek intellect, simplicity, nobility and greatness. Behind the protagonists of the Gothic Revival, too, there were ideas other than simply the reawakening of dead history, for most European countries connected reminiscences of their first national glory with the Gothic epoch. Disregarding the fact that English and German Gothic were unthinkable without Saint-Denis and Chartres, neo-Gothic buildings like the Houses of Parliament in London (1840–65) and the reconstructed Cologne Cathedral became memorials to a national consciousness which had grown stronger during the romantic age. Karl Friedrich von *Schinkel's design for a Prussian national

Ferdinand Dutert and Contamin. Machinery Hall at the International Exhibition. Paris, 1889

cathedral, of course, is in the most romantic fairy-tale Gothic.
Such arguments did not apply to the attempts to revive the other styles. The town became a populated museum, a permanent exhibition. The great architects of the century already built in heterogeneous styles. John *Nash was not only responsible for magnificent Ionic columns but also for the bizarre effects of the Brighton Pavilion (1815–23) with its oriental trappings.

John Nash. Brighton Pavilion, 1815–23

John Nash and James Thomson. Cumberland Terrace, Regents Park. London, 1826–7

Schinkel supplied Gothic and Renaissance schemes to choose from for his Werdersche Church in Berlin (built from 1825 to 1831). Eventually not only were alternative proposals such as these possible, but even the combination of different styles in the same building. Friedrich Schmidt, architect of the Vienna Town Hall (started 1872) declared in reply to the question whether the building was conceived more in the Gothic or the Renaissance vein: 'It is the accomplishment of an artist who has absorbed the architecture of past centuries.' The 'cold synthesis', in which the elements do not merge but remain separate and recognizable with their different origins, became the ideal. It was typical of the arrogance of the age to force successive periods to exist side by side.
The 19th century not only had styles, it had a style—*its* style. Development may appear to have resolved itself into an endless reprise of architectural fashions, but in reality this carnival of imitation followed consistent rules. The 18th century bequeathed its successors an architecture that loved large stereometric buildings, used decoration with restraint and tried to preserve continuity of surfaces. The classical motifs of column, entablature and arch were set off by plain wall surfaces or confronted by them. The pillars on John *Soane's Bank of England (1803) look like cut-out vertical wall panels. On twin-tower façades of churches (The Ludwigskirche in Munich by Friedrich von Gärtner, 1829–40; Saint-Vincent-de-Paul, Paris, 1824–44, by Lepère and Hittorff) the individual towers remain tied in by surface continuity and only appear as separate parts of the building in the upper storeys.
The historic styles employed by architects at this time were interpreted in this sense. Klenze and his contemporaries at Munich at the time of Ludwig I built Renaissance palaces in the new Ludwigsviertel part of the town, but they took as their model the Early Florentine Renaissance, not the Roman High Renaissance with its strongly accentuated wall relief. And Gothic examples fascinated them not primarily by their spatial interpenetration. A late building by Schinkel, the neo-Gothic castle of Kamenz in Silesia (1838–65) still shows an unsurpassed refinement in its treatment of wall surfaces. The unpierced walls make up a sculptural whole—the purer and more

severe in style the earlier the masters are of this romantic classicism. It was not without reason that the twenties and early thirties of this century, with their inclination to stereometric form, discovered an affinity with Ledoux, Boullée, Durand, Sobre, Lequeu, Soane, Gilly, Weinbrenner, Haller von Hallerstein and partly even with *Schinkel! It is significant that a book by Emil Kaufmann which came out in 1933 was called *From Ledoux to Le Corbusier*.

As the century progressed, so did the tendency to carve up surfaces. Architecture became picturesque. Clearly defined massing gave way to something that looked as if it had been nibbled at from outside, and plebeian wealth replaced noble poverty. Details that were formerly precise and clearly legible became clumsy, complicated and restless, and could only be understood as part of the whole building—and sometimes not even then. Picturesque arrangements took over from the—still valid—symmetrical plan. A large structure was now subdivided into so many main and subsidiary parts that the orderly effect of symmetry, especially as seen from a narrow street, was considerably weakened. What applies to the exterior also applies to the inside. Niches and bays hived off the drawing-rooms to conform with late-bourgeois notions of comfort and ease. If multiplicity of forms was a tacit demand, then the mixture of heterogeneous forms was its consequence. At the beginning of the 19th century architects selected their models from the stylistic conceptions of their time. In the second half of the century anything goes: distinguished antique, heavy Romanesque, riven Gothic, opulent Renaissance and, finally, Baroque, whose hour struck only when the plastic treatment and spatial exploitation of the walls had sufficiently progressed.

In the field of town planning 19th-century architecture failed almost completely. The romantic classicism prevalent around 1800 already had a tendency to break down the walls of the 'place' and isolate buildings that were of any significance in the design of the town. Open space was no longer

Friedrich Gilly. Theatre. Berlin, 1800. Project

Gottfried Semper. Opera House. Dresden, 1837–41

Charles Garnier. Opera House. Paris, 1861–74

considered as a positive shape, a spatial concept, which created its own limits as it were, in the way the Baroque squares had done so admirably. Open space was now an element pressing in from an undefined distance, which was framed by architectural shapes, but was not moulded by them.

The transition to such town planning layouts was an early development. Already the Place de la Concorde in Paris (since 1753) is no longer formed by its peripheral buildings, by its architectural frame, but is open in several directions. A generously proportioned plan like that by Ludwig Förster for the Vienna Ringstrasse (1857–8)—the highest level of spatial luxury that town planning afforded itself in this economical century—strings together a series of open spaces and groups of buildings. The open spaces are arranged axially about each part of the polygonal Ring avenues, but are not in any relationship to each other, nor do they set each other off. Undefined open space surrounds the prominent buildings, which are grouped as though at an exhibition. This scheme, dismantled ramparts done up as boulevards with prestige buildings strung out alongside, was a customary town-planning recipe of the 19th century and in line with the contemporary need for display. More rigorous measures, such as the breaches driven by Baron *Haussmann at the time of Napoleon III through the chaos that was Paris, are among the few effective solutions. These sanitary measures, however, did not develop any new conception of town life, and behind the new façades everything remained the same. The outer peripheries of the towns were completely left to look after themselves and spread along the traffic arteries.

The rapid growth of cities was the worst problem. In 1860, the USA had nine

Ludwig Förster. Project for the Ringstrasse. Vienna, 1857–8

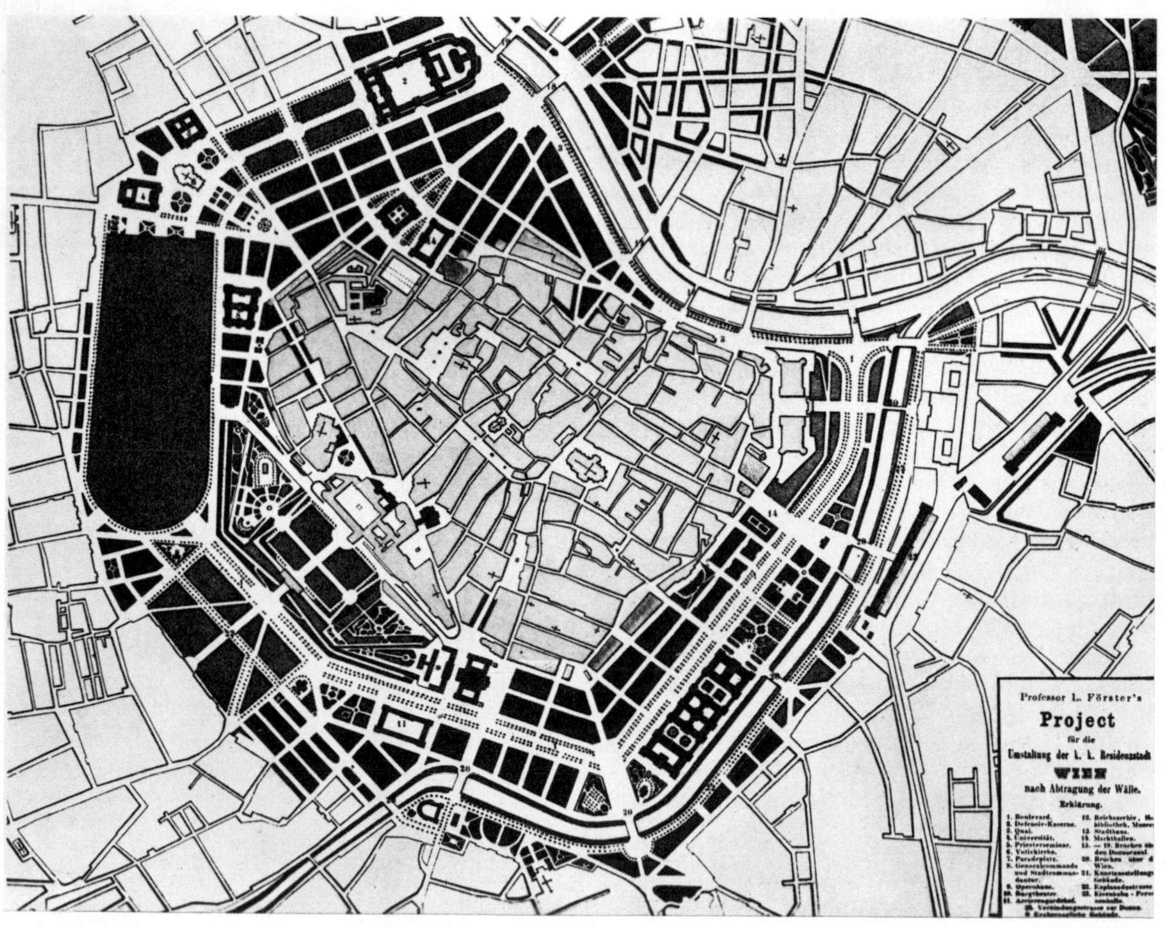

cities with more than 100,000 inhabitants; by 1910 there were fifty. London increased its size eightfold within a hundred and fifty years, Mannheim and Düsseldorf went up by more than fourfold in forty years, while Chicago doubled its size in a single decade from 1880 to 1890. Building regulations were restricted to a minimum. The Berlin by-laws allowed any height of building in streets over fifty feet wide and permitted back yards seventeen feet square! The old town centres had to assume the civic functions of vastly increased living conglomerations. The attention of architects was focused on the monumental buildings; for the decorative treatment of apartment house façades there existed pattern books. Structural engineers were kept fully occupied with the enormous task of maintaining the services for this mammoth organization. When the buildings they erected needed an architect's touch, details familiar from other types of edifice were employed to meet the new requirements as far as was practical. But for factories, abattoirs, power stations, market halls, and water towers the academies had no models.

The reaction to these circumstances, which was especially marked in England in the *Arts and Crafts movement, was as heroic as it was helpless. Especially as the understandable discontent with the industrial age often went together with an antagonism towards machinery and thus seemed to rule out in advance any hopes of far-reaching efficiency. The diagnosis was correct, the cure imperfect. The furniture, furnishing materials and wallpapers made by William *Morris in his workshops with the help of his Pre-Raphaelite friends were new and original creations which contrasted favourably with the stylistic imitations of the eclectics. But the era of the machine could only be successfully combated by the use of machinery—not without it. The distrust of the division of labour and the manufacturing methods of industry survived until late in the present century; it echoes still in the slogan of the early *Bauhaus days: 'Architects, sculptors, painters, we must all return to handicraft!'

A great change in attitude to the machine had by no means yet occurred around 1900 when enthusiasm for 'the beauty in the tremendous force of its vast but calm outlines' and 'the clean, smooth, polish of the machine' inspired progressive spirits.

Charles Annesley Voysey. Perrycroft House. Colwall, 1893

Obrist and van de *Velde praised the 'wonderful fitness for purpose' of ocean liners, locomotives, and aeroplanes, and yet Obrist's embroideries and van de Velde's silver service were not intended for mass production by machinery but required the tools of a craftsman. *Le Corbusier, for example, talked of *prefabrication early on in his career, but when he called the house 'a machine for living in' he was not only thinking of the smooth functioning of these buildings but of the formal properties of the machine as well. What fascinated him in the motor-car to such an extent that he called his projects after motor-car marques, and what he tried to achieve in his houses, was not least the 'simple shell, which creates space for manifold organs'. The smooth and perfect shapes, the dynamic appearance and the sound of speed appealed to his aesthetic senses, which carefully selected the objects of his admiration. A typewriter or a sewing-machine with their visually complex mechanisms had to wait for the Surrealists before they were aesthetically acceptable. And it was but one step further from aesthetic appraisal to the recognition that the new and rational methods of construction, already long employed by structural engineers, were eminently compatible with 'great' architecture, the architecture of architects.

This step was not yet taken by the *Art Nouveau. But at least it combined the various tendencies towards a new architecture within a consistent style. Scant justice is done to the era between 1880 and 1910 when it is merely looked on as a transitional period to modern art and architecture, for within it lay the presuppositions of the

Joseph Olbrich. Ernst-Ludwig-Haus. Darmstadt, 1901

20th century. The awareness of what the functions of a house should be that characterized the pioneers of the Arts and Crafts movement, led to the epoch-making houses of *Voysey and *Mackintosh; parallel development in North America was due to the work of the young Frank Lloyd *Wright and a number of Californian architects. The elegant surface treatment which the anonymous London town house had preserved since the beginning of the 19th century entered into a fascinating combination with the idiosyncratic sense of proportion of the nineties (Ashbee, Godwin, *Shaw, Voysey). The cubic building fantasies of the time of Soane and the architects of the French Revolution were echoed in the Late Art Nouveau period, by Viennese practitioners in particular. Iron and glass, which structural engineers had boldly introduced into their designs time and again in the course of the century, were made to serve the new style's need for ornamental expression, and employed to perform tricks of decoration (*Horta, *Guimard).

But above all Art Nouveau starting from

Frank Lloyd Wright. Martin House. Buffalo, N.Y., 1904

Page 13. Antoni Gaudí. Casa Milà. Barcelona, 1905–10

Jacobus Johannes Pieter Oud. Workers' housing. Hook of Holland, 1924

Michael de Klerk. De Dageraad housing estate. Amsterdam, 1920–2

mere surface decoration advanced to a fully three-dimensional expression of architecture which formed a direct link with *Expressionism. The transition from Art Nouveau to Expressionism is everywhere fluid. Expression was aimed at by both movements, even if Expressionism hardly took over the flowing contours and the ostensibly soft masses of Art Nouveau, with its manifold reminiscences of and associations with the organic world of nature. But the darkly menacing cubic forms of Mackintosh's Glasgow School of Art (1893–1909), the unadorned blocks of Adolf *Loos, betraying so much of Art Nouveau proportions, Rudolf Steiner's Goetheanum at Dornach near Basle (1925–8) or the phantasmagoria of Antoni *Gaudí's late work can be interpreted both as products of Art Nouveau and as manifestations of Expressionism.

It is much more difficult to find connections between Expressionism and the style of the twenties, although they were close and manifold. Only in the *Netherlands was the situation sharpened by controversy as the School of *Amsterdam opposed the Rotterdam Group. **Wendingen* on the one side, *De *Stijl* on the other; picturesque individual homes here and rows of whitewashed disciplined houses there; picturesque-plastic thinking as against fascination with objective form; this was the sharply defined antithesis despite a common derivation from the forerunner of modern Dutch architecture, Hendrik Petrus *Berlage, and despite the great impact made by Frank Lloyd *Wright on both *Wendingen* and *De Stijl*.

But in Central Europe, the fronts overlapped, just as did Art Nouveau and Expressionism. Nearly every great architect of the twenties went through an Expressionist phase. Peter Behrens's Turbine Factory in Berlin (1908–9), which is looked on as the manifesto of functional architecture, has massive corner piers, a huge cornice formed by the side windows canting inwards, and a heavy roof, features dictated by an urge for Expressionism—not by structural necessity. The glazed façades of the factories by Walter *Gropius have exerted a revolutionary effect. They did not preclude the fact that the model factory at the Cologne Werkbund Exhibition of 1914 was built on a strictly axial plan and confronts

Adolf Loos. Small house. 1923. Model

the viewer with a heavy Egyptian-type façade, properties that seem to be out of keeping with the modernity of the staircase towers. Bruno *Taut's pavilions at various exhibitions set out to demonstrate not so much the practicality as the poetic magic of the new building materials, steel and glass. The first *Bauhaus Manifesto is decorated with a woodcut by Lyonel Feininger, which idealizes the Gothic cathedral and expresses the affinity of the Bauhaus idea with the thinking of medieval building craftsmen—Expressionism of the purest water. In the years immediately after the First World War, when commissions were hard to come by, visionary drawings were made by numerous architects who later played a part in the Berlin association *Der *Ring*, and these, together with those of *Sant'Elia are among the most beautiful architectural esquisses of our time. *Mies van der Rohe's glass-house projects with their poetic quality are a part of this trend no less than the avowed expressiveness of *Poelzig's space caverns and *Mendelsohn's architectural sculpture.

A new development in the twenties, which affected Expressionism as well, is the involvement of time in the experience of a

Walter Gropius and Adolf Meyer. Model factory at the Werkbund Exhibition. Cologne, 1914

Lyonel Feininger. Woodcut from the first Bauhaus Manifesto. 1919

work of architecture. Three-dimensional shapes, whether sculpture or architecture, are only revealed in all their aspects when the viewer moves around them, i.e. after the passage of a certain time. But the plastic buildings of Expressionism were uniformly constructed; Gaudí's Casa Milà does not reveal new vistas from whatever side it is looked at. An outstanding building of the twenties, on the other hand, such as the Bauhaus at Dessau (1925) or Le Corbusier's project for the League of Nations (1927), is only fully appreciated if the observer constantly changes his viewing position. The intersections of different parts of the building, the ever-changing perspectives, the constant variations in visual scale, and the alternation from high to low, large to small, nearness to distance, horizontal to vertical have been carefully worked out in the design. As the eye can only make what is meant to be a three-dimensional

Le Corbusier. League of Nations Palace. Geneva, 1927. Project

composition into a flat picture from a fixed viewpoint, the original aesthetic intent of the building can only be fulfilled by a person in motion. 'It is essential to walk round a building in order to grasp its shape and the function of its parts' writes Gropius in relation to the Bauhaus scheme.

From this a new vocabulary of shapes emerged: in particular the dissolution of the mass into slender members of changing dimensions; asymmetry of plan; locating individual wings at angles apart; and the creation of vistas by means of ground floor columns or space-spanning bridges. No part of the building demands prior attention, so special features and wall reliefs are dispensed with. The eye travels over white, smooth walls and is led on by horizontal strips of window, rows of columns or wall openings. Baroque architecture also 'led the eye', but by means of intersecting streets which revealed a building at right angles or diagonally; oval or circular open spaces, parterres or fountains were obstacles on the prescribed route. The architecture of the twenties knows no such routes. The spectator goes his own way, and the building is meant to be seen from any angle.

Already the '*Città Nuova*' by the Italian Sant'Elia had included movement as part of its architectural and urbanistic conception, in conformity with the Futurist delight in the dynamics of modern city traffic. But Sant' Elia was not so much concerned with the movement of the spectator and not at all with the free rhythm and calmness of tempo which are the prerequisites of such building schemes of the twenties as the Bauhaus or the Weissenhof housing estate at Stuttgart. Sant'Elia was concerned with the movement of the object, not of the beholder: the rushing traffic on several levels, arriving and departing trains, escalators and elevators, motor cars, and aeroplanes landing and taking off. Sant'Elia, and not Le Corbusier, first wrote of the modern house that was to resemble a gigantic machine. Sant' Elia's architectural shapes are compact and monumental, as though rooted in the ground; they are often symmetrical, and can be grasped from one viewpoint.

Many practitioners of modern architecture were only concerned with the new aesthetic inasfar as it served a new social attitude. 'We know no problems of form, only problems of building', Mies van der Rohe said in 1923. There have probably seldom been times in which architects were less aware of an aesthetic ideal. The aims of the spatial organization of a house were correct exploitation of the site, appropriate orientation, sound insulation, short, time-saving circulation for the housewife, and clear distinctions between individual zones of function. The preoccupation with these basic problems of human habitation was accompanied by growing scientific precision, and by no means only in Europe but in South America, for example, too.

The key word of this era is a concept whose history reaches back into the 19th century but which ultimately lies behind every type of architecture in some form or other: *Functionalism. The relationship of building to function has been the subject of many interpretations, in the light of the purpose for which the building is to be used, its materials, structure and environment. The opinion has often been voiced that the expression of function is beautiful in itself. As Bruno Taut said in 1929: 'Serviceability becomes the actual content of aesthetics.' The second assumption, which remained unspoken at the time, was that the factors determining functional architecture are themselves unchangeable and are not for their part postulated by any one style. Philip *Johnson recounted to students at Harvard University the reaction of visitors to his Barcelona chairs, designed by Mies van der Rohe: 'When people come who like them, they exclaim "What wonderful chairs!" Which they really are. And when they sit down, they remark ". . . and how comfortable!" But if someone comes who dislikes chairs made from strips of curved steel, he will generally say: "How uncomfortable!"'

In the twenties we find numerous examples of people thinking their chairs comfortable because they liked their design. Architecture was then expressing functions founded on aesthetic ideals. Thus extensive use of glass walls met the demand for well-lit living and working areas and for close contact between interior and exterior, but the practice was unwisely introduced before the problem of protection from the sun had been solved. Sun louvres only appeared again during the thirties in the wake of new aesthetic ideas for enlivening façades three-dimensionally.

The twenties were a great Utopian period. The new architecture had to be quite different from the historical styles of the past. Divorced from art-historical development, this architecture was meant to be timeless and valid in the encounter between purpose and material. That is why the functional argument carried such weight. It seemed to guarantee that architecture was now orientated towards viewpoints that were constant and lay within the nature of man or the characteristics of materials. 'The objectivization of personal and national features is clearly recognizable in modern architecture' (Gropius, 1924). An international agreement seemed possible. For the attribute 'international' also appears among the designations which the period conferred upon itself. Gropius called his 'picture book of modern architecture' in 1924 *Internationale Architektur*, and the tag **International Style*, coined in a publication of the year 1932 by Hitchcock and Johnson, took its place beside Rationalism or *Neue Sachlichkeit*. Regional variations of this general canon were permissible, but only as voices that were part of a polyphonic harmony. Team-work like the Weissenhof housing estate of the *Deutscher Werkbund, to which sixteen architects from different countries contributed, the founding of the architectural organization *CIAM and the work submitted in the large international competitions of the twenties, forcefully demonstrated the new spirit of unity, even if the judges themselves still awarded the prizes to reactionaries.

It was not only Central Europe—the *Netherlands, *Germany and *Switzerland—that was in the throes of the new movement. When Gropius compiled the first Bauhaus book in 1924, the *Internationale Architektur*, more than half of the eighty-five examples of the new style were designs or models only. But in the course of one decade, the International Style established itself. In *Italy, the young **gruppo 7* was formed. In *France an avant-garde emerged whose clients were generally private patrons. In *Finland there were promising beginnings. *Sweden's eminent architect Erik Gunnar *Asplund wheeled round and openly joined the new movement with the Stockholm Exhibition of 1930. Modern architecture emerged in Hungary, Poland and above all in Czechoslovakia.

But already the two enormous reservoirs of power were considered to be the United States and the Soviet Union. The *United States had silos and factories whose sober pathos delighted Gropius, Le Corbusier and Mendelsohn. Even though architects such as *Schindler or *Neutra only concerned themselves with private building, the victory of the new idea was only a question of time in this land of phenomenal activity. Russia made such remarkable contributions as *Constructivism. With his 'suprematist architectures' *Malevich created abstract compositions in which the interplay and spatial relationship between rectangular shapes is explored; the Bauhaus published his work in the Bauhaus Books series which as a rule were reserved for their own products.

The ideas of the Russian architects at this time were informed by a technological mystique. Structure is exposed. El *Lissitzky projected multi-storey buildings as 'Cloud Props'; in a scheme for the Lenin Institute, Moscow, in 1927, J. J. Leonidov designed a glass sphere suspended by steel ropes to house an auditorium for 4,000 people. Even the less ambitious designs for offices and industrial plants show a graphic

Chemical works. Detail. Moscow, before 1929. Project

brilliance and precision which betray a fascination for all that is technical. The defeat of the huge but badly equipped Russian army in the First World War had relentlessly revealed the need for technology: now technology was looked on as the means of salvation that would safeguard the future of the new order. Erich Mendelsohn, who knew the architecture of the USSR and the USA at first hand, saw the problem as a need to create a synthesis of America's 'rational intelligence' and Russia's 'vehement feeling', and he thought such a task was capable of achievement. Perhaps the attraction which big competitions had for the world's greatest architects, like the one for the Chicago Tribune Skyscraper (1922) on the one hand and those for the Kharkov Theatre (1930) and the Palace of the Soviets in Moscow (1931) on the other, stemmed from similar considerations! America and Russia were the lands of promise for modern architecture.

But this ideal of international unity was impossible without some simplifications. Already two of the greatest exponents did not fit into the picture which the new movement had of itself. Frank Lloyd Wright, who had been of great influence since the turn of the century, possessed too much poetry, pathos and stubbornness to allow his work to be derived from 'utilitarian elements'. *Oud, the Dutch protagonist of the new architecture, called Wright one of the greatest architects of his time. But he also gave a warning that the 'lyric enchantment that sounded from the pipes of this architectural pied piper was at the same time damaging the purity of tone' of the new architecture. How little inspiration Wright's work derived from the strict and disciplined architecture of that period is borne out by the fact that there is a temporary falling off in his industry in the twenties. Le Corbusier, too, aroused some misgivings, although his individual forms (the features on his villa

Alvar Aalto. Sanatorium. Paimio, 1929–33

roofs) at this time could not yet be understood as anticipations of his later sculptural play with forms. Bruno Taut wrote that it was Le Corbusier's greatest weakness that 'he was an abstract painter as well and that he mixed up architectural problems with those of painting', and Mendelsohn reproached him with lack of economy in his Weissenhof flats.

To the extent that the architecture of smooth white surfaces, rectangles, clearly articulated groupings, lightness and transparency, encountered new and hitherto unexplored fields, it changed. Alvar *Aalto's early buildings indicate already how design determined by function leads to a new style image, as soon as stylistic attitude is freer and gesture more liberal. For example, Le Corbusier's design for the League of Nations Palace at Geneva (1927) envisaged a curved ceiling above the auditorium descending in great waves, clearly breaking back from each other, to the speaker's desk. The lecture hall in Aalto's library at Viipuri (1927–35) also has a ceiling suspended from the structural roof for the same acoustic reasons, but it is now developed in a freely undulating flow, sometimes rising, sometimes flat, a shape that only a few years earlier would not have been acceptable in the citadels of the International Style.

Aalto's architecture with its organic materials, its adaptation to the surrounding countryside and its avoidance of all dogma is the most conspicuous example of this change, because it is the work of a great architect. The new relationship to nature, as shown by his buildings, is not confined to him. The architects of the twenties had a preference for unadorned precise technological shapes. Their buildings, too, showed a fruitful relationship to exterior space and to nature; the opening up of the wall, the way a building's parts reach out to the open air and the invasion of the living areas by nature (Le Corbusier's buildings on *pilotis*, and his roof gardens!) all bear witness to it. But this relationship was one of contrasts. Here stood the man-made structure with its taut, clean lines and pure homogeneous surfaces, while there lay luxuriant untamed nature. As Oud put it in 1921: 'Instead of the natural charm of uncultivated material, the broken effect of glass, intricately textured surfaces, clouded colours, fused enamels and the weathering of walls we now have the attraction of cultivated material, clear glass, shining curved surfaces, the sparkling and brilliance of colour and the glitter of steel.' After 1930 and again after 1950 'natural charm' began to break through again.

Le Corbusier. Villa Savoye. Poissy, 1927–31

Frank Lloyd Wright. Offices for S. C. Johnson and Son. Racine, Wis., 1936–9

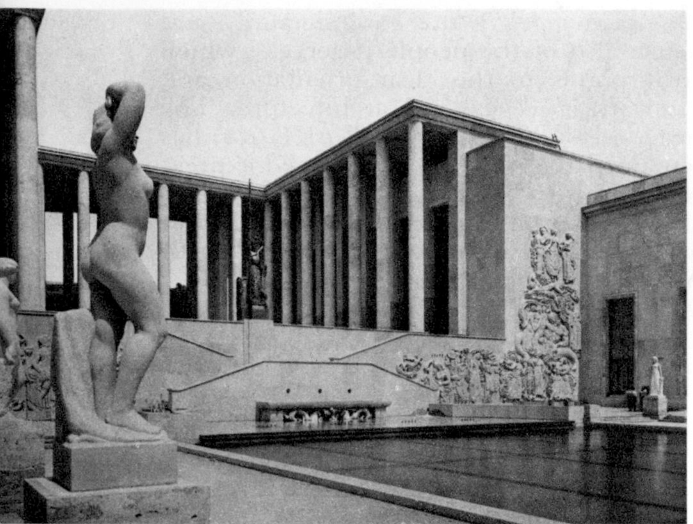

A. Aubert, J. C. Dondel, M. Dastugue, P. Viard. Musée d'Art Moderne Paris, 1937

A new appreciation of the lively rather than the stylized surface, as expressed by Aalto's choice of building materials, gained ground in many places. In southern countries the necessity for protection from sun and glare provides a functional reason for this. Le Corbusier put honeycombed screens on the elevations in his designs for multi-storey blocks. In *Denmark, the new University at Aarhus founded in 1932 affords an example of the effects that can be achieved

Frank Lloyd Wright. Kalita Humphreys Theater. Dallas, Texas, 1960

by the use of bricks without any detriment to the modernity of its idiom. Lively surface textures are featured at *Gardella's elegant clinic at Alessandria (1936–8) and at the entrance to the Finsbury Health Centre, London (1938). The aptitude of Brazilian architects in the field of plastic and free-form inventions first revealed itself before a great public at the New York World's Fair of 1939 in the pavilion by *Costa and *Niemeyer. Modern architecture was no longer essentially confined to a small area in Central Europe but made its appearance now all along the periphery of its former centre.

The geographic decentralization coincided with a stylistic one. Architecture in the thirties is more divided, perhaps richer in possibilities, but also less grandiose than in the preceding period. The stylistic formula of the twenties would no longer wear. Frank Lloyd Wright's individual type of art, which had derived little benefit from a climate of spiritual sobriety and ascetic poetry, now flourished, but concerned itself with the large-scale disposition of masses and with less detailed ornament. The other great architects of the older generation did not build much, mainly for reasons beyond their creative powers. Le Corbusier received only a few commissions, as measured against the wealth of his ideas. Gropius, forced into exile after 1933, had to adapt himself twice to new surroundings, first in England and then in America. Finally, Mies van der Rohe did not succeed in building a single large project between his Tugendhat House at Brno in 1930 and the Illinois Institute in Chicago, started in 1940!

Just as in the 19th century, the architecture of the engineers was separate from that of the architects. *Shell constructions, which have played an important part since the end of the Second World War, were mainly used for industrial schemes, and not as yet for public buildings except by *Torroja. *Nervi's large-span steel or reinforced concrete halls were at first only used as aircraft hangars; his world-wide reputation was only established after the war.

Periods of modern architecture when the contemporary style's powers of expansion flag for a while, are usually characterized by an emergence of classicism. Classicism is the temptation of the century. Architects of all generations gave in to it: Peter Behrens as well as Walter Gropius, and both with buildings of national prestige to their credit, the German Embassy in St Petersburg (1911–12) and the United States Embassy in Athens (1961). Fascists everywhere under the sun encouraged this more or less secret leaning, and made classicism the official style of architecture. The accessories of the style such as columns, pillars, pilasters, cornices, and flights of steps were raised to an imperial pseudo-grandeur and, in their violation of human scale, personified the inhuman power that raised these buildings. Fascist, National Socialist, and Soviet types of government architectures were presented at the Paris International Exhibition of 1937; their declamatory gesticulations laid bare the ideology behind the style. Even nations that had no need of such hollow forms of self-assertion succumbed to the attractive force of neo-classicism. The buildings which were put up in Paris at the same time on the opposite bank of the Seine, the Musée d'Art Moderne and the Palais Chaillot, were close behind the concrete pamphlets of the dictatorships for dreary amplitude.

Classicism was not only a temptation but also a legitimate possibility. Nobody will deny the respect due to Asplund's Stockholm Crematorium (1935–40) which the quiet dignity of this building deserves. The Lincoln Memorial in Washington (1914–22) and the National Gallery of Art there (1937) are honest examples which are all the more justified as the first public buildings of the newly created country were in this style at the very beginning of the North American tradition in building. Classicism in America meant memories of independence and the Revolutionary War. Apart from the imitation of column and pillar, gable and abacus, latent classicism is evident in more than one important modern building (*neoclassicism). Mies van der Rohe has built in an unmistakable idiom, free of all imitation, after his early villas with their reminiscences of Schinkel. But the way he places steel sections in front of a wall in order to reveal the play of forces in the framework hidden in the wall, recalls the symbolism of forces expressed by the individual parts of a building in classical architecture. In the designs for the layout of the Illinois Institute of Technology in Chicago, which preceded the final scheme of 1940, there is an axial arrangement of the architecture—and hence also of the people it serves—which corresponds to the clear orientation and axial stress of classical architecture. The Seagram Building in New York (1958) has remained the most clearly defined expression of this style so far. Related tendencies, albeit less strongly marked, are to be found in the decorative variants of current North American architecture.

What is modern architecture? Is it architecture based on the latest possibilities of building technique, from the earliest cast-iron structures to prestressed reinforced concrete? Architecture that aims at realizing a new style of living, perhaps in the manner of CIAM's ideals? Architecture which believes in a new spatial conception, the open plan that links indoors and outdoors and combines both in a single continuum? Or is modern architecture a provisional expression that will pass away by itself, because only after a period of time can clear and precise notions of style develop?

The situation became clear four or five years after the end of the Second World War. Around 1950, Olympus was unanimous and the gods distributed their gifts. Walter Gropius had trained himself a team of young American architects. Mies van der Rohe's ideal of the clear and crystalline

Ludwig Mies van der Rohe. Alumni Memorial Hall, Illinois Institute of Technology. Chicago, 1945–6. Detail

cube was accepted by the great American architectural firms and eventually by post-war European architects also. An unpleasant episode, that of the erection of the United Nations Secretariat in New York (1950–1), indicates how effortlessly the conceptions of the great authorities—in this case Le Corbusier's—could be carried out, even if association with the great masters of modern architecture was uncomfortable, as association with genius has always been. International Style, Functionalism, Rationalism or whatever they were called, were of equal importance in 1950. This kind of architecture, however, was no longer as dogmatic as it had been in the twenties, and regional and personal variations were admitted in considerably greater measure. Surfaces were more lively and textured and natural materials held their ground against the smooth white planes of the twenties—tendencies that continued from the thirties into the fifties. Colour began to assume a greater importance; but after all Le Corbusier and Bruno Taut had already pleaded for colour in building in the twenties.

In all, there was a mandatory stock of forms in 1950, which could be summarized, as they had been twenty-five years before, under headings such as transparency, visual lightness, and apparent weightlessness. Only a few years after the middle of the century the scene changed. There are times that favour the formation of traditions and those that react with neurotic vehemence to its every onset. Wright, Gropius, Mies van der Rohe, Le Corbusier: at what time did a new generation have the opportunity to build alongside their own forebears and to debate with their living exemplars? Frank Lloyd Wright, however much he had acted as a motive force at decisive moments, was no teacher in the sense of being a schoolmaster; his protean individualism did not lend itself to ready transference. Le Corbusier, in his Unité d'Habitation at Marseilles (1947–52), had thereby created the prototype of the slab-shaped high apartment block, with

Ludwig Mies van der Rohe. Chemotechnics and Metallurgy Building, Illinois Institute of Technology. Chicago, 1946

Edward Durell Stone. Gallery of Modern Art. New York, *c.* 1957. Model

internal service passages and two-storey flats; a building that had, or could have had, the force of a model. But since Ronchamp (1950–4) at the latest, his architecture has assumed an individual look, even to the untrained eye, that is unrepeatable. Gropius seems to have become a victim of his own pedagogic virtue in giving his pupils and collaborators a clear field for their own development; the University at Bagdad (under construction), which he designed with his *TAC team, is not likely to become such an important example as the Dessau Bauhaus (1926) and the Harvard Graduate Center at Cambridge, Mass. (1949–50) had been.

The most spectacular is the decline of van der Rohe's pupils. Mies himself has probably built more since 1950 than during the first four decades of his creative life. Each year, these apparently simple structures spring up, standing or reclining boxes of sublime proportions and finely modelled profile. But his former disciples have long since renounced his ideal of ascetic nobility. In 1952 the large firm *Skidmore, Owings and Merrill, which has an exceptional feeling for the trends of the time, completed Lever House, the model prototype of the multi-storey office block in which the load-bearing frame remains concealed and a fully glazed outer skin forms a *curtain wall. With its precise rectilinear shape in the thoroughgoing Miesian tradition, and free of all decoration, this building proved the starting point of a new tendency in architectural decoration. Verticals and horizontals are equally distributed in the treatment of the glass façade; the surfaces which envelop Lever House are completely devoid of directionality. The division by storeys is shown up clearly and the structural frame is discernible through the transparent panes. More recent buildings play decorative tricks with the curtain walling. The walls, which are not load-bearing, consist of pressed aluminium panels, handicraft-type metal grilles, or prefabricated concrete or plastic units which are assembled in monumental patterns. In

Skidmore, Owings and Merrill. Lever House. New York, 1952

Vittoriano Viganò. Istituto Marchiondi. Milan, 1957

the American Pavilion at the Brussels International Exhibition by Edward D. *Stone (1958) this divagation received the accolade of official prestige.

The excessively smooth form of this boneless type of decorative architecture is confronted by the rugged forms of a number of others, mainly the work of Italian architects. This faction, to which the architecture of *Japan and the later Le Corbusier also belongs, has declared its opposition to the jewel-like wall mem-

Eero Saarinen. TWA Terminal Building. Kennedy Airport, New York, 1962. Model

branes of the Americans. The wall becomes heavy and solid even where it is not load-bearing. Building materials are preferred with rough, granular, and contrasty textures such as brick and exposed concrete with the shuttering marks showing up as coarsely as possible. The predilection for weighty loads is carried to such extremes that the Torre Velasca in Milan (1957) has been provided with a huge crown-like top. Acute or obtuse angles reign supreme, with a tendency to hard, dissonant articulation of the individual parts of a building. The visual scale is constantly jumping and small units are abruptly confronted with large ones. Detail, like overall form, is block-shaped and heavy in appearance. The cultivated elegance of the decorator-architects is faced with brutal Expression, while the hedonists confront men wrestling with problems.

In all this antagonism between the two camps, a form of unity subsists in more than just the affront towards the classical concept of balance between load and support found in the creations of a Mies van der Rohe. Both parties exist in a deeply thought-out relationship to the history of architecture. Even the classic phase of modern architecture, the twenties, was not divorced from history, however much its protest against the style-imitations of the 19th century would have us believe it. Gropius sold Napoleon's table linen which his family had owned, in order to acquire building land for the Bauhaus in Weimar: an act which has its symbolic overtones. At least the twenties did not sell history completely for the sake of the present. Then, too, there was a historic revival but it was, so to say, ahistoric: it preferred those periods of time that had an anonymous character: the classical temples of Greece, which Le Corbusier had learnt to admire on his travels, the grain silos of the 19th century in North America, the farmhouse.

In the architecture of 1960, on the other hand, the past is admitted in almost every shape. In Italy, silhouettes appear that recall the baptistries of Parma and Cremona, and office blocks which recall medieval fortress towers. The Americans build semicircular structures amid gardens which invite comparison with the English 18th-century 'crescents', and there is constant borrowing from various exotic styles, mainly the Islamic ones but also from late

BBPR. Torre Velasca. Milan, 1957

Gothic. *Yamasaki attempted to combine 'the typical English character of the Palace of Westminster with the elegant lightness of the Doge's Palace' in his design for the American Embassy in London. His project was completely in accord with the ideas behind the huge building programme of the United States. A decade earlier, a country that erected prestige buildings abroad would have wanted these to reflect its own way of living and building. As a matter of fact, the American consulates in post-war Germany were images of what had just manifested itself in the Lever Building, New York, as the most recent tendency in United States architecture. The new buildings of the US State Department, over fifty diplomatic missions, reflect on the contrary the environment in which they are erected; a case of applied diplomacy. The competition for the Embassy in London explicitly demanded 'an architectural style which creates an atmosphere of good will by its intelligent appreciation and consideration of the site and by its adaptation of the architecture to its surroundings'.

The relationship of modern architecture to itself is already being reflected on—a situation that is alien to the historic styles. High and Late Renaissance knew no reversions to Early Renaissance; but modern architecture reminds itself with verbal quotations of Art Nouveau ('neo-Liberty'), De Stijl ('neo-neoplasticism') or the functionalism of the twenties, an

Minoru Yamasaki. McGregor Memorial Community Conference Center. Detroit, Mich., 1959

important phase of its own evolution. A new eclecticism is in the air.

The tendency to a literary programme is hence boundless. It stretches from an expression of certain psychological states to pure symbolism of form. Paul *Rudolph, one of the most talented of the younger American architects, demands that architects should concern themselves 'with considerations of vision, symbolism, and content'. Yamasaki advocated a 'friendly, more gentle kind of building', and attacks 'muscular boasting' in architecture; Edward D. Stone talks of a 'need for richness, exuberance and pure unadulterated freshness'. A picturesque character has been more and more demanded for buildings in recent years. The famous south-east corner of Le Corbusier's Ronchamp Chapel (1950–4) suggests the bold curve of a ship's bow by legitimate means, i.e. through the expressiveness of its abstract shape. Eero *Saarinen's TWA Terminal Building, Kennedy Airport (1962), was probably inspired by the thought of a bird in flight. But it is pushing architecture too far if it has to express freedom of speech (*Stubbins's Congress Hall, Berlin, 1957) or if the pools on the model of a Capitol for the fiftieth State of the USA are meant to represent the sea surrounding the Hawaiian Islands.

Carlos Raúl Villanueva. Building for the Faculty of Architecture and Town Planning, University City, Caracas, 1957

It is the eternal privilege of contemporaries to think of their own times as being particularly complex and involved. Hence modern architecture, too, is a mass of contradictions. A revaluation of the historic styles has led to a plurality of expression that would have been unthinkable even as recently as 1950. Countries that were on the periphery of architectural development before, now offer individual and unmistakable solutions of their own—South America, Japan. The great architects have lost much of their power to serve as models. Art form seems to triumph over residential form, and architecture as formal expression over architecture as social design. At the same time the problem of the modern city is becoming ever more pressing, while the demand for prefabrication and the industrialization of building is undeniable.

Architectural critics from all over the world have their say in this book. They would probably not agree on all points as regards matter, method and even basic conceptions if they came together round a table. But they would be unanimous in their belief that the forms and problems of contemporary architecture must be debated passionately. It is right to take an interest in the history of modern architecture not only because modern architecture has arrived at a stage in its development where architects themselves have again become interested in history, but above all because modern times have lasted long enough to provide the answers to many questions.

WOLFGANG PEHNT

Page 27. Le Corbusier. Notre-Dame du Haut, South-east Angle. Ronchamp, 1950–4

Aalto, Hugo Henrik Alvar, b. Kuortane, Finland, 1898. Aalto studied under Sigurd Frosterus at Helsinki Polytechnic, where he graduated in architecture in 1921. In the years immediately following he travelled in Scandinavia and Central Europe, worked for a short time in the planning office of the 1923 Gothenburg Fair, and made his official début with the Tampere Industrial Exhibition of 1922, though his first work was really the remodelling of his mother's house, the Mammula of Alajärvi, carried out when he was still a student. He opened his first office in Jyväskylä, and in 1925 married Aino Marsio, who until her death in 1949 was his principal collaborator, especially in the work connected with the organization and production of Artek timber furniture, first designed in 1928 for Paimio Sanatorium.

In Jyväskylä Aalto erected a number of 'pre-functionalist' buildings including the Trade Union Theatre (1923–5). He moved to Turku in 1927, and collaborated with Erik *Bryggman in 1929 on the Jubilee Exhibition organized to celebrate the seventh centenary of the city. This exhibition displayed an exemplary feeling of coherence, and considerable originality as a graphic structure. It also marks an important stage in the history of *Finnish architecture, for with it both Aalto and Bryggman reached the culmination of their development towards *Functionalism, abandoning the decorative elements of their former classic style to produce the first expression of modern architecture in Scandinavia. (*International Style)

The works which Alvar Aalto carried out over these years already reveal the fully developed character of his art, which may be set beside that of the greatest artists, because it succeeds both in being of its time and, simultaneously, timeless. They include the Library at Viipuri (1927–35), newspaper offices for the Turun Sanomat (1929–30), and Paimio Sanatorium (1929–33). This first 'white' period continued right up to the Second World War, and is

Alvar Aalto. Municipal Library. Viipuri, 1927–35

Alvar Aalto. Sunila cellulose factory. Kotka, 1936–9

Alvar Aalto. Town Hall. Säynätsalo, 1950–2

Page 29. Alvar Aalto. Church. Vuoksenniska, near Imatra, 1956–8

Alvar Aalto. Church. Vuoksenniska, near Imatra, 1956–8

rich in projects such as those at Paimio and Viipuri, which will always be considered among the classics of modern architecture: the architect's own house at Riihitie 10, Helsinki (1935–6), a delightful and little-known masterpiece; the Finnish Pavilions at the International Exhibitions in Paris (1937) and New York (1939); the terraced house of Kauttua and the Villa Mairea (1938–9); and a number of industrial buildings such as the cellulose factory at Toppila (1930–1), and the huge industrial

Alvar Aalto. Maison Carré. Bazoches, 1956–8

and residential Sunila complex (1936–9, completed 1951–4) near Kotka.

After the intermission of the war years, Alvar Aalto applied himself to rebuilding his native land. In 1944–5 he drew up a master-plan for the development of Rovaniemi, the capital of Finnish Lapland, in conjunction with Y. Lindegren, B. Saarnio, M. Tavio, and K. Simberg. The works built or projected in the first ten years after the war may be ascribed to what we shall call the artist's middle or mature period. It may also be referred to as his 'red' or 'Cézanne' period, from the intense hues of the bricks he employed and his manner of handling volumes, but above all from the way that light is broken into facets in the manner of Cézanne; or his 'Italian' period, from the affectionate memories that are embodied of the severe Tuscan contours of towers and strongholds, and from the way he contrives internal courtyards, often raised at a higher level, where the explicit feeling of authority is tempered to a human scale. The work which embodies and concludes the structural and spatial experiments of this period, while constituting its highest and most perfect expression, is the Town Hall at Säynätsalo (1950–2). Mention should also be made of the imposing campus of Jyväskylä Teachers' Training College (1952–7), and the Funeral Chapel for Malmi, near Helsinki, a fine design that has remained unbuilt. (*USA)

It was at this time that Alvar Aalto's intense work on civic schemes began, which are altering the face of Helsinki. His buildings of the fifties, such as the Rautatalo office block, 1952–4, one of his greatest projects; the Engineers' Institute, 1952; the National Pensions Institution, 1952–6; and the Cultural Centre, 1955–8, are of an intermediate stage between his 'red' and second 'white' periods, which may be literally referred to as 'bronze'. Aalto's command of plastic design had become enriched to an extraordinary degree, backed as it was by thirty years of building experience. The butterfly roof of Säynätsalo Town Hall and the great hull of the Stadium at Otaniemi may serve as symbols of this supreme mastery of technology and three-dimensional design in the handling of wood: Finland's most typical and traditional, if modest, building material. The following schemes date from the same years: the design for Seinajoki Episcopalian

Church (1952), completed in 1958 as part of a more extensive town-planning layout currently in course of realization; the Enso-Gutzeit paper mill at Summa (1953); the cemetery and chapels for Kongens Lyngby, near Copenhagen, in collaboration with Jean-Jacques Baruel (not built); the design for Vienna Municipal Hall (1953, not built); the Oulu Theatre project (1955); Otaniemi Polytechnic (1955, under construction); the development plan for Imatra (1947–53) and the regional plan for Lapland (1950–7).

Meanwhile, Aalto's second 'white' period begins in 1953, with the country house he built himself, of a somewhat experimental character, on the island of Muuratsalo. In 1955 came his masterly studio, completely in white, where Aalto's habitual attention to the psychological effects of colour reaches its ultimate stage in surroundings with no colour at all, intended to be conducive to work and quiet meditation. His eight-storey block of flats for the Berlin Interbau dates from 1955–7; then came the project for the Municipal Centre at Gothenburg (1956), the Church at Vuoksenniska near Imatra, and the Maison Carré, in the neighbourhood of Paris (both between 1956 and 1958). The latter work was carried out in collaboration with Elissa Makkinheimo, whom Aalto married in 1952. The almost 'Mycenaean' articulation of spaces gives the interiors of these buildings less volumetric definition, as grouping becomes ever more complex. Space is no longer simply fluid in the way it was at Viipuri, but grows, and, as it were, breathes in every direction around man. This treatment characterizes Aalto's most recent works, in course of construction or projected: the museums for Aalborg (Denmark) and Bagdad; Kiruna Town Hall; the Volkswagen Cultural Centre at Wolfsburg, and the tower house at Bremen. All these schemes were drawn up in 1958, and the last two are under construction. Later works include the Enso-Gutzeit office block at Helsinki (1959–62), the Opera House at Essen, and the Cultural Centre in Helsinki. Numerous other schemes are at the planning stage.

No other architecture of the present day exerts quite the same fascination as Alvar Aalto's: rich in allegory, unforeseeable, at once mystical and sensual, rationalist and anti-rationalist. As an outstanding practitioner of *organic architecture, he is aristocratically remote from all the mannerisms that have appeared due to a misunderstanding of this term. In the present state of architecture, where the need to provide accommodation for ever-increasing masses of people has led, and too often still leads to a frightful deterioration in the human and psychological qualities of housing and urban environments, to say nothing of the aesthetic considerations involved, the work of this poet amongst architects, so rich in affectionate attention to all human needs, expressed and latent, recognized or forgotten, is a source of comfort and hope. With the current spread of 'new' materials, whether used with greater commercial brashness or more barbarous insipidity it is difficult to say, Aalto's lamps and chairs, and the materials he employs, speak to us

Alvar Aalto. Cultural Centre. Helsinki, 1955–8

with an ancient wisdom whose very memory we seem to have lost. His work is a protest against everything stupid, unnatural and impoverished that goes under the name of 'modern', against fashionable clichés and trick photography. It is the contradictory and coherent work of a genius who does not adapt himself to the conventions of today or yesterday, because he is one of the men of our time who understands with the greatest clarity what the word tradition really means, and how, having grasped its spirit perfectly, one becomes part of it: without nostalgia, or complexes, though with all the respect due to it: in fine, a free man.

Bibliography: Alvar Aalto, 'Zwischen Humanismus und Materialismus', in *Der Bau*, No. 7/8, Vienna 1955; reprinted in *Baukunst und Werkform*, Volume IX, No. 6, Darmstadt 1956; Alvar Aalto, 'Problemi di architettura', in *Quaderni* ACJ, Turin 1956; Alvar Aalto, RIBA Annual Discourse, London in *RIBA Journal*, May 1957; Ed. and Cl. Neuenschwander, *Alvar Aalto and Finnish Architecture*, London 1954; Pier Carlo Santini and Göran Schildt, 'Alvar Aalto from Sunila to Imatra: Ideas, Projects and Buildings' in *Zodiac 3*, Milan 1958; Frederick Gutheim, *Alvar Aalto*, New York 1960; Göran Schildt and Leonardo Mosso, *Alvar Aalto*, Jyväskylä 1962.

LEONARDO MOSSO

Aberdeen, David du Rieu, b. 1913. Studied at Bartlett School of Architecture, London University; later lecturer at the Atelier of Advanced Design there (1947–53). Won the open competition for the TUC Memorial Building, London (1953–56). Housing at Basildon, Harlow and N. Southgate (London), the latter featuring a thirteen-storey point block. Redevelopment of Paddington Hospital; commercial buildings; aircraft hangars.

Abramovitz, Max, b. Chicago 1908. Studied at the University of Illinois and at Columbia University. In partnership with Wallace K. *Harrison.

Adler, Dankmar, b. Stadt Lengsfeld, Germany 1844, d. 1900. He was the son of a cantor. Began his drawing studies at fifteen. Immigrated to Detroit, 1854. Associated with A. J. Kinney, 1869–71; Edward Burling, 1871–9; Louis H. *Sullivan, 1881–95. (*USA) With Burling he collaborated on numerous designs during the building boom in Chicago, following the great fire of 1871. In 1879, he set up independent practice and was joined two years later by Sullivan. His most important work was the Central Music Hall in Chicago (later torn down to provide space for the present retail store of Marshall Field and Co.), which was entirely Adler's work except for Sullivan's decorative organ grilles. Finished in 1879, it was the prototype for a subsequent series of theatres by the firm. The planning, layout and lighting were noteworthy, although Adler was praised primarily for his instinctive mastery of acoustics. After completion of the Central Music Hall, Sullivan rose rapidly to the position of chief draftsman. Adler, during his later years, managed the engineering and business aspects of the firm and was active in various architectural organizations, introducing many progressive reforms and attempting to improve the position of architecture in American society. Among his works were a series of interesting synagogues, one, Anshe Ma'arev, for his father's congregation.

Albini, Franco, b. Robbiate, Como 1905. Graduated 1929 at Milan, where he now lives. His first essays in architecture were made during the thirties, in connection with the Milan Triennali and Trade Fairs. The fine pavilion for the Istituto Nazionale delle Assicurazioni dates from 1935. It was the first of his designs to be built, and already unmistakable. Having come to maturity of outlook and architectural practice during the years when Persico and Pagano were conducting their polemics in the pages of *Casabella* on behalf of a rationalist architecture in the European manner, and against the current of the *Novecento Italiano*, Albini has kept faith with those distant premisses to a greater degree than perhaps any other of his companions. This will be readily perceived if his entire work is analysed; in this way it would be seen how he likes thinking of architecture in essentially rational terms, to which he restricts the emotions of fantasy. Of course, there is more to it than that: there is his consciousness of profound underlying reasons, social and historic order and architectural rationalism.
For many years Albini's fantasy played on

the contrast between his lively, spatial intuitions (as expressed by his frequent clever use of transparent, i.e. luminous, diaphragms, and reticulated panels, i.e. openwork panels which let the light flow in) and the clear orthogonal geometry of his structures. The contrast was finally resolved by identifying the formal element in the structure itself and from then onwards Albini's style has been more strongly expressed. This is exemplified in the field of architecture from his first villa in Milan, 1938, and his workers' flats there, 1936–8, to the Palazzo INA at Parma, 1951, the new municipal offices at Genoa, 1959 and on through to the large department store La Rinascente in Rome, 1961, his most recent and most discussed work. In the field of town planning, it may be traced from his first studies and projects, produced in conjunction with Pagano, Camus and Palanti before the war, down to the development plan for Reggio Emilia (1947–8, in collaboration); in industrial design: from the metal chair, in whose design he collaborated for the 1936 Triennale, to the circular armchair, designed in collaboration with Franca Helg for the Triennale of 1960; in the fitting out of shops, houses and museums: from the Museo di Palazzo Bianco at Genoa in 1951, a high-water mark in international museology, to the Museo del Tesoro di San Lorenzo at Genoa, 1954–6, which is one of the most intense and interesting works of recent Italian architecture, starting from its plan, laid out with a pure organic geometry, like that of a crystal.

Franco Albini. Museo di Palazzo Bianco. Genoa, 1951

Albini, who has attained world stature as a museum architect, has been entrusted with the project for the great new museums of Egyptian art at Cairo, currently under construction. He was a member of the executive committee of the 1951 Triennale; has lectured for some years at the Venice Istituto Universitario di Architettura; and was awarded the Olivetti national prize for architecture in 1957.

Bibliography: Giuseppe Samonà, 'Franco Albini e la cultura architettonica in Italia', in *Zodiac 3*, Milan 1958; G. C. Argan, *Franco Albini*, Milan 1962. See also: *Architectural Review*, March 1957 and December 1960.

GIULIA VERONESI

Almqvist, Osvald, b. Trankil near Karlstad 1884, d. Stockholm 1950. Studied at Stockholm Technical College. The 'first Swedish functionalist'. He founded a School of Architecture in 1910, together with *Asplund, Bergsten, *Lewerentz, and other young architects, which lasted only a short time but contributed to a clarification of the situation in Sweden. Housing, power stations.

Amsterdam, School of. Group of architects that started from the break with *Berlage and provided a parallel movement in the twenties and thirties of this century to contemporary German *Expressionism. Their mouthpiece was the journal **Wendingen*. The plastically conceived shapes of their brick buildings were in sharp contrast to the buildings of De *Stijl. Most eminent exponents were Kramer, van der Mey, and Michael de *Klerk.

Antonelli, Alessandro, b. Ghemme, Novara 1798, d. Turin 1888. Professor at the Accademia di Belle Arti at Turin. He built the multi-shell cupolas of St Gaudenzio at Novara (1841–81) and of the Mole Antonelliana at Turin (1863–88), bold feats of engineering, which relied in the main on Classic Revival forms of decoration.

Architects' Co-Partnership. Practice originally founded by C. K. Capon, P. L. Cocke, M. H. Cooke-Yarborough, L. M. de Syllas, J. M. Grice and M. A. R. Powers. Their rubber factory at Brynmawr, South Wales (1949) with its repetition of simple but powerful shapes gave the first indication of the feeling for sculptural effect which characterizes the firm's style. This has been displayed since in a series of educational buildings, including schools in London, Warwickshire, Hertfordshire and Dorsetshire, and university premises at Leicester, Carmarthen and Cambridge. Their hall of residence for undergraduates at St John's College, Oxford has an ingenious plan comprising a series of related hexagons, whose cellular character provides an interesting silhouette in sympathy with the existing medieval building.

HAROLD MEEK

Aronco, Raimondo d', b. Gemona, Udine 1857, d. Naples 1932. Graduate of Venice Academy. Together with *Basile and *Sommaruga he was the most important exponent of *Art Nouveau in Italy. D'Aronco designed the main building of the Turin Industrial Exhibition (1902), a bizarre mixture of the most varying influences including the Viennese. Worked in Turkey. Later, like *Horta and partly also *Behrens, he turned to designing in the Classic Revival style.

Art Nouveau. Extensive romantic, individualist and anti-historical movement which affected the whole of Europe between 1890 and 1910. It was known in England at the time as the 'modern style'; in Belgium as the *coup de fouet* (whiplash) or *paling* (eel) style (from the flexible line introduced by *Horta), or the *style des Vingt* (in view of the important part played by a group of this name led by Octave Maus); in Germany it was called the *Jugendstil*, from the Munich periodical *Jugend*; in France the *style nouille* (noodle style) or *style Guimard* (after the architect Henri *Guimard, who designed the decorative entrances to the Paris Métro in 1899). The Austrians named it the *Sezessionsstil* (after the Viennese *Sezession* group, led from 1897 on by the painter Klimt and the architects *Hoffmann and *Olbrich); in Italy it was the *stile Liberty* or *stile floreale*, and in Spain *modernismo*.

Known more generally as the *style 1900*, Art Nouveau expresses an essentially decorative trend that aims to highlight the ornamental value of the curved line, which may be floral in origin (Belgium, France) or geometric (Scotland, Austria). This line gives rise to two-dimensional, slender, sinuous, undulating and invariably asymmetrical forms. The applied arts were the first to be affected (textiles by William Morris, 1880; wood-engraved title page to *Wren's City Churches* by Arthur H. Mackmurdo, 1883; vases by Émile Gallé, 1884; ornamental lettering by Fernand Khnopff and Georges Lemmen, 1890–1; mural tapestry *The Angels' Vigil* by Henry van de Velde, 1893; furniture by Gustave Serrurier-Bovy, 1891; title page for *Dominical* by van de Velde, 1892).

Next came architecture, represented by the house which the architect Victor *Horta built at Brussels in 1892 for the engineer Tassel, a key-work of the new style, which was to find a dazzling counterpart a few years later in the Elvira studio at Munich by August *Endell (1897–8, destroyed). Among the most characteristic architectural products of Art Nouveau, albeit widely differing in purpose and plastic expression, may be counted the houses built by Paul *Hankar in Brussels (1893–1900); the works of Willem Kromhout (1864–1940), Th. Sluyterman (1863–1931) and L. A. H. Wolf in the Netherlands; Guimard's Castel Béranger (1897–8), Métro stations and the auditorium of the Humbert de Romans building (1902, destroyed) at Paris; Horta's Maison du Peuple (1896–99) and the former Hôtel Solvay (1895–1900) in Brussels; the overhead Stadtbahn station at the Karlsplatz, Vienna (1897) by Otto *Wagner; and the Osthaus Museum laid out by van de Velde at Hagen (1900–2). All these works are the result of a deliberate attempt to put an end to imitations of past styles; in its place is offered a florid type of architecture which exploits craft skills, using coloured materials (faience cabochons, stoneware, terracotta panels, stained glass), exotic veneers, moulded stonework, grilles, balconies, and tapered brackets in wrought-iron; and burgeoning with asymmetrical door- and window-frames, bow and horseshoe windows, etc. We are in the presence of a type of architecture which is seeking a relationship between surface and ornament, rather than a spatial expression of plan. An exception to this may be found in buildings designed in the tradition of the English country house (*Voysey, *Mackintosh), with their principle of building from inside to out; and the Continental examples based on them (Olbrich's houses on the Mathildenhöhe at Darmstadt). In the later phases of Art Nouveau, façade decoration was accompanied by a powerful plastic treatment of the whole building, either by the dramatic accentuation of individual parts of the structure (Glasgow Art School, 1898–1909, by Mackintosh) or by the sculptural modelling of the whole building mass (Werkbundtheater, Cologne, 1914 by van de Velde; Casa Milà, Barcelona, 1905–10, by *Gaudí).

Art Nouveau was first and foremost an aesthetic undertaking, based on social theories and inspired by aesthetes such as Ruskin, Morris and Oscar Wilde. It was born from a panic fear of the rise of industrialism, and from a determination to create a new style, in view of the 19th century's stylistic bankruptcy, which would affect the design of objects of everyday use and leave its mark ultimately on the décor and surroundings of daily life.

In theory, from the ethical and political point of view, it appears as an attempt to integrate art with social life; in practice, and from the cultural point of view, it assumes the manner of a reactionary bourgeois movement. Art Nouveau tried, in effect, to relieve man from the pressures of a technological milieu. Faced with the machine, which it regarded as the work of the devil, it aimed at renewing contact with nature and rehabilitating the tool in its rôle of the 'lengthener of the hand'; by the same token, it obliged the artist to express himself in the margin of the living forces of technology. On the other hand, it claimed to be able to fashion a three-dimensional universe, independent of the fundamental support of the true creators of the epoch (Cézanne, Gauguin, Van Gogh, Munch) or rather, only borrowing the most external trappings of their inspiration. The point may thus be seen at which Art Nouveau (in the midst of its romantic, sentimental and social outbursts) posed in contradictory terms the problem of the social relations of art. It may also be seen how it brought about, in all fields, a real severance between life and thought, and partially destroyed the 'relation between plant and soil'.

August Endell. Elvira photographic studio. Munich, 1897–8

Art Nouveau may thus be compared to a short circuit; by confounding style and surface ornament, and by basing all its efforts on theories of decoration, it appeared as a parenthesis in the organic development of history. At a time of the most prodigious industrial development, which saw the works of *Eiffel, Contamin and Dutert, and the early *Gropius, Art Nouveau kept painters, sculptors and architects at a respectful distance from the complex of technology, and inveigled them into a concern for virtuous craftsmanship rather than for machines and machine

Hector Guimard. Entrance to a Métro station. Paris, 1900

Victor Horta. Hôtel Tassel. Brussels, 1892–3

products. Hence, despite the ever-increasing tempo of human life, Art Nouveau wished to protect the quiet little world dreamt of by Ruskin, Morris, Tolstoy, Dickens, Renan, Zola and many others. Distinguished architects of the Art Nouveau style, such as Mackintosh, *Behrens and the Viennese masters became pioneers of modern architecture, it is true, but with their forward-looking buildings they overstepped the frontiers which the style had imposed upon its adherents.

Bibliography: Fritz Schmalenbach, *Jugendstil. Ein Beitrag zu Theorie und Geschichte der Flächenkunst*, Würzburg 1934; Stephan Tschudi Madsen, *Sources of Art Nouveau*, New York 1956; Helmut Seling (editor), *Jugendstil. Der Weg ins 20. Jahrhundert*, Heidelberg 1959; Peter Selz and Mildred Constantine (editors) *Art Nouveau. Art and Design at the Turn of the Century*, New York 1959; Louis Gans, *Nieuwe Kunst. De Nederlandse Bijtrage tot de 'Art Nouveau'*, Utrecht 1960; Jean Cassou, Emil Langui, Nikolaus Pevsner, *Durchbruch zum 20. Jahrhundert, Kunst und Kultur der Jahrhundertwende*, Munich 1962; Robert Schmutzler, *Jugendstil-Art Nouveau*, Stuttgart 1962.

ROBERT L. DELEVOY

Arts and Crafts. In 1861 William *Morris, together with a group of Pre-Raphaelite painters and architects in London, founded the firm of Morris, Marshall and Faulkner, Fine Art Workmen in Painting, Carving, Furniture and the Metals. He thus took the first step in a movement that was to lead over the next thirty years to an ultimate crystallization in C. R. Ashbee's Arts and Crafts Exhibition Society of 1888. The route was marked by a series of experiments, researches and battles, including the foundation of various other associations for the purpose of reviving craft production and fighting the encroachments of machinery on life. In its progress, the movement was to exercise a profound influence on the development of new ideas, tastes and methods of work over the whole of Europe. Inspired by the example of medieval craftsmen, Morris conducted a passionate campaign throughout these years to restore a genuine feeling of creativity to the decorative arts (i.e. those pertaining to domestic interiors), and indirectly to architecture as well. He fought against the

Antoni Gaudí. Casa Batlló. Barcelona, 1905–7

Charles Robert Ashbee. House in Cheyne Walk. London, 1904

lowering of standards that had been brought about when the market was flooded with cheap mass-produced goods which brought not truth and beauty, but falsehood and ugliness into everyday life. Behind this attitude lay the moralizing aesthetics of John Ruskin.

But in the years that had passed since Morris & Co. was founded, the rise of industrial mass-production methods and the abhorred machine were facts that could no longer be suppressed or ignored. Ashbee, indeed, took account of them, and accepted, at least in theory, the need for collaboration with industry. In this may be seen the beginnings of industrial design, which ever since the time of the Crystal Palace had been a desideratum of the machine age.

The social, or even Socialist, presuppositions of this process are clear: to raise to the dignity of art the cheap, widely distributed, mass-produced standard product. Its influence is clear, too, especially on van de *Velde's work in this sphere, and in the developments which gave rise to the *Deutscher Werkbund. An important rôle in this respect was played by the German architect Hermann *Muthesius, who spread the knowledge of modern English domestic architecture throughout Germany in the early years of this century with his numerous well-documented books on the English house and the exhibitions he organized abroad of English furniture and decorative schemes.

With the question of taste, however, things were more complex and difficult, not least because Walter Crane, the first president of the Arts and Crafts Society was still personally bound up with the old Pre-Raphaelite aesthetic, and sometimes opposed a greater 'opening-up' of the movement, although some of the most advanced architects of the day were to be found amongst the first members and exhibitors, men such as C. F. A. *Voysey, C. R. Ashbee, W. R. Lethaby, George Walton and E. L. Lutyens. Crane, in fact, always categorically excluded from the Society's exhibitions the works of the young C. R. *Mackintosh, and the whole Glasgow School, which was to exert such an influence on the Continent, particularly in Vienna.

It may nevertheless be affirmed that the Arts and Crafts movement made a lasting impression in both the aesthetic and technical spheres. Its abandonment of the

Philip Webb. Red House. Bexley Heath, Kent, 1859

stylistic imitations of the 19th century, its disavowal of illusionistic patterns and its preference for continuous forms laid the basis for the creative fantasies of *Art Nouveau and Jugendstil, and for the break with the aesthetic outlook of the 19th century, which the art of the present century was to consummate.

Bibliography: Nikolaus Pevsner, *An Enquiry into Industrial Art in England*, New York 1937; Nikolaus Pevsner, *Pioneers of Modern Design from William Morris to Walter Gropius*, New York 1949; Jean Cassou, Emil Langui, and Nikolaus Pevsner, *Durchbruch zum 20. Jahrhundert, Kunst und Kultur der Jahrhundertwende*, Munich 1962.

GIULIA VERONESI

Aslin, Charles Herbert, b. Sheffield 1893, d. 1959. Studied at Sheffield University Department of Architecture. After a career in various local authority offices Aslin became County Architect for Hertfordshire in 1945, where he stayed till his retirement in 1958.

At the end of the Second World War, acute shortage of school places in Hertfordshire, together with lack of manpower and craftsmen in the building trade moved Aslin to tackle the problem as a quasi-military 'planned operation'. Taking advantage of the production potential of light industry, built up during the war, he organized a system of school *prefabrication from factory-made parts, of sufficient flexibility to allow each school to be treated individually.

The prototype was Cheshunt Primary School, built in 1946 on an 8 foot 3 inch grid. In 1947, eleven schools were projected on a serial production basis, with flat roofs, solid floors, and standardized stanchions and beam connections; in 1948–49, development proceeded on twenty-one primary schools, while the 1947 schools were being completed. Development on these lines has continued ever since, with the 8 foot 3 inch grid successfully applied to multi-storey buildings, though a later development has led to the introduction of a 2 foot 8 inch planning module. The hundredth school of this type was opened in 1955. (*Great Britain)

Aslin also pioneered the use of bold clear colours in schools. He was President of the RIBA in 1954–6.

Bibliography: C. H. Aslin, 'Specialized developments in school construction' in *Journal of the RIBA*, November 1950; K. C. Twist, J. T. Redpath and K. C. Evans, 'Hertfordshire Schools Development' in *Architects' Journal* (London), 12 and 26.5.1955, 11.8.1955, 19.4.1956 and 2.8.1956.

HAROLD MEEK

Asplund, Erik Gunnar, b. Stockholm 1885, d. Stockholm 1940. The architecture of Erik Gunnar Asplund, one of the most prominent of Swedish architects of the first half of the twentieth century, is of historical significance because it shows the transition from traditional to modern architecture. Asplund received his architectural training at the Technical High School and the Academy of Art, Stockholm. He completed his training and began practice in 1909. His early work consisted mainly of houses. In 1913–14 he went to Italy and Greece to study the architecture of these countries; the visit made a profound impression on him and the influence of classical architecture can be discerned in almost all his work. (*Sweden)

Among the buildings for which he was responsible on his return, from about 1914 to 1928 which represents his early period, were the layout of the Stockholm South Cemetery in collaboration with Sigurd Lewerentz, the Woodland Chapel in the same cemetery (1918–20), the Snellman villa, Djursholm (1917), the Skandia Cinema (1922–3) and the Stockholm City Library (1924–7). The last two mentioned

Erik Gunnar Asplund. Law Courts Extension. Gothenburg, 1934–7

are among Asplund's most important works, and they are both strongly classical in design. The Skandia Cinema, which was much admired at the time it was built, is rectangular in shape with side balconies and a design that depends for its aesthetic effect on a balance of verticals and horizontals, with a restrained use of classical decoration. The City Library is symmetrical in plan with a large cylindrical lending hall enclosed on three sides by rectangular blocks containing reading and study rooms and offices. The central part was originally designed to be surmounted by a dome, but this was abandoned for a flat roof over the cylinder. The whole work is a classical conception with an accent on simplicity and severity which was a trend of the time. If Asplund had continued designing in the style of the Skandia Cinema and the Stockholm City Library, he would have been regarded as another competent traditional architect, but with the buildings of the Stockholm Exhibition of 1930, for which he was responsible, he showed himself a modern architect expressively handling glass and steel with the lightness of effect that these materials create. This is seen especially in the Paradise Restaurant with its slender supports, its glass walls, its circular glass tower, and large coloured sun blinds, the very epitomization of the new architecture in Europe.

After this exhibition Asplund designed the Bredenberg store in Stockholm (1933–5), which has something of the lightness of the exhibition buildings; the State Bacteriological Laboratory, Stockholm (1933–7); the Gothenburg Law Courts Extension (1934–7), the design of which is modern in spirit yet harmonizes in scale with the original building in the classical style; and lastly the Forest Crematorium, Stockholm South Cemetery, begun in 1935 and completed in 1940. This building is generally regarded as his masterpiece. The work involved the remoulding of the site: the transformation of a gravel pit to a wind-swept hill on the summit of which the crematorium was built. Near it is a large pool, to reflect the sky, and a large marble cross. The group of buildings consists of three chapels, the crematorium and the columbarium; at the main entrance is a large portico with numerous plain shafts. Simple, dramatic and original as is the

Erik Gunnar Asplund. Stockholm Exhibition, 1930

Erik Gunnar Asplund. Forest Crematorium. Stockholm, 1935–40

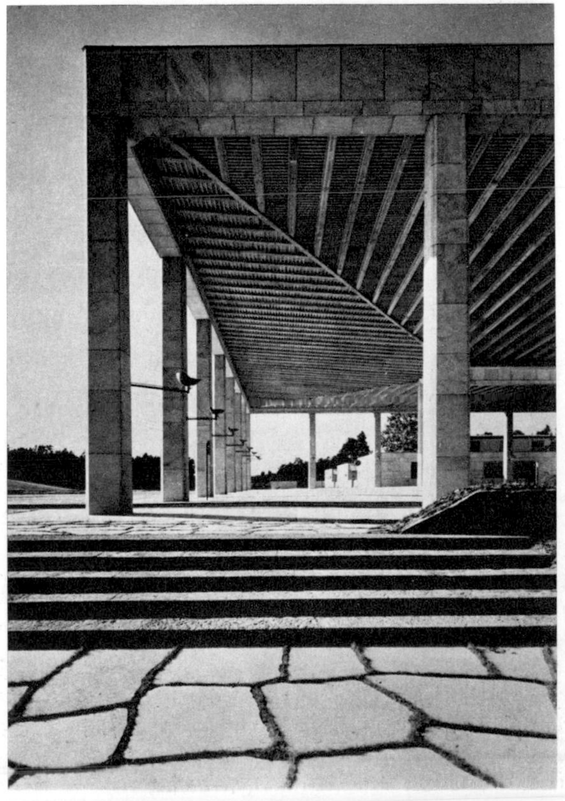

design for a purpose of this kind it is essentially Greek in conception, the feeling of repose that it creates depending on the relation of verticals and horizontals; it demonstrates how Greek architectural feeling can live in architecture that seems to be imbued with the modern spirit.

Bibliography: Bruno Zevi, *E. Gunnar Asplund*, Milan 1948; Holmdahl and Odeen (eds), *Gunnar Asplund, Architect*, Stockholm 1950; Eric de Maré, *Gunnar Asplund —A great modern architect*, London 1955.

ARNOLD WHITTICK

Athens Charter. A manifesto published by the international architectural organization *CIAM in 1933, setting out data and requirements connected with the problem of the modern city under five main headings (Dwellings, Recreation, Work, Transportation, Historic Buildings).

Austria. The wealth and power of the old monarchy on the Danube found its chief expression in the concentration of culture at Vienna, which reached a climax around 1900 in *Art Nouveau. The extensive diffusion of Austrian architecture, arts and crafts to other countries has never been achieved again. *Wagner, *Hoffmann, *Olbrich and *Loos triumphed over senseless eclecticism and produced outstanding examples of new conceptions of space. It is characteristic of the Vienna School that it never quite cut itself loose from tradition, whether it condemned ornament radically like Loos, or sought to give it a new purpose like Hoffmann. It always adhered to the native tradition, especially to Kornhäusel.

Otto Wagner. Station building for the Vienna Stadtbahn. Vienna, 1896–7

Adolf Loos. Steiner House. Vienna, 1910

Decimated Austria was hit harder by the consequences of the First World War than any other country. The new style in building, that second great attempt to do away with the influences of the past, had only met with a weak response in Austria. Furthermore, the puritanical and ascetic features of the movement, of the kind the Bauhaus embodies for example, are properties that are alien to the Austrian mentality. That is why significant Austrian architects became successful only when they went abroad: *Schindler, *Neutra, Bieber, Brenner, Schuster, Gottwald, Steinbüschel, *Seidler and Petschnigg.

Others transformed the influences entering from the north and west to achieve a charming compromise, as did Lichtblau and Haertl, or Strnad, who started off with classical shapes and modified them subjectively. Frank produced typical examples with a clear directness and cultivated the Viennese arts and crafts in new shapes.

Roland Rainer. Municipal Hall. Vienna, 1954–8

Schuster revived the Biedermeier tradition. *Holzmeister, too, starting off in the traditional idiom, developed strong and capricious forms (churches and Salzburg Festival Theatre).

After the Second World War, economic stagnation was even more paralysing than between the wars. It is largely due to the vitality of Roland *Rainer and his school that this lethargy has been overcome.

Karl Schwanzer. Austrian Pavilion at the International Exhibition. Brussels, 1958

Arbeitsgruppe 4. Parish Church. Salzburg-Parsch, 1955–6

Rainer combines strict economy and rationality with a sure feeling for the expression of any building function. His Vienna Municipal Hall (1954–8) for 16,000 people, a steel structure with aluminium cladding, is of a new type for this class of building; one which he has employed again for halls at Bremen and Ludwigsburg. In conscious contrast to the fortress-like blocks of flats built in Vienna during the twenties, Rainer, in conjunction with Auböck, put up an experimental estate of detached prefabricated houses adjoining the old Vienna Werkbund estate. These examples, like others inspired by him in housing estates by younger architects (Windbrechtinger/Ketterer, Sekler, Freyler), propagate his theories on low buildings in cities. Only after a hard struggle has Rainer been able to carry into effect his general plan for rebuilding in Vienna.

A characteristic combination of the principles of modern architecture with the traditions of the Vienna School of 1900 has been achieved by architects such as Lorenz, who combines restraint in outer shape with a three-dimensional feeling for space, or Gottwald, a typical engineer-architect who has built some remarkable schools and industrial buildings in Germany. His four-storey block of flats in the Hansa district of Berlin is an interesting solution of the problem of flexibility in the provision of dwelling space. A lucid demonstration of Austrian architecture is afforded by the exhibition pavilion at Brussels (1958) by Schwanzer which was re-erected in Vienna for the Museum of the Twentieth Century. Strict logicality in the manner of Loos is perpetuated in the work of Arbeitsgruppe 4 (Holzbauer, Kurrent, Spalt): church near Salzburg, shops. There are also manifestations of individuality in sports buildings such as the Gänshäufel Baths, Vienna, by Fellerer and Wörle, and in the simple and clear shapes of the airport buildings at Schwechat by the architects Klaudy, Pfeffer, Hoch and Schimka.

HUBERT HOFFMANN

Bakema, Jacob B., b. Groningen 1914. Studied architecture and hydraulic engineering in his home town, graduated at evening classes in advanced architecture in Amsterdam (HBO), and attended lectures part-time at the Delft Technical College. After that he worked for a few years under

J. H. van den Broek and Jacob B. Bakema. Lijnbaan pedestrian precinct. Rotterdam, 1953

Professor Cor van *Eesteren, in the *town-planning department of the City Architect's office in Amsterdam, and in the office of Van Tijen and Maaskant. Went into partnership with J. H. van den *Broek in 1948. Solely responsible for the art centre 't Venster in Rotterdam (1947) and the civic center plan for St Louis, Missouri (1955). (*Netherlands)

J. J. VRIEND

Baldessari, Luciano, b. Rovereto near Trento 1896. Graduated Milan 1922. Architect, painter, stage designer. Exhibition architecture, including the free forms of the Breda Pavilion, Milan (1951).

Bartning, Otto, b. Karlsruhe 1883, d. Darmstadt 1959. Studied at the Technical Colleges of Berlin and Karlsruhe. Industrial, administrative, domestic and hospital buildings and, in particular, Protestant churches. *Steel church on the Pressa, Cologne (1928); Church of the Resurrection, Essen, on a circular plan (1930); emergency churches of prefabricated timber construction for the German Evangelical Relief Organization (designed 1946).

Basile, Ernesto, b. Palermo 1857, d. Palermo 1932. Built shortly after the turn of the century in the Italian *Art Nouveau style (Casa Basile, 1904; Casa Frassini, 1906, both at Palermo). Later changed over to a Classic Revival style and opposed the *Functionalist architecture of the twenties.

Baudot, Anatole de, b. Saarburg 1834, d. Paris 1915. Pupil of *Labrouste and *Viollet-le-Duc. De Baudot, 'Romantic of *Reinforced Concrete', introduced the new building material to ecclesiastical architecture (St Jean-de-Montmartre, Paris, 1894–7). Besides designing buildings he carried out restorations and worked as an architectural writer.

Bauhaus. The Bauhaus was a school of design, building, and craftsmanship founded by Walter *Gropius in Weimar in 1919. It was transferred to Dessau in 1925, where it continued until 1928, and then transferred to Berlin, ultimately closing in 1933. The ideas and teaching of the Bauhaus have exercised a profound influence throughout the world.

Oskar Schlemmer. Bauhaus symbol, 1922

Before the First World War the Belgian architect Henry van de *Velde had been director of the Grossherzogliche Sächsische Kunstgewerbeschule and the Grossherzogliche Sächsische Hochschule für Bildende Kunst at Weimar, and he had recommended to the Grand Duke of Saxe-Weimar that Walter Gropius should be his successor. The Grand Duke summoned Gropius for an interview in 1915, and Gropius asked for and was given full powers to reorganize the schools; when he took up his appointment in 1919 he united the two schools under the name of Das Staatliche Bauhaus Weimar. This was of profound significance because it made clear at the outset that one of the main purposes of the new school was to unite art and craft which had for too long been divorced from each other. Gropius contended that the artist or architect should also be a craftsman, that he should have experience of working in various materials so that he knew their qualities and that he should at the same time study theories of form and design. The traditional distinction between artist and craftsman should, Gropius thought, be eliminated. He also believed that a building should be the result of collective effort, and that each artist-craftsman should contribute his part with a full awareness of its purpose in relation to the whole building. Gropius was therefore an advocate of team-work in the creation of a building and in the production of furniture,

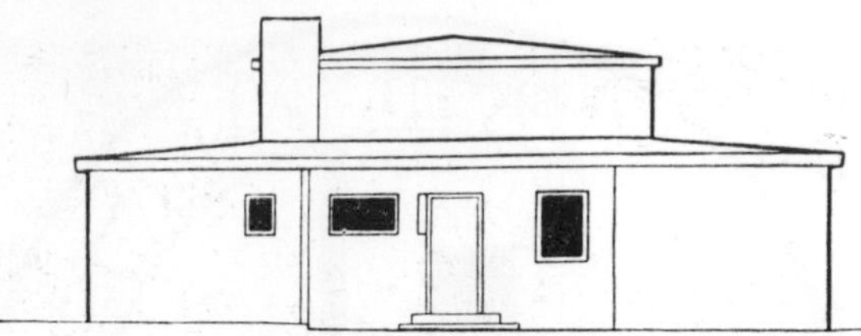

Georg Muche. Bauhaus experimental house. Weimar, 1923. Elevation and plan

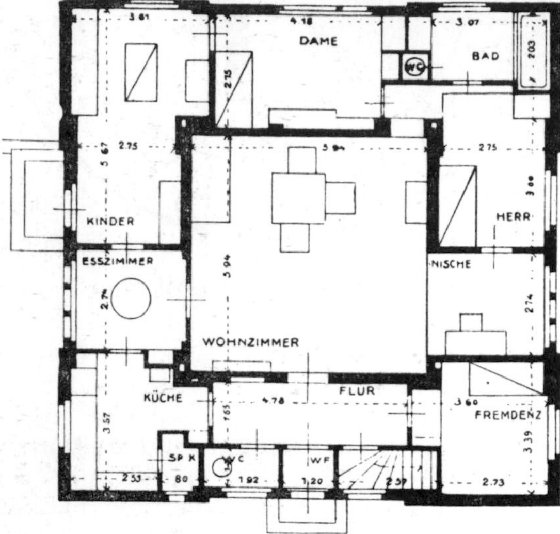

pottery, and all the various architectural arts.

The teaching thus comprehended industrial production. Gropius was not opposed, as was William *Morris, to the increasing use of machinery in the production of well-designed objects, but he believed that the machine should be made absolutely subservient to the will of the creative designer. This part of Gropius's teaching has perhaps been most difficult for many people to understand. Many critics have asked why it is necessary for students to master a craft in a material and yet acquiesce in industrial production. But Gropius regarded machinery merely as an elaboration of the hand tool of the craftsman, and thought it was necessary to know the nature of the material and all its potentialities before the tool or machine could be used to the best advantage.

There is obviously a correlation of teamwork in building and the necessary division of labour in industrial production, but the best results are likely to be obtained in both if members of the team not only master their own particular part but grasp its relation to the complete building or industrial product. By thus using the machine to the best advantage the training at the Bauhaus was directed not to works of hand craftsmanship but to the creation of type-forms which could serve as models for mass production. And in the creation of this type-form the artist himself produces the prototype, that is if it is a teapot he makes this in the clay with his own hands as the model for mass production; he is no longer merely the drawing-board designer, but the designer-craftsman.

The curriculum of training consisted of two parallel courses of instruction, one devoted to the study of materials and craft (Werklehre) and the other to the theories of form and design (Formlehre). In the early years of the school it was necessary for the student to be taught by two masters, one in each section, an artist and a craftsman, because of the difficulty at that time of finding teachers who were sufficiently masters of both. These two teachers worked in close collaboration. Instruction at the school began with a preliminary course of six months, during which period the student worked with various materials—stone, wood, metal, clay, glass, pigments, and textiles—while he received elementary instruction in the theory of form. The purpose of working and experimenting with materials was to discover with which particular material the student had naturally the most creative aptitude, for it was an essential purpose to bring out the latent creative faculties of the individual. It might be that one student had a strong feeling for wood, another for the harder materials, stone and metal, another for textiles, another for pigments and colour. He was instructed in the use of tools and later in the use of machines that in industry have supplanted these tools. In the school devoted to form and design, instruction was given in the study and representation of natural form, in geometry and principles of building construction, in composition and the theories of volume, colour, and design.

Gropius was fortunate in gathering together some very able teachers, many of whom afterwards became famous in their various spheres. Among the first was Johannes Itten, who joined the school in 1919 and whom Gropius had first met a year earlier teaching in a private school in Vienna. Gropius was impressed with Itten's methods of education and invited him to the Bauhaus to direct the preliminary course. Itten's teaching included the study of the physical character of natural materials by representation and experiment, for it was contended that representing a material intelligently was one way of appreciating its structure. And in working in a particular material the student must not only develop a feeling for it in all its aspects, but he must appreciate its relation to other materials so as to be aware of its qualities by comparison and contrast. Other teachers at the Bauhaus at Weimar were Lyonel Feininger, printer and graphic artist, and Gerhard Marcks, sculptor and potter, both of whom joined in 1919; Georg Muche, painter, weaver, and architect, joined 1920; Paul Klee (painter, graphic artist, writer) and Oskar Schlemmer (painter, stage designer), both joined 1921; Wassily Kandinsky, painter and graphic artist, who joined in 1922; and László Moholy-Nagy, painter, theatrical designer, photographer, and typographer, who joined in 1923.

In 1923, at the request of the Thuringian Legislative Assembly, the Bauhaus held an exhibition of its work which was to serve as a report on the four years of the life of the Bauhaus. Gropius felt that this was a bit premature; he would have preferred to wait until more mature results could be presented. The theme of the exhibition was 'Art and Technics, a New Unity', and included in the exhibition were designs in various materials, various products of the different workshops, examples of theoretical studies, and a one-family house called 'Am Horn' which was built and furnished by the Bauhaus workshops. This house was planned as a large square with several small rooms arranged round a central larger one; it was enthusiastically acclaimed by many critics, among them Dr E. Redslob, the National Art Director of Germany, who praised its organic unity.

In spite of the progress and success of the Bauhaus it met with much local opposition from the more conservative members of the community, while the whole enterprise was associated with Socialism in the minds of many because it happened to be established at a time when there was a Socialist régime. It also met with considerable hostility from the Thuringian Government, which more or less forced Gropius to a decision at the end of 1924 to close the school. Both teachers and students wholeheartedly supported Gropius; the Director and masters notified the Government of Thuringia on 26 December of their decision to close the institution, created by them, on the expiration of their contracts on 1 April 1925.

Walter Gropius. Bauhaus. Dessau, 1925–6

Various cities discussed the possibility of transplanting the Bauhaus, among them Frankfurt, Hagen, Mannheim, Darmstadt and Dessau. The Mayor of Dessau succeeded in securing the transfer of the Bauhaus to his town. He appropriated seven houses for the use of the school while a new building was being erected. This building, designed by Gropius in response to the request of the City Council, was begun in the autumn of 1925 and completed in December 1926. It consisted of three principal wings, a school of design occupying one, workshops another, and a students' hostel a third. The first two were linked by a bridge over a roadway, and in

Walter Gropius. Bauhaus. Dessau, 1925–6

this bridge were administrative rooms, club rooms, and a private atelier for Professor Gropius. The students' hostel was a six-storey building consisting of twenty-eight studio-dormitory rooms. The building was constructed partly of *reinforced concrete. In the workshops' wing reinforced concrete floor slabs and supporting mushroom posts were employed with the supports set well back to allow a large uninterrupted *glass screen on the façade extending for three storeys. This was probably the first time so ambitious a use of glass screen was employed in an industrial building, and it helped to lead the way to similar constructions throughout Europe and America.

With the re-establishment of the Bauhaus at Dessau, the opportunity was taken to revise the curriculum. The earlier method of joint instruction by two masters, an artist and a craftsman, was abandoned and was supplanted by that of one master who was trained as both. This was becoming increasingly possible because several former Bauhaus students were now appointed masters: Josef Albers, Herbert Bayer, Marcel *Breuer, Hinnerk Scheper, and Joost Schmidt. Seven of the masters who had been with the Bauhaus at Weimar continued at Dessau. Gerhard Marcks left because there were not sufficient funds to install his pottery workshop at Dessau. Johannes Itten had left in the spring of 1923 owing to differences of opinion on the conduct of the preliminary course, and his work was continued by Moholy-Nagy and Josef Albers, who jointly broadened its scope. In revising the course at Dessau the opportunity was also taken to reaffirm the principles which guided the Bauhaus system of education: these could be summarized as training in design, technics, and craftsmanship for all kinds of creative work, especially building; the execution of experimental work, especially building and interior decoration; the development of models or type-forms for industrial production and the sale of such models to industry. As a general doctrine the Bauhaus sought to establish the common citizenship of all forms of creative work and their interdependence on each other.

The Bauhaus continued at Dessau under the direction of Walter Gropius until early in 1928, when he resigned because he wished to devote himself more freely to his creative work without being restricted by official duties; on his recommendation Hannes *Meyer, the Swiss architect, who had been head of the department of architecture, became director. Meyer resigned in June 1930 as the result of differences with the municipal authority, who then tried to persuade Gropius to take over again. Instead, Gropius recommended the appointment of Ludwig *Mies van der Rohe, who accepted the position. In October 1932, after the National Socialist party had taken over the Government of

Anhalt, the Bauhaus moved to Berlin; in April 1933 it was closed by the National Socialists. From April 1933 the building at Dessau was used for the training of political leaders.

Although the school was closed, its teaching and methods were by no means dead, and they continued to exercise a wide influence throughout the world. Indeed, it may be said that its influence has been strongest since it ceased to exist, probably because it takes time for such ideas to spread. Many art schools in Europe and America have adopted in part its methods of teaching, especially as many of its masters and students have taken positions in art schools and institutes throughout Europe and America. For example, Moholy-Nagy became director of the New Bauhaus—now the Institute of Design—at Chicago, where Bauhaus methods were employed. They have also been introduced partially at the school of architecture at Harvard University, the Laboratory School of Industrial Design in New York, and in the Southern California School of Design. It would be a mistake to think that the ideas that prompted Bauhaus training are universally accepted, but it is doubtful whether any method of art teaching of the century has had quite the same impact.

Bibliography: Walter Gropius, *Idee und Aufbau des Staatlichen Bauhauses*, Weimar 1923; *Neue Arbeiten der Bauhauswerkstatten*, 1925 (English translation, *The New Architecture and the Bauhaus*, London 1935, reprinted 1955); Herbert Bayer, Walter Gropius, and Ise Gropius, *Bauhaus 1919–1928* (London 1939, Boston 1952); Hans Maria Wingler, *Das Bauhaus, Weimar, Dessau, Berlin*, Cologne 1962.

ARNOLD WHITTICK

BBPR. Partnership of architects Lodovico Barbiano di Belgioioso, Enrico Peressutti, Ernesto N. *Rogers, and (until his death in 1945) Gian Luigi Banfi. The team achieved international fame with its Sanatorium at Legnano (1937–8); more recent buildings such as the Torre Velasca, Milan (1957; *p.25), try to establish a poetic style by reference to tradition and local atmosphere. Housing and industrial buildings; exhibition architecture (children's maze at the Milan Triennale 1954); restoration work; interior decoration (Museum at the Castello Sforzesco, Milan, 1952–6). (*Italy)

Beaudouin, Eugène, b. Paris 1898. Student at the French Academy in Rome. In collaboration with Marcel *Lods he designed, in 1933, the Cité de la Muette at Drancy, near Paris, a mixed development estate where prefabricated reinforced concrete units were used; the Pavilion School at Suresnes (1932–5); and the Maison du Peuple at Clichy (1939). Cité Rotterdam suburb at Strasbourg (1951–3). Town and regional planning. (*France)

Beaux-Arts. *École des Beaux-Arts.

Behrens, Peter, b. Hamburg 1868, d. Berlin 1940. In a society torn between archaic mental attitudes and a blind faith in the lightning progress of technology, Behrens was one of the first architects of the 20th century to develop a form of architectural thought that would answer to the demands of an industrialized civilization. At a period when the moral and social demands put forward by the Expressionist painters of Dresden (*Die Brücke*) were leading to new directions in the graphic arts, he was in at the birth of modern architecture in Germany, where he exerted a leading influence between 1900 and 1914. Furthermore, the sidelines derived from architecture in which he engaged inaugurated (1907) a form of specialization that has become widely known in our times under the name of Industrial Design. Here, too, he deeply influenced the development of technology and style at a time when the propagation of craft-derived forms by the exponents of *Art Nouveau was threatening to undermine any attempts to formulate design principles in conformity with new ways of living.

Behrens did not discover his true vocation from the first. Like *van de Velde and *Le Corbusier, he was a painter at first, and came to architecture via the so-called applied arts. From 1886 to 1889 he attended painting classes at the art schools of Karlsruhe and Düsseldorf. In 1890 he was impressed by the work of the *luministes* (Israels) in Holland, and the work of painters such as Leibl in Munich; he was a founder-member of the Münchner Sezession in 1893. Already interested in the graphic arts, his early compositions (coloured woodcuts, frontispieces for books, etc.) are still permeated by the decorative influence of Art Nouveau.

Peter Behrens. Behrens House. Darmstadt, 1901

After travelling in Italy (1896), Behrens turned in 1898 to problems of industrial production and designed a number of prototype flasks for mass production by a large glass works; these are already notable for their plain, straightforward shapes. In 1899 the Grand Duke Ernst Ludwig invited him to stay at Darmstadt and join a group of young artists (the architect Joseph M. *Olbrich, the interior decorators P. Huber and P. Bürck, the painter H. Christiansen, and the sculptors L. Habich and R. Bosselt) who under the name of *Die Sieben* (The Seven) had as their aim the establishment of effective relationships between all the plastic arts. It was then that

Peter Behrens. AEG Turbine Factory. Berlin, 1908–9

Behrens took up architecture and, as van de Velde had done at Uccle five years before, he built his own house and fitted it out completely in a unitary style that betrayed the influence of both van de Velde and *Mackintosh. At the instance of *Muthesius, he was appointed head of the Düsseldorf School of Art in 1903, a post he held until 1907. From this period onwards his classical temperament led him to design sober, powerful and massive works, of mathematical severity and uncompromisingly functionalist in style. The houses he built for Obenauer (Saarbrücken, 1905–06), Cuno and Schroeder (Eppenhausen near Hagen, 1908–10) express this rationalistic tendency, that was ultimately to distinguish the work of Behrens from the plastic dynamism and lyricism of *Poelzig and *Mendelsohn.

In 1907, the year the Deutscher Werkbund was founded, Behrens was summoned to Berlin by the AEG (the German General Electrical Company). His duties comprised the design not only of pieces of electrical equipment (cookers, radiators, ventilators, lamps, etc.) but also of the firm's packaging, catalogues, leaflets, posters, letterheads, showrooms, shops, and, to boot, factories and workshops. The circumstance is of much importance: it marks the emergence, in the midst of industry, of a desire to humanize technology. By employing an architect to ensure a good visual appearance for their products, the AEG was bringing objects into daily life that were not only functionally efficient, but were harmoniously and sensitively designed as well, permeated as they were by an authentically creative style which, in the last analysis, projected the brand image of an industrial power. At the same time, and under the same auspices, Behrens introduced a new expression of monumentality to European architecture with his turbine factory for the AEG (Berlin, 1908–9)—the first German building in glass and steel—the high tension plant (1910) and the factory for small motors (1910–11), etc. Behrens also built a complete district of flats for AEG workers at Hennigsdorf, near Berlin (1910–11). Apart from numerous factories which he erected throughout his career, mention should be made of certain other

Page 49. Peter Behrens. Entrance hall of the Hoechst Dyeworks offices. 1920–5

Peter Behrens. Offices of the Hoechst Dyeworks, 1920–5

major works of his, designed in a neoclassic style that expressed their owners' need for prestige. These include the Mannesmann offices at Düsseldorf (1911–12), those for the Continental Rubber Company at Hanover (1913–20), and the German Embassy in St Petersburg (1911–12).

In 1922 Behrens was appointed director of the School of Architecture at the Vienna Academy; some of the buildings he designed in the following years may be considered as examples of German *Expressionism (Hoechst Dyeworks, 1920–5). In 1936 he became head of the department of architecture at the Prussian Academy of Arts, Berlin. His most outstanding pupils are: Le Corbusier, who worked in his Berlin office from 1910 to 1911; Gropius, from 1907 to 1910; and Mies van der Rohe, from 1908 to 1911.

Bibliography: Peter Behrens, *Feste des Lebens und der Kunst*, Jena 1900; Fritz Hoeber, *Peter Behrens*, Munich 1913; Paul Joseph Cremers, *Peter Behrens, Sein Werk von 1909 bis zur Gegenwart*, Essen 1928; K. M. Grimme, *Peter Behrens und seine Wiener akademische Meisterschule*, Vienna 1930

ROBERT L. DELEVOY

Belluschi, Pietro, b. Ancona 1899. From 1927 chief designer in an architect's office at Portland, Oregon; since 1943 has intermittently run an office of his own. Now mainly a consultant and designer in collaboration with other architects. Residential and office buildings, shopping centres, ecclesiastical buildings. Equitable Savings Building at Portland, Oregon (1948), in which all façade units together with the aluminium-clad stanchions are arranged flush with the wall plane. (*Curtain Wall)

Berg, Max, b. Stettin 1870. Studied at Technical College, Berlin-Charlottenburg. City Architect, Breslau (1912–13). His Centenary Hall at Breslau, a huge cupola with exposed ribs, was one of the boldest *reinforced concrete structures of its time. Exhibition Hall Messehof (1925) and hydroelectric station at Breslau. (*Germany)

Berlage, Hendrik Petrus, b. Amsterdam 1856, d. The Hague 1934. Berlage studied at Zurich, and had his own practice in Amsterdam from 1889 onwards; he is regarded as one of the great innovators of architecture around the year 1900. Reacting against 19th-century eclecticism, he aimed at an 'honest awareness of the problems of architecture' and a craftsmanlike approach to materials and construction. Berlage revealed once more to his contemporaries the meaning and magic of brickwork. Plastering a wall was tantamount to falsification in his eyes, and he eschewed its use even in the rooms of private houses. Berlage's 'moral' outlook was in harmony with the social climate of the times, which since *c.* 1895 was strongly influenced by the rising labour movement.

Despite his rejection of all historic styles, Berlage felt attracted by the massive gravity of the Romanesque, which is reflected in his semicircular arches and his large unbroken wall surfaces. These features also recall the work of the American architect H. H. *Richardson, which probably influenced him during his trip to America. Characteristic works of his include the Diamond-workers' House, Amsterdam (1899–1900), Holland House, London (1914), and above all Amsterdam Stock Exchange, completed in 1903. The Stock Exchange was the outcome of a competition held in 1897, which Berlage won with a design he subsequently altered in many details. In this monumental work, Berlage used a light-coloured stone for special features, in addition to brick. The steel roof structure over the main hall is left exposed. There is a certain aridity of conception here which cannot be overlooked; it appears also in Berlage's earliest designs for furniture.

As an architectural writer, Berlage exerted great influence through his numerous publications and lectures. Many buildings, especially in the *Netherlands, are based on Berlage's work, even though they differ formally from it. He himself, in his later years came under the influence of the young *Expressionist architects. In 1928 he attended the first congress of *CIAM at La Sarraz, but felt himself too committed to a more traditional conception of architecture to be able to join the CIAM.

Bibliography: Hendrik Petrus Berlage, *Gedanken über den Stil in der Baukunst*, Leipzig 1905; Hendrik Petrus Berlage, *Grundlagen und Entwicklung der Architektur*, Berlin 1908; Hendrik Petrus Berlage, *Studies over Bouwkunst, Stijl en Samenleving*, Rotterdam 1910; Jan Gratama, *Dr. H. P. Berlage Bouwmeester*, Rotterdam 1925.

J. J. VRIEND

Hendrik Petrus Berlage. Stock Exchange. Amsterdam, 1897–1903

Bill, Max, b. Winterthur 1908. Painter, sculptor, exhibition designer, architect. Studied at Zurich Art School and (1927–9) at the *Bauhaus. From 1951 to 1956 rector of the Hochschule für Gestaltung at Ulm and head of the departments of architecture and industrial design. Private houses, offices. The buildings of the Ulm Hochschule (1953–5) embody a complex scheme in an open, easily graspable layout, which harmonizes well with its setting. (*Switzerland)

Bibliography: Tomás Maldonado, *Max Bill*, Stuttgart 1956; Margit Staber, 'Max Bill und die Umweltgestaltung', in *Zodiac 9*, Milan 1962.

Hendrik Petrus Berlage. Stock Exchange. Amsterdam, 1897–1903

Bogardus, James, b. Catskill, New York 1800, d. New York 1874. Manufacturer and inventor, who built multi-storeyed factory buildings in the mid-19th century, where the outer walls were assembled from cast-iron units (his own factory in New York, 1848–9; Harper and Brothers Building, New York, 1854). The publicity Bogardus gave his buildings resulted in the widespread adoption of cast-iron façades, which paved the way for steel-frame structures (*Steel).

Böhm, Dominikus, b. Jettingen, Bavaria 1880, d. Cologne 1955. Studied at Stuttgart Technical College under Theodor *Fischer. Catholic ecclesiastical buildings

Rino Levi. Art Palacio Cinema. São Paulo, 1936

(e.g. Church at Mainz-Bischoffsheim, 1926; St Engelbert at Cologne-Riehl, 1930; St Maria Königin at Cologne-Marienburg, 1954).
Bibliography: August Hoff and H. Muck, *Böhm, Leben und Werk*, Munich and Zurich 1962.

Bonatz, Paul, b. Solgne, Lorraine 1877, d. Berlin 1951. Pupil and successor of Theodor *Fischer at Stuttgart Technical College. Main station at Stuttgart (1913–27, with F. E. Scholer). Cultural, commercial, and industrial buildings. (*Expressionism)

Bourgeois, Victor, b. Charleroi 1897, d. Brussels 1962; 1914–19 student at the Académie Royale des Beaux-Arts, Brussels. His conception of architecture as the mirror of society led him early in his career to the problem of municipal housing. The Cité Moderne at Berchem-Ste-Agathe near Brussels (1922–5) seeks to relieve the monotonous character of the estate by varying the articulation of terraced housing and by the use of open squares and courtyards and lively façade elements. Social buildings, schools, estates, town planning. Professor at the École Nationale Supérieure d'Architecture.
Bibliography: Georges Linze, *Victor Bourgeois*, Brussels 1961.

Attilio Correia Lima. Santos Dumont de Hidros Airport. Rio de Janeiro, 1938

Brazil. When in 1943 the Museum of Modern Art of New York presented its exhibition on old and new architecture in Brazil, the world was suddenly made aware that in a faraway country the International Architecture of the 1920s had blossomed into a tropical version. Characterized by its daring formal expression, its lyrical content, and its regional connotations, it also had strong spiritual links with the colonial past of the country. As a matter of fact, it had sprung up in the wake of two rebel movements, the Modern Art Week in São Paulo, 1922, and the Regionalist movement in Recife, 1926, led by Gilberto Freyre, which aimed at giving new shape to Brazilian intellectual and artistic life, not only by bringing it up to a truly contemporary outlook, rooted in the most genuine sources of Brazilian life, but also by attempting to destroy the alien influences which had dominated the country since the arrival in 1806 of the King of Portugal, D. João VI, when he fled the Napoleonic invasion and transferred his court to Rio de Janeiro. In 1816 D. João VI invited a French mission of painters, sculptors, and architects to 'civilize' the country, with the result that the organic development of a local architecture, brought about throughout the colonial period by an ecological assimilation of the Portuguese Baroque style, was disrupted, and all kinds of foreign pseudo-styles were introduced, turning the 19th century into an uncharacteristic interval, chiefly taken up by copies of whatever might be done abroad—not only in architecture but in all the arts.

Page 53. Lúcio Costa, Oscar Niemeyer, Jorge Machado Moreira, Affonso Eduardo Reidy, Ernani Vasconcellos and Carlos Leão; consultant architect, Le Corbusier. Ministry of Education. Rio de Janeiro, 1937–43

Jorge Machado Moreira. House for Antonio Ceppa. Rio de Janeiro, 1958

A few years before these two movements, scientific studies of the effect of sunlight on buildings had been started by Alexandre Albuquerque, who in 1916 succeeded in incorporating into the Building Code of the city of São Paulo precise requirements as to the minimum provision of sunlight in a new building. There existed thus in the 1920s not only an intellectual atmosphere receptive to the new ideas in architecture but also a sound regional approach to the basic problem of the exposure of buildings, both in order to assure a minimum of sunlight and also to control its excess. In 1927 in São Paulo, G. *Warchavchik, a newcomer from Russia, presented his first cube-like houses to the public, and was later joined in partnership by Lúcio *Costa. When the Revolution of 1930, led by Getulio Vargas, upset all the conventional political and cultural values of the country and launched a programme of important new public works, the younger architects were in a way prepared for the decisive, if paradoxical, episode of the new building for the Ministry of Education and Health. A competition was held for the design of this building, and all the modern projects were disqualified by a conservative jury. But the Minister of Education, Gustavo Capenema, who was surrounded by a group of far-seeing collaborators, had the daring, after paying the prizes awarded by the jury, to invite Lúcio Costa, one of the disqualified competitors, to design the final project. Lúcio Costa insisted on a team of all the other rejected candidates being formed, and this was done. Lúcio Costa, Oscar *Niemeyer, Jorge Machado Moreira, Affonso Eduardo *Reidy, Ernani Vasconcellos, and Carlos Leão were thus responsible for the development of the final design. In 1936, *Le Corbusier was invited as a consultant on this project, as well as on one for the new University City. He stayed in Brazil only three weeks, working with the group and giving a few public lectures, but during this short stay the turning-point was reached and modern architecture was irrevocably established. Le Corbusier's main ideas fell on fertile ground. The concept of *pilotis* was especially good for the Brazilian climate, the *brise-soleil* were in many cases an absolute necessity, and his basically lyrical formal approach was thoroughly suited to the Brazilian spirit. A local version of International Architecture thus emerged. Prior to this, Warchavchik's houses, from 1928 on, and Rino Levi's outstandingly direct Art Palacio Cinema in São Paulo (1936) must of course be mentioned.

In the years that followed, i.e. from 1937 to 1943, an impressive number of distinguished jobs show how quickly maturity was achieved. They include: Oscar Niemeyer's Day Nursery in Rio (1937), his Ouro Preto Hotel (1940), his Casino, Yacht Club and Dance Hall (1943), and the São Francisco Chapel (1944) at Pampúlha; Luiz Nunes's (with Fernando Saturnio de Brito) Water Tower at Olinda (1937); Attilio Correia Lima's Santos Dumont de Hidros Airport in Rio (1938), with Jorge Ferreira, Thomaz Estrella, Renato Mesquita dos Santos and Renato Soeiro; Lúcio Costa's and Oscar Niemeyer's (with Paul Lester Wiener) Brazilian Pavilion at the New York World's Fair (1939); Marcelo and Milton Roberto's ABI—the Brazilian Press Association Building (1938), the Instituto de Resseguros Building (1942), and the Santos Dumont Airport Building (1944), all in Rio; Alvaro Vital Brasil's Edificio Esther apartment building (with Adhemar Marin-

Henrique E. Mindlin. Avenida Central Building. Rio de Janeiro, 1961

ho) in São Paulo (1938) and his Vital Brasil Institute, in Niteroi (1941); Olavo Redig de Campos's Social Centre in Rio (1942); Firmino Saldanha's Mississippi (1938) and Mossoró (1940) apartment buildings in Rio, not to mention the Ministry of Education and Health itself, started in 1937 and finished in 1943. All these are landmarks which have already endured the test of time.

After the war years the country entered into a phase of fast industrialization which helped to raise the level of construction, also of tremendous real estate speculation, which of course resulted in a number of second-rate jobs. However, the initial impulse persisted and today a large number of good buildings may be credited to the movement. To the architects whose work has become better known abroad belong Paulo Antunes Ribeiro, João Vilanova Artigas, Sergio Bernardes, Francisco Bolonha, Oswaldo Bratke, Icaro Castro Mello, Ary Garcia Roza, Henrique E. Mindlin, and Giancarlo Palanti. The most important events in the history of Brazilian architecture since 1950 are Oscar Niemeyer's Ibirapuéra Exhibition Pavilions in São Paulo (1953); in Rio, Lúcio Costa's Parque Guinle apartment buildings (1948–50–54); Affonso Eduardo Reidy's Pedregulho Housing Estate and his Museum of Modern Art in Rio de Janeiro (1954 –); Jorge Machado Moreira's University City (1953–), as well as, of course, Niemeyer's superb buildings in Brasilia.

In spite of obvious individual differences, there is in most Brazilian work a deliberate formal research, an attempt at lightness and airiness and, in many cases, a transliteration into contemporary terms of old elements from the colonial past (such as open ceramic tile work, various forms of 'jalousies', or the renewed use of ceramic murals in tiles, i.e. *azulejos*, or in mosaic) which give it a common character. There is in general, however, much less use of colour in the exterior than might be expected by the foreign visitor. It is

Oscar Niemeyer, Zenon Lotufo, Helio Uchôa and Eduardo Kneese de Mello. Palace of Industry, Ibirapuéra Park. São Paulo, 1951–4

Affonso Eduardo Reidy. Museum of Modern Art. Rio de Janeiro, commenced 1954

Oscar Niemeyer. President's Palace. Brasilia, completed 1959

probably felt that the brilliance of the sky and of the sunlight, as well as the gorgeous landscape, need no further reinforcement. A great deal of the colour which serves to emphasize the best architectural jobs is due to the surrounding gardens, in connection with which the immense contribution of Roberto Burle Marx must be stressed. The rôle played by Brazilian painters, starting with Candido Portinari's murals and *azulejo* designs for the Ministry of Education must also be noted.

Modern architecture in Brazil has had a paradoxical development, leading it to the summits of creative achievement almost from the start, a result perhaps of the fact that it was handed down and imposed from above by an intellectual *élite* under exceptionally fortunate circumstances. Monumental buildings were put up before any real attempt had been made at solving the urgent problems of providing schools or hospitals or low-cost housing. Until recent times city planning and interior decoration were neglected in favour of more spectacular undertakings. Architects were satisfied with traditional Brazilian furniture or the best that could be brought from Europe, contemporary if possible.

The most striking example of this peculiar development is the dramatic creation by President Juscelino Kubitschek of Brasilia, the new capital for the country, about 1,000 kilometres from the Atlantic coast, in a hitherto virgin territory. Located on gently sloping highlands, half surrounded by a huge artificial lake, this new city, planned for 600,000 inhabitants, was formally inaugurated as the new seat of the Federal Government on 21 April 1960, only three years, one month, and five days after an international jury had selected Lúcio Costa's deceptively simple plan in an open competition among Brazilian architects. In a general outline reminiscent of an aeroplane, the wings are devoted to the super blocks of apartment dwellings; the main axis, along what would correspond to the body of the plane, to the monumental distribution of the Ministries and the Plaza of the Three Powers (Presidential Palace, Supreme Court, and Congress), with the business and entertainment districts round the intersection, which is emphasized by the bus depot, arranged on several levels. Thoroughly planned with deep human concern, yet deliberately aiming at a clear symbolic expression of the city's unique function, Brasilia has carried to the man-in-the-street the concept of planning to an unsurpassed degree, especially through the total elimination of traffic intersections, one of the aspects of planning most easily grasped by the general public.

The unity and integrated character of Brasilia derive not only from Costa's lucid plan but also from Oscar Niemeyer's striking design for most of the buildings carried out to date. There can be no question that the building of Brasilia, in very difficult economic and financial circumstances and involving considerable sacrifices for the country as a whole, constitutes a magnificently constructive statement of the collective will of the people.

Bibliography: Philip L. Goodwin, *Brazil Builds*, Museum of Modern Art, New York 1943; Henry-Russell Hitchcock, *Latin American Architecture since 1945*, New York 1955; Henrique E. Mindlin, *Modern Architecture in Brazil*, Colibris, Amsterdam 1956.

HENRIQUE E. MINDLIN

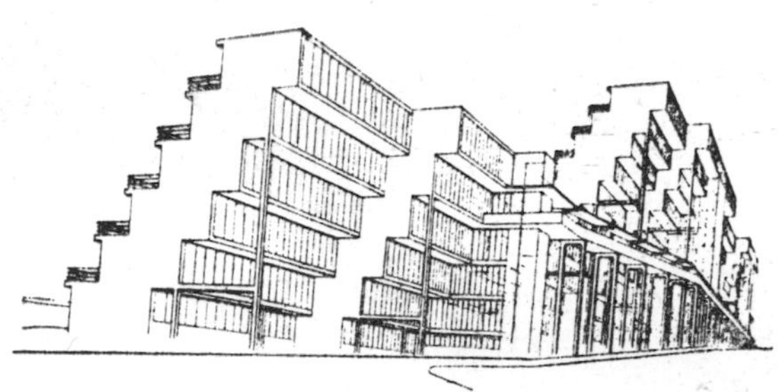

Marcel Breuer. Elberfeld Hospital, 1928. Project

Breuer, Marcel, b. Pecs, Hungary 1902. In 1920 Breuer moved to Vienna, intending to become a painter and sculptor. After a brief attendance at the Art Academy he became disillusioned with its 'tired eclecticism' and looked around for a practical apprenticeship in one of the crafts, which would bring him into direct contact with tools and materials. Before long, he heard of Walter *Gropius's *Bauhaus, then located in Weimar; and, late in 1920, he left Vienna for Weimar and became one of the youngest members of the first generation of Bauhaus students. Under the influence of Breuer and others then at the Bauhaus, the emphasis of the school began to shift from 'arts and crafts' to 'art and technology'—or from romanticism and impressionism to rationalism and objectivity in design. Breuer's principal interest, from the start, was in the area of furniture design, and by 1924, at the age of twenty-two, he took over the direction of the Bauhaus's furniture department. Before long his preoccupation with standardized, modular unit furniture led him to interior design and standardized, modular unit housing—and, thus, to architecture.

Breuer's most notable contribution to contemporary design in the 1920s was in the field of furniture, for he had invented, as early as 1925, a series of systems that employed continuously bent steel tubes (painted or chromium-plated) to form the structural frames of stools, chairs, and tables. Indeed, between 1925 and 1928 Breuer literally designed almost every single piece of modern, tubular steel furniture in use today all over the world. Among his finest designs was the S-shaped cantilever chair of 1928, which remains the most commonly used modern commercial chair in the world today. Much of this important experimental work in furniture design was made possible by the move, in 1925, of the

Marcel Breuer, Alfred and Emil Roth. Doldertal apartments. Zurich, 1935–6

Marcel Breuer. Breuer House. New Canaan, Conn., 1947

Marcel Breuer. Gymnasium, Litchfield High School. Litchfield, Conn., 1954–6

Bauhaus to Dessau, and the construction of the new Bauhaus by Gropius. Breuer was commissioned to design all the furniture needed in the new buildings, and this commission provided an important stimulus to his work in this field. In later years—especially in Switzerland and in England—Breuer again advanced the art of furniture design by developing some of the first bent and moulded plywood chairs ever manufactured in quantity, as well as some of the first chairs using aluminium as a structural supporting frame.

Meanwhile his interest in architecture had grown, and he left the Bauhaus in 1928 to practise as an architect and interior designer in Berlin. During the next half-dozen years Breuer built several houses and apartments easily as radical as—and often more practical than—the contemporary work of the time by *Le Corbusier and others. Moreover, he entered a number of competitions and otherwise prepared theoretical projects for cities, theatres, factories, etc., that greatly influenced his contemporaries. With the advent of Hitler in 1933, Breuer made preparations to leave Germany and soon entered into partnership with F. R. S. *Yorke in London. The partnership lasted until 1937, when Walter Gropius, who had been appointed Chairman of the Department of Architecture at Harvard, asked Breuer to join him on that faculty. At the same time, Gropius and Breuer formed an architectural partnership in Cambridge, Massachusetts. This partnership lasted until 1941.

While it is difficult, if not impossible, to separate the individual contributions of Gropius and Breuer both to the teaching at Harvard and to the houses designed in their office, it is fair to say that Breuer's contact with individual Harvard students was especially close (he was closer to them in age, and he tended to be extremely practical in his approaches to design problems); and it is fair, also, to say that much of Breuer's attention to detail is evident in the work completed by the Gropius and Breuer partnership. In any event, both Breuer's teaching and Breuer's completed buildings left a profound impression on a new generation of American architects. Among his students, for example, were such men as Philip *Johnson, Paul *Rudolph, John *Johansen, Edward L. Barnes, Landis Gores, and Willo von Moltke—all of them prominent in American architecture and planning today.

In 1946 Breuer moved to New York City, and he has practised there ever since. For the first few years of that practice, Breuer's work was limited largely to houses and smaller, institutional buildings; but in 1952 he was selected to be one of the three architects for the new Headquarters for UNESCO, in Paris. (The other two were the Italian Pier Luigi *Nervi, and the Frenchman Bernard H. *Zehrfuss.) From that moment on, Breuer's work became increasingly important internationally, and larger in scale: his UNESCO Headquarters were completed in 1958; a monastery in Minnesota was under construction at the same time; college buildings all over the

Page 59. Marcel Breuer. St John's Abbey Church. Collegeville, Minnesota, 1953–61

US, large urban projects in South America and in Asia, factories and office buildings in Europe and the US all came his way. At long last he had arrived.

In a sense, Breuer is the last of the true functionalists. In the early 1920s he was greatly influenced by the spirit of the *Constructivist movement, both in Russia and in Western Europe. All his designs were highly articulated: a Breuer chair would express every element separately, both in form and in material; a Breuer house would express different areas of activity in different and separate forms (his H-plans for houses, which separate the day-time areas from the night-time areas, are especially well known); in his construction details, every element of the structure was always clearly defined and separately articulated; and even in his large buildings, such as the UNESCO Headquarters, there was always a clear distinction and separation of functionally different elements—whether different kinds of buildings or different parts of the same building. The resulting clarity in his work has done much to keep modern architecture from becoming eclectic and formalistic. Although some of Breuer's separately articulated elements tended to be poetic rather than purely practical, they always did describe, very literally, what was happening in plan, structure, or building equipment. Still, this clarity of organization has certain drawbacks, for it is often difficult to create a coherent architectural grouping if each part of the group is given separate and equal importance. For this reason, some of the larger projects Breuer undertook in the years after 1952 have consisted of buildings which were individually impressive but failed to add up to truly significant architectural groupings. The UNESCO Headquarters, for example, consists of several separate structures, each of which is highly successful in itself; but as a group these separate structures do not, at present, form a successful architectural unity.

It is too early to evaluate Breuer's work in its entirety, but it is possible to evaluate his influence upon his contemporaries and upon younger generations of architects. Because of the great clarity of his structures and the great clarity of organization of his plans, he has become an enormously successful teacher, for in his work all the fundamentals of modern architecture are clearly distinguishable and presented with imagination and with art.

Bibliography: Peter Blake, *Marcel Breuer, Architect and Designer*, New York 1949; Marcel Breuer, *Sun and Shadow, the Philosophy of an Architect*, New York 1956; *Marcel Breuer, 1921–1962*, Stuttgart 1962; *Marcel Breuer: 1921–1961, Buildings and Projects*, ed. Cranston Jones, London 1962.

PETER BLAKE

Brinkman, Johannes Andreas, b. Rotterdam 1902, d. 1949. From 1925 in partnership with L. C. van der *Vlugt. The Van Nelle tobacco factory in Rotterdam (1928–30), to whose design Mart Stam also contributed, is, with its transparent structure, one of the most important industrial buildings of the twenties. The slab-shaped Bergpolder point block in Rotterdam was built in 1933–4 (Brinkman, van der Vlugt and W. van Tijen), an early prototype of buildings on stilts. Partnership with J. H. van den *Broek (1937). (*Netherlands)

Broek, J. H. van den, b. Rotterdam 1898. The names of J. H. van den Broek and Jacob B. *Bakema are inseparably connected with post-war building in the *Netherlands, and the reconstruction of Rotterdam in particular. Van den Broek is a professor at Delft Technical College, where he himself graduated in 1924. He started his own practice in 1927 at Rotterdam, entering into partnership with J. A. *Brinkman in 1937 and J. B. Bakema in 1948.

Architecture and social outlook are closely linked in the work of van den Broek and Bakema. The Lijnbaan shopping centre in Rotterdam (1953), a systematically laid-out pedestrian street with low-built shops, was a distinctive contribution to current *town-planning practice. The civic centre at Marl (under construction) gives a modern interpretation to the old idea of a citadel, while providing a comprehensive centre for a rising industrial town. A considerable proportion of the two architects' practice is taken up with housing and schools (school buildings at Brielle, 1948–57; Montessori Lyceum, Rotterdam, 1958).

Van den Broek and Bakema have carried out other projects also, in which Bakema's description of architecture as the three-dimensional expression of human activity has been realized. These include exhibition buildings (Dutch pavilions at the International Expositions at Paris, 1937, and Brussels, 1958), offices (Van Ommeren, Antwerp, 1939; N. B. ten Cate, Almelo, 1954), department stores (Wassen van Vorst, 1951; Galeries Modernes, 1956, both in Rotterdam), and industrial layouts, laboratories, and research buildings for the Technical High School at Delft. The two churches at Schiedam (1957) and Nagele, in the Nordostpolder (1959) are severely rectilinear buildings which achieve their effects through the interplay of large glazed areas and plane surfaces.

Bibliography: J. H. van den Broek, *Creative krachten in de architectonische conceptie*, Delft 1948; Jürgen Joedicke, *Architektur und Städtebau, Das Werk der Architekten van den Broek und Bakema*, Stuttgart, in preparation.

J. J. VRIEND

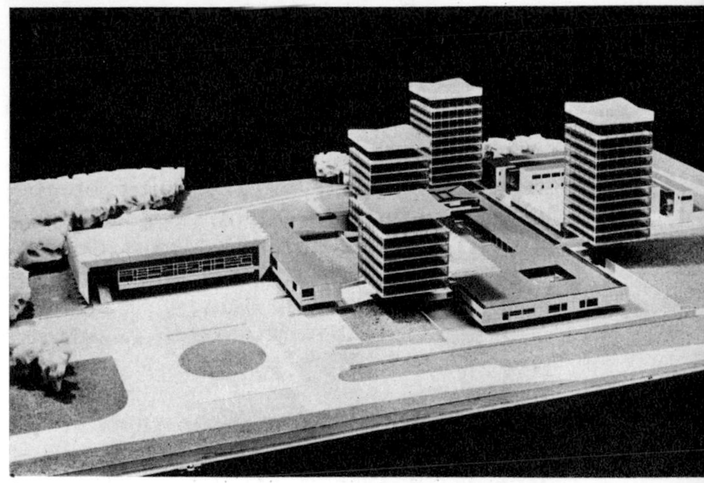

J. H. van den Broek and Jacob B. Bakema. Town Hall Complex. Marl, under construction. Model

Brutalism. Brutalism gave conscious form to a mood that was widespread among younger architects in the 1950s, but in spite of the fact that it expressed a sentiment that was felt in most parts of the Westernized world its origins can be pinpointed in space and time with some precision. Although Giedion is wrong in his etymology ('Brute + Alison') he is right in identifying the Smithson family as the source of the word—either Alison *Smithson or the Smithson's family friend Guy Oddie (who used to call Peter Smithson 'Brutus') was the first person to utter the phrase *The New Brutalism*, some time in the early summer of 1954.

This much being established, what was the intended content of the phrase? The basis was a mood of frustration brought on partly by the difficulties of building in Britain after the Second World War, and partly by disgust at the smugness of the compromising elders who were still able to build because they were well placed with the 'Establishment'. The stylistic preferences of these elders were known as 'The New Humanism' by the political Left, 'The New Empiricism' by the political Right. 'The New Brutalism' as a phrase was intended as a mockery of both, but it also drew attention to certain real qualities in the architecture that was being admired or designed by the Smithsons and their generation.

They set as their standard the uncompromising ruthlessness of *Mies van der Rohe and *Le Corbusier, their intellectual clarity, their honest presentation of structure and materials. At the same time, they sensed in the work of these masters a continuing tradition, an architecture that lay above and beyond styles and fashions—among the work of the past they admired the clarity and formality of Palladio, the heroic scale of the Anglo-Baroque architects Vanbrugh and Hawksmoor, and the clear-cut and massive forms of early 19th-century engineering structures.

J. H. van den Broek and Jacob B. Bakema. Church of the Resurrection. Schiedam, 1957

But the architecture that emerged from these admirations was, in the beginning, purely Miesian. No doubt a streak of English puritanism accounts for this initial selection of a simple, elegant structural system, for it was allied to an absolute horror of any pretence or concealment; not only were structure and materials honestly expressed, but services as well. In the school at Hunstanton, England, the first true Brutalist building, not only are steel and brick expressed with an honesty that goes even beyond the acceptable subterfuges of Mies, but pipe runs, electrical conduits, and other services are exposed to view. The austerity of this design was so remarkable that it attracted world-wide attention, and international comparisons were sought. Of these, Louis *Kahn's Art Centre at Yale University was in some ways more convincing than Mies's own work, because Kahn seemed equally preoccupied with the raw nature of the materials and concerned with the expression of the services.

By the time that this was happening, however, the original puritanical extremism of the English Brutalists was beginning to merge with an international movement of different origins and only remotely comparable aims. This movement could be characterized by developments as diverse as the a-formal painting of Jackson Pollock and the a-formal planning of the Chapel at Ronchamp, the *art brut* of Dubuffet and the *béton brut* of the *Unité* at Marseilles. The Brutalism of the uncompromising exhibition of materials became allied to a Brutalism of form; the expressed symmetry of the Hunstanton School and the concealed symmetry of the Yale Art Centre were abandoned in favour of a ruthless honesty in expressing the functional spaces and their inter-relationships. Even that adaptable rectangular geometry, derived from abstract painting, that the older functionalists had been able to accept, was now cast aside, in favour of modes of composition based on the topography of the site and the topology of internal circulation—as may be seen very clearly in the siting and planning of Park Hill, Sheffield, designed in the city architect's office by the newly graduated Jack Lynn and Ivor Smith.

Jack Lynn and Ivor Smith. Park Hill Housing Estate. Sheffield, 1955–61

Le Corbusier. Unité d'Habitation. Marseilles, 1947–52. Detail of piers at ground floor level

Once the Brutalism of a building such as Park Hill is understood it becomes clear that the application of the term to such fashionably sentimental architecture as that of Leonardo Ricci is improper, as is any attempt to make 'Brutalists' out of—say—Juan *O'Gorman or Paolo *Soleri. Brutalism implies some sort of attempt to make manifest the moral imperatives that were built into the tradition of modern architecture by the pioneers of the 19th century, and the use of shutter-patterned concrete or exposed steel-work is only a symptom of this intention—as Peter Smithson has said, 'We also admire the nature of gold paint, where it is necessary.' The fundamental aim of Brutalism at all times has been to find a structural, spatial, organizational and material concept that is 'necessary' in this metaphysical sense to some particular building, and then express it with complete honesty in a form that will be a unique and memorable image. In the creation of this definitive image the other plastic arts provide, not an aesthetic, but an exemplar of method or a standard of comparison—thus, the admirations of the Brutalists have covered subjects as diverse as US car-styling and the Ise shrines in Japan. Neither have had any visible influence on Brutalist architecture, but both are examples of images created out of the kind of necessary conditions the Brutalists believe to be fundamental, also, to the conception of buildings today. It is this insistence on the primacy of the given and necessary factors in the conception of a building that has caused Sir John Summerson to compare the beliefs of the Brutalists to the Rigorism of Lodoli and other radical theorists of late 18th-century Italian Illuminism.

On this ground, the only Brutalist building in Italy is the Istituto Marchiondi by Vittoriano Viganò, even though at first sight its departures from the common practices of the modern movement appear less extreme than those of the neo-Libertarian sentimentalists. Stylistically, the

Alison and Peter Smithson. Hunstanton School. Norfolk, 1954

Alison and Peter Smithson. Economist Building. London, under construction. Model

Vittoriano Viganò. Istituto Marchiondi. Milan, 1957

Istituto Marchiondi consciously echoes the ideas, if not the work, of Giuseppe *Terragni and the period of *l'architettura razionalista*, which provide an image that is entirely expressive of the stern, reformative necessities that underlie the conception of this building.

Nevertheless the Istituto Marchiondi draws attention to the relationship of Brutalism to the traditions of architecture. For all its aggressive tone and uncompromising attitudes, Brutalism does not represent a radical departure from the traditional conception of architecture—it is in no way comparable to the technological extremism of Buckminster *Fuller, nor even to the methods of radical functional analysis developed in England by the Nuffield Trust. The most instructive comparisons to be made on this subject are with action-painting and *musique-concrète*. Action-painting abandoned the last vestiges of formal composition but still accepted such 'outworn' traditions as paint, canvas, and a rectangular format for the picture, all of which had been previously rejected at various times by modern painters; *musique-concrète* abandoned the polite fictions of the sounds made by artificial musical instruments in favour of recordings of 'real noises', but it abandoned very little else of what had been left of the traditions of music by earlier modernist composers. Similarly the Brutalists, while abandoning fictitious surface for the 'reality' of steel and concrete and the concept of formal composition as necessary to the art of architecture, have still practised and theorized within the basic traditions of architecture.

To make another comparison between the Brutalists and one of the architects whom they admire, without now imitating his forms: the Smithsons's project for the Economist Building in London has the three component buildings informally grouped around an irregular piazza, whereas the Seagram Building in New York is a single classicist slab, axially sited behind a formal forecourt. The irregular Economist piazza gives a truer image of the organizational and topological necessities of that particular functional programme than an imitation of the Seagram composition would have done, and yet this project accepts the siting of the main built volumes on a pedestrian platform from which vehicles are banished, as does the Seagram, rather than providing some radical solution of the relationship between building, pedestrians and wheeled traffic.

Brutalism, then, is a tough-minded reforming movement within the framework of modern architectural thought, not a revolutionary attempt to overthrow it. On the other hand, the implicit intention of the Brutalists to return to fundamental functionalist principles in order to make them fulfil their apparent promise may involve the refusal of so many marginal compromises that an effective revolution may unintentionally result.

REYNER BANHAM

Bryggman, Erik William, b. Turku 1891, d. Turku 1955. Bryggman studied at the Design School of the Turku Art Society from 1906 to 1909, and later at Helsinki Polytechnic, where he graduated in architecture in 1916. Directly afterwards he began his professional career with a series of important works in collaboration: the Helsinki War Memorial, with the sculptor Ilkka; the Monument to Liberty at Oulu, with the sculptor Sakselin; and the restoration of the medieval Cathedral at Turku, carried out from 1921 to 1923. In the same year Bryggman opened his own office in the old capital, where he always lived, and where he was joined a few years later by Aino and Alvar *Aalto. The Aaltos's propinquity and collaboration with Bryggman did not last long, however, as the former afterwards moved on to Helsinki, but it came during the most critical period in the development of their architectural thought and resulted in a unique work of collaboration, of great importance in the history of Finnish architecture: the Seven Hundredth Anniversary Exhibition of the City of Turku, which took place in 1929 and is considered to be the first example of modern architecture in Scandinavia.

Bryggman, who was seven years older than Aalto, had carried out a good many works before the Turku Exhibition; they mark the most important stages in that process leading to *Functionalism which was silently developing in the architecture of the young nation. Amongst them may be noted a block of flats for employees of the Finnish Sugar Company at Turku (1923–4), some houses in Turku and elsewhere, and two hotels in Turku: the Seurahuone, with very sophisticated décor (1928), and the Hospitz Hotel (1927–9). His finest work was carried out, however, between 1930 and 1940, starting with Parainen Cemetery Chapel, the Kinopalatsi Cinema at Turku, and the Finnish Pavilion at the Antwerp International Exhibition, all dating from 1930. Next came a series of delightful white country houses, set like crystals amid the virgin nature of the islands in the archipelago: those at Ruissalo and Hirvenssalo (1933); the Villa Kaino at Kaskerta (1935); the Villa Jaatinen (1939); and Vierumäki Sports Club, another work in a purely rationalist style (1930–6). Finally, in this period, we may mention the Library of Turku Academy (1935), and the cemetery chapel in the same city, built between 1938 and 1941. The book tower of the Academy rises in a district of the old city, over which the dark mass of the Cathedral looms in the distance. It is remarkable for the balance of its voids in the large white walls, and for the perfect way it fits in with its surroundings, via a subtle handling of proportions and a complete understanding of the *genius loci*. Turku Cemetery Chapel is Bryggman's best known work, and it is undoubtedly a very fine one, especially in the magical lightness of its internal space, but taken as a whole it is certainly less great, already revealing in certain points the germ of that progressive decline that ultimately affected his performance. The chapel was built to replace one originally erected in 1877 to the designs of F. A. Sjöstrom. Construction commenced in 1938, and was finished with much labour in 1941, despite the war and the great difficulties of supply. In this project more than any other of Bryggman's designs, one feels that the architect has reached deeply into himself and brought to the surface all his most intimate and painful sensibility, but that in doing so he has passed the inexorable limit beyond which it becomes a weakness not to control one's own powers of suggestion. Nevertheless, Turku Chapel is the work in which the architect's personality is expressed most fully, through the medium of a serene rationalism, rarefied and infused by the subtle *frisson* of a pervading romanticism, in a placid and almost still atmosphere, where the dominating whiteness finds its essential complement in the light, which, as it varies, alters the weight and the consistency of the architectural elements.

Erik Bryggman. Cemetery Chapel. Turku, 1938–41

Bryggman's post-war works, in the decade from 1945 to 1955, the year of his untimely death, confirm that Turku Chapel marked the end of his rationalist period in the thirties, just as the 1929 Exhibition proved the turning point between his previous classicism and the functionalism which followed. The buildings of this final period, which we may call one of romantic decline, are numerous, and often very good: they include an estate of timber houses at Pansio, near Turku (1946), the Students' Union and the chemistry laboratory of Turku Academy (1948–50), the Villa Nuuttila on the island of Kuusisto, finely tailored to the site (1947–51) and Riihimäki Water Tower (1951–2).

The last designs which bear Bryggman's

name are probably, in part at least, the work of his office, over which the architect, by now a sick man, gradually lost control. They show a decline towards more complex forms, at times tending to *organic practice, with the careful siting of buildings in the landscape, at others showing a more strictly 'national' inspiration in the handling of volumes, materials and colours, as in his last cemetery chapels. Then his life drew to a premature close, leaving us as a consolation for his loss those authentic works of art, reflecting in their essential forms of line and volume the clear simplicity of his own life and spirit, which have made Turku, already famous for its ancient architectural traditions, Erik Bryggman's city.

Bibliography: Leonardo Mosso, 'L'opera di Erik Bryggman nella storia dell' architetture finlandese', in *Atti SJA*, Turin December 1958.

LEONARDO MOSSO

Bunshaft, Gordon, b. Buffalo, New York 1909. Studied at the Massachusetts Institute of Technology, Cambridge, Mass. In 1937 he joined the architectural firm of *Skidmore, Owings and Merrill; since 1946 partner. Bunshaft was responsible for the design, among others, of the Lever Building (New York, 1952), one of the most influential buildings of the last two decades, and the Connecticut General Life Insurance Building (Bloomfield, Conn., 1957).

Félix Candela. Church of the Miraculous Virgin. Mexico, 1954

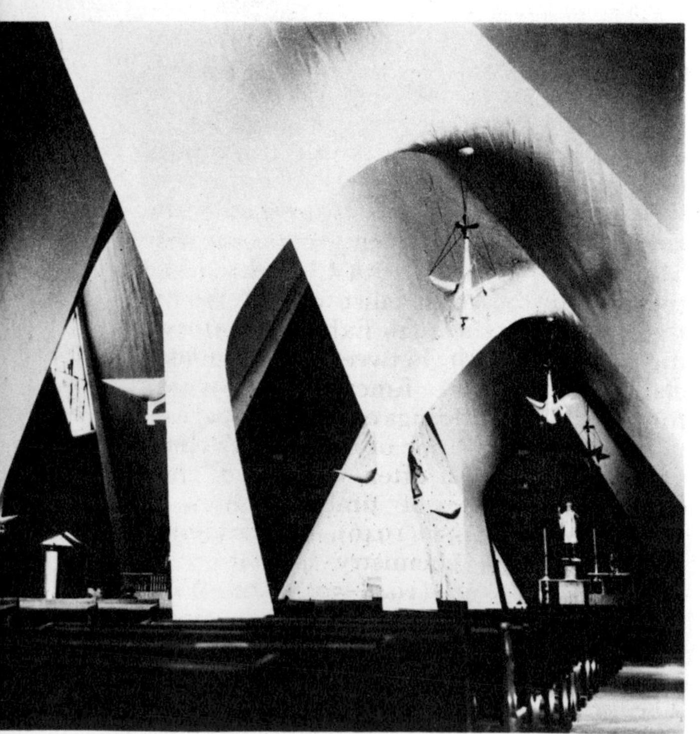

Burnham, Daniel Hudson, b. Henderson, New York 1846, d. Heidelberg 1912; 1873–91 in partnership with John W. *Root. Burnham and Root designed the Reliance Building at *Chicago (1890–4), a classical example of early American steel-frame construction, and the Monadnock Building (1889–91), a skyscraper with load-bearing outer walls of gently modulated profile. After Root's death in 1891, the firm, which had been entrusted with the preparation of the World's Columbian Exposition at Chicago in 1893, veered towards an academic eclecticism. Planning of city centres with axial layouts (Washington, Cleveland, San Francisco, Chicago).

Candela, Félix, b. Madrid 1910. Studied at the Escuela Superior de Arquitectura, Madrid. Towards the end of his studies, Candela had the opportunity of watching one of the best known structures by *Torroja, the Frontón Recoletos, being built. This double barrel-vault spanning 197 feet by 118 feet, or other works by Torroja, probably awakened Candela's interest in *shell vaulting. At all events, he was determined to visit the German shell vaulting specialists Dischinger and Finsterwalder, when the outbreak of the Spanish Civil War in July 1936 prevented his trip. It is anybody's guess if Candela and the exponents of the highly developed German methods of calculation would have seen eye to eye. After Candela had fought in the Civil War on the Republican side, he came to *Mexico in the summer of 1939 via the refugee camps at Perpignan. After twelve years in his adopted country, during which time he, and later his brother Antonio, picked up a living as architects and builders, he began advocating the use of shell vaulting, at first in articles and lectures. The building of the University City gave him an opportunity to construct the first hyperbolic paraboloids, which enabled him to reduce the roof of the Cosmic Ray Building to a thickness of $\frac{5}{8}$ inch.

A special advantage of this shape as compared with the sphere or other types of vault, is that the shuttering for hyperbolic paraboloids can be made from straight boards. Due to the relative simplicity of this process, and the great saving in material, Candela's constructions are more economical than other rigid roofs, and this fact alone won his firm numerous industrial commissions. Candela increased his spans with every project and became increasingly bolder in the exploitation of shell vaulting. When he maintains that he is guided less by exact calculation than by an intuitive feeling 'in the manner of the old master builders of cathedrals' we must recall that his intuition has a very firm foundation in his knowledge of materials and stresses, which grows with each new building. As an architect and designer, Candela has distinguished himself with his Church of the Miraculous Virgin in Mexico City (1954) which shows the unmistakable influence of *Gaudí, even though Candela departs widely from the building methods of the lonely Catalan. Later buildings of a non-industrial nature such as the Stock Exchange, several churches and pavilions in Mexico and Cuernavaca and a restaurant in Xochimilco were executed in collaboration with different architects, who were glad to avail themselves of the free outlines of his structures in their search for organic or baroque shapes.

Candela is not lacking in official recognition these days. In 1961 he was awarded the gold medal of the Institute of Structural Engineers in London and almost simultaneously the Auguste Perret Prize of the Union Internationale des Architectes. Shortly afterwards, Harvard invited him to give the Norton Lectures.

Bibliography: Max Cetto, *Modern Architecture in Mexico*, Stuttgart and New York 1960; Colin Faber, *Candela, the architect of shell construction*, New York and Munich, in preparation.

MAX CETTO

Candilis, Georges, b. Baku, Russia 1913. Studied in Greece where he met *Le Corbusier in 1933 at the *CIAM Congress in Athens. A scholarship made a stay in Paris possible (1945), and after that (until 1950) he worked for Le Corbusier. Residential buildings in Morocco (with Dony, Josic, and Woods). Planning for Le Mirail near Toulouse. The new town of Bagnols-

Félix Candela and Enrique de la Mora. Chapel of the Missionaries of the Holy Ghost. Coyoacán, 1956

sur-Cèze in the Rhône valley (started in 1956, with Bodiansky, Woods and Piot), adjoining an old urban centre with which it shares a cultural and sports area. (*France)

Casson, Sir Hugh Maxwell, b. Southampton 1913. Studied at Cambridge; Craven Scholar, British School at Athens. In private practice from 1937 with the late C. Nicholson; resumed 1946, after war service, latterly with Neville Conder. Professor of Interior Design, Royal College of Art, since 1953. His directorship of architecture at the *Festival of Britain, 1948–51, ensured its remarkable triumph as a piece of organized *townscape; the same powers of urbanistic control are evident in his schemes for Cambridge University (with N. Conder). His Youth Hostel at Holland Park, London, blends sympathetically with the remains of Holland House (17th century), while making no concessions to historicism.

HAROLD MEEK

Castiglioni, Enrico, b. Busto Arsizio near Milan 1914. Designs for complex sculpturally modelled shell constructions, which vault wide areas and mould spaces with the help of light. (Project for the main station in Naples, 1954; for the pilgrimage Church of the Madonna delle Lacrime at Syracuse, 1957.)

Chamberlin, Powell and Bon: Peter Chamberlin, Geoffrey Powell, and Christof Bon. First attracted attention in 1952 with their prize-winning scheme for high-density housing at Golden Lane, London (1953–7), a controversial layout with interesting treatment of multiple ground levels, a preoccupation later (1957) developed in their plan for the Barbican district of London, with separate routes for traffic and pedestrians. Their Bousfield Primary School with its *Miesian exteriors, was awarded the London Bronze Medal for Architecture in 1956; Newington Secondary School, also in London, features a complex folded roof over the assembly hall. Among their other schemes mention may be made of the Sports Centre for Birmingham University, with sculpturesque buildings atop a large podium, and the development plan for Leeds University, which closely integrates the academic layout with the city centre.

Bibliography: 'Detailed Proposals for the Barbican Redevelopment', in *Architects' Journal* (London), 4.6.1959. HAROLD MEEK

Chiattone, Mario, b. Lugano 1891. Studied architecture and painting at the Brera, Milan. Became a member of the *Futurist movement and together with his fellow-student *Sant'Elia exhibited a collection of drawings at Milan in 1914 under the heading 'Structures for a modern Metropolis'.

Daniel Hudson Burnham and John Wellborn Root. Monadnock Building. Chicago, 1889–91

Chicago School. This is a term conventionally applied to the characteristic commercial architecture of the American mid-west, especially Chicago, in the last quarter of the 19th century. It has also occasionally been used, but inappropriately, to cover the domestic Prairie style of 1900 that was evolved by Frank Lloyd *Wright and his followers in the same region. The Chicago style of commercial architecture is dominated by two features: the metal frame, as the basic structural system, together with its clear expression

Henry Hobson Richardson. Marshall Field Warehouse. Chicago, 1885–7

on the building's exterior in a simple, often non-historical vocabulary. The Chicago fire of 1871 demonstrated the importance of fire-proof construction and the inability of exposed cast-iron structures to withstand the heat, but the definitive solution to this problem, the protective combination of a metal frame sheathed by brick or masonry, was not arrived at until the construction of the Home Insurance Building, 1883–5, by William Le Baron *Jenney, a ten-storey structure which was subsequently extended. However, this building's structural system was only tentatively expressed in the somewhat conventional detailing and awkward articulation of the exterior, which has none of the suavity of subsequent skyscrapers of the 1890s by *Adler and *Sullivan, *Burnham and *Root, or *Holabird and *Roche. Indeed, the outward appearance of Jenney's pioneer structure does not break with the eclectic Victorian and Second Empire vernacular modes that had been employed previously in Chicago by H. H. *Richardson in the American Express Building, 1872, and by Dankmar Adler in the Central Music Hall, 1879, both typical examples of Chicago architecture before the advent of the skyscraper. Furthermore, a significant stylistic predecessor (though not a specific inspiration) for the Home Insurance Building is the ten-storey mansarded Tribune Tower, New York, 1872–5, by Richard Morris Hunt (1827–95). While this earlier instance of eastern commercial architecture did not employ the metal frame, its pronounced vertical conception certainly is as deserving of the label 'skyscraper' as are the later, more structurally sophisticated towers in Chicago.

If Jenney's structure helped to provide the freedom from height restrictions that were imposed by load-bearing masonry construction, the 'style' of the Chicago School was reoriented by the simple monumentality of Richardson's rusticated, round-arched, but only nominally revivalistic Marshall Field Warehouse, 1885–7, a building which depended for its effect upon an epic expression of its surface material. At first its forms were imitated, as in Adler and Sullivan's Auditorium Building, 1886–9, or in Burnham and Root's Rookery, 1885–7. These derivative structures were rather more elaborate and historically detailed versions of the Richardsonian paradigm, and the external walls of both were of conventional masonry construction. Subsequently the letter of Richardson's style was dropped, but his direct, expressive compositional principle was transformed into a mode fit for the metal frame and the large glazed openings which now became possible. Jenney's second Leiter Building (now Sears, Roebuck & Co.), 1889–90, is a bold, regular eight-storey volume in which the lines of the structure and the regular window rhythms dominate the almost invisible touches of classicizing detail. Similar qualities are to be observed in the pronounced verticality of the Reliance Building, 1890–4, by Daniel H. Burnham and

Daniel Hudson Burnham and John Wellborn Root. Reliance Building. Chicago, 1890–4

John W. Root, one of the most startling anticipations of the metal and glass style of the mid-20th century. The lower floors of the Reliance Building were built at the same time as Burnham and Root were completing the last masonry skyscraper, the sixteen-storey Monadnock Building, 1889–91, whose simple, rugged elevation contrasts with its light if somewhat inelegant contemporary. Two of Sullivan's finest Chicago School metal-frame skyscrapers of this period were built in St Louis (Wainwright Building, 1890–1) and Buffalo (Guaranty Building, 1894–5), but his most characteristic efforts of the late 1890s are in Chicago: the Carson, Pirie and Scott Store, 1899, and his portion of the façade of the tripartite Gage Building, 1898–9. The Gage Building was the work of William Holabird and Martin Roche (who had made a skeleton framed addition to Burnham and Root's massive Monadnock Building in 1893), and Sullivan was employed to design the façade of the larger right third of the building, accommodating himself to the established structural grid. A comparison of the differing parts of this façade points up the multiple virtues of the Chicago School: the directness and simplicity of the Holabird and Roche portions is in contrast to the more refined, complicated, yet beautifully integrated Sullivan design.

The expressive originality of the Chicago School did not outlast the beginning of the 20th century. The admiration for the academic modes of design, popularized by the Columbian Exposition of 1893 (originally projected in a romantic, almost Richardsonian mode by Root in 1891, but finally executed in a frigid *beaux-arts* manner), did not take hold immediately, but by 1900 the great period of Chicago commercial architecture was over. It did, however, produce a notable, if somewhat isolated, aftermath in such works as Richard E. Schmidt's (b. 1865) Nepeenauk Building, 1901–2, and Montgomery Ward Warehouse (actually by the firm Schmidt, Garden and Martin), 1906–8, in Dwight Perkins's Carl Schurz High School, 1910, and, most provocatively, in Frank Lloyd Wright's Larkin Building, Buffalo, 1904.

Bibliography: Early Modern Architecture: Chicago 1870–1910, New York 1940; Thomas S. Tallmadge, *Architecture in Old Chicago*, Chicago 1941; F. Randall, *History of the Development of Building Construction in Chicago*, Urbana, Illinois 1949; G. Condit, *The Rise of the Skyscraper*, Chicago 1952.

JOHN M. JACOBUS, JR

CIAM (Congrès Internationaux d'Architecture Moderne). The foundation of CIAM in 1928 has been called the beginning of the 'academic' phase of modern architecture: the time certainly appeared propitious for the introduction of some kind of international order into the scattered and independent essays towards a new architecture whose international unity of intention and style had been demonstrated at the Weissenhof exhibition of the previous year.

The effective impetus towards the foundation of CIAM came from Hélène de Mandrot, a sincere and intelligent woman who had aspirations towards being a patroness of the arts. She proposed in the first place a reunion of creative spirits at her château at La Sarraz, Switzerland, but this romantic project was turned to something more purposeful after consultation with Sigfried Giedion and *Le Corbusier. The preparatory document, issued to intending delegates, stated: 'This first congress is convened with the aim of establishing a programme of action to drag architecture from the academic impasse' (it was, in fact, to drag it into another) 'and to place it in its proper social and economic milieu. This congress should . . . determine the limits of the studies and discussions shortly to be undertaken by further congresses.' Although a distinction was thus made between the preparatory congress and later meetings, the date of 26, 27, and 28 June 1928 at La Sarraz is remembered and recorded as CIAM I, in spite of the fact that the properly constituted series of *Congrès Internationaux d'Architecture Moderne* did not begin until after the declaration of 28 June. The contents of the declaration embodied most of the best aspirations as well as the most fashionable fetishes of the architecture of the time. Sample statements read: 'It is only from the present that our architectural work should be derived', and 'The intention that brings us together is that of attaining a harmony of existing elements—a harmony indispensable to the present—BY PUTTING ARCHITECTURE BACK ON ITS REAL PLANE, THE

ECONOMIC AND SOCIAL PLANE; therefore architecture should be freed of the sterile influence of the Academies and of antiquated formulas', and again, 'The most efficacious production is derived from rationalization and standardization.'

The historical irony of these repeated invectives against the Academies is underlined by the dry, formalistic statement of aims that appears as the preamble to the statutes drawn up at Frankfurt-am-Main in 1929 (CIAM II). The aims are given as: (*a*) to state the contemporary architectural problem; (*b*) to restate the idea of modern architecture; (*c*) to disseminate this idea throughout the technical, economic and social strata of contemporary life; (*d*) to remain alert to the problems of architecture.

The Frankfurt Statutes also gave CIAM three operative organs: (1) the *Congrès* or general assembly of the members; (2) CIRPAC (Comité Internationale pour la Résolution des Problèmes de l'Architecture Contemporaine) to be elected by the *Congrès*; and (3) working groups, to apply themselves to specific subjects in collaboration with non-architectural specialists. At the same time the hierarchy of membership was stabilized in the form of national member-groups, to which individuals belonged.

It must be stated that this academic flavour (doubtless given by the 'clerics' such as Giedion, rather than the practising architects) was in no way representative of the work actually being undertaken in these years. The Frankfurt Congress had been called under the auspices of Ernst *May, the city architect and Europe's greatest expert on low-cost housing, and its outcome was a serious report, *Die Wohnung für das Existenzminimum.* CIAM III was held in Brussels in 1930, through the good offices of Victor *Bourgeois, and applied itself to basic problems of land-organization for housing, publishing an equally important report, *Rationelle Bebauungsweisen.* Both reports were at once dogmatic and realistic, somewhat in the manner of the town-planning studies being pursued at the Bauhaus under Hannes *Meyer, and these documents close the 1920s with the last genuine group-efforts of the architects who had met together to build Weissenhof. The next three years were to see fundamental changes.

Already in 1930 it was becoming apparent that CIAM was neither intellectually nor organizationally prepared for the problem to which the logic of its discussions had driven it—town planning. In order to deal with this situation CIAM set to work to standardize the graphic techniques, scales, and methods of presentation used by its members (an enterprise that was not really completed until the adoption of the *Grille-CIAM* after 1949). The Dutch national group, under Cor van *Eesteren, became the working group entrusted with the evolution of an effective symbol language for town planning. These labours, conducted against a background of growing political tensions and disintegrating international relations, proved to be protracted, and CIRPAC met three times (Berlin, 1931, Barcelona, 1932, and Paris, 1933) before it was felt that work was sufficiently advanced for another plenary *Congrès* to be called. This delay of almost three years proved crucial to the whole future of the movement; CIAM underwent a subtle and irrevocable change and took on the character which it was to preserve until its collapse more than twenty years later.

CIAM IV—theme 'The Functional City'—took place in July and August 1933 aboard the S.S. *Patris*, in Athens, and in Marseilles at the end of the voyage. It was the first of the 'romantic' congresses, set against a background of scenic splendour, not the reality of industrial Europe, and it was the first *Congrès* to be dominated by Le Corbusier and the French, rather than the tough German realists. The Mediterranean cruise was clearly a welcome relief from the worsening situation of Europe, and in this brief respite from reality the delegates produced the most Olympian, rhetorical, and ultimately destructive document to come out of CIAM: the *Athens Charter. The hundred and eleven propositions that comprise the Charter consist in part of statements about the conditions of towns, and in part of proposals for the rectification of those conditions, grouped under five main headings: Dwellings, Recreation, Work, Transportation, and Historic Buildings.

The tone remains dogmatic, but is also generalized and less specifically related to immediate practical problems than were the Frankfurt and Brussels reports. The generalization had its virtues, where it brought with it a greater breadth of vision and insisted that cities could be considered only in relation to their surrounding regions, but this persuasive generality which gives the Athens Charter its air of universal applicability conceals a very narrow conception of both architecture and town planning and committed CIAM unequivocally to: (*a*) rigid functional zoning of city plans, with green belts between the areas reserved to the different functions, and (*b*) a single type of urban housing, expressed in the words of the Charter as 'high, widely-spaced apartment blocks wherever the necessity of housing high densities of population exists'. At a distance of thirty years we recognize this as merely the expression of an aesthetic preference, but at the time it had the power of a Mosaic commandment and effectively paralysed research into other forms of housing. The Paris *Congrès* of 1937 (CIAM V) which was to be the last before the war, did little more than make marginal annotations to the Charter.

By the time the war was over, twelve years had passed since the Charter was drawn up, and its proposals had become the established dogma of progressive town planning. In the first years of peace there could be seen attempts to apply the Charter as a universal blueprint all over the world. But even while the *Système-CIAM* was being enforced in the schools and in planning offices its fatal weakness had been recognized, as is made clear by the insertion of a section in *Can Our Cities Survive*? that had no warrant in the Charter: the Civic Centre. At first this appears to be little more than a place where the citizen can go to escape from the Cartesian prison of Dwelling / Work / Recreation / Transportation, but as the study of centres proceeded it became apparent that CIAM's Functional City had been conceived in ignorance of the city's specific functions. Thus the Charter defines Dwelling as the first urban function; but it is also the first rural function; Work and Transportation are functions even of the nomadic life of the desert; Recreation is not specific to cities. The attempt to isolate the specifically urban functions of the city was to be the prime task of CIAM after the war, and since it led to the overthrow of the categories and categorical imperatives of the Athens Charter it was to lead to the destruction of CIAM, to which the Charter had become more central than either the preparatory document of 1928 or the Statutes of 1929. At first there was no sign of trouble. CIAM VI met in 1947 at Bridgwater, England, a joyous reunion of the heroes of Weissenhof and the followers they had collected in the 1930s; its outcome, a review of buildings erected since CIAM V by the members, edited by Giedion and published under the title of *A Decade of New Architecture*. But at CIAM VII, held at Bergamo in 1949, a new pattern was beginning to emerge, with the growing importance of the Italian delegation and the gathering of numbers of war-toughened students on the fringes of the *Congrès* in order to sit at the feet of the men who were, to them, legendary figures, the makers of modern architecture.

At CIAM VIII, held at Hoddesdon in England, in honour of the Festival of Britain, 1951, the new pattern of CIAM was becoming plain—increasing numbers of students, and official recognition of the inadequacy of the Charter, since the theme was 'The Urban Core'. For this theme the delegates were as unprepared intellectually as they had been for town planning in 1930, and the Congress report, edited by Jacqueline Tyrwhitt, José Luis *Sert, and Ernesto *Rogers, is little more than a compendium of fashionable clichés, such as the need to integrate painting and sculpture into architecture, while at the heart of these so-called studies appears an intellectual and urbanistic vacuum: the centre of the city is considered simply as yet another functionally designated area, an open space, to which the citizens were to be attracted by some mysterious quality of 'spontaneity'.

It was not long before the failure of CIAM VIII was recognized, but in the meantime CIAM IX at Aix-en-Provence had taken place; its theme was officially 'Habitat', but the *Congrès* will be chiefly remembered as a mass rally of Le Corbusier's student fan-club and the proceedings, culminating in an impromptu striptease performance on the roof of the Unité at Marseilles, were marked by adolescent *bonhomie* rather than mature cerebration. Yet it was to be the young who undertook to deliver CIAM from the new 'academic impasse' into which it had lapsed. The group who were entrusted with the preparation of CIAM X (who were therefore known as Team-X) took up a position that, though it drew to some extent on the programme documents for CIAM IX, nevertheless represented a clean break with both the mood and the content of the Athens Charter. Against the large-scale diagrammatic generalizations of the Athenian tradition, Team-X set up the personal, the particular, and the precise: 'Each architect is asked to appear with his project under his arm, ready to commit himself. Today we recognize the existence of a new spirit. It is manifest in our revolt from mechanical concepts of order . . . CIAM X must make it clear that we, as architects, accept the responsibility for the creation of order through form . . . the responsibility for each act of creation, however small.'

Though the theme of CIAM X was still nominally 'Habitat', the real business of the *Congrès*, which took place in Dubrovnik in 1956, was the direct challenge presented to the established members by the young radicals of Team-X, *Bakema, *Candilis, Gutmann, the *Smithsons, Howell, van *Eijck, and Voelcker. By the end of the congress, CIAM was in ruins and Team-X stood upon the wreckage of something that they had joined with enthusiasm, and—with equal enthusiasm—destroyed. The sense of the end of an epoch was so strong that the *Congrès* accepted the fact of death with comparative calm; the national groups were instructed to wind up their affairs, and the project of a memorial volume covering twenty-five years of work was seriously discussed. But there were national groups, notably the Italian, who felt that CIAM could still be of service. In addition, Team-X were not averse to international meetings as such, and the combination of these two parties produced, in 1959, a further congress in Otterlo, Holland. In content this was to be similar to what Team-X had intended for CIAM X, and particular projects were indeed discussed, individual responsibility was accepted, and the results, edited by Oscar Newman, were published as *CIAM 59 in Otterlo*. These published documents reveal that close discussion of the particular could often be as trivial as broad discussion of generalities, while the title of the report conceals a bitter dispute among the delegates who, in fact, voted to dissociate their activities from the word 'CIAM'. But the vote was disputed by some of the delegates who left before the final meeting, and as a result accusations of bad faith were launched against Team-X by founder-members Giedion, Sert, *Gropius, and Le Corbusier (none of whom had been in any way involved with the congress).

This was neither a productive nor a dignified outcome to thirty years of international activity, and the blame for the final collapse of CIAM must be laid chiefly on the inability of the founder-members to resist the temptation to *faire école*. They failed to guard against the academic tendencies in their midst, and became the victims of what Cor van Eesteren termed 'a too formal structure' to which work-programmes had to be subordinated. Nevertheless, in two vital periods—1930–4 and 1950–5—CIAM was the major instrument through which the ideas of modern architecture and town planning were made known to the world, while it performed an equally vital function during the war years in maintaining the nucleus of an international network of communications between progressive-minded architects. It is quite possible that these achievements may ultimately prove to be of greater historical importance than any of the documents that CIAM produced, even the Athens Charter.

Bibliography: Die Wohnung für das Existenzminimum, Stuttgart 1930; *Rationelle Bebauungsweisen*, Stuttgart 1931; *Logis et loisirs*, Paris 1938; (Le Corbusier) *La Charte d'Athènes*, Paris 1941; J. L. Sert and CIAM, *Can Our Cities Survive?*, Cambridge, Massachnsetts 1942; S. Giedion, *A Decade of New Architecture*, Zurich 1951; Oscar Newman (ed.), *CIAM 59 in Otterlo*, Stuttgart 1961.

REYNER BANHAM

CLASP. Acronym for Consortium of Local Authorities Special Programme. In 1957, a group of local education authorities in England banded together to exploit a system of *prefabricating schools, originally devised in Nottingham under Donald *Gibson to counteract subsidence in mining areas and later extended, as in C. H. *Aslin's Hertfordshire schools, to allow buildings to be erected rapidly from mass-produced prefabricated units at low cost and with a small labour force. Consortium components amount to about half the cost of CLASP schools; £7 million worth of

CLASP school. West Bridgford, Nottinghamshire, 1962

work was built in 1961–2, and a second Consortium has been formed of other authorities (SCOLA).

A 3 foot 4 inch planning grid is used, with external walls that can change direction at 6 foot 8 inch and 10 foot intervals. An organic grouping of elements with carefully controlled relationships between the spaces creates a deceptive, though usually successful feeling of informality. The same informality, however, when evoked in the choice of external cladding components often appears arbitrary and visually confused, lessening the effect of the carefully related spaces.

A CLASP school was exhibited at the 1960 Milan Triennale, where it aroused great interest.

Bibliography: Ministry of Education (Building Bulletin No. 19): *The Story of CLASP*, London 1960; 'CLASP in Italy', in *Architectural Review*, May 1963.

HAROLD MEEK

Concrete. *Reinforced concrete.

Constructivism. The movement known as Constructivism originated in Moscow just after the First World War in the work and theories of the two sculptor brothers Naum Gabo and Antoine Pevsner, who issued a Realistic Manifesto in 1920 which indicated the aims of the movement. Other Russian artists associated with the movement in those early years were Vladimir *Tatlin, painter, sculptor, and architect; Kasimir *Malevich, painter and sculptor and founder of the Suprematist movement; and El *Lissitzky, painter and architect. The purpose of the group has perhaps been most succinctly indicated by Naum Gabo, writing in *Abstraction-Création* in 1932, when he said that constructivists no longer paint pictures or carve sculptures but make constructions in space. The distinction between painting and sculpture is thus eliminated and both enter the domain of architecture. Thus Constructivism is a movement that affects all the visual arts, but it emanates in the first place from sculpture. This sculpture being constructions of various elements is essentially the same aesthetically as the constructions in architecture.

Constructivist sculpture consists of constructions in various materials—metals, glass, plastic, and nylon—and one work may be composed of many materials. It was the purpose in making such sculpture to express in symbolic forms the conceptions of life and the universe prompted by modern science. Materials provided by modern industry were logically the most appropriate for this purpose, and thus the constructions of Gabo and Pevsner are expressions mainly in abstract or associative forms that stem from modern science. Constructivism has, by some, been closely associated with Cubism. It was regarded as exhibiting the simple relations of geometric forms to which all natural forms can be reduced according to the dictum of Cézanne that 'Everything in Nature is shaped according to the sphere, cone, and cylinder.' Geometric forms were thus, to some Constructivists, the essential structural forms and Cubist painting was, therefore, either symbolical of Constructivism or actual Constructivist painting.

In architecture Constructivism can be regarded as part of the broader movement of *Functionalism, with an accent on constructional expression. Construction in all its aspects was emphasized to the full and in that emphasis all the traditional accessories of a building, such as ornament and style, were discarded so that the aesthetic effect depended on the formal relations of mass and space emanating from the most efficient construction. Any object that was efficiently made for its purpose was

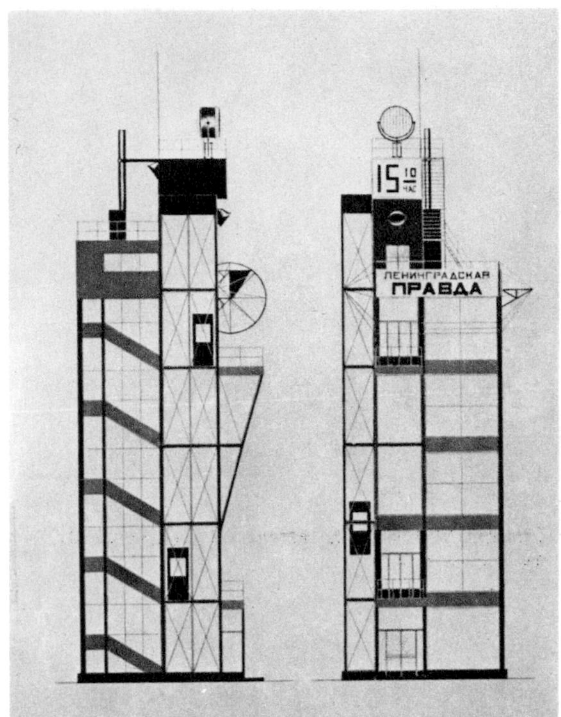

Alexander and Vladimir Vesnin. Pravda Building. Leningrad, 1923. Project

regarded as a model to follow; thus the most modern methods of construction, involving the use of new materials made available by industry, whereby structural efficiency could be secured superior to traditional methods, were encouraged, while the efficient machine was cited as a standard of excellence. In this theory there was a good deal of kinship with the early theories of *Le Corbusier, who in his book *Vers une Architecture* cited modern machines, such as the motor-car and aeroplane, as examples of efficient constructions, involving the logical relations of parts to the whole.

In 1921 El Lissitzky, one of the Russian members of the Constructivist movement, came to Berlin and in the following year a Constructivist International was founded with which, in addition to El Lissitzky, the well-known Dutch artist and architect, Theo van *Doesburg, was associated. The manifesto accompanying the foundation, published in *De *Stijl*, affirms the importance of the machine in modern life, and declares that, being designed strictly for its purpose without irrelevancies, it should form a model for building. The principle of Elementarism is also introduced, a kind of philosophy of the elements that form the structure of a building. The manifesto was not a very profound statement of aims and hardly survives critical examination. For example, in the cult of the machine there is a suggested independence of nature and belief in a 'mechanical aesthetic'. Further thought would have made it clear that all machines originate in natural organisms and their functions, while the manifesto is in part a contradiction of the evolution of Cubism based on the principle that geometric forms are, basically, essentially natural forms.

Other members of the Dutch De Stijl group who were associated with the Constructivist movement were Cor van *Eesteren, Gerrit T. *Rietveld, Mart Stam, the painter Piet Mondrian, and the Belgian artist Georges Vantongerloo. In 1923 a further manifesto was issued under the title of *Vers une Construction Collective*, by Theo van Doesburg, Cor van Eesteren, and G. T. Rietveld. In this manifesto it is asserted that the laws of space and colour have been studied and that it was found that their variations and relationships can be resolved into a definite unity, while the

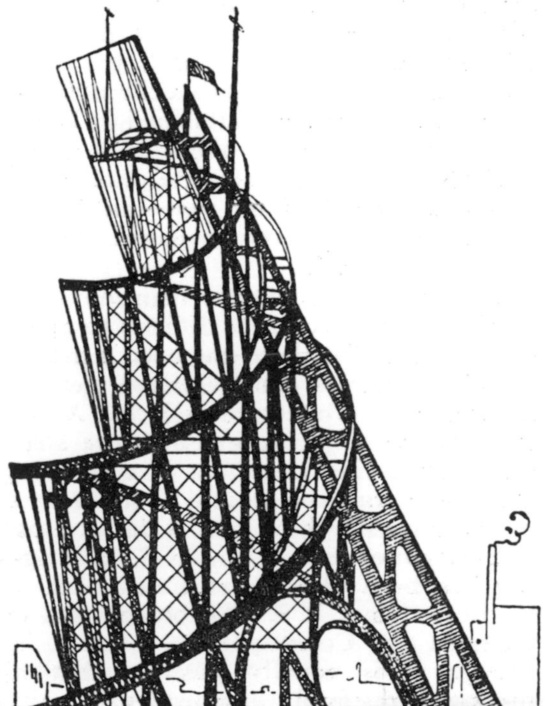

Vladimir Tatlin. Monument to the Third International in Moscow, 1920. Project.

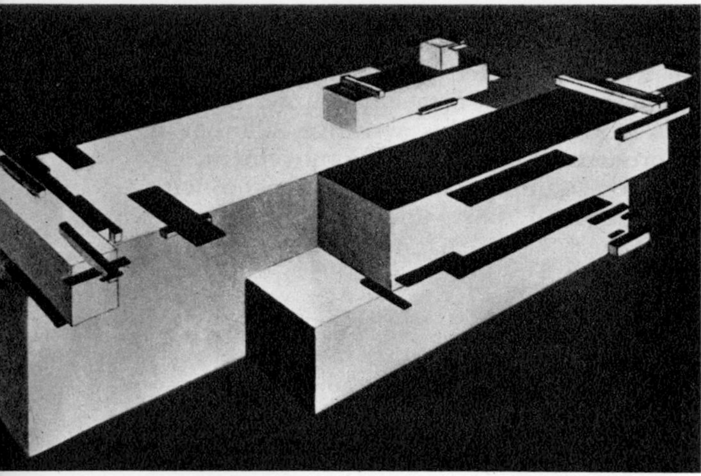

Kasimir Malevich. Suprematist architectural model. 1920–2

El Lissitzky and Mart Stam. 'Cloud Props'. Project. 1924

result of the study of the relation of space and time is that the two through colour give a new dimension, and that means have been secured whereby the duality of the interior and exterior of a building can be eliminated. The main point here is, of course, that all the diverse elements which make a construction in the arts can be composed into a unity satisfying to the human spirit, which was repeating in different words what had been said many times before.

Works that might be cited as examples of Constructivism are many and varied. A significant early example is Vladimir Tatlin's design for a monument to the Third International made in 1920, a design of a spiral character in which the bare bones of steel construction are manifest and which could be regarded as either sculpture or architecture. Very much in the same spirit is a much later work, the immense Construction in Space completed by Naum Gabo in 1957 and placed near the Bijenkorf building in Rotterdam. Many of the most interesting Constructivist architectural works are projects, and include a design for the Leningrad *Pravda* offices by the Vesnin brothers made in 1923; a scheme by El Lissitzky and Mart Stam in 1924 for office blocks erected on huge supports bestriding a city thoroughfare, known as the 'Cloud Props' project; Marcel *Breuer's scheme for a theatre in Kharkov made in 1930; and the many industrial fantasies in Jacob Tchernykhov's *Architectural Fictions*, published in Leningrad in 1933. There is one scheme in this book (No. 74) in which buildings at various points are perched on vast cantilevered structures, suggesting construction for construction's sake.

The influence of Constructivism on modern European architecture is difficult to assess. Certain it is that there has been a marked impulse to stress constructional elements in creating architectural effects. Among these is the emphasis given to the structural supporting members of a building, often by leaving the ground floor wholly or partially open, which play a decided part in the architectural ensemble. Such designing has been chiefly associated with Le Corbusier, and it is possible he was influenced by Constructivist theories, although it is equally possible that his theories, resolved independently, gave

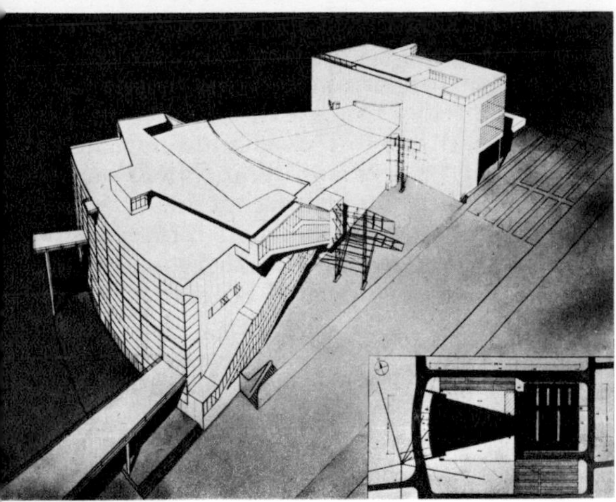

Marcel Breuer. Theatre at Kharkov, 1930. Project

strength to the early Constructivists. The display of structural members in a building, especially large supporting elements, is becoming a more prominent feature of much modern architecture, and formal decorative effects are increasingly dependent on the emphasis on structure. Indeed, in some designs the simulation of structure is actually introduced as a decorative motif and this may be in part due to the movement.

Perhaps the tenet of the Constructivists that has most strongly survived in architectural thought is the identity of efficient construction with beauty, which is a variant of the theory that true and economical fitness for purpose results in beauty. It is a theory held by many noted architects and engineers. For example, the Italian structural engineer, Pier Luigi *Nervi, who has been responsible for some of the most beautiful constructions in concrete, believes that the best chance of a building being beautiful is for it to be structurally right.

Bibliography: El Lissitzky, *Russland, Die Rekonstruktion der Architektur in der Sowjetunion*, Vienna 1930; Jacob Tchernykhov, *Architectural Fictions*, Leningrad 1933; Naum Gabo, *The Constructive Idea in Art*, London 1937; Rex Martienssen, 'Constructivism and Architecture. A new chapter in the history of formal building', *South African Architectural Record*, vol. 26, 1941.

ARNOLD WHITTICK

Costa, Lúcio, b. Toulon 1902. The acknowledged dean of modern architecture in *Brazil as well as its most articulate thinker, Lúcio Costa epitomizes, both in his work and in his writings, all that is more deeply typical of this movement, i.e. the continuing emotional relationship with the colonial past and the lyrical and humanistic approach to the problems of our time.

After graduating in 1924 from the Escola Nacional de Belas Artes in Rio de Janeiro, Costa entered into an early partnership with Gregori *Warchavchik, a Russian architect who had studied in Rome and settled in Brazil and who was responsible for the first modern, cube-like houses built in the country. In 1931, in the wake of the drastic changes brought about by the successful Vargas Revolution of 1930, Lúcio Costa was appointed to the directorship of the School of Fine Arts, which included the School of Architecture, and attempted a renewal of teaching methods, thus bringing to life a whole new generation of young architects oriented in a contemporary direction. Subsequently, in several projects which figure among the most significant milestones of the movement in Brazil, Lúcio Costa was able to express his discriminating good taste and his synthetic vision of the traditional past and the dynamic present of the country. The Ministry of Education and Health, (1937) for which *Le Corbusier was consulting architect and Lúcio Costa for a time the leader of the team of architects, the Brazilian Pavilion at the New York World's Fair, with Oscar *Niemeyer (1939), the Parque Guinle apartment buildings in Rio (1948–50–54), inspire young Brazilian architects to this day.

When in 1937 the DPAHN (National Historical and Artistic Patrimony Department) was formed Lúcio Costa joined it from the start and has never interrupted his devoted study of the history of Brazilian architecture or his work for the restoration and preservation of artistic monuments. Throughout his career, Lúcio Costa has always selflessly supported the work of Oscar Niemeyer, whose extraordinary talent was singled out by him in the early days when the Ministry of Education and Health was being designed, and who thus rose to his decisive role in the development of modern architecture in Brazil.

Lúcio Costa. Parque Guinle apartment buildings. Rio de Janeiro, 1948–54

Recently Lúcio Costa has become more and more involved in city planning. His master-plan for Brasilia, which was selected by an international jury in an open competition in 1956, and which provides a superb framework for Niemeyer's monumental buildings as well as a beautiful and rational setting for a better organized community life in a dignified capital city, is justly famous.

Bibliography: Except for an article on 'The Architect and Contemporary Society' published by UNESCO, and one on 'The New Scientific and Technological Humanism' published by the Massachusetts Institute of Technology, Lúcio Costa has to be read in Portuguese, but the result will be worth the trouble, especially in the case of the articles 'A Necessary Documentation', 'Portuguese-Brazilian Furniture', 'Jesuitic Architecture in Brazil', published in the *Revista do Serviço do Patrimônio Historico Artistico*, nos. 1, 3, 5, and of the publications of the Ministry of Education and Culture of his 'Thoughts on Contemporary Art' and 'A great deal of Building, a bit of Architecture, and a Miracle'.

HENRIQUE E. MINDLIN

Cuijpers, Petrus Josephus Hubertus, b. Roermond 1827, d. Roermond 1921. Studied at Antwerp Academy, follower of *Viollet-le-Duc. Cuijpers stood at the watershed between historicism and the modern movement in the *Netherlands. Numerous Catholic churches in a freely adapted Gothic manner. Rijksmuseum (1885) and main station at Amsterdam (1889).

Curtain wall. In the evolution of structural systems two basic types can be distinguished, deriving at various times from the particular contingencies of place and civilization: massive structures and skeleton ones.

In buildings of the first type (Palazzo Strozzi, Florence, 1489–1507; Notre-Dame du Haut, Ronchamp, by *Le Corbusier, 1954) every part of the walls performs, without differentiation, the functions both of loadbearing and of separation; in the second type (Chartres Cathedral, 1194–1220; Promontory Apartments, Chicago, by *Mies van der Rohe, 1949) on the other hand, a system of high strength units, which may be connected together in various ways, performs the special functions of a loadbearing framework, while the other parts of the wall are devoted exclusively to the tasks of closing off and separation. All nonloadbearing walls, adopted at any time by whatever structural tradition, could in a certain sense be called curtain walls; in fact they possess in some respects both the qualities of a wall (which is immovable, heavy, and definitive) and those of a curtain (which is movable, light, and temporary). In this broad sense the Gothic cathedrals with their large windows between piers, the frame buildings of Japan which close off space with panels of wood and paper, and those of Central and Northern Europe which employ brick walls, sometimes plastered, for partitioning, may be considered authoritative examples of curtain wall architecture.

However, the feature called by the modern name of curtain wall (the English term has universal currency) signifies a particular kind of external, non-loadbearing wall, composed of repeating modular elements, shop-manufactured and erected on site, which performs all the functions (and only these) of separation between indoors and out, and in particular those of defence against external agencies (atmospheric and otherwise), thermal and acoustical insulation, and regulation of view, light and air. This definition, however, is not always strictly adhered to, either because curtain walling is of recent invention, and has thus not yet been the subject of any deep critical examination, or because its typology is being constantly enriched, thanks to the continual efforts of designers and manufacturers to find better methods of production and application.

The curtain wall is the end-product of a process of development that has involved a number of interrelated considerations connected with technical progress, social and cultural factors, and the emergence of the modern style in architecture. The introduction and perfecting of new structural techniques making use of *steel at the beginning of the 19th century and *reinforced concrete in its second half, gave the impulse to a spreading use of framed structures (Chocolate factory at Noisiel-sur-Marne, by Saulnier, 1871–2; second Leiter Building, Chicago, by Le Baron *Jenney, 1889–90; house in the Rue Franklin, Paris, by *Perret, 1903). The increased employment of this type of walling showed the importance of aiming at two characteristics in particular: slenderness, to keep the maximum floor area available for use, and lightness, so that by reducing the load on the steel frame, the latter might be designed with correspondingly smaller members.

The small dimensions of the steel frames and the progress made by the glass industry permitted an increase in window sizes, a development that was also stimulated by the demand for as much natural light as possible in industrial and commercial buildings. Between 1850 and the early years of the 20th century the window gradually turned into the window wall (Chatham Dockyard Museum, 1867; Reliance Building, Chicago, by *Burnham and *Root, 1890–4; Samaritaine department store, Paris, by Jourdain, 1905), sometimes taking over the whole basic area defined by the façade (Maison du Peuple, Brussels, by *Horta, 1896–9; AEG works, Berlin, by *Behrens, 1908–9). The use of large areas of glass had meanwhile become widespread in greenhouses and winter gardens, pedestrian galleries, railway station roofs and large exhibition pavilions (Crystal Palace, London, by *Paxton, 1851; Machinery Hall, Paris, by Dutert and Contamin, 1889).

The transformation of the window into the window wall and the employment of large glazed areas drew attention to a number of problems and evoked the first solutions to them; they included such questions as that of insulation, eliminating condensation, developing the secondary glazing framework (Hallidie Building, San Francisco, by *Polk, 1918) and countering the effects of expansion by the careful design of joints and fixing systems. Large industrial buildings and tall office blocks, conceived as endless repetitions of identical cell units, led to the use of a uniform grid for the structural frames. Between the eve of the First World War and the beginning of the Second, the architects of the modern movement carried out a series of experiments, each of which may be considered as perfecting some particular aspect of curtain walling by the use of modern methods of industrial production (Fagus factory, Alfeld, 1911; model factory at the Werkbund Exhibition, Cologne, 1914; Bauhaus, Dessau, 1925–6, all by *Gropius; Bijenkorf department store, Rotterdam, by *Dudok, 1929–30; Maison Suisse, University City, Paris, 1930–2; Salvation Army Hostel, Paris, 1932; Maison Clarté, Geneva, 1932, all by Le Corbusier).

At the same time the theoretical principles of this new means of architectural

Jules Saulnier. Chocolate factory. Noisiel-sur-Marne, 1871–2

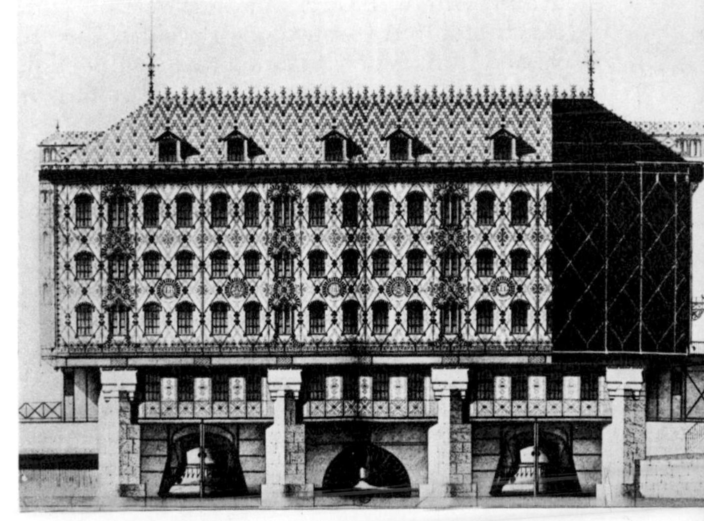

Walter Gropius. Bauhaus. Dessau, 1925–6

Gian Antonio Bernasconi, Annibale Fiocchi and Marcello Nizzoli. Palazzo Olivetti. Milan, 1954.

expression were being formulated via educational experiments (*Bauhaus), writings (Le Corbusier) and projects (various schemes of Mies van der Rohe between 1919 and 1922; Gropius and Meyer's design for the Chicago Tribune competition, 1922). It was only after the Second World War, however, that the first experiments began in the real industrialization of the building trade on a vast scale. It was this period that saw the development and spread of the curtain wall in the United States (UN Secretariat Building, New York by *Harrison and others, 1947–50; Lake Shore Drive Apartments, Chicago, 1951 and Seagram Building, New York, 1956, by Mies van der Rohe) and Europe. Architects experimented with its application to different types of building, and discovered new possibilities of expression, with the close collaboration of manufacturers on the alert for new materials and methods.

The classification of curtain wall types is still in its early stages, though certain criteria based on technical and structural considerations seem to provide a valid instrument for critical inquiry:

1. Presence or otherwise of spatial modelling of the façade, obtained with strongly projecting or recessed units. Some types feature three-dimensional treatment: main elevation of the Palazzo Olivetti, Milan, 1954, by Bernasconi, *Fiocchi and *Nizzoli; others employ a flat or two-dimensional treatment: Phoenix-Rheinrohr Building, Düsseldorf, 1960, by Hentrich and Petschnigg.

2. Relationship to the structure's loadbearing frame. Some types do not bring out the framework at all, but cover it like a sheath: Lever House, New York, 1952 by *Skidmore, Owings and Merrill; some pick out only the verticals: Inland Steel Company Building, Chicago, 1954 by Skidmore, Owings and Merrill; or only the horizontals: headquarters of the Fédération Nationale du Bâtiment, Paris, 1950, by Gravereaux and Lopez. Yet others feature both verticals and horizontals: Equitable Savings Building, Portland, Ore., 1948 by *Belluschi.

3. Differentiation between the wall unit and its frame. Some types are in the form of panels set in a secondary frame, which in its turn is fixed to the loadbearing structure: Crown Hall of the IIT, Chicago, 1955 by Mies van der Rohe. Others use panels of an appropriately rigid section, which is

anchored direct to the main structure: Alcoa Building, Pittsburgh, 1953 by *Harrison and *Abramovitz.

4. Structural make-up of the secondary frame, where it exists. Some types feature vertical elements, others horizontal ones, others again use a grid of both.
5. Method of assembly of individual elements. Some come in single units, others have to be put together from various parts.
6. Method of connecting adjacent units. Some types have edge sections which interlock with the next unit, others use an intermediate feature.
7. Method of packing joints. Some types have rigid joints (welded), others use non-rigid packing (mastic, plastic, etc.).

Bibliography: Curtain Walls, Milan 1956; *Construire en acier*, Zurich 1956; Ian McCallum (editor), 'Machine-Made America' in *The Architectural Review*, London, May 1957, No. 724; W. Dudley Hunt, *The Contemporary Curtain Wall*, New York 1958; R. Schaal, *Vorhangwände—Curtain Walls*, Munich 1961; R. McGrath and A. C. Frost, *Glass in Architecture and Decoration*, London 1961; *Industrial Architecture* (London) 6/1963.

GIUSEPPE GIORDANINO, GIUSEPPE VARALDO, AND GIAN PIO ZUCCOTTI

Skidmore, Owings and Merrill. Inland Steel Company Building. Chicago, Ill., 1954

Left. Pietro Belluschi. Equitable Savings Building. Portland, Ore., 1948

Wallace K. Harrison and Max Abramovitz. Alcoa Building. Pittsburgh, 1953. Erection of a prefabricated unit

Deilmann, Harald, b. Gladbeck 1920. Studied and worked as assistant at Stuttgart Technical College. Architect of the Municipal Theatre, Münster, together with Hausen, Rave, and Ruhnau (1954–6). Nordwest-Lotto offices, Münster (1960). Hospitals, cultural buildings.

Deitrick, William H., b. Danville, Va. 1905. Together with *Nowicki and Severud architect of the arena at Raleigh, N.C. (1952–3). The roof of the arena is carried by steel ropes which are *suspended from two sloping parabolic arcs.

Denmark. Danish people have always drawn inspiration from the major centres of world culture, but have shown a capacity to adapt new ideas to Danish landscape and climate, customs and building practices, adopting what is new with caution and criticism. Thus the process whereby Danish architecture acquired its own character was markedly evolutionary. Securely anchored in their own tradition of craftsmanship, the Danes developed a sense for simple order, natural proportions, and rhythm, first through half-timbered work and afterwards through the *modular brick buildings of the Empire period. Emotionalism in architecture was always distrusted and the worst excesses of eclecticism were avoided. On the other hand the genuine progressive movement was slow to make itself felt.

A functional tradition runs through Danish architecture, from the simple brick buildings of the Empire period, via Gottlieb Bindesbøll onward to neoclassicism, to Ivar Bentsen and Kay *Fisker. Bindesbøll's Medical Association houses and Oringe Hospital (built in the fifties) are simple buildings of yellow brick serving a clear functional purpose. Daniel Herholdt's work of the 1860s has a clearer sense of style, but shows the same respect for simple structures and honest materials. Herholdt was also the first to use cast-iron in a major building—Copenhagen University library (1861). The master builder of Copenhagen town hall, Martin Nyrop, carried the use of this material's special properties further, while Jensen *Klint, securely rooted in the brick-building tradition, thought he had arrived at a new and timeless architecture with Grundtvig's Church (1920–40), a gigantic paraphrase of the Danish country

Gottlieb Bindesbøll. Thorwaldsen Museum. Copenhagen, 1839–48

church. The neoclassicism of 1910–15 was eclecticism's last outburst. Its two chief works were Carl Petersen's Fåborg Museum (1912); and the Police Station (1918–22, by Hack, Kampmann and his two sons, and Åge Rafn. The chief significance of the period for the future lay in a severer artistic discipline and a sharpened sense for the qualities of craftsmanship and material.

Ivar Bentsen carried on the tradition of brick building with small unpretentious houses and good blocks of flats, and since the twenties Kay Fisker has been the leading exponent of traditionalism, playing a leading part in the effort to improve the quality of ordinary housing. The most important product of Functionalism has been Århus University (begun 1931), the first part of which was designed by Fisker in collaboration with C. F. Møller and Povl Stegmann. Its many separate buildings stand skilfully related to one another in a rolling park-like campus. The laconic and precise style of the first yellow brick buildings has been continued by C. F. Møller alone during the past twenty years, without losing the originally projected unity of design. Fisker's strong personality shows to advantage in Copenhagen's Voldparken School and the Maternity Care Building of the mid-fifties. Kåre Klint carried on his father Jensen Klint's ideas in Bethlehem Church (1937) and also became the leading figure of furniture design, with semi-traditional furniture of the highest craftsmanship. In the post-war years an agreeable personal atmosphere has been given to housing developments like Søndergårdsparken (architects P. E. Hoff and Bennet Windinge) by the location of the buildings and their relation to terrain and landscape gardening. There has been especial emphasis on school building in the past decade, with low single- and double-storeyed buildings which create admirable conditions of intimacy for the pupils. One of the finest of these is F. C. Lund and Hans Christian Hansen's Hansted School in Copenhagen.

The *Art Nouveau movement left little of note in Denmark (see, however, the work of Anton Rosen and Thomas Bindesbøll). International *Functionalism first made itself seriously felt after the Stockholm Exhibition of 1930, which was a revelation for young Danish architects. Vilhelm Lauritzen became an outstanding exponent of Functionalism, coping with contemporary problems such as Copenhagen Airport and Broadcasting House. Mogens Lassen built the first *Le Corbusier-inspired villas and Fritz Schleget became the Danish exponent of a freedom from aesthetic preconceptions established by *Perret with his reinforced concrete work (Mariebjaerg crematorium). The young Arne *Jacobsen also belonged to the revolutionary group, with the charming

Vilhelm Lauritzen. Broadcasting House. Copenhagen, 1938–45

Povl Ernst Hoff and Bennet Windinge. Høje Søborg apartment block. Copenhagen, 1949–51

Left. Peter Vilhelm Jensen Klint. Grundtvig Church. Copenhagen, 1920–40

Kay Fisker, C. F. Møller, and Povl Stegmann. Århus University. Commenced 1931

development at Bellevue and later (in collaboration with Møller and Lassen) with the Århus and Søllerod town halls. These edifices were the climax of progressive building in the thirties, before the material shortages of the war and subsequent years brought a return to the cultivation of traditional qualities.

The post-war years have been marked especially by inspiration from the USA, first by *Wright's houses and their adaptation to the landscape, later by *Mies van der Rohe's simplicity. Again Jacobsen was the leading figure, with large administrative buildings and hotels, like Rødovre town hall (1955) and the SAS building in Copenhagen (1959). In his schools and housing Jacobsen convincingly combined foreign inspiration with Danish tradition. Among the younger generation Halldor Gunnløgsson is a fine exponent of a severe classical architecture. Drawing inspiration both from Japanese architecture and from Mies van der Rohe, he has built single houses and (in co-operation with Jørn Nielsen) Kastrup town hall. Jørn *Utzon is the vital, imaginative and original talent whose prize design for Sydney Opera House is now under construction. In Denmark he has so far only completed a number of interesting houses and housing blocks. Utzon is Denmark's most important representative of a dynamic, organic architectural sense. Vilhelm Wohlert and Jørgen Bo have created a delightful background for contemporary art in Louisiana Museum, combining sensitivity with caution towards external effects.

Jørgen Bo and Vilhelm Wohlert. Louisiana Museum. Humlebaek near Copenhagen, 1958

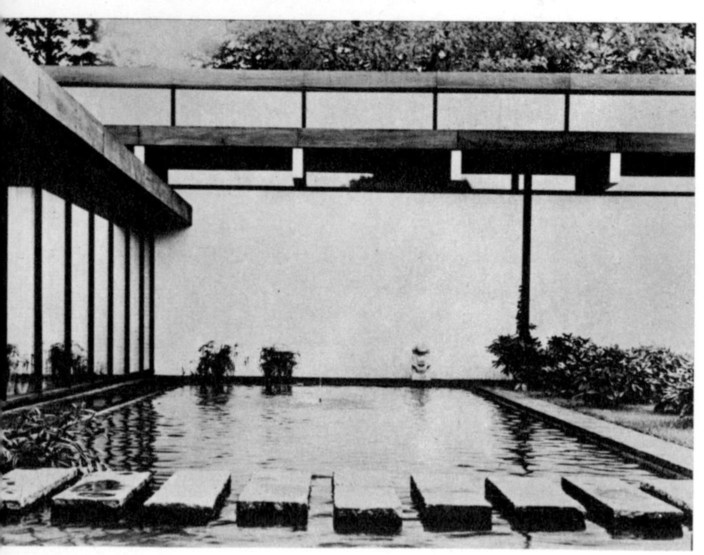

Otherwise it is not so much by individual achievements that Denmark has acquired a certain international recognition as by the conscientious and workmanlike character of her architecture and craftsmanship.

Bibliography: Kay Fisker and Knud Millech, *Danske Arkitekturstrømninger 1850–1950*, Copenhagen 1951; Harald Langberg, *Dansk Byggeskik*, 1955; Monies, Hjort, Røgind, *Contemporary Danish Architecture*, Copenhagen 1956; (Symposium): *The Architecture of Denmark*, London 1949; Esbjørn Hjort, *Housing in Denmark since 1930*, London 1952.

TOBIAS FABER

Deutscher Werkbund. The genesis of the Deutscher Werkbund, which was founded on 6 October 1907 by the German architect Hermann *Muthesius, can be traced back, in part, to the movement in England led by William *Morris and his associates in the middle of the 19th century to revive the standards of craftsmanship in the arts of everyday life that had obtained in the Middle Ages. This movement was associated with the moral requirement that the craftsman should find pride and joy in his labour, and it led to an antagonism to machinery and its crude productions in contemporary industrial art, although it should be emphasized that the antagonism was less to machinery itself than to its bad use by the continual stamping out of crude imitations of historical styles. It must be acknowledged, however, that Morris never really came to terms with machinery, which he felt was responsible for so many of the social and aesthetic evils of the 19th century. Yet the movement led by William Morris revived much of the excellent medieval craftsmanship, with the emphasis on quality of design, of material, and of individual skill. The movement also contributed to the revival of a high standard of domestic architecture which began with the Red House designed by William Morris's architect Philip *Webb in 1859. This was the first of a series of excellent houses designed by Webb, which together with those by C. F. A. *Voysey and Norman *Shaw showed at that time (that is, the last forty years of the century) a new spirit in domestic architecture. Instead of formal symmetrical elevations with planning to match as in Late Renaissance buildings, houses were designed more in accordance with the best fulfilment of their purpose, with rooms in convenient relation to each other, and orientation in accordance with sunlight. This meant design more on medieval lines with often irregular plans, while it was accompanied with an expressive use of the best materials.

From 1896 to 1903 Hermann Muthesius was attached to the German Embassy in London, and during his sojourn he made a thorough study of English contemporary architecture and of industrial art. He returned to Germany with enthusiastic admiration for English domestic architecture and applied art in the Morris tradition and wrote several books on these subjects. He deplored the poor condition of industrial art in Germany, its constant repetition of dead historical styles, and as head of the Prussian Board of Trade for Schools of *Arts and Crafts in 1907 he took steps to effect improvements and to infuse new life into industrial art by forming the Deutscher Werkbund. His criticisms of contemporary German art met with a good deal of opposition, both in art circles and from industrialists, but he was able to exercise some influence on the latter by emphasizing the economic aspect of good design and craftsmanship in industrial production, because without these there was a risk that Germany would lose ground in world markets. Several industrialists seemed to realize this and it is not without significance that they appointed well-known architects and designers as design consultants about the same time as the foundation of the Deutscher Werkbund, the most notable being Peter *Behrens, appointed in this capacity to the AEG.

The avowed objects of the Deutscher Werkbund were to select the best representatives of the arts and crafts, industry and trades, to make all necessary efforts to secure high quality in industrial art, and to form a centre for all who aimed at this high quality in their work. Among those who were associated with the venture in its early years, in addition to Muthesius, were Karl Schmidt, Theodor *Fischer, Richard *Riemerschmid, Hans *Poelzig, Heinrich Tessenow, Josef *Hoffmann, and Henri van de *Velde. There was a great insistence on quality of craftsmanship and

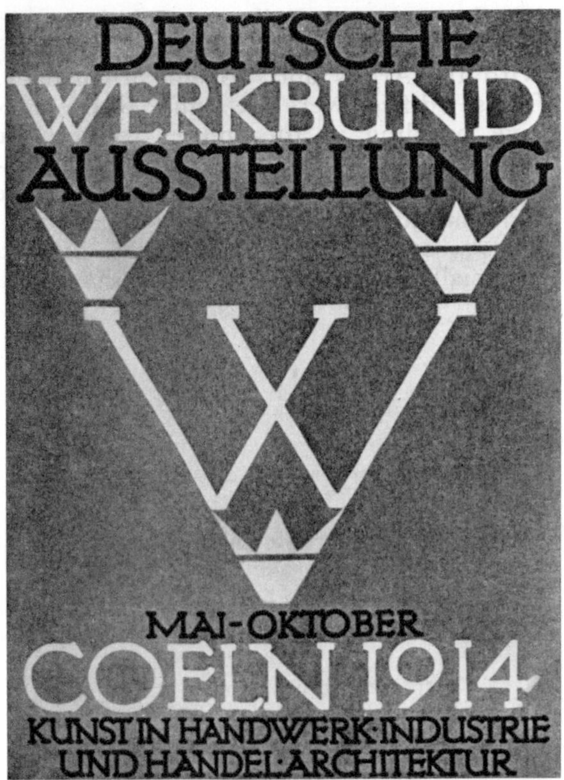

Fritz Hellmut Ehmcke. Poster for the Werkbund Exhibition. Cologne, 1914

material, and it is a question whether aesthetic aspects were sufficiently considered, but this was rectified later when the whole question of aims was considered at the Convention in 1911. The attitude of the members to the use of machinery in production was very different from that of William Morris. They not only came to terms with it, but they welcomed it as a valuable means of large-scale output of quality goods. They viewed machinery as a development of the hand tool, but, like the hand tool, something to be fully controlled and wholly subservient to the artist-craftsman. Another factor that probably influenced the acceptance of the machine by the Deutscher Werkbund was the gradual realization that many machines are beautiful things in themselves, and that such objects as the modern locomotive, motor-car, aeroplane, and modern liner can compare in beauty with the finest of modern buildings.

At the congress held in 1911 Muthesius reasserted the aims of the Deutcher Werkbund, but in addition he placed emphasis on aesthetic qualities and spiritual values which he associated with ideas of form, and he advocated turning for inspiration to that architecture of the past where the realization of form had been of the highest excellence, in the Greek temple, the Roman baths and the Gothic cathedral. This perfection of form was associated, to some extent, in the mind of Muthesius with mathematical calculation, which, together with the acceptance of machine production, led to a belief and advocacy of standardization that he expressed at the annual meeting of the Werkbund in 1914. This point of view, however, met with opposition from Henri van de Velde, a prominent member of the Werkbund, who could not reconcile standardization and the acceptance of canons with the individual creative work of artists. An artist, he contended, was always an individualist, who would never submit to rules and standards. These two lines of thought existed in the ranks of the Werkbund, as indeed they have always existed in discussions of art and architecture.

In this same year, 1914, the Deutscher Werkbund held a very important exhibition of industrial art at Cologne, which some have regarded in retrospect as the most important of the century. Several of the buildings for this exhibition were designed by pioneer modern architects, including Henri van de Velde, Walter *Gropius, Peter Behrens, Josef Hoffmann, and Bruno *Taut, and include some of the most significant early examples of modern architecture in steel, concrete and glass.

Weissenhof Housing Exhibition. Stuttgart, 1927

Van de Velde's contribution was a theatre which contained several innovations. Perhaps the most notable building of the exhibition and that which marked the greatest advance was the model factory administrative block and garage designed by Walter Gropius in collaboration with Adolf *Meyer. The contribution of Bruno Taut was a pavilion for the German *glass industry which consisted of a twelve-sided glass drum with a pointed glass dome. The First World War arrested the work of the Deutscher Werkbund, but it had already exerted considerable influence throughout Europe and many institutions were formed in other countries to follow its example. An Austrian Werkbund was formed in 1910 and a Swiss in 1913. The Swedish Slöjdsforening was reorganized about the same time to conform with the Werkbund, while in England in 1915 the Design and Industries Association was established which was frankly modelled on the Deutscher Werkbund.

The next really great event in the history of the Werkbund was the exhibition of 1927 which included a housing exhibition on a hill in Weissenhof, a suburb of Stuttgart. It was superintended by Ludwig *Mies van der Rohe, then a vice-president of the Deutscher Werkbund, who invited several European architects to submit designs. Those who accepted invitations were the German architects: Peter Behrens, Walter Gropius, Hans Poelzig, Bruno Taut, Hans *Scharoun, Adolf G. Schneck, Ludwig *Hilberseimer, R. Döcker, Adolf Rading, and Max *Taut; the Austrian architect, Josef Frank; the French architect, *Le Corbusier; and the Dutch architects, J. J. P. *Oud and Mart Stam, while Mies van der Rohe himself designed a block of flats for the scheme. He gave the architects complete freedom in their designs with the one proviso that all the houses should have flat roofs. This housing exhibition proved to be one of the most important events in domestic architecture in the period between the two wars. Its historical value is that it demonstrates, in a concentrated form, the stages reached in the evolution of house design and construction in 1927 by the most progressive architectural thought in Europe. In some of the houses a degree of standardization is employed which would make it possible to build them economically on a large scale.

For example, in the two houses designed by Walter Gropius a steel-framed construction is employed on a grid of about one metre, with asbestos cement sheets as external facing on slabs of cork with suitable internal facing, a method which lends itself not only to mass production but to dry assembly. This is also the case with the block of flats designed by Mies van der Rohe constructed of a light steel frame with standardized wall sections and windows. Similarly the house designed by Hans Poelzig consists of timber sheets fixed to a framed structure. Several of the houses are built of reinforced concrete, including those designed by Le Corbusier in which the essential structure consists of reinforced concrete and steel posts or columns placed at intervals on which the houses are suspended. Flexibility in the design and use of the houses was one of the principal motifs in the designs.

The housing exhibition of the Deutscher Werkbund at Stuttgart was in many ways an exemplification of the principles of modern building advocated by the Werkbund's founder, Muthesius, in 1911. It took place in the year of his death, and its success—for it attracted attention among architectural circles throughout the world—was a reward for his early pioneer efforts. A further triumph for the Deutscher Werkbund was its very successful participation in the Paris exhibition of 1930. The German Government entrusted the task to the Deutscher Werkbund, which appointed Walter Gropius to organize the German section. He was assisted by three of his former colleagues at the Bauhaus, L. Moholy-Nagy, Marcel *Breuer, and Herbert Bayer. The exhibition was dedicated to building and the industrial arts and had two main themes, which were a continuation of those of the Stuttgart housing exhibition: standardization in all fields of building and the mass production of well-designed housing units. (*Prefabrication)

With National Socialism the Deutscher Werkbund was disbanded. It was revived after the end of the Second World War.

Bibliography: Die Form, Berlin, especially IX—1927, and VII—1932; Nikolaus Pevsner, *Pioneers of the Modern Movement*, especially chapter 1, London 1936; Reyner Banham, *Theory and Design in the First Machine Age*, 1–5, London 1960.

ARNOLD WHITTICK

Doesburg, Theo van, b. Utrecht 1883, d. Davos 1931. Van Doesburg, whose real name was Chr. E. M. Küpper, began his career as a painter; his pictures were shown for the first time at an exhibition in The Hague in 1912. In collaboration with the architects *Oud and Wils, van Doesburg endeavoured to transfer his painting of the two-dimensional into something spatial and connect it organically with architecture. In 1916 he founded the *Sphinx* group in Leiden together with Oud, but it did not last long. A year later, he joined a group of artists and architects in De *Stijl, a movement set up to achieve a 'radical renewal of art'. Van Doesburg became the spokesman of the group, whose ideology he helped to formulate.

In 1917, together with Oud, he designed the hall of the latter's house at Noordwijkerhout, near Leiden, in which he sought to reinforce and stress the architecture by means of painting. His use of primary colours, tiled flooring and geometrical leading on the windows is in line with De Stijl methods. In the years that followed, van Doesburg was invited to lecture on the movement's activities at the *Bauhaus in Dessau, and in Berlin. The Bauhaus also took over his book on the basic principles of art, originally published in Dutch (Amsterdam 1919), as the sixth publication in the Bauhaus Books series (*Grundbegriffe der bildenden Kunst*, Munich 1924).

When the Aubette, a dance hall and amusement centre in Strasbourg was reconstructed in 1926–7, van Doesburg was able to realize his ideas on space and colour on a larger scale, in collaboration with Hans Arp. Moving to Paris, he built a studio for himself at Meudon-Val-Fleury (1930–1), which soon became the focus of the Stijl movement. He worked once more in collaboration with Cor van *Eesteren, as he had done already in the early twenties, and turned his attention to applying the principles of De Stijl to town planning. Van Doesburg's death in 1931 meant the end of the Stijl group, but its concepts of space, which he helped to define, have remained a living issue to the present time.

Bibliography: Theo van Doesburg, *De Nieuwe Beweging in de Schilderkunst*, Delft 1917; Theo van Doesburg, *Drie voordrachten over de nieuwe beeldende*

Theo van Doesburg. Aubette. Strasbourg, 1926–7

Kunst, Amsterdam 1919; Theo van Doesburg, *Klassiek, barok, modern*, The Hague 1920; Theo van Doesburg, *L'Architecture vivante*, Paris 1925.

J. J. VRIEND

Drew, Jane Beverly, b. 1911. Studied at the Architectural Association School of Architecture, London. In partnership with J. T. Allison, 1934–9. Independent practice, 1939–45. In partnership with Maxwell *Fry (whom she married in 1942) since 1945. Early work in Kenya led to specialization in tropical architecture. Assistant Town Planning Adviser, West Africa, 1944–5. Schools, housing and colleges in Ghana. Joint work with Maxwell Fry on the University of Ibadan, Nigeria. Projects in Kuwait (1,000-bed hospital); India (hospitals, housing, and a large high school; senior architect at Chandigarh in collaboration with *Le Corbusier); Singapore; Ceylon; South Persia (housing, town planning, hospital extensions, cinemas); and Mauritius (hospitals and housing). Jane Drew served as Bemis Professor at the Massachusetts Institute of Technology in 1961, and has lectured widely elsewhere.

Dudok, Willem Marinus, b. Amsterdam 1884. Although deriving something from both the School of *Amsterdam and De *Stijl, Dudok evolved an independent position of his own. The contrast of solid and void areas, horizontals and verticals recalls De Stijl, but Dudok's brick buildings nearly always retain a massive weightiness. Numerous buildings at Hilversum, where Dudok became municipal architect in 1915: Vondel School (1928–9), Town Hall (1928–30). Netherlands House at the Paris Cité Universitaire (1927–8), Bijenkorf department store at Rotterdam (1929–30, now replaced by the new building by Marcel *Breuer). (*Netherlands)
Bibliography: W. M. Dudok, Übersicht über sein Werk, Amsterdam 1954.

Duiker, Johannes, b. The Hague 1890, d. Amsterdam 1935. Studied at Delft Technical College. Member of De *Stijl and the group connected with the journal *De 8 en Opbouw*. Zonnestraal Sanatorium at Hilversum (1928, together with B. Bijvoet); open-air school at Amsterdam (1930–2), a five-storey fully glazed structure with terraces for open-air lessons.

Eames, Charles, b. St Louis, Missouri 1907. Broke off his studies at Washington University, St Louis, after eighteen months. Architect and designer. Together with his wife Ray he undertakes almost any sort of design from toys to furniture. His own house at Santa Monica, California (1949), a steel-frame building constructed from prefabricated units, is reminiscent of an old Japanese house in its proportions and light appearance.

Ecole des Beaux-Arts. Most influential School of Art and Architecture in the 19th century. The Parisian École goes back to its foundation by Colbert in 1671. Its teaching system rests on lectures and practical work in artists' studios and architects' offices. The Grand Prix de Rome offered by the École provides several years of study at the French Academy in the Villa Medici in Rome. The institute's basic conceptions of architecture lie in the composition of well-proportioned elements in a well-proportioned whole. In practice, the École, where many eminent architects have been trained, has often opposed modern trends in architecture.

Eesteren, Cor van, b. Ablasserdam 1897. Studied at the Academy in Rotterdam, the Sorbonne, and the *École des Beaux-Arts. Belonged from 1923 to the De *Stijl movement. Collaboration with van *Doesburg, especially on housing projects in 1923. For many years President of the *CIAM. Municipal buildings (Amsterdam Plan, 1936).

Eiermann, Egon, b. Neuendorf, near Berlin 1904. Together with Hans *Scharoun, Egon Eiermann is among the most discussed architects of post-war Germany. The work of these two men denotes the span of modern German architecture. If Scharoun designs with a feeling for the possibilities of sculptural massing, Eiermann lays stress on perceptible articulation, logical expression of the structural frame and precise detailing. His buildings create an impression of extraordinary clarity and taut organization. Architecture means to him 'making order visible, from town planning to the smallest building'. Structure and function can nearly always be read off, and his industrial plants reveal the aesthetic charm of visibly displayed technical apparatus. Eiermann develops his designs from functional analysis, in the widest sense of the word, including an assessment of the cultural and geographical background. Two office blocks, built over the same period, for the Essener Colliery (1960) and the Müller Steel Works at Offenbach (1960) depend in their different conceptions on the character of their surroundings: relatively blank wall areas with smallish window openings and quiet, dark panel cladding in the Ruhr town; brightly coloured façades with shady galleries and variable protection from the sun on the Upper Rhine. The tendency towards dogmatic preference for certain shapes is less pronounced in Eiermann than in other architects who are still under the influence of *Mies van der Rohe's image of a clear-cut rectilinear architecture.

Egon Eiermann. Handkerchief Mill. Blumberg, 1951

Egon Eiermann. Neckermann Mail Order Company Building. Frankfurt, 1958–60. Detail of elevation

Eiermann, who studied under *Poelzig in Berlin, wrote his thesis on a department store, and worked at first in the architects' office of the Karstadt multiple store company. He retained a liking for this type of work even after the war (Merkur Department Store at Heilbronn, 1951). The Blumberg Handkerchief Mill (1951) represents a culminating point in his work, with the slender tracery of its various viewpoints. Of Eiermann's church designs, St Matthew's at Pforzheim (1953) and the Memorial Church in Berlin (1961) have been built; the war damaged stump of the latter's tower was preserved and surrounded by the simple stereometric buildings of the new church.

For these ecclesiastical buildings Eiermann used pierced blocks with coloured glazing, which the light filters through. Similar textured wall surfaces, which have a purely decorative purpose, occur at his two deparment stores, the Horten at Heidelberg and the Merkur at Stuttgart (1961); they are reminiscent of Edward D. *Stone's work. But these buildings do not stand comparison with that of the export firm of Neckermann at Frankfurt (1958–60). In contrast to the patterned surfaces of the two department stores, the Frankfurt building is vigorously enlivened by external galleries, fire-escapes, and air conditioning and stair towers. Eiermann's buildings for the German government display more delicate outlines and elegant proportions; they include the German pavilion at the Brussels World Fair (in collaboration with Sep Ruf, 1958) and the German Embassy in Washington, which rises in steps on a sloping site (work still in progress).

Eiermann, who lectures at Karlsruhe Technical College, has also made a name for himself as an industrial designer.

WOLFGANG PEHNT

Gustave Eiffel. Truyère Bridge. Garabit, 1880–4

Eiffel, Gustave, b. Dijon 1832, d. Paris 1923. Gustave Eiffel, a Burgundian by birth, was intended to be a chemist and only by chance became a structural engineer. As consultant to several building firms and later as an independent consulting engineer, he had the opportunity of making himself familiar with all the problems occasioned to bridge designers by the advance of the railways into ever more difficult territory. He soon realized that these problems could not be solved if the metal used was, as hitherto, in the form of the comparatively heavy and inelastic cast-iron. New materials, such as rolled iron and *steel had to be used, and these were now being commercially produced in sufficient quantities, but new methods and shapes had also to be invented that did justice to the better static behaviour of these materials.

When Eiffel founded his own firm in 1867 he already commanded a sufficiently extensive experience. He also realized the importance of collaborating with outstanding men such as Nouguier and Koechlin, and he introduced new methods, whose precision gave his firm great advantages over his mostly foreign competitors. Soon after the end of the Franco-Prussian war, commissions came in from all over the world (France, Switzerland, Austria, Hungary, Russia, Portugal, Peru, etc.). Thus he had ample opportunity of testing the versatility of the lattice beam he had developed and which he made the most important component of a novel structural system. Apart from numerous bridges, stations, roof projects, and other structures, nearly all of which brought technical advances, his three main designs were: the Maria Pia Bridge over the Douro near Oporto (1877–8), the Truyère Bridge near Garabit in the French Massif Central (1880–4), and the Eiffel Tower in Paris (1887–9). These three enormous structures are all closely related. All three rely throughout on the application of the principle on which the lattice beam is based, viz. the subdivision of beams into three-dimensional space frames built up from individually small members and riveted together from commercially available angle irons or flats, which afford maximum rigidity for minimum weight. The Eiffel Tower is nothing but an extension of the solution tried out at Oporto and Garabit for extremely tall bridge supports.

The Tower, in particular, marks an important stage in the development of modern architecture for the impressive proof it gives of the fecundity of the engineering approach: intuitions, substantiated by calculation, led to entirely new shapes. The Tower brought the realization of a new spatial image, made up of joints and fields of force, to which indeed only graphic artists like Robert Delaunay and Antoine Pevsner were receptive, and then hardly before 1910. Through their intermediation, and thanks to the interpretations they gave

Gustave Eiffel. Eiffel Tower. Paris, 1887–9

of this spatial image, it was beamed back to architecture. The work of *Wachsmann and Le Ricolais on space structures has aroused the interest of architects and for some years now they have been working on Eiffel's multi-centred conception of space.

Eiffel himself pursued the logical direction of his research on the greatest adversary his giant constructions had to contend with: the wind. From 1910 on, he devoted himself to aerodynamic studies, which led to the building of the first wind-tunnel to meet the needs of the aircraft industry (1911), and to the development of the first aeroplane tested in a wind-tunnel (Bréguet LE, 1918).

Bibliography: Gustave Eiffel, *Mémoire présenté à l'appui du projet définitif du Viaduc de Garabit*, Paris 1889; Gustave Eiffel, *La Tour de Trois Cents Mètres*, Paris 1900 (2 folio vols.); Gustave Eiffel, *La Résistance de l'air et l'aviation*, Paris 1913 and 1914; Jean Prévost, *Eiffel*, Paris 1929; Maurice Besset, *Gustave Eiffel*, Milan 1957, Paris 1959.

MAURICE BESSET

Eijck, Aldo van, b. Driebercen 1918. Eijck, who has shown particular interest in problems of education (children's playgrounds at Amsterdam), created 'a house like a small town' when he built the Municipal Orphanage at Amsterdam (1955; *Netherlands). This consists of square space units which make up a growing complex of buildings. Municipal work (collaboration in the Nagele Plan).

Ellwood, Craig, b. Clarendon, Texas 1921. Mainly private dwellings of unusually elegant proportions and careful detailing which are reminiscent of *Mies van der Rohe with their slender sections. Carson-Roberts Building, Los Angeles (1961).

Endell, August, b. Berlin 1871, d. Breslau 1925. Self-taught. Designer and architect in the *Art Nouveau style. His most important buildings, the Elvira Photo Studio at Munich (1897–8) and the Buntes Theatre at Berlin (1901), are both distinguished by ingenious surface decoration. (*Germany)

Ervi, Aarne, b. Tammela, Finland 1910. Tapiola Garden City near Helsinki was based on Ervi's 1953 plan, and he himself carried out several of the projects there. Buildings for Turku University (1956–9).

Expressionism. Expressionist architects, like Expressionist painters, had no cultural groupings, with unified programmes and activities, and most architects who came within the ambit of Expressionism did so only for a short period of their development, although this often proved to be the zenith of their artistic careers. In the work of the best of them, various influences must be recognized as existing simultaneously side by side, or at different levels; these may vary from *Art Nouveau to romantic nationalism, from Expressionist art to a kind of late-romantic surrealism, and from rationalism and a search for objectivity to a view of the creative act as an unrepeatable gesture of self- and world-knowledge.

In Germany, during the years immediately prior to 1914, the true artistic avant-garde consisted of architects who owed their allegiance to the *Jugendstil, the course of whose history overlaid that of Expressionism for upwards of ten years. If we look more closely at the anti-classical, anti-internationalist traits that characterize the German version of Art Nouveau, its considerable hang-over from the historical styles and its general tendency to picturesqueness and a taste for organic forms, not projected on to plane surfaces but conceived plastically almost from the start, we shall readily perceive the numerous connecting links with avant-garde German Expressionist movements such as the *Brücke* and the *Blaue Reiter*. In this context one thinks of the work of Eckmann, Pankok, Obrist, *Endell, Joseph Maria *Olbrich, who played a key role at this period with his activities at Darmstadt, and above all of Richard *Riemerschmid with his Hellerau factory (1910) and Henry van de *Velde, for their direct influence on the architects of Expressionism.

A typical feature of the situation in Germany at the time was the way the country was divided up between different cultural centres, each with a strong individual character and relatively independent of all the others, with its own schools of architecture and the applied arts. Efforts were being made to develop a romantic-national style, as a form of escape from eclecticism, that would provide the new German nation with a suitable form of architecture. With Alfred Messel's Wertheim department store (1896) a series of attempts began at simplifying the eclectic Wilhelminian language of the times which implicated all the most distinguished architects currently practising: Theodor *Fischer who taught at Munich (Ulm Garrison Church, 1911), Ludwig Hoffmann, Paul *Bonatz (Main Railway Station, Stuttgart, 1913–27, with F. E. Scholer), and Fritz Schumacher, Professor at Dresden, and later at Hamburg, who had already before 1914 clearly worked out and established an expressive style of his own.

It was Peter *Behrens who achieved the transition to Expressionism with his buildings for the AEG in Berlin (1908–13). We are not concerned here with those elements which clearly anticipate the rationalist style. Behrens's factories are not designed with the kind of utilitarian character associated with the functional tradition, but rather as the representation of a new power, one that directly multiplies nature's goods. In his work may be seen that process of deformation of the national romantic style which is one of the fundamental sources of Expressionist architecture.

Apart from Behrens, there are only two architects before the First World War clearly distinguishable as Expressionists: Hans *Poelzig and Max *Berg. The conventional exterior of Berg's reinforced concrete Centenary Hall in Breslau (1912–13) gives no indication of the exciting three-dimensional treatment inside the enormous dome, 213 feet in diameter. It is impossible to find any reinforced concrete building before this date equally as compelling, and with as little of the schematic about it. Of these three architects, however, it is Hans Poelzig who seems to have adhered most consciously to Expressionism. His large industrial complex at Luban (1911–12) seems even more unprejudiced in design than the best works of Behrens at this period. His volumes are built up of asymmetrical blocks, whose organic unity seems to underline the peculiar individuality of the design. Three years previously, Poelzig had built a large house near Breslau, where the plastic fusion of all the elements towards a volumetric continuity recalls some of van de Velde's villas of the same epoch.

Thanks to the absence of preconceived types, it was industrial architecture that offered the line of least resistance to progressive experiments at the time. This may be seen in the celebrated scheme for a water mill at Weider (1906), and above all in the great structure built by Poelzig at Posen (1911), with a water tower above and an exhibition hall below; brick is used here to clad a steel framework. The bold handling of volumes makes it one of the

Hans Poelzig. Water tower. Posen, 1911

Hans Poelzig. Salzburg Festival Theatre, 1920–1. Project

Glashausproblem:
Raum bricht Raum.
Gedanke – Feininger –
Wirklichkeit?

Mies van der Rohe. Office building, Friedrichstrasse, Berlin, 1919. Project (first version)

Fritz Höger. Chilehaus. Hamburg, 1922–3

most significant German buildings of its day—the 'total transposition of a personal idea into a work' which Kirchner demanded as the basis for art. A series of sketches dating from this period are clearly influenced in conception by certain drawings of Kokoschka, and show a desire to model a building with an aggressive immediacy that leaves no part of its surface unmarked by its author's will.

German culture in the years after the First World War became progressively more political in character. The Socialist revolution accompanied Expressionism as a form of protest for at least ten years, in an ideologically hybrid identification between cultural avant-gardism and progressive politics. Examples of this tendency may be seen in the Berlin *Arbeitsrat für Kunst* and *Novembergruppe*. The latter group, descended from pre-war anarchist papers such as *Aktion* and *Revolution*, attracted to it all the foremost representatives of German artistic life in the years 1918–20; many architects were members, including *Gropius and *Mendelsohn. The *Novembergruppe*'s programme attributed particular importance to architecture, regarded as a direct instrument for raising social standards. The group was dissolved after the bloody suppression of the Sparticist rising, and the ensuing disillusion among the progressive spirits of the Weimar Republic contributed decisively to the emergence of *Neue Sachlichkeit*, which became the focus of much Expressionist activity.

The *Bauhaus, too, especially during its Weimar period, absorbed many features of Expressionism. The crude pragmatism; the stark expressive simplicity; a tenacious grip on reality combined with an ethical sense of human obligation; all accord well with the School's methodological programme as also with a type of design that was a frequent outcome of Expressionist theory. It is in this light that some of the works of the protagonists of rationalism built at this period may be clearly explained; works carried out in a style with close affinities to Expressionism. They include *Mies van der Rohe's design for a skyscraper (1919) and his memorial to Rosa Luxemburg and

Page 94. Hans Scharoun. Sketch. 1920

Michael de Klerk. Eigen Haard estate. Amsterdam, 1921

Paul Bonatz. Head Office, United Steel Works. Düsseldorf, 1922–4

Karl Liebknecht (1926), and Gropius's War Memorial at Weimar (1922) and his theatre at Jena (1923).

Numerous other buildings at this time, however, were built under the direct influence of pre-war Expressionism, thus displaying a cultural lag of about ten years. They may be roughly divided into two distinct groups: one pushing the Expressionist protest in the direction of a progressive intensification of its idiom, either in a lyric vein with Art Nouveau reminiscences, or in a desperate manner leading to the destruction of volume; the other tending towards a national-romantic style. This kind of ambiguity is typical of Expressionism, which proved a fertile source of progressive drives and rationalist activity. Emil Fahrenkamp, for example, built a series of interesting factories in 1923, but later went over to a nationalist style. Wilhelm Kreis, with his Düsseldorf skyscraper, the Wilhelm-Marx-Building (1922–4), and the interior of the planetarium in the same city, produced two works of the highest merit in a near-Expressionist idiom, but later developed a heavy simplified neoclassic manner. *Scharoun, Schneider and the *Luckhardt brothers made use of the figurative manifestations of Expressionism within the orbit of rationalist practice. Rudolf Steiner's Goetheanum at Dornach (1925–8) is linked to Expressionism by its picturesque treatment, but occupies a place apart, as it was designed in accordance with the principles of Anthroposophy.

The School of *Amsterdam, too, whose mouthpiece was the journal **Wendingen*, displayed an intensification of the national style; but the situation was somewhat different here from that in Germany, as social contrasts were less extreme. In point of fact, the largest scheme carried out by these architects was the development of low-cost housing estates in South Amsterdam. Hence the Expressionist character of the work is not a manifestation of protest; it derives from a peculiar ability to evolve an endless variety of forms, in a three-dimensional treatment that often achieves almost fairy-tale effects.

The most important Expressionist buildings erected in Germany in the first years after the war comprise: the Chilehaus (Fritz Höger), Ballinhaus (brothers Hans and Oskar Gerson) and Sprinkenhof

Rudolf Steiner. Goetheanum. Dornach, 1925–8

(Höger and the Gerson brothers), at Hamburg (1922–3), all influenced by Fritz Schumacher; the Einstein Tower by Erich Mendelsohn at Potsdam (1920); and the entrance hall of the Hoechst Dyeworks by Peter Behrens (1920–5). In Behrens's building, the wall surface features continuous punctuation by varying textures and materials, which emphasizes a feeling of unrest and instability that seems to lurk beneath the severe overall design. The brickwork is in shades which range from blue to orange and yellow, a palette which recalls the water-colours of Nolde or Kirchner. Mendelsohn, on the other hand, was influenced by the *Blaue Reiter* movement—he knew Franz Marc and Kandinsky when a student at Munich in 1911—and his Jugendstil reminiscences derive from that source. His sketches, executed between 1914 and 1920, display the same stylistic idioms, and that character of cosmic and stylistic search and lyric effusion as an act of liberation, and at the same time mystical union with the world, that is typical of the *Blaue Reiter's* spiritual posture. His use of sketches to work out his approach to a theme, without reference to structure, is typically Expressionist.

Two other architects deserve special notice: Hugo *Häring and Otto *Bartning. For Häring adherence to the Expressionist aesthetic was tantamount to a recognition of German Gothic as an anti-illuminist culture that shunned the laws of geometry and was hence organic in form (farm buildings, Garkau, 1923). For Bartning, however, architecture is growth and activity, the force of nature itself (Star church project, 1922). Poelzig's development between 1919 and 1930 is in two phases. The rebuilding of the Grosses Schauspielhaus in Berlin, the designs for the Salzburg Festival Theatre and a festival hall at Dresden carry the process of

Erich Mendelsohn. Einstein Tower. Potsdam, 1920. Project

dissolving not only the classic rules of composition but the very constituent elements of the structure itself to extraordinary lengths. A second phase witnesses the reassertion of volumetric values, with a soberer and more monumental style, as exemplified by his designs for the IG-Farben offices at Frankfurt (1928–31) and his broadcasting studios in Berlin.
Under the stress of the menacing political situation in the early thirties, the artistic forces of the time tended to crystallize into groups centring around the democratic opposition or the Nazi party. The sharpening of this crisis betokened the end of Expressionism, which by its intrinsic nature could not tolerate extreme ideological conditions, although it tended to promote and educe them. The 'white architecture of the twenties' became a symbol of the democratic opposition, while Expressionism began to acquire pan-Germanic and nationalist traits, and in its ideological uncertainty was relegated to a position of cultural insignificance.
Bibliography: Walter Müller-Wulckow, *Deutsche Baukunst der Gegenwart*, Leipzig 1929; E. M. Hajos and L. Zahn, *Berliner Architektur der Nachkriegszeit*, Berlin 1928; Vittorio Gregotti, 'L'architettura dell' espressionismo', in *Casabella Continuità*, No. 254, Milan 1961; Arnold Whittick, *European Architecture in the Twentieth Century*, Vol. 1 (up to 1924), Vol. 2 (1924–33), London 1950 and 1953.

VITTORIO GREGOTTI

Festival of Britain, South Bank Exhibition. London, 1951. Aerial view of site

Farmer and Dark. Frank Quentery Farmer, b. 1879, d. 1955 and Bernard Franklin Dark. Practice founded 1934, specializing in industrial buildings, where effects are achieved by essentially simple but carefully developed methods of planning and close attention to details; factories, mills, power stations. In 1957 a 75-inch module system was developed for one- or two-storey timber buildings (Sconce Hills School, Newark, Notts.).

Festival of Britain. A national manifestation organized throughout the United Kingdom in 1951, at the original suggestion of Sir Gerald Barry, to mark the centenary of the Great Exhibition of 1851. Its most important architectural expression was the exhibition laid out on the south bank of the Thames in London (Director of Architecture: Hugh *Casson). This was significant not only for the opportunity it afforded millions of people to see stimulating modern architecture of an almost uniformly high level of design, but because it provided an occasion for displaying the principles of *townscape which had been developing and clarifying themselves over the previous years. Eschewing the formal layouts that had been usual in earlier major exhibitions, recourse was had to a subtly planned disposition of buildings and features, an exploitation of changes of level, progressively evolving views and the dramatic long-distance backdrop of the north bank of the Thames to give an impression of exciting complexity and size that was quite extraordinary for so small a site.
Notable contributions were made by Ralph Tubbs (Dome of Discovery), Arcon (Transport), Maxwell *Fry and Jane *Drew, Edward *Mills (Administration building), R. Y. Goodden and R. D. Russell (Lion and Unicorn), H. T. Cadbury Brown (Land of Britain), Brian O'Rorke and F. H. K. Henrion (The Natural Scene and The Country), *Architects' Co-Partnership (Minerals of the Land), G. Grenfell Baines and H. J. Reifenberg (Power and Production) and Basil *Spence (Sea and Ships).
Bibliography: H. Casson, 'The 1951 Exhibition' in *Journal of the RIBA*, April 1950. See also *Architectural Review* for May 1951.

HAROLD MEEK

Misha Black, Alexander Gibson, and Design Research Unit. Regatta Restaurant. Festival of Britain, South Bank Exhibition. London, 1951

Figini, Luigi, b. Milan, 1903. Graduated there 1926. Founder member of **gruppo 7*. Collaboration with Gino *Pollini. Residential buildings, factories (for Olivetti in Ivrea), exhibition architecture, and interior decoration. The Church of the Madonna dei Poveri erected on a basilica plan (Milan 1952–6) attempts to create an atmosphere of mystical faith with its exposed concrete frame, narrow light slits in the nave and its deliberate impression of a rough, unfinished state. (*Italy)

Finland. The counter-movement to eclecticism began to take shape in Finland in the course of the 1890s. Although preliminary development was gradual, the actual breakthrough in 1900 proved stormy. Following it, virtually no classical shapes emerged again for a long time. The victor was not *Art Nouveau in its true sense, but a Finnish version of it, the so-called National Romantic style, which was inspired by the tradition of primitive Finnish architecture. Axial symmetry was done away with and replaced by the free plan and free massing. Façade architecture gave way to layouts with separate blocks and wings. One of the essential problems of modern architecture had already been encountered: that of the continuity of space. These problems were solved in such an original way in Finland that the best examples have preserved their freshness throughout the past decades. While Art Nouveau often relied on decorative details for its artistic effect, the Finnish National Romantic style depended more on the effect of its materials as such. Timber and granite were favourite media from which strong and expressive effects were derived. The painter Akseli Gallén-Kallela may be regarded as the spiritual father of the National Romantic movement in Finland, and his studio built in the Wildmark (1894) was the first achievement of the new style. Three architects, Gesellius, Lindgren and Eliel *Saarinen, soon took their place at its head. It was their design for the Finnish pavilion at the Paris International Exhibition of 1900 which precipitated the breakthrough, and their fortress-like loghouse building at Hvitträsk near Helsinki (1902) still makes the strongest impression on a spectator to this day. Lars Sonck, the builder of Tampere Cathedral (1902–7) is currently regarded as the most brilliant exponent of the real romantic style. By its side, International Art Nouveau also made its appearance in Finland, assuming the tasks of a rationalist school in comparison with the picturesque romantic style. Its representatives are Selim Lindquist, Onni Tarjanne and Usko Nyström, whose aims were closer to present-day architecture than those of the romantics although they did not always measure up to them as artists.

Lars Sonck and Valter Jung. Bank. Helsinki, 1904

Sigurd Frosterus, a pupil of van de Velde's, and Gustaf Strengell were the leaders of the rationalist opposition and modern architectural ideas emerge in their writings around 1904. Even if they did not manage to defeat the romantics, the rationalists dealt them a decisive blow. The reaction was mainly due to the example set by Eliel Saarinen. He developed his own monumental style, whose fundamental idea is a vertical movement breaking through from the central feature of a horizontal mass; a subject whose pathos greatly appealed to his contemporaries. Saarinen's most important building in Finland is the main station at Helsinki (1904, built 1910–14), but it is less attractive than his general plan for the town—a fully consistent decentralization plan, conceived as early as 1918.

After the end of the First World War, it became apparent that belief in the birth of a new art and a new architecture had been vain. Classical motives, albeit freely handled, returned to architecture. Coupled with this tendency now was the influence of Swedish classicism, which prevailed among the young generation. Striving for monumentality during the classicizing intermezzo of the twenties reached its peak in J. S. Sirén's Parliament Building. For many others, such as Erik *Bryggman and Gunnar Taucher, this trend meant a process of simplification, which banished every last moulding from their smooth surfaces. The timeless, functional architecture of the Mediterranean countries was the main exemplar adduced, and in this respect classicism too paved the way for the new architecture. Furthermore, the social thought of the twenties introduced a new element, as shown in the garden suburb of Käpylä at Helsinki (1920–5), planned by Martti Välikangas and others, which is based on old Finnish traditions as much as on the teachings of Ebenezer *Howard.

The new architecture, *Functionalism, only reached Finland in the late twenties. The exhibition at Turku, designed by Alvar *Aalto and Erik Bryggman in 1929, became the manifesto of the movement. The great Stockholm Exhibition of the following year assured the victory of Functionalism in Finland too. Compared with most other countries, the change in Finland was rapid and complete. The first new works by Bryggman, Erkki Huttunen, Yrjö Lindegren, and others showed great maturity, quite apart from Aalto's sanatorium at Paimio (1929–33) and the library at Viipuri (1927–35), which are among the classic masterpieces of modern architecture.

This 'white' Functionalism in Finland does not lack individuality despite its internationalism. A certain stress of solidity is characteristic of most of its products and gives them an expression of real monumentality, which often achieves pathos as in P. E. Blomstedt's work. Bryggman displays an outward lightness which is reminiscent of Continental rationalism but always preserves a romantic colouring.

Although the thirties were so uniform in Finnish architecture, new ideas did develop

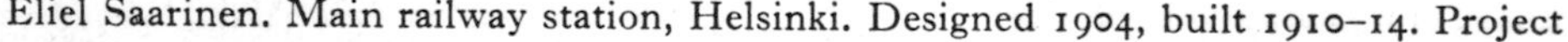

Eliel Saarinen. Main railway station, Helsinki. Designed 1904, built 1910–14. Project

during this period, and more diverse artistic expressions resulted. Aalto above all, whose works from the outset attracted attention outside Finland, demonstrated new powers of design. His cellulose factory at Sunila (1936–9) and the house built along terraces at Kauttua (1938–40) are studies in adapting architecture to landscape. Free shapes and careful use of building materials (in particular of timber) characterize his work from the start (Finnish Pavilion at the New York World's Fair, 1939).

The forties brought a reaction against the severity of Functionalism. The Olympic Village by Hilding Ekelund and Välikangas (Helsinki 1940) marks the retreat of the cube in favour of less demanding functional shapes and the memorial chapel at Turku cemetery (1938–41) by Bryggman appeals to the spectator's emotions. Throughout the war building activity was very limited and the artistic results were modest. The romantic reaction took refuge in eclecticist and decorative motives, so that the fundamental character of the new architecture seemed in some ways to be already as good as lost.

The fifties saw a new upsurge of activity, once more beneath the banners of rationalism and Constructivism. American influences were apparent in the work of Aarne *Ervi and Viljo *Revell. Revell's studio became a kind of headquarters of the rationalist school, from which many of the leading architects of today have emerged. The bright and simple Kudeneule factory at Hanko (1955) may be regarded as Revell's most typical design. He has become widely known as the leader of the team that won the Toronto City Hall competition. Although the fifties were so rationalistic, the trend that started in the thirties still continued. The heavy, vigorous shapes of Finnish architecture are very different from the precise purism of the *International Style; feeling for materials and adaptability to natural surroundings have remained constant. Even in such purist examples as the chapel at Otaniemi (1957) by Kaija and Heikki *Siren, it is for just these reasons that a warmth has been preserved which we generally call 'human'.

These properties are most pronounced in Alvar Aalto's buildings. Although at first he renounced free shapes, his designs preserve a plastic unity despite their

Gunnar Taucher. Housing. Helsinki, 1926

Jorma Järvi. High School. Helsinki, 1955. Assembly Hall

Alvar Aalto. Boarding School. Helsinki, 1952–6

Page 102. Yrjö Lindegren and Toivo Jäntti. Olympic Stadium. Helsinki, 1934–40 and 1952

Kaija and Heikki Siren. Chapel, Otaniemi Technical College, 1957

rectangularity (Town Hall at Säynätsalo, 1950–2; boarding school at Helsinki, 1952–6). Later he returned to free shapes and transferred them from the interiors to the way his buildings were massed (Cultural Institute at Helsinki, 1955–8; church at Vuoksenniska near Imatra, 1956–58). His palette as always is built up from natural materials and has become still richer. Apart from timber he now employs exposed brickwork, copper, ceramics and marble. Aalto has not founded a school of architects but his influence on Finnish architecture is none the less extraordinarily great, thanks to his ability to point out new directions and to serve as a criterion of architectural quality.

Lindegren (extensions to the Olympic Stadium at Helsinki, 1952; 'Snakehouse' residential district at Helsinki, 1951) and Aulis Blomstedt have also gone their own roads. The less numerous and more modest works of Blomstedt achieve their effect by their outstanding sureness of proportion to which he has devoted special research.

New trends reached Finland, too, towards the end of the fifties. The free shapes of *shell vaulting have remained more or less at the design stage, however, and this situation is not yet resolved.

Bibliography: Nils Erik Wickberg, *Byggnadskonst i Finland*, Stockholm 1959;

Viljo Revell. Kudeneule Textile Works. Hanko, 1955

Aulis Blomstedt. Extension to a Workers' Club. Helsinki, 1959

Hans J. Becker and Wolfram Schlote, *Neuer Wohnbau in Finnland*, Stuttgart 1958, Milan 1960.

KYÖSTI ÅLANDER

Fiocchi, Annibale, b. Milan 1915. Director of the architectural department of Olivetti's. Housing estates and factories in Ivrea (together with *Nizzoli, *Figini and *Pollini and Mario Oliveri), Palazzo Olivetti, Milan (with G. A. Bernasconi and Nizzoli, 1954). (*Curtain Wall; *Italy)

Fischer, Theodor, b. Schweinfurt 1862, d. Munich 1938. Collaborated with Paul Wallot on the Reichstag Building, Berlin. Taught and built in Stuttgart, Munich, and elsewhere. Evangelical Garrison Church at Ulm (1911), numerous offices, schools, museums.

Fisker, Kay, b. Copenhagen 1893. Studied at the Academy of Fine Arts, Copenhagen. The influence of international Functionalism is evident in Fisker's buildings, but he has not abandoned the tradition of Danish brick architecture. Considerable teaching activity. Architect of Århus University, together with Povl Stegmann and C. F. Møller (work commenced 1931), school at Husum (1949–51), large housing estates. *Bibliography:* Hans Erling Langkilde, *Arkitekten Kay Fisker*, Copenhagen 1960.

Floorscape. The use of patterns and textures in the ground as a design element, either contributing to overall visual appeal, suggesting lines of directivity to the pedestrian, or simply emphasizing space.
Bibliography: Elizabeth Beazley, *Design and detail of the space between buildings*, London 1960; Gordon Cullen, *Townscape*, London 1961.

France. The history of modern architecture in France is characterized by the tenacious resistance to new ideas put up by the reactionary forces and the continuance of a type of thought aiming at reform, which has been asserting itself equally stubbornly for a hundred years. From this polarity a fascinating historical picture emerges and, at the present time, a conflicting situation that can only be surveyed with difficulty. Academic resistance has centred round the Paris *École des Beaux-Arts, with practically all the means of a centralized, official apparatus at its disposal. The attitude of this court of official opinion was not only of importance to France; European and American reaction took its cue for decades from the example of the École des Beaux-Arts. Though the academicians succeeded in keeping commissions away from the younger generation and withholding from them the opportunity for experimentation, they could not prevent men in every generation who had espoused a revolutionary attitude from making their influence felt even far beyond the frontiers of their own country.
The conflict flared up when *Viollet-le-Duc, in his own feud against the Beaux-Arts, professed a doctrine relating form to material and function, which his investigations into Gothic architecture had suggested to him (*Dictionnaire de l'Architecture*, 1854 ff., *Entretiens sur l'Architecture*, 1863–72, American translation 1875–1881). This doctrine has influenced practically all pioneers of modern architecture, from *Richardson, via *Berlage and *Horta, to *Perret, *Le Corbusier and even F. Ll. *Wright. It met with most approval from the engineers, who saw in the return of architecture to structural form an ideal

which they themselves did not dare to proclaim publicly. Their colossal structures (Douro and Garabit bridges by *Eiffel, 1877–84; Eiffel Tower and Contamin's Machinery Hall, 1889; Arnodin's Ponts Transbordeurs at Nantes and Marseilles, 1900–5) seemed to confirm the doctrine of the essential dependence of form on function, and the new formal and spatial concepts were indeed traced back to a strict adherence to this thesis. The prestige of such works has outlasted the change of generations. No wonder then that Choisy's still influential *Histoire de l'Architecture*, which was published towards the end of that golden age of construction in 1898, tackles the history of form in a purely engineering spirit.

The iron style had just reached its Baroque phase in Art Nouveau (*Guimard's Métro station entrances, 1900, Frantz Jourdain's Samaritaine department store, 1901) when a new generation tried taking the new material of reinforced concrete as the starting point for a new style, based on the same functional principles. A clear, strictly geometrical vocabulary of form, with classical overtones in the case of Perret, takes the place of the spatially complicated iron structures. Until the First World War the architectural use of reinforced concrete was restricted to a few examples (Perret, *Garnier). But these pioneers deserve the credit for having made the new material fit for architecture, while restoring validity again to the principle of truth to structure. The conflict with official architecture now assumed a sharper character than at the time of the iron engineers whose sphere of activities only overlapped with academicism at the edges.

Only after the war did the 'new style' emerge from a combination of architectural form with the new spatial concept that had crystallized between 1907 and 1914 in the graphic arts: Cubism. Since then Le Corbusier's genius towers over the horizon of French architecture. Around him and beside him, however, though seldom quite independent of him, new paths were explored. During the twenties the interchange of ideas with other centres of the movement —Germany and Holland—was particularly active. It was promoted by such journals as *L'Esprit Nouveau* (edited by Le Corbusier and Ozenfant, 1920–6) *Les Cahiers de l'Effort Moderne* (edited by Léonce Rosenberg, 1925–7) and the *Architecture Vivante* series (edited by Badovici and Morancé from 1923); by exhibitions such as the International Exhibition of Applied Art, Paris, 1925, the unequalled exhibition of the Deutscher Werkbund (with the *Bauhaus as a focal point) in the Salon des Artistes Décorateurs, Paris, 1930, and the participation of French architects at the Werkbund Exhibition in Stuttgart, 1927, and at the International Building Exhibition, Berlin, 1930, etc. Adolf *Loos worked in Paris from 1923 till 1928 (Maison Tzara, 1926) and exerted a deep influence

Hector Guimard. Métro entrance. Paris, 1900

Henri Labrouste. Bibliothèque Ste Geneviève. Paris, 1843–50

Le Corbusier. Salvation Army Hostel. Paris, 1931–2

on the younger architects. Le Corbusier and Jeanneret, André *Lurçat, Robert *Mallet-Stevens, Gabriel Guevrekian, Jean Badovici, Michel Roux-Spitz built houses and villas for avant-garde patrons, all typical examples of the *International Style; suffice it to mention the steel and glass house built by Pierre Chareau for Dr Dalsace, 1931.

The exponents of the new architecture, however, lacked the powerful support which their colleagues in Germany and Holland enjoyed in the form of major commissions from municipal authorities for the design of housing estates. It was only as late as 1930–5 that opportunities for other work arose on a limited scale. Thus besides a few blocks of flats (preceded twenty years earlier by those of Henri Sauvage in the Rue Vavin which had not received the attention they merited), the Hôtel Latitude 43 was built at St Tropez in 1933 by Pingusson and the school at Villejuif by Lurçat in 1931–3. The housing estates of Eugène *Beaudouin and Marcel *Lods at Drancy (the first point blocks) and Bagneux followed, with their open air school at Suresnes (1932–5) and the Maison du Peuple at Clichy (in collaboration with Jean *Prouvé). A development opened up that might have led to a kind of 'Scandinavian style' if stagnation on the property market, the hostility of the authorities and the deplorable success of the compromise-architecture at the Paris International Exhibition of 1937 had not barred the way.

The years following the Second World War created a completely new situation: a building boom, shifting the emphasis to State-backed housing schemes (annual target: 350,000 dwellings), with the problem extended to dimensions that required the creation of mixed teams of architects, engineers, and sociologists, and the emergence of town- and country-planning projects to a position of major importance. The unique opportunity of this first reconstruction period has been missed in France as thoroughly as elsewhere. Le Corbusier's advanced scheme for St Dié was not carried out; the aged Perret created a grandiose urban abstraction at Le Havre, but his pupils can breathe no life into it. Pison's research into contemporary farm buildings was not followed up. The remainder is mediocrity. It looks above all as if French architecture has succumbed to an empty inhuman geometry, from which it can at best only save itself by recourse to an inadequate, if technically brilliant, formalism in ostensibly purpose-free buildings (French Pavilion at Brussels, 1958).

Eugène Beaudouin and Marcel Lods. Cité de la Muette, Drancy near Paris, 1933

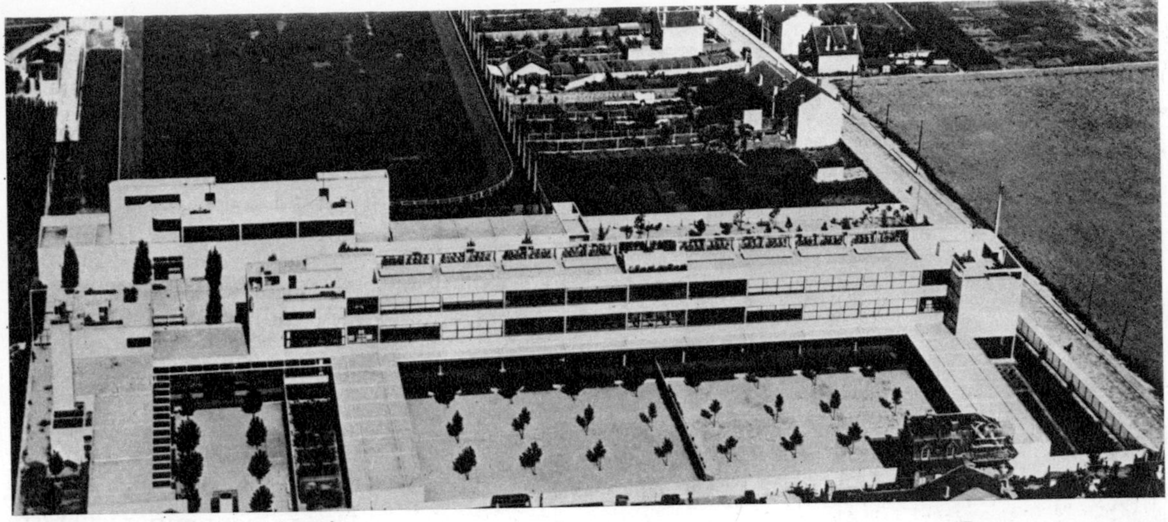

André Lurçat. School. Villejuif, 1931–3

A new generation, whose most outstanding representatives have been trained by Le Corbusier or who at least acknowledge allegiance to him has led to a marked change since about 1955. These younger men show a common tendency, which may be traced back to Le Corbusier, to consider all architectural problems in the light of a 'humanisme total', whether it is a matter of individual buildings or of town planning. In the manipulation of technical resources, apart from the influence of the masters of reinforced concrete such as *Freyssinet, André Coyne and Bernard Lafaille, the work of Jean Prouvé is exerting an increasingly more marked effect. His example makes up for the temptation offered to their followers by the monumentality of Le Corbusier's later works and the abstract transparency of Mies. Hence an original French style is beginning to establish itself, whose principal features can already be recognized in numerous buildings and projects. These include the new town of Bagnols-sur-Cèze and the planning for the Toulouse satellites at Le Mirail (*Candilis team), the blocks of flats at Croix and St Germain (Shape-Village), the Paris Museum of Folk Art (Dubuisson), the Vieille-Église housing estate at Croissy (Chemineau and Mirabaud), tall blocks of flats, shops and district heating plant at Bagneux (Gomis, Bodiansky, Gillet), residential and school buildings, the cathedral at Algiers (Herbé and Le Couteur), the Les Bureaux housing estate at Sceaux and the Museum at Le Havre (Lagneau team), the experimental plastic house by Schein and Magnant, the studio house at St Rémy, the 'Mex' type adaptable prefabricated houses and the St Antoine University Clinic by A. Wogensky, who was the architect in charge of building the Unités d'habitation when head of Le Corbusier's office.

Men of the older generation have also contributed to this renaissance, e.g. Lods with his large housing estate, Marly (with Honegger and Beuté), André Sive with several housing schemes, Beaudouin with the Cité Rotterdam at Strasbourg and the point blocks in Berlin (Hansa district) and Pantin (with Lopez), Emile Aillaud with industrial buildings in Lorraine and the ribbon and round tower housing estates at Aubervilliers and Bobigny, Pierre *Vago with the Basilica at Lourdes (with Freyssinet), and Ecochard with town planning and large-scale buildings in North Africa and the Near East. Mention should also be made of the office buildings by Lopez and Gravereaux (Rue Lapérouse and Rue Viala in Paris, with Prouvé) and by Edouard Albert at Paris and Orly, the Technical College (INSA) at Lyons (Jacques Perrin-Fayolle with Prouvé), the Faculty of Philosophy at Poitiers (Ursault), the medical faculty at Marseilles (Egger), the training workshops of the Electricité de France near Soissons (P. and P. Sirvin), Ginsberg's residential blocks in the west of Paris, and several shopping centres and

Georges Candilis, Bodiansky, Woods and Piot. Bagnols-sur-Cèze. Commenced 1956

Eugène Beaudouin. Cité Rotterdam. Strasbourg, 1951–3

industrial and exhibition buildings. The churches form a group of their own: Rueil (Sonrel and Duthilleul), Neuilly (Coulon), Mazamet (Belmont), Baccarat (Kazis), Fontaine-lès-Grès (Marot), Pontarlier and Villejuif (Rainer Senn), the Franciscan Monastery at Orsay (Brothers Arsène-Henry) and the Dominican Monastery at Lille. The influence of the Dominican journal *Art Sacré* played a decisive rôle here.

Since 1925, Charlotte Perriand has been in the forefront of the fight for functional equipment in the home. The feud between *Formes Utiles* (André Hermant) and *Esthétique Industrielle* (Jacques Viénot) has led to the solution of many minor problems in the field of industrial design. The *Architecture Mobile* Association is carrying out basic research, the sculptor H. G. Adam encourages his pupils to co-operate with architects, and the Cercles d'Études Architecturales have become a forum for modern architecture and an important centre for international exchange. This revival of the spirit of experimentation on which the best French tradition has always been based can be furthered by the reform of architectural education, which was at last taken in hand in 1962 and which should lead to the suppression of the *de facto* monopoly of the Beaux-Arts.

Bibliography: S. Giedion, *Bauen in Frankreich, Eisen und Eisenbeton*, Leipzig 1929; Marie Dormoy, *L'Architecture Française*, Paris 1938; *25 Années UAM* (*Union des Artistes Modernes*), Paris 1956; J. Schein, *Paris construit*, Paris 1961.

MAURICE BESSET

Guillaume Gillet. Notre Dame de Royan, 1954–9

Camelot, De Mailly and Zehrfuss. Centre Nationale des Industries et Techniques. Paris, 1958

Freyssinet, Eugène, b. Objat, France 1879, d. 1962. Freyssinet was a pupil of the reinforced concrete pioneer Charles Rabut. In 1907, when just twenty-eight years old and employed as an engineer by a road-works authority in Central France, he built the bridges of Boutiron and Le Veurdre (destroyed 1940–4), which together with the contemporary early works of the Swiss *Maillart are considered among the boldest and most elegant creations of the early days of *reinforced concrete bridge building. A design for an arched bridge with a span of 607 feet (1913) was not executed due to the outbreak of war, but served as a basis for a number of later bridges by Freyssinet, right up to the Traneberg Bridge in Stockholm (1932, 597 foot span) and the bridges on the Caracas-to-La Guaira motorway (1950–5, average spans 476 feet). The St Pierre-du-Vauvray Bridge was built in 1922, its thin deck slab borne by a daring twin-arch 433 feet in span (destroyed 1940–44). Apart from the road and railway bridge over the Elorn estuary in Brittany, with three piers (1926–9, span 3 by 564 feet, partly destroyed 1944, since then rebuilt), Freyssinet's most popular works were the two airship hangars at Orly (1916–24, each 984 foot long and 205 foot high, destroyed 1944). These giant structures are important in the history of architecture not just because of their tremendous size and their technical innovations, but perhaps even more because of the matter-of-factness with which harmony of forms results from the choice of rational, albeit unusual, structural solutions despite unfamiliar dimensions. St Pierre-du-Vauvray and Orly are examples of pure functional beauty raised to the highest pitch of drama. Exceptionally bold intuitions of form were realized in them without their effect being weakened by any later 'cosmetic' alterations.

Eugène Freyssinet. Elorn Estuary Bridge. 1926–9

Apart from bridges, Freyssinet designed mainly industrial buildings, warehouses, etc., in his 'industrial period' (he was technical director of the Entreprises Limousin from 1913 to 1928). During this time he produced a series of now famous examples in the field of *shell and vaulted structures. Due to the difficulty of shuttering, the execution of curved shapes in reinforced concrete is troublesome and expensive. Freyssinet therefore attempted, on the one hand, to achieve extensive standardization of these shapes, and on the other hand to improve the static behaviour of reinforced concrete by means other than stiffening deformations. He had the idea of subjecting the reinforcement to tensile stresses. These tensile stresses were intended to compensate for the compressive stresses which are engendered in the finished building by the self-weight of the concrete and the additional live loads. This led to the invention of pre-stressing, as it is now called, in experiments which go back to 1926 (his 'scientific period'). Freyssinet used it from 1933 onwards for the most varying tasks in multi-storey and underground structures (dam building in North Africa and harbour construction at Brest, 1937–9, and in particular Le Havre, 1946–52, runways at Orly, 1946–7, bridges and water tanks of up to 9,000 cubic yards capacity).

Eugène Freyssinet. Airship hangar. Orly, 1916–24

The shapes resulting from pre-stressed concrete are considerably flatter, slenderer and more highly stressed than those of normal reinforced concrete. The Marne bridges Freyssinet rebuilt with an average span of 230 feet thus have a stress ratio of 1:45. The strength of the units, which are prefabricated on the bank and assembled like steel beams, depends on the centrepiece of the bridge which is 2 feet thick. This type of construction, which was tried out on bridges, could be taken over for the underground Basilica of Pius X at Lourdes, where a maximum clear width had to be achieved for a minimum overall height. Here, as at Orly, repetition of a single technical shape worked out to the last detail, resulted in a monumental effect of

a truly architectural nature. As in certain designs by Pier Luigi *Nervi, pure structure becomes most impressive architecture.
Bibliography: Maurice Besset, *Eugène Freyssinet*, in *Les Architectes Célèbres*, Vol. 2, Paris 1959.

MAURICE BESSET

Fry, Edwin Maxwell, b. 1899. Studied at Liverpool School of Architecture. Partnership with Walter *Gropius, 1934–6; with Jane *Drew, 1945–50. From 1951 to 1958 practised as Fry, Drew, Drake and Lasdun; since 1958, Fry, Drew and Partners. A pioneer of modern architecture in *Great Britain; his Kensal House housing scheme at Ladbroke Grove, London (1936, in collaboration) was the nearest British prewar approach to a continental *Siedlung*. Schools, hospitals, housing, offices; educational buildings in West Africa, where he worked as a town planner from 1943 to 1945. Senior Architect at Chandigarh, 1951–4, in collaboration with *Le Corbusier.

Fuller, Richard Buckminster, b. Milton, Massachusetts 1895. Not an architect in the usual sense of the word, but instead a unique reflection of those 20th-century concepts related to the machine aesthetic, Fuller has received recognition from the architectural profession for his unique gifts only in the last few years. His formal education was sketchy and did not progress much beyond two years at Harvard, 1913–15. After service as a naval officer during the First World War and after occupying a number of positions in business and industry, he perfected a kind of machine for living in which he called the 'Dymaxion (dynamic plus maximum efficiency) House' in 1927. In contrast to the poetic expressions of the machine age which were so frequently manifested in the buildings of the 1920s in Europe, and especially in *Le Corbusier's lyrical Villa Savoye, 1929, Fuller's product was a machine for living in in a literal rather than in a metaphorical sense. Unlike the contemporary masterpieces of European Purism and related movements, Fuller's Dymaxion House was not in any consequential way an object for aesthetic contemplation, but is more correctly viewed as an assemblage of mechanical services in conjunction with living areas. In 1932–5 Fuller developed a motorized version of this idea in his 'Dymaxion Three Wheeled Auto'.
Since then Fuller has devoted much time and effort to the art of structures, and these studies have led to his Geodesic Domes (*Space Frames), structures of metal, plastic, or even of cardboard based upon octahedrons or tetrahedrons. He came to use the domical shape not for a traditional, architectural reason—not, for instance, because it was an 'ideal' form—but because of its natural efficiency in providing the greatest space enclosed in relation to the surface area of the enclosing form. In their use of standardized parts, these Geodesic Domes are, in a sense, the most recent descendants of the assembly techniques that were first employed by Sir Joseph *Paxton in the Crystal Palace, London, 1851. The largest of these domes that has been erected was the repair shop for the Union Tank Car Co., Baton Rouge, La., 1958, with a diameter of 384 feet, a span that exceeds those of the mammoth 19th-century exhibition halls, such as the Machinery Hall at the World Exhibition, Paris, 1889 (362 feet). More recently Fuller has produced a new system known as

Richard Buckminster Fuller. Dymaxion House, 1927. Model (*Prefabrication)

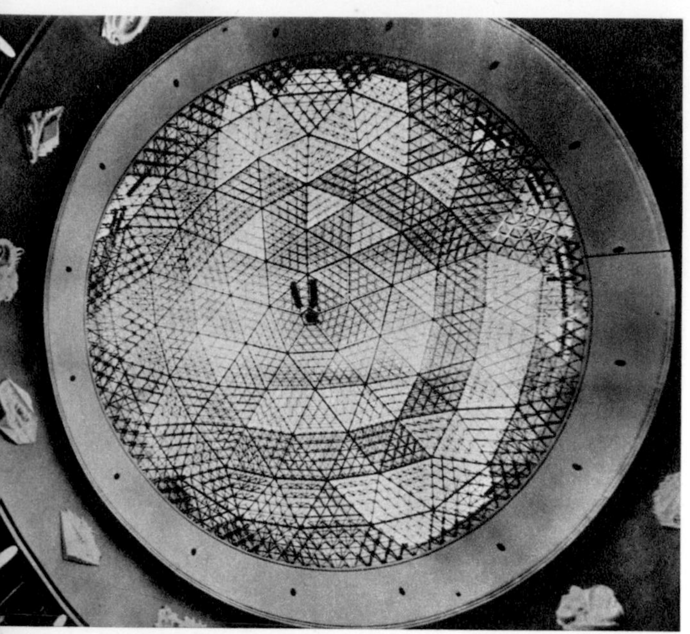

Richard Buckminster Fuller. Ford Motor Company. Dearborn, Mich., 1953. Dome

Tenegrity Structures (a contraction of Tensional Integrity), examples of which were exhibited at the Museum of Modern Art, New York, in 1960.

Understandably more popular with students than with the established elements in the architectural profession, Fuller has enjoyed notable success as a visiting lecturer in various architectural schools in the USA, among them being Cornell, Massachusetts Institute of Technology, University of California, University of Pennsylvania, Princeton University, University of Michigan and Yale University. In 1952 Fuller received the Award of Merit of the New York Chapter of the AIA, and in 1959 the national organization of the same body recognized his work with the award of an honorary membership.

Bibliography: Robert W. Marks, *The Dymaxion World of Buckminster Fuller*, New York 1960.

JOHN M. JACOBUS, JR

Functionalism. 'Form follows function' is the catchphrase that spells modern architecture to most laymen. In the 1920s it seemed like a strange idea, cold and forbidding; today, although widely accepted (and even more widely misunderstood), 'form follows function' continues to evoke the image of modern as opposed to traditional architecture more readily than any other slogan. Yet there is no architectural principle that can claim a more ancient and distinguished tradition. Form has followed function from the paleolithic cave-dwellers to the neolithic lake-dwellers; it followed function in Roman forts and aqueducts, in medieval castles and the Great Wall of China, in 18th-century English warehouses, and in 20th-century Manhattan office piles. Functionalism, in short, is as old as building itself.

Critics of functionalism sometimes suggest that functionalism stops where architecture begins. This is unfair both to functionalism and to architecture. The functionalist period in the development of a new architecture is much like the formative childhood period in the life of a man. As he matures, he may reject many of the fads and prejudices of his teen-age; none the less, the basis of his personality was laid during those earlier years.

The personality of modern architecture had its genesis in the 1850s, the formative years of present-day Functionalism. Both the followers of *Le Corbusier and of Frank Lloyd *Wright—now apparently poles apart—derived much of their early inspiration from the 19th-century doctrines of Eugène *Viollet-le-Duc, the French architect and theoretician, who is best known for his restorations of medieval castles. Less well known, but more important, are his attempts to rationalize (or 'functionalize') the art of architecture into a logical system with simple rules. Le Corbusier's writings of the early twenties—for example, his *Vers une architecture*—read like Viollet-le-Duc brought up to date; and Wright told his architect-son to read Viollet-le-Duc, because his writings would give him all the basic education he needed.

The first rule of Functionalism grew directly out of the credo that form must reflect function—or 'express' function, as architects like to say. This was paraphrased to mean that all the different elements in a building should be separately 'expressed': for example, the structural columns and beams should be made clearly visible, inside and out, and separated from non-structural wall panels and partitions, so that the structural frame would clearly 'express' its function of holding up the floors and the roof.

The second rule of Functionalism came about in a more roundabout way. Because the early Functionalists got much of their inspiration from the machine itself, machine forms became greatly admired. The fact that such forms did not always make much sense in buildings did not matter; after all, Louis *Sullivan used plant forms for terracotta ornament because natural organisms were something that *he* admired—so why should not machine forms like cylinders, cones, cubes, and other geometric shapes be used by the admirers of machine organisms? None of this need have come as a surprise. As early as 1920, Le Corbusier had written jubilantly: 'Thus we have the American grain elevators and factories . . . the American engineers overwhelm with their calculations our expiring architecture.' However, Le Corbusier was not quite so overwhelmed as he may have seemed. For while he was praising functional buildings put up by practical men, he also announced, in the same breath, that 'architecture is the masterly, correct, and magnificent play of masses brought together in light . . . cubes, cones, spheres, cylinders, or pyramids are the great primary forms which light reveals to advantage . . . these are *beautiful forms, the most beautiful forms* [his italics]'. In other words: Functionalism is wonderful—as long as it produces beautiful forms.

But while these sophisticated Functionalists were busy in the 1920s and 1930s developing a style out of the raw material of engineering, there grew up, on the sidelines, another kind of functionalist. He was the builder, the businessman, the engineer, who really believed all that he had read in the papers about cheaper, more practical, more form-fitting architecture. If 'form follows function', he argued, does not efficient function automatically produce beautiful form? Well, it seemed to—in some instances at least: How about aeroplanes? How about some bridges, ships, tools, factories, dams? And if you can produce beauty by some kind of automatic function-computer, why bother with all the talk about art? The output of these literal functionalists is all around us today, for everyone to see. Every big American city is studded with office and apartment buildings designed—if that is the word—by some sort of automatic 'functional' process: the exterior shape is determined by zoning laws; the exterior surface is papered with *curtain wall patterns picked out of a manufacturer's catalogue; the interior layout is determined by rental experts, the core by the stop-watches of elevator specialists; the roof is designed by the cooling tower fabricators; and the lobby by the newspaper distributors. Result: chaos—in the name of 'functionalism'.

Unfortunately, the 'sophisticated Functionalists' have only themselves to blame. They laid the trap when they began to apologize for the new style by claiming it was less expensive to build and less expensive to maintain. Few, if any, ever came out and said publicly that Functionalism was a coherent system of organization, a completely integrated method of putting a building together, and that it should be judged entirely on its own merits.

The present confusion over Functionalism has not been caused entirely by the innocent or the opportunistic. Functionalism needs to re-examine its own premises to see how many of them still make sense. Is it really justifiable to adhere so rigidly to a machine aesthetic? Does it really make sense to articulate and to express all things—to separate a building's elements only to have to link them together again afterwards? 'Expressing structure' is fine in many kinds of buildings; in many others, however, expressing the structure may turn out to be a big headache. And when you come to expressing mechanical equipment—elevators, or cooling towers—then the question arises, why not express the plumbing, the wiring, and the heating, too? Moreover, as the need increases for flexible space uses (in schools, offices, factories, almost any type of building), the urge to articulate each plan element must be suppressed; for, after all, the plan requirements may change overnight.

Functionalism, however, though in transition, is far from dead. It remains a rigorous and demanding discipline, an excellent textbook for young architects, a fine standard by which to judge many a building put up today.

Bibliography: E. R. de Zurko, *Origins of Functionalist Theory*, New York 1957.

PETER BLAKE

Furness, Frank, b. Philadelphia 1839, d. 1912. In buildings such as the Provident Trust Co. Building (Philadelphia, 1879)

Furness employed neo-Gothic features to create an architecture of powerful gravity and impressively integrated massing. His decoration is entirely original and employs free geometric or organic shapes derived from nature. Louis *Sullivan worked in his office in 1873. (*USA)

Futurism. The Futurist movement, which began in 1909, ignored architecture until 1914. In that year two young architects, Antonio *Sant'Elia and Mario *Chiattone, presented a revolutionary picture in Milan of the *Città Nuova*, the city of the future, in a series of designs and projects. In the catalogue of the exhibition a powerful harangue by Sant'Elia was published, which pleads the historical and human necessity for a radical renewal of Italian architecture, that had fallen into an academic eclecticism lacking any vital spark. The author was clearly familiar with the writings of Boccioni and Marinetti, although he had not joined the Futurist movement himself, and his proposals to 'harmonize the environment with man', in the light of the extraordinary and decisive developments of science and technology, frequently chime in with the views expressed in Futurist manifestoes on the other arts.

Marinetti, discovering the Futurist elements in Sant'Elia's thought, determined to integrate the movement's programme with this fascinating and open-minded piece of writing on architecture. He persuaded Sant'Elia to join the group, introduced some modifications to his text (which made no mention of Futurism in the original version) and published it again in July of the same year, 1914, under the title of *Manifesto dell'Architettura Futurista.* The manifesto proclaimed that 'everything must be revolutionized. Architecture is breaking loose from tradition. It is forcibly starting from scratch again', and a 'preference for what is light, practical, ephemeral and swift' was praised as being Futurist, in accordance with Boccioni's aesthetic theories on 'plastic dynamism'.

Mario Chiattone. Block of flats. 1914. Project

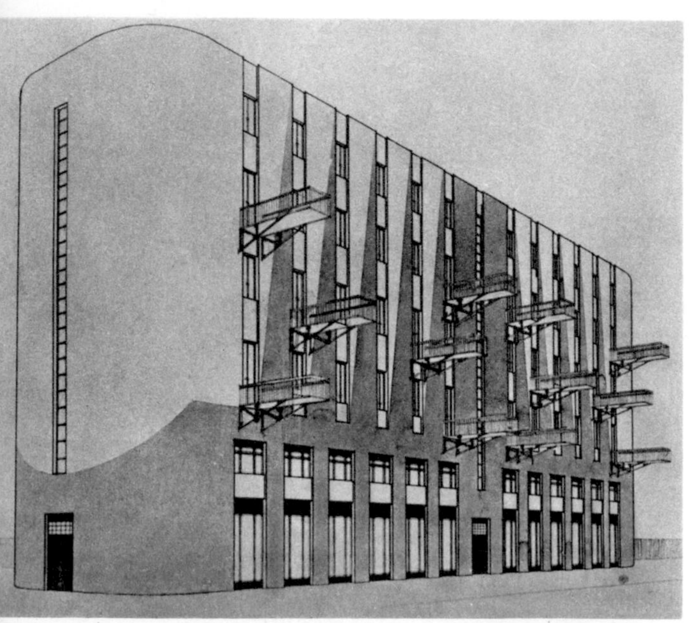

This manifesto was the most important objective that Futurism achieved in the field of architecture. It has become famous and has acquired great historical value because in its way it helped to bring *Italy into the mainstream of modern developments in European architecture. In actual fact, it was only a matter of words: no important Futurist work was ever built in Italy. The finest thing that has come down to us from this period of lively controversy is simply the series of splendid drawings by Sant'Elia himself, which portray, in part at least, the architecture of Futurism. To these may be added the designs of Chiattone, most of them unpublished until 1962, and based furthermore on a static system that foreshadows the aesthetics of the *Novecento Italiano*, far removed from the 'plastic dynamism' that is at the basis of Futurism.

Fourteen years had to pass before Futurist architecture was thought of again. In 1928 one of the keenest and most convinced supporters of the idea of Futurism in architecture, the painter and journalist Fillía, organized the 'First Exhibition of Futurist Architecture' (it was also to be the only one) 'under the high patronage of His Excellency Mussolini'. The artists who took part were of various origins and tendencies: Antonio Sant'Elia, Mario Chiattone, Alberto Sartoris and Virgilio Marchi (architecture); Ivo Pannaggi, Giacomo Balla and Fillía (interior decoration); Enrico Prampolini, Fillía and Nicola Diulgheroff (stage designs); Fortunato Depero, Diulgheroff and Prampolini (exhibition architecture); and various other artists with posters and objects of daily use. Most of the schemes illustrated were only

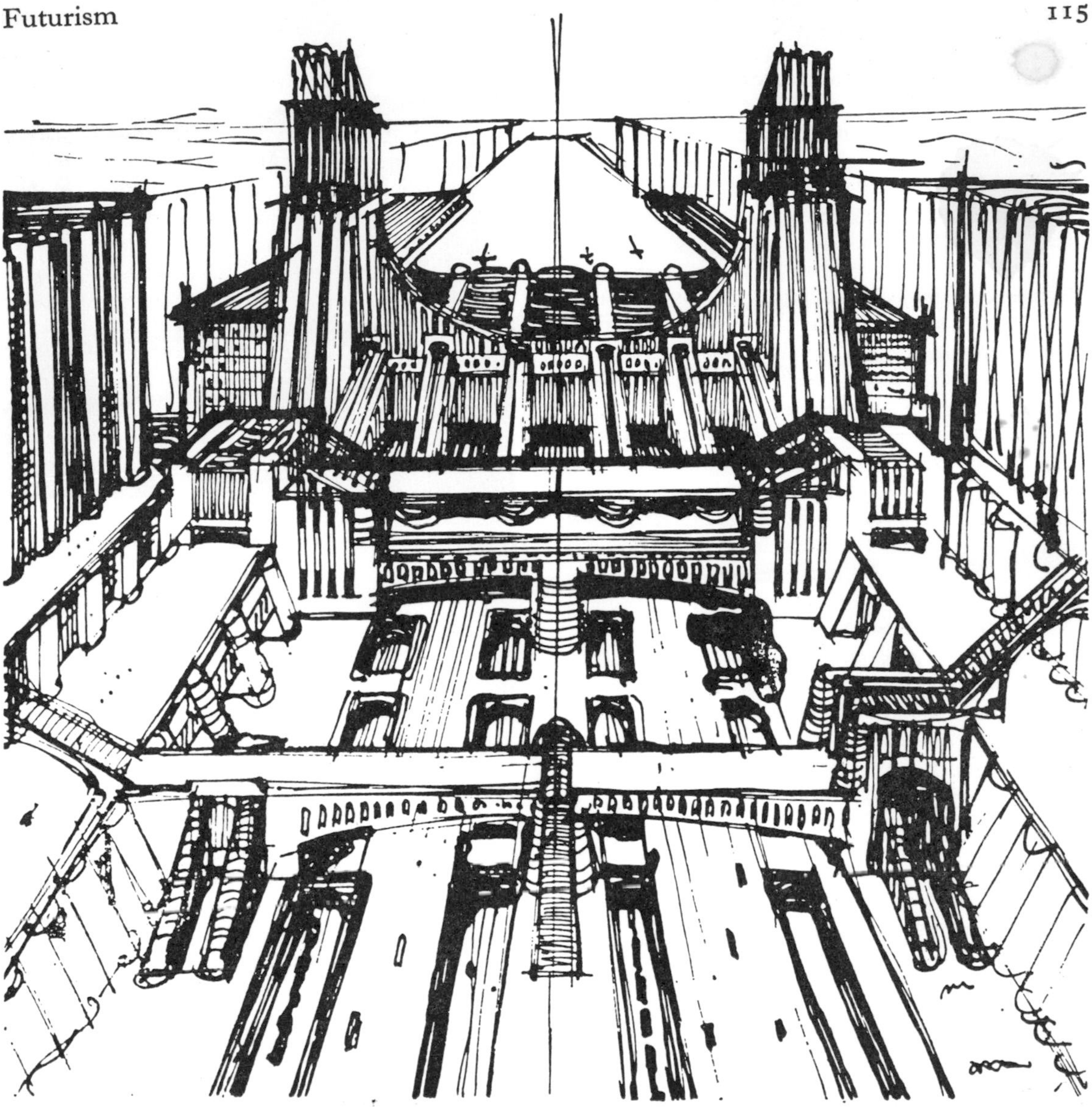

Antonio Sant'Elia. Città Nuova. 1914. Project

projects. The sole works of architecture, apart from exhibition designs, built up to then (by Sartoris) were tied in with the European rationalist movements and ignored 'plastic dynamism'. But Fillía continued to believe in the possibility of Futurist architecture developing as Fascist architecture, and to promote and spread this idea he founded and edited a number of journals (*La città futurista*, *La città nuova*) and wrote articles and books (*Arte Fascista*, 1928; *La nuova architettura*, 1931).

Of works that were actually built a few 'Futurist villas' may be mentioned (at Turin and Albisola), and some exhibition pavilions (by Depero at Monza, 1924; by Fillía at Turin and Florence, 1928). Stage designs were carried out by Enrico Prampolini, Virgilio Marchi and Anton Giulio Bragaglia, amongst others, for the Teatro degli Indipendenti in Rome, which was run by Bragaglia.

The work in which Futurism, with all its poetry, culminated was the 'Exhibition of the Fascist Revolution' held in Rome in 1932. Organized by architects, painters and designers who were mostly drawn from the ranks of Futurism, it was the only manifestation of Fascist art that achieved any historic *rapport* with the rest of Europe, by displaying a kind of *Constructivism which could be compared with that of Russia. While the Futurist requirements of plastic dynamism, simultaneity and speed ('empty words in architecture' Mario Chiattone wrote) were being met by stage design techniques at the Exhibition, the principles of the *Novecento Italiano* were winning acceptance in architecture: 'plastic values' taken from national tradition, and accepted by Fascism as those truly expressive of the times. Sant'Elia had died twenty years before, shortly after *Gropius's Fagus factory was built. Now Marinetti, the leader of Futurism, was appointed by Mussolini to the Accademia d'Italia.

Bibliography: Virgilio Marchi, *Architettura futurista*, Foligno 1924; F. T. Marinetti, Enrico Prampolini and Escodame, *Sant' Elia e l'architettura futurista mondiale*, Milan 1931; Alberto Sartoris, *Sant'Elia e l'architettura futurista*, Rome 1944; Fillía, *La Nuova Architettura*, Turin 1931; Reyner Banham, 'Futurism and Modern Architecture' in *RIBA Journal*, February 1957; Rafael Benet, *Futurismo y Dada*, Barcelona 1949; Drudi Gambillo and Teresa Fiori, *Archivi del Futurismo*, Rome 1958; Reyner Banham, *Theory and Design in the First Machine Age*, London 1959.

GIULIA VERONESI

Ignazio Gardella. Block of flats for employees. Alessandria, 1952

Gardella, Ignazio, b. Milan 1905, first winner of the Olivetti National Prize for architecture, is a lecturer at the University Institute of Architecture, Venice. In the current architectural scene in Italy, Gardella is a figure of particular importance. In contrast to the other architects of his generation, he has not had recourse to any social or aesthetic ideologies for the genuine rationalism he has displayed from his first works. This attitude, nevertheless,

Ignazio Gardella. Mensa Olivetti. Ivrea, 1959

has permitted him to work quite naturally by the side of the most committed of his colleagues. He has collaborated with them fruitfully at the various Triennali, in architectural and town planning competitions and in projects of all kinds. His work is characterized by its elegance and purity of composition, in a lyric vein which he has used to provide magisterially free and simple solutions to the most complex problems.

He began his career with interior decoration and rebuilding schemes. The most noteworthy among the latter are: the renovation of the theatre at Busto Arsizio in 1934, and an extension of the Villa Borletti in Milan (1935), which first brought him to notice. In the following year came his finest work to that date, and one that remains 'an outstanding example of Italian rationalism' (Mazzariol): the Anti-tuberculosis Dispensary at Alessandria (1936–8), in which the most interesting lines of Gardella's architecture are defined: clarity in the handling of plane surfaces and a judicious use of materials as essential instruments of expression. In this connection, the extensive employment of brick to face a reinforced concrete building shows Gardella's tendency to respect local traditions, at least as far as the use of colour goes.

The splendid Dispensary (soon to become dilapidated through neglect on the part of the city authorities) was the first and most significant of Gardella's architectural activities in Alessandria, where he has left a distinctive imprint, building the major part of his own most important works there: the Provincial Laboratory for Hygiene and Prophylaxis (1937–9); a block of flats for employees (1952), in which he tried, by an interesting play of movement on the elevation and the use of deeply projecting eaves, to go beyond a purely 'rationalist' scheme; a building for the Borletti works, in 1951; the Children's Hospital, in 1955; and finally, a Vocational School, currently under construction. During the same period Gardella was building elsewhere too. In 1946, in a block of flats he designed at Castana, particular emphasis was laid on an attempt to reinterpret regional and traditional elements in a modern key. This characteristic has led Gardella little by little a long way from his initial standpoint; his architecture, diverging as it does sometimes from strict rationalism has sparked off a good deal of controversy, though no one disputes his taste or technical skill.

Tony Garnier. Residential district. Cité Industrielle. 1901–4. Project

He has built blocks of flats and villas, and a group of terraced houses (1952) in the new suburb of Cesate Milanese, where he also plans to erect a brick-built church with historic overtones and a layout of subtle geometric invention in the contemporary spirit. He returns again to the poetic 'rationalist' manner, albeit exceptionally, with the white annexe he designed for the Museum of Modern Art in Milan (1953). Thereafter he often subordinates the free workings of his own imagination to the promptings of the environment in his schemes, which include a house on the Grand Canal in Venice, and a villa on the Riviera, His most significant design currently under construction, apart from the Vocational School at Alessandria, is the Olivetti Studies Centre at Ivrea.

Gardella was a member of the executive committee of the 1959 Milan Triennale.

Bibliography: G. C. Argan, *Gardella*, Milan 1959; Giuseppe Mazzariol, 'Umanesimo di Gardella' in *Zodiac 2*, Milan 1957.

GIULIA VERONESI

Garnier, Tony, b. Lyons 1869, d. La Bédoule 1948. Tony Garnier is a unique case. His first job, the project for an industrial town designed in 1901–4, when he was a Rome Scholar of barely thirty, contains not only a wealth of fertile, revolutionary ideas but so many concrete suggestions as well for the most diverse architectural

Tony Garnier. Railway station. Cité Industrielle. 1901–4. Project

problems of the modern town that as a mature master later on he had only to dip into it to cope with his manifold commissions: in particular the 'Grands Travaux de la Ville de Lyon', the abattoir of La Mouche (1909–13), the Olympic Stadium (1913–16), the Grange Blanche Hospital (1915–30), the War Memorial (1924), the telephone exchange (1927) and the residential district known as 'Les États Unis' (1928–35). Even the still much-copied town hall of Boulogne-Billancourt (1931–4, in collaboration with Debat-Ponsan) can be traced back to the 'Cité Industrielle'. But this does not mean that the untiring, ever-searching Garnier even considered resting on his early-won laurels.

Even the idea that lies at the basis of Garnier's 'Cité Industrielle' is revolutionary in its novelty. The town planning of his time had not progressed beyond Camillo Sitte's *Stadtbaukunst* (1889) and the English garden city, both of which only cope with certain aspects of the problem. Thanks to his Socialist leanings, Garnier conceived a town organism which—without churches and barracks!—fully serves the human needs of an industrial age. His choice of material which determines the shape of the individual buildings is no less bold; only a few experimental buildings were erected in reinforced concrete in 1901. In addition, Garnier invented the shapes best suited to reinforced concrete, which have become standard features in modern architecture: continuous strips of glazing, glass walls, *pilotis*, and flat roofs. The 'free plan' derives from his cantilevered structures, which (with the exception of *Perret, 1903) he was the first in Europe to achieve. In addition, there are surprising technical innovations such as electric heating, thermostats, service cores, and a novel system of ducting worked out to the last detail. The shapes are of a baffling modernity. Their ascetic geometry recalls the harmonious cuboid houses of Adolf *Loos (e.g. Garnier's own house at St Rambert, 1911). No less advanced are the designs of the buildings and the general disposition of the town: a residential district without enclosed courtyards but featuring continuous green areas and traffic-free pedestrian precincts; single-storey schools in open layouts; hospitals planned in separate blocks; numerous sports stadia;

a community centre that anticipates contemporary social centres; separation of vehicular and pedestrian traffic; clear distinction between the different functions of a town (living, work, leisure, education, traffic), in a way that has only been theoretically planned by *CIAM since 1928. All the fundamental ideas of modern architecture and town planning have not just been hinted at in Garnier's project but are carefully thought out in detail. Only the outbreak of the First World War prevented their actual realization at Lyons from 1915 to 1920.
Garnier's name was little known outside Lyons up to the time of his death. His influence, however, extended far beyond the circle of faithful pupils who had gathered round him. Long before the publication of *Une Cité Industrielle* and its later shortened version, Garnier's ideas were known in progressive architectural circles; they played a considerable part in *Le Corbusier's ideas on town planning. Only after his death was Garnier's importance fully recognized as one of the key figures of the start of the century.
Bibliography: Tony Garnier, *Une Cité Industrielle*, Paris 1917; Tony Garnier, *Les Grands Travaux de la Ville de Lyon*, Paris 1919; Jean Badovici and Albert Morancé, *L'œuvre de Tony Garnier*, Paris 1938; Giulia Veronesi, *Tony Garnier*, Milan 1948.

MAURICE BESSET

Gaudí, Antoni, b. Reus, Catalonia 1852, d. Barcelona 1926. Gaudí, who came from a family of coppersmiths, began his architectural studies in Barcelona at the age of seventeen and graduated in 1878. At school his radical nonconformity often earned him bad marks in his examinations. He felt little attraction for the official courses, whereas, during his years as a student, he was an assiduous frequenter of the philosophy classes of Llorens y Barba and the lectures on aesthetics by Pau Milà y Fontanals. In his youth Milà y Fontanals had lived in Rome during its romantic period, where he had moved in the circle of the Nazarenes, Overbeck and his fraternity. As a consequence he had developed in a direction parallel to the English Pre-Raphaelites, with a passionate attachment to the Middle Ages, symbols, mystery and a certain esotericism. In Catalonia this kind of mentality had been brought about by the nationalist movement, some seeing in a return to the Middle Ages a return to Catalonia's Golden Age, others displaying a primitivist reaction which sought the fount of life in the realm of folk-lore and in communion with the nature of one's native land.
Gaudí's ideas were decisively influenced by this school of thought, which led him to a veneration for craftwork and the honesty of medieval art; to a mechanistic logic inspired by *Viollet-le Duc's conception of medieval architecture; and to nature as a source of inspiration, not only for decorative details but for structures as well. While he was a student, he worked as an assistant to Villar and Fontseré on the

Antoni Gaudí. Palau Güell. Barcelona, 1885–9

church at Montserrat and on the waterfall in the Ciutadella Park in Barcelona. His contribution consisted of decorative details derived from a stylization of themes from nature in the Japanese manner and from the use of ironwork features with strongly accentuated joints. His workshop experience marked him off from those architects who were merely academic draughtsmen and helped him to grasp three-dimensionally the way things are made, with tangible material.

In 1878, shortly after graduating, he designed the Casa Vicens, in the Carrer de les Carolines at Barcelona, a building suggestive of Islamic prototypes with its stepped prismatic blocks, its alternations of stone and brick, and its brilliant decoration in polychrome tiles. Constructed as it was at a period when revivalism was in full flood, it had the merit of belonging to no known style. This recourse to Islamic details was one of the levers Gaudí used, in conjunction with neomedievalism, to throw off the weight of academic prejudices and try to arrive at his own means of expression, which was characterized by a feeling for the modulation of indirect light in interiors, and something that was to be as much part and parcel of his architecture as it was to be opposed to the colourless art of the academics: his polychrome use of ceramics, mosaics, glazing and painting. Although naturalism was limited at the Casa Vicens to palm leaves featured in the wrought-iron work and the decorative ceramics which displayed ivy and raspberry tendrils, Gaudí took a step further with the street lamps he designed for the Plaça Reial in Barcelona, where he imitated forms derived from the growth of plants. The same period marks the beginning of his interest in structural problems, with the parabolic arches he employed in warehouses built for the Mataró Workers' Cooperative (1878–82), and in social questions with his schemes for workers' housing drawn up for the same co-operative.

In 1883, Gaudí was commissioned to continue the work on the Church of the Sagrada Familia, a building of great size that was progressively to monopolize his activities. A neo-Gothic design by Villar was already in existence, which Gaudí

Antoni Gaudí. Church of the Sagrada Familia. Barcelona, 1883–1926

Antoni Gaudí. Casa Milà. Barcelona, 1905–10

abandoned, but the lines of the apse, the first part he built, still contain many Gothic reminiscences, although the mouldings and decorative details are drawn much more closely from nature. It is to this period that the Palau Güell belongs in the Carrer Nou de la Rambla, Barcelona, now the calle Conde del Asalto (1885–9), where Gaudí's structural experiments—the use of parabolic arches is the most evident one—create a personal style, adapted to the exclusive use of stone, timber and wrought-iron. This palace, and his designs for a large building for Catholic missions in Tangiers, with towers that recall the parabolic cupolas of villages in the Chad, formed the basis of his complete liberation from the historic styles, and his approach to a 'biological' style.

Work on the Sagrada Familia continued with the Nativity façade of the east transept. This consists of three open portals between four interpenetrating square-based towers, set diagonally, which rise to a height of 351 feet and terminate in thin, curved, circular features crowned by a piece of capricious play with intersecting surfaces, covered in mosaic. A complex and lively world, modelled for the most part by Gaudí himself and comprising an immense variety of plants and animals, throngs the great concavities below the gables, which are covered in imitation snow carved out of stone and carry a series of sculptures depicting the childhood of Christ. While in his previous works naturalism was used purely decoratively, in this instance the sculptures of living forms, connected up by a series of continuous curved surfaces, make up a form of cladding that covers the structure completely and models it independently.

Henceforth, as in the Casa Batlló in the Paseo de Gracia, Barcelona (1905–7), natural and organic forms no longer simply comprise a kind of ornament superimposed on the building but go on to constitute essential structural elements, as in the case

of the bone-shaped columns, the undulating façade covered with polychrome mosaics like a sheet of sea-water set on end, and the imbricated roof like an armadillo's back. This type of effect is a transitional one between the sculptural plasticity of Gaudí's earlier years (1878–91), and that of his later period. (*Art Nouveau)
This structural plasticity has as one of its chief features the system of design Gaudí used for the Colonia Güell Church (1898–1914), which was planned by means of a string model representing the structural ribs of the building, from which were hung weights proportional to the loads which each member would have to carry. The polygons formed by these strings gave the inverted shape of the building's columns. It permitted a type of vaulted structure without buttresses of any kind, since all thrusts are taken up by suitably inclined pillars. This method was later used in designing the naves of the Sagrada Familia.
In the Güell Park (1900–14) Gaudí made systematic use of inclined supports of unwrought stone for retaining walls and bridges, where he raised great masses of stone on flimsy columns in a tense desire to flaunt gravity. An important feature in this park is the abundant employment of ceramic and glass mosaic, which presents an extraordinary ensemble of powerfully expressive abstract compositions, in which Gaudí makes frequent use of broken plates, china dolls, bottles, etc., in a fabulous fantasia, like the elements of a collage.
The Casa Milà (1905–10), called *la Pedrera* (the quarry) is perhaps Gaudí's most original work. An interesting structural feature is the way the entire weight is carried between the external elevations and the columns which surround the patios. The handling of the internal space is also noteworthy, with its numerous acute and obtuse angles and undulating walls. Plastically speaking it constitutes a great stone sculpture of organic shape, with a rhythm of undulating horizontal edges, comparable to eyebrows or lips, pierced by windows, which preserve the expression of human eyes or mouths, somewhat in the manner of sculptures by Henry Moore or Barbara Hepworth. Gaudí's structural masterpiece was reached in 1909 with his Sagrada Familia schools, walled and roofed by undulating membranes of thin brick.
Towards the end of his career, Gaudí asserted that the straight line belonged to men, the curved one to God. Shortly before his death he invented a system of well-nigh universal application, based on hyperboloids and paraboloids, though his designs were never purely geometrical. They always preserved a close tie with familiar living shapes: bones, muscles, wings and petals, and at other times with caves and even stars and clouds.
Terrifying and idyllic features may be encountered side by side in Gaudí's work, in a way that closely recalls Surrealism. This impression is accentuated by the fortuitous objects in his collages, and gives Gaudí's architecture, despite his profoundly rational approach to structure, a character that is impassioned, savage and poetical to the point of frenzy.
Bibliography: Alexandre Cirici-Pellicer, *El arte modernista catalán*, Barcelona 1951; J. F. Ràfols, *Gaudi 1852–1926*, 3rd edition, Barcelona 1952; Joan Bergós, *Antoni Gaudí, L'home i l'obra*, Barcelona 1954; George R. Collins, *Antonio Gaudí*, New York 1960; James Johnson Sweeney and Joseph Lluis Sert, *Antoni Gaudí*, London 1960.

ALEXANDRE CIRICI-PELLICER

Germany. In 1828 the architect Heinrich Hübsch published a brochure with the title *In which style should we build*? In it he put forward the thesis that it was impossible to create new and beautiful forms in architecture. But the combination of these forms, and the 'arrangement of the parts . . . could reveal much that was individual'. These words sum up the malaise of the 19th century. The romantic period in German architecture after Friedrich Gilly had omitted to develop an exclusive manner in which the whole was subjected to a common rule like its parts. In practice, of course, the combination of adopted antique or Gothic features led to a new kind of style. The German romantic period was already familiar with unlimited repetitions of particular forms, the renunciation of dominating axes, flowing plan forms and the alternating interpenetration of space and buildings, and it already took account of the optical displacements and intersections that ensue when the spectator moves about. It is not by chance that the early *Mies van der Rohe was influenced by the country house projects of *Schinkel.

In the face of the tasks confronting the 19th-century architect this anticipation of the principles of modern architecture seems to lack binding force or significance. Infinite space was one thing, back yards in the Ackerstrasse, Berlin, another. Industrial expansion and increasing population created an inescapable situation in the second half of the 19th century. There were no models for factories, commercial buildings or above all for apartment blocks on a large scale; there was a reluctance at first to accept these tasks as worthy of architecture. The readiness for technical experimentation which led to revolutionary solutions in building with iron and *steel in *Great Britain, *France and the *United States, was less pronounced in Germany. Internationally important innovations in building technique only appeared in the 20th century with the glass architecture of the years around 1910, Max *Berg's reinforced concrete dome (Centenary Hall, Breslau 1912–13), the *shell structures of the twenties and the scientific study of building as developed by the *Bauhaus.
*Art Nouveau, which marked the beginning of extensive reform movements, began with private houses. *Muthesius studied English country house styles while serving as an attaché at the German Embassy in London, *Riemerschmid and *Behrens started their architectural careers by building their own houses. This limitation was not meant as a renunciation, for the new style was not going to be determined by popular taste but, as Henry van de *Velde expressed it, by the 'ethos of the most intimate of man's possessions', the ethos of his own home. The Darmstadt Exhibition on the Mathildenhöhe (1901) which mainly featured such individual homes was thus not a private but a public event of considerable significance.
German Jugendstil had a higher moral content than Art Nouveau in France or Belgium. Appreciation for what was good and solid, honesty in the expression of materials and functions and the craft mentality were able to continue in force even when these new art forms had ceased to bloom. Enterprises such as the Vereinigte Werkstätten at Munich, the Werkstätte für Handwerkskunst at Dresden and above all the *Deutscher Werkbund founded in 1907, to which the most significant practitioners of Art Nouveau belonged, carried on the message. Parting from Art Nouveau proved the easier since no German architect had fulfilled the intentions of the new style as had Victor *Horta in Brussels, *Mackintosh in Glasgow, *Gaudí in Barcelona or even *Guimard in Paris. August *Endell's buildings, the wittiest creations of German Art Nouveau in architecture, remained examples of decorative art, two-dimensional surfaces attached to three-dimensional buildings. The Belgian Henry van de Velde built too late in Germany to exert a significant influence on architectural developments there.

Karl Friedrich Schinkel. Playhouse. Berlin, 1818–31

August Endell. Buntes Theater. Berlin, 1901

Max Berg. Centenary Hall. Breslau, 1912–13

The Werkbund Exhibition at Cologne in 1914, where van de Velde erected a theatre in the generous flowing lines of the latest Art Nouveau, featured two buildings that anticipated the future: Bruno *Taut's pavilion for the German glass industry and the model factory by Walter *Gropius. A new building material, *glass, and a new building assignment, the factory, had led to a new aesthetic. Both buildings exhibit the close connection between function and expressive form which lasted until well into the twenties. Peter Behrens's turbine factory in Berlin (1908–9) with its heavy roof and Hans *Poelzig's chemical factory in Luban (1911–12) with its decorative masonry and carefully proportioned fenestration are not the monuments of a purely objective architecture which they have been made out to be. Nearly all important architects who played a significant rôle in the twenties have gone through an Expressionist phase: *Mendelsohn, Poelzig, the brothers *Taut and *Luckhardt, *Scharoun, Mies van der Rohe with his glass-tower visions and the memorial to Karl Liebknecht and Rosa Luxemburg (1926) and Gropius with the sharply thrusting architectural sculpture of his War Memorial (Weimar, 1922).

The Bauhaus at Weimar and later at Dessau became the high school of 'Neues Bauen' (a name coined by Hugo *Häring). If the educational foundations were laid here, and the Dessau school buildings themselves were examples of the most avant-garde type of architecture, the real testing of the new architecture took place in the big cities. Berlin was the centre. Ever since Martin Mächler's new zonal plan of 1920, a kind of creative activity prevailed here, which did not confine itself to individual buildings but pursued a town planning concept. The 'white towns', Berlin's urban estates amid green settings, bear witness to this even today. The Weissenhof estate at Stuttgart, 1927, was largely built by Berlin architects, who moreover—despite stylistic differences—had joined together in an association, the *Ring. The new ideas radiated from Berlin. Bruno Taut, who was city architect in Magdeburg for a time, Ernst *May, who built excellent housing estates at Frankfurt, Richard Döcker in Stuttgart, Otto Haesler in Celle and Kassel were in the forefront. Contacts with Holland and France strengthened the avant-garde. Mies van der Rohe's German pavilion at the Barcelona International Exhibition of 1929, a subtle composition of space-creating planes, proved that this type of architecture was recognized by the government too as representative of the new republic. Northern Germany, where Fritz Schumacher in Hamburg laid the foundations for a type of country planning that reached beyond the limits of civic design, was the home of an architecture which rested on the local tradition of building in brick and kept its expressive character somewhat longer.

The advent of National Socialism called a sudden halt to the 'New Architecture'. The Bauhaus was dissolved and architects such as Gropius, *Hilberseimer, *Breuer, *Wagner, Mies, Mendelsohn, May and Hannes *Meyer emigrated. In contrast to Fascism, National Socialism tolerated no modern architecture within the State. The official style was a monumental, sterile, *neo-classicism. For residential buildings, a Biedermeier-like native style supervened, which had already gained ground shortly after the turn of the century and had put up a considerable proportion of all buildings even during the heroic period of the modern movement. Only industrial buildings continued to permit functionally justified and aesthetically pleasing designs to be carried out; it amounted to a kind of internal emigration.

The tabula rasa after 1945 was complete. The character of German architecture in the twenties had been largely formed by the pioneer work carried out before the First World War; that after the Second World War stood alone. The task was immense. The demand for homes in the Federal Republic was estimated at 6.5 millions in 1948. Even at the end of 1960 the deficit was still estimated at 1.3 millions, to which another 1.5 millions must be added, to replace condemned property. Of the present 14 million living units less than half include a bath!

550,000 new homes a year is an achievement. But it has not brought with it a new way of living. There is nothing equivalent to the English New Town movement or

Hans Scharoun. Siemensstadt housing estate. Berlin, 1930

Mies van der Rohe. German pavilion at the International Exhibition. Barcelona, 1929

*Le Corbusier's *Unités d'Habitation*. German architects had to build before they had time to think. The costly relief measures that have been devised for nearly all the larger cities nowadays to prevent their centres from becoming completely choked are more concerned with traffic restrictions than town planning. Only in individual cases such as Hanover have planning measures proved more far-sighted. Hamburg is considering building a second centre. New satellites like Sennestadt near Bielefeld by Bernhard Reichow (where there are no traffic crossings), the Neue Vahr near Bremen or the planned Nordweststadt near Frankfurt offer more pleasing prospects. In the Hansa district of Berlin, a central area in a parkland setting, major international architects have left their mark. But this enterprise which was opened in 1957 as the Interbau-Exhibition has remained a medley of remarkable individual buildings; no town planning principle can be deduced from the layout, rudely bisected as it is by a tarffic artery. Even the much publicized *Haupstadt Berlin* competition has remained without visible effect.

Helmut Hentrich and Herbert Petschnigg. Phoenix-Rheinrohr skyscraper. Düsseldorf, 1957–60

If any force towards integration in urban or country settings has hitherto been lacking, the isolated achievements of individual architects are admirable. Individual projects rate differently. High points are the prestige buildings of industry or communities: administrative buildings like the three-slab point block of the Phoenix-Rheinrohr at Düsseldorf by Hentrich and Petschnigg (1957–60) whose elevational treatment does not come up to the standard of the splendidly articulated massing; cultural buildings such as the municipal theatre at Münster (1954–6) whose team of architects have intelligently incorporated a neoclassic ruin into the building complex; or the municipal theatre at Gelsenkirchen (1958–9) with its transparent theatre mechanism. Extensive re-thinking on the subject of concert halls has gone into the Stuttgart Liederhalle (by Abel and Gutbrod, 1955–6) with its somewhat over-lavish décor, and especially into Scharoun's Berlin Philharmonic, with the audience orientated towards the centrally placed orchestra (under construction). Church buildings are on a high level with designs by Dominikus *Böhm, *Bartning, Baumgarten, Lehmbrock and Oesterlen; the churches of the archdiocese of Cologne stand out by their special quality. This is where Rudolf *Schwarz built many of his churches, three-dimensional images of an incontestably timeless quality.

Modern German architecture has no claim on any of its great masters any more. Gropius has built one private house and a block of flats for the Interbau in Berlin since the last war. Mies did not get his first German commission until 1960, an office block for Krupp's of Essen. But his influence above all can be felt in Germany either directly or indirectly in the way that his ideas have been treated by American architects such as *Skidmore, Owings and Merrill. The rectangular cube, the dissolution into glass, the narrow profile and the separation into load-bearing members and infill areas are features which are met with in many of the buildings by Friedrich Wilhelm *Kraemer, Johannes Krahn,

Gerhard Weber and Otto Apel. In this middle generation, which was young in the twenties and today occupies chairs at the colleges and academies, Egon *Eiermann and Hans Scharoun represent extreme positions: Eiermann who is concerned with the lucidity and perspicuous arrangement of the formal image and with elegance of design; Scharoun who works on each assignment as though the planning problem it exemplifies had never occurred before.
In the youngest generation freedom of conception, psychological command and originality of design are manifestly gaining ground. Wolske with his Beethovenhalle in Bonn (1959) has built a vast festival hall in the spirit of Scharoun. The Berlin Academy by Düttmann (1959–60) is a lively organism free from chilly reserve. Blocks of flats and houses by Oswald Mathias Ungers or houses by Reinhard Gieselmann seem to provide a parallel to international *neoplasticism or *Brutalism, but in actual fact they should be regarded rather as playing with plastic forms in the course of fulfilling the building programme.
Buildings by engineer-architects often determine the aspect of an extensive environment more strongly than architecture, in its narrower sense, is able to. Amongst television towers, the one in Stuttgart by Fritz Leonhardt (1954–6) has remained unequalled in its slender grace. The Nord bridge in Düsseldorf and the Severin bridge in Cologne are bold, suspended structures, the one at Cologne having been suspended asymmetrically from a single pier, out of planning consideration for the nearby Cathedral towers. Despite their international renown, Frei *Otto's tent roofs have not yet assumed the position in Germany that they may one day occupy, since they have been labelled as exhibition architecture. It would not be the first time that structural innovations had left their stamp on a new style.
Bibliography: Hermann Beenken, *Schöpferische Bauideen der deutschen Romantik*, Mainz 1952; Fritz Schumacher, *Strömungen in deutscher Baukunst seit 1800*, Leipzig 1935; G. Hatje, H. Hoffmann, K. Kaspar, *New German Architecture*, London 1956; *Planen und Bauen im neuen Deutschland*, Cologne 1960; U. Conrads and W. Marschall, *Modern Architecture in Germany*, London 1962.

WOLFGANG PEHNT

Rudolf Schwarz. St Anne's Church, Düren, 1951–6

Siegfried Wolske. Beethovenhalle. Bonn, 1959

Friedrich Wilhelm Kraemer. Technical and Evening College. Dortmund, 1956–9

Frederick Gibberd. Metropolitan Cathedral of Christ the King, Liverpool. Under construction. Model

Gibberd, Frederick, b. Coventry 1908. Studied at Birmingham School of Architecture; in private practice since 1930. Planning consultant to several borough councils and, since 1947, architect planner of Harlow New Town. Gibberd has designed a wide range of buildings, including flats, housing schemes and hospitals: Scunthorpe steelworks and power house, 1947–9; London Airport, 1955; National Dock Labour Board Offices, London, 1956; Hinkley Point Atomic Power Station, Somerset, 1957; Ulster Hospital, N. Ireland, 1953–62; technical colleges at Hull, Kidderminster and Stourbridge. His prize-winning design for the Roman Catholic Cathedral at Liverpool shows the influence of *Niemeyer's Brasilia Cathedral. Gibberd has written a popular history of English architecture (1938), and a definitive work on town design (1953).

HAROLD MEEK

D. E. E. Gibson. Broadgate House. Coventry, 1953

Gibson, Sir Donald Evelyn Edward, b. Manchester 1908. Studied at Manchester University School of Architecture. He was City Architect of Coventry (1939–55) when it was devastated by German air raids in the Second World War, and his powerful feeling for urban form and unswerving professional integrity succeeded in recreating a city centre there in which fewer opportunities have been missed than in any other city of *Great Britain, whose reconstruction of blitzed areas has generally attained a mediocre standard. From 1955 to 1958 he was County Architect of Nottinghamshire where the *CLASP system of prefabrication for schools was initiated under his auspices. In 1958 he became Director-General of Works in the War Department, where he brought CLASP construction into use for buildings of various types, including the Army's Computer Headquarters at Worthy Down. Since 1962 he has been Director-General of Research and Development in the Ministry of Public Building and Works.

HAROLD MEEK

Gill, Irving John, b. Syracuse, New York 1870, d. 1936. First worked in the office of *Adler and *Sullivan in Chicago; after 1896 in San Diego on his own. His early buildings are in the 'Schindel' style, followed since about 1906 by work in which simple geometric elements assume importance: 'the straight line, the arc, the cube and the circle, the mightiest of all lines' (Wilson Acton Hotel at La Jolla, 1908; Dodge House, Los Angeles, 1916). His whitewashed, flat-roofed asymmetrically disposed *reinforced concrete buildings, which often display no mouldings of any kind, were inspired by Spanish mission stations in California and are markedly similar to the Cubist architecture of Adolf *Loos.

Burton and Turner. Palm House. Kew, 1844

Glass. Glass production has its origins in remote antiquity. The Phoenicians and Egyptians already made objects from molten glass; the Romans had a glass industry capable of producing precious objects, and the introduction of glass-blowing is probably due to them. On the fall of Rome, Byzantium took over the leading rôle in the sphere of glass production. With the end of the eastern empire Byzantine artists in glass transferred to Venice, which soon became one of the most important centres of production. The German glass industry developed during the Middle Ages; from the 15th century Bohemian products began to acquire importance. Between the 17th and 18th centuries glass manufacture spread throughout France, Belgium, England, Spain and Russia; by the beginning of the 19th century it had reached North America as well.

Towards the middle of the 19th century the glass industry entered a period of intensive development; the end of the century saw the introduction of the first mechanized processes, backed by a systematic investigation of the physics and chemistry of glass. Hand manufacture and mouth-blowing are only employed today for special products and *objets d'art*.

The remarkable progress made by the glass and iron industries afforded new techniques for confronting the architectural problems of the early 19th century. The Galérie d'Orléans by Fontaine (Paris, 1829) is the prototype of all large pedestrian galleries, and is probably the first example of a large area with opaque walls covered by a glazed, translucent vault. A number of large greenhouses erected in France and England between 1830 and 1850 (at the Jardin des Plantes, Paris, by Rouhault, 1833; Chatsworth Conservatory by *Paxton, 1838; Palm House at Kew by Burton and Turner, 1844) exhibited a strictly functional character while reaching hitherto unfamiliar dimensions. Such structures became popular and were sometimes transformed into places of public resort (Jardin d'Hiver, on the Champs Elysées). With the Crystal Palace in London (1851) Joseph Paxton, by transferring the structural principles of the great greenhouses to the first exhibition pavilion, demonstrated the high degree of perfection that had been achieved in the manufacture and

Victor Horta. Maison du Peuple. Brussels, 1896–9. Detail of facade

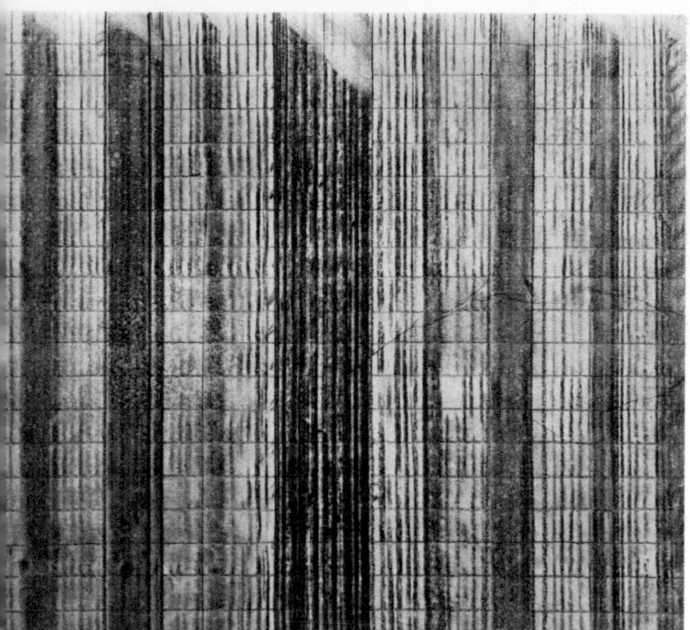

Ludwig Mies van der Rohe. Office block, Friedrichstrasse, Berlin, 1919. Project (first version)

Bruno Taut. Glass pavilion at the Werkbund Exhibition. Cologne, 1914

application of glass. The skill with which he designed in new materials, without harking back to academic tradition, was the result of his habit as a greenhouse designer of pursuing functional ends rather than those of formal prestige.

The large glazed gallery became a basic architectural feature of Paris International Exhibitions in the second half of the 19th century, reaching in Dutert and Contamin's Machinery Hall (1889) the most complete expression of synthesis between a great and original steel structure and its transparent covering. In 1853, Baltard built Les Halles Centrales at Paris, roofed partly in glass on an iron framework. After 1850 the use of huge transparent roofs became common in railway stations (Paddington Station, London, by Brunel and Wyatt, 1854; Lime Street Station, Liverpool, by Turner). In 1876 Boileau and *Eiffel covered the 'Bon Marché' stores in Paris with a complete glass roof. Large glass roofs were adopted by *Berlage for the Amsterdam Stock Exchange (1898–1903) and by Otto *Wagner for the Savings Bank in Vienna (1905) to give top lighting to areas of major importance or prestige. In less than a century the large glass roof had become a definite part of the architect's structural technique and repertory of expression.

'The history of architecture shows that down the centuries an unremitting battle has been joined on behalf of light against the obstacles imposed by the laws of gravity: the history of windows' (*Le Corbusier). Before the introduction of modern structural systems the sizes of vertical load-bearing elements in buildings (especially multi-storey ones) of the traditional type were necessarily so large as to confer on elevations more the character of pierced walls than of surfaces with integrated fenestration.

The process of development whereby the window ultimately extended its dimensions to occupy practically the whole façade began about the middle of the 19th century, when cast-iron, which had already been in use for half a century for internal construction, began to take the place of solid walling on external elevations too (Harper and Brothers' Building, New York, by

Page 131. Frank Lloyd Wright. Laboratory tower for S. C. Johnson & Son. Racine, Wis., 1949

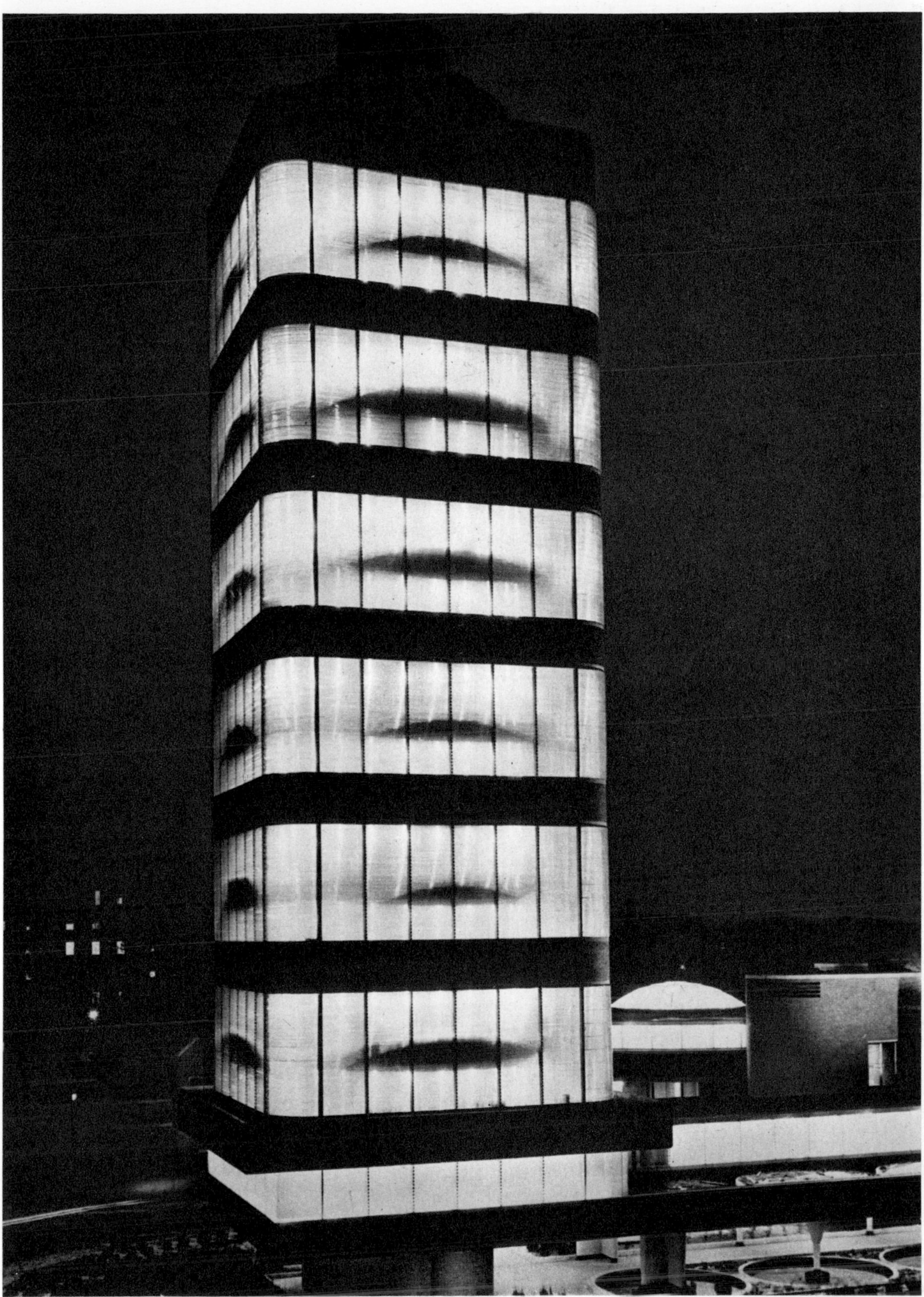

*Bogardus, 1854; riverfront buildings at St Louis, by unknown architects, 1850–80). The tendency to increase the ratio of glass to the total surface area was facilitated by the introduction and perfecting of completely framed buildings, firstly in cast-iron and later in steel, by William Le Baron *Jenney and other architects of the *Chicago School, thus answering the demand for as much natural light as possible for every room in those first large office blocks. With the Reliance Building of *Burnham and *Root (1890–4) and *Sullivan's Carson, Pirie and Scott department store (1899), the façade assumes a modular texture, with continuous rows of closely spaced but ample windows. The so-called 'Chicago window' is rectangular in shape, running horizontally, and features several lights with a large central pane.

*Horta, in his Maison du Peuple, Brussels, 1897, and *Behrens in his AEG works, Berlin, 1909, adopted continuous glass surfaces for almost the whole façade. Le Corbusier in the Pavillon Suisse, University City, Paris, 1930–2, reduced the formal importance of the steelwork, making it seem in the fully glazed wall simply the basic frame for a single great window.

Le Corbusier. Notre-Dame du Haut. Ronchamp, 1950–4. Detail of the south wall from inside

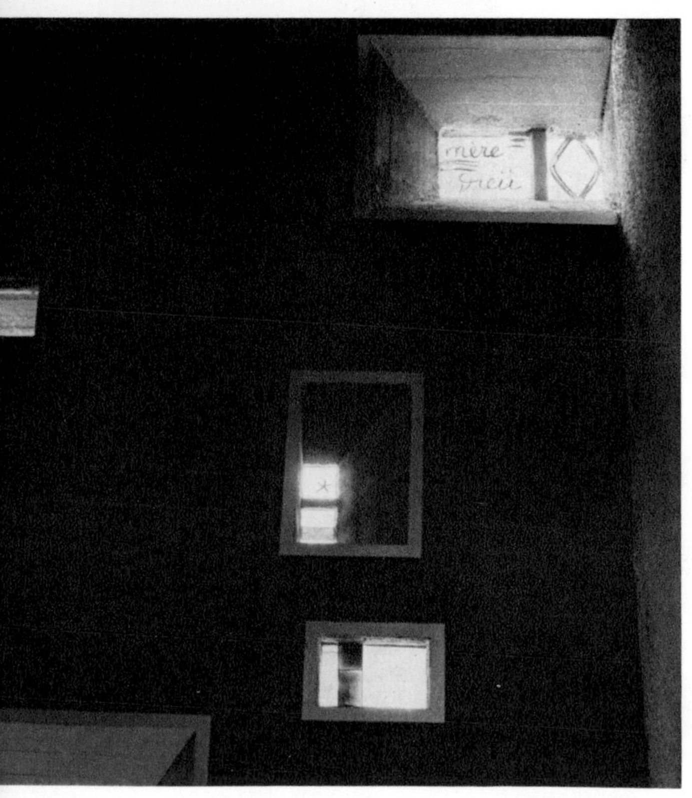

Thus in addition to its traditional functions of providing daylight and view, glass began to be used for all the requirements of separation and insulation between interior and exterior. The window was extended to become the window wall. In the examples cited this is still contained within a single mesh of the structural grid, but elsewhere the continuity of the window units was developed until a continuous glass screen runs in front of the horizontal members (Fagus factory at Alfeld by *Gropius, 1911; Maison Clarté, Geneva, by Le Corbusier, 1932); or in front of the vertical members (model factory at the Werkbund Exhibition, Cologne, by Gropius, 1914; Salvation Army Hostel, Paris, by Le Corbusier, 1932); or in front of the whole structural grid of the façade (Hallidie Building, San Francisco, by *Polk, 1918; Bauhaus, Dessau, by Gropius, 1926; UN Secretariat, New York, by *Harrison and others, 1947–50).

While the window was becoming a glass façade, *Mies van der Rohe was investigating the theoretical bases for skyscrapers completely clad in glass with his projects for a skyscraper at Friedrichstrasse Station, Berlin, 1919, and a tower of glass and steel, 1921. These came to represent a typical manifestation of modern architecture, as defined in particular by two design features: simple volumes and glass surfaces. Outstanding examples of this type became numerous both in North America and Europe: Lake Shore Drive Apartments, Chicago, 1951 and the Seagram Building, New York, 1956, both by Mies van der Rohe; Lever House, 1952, and Union Carbide Building, New York, 1960, by *Skidmore, Owings and Merrill; Torre Galfa, Milan, by Bega, 1959; Mannesmann Building, Düsseldorf by Schneider-Esleben, 1960.

Meanwhile developments were taking place in the design of structural frames; sometimes these were co-planar with the enclosing walls, at others they were set back, with the walls cantilevered out. This was the source of further compositional research on windows. Le Corbusier's 'Five points for a new architecture' (*c.* 1920), Mies van der Rohe's scheme for an office block in reinforced concrete (1922) and other projects led to the introduction and

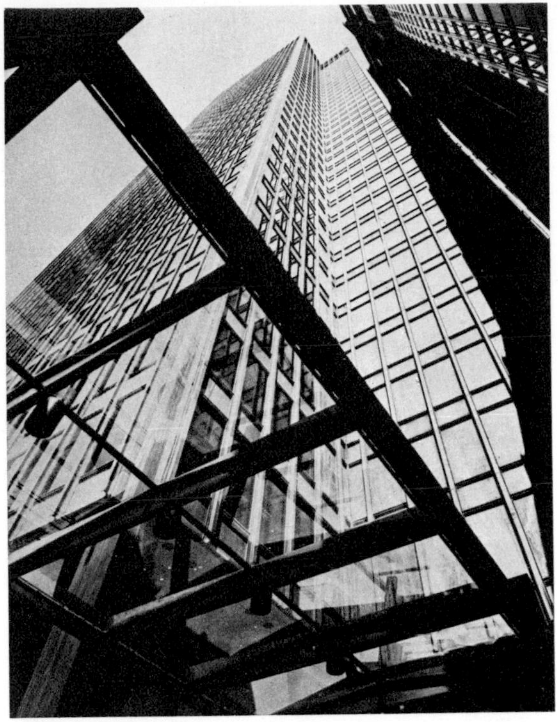

Ludwig Mies van der Rohe. Seagram Building. New York, 1958

widespread use of strip windows (Kiefhoek Estate, Rotterdam by *Oud, 1925; Van Nelle tobacco factory, Rotterdam, by *Brinkman and van der *Vlugt, 1928–30; Schocken department stores, Chemnitz, by *Mendelsohn, 1928; tobacco factory at Linz, by Behrens and Popp, 1930–5) and windows freely shaped and set in elevations (Lovell House, Los Angeles, by *Neutra, 1927; open-air school, Amsterdam, by *Duiker, 1930–2).

The possibility of obtaining ever greater areas of glass, the adoption of slender modern structures with large spans, the boldness with which traditional materials were being used in a new spirit, and the tendency to emphasize spatial continuity between adjacent rooms and between interior and exterior led to the emergence of completely transparent glazed walls with the structural frame reduced to a minimum (Tugendhat House, Brno, by Mies van der Rohe, 1930; pavilion at the Stockholm exhibition, 1930 by *Asplund; Villa Savoye, Poissy, by Le Corbusier, 1929–30). Commercial buildings with special need for transparency (windows of shops and large stores) and the incidence of particular requirements for spatial continuity (partition between the reading room and stacks in the Bibliothèque Nationale, Paris, by Labrouste, 1858–68) had initiated this process already in the 19th century. Modern architectural theory and the new types of glass available have brought this development to its culmination.

The vocabulary of current architectural expression has also been enriched by the unusual, and sometimes fanciful use that has been made of special products of the glass industry: thick slabs of glass for the treads of top-lit stairs (Brewster Apartments, Chicago, by Turnock, *c.* 1890; Maison Clarté, Geneva, by Le Corbusier, 1932); glass bricks for walls and roofs; rows of glass tubing making up walls and ceilings (Johnson Wax offices, 1936, and laboratory tower, 1949, Racine, Wis., by *Wright); polarized glass for heat protection (Van Leer works, Amsterdam, by *Breuer, 1957–8); blown glass polyhedra for spatial compositions (Veneto Pavilion at the 'Italia '61' Exhibition, Turin, by Scarpa, 1961).

A new interpretation has similarly arisen of the ancient tradition of decorative glass, whose forms have been adapted to modern structural and architectural requirements (Steel Church, Cologne by *Bartning, 1928; Cathedral of St Michael, Coventry, by *Spence, 1954–62). Cartoons for stained glass windows were designed by outstanding modern artists (Chapel at Vence by Matisse, 1947), and new techniques for treating the glass (Notre-Dame du Haut, Ronchamp, by Le Corbusier, 1954) or binding the component parts of the design together (Church at Audincourt, by Novarina, Léger and Barillet, 1950–1; Church at Athis-Val by Laurence and Rocher, 1954) were explored. Finally, the task of directly expressing the decorative significance of the glass has been transferred to the design of the framework itself (Robie House, Chicago, by Wright, 1909; Church of Notre Dame, Le Raincy, 1923, and Ste Thérèse, Montmagny, 1926, by *Perret; glasswork in the Italian Pavilion at the Brussels International Exhibition, by *Gardella, 1958).

Bibliography: F. Franceschini, *Il vetro*, Milan 1955; R. McGrath and A. C. Frost, *Glass in Architecture and Decoration*, London 1961.

GIUSEPPE VARALDO
GIAN PIO ZUCCOTTI

Goff, Bruce, b. Alton, Kansas 1904. Designer of houses which clearly show their derivation from Frank Lloyd *Wright. Goff drives poetic impulse to formal caprice (circular and spiral buildings with continuous flowing space; house made up of cubic units).
Bibliography: Progressive Architecture, Dec. 1962.

Gollins, Melvin, Ward and Partners. Frank Gollins, James Melvin, Edmund Fisher Ward. Extensive practice distinguished for ability to handle large masses and exploit the results of careful research. Works include Castrol House, London (with *Casson and Conder), Cleveland Technical College, Redcar, and developments at the Western Bank area of Sheffield University, for which they have designed a library to hold a million books.

Sir Owen Williams. Boots' Factory. Beeston, near Nottingham, 1930–2

Great Britain. Modern architecture developed in France and Central Europe in the first three decades of the century, but it was late in coming to England. It is true that English domestic architecture seen in the work of Philip *Webb, Norman *Shaw, and C. F. A. *Voysey in the late 19th and early 20th centuries eloquently demonstrated designing that was logically and tastefully in answer to needs, and that this had a great influence in Europe, but the task of further development along such lines over a bigger field of building continued first in Germany, Austria, and to a lesser extent in France. Except for rare, isolated, examples it was not until the thirties that development along vigorous functionalist lines, in the broadest sense, was again manifest in England. Among the few exceptions was the Royal Horticultural Hall in London, designed by J. Murray Easton and Howard Robertson in 1923. This hall is constructed of *reinforced concrete parabolic arches, which hold together a step structure with four tiers of windows. It is a functional and expressive use of reinforced concrete and makes a beautiful and impressive interior.
Among the most important, slightly later, examples of modern architecture in England are the early works of a structural engineer, Sir Owen *Williams, of which the most notable are the large factory for Boots the Chemists at Beeston, near Nottingham, completed in 1932, the Empire Swimming Pool at Wembley (1934), and the Peckham Health Centre (1936). All these works are in reinforced concrete, the structure of which largely determines the appearance of the buildings. The Boots factory shows the influence of the *Bauhaus at Dessau, designed by Walter *Gropius. It is a large building and consists of reinforced concrete mushroom columns supporting concrete floors, the whole enclosed in glass walls, the only break in the glass being the edges of the concrete floors. By this simple mushroom-slab construction and the glass walls this building marked a big step forward in factory design in England and it was increasingly imitated. The Swimming Pool at Wembley was, at the time of its completion, the largest covered bath in the world. It was built on the reinforced concrete frame principle on a horizontal grid and vertical unit, which permitted the extensive em-

ployment of standardized parts. The roof is constructed of a series of three hinged arches held by vertical concrete shafts, which project above the plane of the low-pitched roof and perform a similar function to that of buttresses in a Gothic church. The Peckham Health Centre was a pioneer venture of two doctors, and Sir Owen Williams provided them with a modern three-storey structure of reinforced concrete with glass screens for external walls, thus admitting the maximum of light. Design is determined by purpose, and here the newest methods of construction are devised to satisfy that purpose as efficiently as possible. So as to enhance the enjoyment of sunlight and the surroundings the wall on the south-west side becomes in the two upper storeys a series of bay windows. Following similar lines, with extensive use of glass walls, is the Royal Corinthian Yacht Club building at Burnham-on-Crouch designed by Joseph Emberton in 1930. With its long balconies in front of glass walls, giving horizontal emphasis, it harmonizes with its position by the sea.

Some of the most notable contributions to modern architecture in the thirties in England are to be found in individually designed houses, and the torch of Webb, Voysey and Shaw seems to have been recovered by architects like Amyas Connell, Basil Ward and Maxwell *Fry, although the torch burns a somewhat different flame. What they have in common are plans and sequence of rooms, determined by convenience, ignoring any preconceived ideas of balance and symmetry. They are mostly built of reinforced concrete, with irregular plans, large windows towards the sun and flat roofs. The first of these houses was the famous 'High and Over' at Amersham, Buckinghamshire, designed by Amyas Connell in 1929. The house has three storeys, consisting of three arms radiating from a central octagonal hall which extends the whole height of the house. Another house built at Grayswood in 1933 by Connell in association with Basil R. Ward has a very irregular plan rather like an irregular triangle, but a perfect orientation is secured with the three principal ground-floor rooms—living-room, study, and dining-room—and the three bedrooms on the front floor all facing south. The irregular plan is reflected in the general appearance which composes

Tecton. Finsbury Health Centre. London, 1938–9

into a very agreeable relation of masses. This was one of the most ingeniously designed modern houses in Europe. It was followed by several other houses by the same architects, and these, and the stimulus given to English architects by the migration of famous German architects to England between 1933 and 1936, including Walter Gropius, Marcel *Breuer, and Erich *Mendelsohn, led several architects to design houses in a similar progressive manner. Among them was Maxwell Fry, who was Gropius's partner for a few years. After Gropius left for America, Fry built several houses on the most modern lines, one of the most effective being a house in Frognal, Hampstead (1938), which has a glass wall on the first floor opening on to a balcony. Fry was also responsible for a working-class housing scheme in Ladbroke Grove, London, which was, from the standpoint of light, good planning and spacing, the most advanced scheme of its kind in London at the time of its erection. Other architects who produced good modern work in which the new methods of construction were employed expressively were the *Tecton Group, who built the Highpoint block of flats at Highgate and the Finsbury Health Centre, both works in the modern idiom, but who became known chiefly for their constructions for the London Zoo: the Gorilla House and the Penguin Pool, where

concrete has been used with good effect in a sculptural manner to show off the comic antics of the penguins. Mention should also be made of the Peter Jones Department Store in Sloane Square, London, designed by William Crabtree in association with Slater and Moberley and C. H. Reilly. Here the main supports of the building are set back from screen walls and the whole has a very light appearance.

In the early post-war period a great deal of experiment was conducted with new methods of house construction, but only a few of the many types survived and led to further developments. Probably the most outstanding post-war architecture in which the resources of modern building were used most intelligently was in schools, particularly those built in Hertfordshire. In these early post-war days materials were difficult to obtain in adequate quantities, and there was a shortage of skilled labour. Techniques were therefore adopted that permitted a fair degree of prefabrication and standardization which would contribute to speedy building. By these methods and designing that aimed at good lighting, large windows and cross-ventilation, some excellent school buildings were erected rapidly.

A notable and typical example of the Hertfordshire schools is the Hampden Secondary School for which the County Architect, C. H. *Aslin, was responsible with W. A. Henderson as the architect in charge. It was built in 1949–51 to accommodate 450 children, with a grouping of buildings according to the functions of general teaching, assembly, crafts and science, physical training and administration. The buildings are mainly two-storey, thus representing a departure from the previous post-war one-storey school building; yet the standard steel-frame structure employed in the latter was used in the Hampden School with cladding of concrete blocks. The irregular yet functional grouping and the long horizontal rectangular massing composes well with the landscape. Other

Tecton. Penguin Pool, London Zoo, 1938

William Crabtree, Slater and Moberley and C. H. Reilly. Peter Jones Department Store. London, 1938

C. H. Aslin. Junior School. Croxley Green, Hertfordshire, 1947–9

notable post-war schools in Great Britain are the secondary school at Hunstanton in Norfolk, completed to the design of Alison and Peter *Smithson in 1954, another functional grouping where the assembly and administration are on the ground floor and classrooms on the upper floor, mostly with glass walls. A notable example in London of a well-planned school characterized by lightness and large glazed areas is the Bousfield Primary School, Old Brompton Road, designed by *Chamberlin, Powell and Bon.

In 1951 three notable concert halls were built: the Royal Festival Hall in London, the Colston Hall in Bristol, and the Free Trade Hall in Manchester, the last two being rebuildings. In all these halls very special attention was paid to acoustics. In the Festival Hall designed by Robert *Matthew, the architect of the London County Council, a large area of slate is incorporated in the floor between the steeply raked auditorium and the orchestra so as to reflect sound. Vision is extremely good from every seat, and the whole building is an excellent design for its function, with a clever use of materials, while the large glass walls of the landings and rear corridors afford views over London and its river.

Some of the best large-scale housing in Britain is to be seen in certain blocks of flats in London and the vicinity, and in some of the two- and three-storey blocks in the new towns, such as Stevenage, Harlow, Basildon and Crawley near London, in Peterlee, Durham and the Scottish new towns of East Kilbride, Glenrothes and Cumbernauld.

The LCC Roehampton estate is one of the largest and most impressive of local authority developments. It accommodates nearly 10,000 persons, and consists of ten-storey tower blocks, six-storey slab blocks, four-storey maisonette blocks, and rows of two- and three-storey dwellings. The estate is situated in wooded undulating country, and the diverse buildings group pleasantly and look well in the landscape. The treatment of the slab blocks with their open ground floors is influenced by the work of *Le Corbusier, but they are marred by gallery access. Other notable housing estates in London are the Spa Green Flats in Finsbury by Tecton (1946–50); Churchill Gardens by *Powell and Moya (1947–53);

Robert H. Matthew. Royal Festival Hall. London, 1951

and the Golden Lane estate in the City of London by Chamberlin, Powell and Bon (1953–7). The dominating buildings in all these groups are tall slab blocks, seven to ten storeys, and they all succeed in being aesthetically pleasing because of well-designed patterns made by the windows and balconies, and by the relation of the blocks to the spaces between. Although they are all low-cost housing there is an agreeable effect of spaciousness between the blocks, while at the same time an effect of intimacy is occasionally obtained as in a group of shops and public house within the Churchill Gardens development.

Two interesting schemes with very different purposes have a strong architectural kinship: a tower block with four wings of small low-cost flats in Bethnal Green (1959) and a block of luxury flats in St James's Place, overlooking Green Park (1961), both by Denys Lasdun & Partners. The architectural idiom is similar in both: large glazed areas related to plain flat rectangular shapes of walls and balconies. The effect is particularly felicitous in the views of the St James's Place flats from various points in Green Park.

The best low-cost two- and three-storey housing during the fifties is undoubtedly in the new towns; one of the reasons for this is that many of the new town development corporations have commissioned well-known architects to design for them. Examples typical of the best are some parts

Denys Lasdun and Partners. Cluster Block. Bethnal Green, London, 1958–60

of Basildon which, in the layout, are adaptations of the Radburn planning of residential areas. In these, by rear access of vehicles to houses, some degree of segregation of vehicular traffic and pedestrians is secured. Three areas: Barstable planned by the development corporation architect Anthony B. Davis; Vange by Sir Basil *Spence; and Kingswood by William Crabtree are examples where this segregation has been achieved with some varied and attractive housing. In Peterlee new town some very compact housing was designed by two development corporation architects, Peter Daniel and Frank Dixon in collaboration with the painter Victor Pasmore. Some of the patterns of the rectangular façades are reminiscent of Pasmore's abstract pictures.
As a whole industrial architecture of the fifties shows a decided improvement on that of the thirties where the custom of having a symmetrically designed Georgian office in front of a series of sheds was all too common. In the fifties there has been a more marked tendency to integrate the various parts into a satisfactory architectural ensemble; some of the best examples can be seen in the spacious industrial areas of the new towns, four of the most notable being at Stevenage, Hemel Hempstead and Crawley round London, and East Kilbride near Glasgow.
Perhaps the most original industrial architecture of the post-war period is seen in power stations, in both the conventional stations using coal or oil and the nuclear power stations, a type of building of which Britain has been a pioneer. In the early thirties most power stations were built with heavy walls of brick, but this was felt to be unnecessarily substantial, and the tendency has been towards a much lighter cladding of glass, aluminium, asbestos and other thin, light materials. Some well-designed power stations have resulted, a number of which are by *Farmer and Dark. A good example is the Marchwood Power Station on the Hampshire coast near Southampton. This building in which aluminium *curtain walling is employed forms a long horizontal mass by the sea with two tall chimneys. With nuclear power stations different problems of design are presented because they include immense reactor buildings which have to be of very sturdy construction. All the massive nuclear power stations so far built—those at Berkeley and Hinkley Point near the Bristol Channel are examples—are different in design. The most recent, that at Sizewell in Suffolk, designed by Frederick *Gibberd, has something of the massive character of a medieval fortress or defensive castle. Instead of the nuclear power stations spoiling scenic beauty, as was feared, they have become interesting features in the landscape.

A main development in British architecture during the fifties can be seen in office and apartment blocks. Consent is now given for higher buildings in certain circumstances, and this has resulted in many office blocks in London being built well above the previously permitted 100 feet (generally about nine or ten storeys) to fifteen, twenty, thirty storeys or even more. The chief distinguishing architectural feature of office blocks since about 1952 is the curtain wall, and a tower block of about fifteen or twenty storeys rising from a lower block of about two or three storeys. Notable buildings of this kind in London are Castrol House, designed by *Gollins, Melvin Ward & Partners; Thorn House, designed by Sir Basil Spence; and the Vickers Building, designed by Ronald

Ward & Partners, which is the highest office block built in London, having thirty-four storeys. There is a danger that the pattern of tower and low podium block if not designed with some originality may become monotonous, and thus architects, alive to this, are introducing more varied treatment such as the curved facade of the Vickers tower, and the Y plan of the new multi-storey Hilton Hotel in Park Lane. This plan serves the function of giving a maximum number of bedrooms views over Hyde Park. With parts of the building of various heights combined with a tower block, the architecture of office buildings is becoming a matter of the large-scale relation of masses, while in the treatment of curtain walls and end walls architecture is moving closer to the art of the painter with effects that depend on the abstract pattern of colours and textures.

Bibliography: J. M. Richards, *An Introduction to Modern Architecture*, 1st edition, London 1940, 3rd edition, London 1961; Edward D. Mills, *The New Architecture in Great Britain 1946–1953*, London 1953; John Summerson, *Ten Years of British Architecture*, London 1956; Trevor Dannatt, *Modern Architecture in Britain*, London 1959.

ARNOLD WHITTICK

Greene, Charles Sumner and Henry Mather. Charles Sumner, b. St Louis 1868, d. Carmel 1957. Henry Mather, b. Cincinnati, Ohio 1870, d. Altadena, Calif. 1954. Studied at Massachusetts Institute of Technology, Cambridge. The Greenes' houses are among the best examples of Californian regionalism at the turn of the century, with their interpenetration of internal and external space, projecting roofs, flat gables and warm materials (timber, shingled walls, coloured windows). Blacker House (1907) and Gamble House (1908–9) at Pasadena, Calif. (*USA)

Gropius, Walter, b. Berlin 1883. One of the outstanding architects and teachers of the 20th century, Walter Gropius is the son of an architect who occupied an important official position in Berlin. It is not without significance that his great-uncle, Martin Gropius (1824–80) was an architect of some reputation who designed, among other notable buildings, the great hall of the new Gewandhaus at Leipzig, and who

Walter Gropius

was also Principal of the Arts and Crafts School in Berlin and Director of Art Education in Prussia. (*International Style) Walter Gropius received his training in architecture first at Munich from 1903 to 1905 and then in Berlin to 1907, when he entered the office of Peter *Behrens where so many young architects later to become famous had also worked, among them Mies van der Rohe and *Le Corbusier, who, however, stayed only for a short time. In 1910, after three years in Behrens's office, Gropius started on his own as an industrial designer and architect. His designing covered a wide range and included interior decoration schemes, wall fabrics, models for mass-produced furniture, motor-car bodies, and a diesel locomotive. His first important building was the Fagus shoelace factory at Alfeld-an-der-Leine, built in 1911 in collaboration with Adolf *Meyer. This building marked a step forward in steel and glass construction. It is three-storeyed, the steel frame supports the floors, and the walls have become glass screens, the non-structural character of which is emphasized by the absence of vertical supports at the corners. At the famous *Deutsche Werkbund Exhibition at Cologne in 1914 Gropius and

Walter Gropius and Adolf Meyer. Fagus factory. Alfeld-an-der-Leine, 1911

Meyer designed the Administrative Office Building which proved to be a very notable contribution to modern architecture. The building is symmetrical, the central portion of the front façade is faced with brick, and at the ends are spiral staircases enclosed for two storeys by glass towers. The glass screen held by a very light steel framework continues on the first floor along the narrow sides and for the whole length of the rear of the block, thus imparting the character of unusual lightness (*p.15). The glass towers enclosing the staircases represent the first use of an architectural motif that was to become an important feature in many modern buildings, especially departmental stores. It was often used by Erich *Mendelsohn with fine effect. Gropius and Meyer also designed the hall of machinery and open garages at

Walter Gropius and Adolf Meyer. Model factory at the Werkbund Exhibition. Cologne, 1914

Walter Gropius. Bauhaus. Dessau, 1925–6

the back of the office block. The former had a slightly pitched roof with steel stanchions curving from the walls.

From 1914 to 1918 came the break of the First World War when Gropius served in the German Army. In 1915 he was given the position by the Grand Duke of Saxe-Weimar of Director of the Grossherzogliche-Sächsische Kunstgewerbeschule and the Grossherzogliche-Sächsische Hochschule für Bildende Kunst at Weimar, and after the cessation of hostilities in 1919 he combined the two under the name of Das Staatliche *Bauhaus, Weimar, because Gropius believed in the unity of design and craft, of art and technics. He was Director first at Weimar from 1919 to 1925 and then at Dessau from 1925 to 1928 when he resigned because he wished to devote his energies more wholeheartedly to architecture untrammelled by official duties.

While at the Bauhaus, however, he was the architect of several buildings and the designer of several projects, his most important building during this period being the world-famous group of buildings for the Bauhaus at Dessau, which was completed towards the end of 1926. Among other works was the rebuilding of the Municipal Theatre at Jena in 1923, designed in collaboration with Meyer, and two very interesting projects, one a building for an international academy of philosophical studies and the other a 'Total Theatre'. The former, designed for a site near the University of Erlangen, belongs to 1924 and shows the tendencies in his planning that two years later resulted in the Bauhaus building. The 'Total Theatre' design was made in 1927 in collaboration with Erwin Piscator, the Berlin theatrical producer. The purpose was to design a theatre that could be changed to accord with the type of play, changed, that is, from the Greek theatre with the semicircular orchestra, to the circus with the central arena and to the modern picture-frame stage. The theatre was so designed that the tiers of seats could be revolved in sections to enable the change from one form to another to be effected quickly. A model

Walter Gropius. Siemensstadt housing estate. Berlin, 1929

was exhibited at the 1930 Paris Exhibition, but it was never built. The movement towards building theatres of flexible construction, however, has grown considerably during the century, and Gropius's project has been a significant contribution towards the feasibility of the idea.

Gropius was not only an architect and industrial designer, but a sociologist who wanted to build on the basis of a rational interpretation of the needs of people. During the latter part of his directorship at the Bauhaus he studied the problem of obtaining the best living conditions in cities while preserving their urban character. He aimed to produce city dwellings in which the inhabitants obtained as much sunlight, space, and air and trees and lawns as possible at very much the same density as then existed. To achieve this he evolved the tall slab-like apartment block of about ten storeys, arranged, not parallel with the street but transversely with it, orientated according to the sun, with cross-ventilation and with broad stretches of garden between the blocks and open at both ends. He showed that with higher blocks housing people at the same density there is far more space and the angle of light is less.

Gropius was able partially to realize his ideas in the Dammerstock housing scheme near Karlsruhe in 1927–8, where he not only designed some of the five-storey blocks but acted as a co-ordinator for eight other architects. In this scheme several blocks are arranged in parallel lanes transversely with the streets. A more ambitious realization was in the large Siemensstadt estate near Berlin, in which Gropius was the supervising architect with several others collaborating, while he was himself responsible for two of the blocks. The general layout consists of long five-storey blocks, orientated north–south so as to get the maximum sunlight, widely spaced with stretches of grass and tall trees with light, delicate foliage between. The blocks have pale plain walls with large windows, and they are planned with two flats per landing. These Siemensstadt flats have exerted a wide influence and have been much imitated.

With the accession to power of the National Socialists in 1933 conditions became difficult for liberal and modern minded architects, so in 1934 Gropius left Germany for England. He settled in London and entered into partnership with E. Maxwell *Fry, one of the most successful of the younger British architects. Together they designed several interesting schemes, the work actually completed including the film laboratories for London Film Production at Denham (1936); two houses, one in Sussex (1936) and one in Old Church Street, Chelsea (1935); and Impington Village College, Cambridgeshire (1936), one of four village colleges erected by the County Council. This was Gropius's most important contribution to architecture in England. It is a one-storey building with single depth classrooms, fan-shaped hall, and club amenities, all very happily sited amongst lawns and trees to serve the dual purpose of a secondary school and community centre for adults.

Early in 1937 Gropius accepted an invitation to become Senior Professor of Architecture at Harvard University, USA, and the following year he became Chairman of the Department of Architecture. He very quickly demonstrated his practical ability as an architect by building his own house, which was completed in the year of his arrival. It has much of the classic restraint of the houses that he had designed for himself and the Bauhaus leaders in 1926. This was followed by a large number of private residences that he designed in collaboration with other architects in America. In the year of his arrival he entered into partnership with the Hungarian architect, Marcel *Breuer, who had been a student and master at the Bauhaus. In the years of their partnership in addition to several houses, including one for Breuer himself, they designed the Pennsylvania Pavilion, New York World's Fair in 1939, and an interesting housing scheme at New Kensington near Pittsburgh in 1941, in which year the partnership with Breuer terminated. The New Kensington housing was for the workers in an aluminium factory, and the houses were built on the slopes of the hills above the factory. They were irregularly sited and in accordance with the best orientation, following the contours of the hills; they were reached by winding paths.

Page 143. The Architects Collaborative. Harvard Graduate Center. Cambridge, Mass., 1949–50

When in Germany, in 1932, Gropius had begun experiments with standardized building elements for mass-produced housing, and he resumed these experiments during the war years 1943–5. The earlier ideas were concerned with copper-sheet houses, but these later developments were with timber panels based on a module both horizontally and vertically of 40 inches. After experiments made in collaboration with Konrad *Wachsmann in Long Island, these houses were erected on a considerable scale in California.

In 1945 Gropius went into partnership with several architects of the younger generation forming a team of eight under the name of 'The Architects Collaborative' (*TAC). In this enterprise Gropius was the guide and leading spirit. That he was able to enter with enthusiasm into so large a group demonstrates his great belief in the value of team-work which he had always felt to be necessary in modern building. The team was responsible for much interesting work which made a noteworthy contribution to mid-20th-century American architecture. It includes several private residences, all of which are worthy of study for their planning and siting; the Junior High School, Attleboro, Mass. (1948); the Harvard University Graduate Center, Cambridge, Mass. (1949–50), which consisted of a group of seven dormitory blocks in relation to the social centre; and the Harkness Commons, a grouping in which the open spaces between the buildings were very carefully related to function. In 1953 the team built the McCormick Office Building. In 1961 Gropius was invited to London to design a building for the Monico site in Piccadilly Circus, the former scheme for which had been rejected by the authorities as not being of sufficient architectural merit for this important site.

Gropius's buildings are distinguished by an adventurous use of the modern materials of steel, concrete and glass, while he may be regarded as perhaps the principal innovator in the utilization of the complete

Walter Gropius and Wils Ebert. Block of flats. Interbau Exhibition. Berlin, 1957

The Architects Collaborative. US Embassy. Athens, 1961

The Architects Collaborative. Bagdad University, 1960. Project

glass *curtain wall for the outer shell of a building, thus admitting the maximum of light. Architecturally his work is always distinguished by a classic restraint and excellence of proportion of which the houses for the staff at the Bauhaus at Dessau are an example. But important as Gropius is as an architect, he is possibly even more important as a teacher and an influence. He was a great believer in the intelligent application of standardization and *prefabrication, but mostly he wanted a building to be the product of team-work in which each member of the team appreciated fully the relation of his contribution to the whole design. Gropius regarded this as a symbol of community living and the intelligent integration of society.
Bibliography: Sigfried Giedion, *Walter Gropius*, Paris 1931; Sigfried Giedion, *Walter Gropius: Work and Teamwork*, Stuttgart, Paris, New York and London 1954; J. M. Fitch, *Walter Gropius*, New York 1960. See also Bauhaus.

ARNOLD WHITTICK

Gruen, Victor, b. Vienna 1903. Studied under Peter *Behrens. Emigrated to the United States in 1938. Mainly town and country planning (e.g. Fort Worth, Texas). His conception of 'shopping centres' was epoch-making, sited out of town and catering for the needs of modern street traffic (Northland Shopping Centre, Detroit, 1952).

gruppo 7. Architectural co-operative of seven (predominantly Milanese) architects, Luigi *Figini, Guido Frette, Sebastiano Larco, Adalberto Libera, Gino *Pollini, Carlo Enrico Rava and Giuseppe *Terragni. The group, founded in 1926, appeared publicly in 1927 with an exhibition at the Biennale in Monza and was invited in the same year to the Werkbund Exhibition at Stuttgart. It stood for an architecture founded on the regional analysis of building functions and attempted to create an Italian tradition in modern building. 'The desire for sincerity, order, logic and clarity above all, these are the true qualities of the new way of thinking.' (Series of articles in *La Rassegna Italiana*, December 1926 to May 1927.)

Guimard, Hector, b. Paris 1867, d. New York 1942. Studied at the École des Arts Décoratifs and at the École des Beaux-Arts in Paris, where he later taught. Guimard was influenced by Victor *Horta, the most gifted and eminent architect of the French *Art Nouveau. His main work consists of the Castel Béranger, Paris (1897–8), the imaginative entrances to the Paris Métro, reminiscent of the organic forms of nature (1900), and the Humbert de Romans Building, Paris (1902), a large auditorium with a steel frame.

Hankar, Paul, b. Frameries 1859, d. Brussels 1901. The architect Paul Hankar was one of the moving figures in Belgian *Art Nouveau, together with Victor *Horta and Henry van de *Velde. He learnt his profession in the office and on the building sites of the architect Henri Beyaert from 1879 to 1894, when Beyaert died. During this period Hankar was personally responsible for the restoration and interior

Paul Hankar. Maison Kleyer. Brussels, 1898

decoration of the Church at Everberg in Brabant.

Hankar took over from his master certain elements of his style, such as the harmonious blending of white stone, blue stone and brick, but introduced modernist details into this traditional type of structure: wrought-iron grilles, consoles, handrails and balconies, and sgraffito murals. A number of medieval and oriental reminiscences are incorporated in his work, too: openings set asymmetrically, stilted arches, battlements, penthouses, broad cornices and heavy modillions, which conspire to produce a picturesque effect. He conceived of architecture as a synthesis of the plastic arts and designed the interior decoration and furniture for most of the private houses he built. He originated an Art Nouveau type of shop-front and fittings which gained rapid acceptance in Europe. He died before being able to carry out a major project, the *Cité des Artistes*, for which he had drawn up the plans.

Bibliography: Charles de Maeyer, *Paul Hankar*, Brussels 1962.

ROBERT L. DELEVOY

Hugo Häring. Farm buildings at Garkau, near Lübeck, 1923

Häring, Hugo, b. Biberach 1882, d. Biberach 1958. Häring advocated in his writings and buildings a theory of organic building which differs from the *organic architecture of Frank Lloyd *Wright.

Häring studied at Stuttgart Technical College (under Theodor *Fischer) and at Dresden. In 1912 he established his own architectural practice in Berlin. In 1924 the *Zehnerring* was founded to fight the tendencies propagated by the then city architect Ludwig Hoffmann, and this group was later enlarged to become *Der *Ring*. The *élite* of the modern architects of Germany belonged to it, and Häring, as its secretary, was the leader of the association. In 1933 the *Ring* was dissolved by the Nazis. Though *Gropius and *Mies van der Rohe emigrated, Häring remained in Germany; he was the head of a private art school. In 1943 he returned to his native town of Biberach, where he died in 1958 after a long, painful illness.

Häring was responsible for a number of important works, of which the Garkau farm buildings (1923) have become particularly famous; his real importance, however, lies in the theoretical field. He expounded his views on organic building in numerous articles and lectures. He maintained that the work of rejuvenating architecture had to proceed in two stages. The first is concerned with research into changing needs, and aims at fitness for purpose and the 'organism'; the second, on the other hand, deals with 'design'. While other contemporary trends in the twenties (*Le Corbusier, for example) determined what shape fitness for purpose would take by using geometric forms accepted as *a priori* beautiful, Häring attempted to develop the design from its fitness for purpose without preconceived ideas of shape. 'We want to search for things and let them unfold their own design. It goes against the grain . . . to determine their shape from the outside, to subject them to a set of derived laws' ('Wege zur Form'). Häring emphasized that organic building did not mean copying the forms of nature but that—as in nature—shape arose from function.

The thesis sometimes propagated by his followers, that organic building demanded curved shapes, not based on orthogonal principles, was rejected by Häring. 'The identity of an object must determine the type of form appropriate to the individual building' ('Geometrie und Organik'). The

decisive criterion in organic building is the determination of form from an object's identity. A building derives its shape from the function which it has to discharge as the tool (or 'organ' as Häring called it) of man. The house as the tool of its inhabitants is the starting point of his thinking.
Häring's ideas, which in the twenties were limited to a small circle, became increasingly important with the new phase of modern architecture that started about 1930. Today, architects as distinct as Alvar *Aalto, Louis *Kahn and Hans *Scharoun hold similar views.
Bibliography: Hugo Häring, 'Wege zur Form', in *Die Form*, No. 1, 1925; Hugo Häring, 'Geometrie und Organik', in *Baukunst und Werkform*, No. 9, 1951; Heinrich Lauterbach and Jürgen Joedicke (editors), *Organhaftes Bauen* (=Dokumente der Modernen Architektur 4), Zurich and Stuttgart in preparation.

JÜRGEN JOEDICKE

Harrison, Wallace Kirkman, b. Worcester, Mass. 1895. Studied at the École des Beaux-Arts, Paris. Worked on the Rockefeller Centre (1931–47). Partnership first with *Hood then with Fouilhoux and Max *Abramovitz. Harrison and Abramovitz are among the greatest American architectural firms and have specialized in office buildings. Storey-high units of aluminium or steel were used for the *curtain walls of such buildings as the Alcoa Building in Pittsburgh (1953) and the Socony Mobil Building in New York (1956). Harrison, who possesses excellent organizational ability, was principal architect for the United Nations Buildings, New York (1947–50, esquisse by Le Corbusier). As coordinator he is directing the construction of the Lincoln Center, a cultural project in New York (building in progress).

Haussmann, Georges-Eugène, b. Paris 1809, d. Paris 1891. As prefect of the Seine department under Napoleon III, Haussmann executed a series of *town-planning schemes in Paris that determined the present face of the city: construction of bridges and prestige buildings, opening up of streets and boulevards to meet military, ceremonial, hygienic and traffic requirements.

Havlíček, Josef, b. Prague 1899, d. 1962. Studied at the College of Technology and the Academy of Fine Arts at Prague (1916–26). Housing, offices, hospitals, large-scale urban works. His 1930 buildings, white blocks with continuous horizontal strips of windows, are amongst the most disciplined examples of the *International Style.

Hilberseimer, Ludwig, b. Karlsruhe 1885. Worked in Berlin till 1928, then at the *Bauhaus in Dessau; since 1938 at the Illinois Institute of Technology in Chicago. Town-planning work of fundamental significance.
Bibliography: Ludwig Hilberseimer, *Grossstadt-Architektur*, Stuttgart 1927.

Hoffmann, Josef, b. Pirnitz, Moravia 1870, d. Vienna 1956. Hoffmann studied architecture in Vienna under Otto *Wagner, whose most faithful and convinced disciple he became. The rationalistic theories that underlay Wagner's teaching had a decisive influence on the course steered by Hoffmann, but the latter's famous elegance and refinement of taste was far removed from the severity of *Loos. He did not, in fact, despise ornament and this led him to show particular interest in the production of craft objects. He taught at the School of Applied Arts from 1899 onwards, and together with Koloman Moser set up a group of studios and workshops, which under the name of *Wiener Werkstätte* enjoyed widespread success and fame for thirty years.
In 1897 he joined with other young artists, including Joseph *Olbrich in founding the Wiener Sezession. Under the influence of the Glasgow School and of Belgian and French *Art Nouveau, its aims were more radically modernist than those of Wagner's school. Ten years later, he moved towards a new cultural avant-garde that centred round the painter Gustav Klimt, with whom Hoffmann founded the *Kunstschau* called 'the Secession from the Secession'. Meanwhile Hoffmann's first works of architecture gave him a European celebrity, which was confirmed by the commission he received to build a large house in Brussels for the Stoclet family. In the opening years of the century he had designed exhibition pavilions, schemes for internal decoration and four houses (Moser, Moll, Henneberg and Spitzer). With the Purkersdorf Sanatorium (1903) he became one of

Josef Hoffmann. Palais Stoclet. Brussels, 1905

the foremost exponents of the new style in architecture. His Palais Stoclet (1905) is an architectural masterpiece that evokes the exquisite poetry of Post-Impressionism and Symbolism. Although completely based on rationalist theories it is rich and refined to the point of decadence, a monument of the last bourgeois age which represents a milestone in Hoffmann's own career, and in the history of European architecture, at the moment when it was turning towards the new century.

In the years that followed, up to the eve of the First World War, Hoffmann built dozens of villas in Vienna with only a few basic variations. At the 1914 *Deutscher Werkbund Exhibition in Cologne, for which he designed the Austrian Pavilion in an elegant style of vaguely neoclassic derivation, he encountered in the work of *Gropius a new and more vigorous form of architectural modernity: one which was to mark, inevitably, the decline of his own, with its exquisite refinements of 'taste'.

In 1912 he began the construction of a villa colony at Vienna-Kaasgraben, which was interrupted by the war; his architectural work was only resumed in 1920, though the activity of the *Wiener Werkstätte* had continued. In 1920, too, he was appointed city architect of Vienna. But with the rise in Europe of De *Stijl, the *Bauhaus and *Le Corbusier's *Esprit Nouveau*, something a little anachronistic in Hoffmann's work was to leave it henceforth slightly on the margin of modern architecture, whose social content was also radically new. Hoffmann himself was aware of this. The housing schemes he carried out in 1924 and 1925 for the City of Vienna, and his terrace houses in particular for the 'Internationale Werkbundsiedlung' of 1932, are built in a style of extreme architectural purity that recalls the houses of *Neutra, Loos, *Rietveld and *Lurçat. They are the last proofs of Hoffmann's conscious and

Josef Hoffmann. Design for an auditorium. 1922

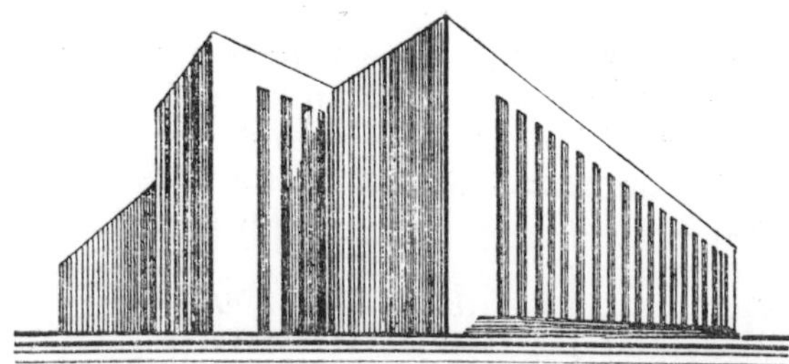

deliberate 'presence' in the process of total revolution through which architecture was passing in those years of unmitigated controversy. The next year, 1933, he decided to close down the famous *Wiener Werkstätte* for good. He designed the Austrian Pavilion for the 1934 Venice Biennale, and, after the last war, some blocks of workers' housing. He died in Vienna in 1956, while a large exhibition devoted to his work was on show in Brussels.

Bibliography: Ludwig Hevesi, *Acht Jahre Sezession*, Vienna 1907; Leopold Kleiner, *Josef Hoffmann*, Berlin, Leipzig and Vienna 1927; Armand Weiser, *Josef Hoffmann*, Geneva 1930; L. W. Rochowanski, *Josef Hoffmann*, Vienna 1950; Giulia Veronesi, *Josef Hoffmann*, Milan 1956.

GIULIA VERONESI

Holabird, William, b. Amenia Union, N.Y. 1854, d. Evanston, Ill. 1923. Trained in the office of William Le Baron *Jenney, later in partnership with Martin Roche. The Tacoma Building (Chicago, 1889) by Holabird and Roche is the aesthetic consequence of the introduction of steel frames for tall buildings; an extensive dissolution of the façade into glass, punctuated by projecting bays, and the abandonment of historical ornamentation.

Holford, Sir William, b. S. Africa 1907. Studied at Liverpool University School of Architecture. Rome Scholar, 1930. Professor of Civic Design at Liverpool, 1937; Professor of Town Planning, University College, London, 1948. Houses, factories, public buildings. Planning proposals for the County of Cambridge, 1950. Report on St Paul's precinct, 1956; three-level plan for Piccadilly. His fourteen-storey block of flats at Kensal (1958) has been called the first large-scale *modular building. President of the RIBA, 1960–2.

Holzmeister, Clemens, b. Tirol 1886. Churches, residential and public buildings. Worked in Turkey (Ministry of War, Summer Palace for Kemal Pasha). New Salzburg Festival Theatre (1960).

Hood, Raymond M., b. Pawtucket, R.I. 1881, d. Stamford, Conn. 1934. Gained first prize in the competition for the Chicago Tribune Building (1923–5, a neo-Gothic design); in 1931, in collaboration with Fouilhoux, he built the McGraw-Hill Building, New York, no longer revivalist in style, and the Daily News Building (1930) with J. M. Howells, anticipating the vertical stress of Rockefeller Center. (*USA)

Horta, Victor, b. Ghent 1861, d. Brussels 1947. A keen disciple of *Viollet-le-Duc, Horta was a leading figure of continental *Art Nouveau and the creator of an original vocabulary of ornament. He helped to open up new paths to 20th-century architecture by doing away with the traditional plan of the private house and providing an architectural expression for the new building programmes set in train by the social and cultural developments of his time. He was also instrumental in devising a number of subtle structural forms that drew on the resources of iron and glass.

Horta began his architectural studies at Ghent Academy (1876) and continued them at the Académie des Beaux-Arts at Brussels. After spending some time in the office of Balat, a neoclassic architect of repute, he built a group of three little houses in the Rue des Douze Chambres at Ghent (1886), where his great architectural ability is already obvious despite the modest scale

Victor Horta. Hôtel Tassel. Brussels, 1892–3

of the project. This first design of his, honest, straightforward and economical, gave little indication of a work that was to appear six years later, whose astonishing architectural and decorative richness revealed its author as someone of great creative maturity, albeit still young (thirty-one): the Hôtel Tassel, built between 1892 and 1893 at 6 Rue P. E. Janson, Brussels. This house, a veritable manifesto of Art Nouveau, is revolutionary in form and structure and is regarded today as one of the classic monuments in the history of architecture. It is the product of an expanding bourgeois economy, strong craft traditions and a country that has achieved a high degree of industrialization; but above all, the Hôtel Tassel is remarkable for the novelty of its plan: instead of the corridor usual in Belgium, Horta substituted an octagonal hall, from which a broad staircase leads off, giving access to the various rooms at different levels. This arrangement breaks with the practice of uniform layout floor by floor, foreshadowing the 'plan of volumes' conceived by *Loos in 1910 and *Le Corbusier's two-storey system of 1930.

Victor Horta. Hôtel Solvay. Brussels, 1895–1900

The Hôtel Tassel is also remarkable as being the first private house to make use of iron, both as a structural material (a huge winter garden on the ground floor is carried on an exposed iron frame, while an elegant iron column supports the staircase) and to supply decorative elements in a flexible linear style, exemplified by the wrought-iron handrails of the staircase and balconies. It is in this building, too, that an impressive repertoire of two-dimensional forms was initiated, based on a close study of plants and flowers: the 'whiplash line' or 'Horta line' literally covers the floors, walls and ceilings; it lashes out everywhere, coiling, interlacing, flying loose, climbing across glazing bars, encircling the feet of furniture, branching out in chandeliers and outstripping, often to excess, every structural requirement.

In the Hôtel Solvay (224 Avenue Louise, Brussels), built between 1895 and 1900, Art Nouveau can be seen in its maturity: it is an astonishing symbiosis, of Baroque and classical, sentiment and reason, craftsmanship and industry, colour and form, with aesthetics dominating technology. This building, wholly fitted out and furnished by Horta, is undoubtedly the most significant and complete example of its period. Horta built numerous houses in Brussels before the First World War in the same style (Autrique, 1893; Winssinger, 1895–6; Van Eetvelde, 1897–1900; Aubecq, 1900). The Maison du Peuple he designed for the Brussels branch of the Socialist Party (1896–9), and the department stores 'A l'Innovation' (Brussels, 1901) and 'Grand Bazar' (Frankfurt, 1903) all employ the structural resources of iron in the service of a new programme. The large glazed façades of these three buildings prefigure the light transparent envelopes that have led to the disappearance of the load-bearing wall. (*Glass; *Steel)

In 1912 Horta was appointed a professor at the Académie des Beaux-Arts, whose head he eventually became (1927–31). After a stay in the United States (1916–19), his architecture assumed an austere, classical direction; the picturesque and calligraphic tendencies of Art Nouveau were conclusively superseded by the straight line. The Palais des Beaux-Arts in Brussels (1922–8) is the principal work of this period; well laid-out and designed in concrete, it was the first cultural centre of

a type that was to gain wider diffusion after the Second World War.
Bibliography: Robert L. Delevoy, *Victor Horta*, Brussels 1958.

ROBERT L. DELEVOY

Howard, Ebenezer, b. London 1850, d. Welwyn Garden City 1928. In his book *Tomorrow: A peaceful path to reform* (London 1898) Howard advocates garden cities to counter flight from the land and the overpopulation of towns. His idea of an economically independent garden city surrounded by an agricultural belt and numbering approximately 30,000 inhabitants led to the foundation of the Garden Cities Association. First garden city: Letchworth near London (1903).

Howe, George, b. Worcester, Mass. 1886, d. Cambridge, Mass. 1955. Studied at Harvard, 1904; Ecole des Beaux-Arts, 1907. Partner in Mellor, Meigs, & Howe, 1913–16. Howe and *Lescaze, 1929–34, Howe and Bel Geddes, 1935, Howe and *Kahn (Louis) 1941, Howe, Stonorov and Kahn, 1941–4, Howe and Brown, 1950–5. Howe's major work, with William Lescaze, was the Philadelphia Savings Fund Society (PSFS) Building, built 1931–2. PSFS is noteworthy for its strong expression of horizontal and vertical structuring and its T-shaped plan, packaging the services separately from the office spaces. Elements such as the curved corner of the banking room set a trend for skyscraper clichés of the later 1930s. Expensive materials were used and all desks and fittings were custom-made; particularly luxurious in the banking hall and the top-floor executive suite, they surpass those in the recent Seagram Building in New York. The PSFS Building marked a transition from the first European phase of the *International Style to the second American phase. Howe's original, basically Beaux-Arts scheme was later modified to conform to International Style concepts.
Other notable works by Howe are: High Hollow, his own house in Chestnut Hill, Pa. (1914–16); the Newbold Farm, Laverock, Pa. (1922–8, since destroyed); the Oakland School, Croton-on-Hudson, N.Y. (1929, the first International Style building on the east coast of the USA); Carver Court Housing, Coatesville, Pa. (1942–4); the Philadelphia Evening Bulletin Building (1954).
Square Shadows, in Whitemarch Valley, Pa. (1934), marked a departure from the stuccoed boxes of European modernism by its use of local materials. One of Howe's most interesting houses is Fortune Rock (1938–9), the Thomas House on Soames Sound, Maine: this was built entirely of local materials by local craftsmen. It is noteworthy for its sensitive siting and for its dramatic double reinforced concrete cantilever which projects the living-room 40 feet over the water.
In the 1940s Howe was Supervising Architect for the Public Buildings Administration and, later, Deputy Commissioner for Design and Construction. He was Hoppin Professor and Chairman of the Department of Architecture at Yale University from 1950–4. He was a unique figure who renounced a career in building Beaux-Arts country houses and successfully adopted the principles of modernism. His PSFS Building is a key monument: the only International Style skyscraper produced until *Mies van der Rohe's work after the Second World War.

Howell, Killick, Partridge and Amis. William Gough Howell, John Alexander Wentzel Killick, John Albert Partridge, Stanley Frederick Amis. Practice with a style characterized by a powerful striving after plastic originality. Their project for the Department of Commerce and Social Science at Birmingham University features *Gaudí-like façades of precast concrete balcony units; a redevelopment plan for St Anne's College, Oxford, consists of a series of curved blocks with highly modelled surface treatment, set in a wide oval round the college garden.

International Style. The term International Style, although recurrently under attack since it was first introduced in the book of that name (New York 1932; *Johnson), has become—in considerable part by default—perhaps the most useful name for the dominant architectural current of the second quarter of the 20th century. Within the broad historical range of modern architecture, from the European and American modes of such men as *Voysey, *Horta and *Sullivan in the 1890s to the present 1960s, it defines a type of architectural design which came into existence in the early 1920s, developed at the hands of a few leaders to classic expression by 1930, and from that time on found wider and wider acceptance throughout the world.

Foreshadowed by the domestic building of Adolf *Loos, the early industrial constructions of *Perret, *Behrens and *Gropius, much work by engineers, European and American, and even the Futurist visions of *Sant'Elia, the new architecture of the pioneers among the second generation of modern architects, particularly the French-Swiss *Le Corbusier, the German Gropius and *Mies van der Rohe, and the Dutch *Oud and *Rietveld, representing a convergence of social and aesthetic aspirations characteristic of the second decade of the century, found early expression, mostly in projects, in the years 1919–23 immediately after the First World War. The large-scale projects of Mies (his glazed towers of 1919 and 1921), the Chicago Tribune Tower design of Gropius and Meyer (1922), and the spaced cruciform skyscrapers of Le Corbusier's 'City of Three Million', also projected in 1922, indicated a generic debt to American achievement in building, and by the mid century the International Style would even come to seem to many a characteristically American style. But for all the debt of younger architects outside America to *Wright, especially in Holland and Germany in the fifteen years following 1910, the initiation of the new style—if style it be—was Western European, even specifically French, Dutch, and German; and it did not even begin to be accepted in other European countries—England, Sweden, Denmark, Finland, Russia and Italy—or in the New World until the late 1920s. As it spread internationally in the 1930s, however, political reaction and economic stagnation interrupted further development in several countries of Europe, notably Germany, Russia and France. On the other hand, by the late thirties, notable work was under way from Helsinki to

Walter Gropius and Adolf Meyer. Chicago Tribune Tower. 1922. Project

Le Corbusier. Second Citrohan House. 1922. Model

Ludwig Mies van der Rohe. Block of flats on the Weissenhof Estate. Stuttgart, 1927

Rio de Janeiro; and when building revived in the late 1940s after the Second World War the International Style had come to be almost universally accepted throughout the whole non-Communist world wherever modern technological advances were already an accomplished fact or even a relatively new importation.

As late as 1952 it was possible to claim (see the article 'The International Style Twenty Years After' in the *Architectural Record*) that, despite all the modulations, reactions and divagations up to that time, the International Style was still the essential core of international architectural practice. A decade later, now that the stylistic divergences of the last thirty years have become more strikingly apparent, the International Style probably still remains the basis of further architectural development since it was, very definitely, the discipline under which almost all architects under sixty were formed. To offer historical parallels not too pretentiously disparate in their chronological range, the divergent aspirations and achievements of the later 1930s, 40s, and 50s bear somewhat the same relation to the classic stage of the International Styles of the 1920s as the modulations that followed the High Gothic in the mid and late 13th century or those that followed the High Renaissance in the mid and late 16th century. On these analogies the International Style, as the 'high' phase of modern architecture, may indeed continue to provide the basis of architectural developments for several generations—and even centuries—to come.

Returning to the book of 1932 which attempted at the end of the classic phase to formulate the International Style which had come into being through the preceding decade since 1922, certain quotations may still be relevant: 'The unconscious and halting developments of the 19th century, the confused and contradictory experimentation of the beginning of the 20th have been succeeded by a diverted evolution. There is now a single body of discipline, fixed enough to integrate contemporary style as a reality and yet elastic enough to permit individual interpretation and to encourage general growth. . . . The idea of style as the frame of potential growth, rather than a crushing mould, has developed with the recognition of principles such as archaeologists discern in the great styles of the past: . . . There is, first,

Alvar Aalto. Building for the newspaper Turun Sanomat. Turku, 1928–30

a new conception of architecture as volume rather than as mass. Secondly, regularity rather than axial symmetry serves as the chief means of ordering design. These two principles, with a third proscribing arbitrary applied decoration, mark the productions of the International Style. This new style is not international in the sense that the production of one country is just like that of another. Nor is it so rigid that the work of various leaders is not clearly distinguishable. . . . In stating the general principles of the contemporary style, in analysing their derivation from structure and their modification by function, the appearance of a certain dogmatism can hardly be avoided. (But) the international style already exists in the present; it is not merely something the future may hold in store. Architecture is always "a set of actual monuments, not a vague *corpus* of theory".'

Some of those actual monuments may well be named, in addition to the skyscraper projects mentioned earlier. These, however, it should be noted, have proved especially premonitory of what may be considered the 'American' phase of the International Style of the 1950s, which could now be illustrated with monuments as far apart geographically as the Edifico Polar in Caracas, Venezuela, by Vegas and Galia and the SAS building in Copenhagen, Denmark, by Arne *Jacobsen, not to speak of prominent examples in countries such as England, Germany, Italy, Belgium and South Africa.

Eero Saarinen. General Motors Technical Center. Warren, Mich., completed 1955

Perhaps the first modest realization of the ideals of the still unformulated International Style was a jewellery shop of 1921 in the Kalverstraat in Amsterdam by G. T. Rietveld inspired by the Dutch *neoplasticism. Parallel with this came the unrealized projects of Le Corbusier for 'Citrohan' houses (1919–21) and those by Mies van der Rohe for a brick country house and for a concrete office building (1922). Major works of the mature International Style followed, with Gropius's *Bauhaus at Dessau (1925–6), Le Corbusier's Cook and Stein houses (1926 and 1927), Oud's low-cost housing at the Hook of Holland (1926–7), Gropius's housing at Törten, Siemensstadt and Dammerstock (1928 and 1929), not to speak of his Dessau Employment Office (1928), perhaps his most perfect work; and finally Mies's German Pavilion at the Barcelona Exposition (1929) and his Tugendhat house in Brno, Czechoslovakia, and the Savoye house at Poissy outside Paris by Le Corbusier (both 1930).

Immediately after 1930 definite modulations began to appear away from some of the austerities of the classic phase, particularly in Le Corbusier's Swiss Hostel (1931–3) at the Cité Universitaire in Paris with its rubble rear wall of irregular curvature and its somewhat sculptural *pilotis* of rough concrete. Thus in the very years of the early 1930s, when the new style was spreading most rapidly throughout the world on the way to its almost universal acceptance after the Second World War, one at least of the founders was still in the lead in moving away from the rigid machinolatry implicit in the most advanced aspirations of the 1920s. But this should not be overemphasized. In the very years of the early 1950s, when Le Corbusier in his Church of Notre-Dame du Haut at Ronchamp in France and his High Courts of Justice at Chandigarh in India was reaching the extreme point of his reaction against the International Style, Mies van der Rohe in his Lake Shore Drive apartments was providing a new model of the tall building, based on his projects of the 1920s, destined to be enormously influential internationally; while Eero *Saarinen, whose early death in 1961 deprived the post-war world of one of its most typically versatile and divergent designers, was still faithful to the Miesian version of the International Style in his first major work, the General Motors Technical Center at Warren, Mich.

It still seems just, therefore, to return to the initial paragraph of this article and to state once more that the International Style was the dominant architectural development of the second quarter of this century, and that its core of tradition, at least, as well as its continued employment in vulgarized modes—to which the term is by some derogatorily restricted—is still the basis of the world's architecture even in the 1960s and may well remain so for many decades.

HENRY-RUSSELL HITCHCOCK

Iron. *Steel.

Italy. 'Since the 18th century there has been no architecture': it is with these words that *Sant'Elia opened his Manifesto of 1914. It would have been truer to say that since the 18th century Italy had produced no great architect, no new directions in architecture and no great school. Nevertheless, there has not been any substantial change from 1914 to the present day, despite Sant'Elia and despite *Nervi: for two centuries now, Italian architects, when they have not built like the ancient Romans, have trodden in the steps of foreigners; only *Terragni has dared to strive for independence. The few interesting architects of the *Stile Liberty* (the Italian *Art Nouveau), *Basile, D'*Aronco and *Sommaruga looked to the Belgians and French; while Vienna provided the models for Sant'Elia himself (influenced by the school of Otto *Wagner) and the Lombard rationalists prior to 1927, who were followers of *Loos and *Hoffmann. After 1927 the young 'Europeanists' of the modern movement reorientated themselves to *Le Corbusier, *Mies van der Rohe or *Gropius. This generation, which is now fifty or sixty years old, still represents the best in Italian architecture today.

Naturally, in the work of each of them, from Basile to *Albini, and from Sant'Elia to Nervi, the personal imprint is stronger than the foreign one; but it has not been as determinative either of the essential content or the original form as the foreign sources have; it is the latter, revived and worked over again, that one sees reflected there. One original element, in the years between the wars however, intervened amid the various foreign influences, as a dangerously suggestive constant: the *Novecento Italiano*, the only cultural movement that was typically Fascist (hence the 'Italiano'), recruited from the 'reactionaries of the modern revolution' (as one of its founders wrote), or rather from the 'revolutionaries of the Fascist reaction' as its critics saw it. But unlike the revolutionary architects of *Germany and the *Netherlands, the protagonists of the *Novecento Italiano* did not start from scratch. They carried out a modernist reform based on the principles of neoclassical architecture and the aesthetics of *valori plastici*, modified in the light of Cubism, or its Italian derivative, *Futurism. Giuseppe Terragni revivified this movement by the support of his artistic genius; he was its most important architect, not only by reason of the absolute value of his works, and of the Casa del Fascio (Como, 1936) in particular, but above all because of the complexity of the problems he set himself in attempting to break down the 'national' barriers to his lively historical feeling for architecture; and by historical we mean European. Luciano *Baldessari worked with similar aims, building the fine Press Pavilion at the Vth Milan Triennale (1933).

Raimondo d'Aronco. Main Building at the Applied Art Exhibition. Turin, 1902

Matté Trucco. Fiat Works. Turin, 1927. Car ramp

The ferment of new ideas came to the boil in 1927, in particular with the work of the seven young architects united under the banner of **gruppo 7*, who formulated their ideas in a number of publications and helped to promote the foundation of the *Movimento Italiano per l'Architettura Razionale*. But as architecture, more than any other art, was tied up with politics, the ambiguous attitude of the *Novecento Italiano* was passed on to the new movement. The subsequent confusion was great, since both opposing trends, the 'modern' and the 'ancient Roman' (whose leader was Piacentini) declared for Fascism. In reality the interests and claims of both sides were equally demagogic, and periods of inauspicious alliance were not lacking either. The journal *Quadrante*, edited by P. M. Bardi, supported the Fascist version of rationalism. Meanwhile, some architecture of note did get built: the Fiat Works by Matté Trucco (1927) and Pagano's Casa Gualino, both at Turin; some houses by Lingeri on Lake Como; and Terragni's Novecomum at Como.

The position was soon clarified, however, by Edoardo Persico, a young critic who since 1929 had been the editor of Giuseppe Pagano's *Casabella*. He showed that rationalist architecture was essentially anti-nationalist, according to the tenets of the *Bauhaus, itself the most rigorous expression of it. Persico had to fight within the editorial board itself of *Casabella* against Pagano's Fascist illusions and his own noble errors, for which he ultimately paid with his life, dying at Mauthausen in 1943.

In 1933 Gio *Ponti took over the direction of the Vth Triennale. Ponti was of modernistic neoclassical provenance, but anti-monumental, and never taking his standpoint to extremes; this made him the favourite architect of the Milanese bourgeoisie. In a spirit of free experimentation, and without any polemical intent, he invited the 'rationalist' group of architects to take a large part in the Triennale, and published their work in his journal *Domus*, thus paving the way to success for them. Their contribution to the Triennale, a series of villas and small houses erected in the park, was of a splendid precision and uniformity; but on the moral plane, though they were not aware of it, the compromise was grave. It was only with the war and the end of Fascism that nearly everybody, starting with Pagano, understood the cause that Persico had defended: they understood, that is to say, that a revolutionary architecture is incompatible with a reactionary government, which is always willing to exploit alliances and compromises. But by that time, Piacentini, the leader of Fascist architecture, and certain Novecentists like him, such as Muzio in Milan, had already sown their colonnades, lictoral towers and 'Roman' arches up and down the length of Italy. It was the same with town planning: Mussolini founded new cities, only one of which had any architectural feeling: Sabaudia (by Cancellotti, Montuori, Piccinato and Scalpelli); and it was only Adriano Olivetti who called in some bright young architects—*Figini and *Pollini—to draw up a plan for the Val d'Aosta.

After the war, the reconstruction drive was beginning to bear fruit, when Bruno Zevi, back in Rome after many years' residence in America (where he had not seen Italy's difficulties and problems), thought he recognized an error in the general alignment of Italian architects, victorious at last, along the front of 'rationalist' aesthetics. But although he performed a task of cultural value in spreading, with polemical ardour, a knowledge of Frank Lloyd *Wright and his campaign for 'natural', i.e. *organic as opposed to 'rational' architecture, he nevertheless helped to confuse once more the ideas of Italian architects who had only recently managed to sort them out, and who in any case found rationalism in architecture congenial. Zevi had the greatest effect on the School of Rome, which counted some of the best architects in Italy amongst its members, including Piccinato, Quaroni (who built some experimental villages at Matera), Montuori, the designer of the new station in Rome (1950, with Calini and others), the whimsical Ridolfi, Moretti, Monaco and Luccichenti. But above all, the architects of Milan were disorientated. They had been induced to re-think their architecture from scratch, sometimes altering their whole style, and it was this lack of ideological clarity that later gave rise to the strange form of the Torre Velasca (1957) and the rising tide of 'neo-Liberty' (Art Nouveau revival) which has almost drowned some young architects and stirred up a scandal

Gian Antonio Bernasconi, Annibale Fiocchi and Marcello Nizzoli. Palazzo Olivetti. Milan, 1954

Eugenio Montuori, Leo Calini, Massimo Castellazzi, Vasco Fadigati, Achille Pintonello and Annibale Vitellozzi. Main Railway Station. Rome, 1950. Booking Hall

Pier Luigi Nervi and Annibale Vitellozzi. Palazzetto dello Sport. Rome, 1956–7

abroad out of proportion to the episode's size and significance.

In and around Milan however, innumerable buildings have arisen: workers' flats, factories, houses, office blocks, churches and a number of skyscrapers (the Pirelli Building by Gio Ponti; the much discussed Torre Velasca by *BBPR; the Torre Galfa by Bega; and the Torre al Parco by Magistretti). In addition to the architects of the first rationalist school, such as *Albini, Figini, Pollini, Sartoris, Lingeri, Belgioioso, Banfi (who died in a concentration camp), Peressutti, Rogers, *Gardella, Bottoni, Mollino, Astengo, Zavanella and *Nizzoli, may be named the younger generation of *Zanuso, Pagani, Castiglioni, Caccia Dominioni, Latis, *Fiocchi, Bernasconi, Morandi, Bassi, *Viganò and Mangiarotti (known for his 'glass church' at Baranzate) among others. But every city and every region is a centre where interesting architects are at work: Cocchia at Cosenza (Naples); Samonà at Minchilli (Bari); Michelucci, designer of the fine station in Florence (1936, in collaboration); the builders of the Market at Pescia in Tuscany (1951); *Scarpa in Venice, where the best school of architecture is situated; and Albini, himself a Milanese, in Genoa, where he has built the two splendid museums of the Palazzo Bianco (1951) and San Lorenzo (1954–6). Works of great interest may often be found in small towns, such as Terragni's Casa del Fascio at Como (1936), Gardella's buildings at Alessandria, those of Baldessari at Rovereto, Gellner's at Cortina, D'Olivio's at Trieste, Nervi's at Chianciano and Bologna, and those by Nizzoli, Fiocchi, Gardella, Figini and Pollini at Ivrea.

The nerve centre of the new Italian architecture is Milan, with its journals, its Triennali, its recently founded Museum of

Architecture, and the economic opportunities afforded by its industries. It was in Milan that culminated the activity of that generous and intelligent patron of modern Italian architecture, Adriano Olivetti; it is being continued by his son Roberto today. On the cultural plane, Rome competes for primacy; it is the home of the *Istituto Nazionale di Architettura*, headed by Bruno Zevi, who also edits *L'Architettura*, published in Rome. Architectural criticism, too, is very active in Italy, backed by an intelligent editorial policy (Argan and Zevi in Rome, Ragghianti in Florence, and Dorfles and Veronesi in Milan). Our general panorama may conclude on a positive note with the name of the greatest and best known amongst living Italian designers, the engineer Pier Luigi Nervi whose superb structures, which for the last thirty years have been rising throughout Italy and the world, have won for him universal renown.

Bibliography: Paolo Nestler, *Neues Bauen in Italien*, Munich 1954; Piero Bottoni, *Edifici Moderni in Milano*, Milan 1954; G. E. Kidder Smith, *Italy Builds*, London 1955; Carlo Pagani, *Italy's Architecture Today*, Milan 1955; Agnoldomenico Pica, *Architettura Italiana Recente*, Milan 1959.

GIULIA VERONESI

BBPR. Torre Velasca. Milan, 1957

Luigi Figini and Gino Pollini. Church of the Madonna dei Poveri. Milan, 1952–6

Jacobsen, Arne, b. Copenhagen 1902. Arne Jacobsen is an architect who has been to a notable degree open to new impulses without losing his attachment to the Danish tradition. The same sense for order, modular rhythms and natural proportions, which developed first in Danish half-timbered construction and later in the brick buildings of the classical revival, characterizes Jacobsen's architecture. Artistic discipline, together with an avoidance of sentimentality and theatric effects, led to a restraint which, combined with a sense for precision in detail and excellence in workmanship, pervades all Arne Jacobsen's later building.

Jacobsen grew up with *Functionalism. When he was a student *neoclassicism

Arne Jacobsen. Bellavista Housing Estate near Copenhagen, 1933

still dominated Denmark and the architecture of about 1800 was greatly admired, in particular that of the architect Nicolaj Abildgård. But his encounter with the architecture of *Le Corbusier and *Mies van der Rohe in exhibitions at Paris (1925) and Berlin (1927–8) was important both for Jacobsen himself and for the whole development of Danish architecture.

Jacobsen was trained in the architectural school of the Academy of Arts, from which he graduated in 1928. He had already attracted notice with the first of a long series of single houses, reminiscent externally of Abildgård and his period, with yellow bricks and a tiled roof. The ease and flexibility of his talent enabled him at the same time to try his hand at Functionalism's cubist style. Together with Flemming Lassen he created a sensation at an exhibition in 1929 with a circular 'house of the future' with helicopter landing-place on the roof.

In his earliest Le Corbusier-inspired villas the smooth whitewashed walls concealed technical faults which followed from the over-hasty adoption of the new style. In 1930–5 he created a harmonious group of buildings in the Bellevue area near Copenhagen, beginning with the baths, whose cabins and kiosks were designed with elegance. These were followed by the three-storey Bellavista housing blocks, whose staggered perspectives gave all flats an equal share of sun and view. Finally came the Bellevue Theatre, which was thought of primarily as a summer theatre and therefore given a sliding ceiling which could make the night sky serve as a roof. Unfortunately both the theatre and the adjoining restaurant have been altered beyond recognition.

It was through his friendship with the Swedish architect Gunnar *Asplund that Jacobsen reached maturity as an artist. From Asplund he learned what it is to *work* at a building, both technically and architecturally, and to respect detail. Asplund's influence shows clearly in Stelling House in Copenhagen (1937–8) and the town halls of Århus (1937) and Søllerød (1940–2), designed in collaboration with Erik Møller and Flemming Lassen respectively. Gradually Jacobsen was able to free himself from Asplund's imprint without forgetting the lessons he had learned from him.

Wartime isolation and the conditions prevailing until 1950 allowed Denmark no opportunity to make use of the new impulses arriving from abroad. Then with the Søholm housing scheme Jacobsen won back his position among the leaders of Danish architecture. In Munksgård's School (1952–6), a single-storey construction with numerous bays and courtyards, he combined a sense for total unity of design and quality with an atmosphere of intimacy. In a series of new offices and administrative buildings he tried to introduce the largely American-developed principle of construction with internal supporting columns and *curtain-wall façades. He appreciated the fact that the aesthetic qualities of so simple, almost anonymous, an architecture must be based on proportions and detail, and designed accordingly [Jespersen's Building in Copenhagen (1955); Rødovre town hall (1955); the SAS Building in Copenhagen (1959)].

Since the war Jacobsen has also constructed a series of handsome private houses, which show to a marked degree his ability to fit buildings into the landscape, such as the houses for C. A. Møller (1951) and Ruthwen Jürgensen (1956), lying in attractive surroundings near the Sound. Exclusive residences were constructed in Jægersborg and Gentofte and blocks of flats in Rødovre (1951). On the industrial side mention should be made of Odden Smokehouse (1943), built with traditional materials, the Massey Harris exhibition and works building (1952), which was awarded the grand prix in São Paulo, Brazil, and Tom's Factories (1961). Arne Jacobsen does not wish to be a specialist. Not only does he range over the entire field of architecture, but he is just as willing to plan silverware, gardens, furniture, and fabric patterns.

Jacobsen has been invited to take part in a number of international competitions [town halls of Marl (1957) and Cologne (1959), World Health Organization's building in Geneva (1960)]. He has received first prize in many Danish and Swedish competitions, including Denmark's National Bank (1961) and Landskrona town hall and sports hall (1957). Since 1959 he has been engaged on St Catherine's College, Oxford. He has been Professor of Architecture at Copenhagen Academy of Arts since 1956.

Bibliography: J. Pedersen, *Arkitekten Arne Jacobsen*, Copenhagen 1954.

TOBIAS FABER

Japan. It was in the year 1868 that a decisive new era dawned for Japan under the rule of Emperor Meiji, putting an end to the long feudal age of the Tokugawa Shogunates which had lasted for 260 years. The isolation policy of the Shogunates was abandoned and the country opened its doors to the world, absorbing Western civilization with eagerness.

Arne Jacobsen. Housing. Søholm, 1950–5

Arne Jacobsen. Jespersen Offices. Copenhagen, 1955

Tetsuo Yoshida. General Post Office. Tokyo, 1931

In Japan wood had always been the main building material. After the restoration the Japanese invited architects from Germany, England, Italy and the United States to help them build Western style architecture of stone and bricks. Japanese architects then copied these examples and soon began to give birth to a Japanese-European style, introducing elements of Renaissance, Gothic and Italian into the traditional native architecture.
Japan is naturally very receptive and liberal in adopting foreign cultures and has been much influenced by them. But she also values and preserves her own age-old culture and blends it harmoniously with imported cultures, though the process of assimilation often takes a long time. The rapid introduction of Western architecture at the beginning of the Meiji period was a challenge to Japan's architectural circles. Scholars such as Professor Chuta Ito and Professor Tei Sekino turned their attention not only to the study of Western architecture but also to the traditions of their own country and other Asiatic lands.
Towards the end of the 19th century steel-framed structure and *reinforced concrete were introduced, bringing a rapid development in the Japanese building industry. Together with this innovation in building technique came the influence of modern movements in Europe such as *Art Nouveau and the Wiener Sezession. In 1920, under the prosperous conditions following the end of the war and with a call for humanism, the Japanese group Secession was formed by a number of younger architects, including Sutemi Horiguchi, Makoto Takizawa, Mamoru Yamada, Kikuji Ishimoto. In 1922 Japan's modern architecture was presented by this group at the Peace Exposition, Tokyo, for the first time. Of its members Mamoru Yamada designed the Central Telephone Office, Tokyo (1926); Kikuji Ishimoto, the Tokyo Asahi News Press Building (1927), and the Shirokiya Department Store, Tokyo (1929). Sutemi Horiguchi devoted his time to a re-examination of the traditions of Japanese architecture and received a doctor's degree for his thesis on Kundaikan-Sochoki, which is an historical document concerning interior decoration in 15th-century Japan.
Japanese modern style is best represented in works built for the Communications Services. Mamoru Yamada was first in this field. He was followed by Tetsuo Yoshida, *Functionalist in the best sense of the word, who designed the Tokyo General Post Office (1931); and later by Hideo Kosaka (Post Office Savings Bank, Kyoto, 1954).
The *International Style found its way into Japan through contacts made by her younger architects and critics with modern groups in Europe. Kenji Imai, a professor at the Waseda University, went to Europe in 1926 to study modern architecture and became personally acquainted with *Gropius, *Le Corbusier, *Mies van der Rohe,

Hideo Kosaka. Post Office Savings Bank. Kyoto, 1954

and others. On his return he published reports on their activities. Kunio *Maekawa went to Paris to work under Le Corbusier; Iwao Yamawaki and Takehiko Mizutani studied at the *Bauhaus in Dessau. About this time two foreign architects visited Japan who had a great influence on her modern movement. One of them was Frank Lloyd *Wright, whose famous Imperial Hotel (1915–22) had very much impressed Japan's architectural circles. The other was a German architect, Bruno *Taut, who travelled all over Japan, seeking out the wonderful treasures of her architectural tradition.

At this stage of their development Japanese architects were confronted with many difficult problems. They were not only concerned with the basic principles of modern building; they were also trying to find answers to the demands of modern living in a new age. In 1937 they founded the *Kosaku Bunka Renmai* (Japanese Werkbund) and issued a publication, *Kosaku Bunka*, in which they outlined their proposals and described the experiments they had made. Hideo Kishida, Shinji Koike, Sutemi Horiguchi, Yoshiro Taniguchi, Takeo Sato, Kunio Maekawa were the leading members of the group. But soon

Kunio Maekawa. Harumi Flats. Tokyo, 1957

Kenzo Tange. Sogetsu Hall. Tokyo, 1960

Kiyonori Kikutake. Sky House. Tokyo, 1958

the time became unfavourable to the growth of such a movement; with the rise of Fascism in Europe, militaristic nationalism took the lead in Japan, and finally the outbreak of war brought the activities of the Japanese Werkbund to an end. Their only chance lay in the rationalization which was necessitated during the war because of the shortage of material and labour.

After the signing of the San Francisco Peace Treaty in 1951 architecture began to develop again under the new democratic constitution. First came the construction of quarters for the occupation forces, then gradually the work of reconstruction in general. The leading architects were Mamoru Yamada, Kunio Maekawa, Kameki Tsuchiura, Kenzo *Tange, and Yoshiro Taniguchi, who had all formerly been connected with the Japanese Werkbund. Examples of their work are the Welfare Hospital by Mamoru Yamada (1953), the International House by Maekawa, Sakakura and Yoshimura (1955), the Peace Centre in Hiroshima by Kenzo Tange, and the Nagasaki Cultural Centre by Takeo Sato (1955). Isoya Yoshida, who remained deeply attached to the traditional styles of Japanese architecture, attempted a modern interpretation of these traditions in his building for the Japanese Academy of Art and several private houses. Kenzo Tange adopted a new curtain-wall technique for the Metropolitan Government Office in Tokyo. He also approached a traditional Jomon style in his use of reinforced concrete for the Sogetsu Hall and Kagawa Prefectural Office.

One of the most important problems for Japanese architects today is rationalization. They are encouraged by large-scale housing projects under the sponsorship of public corporations. Sky House, Kikutake's own house (1958), is an experiment pointing in the right direction for the future.

It is in the last ten years that Japan has given serious thought to the problems of her own cultural heritage. Younger architects such as Kiyonori Kikutake, Masato Otaka, Yoshinobu Ashihara are making great efforts to re-examine and revive Japanese architectural tradition and the Japanese way of living in terms of modern technology. The Kirishima Kogen Hotel, designed by Masachika Murata, is an attempt to achieve a harmony between the building and its natural environment, and the interior is perfectly in keeping with the traditional way of living (chopsticks and kimonos).

Bibliography: Shinji Koike, *Contemporary Architecture of Japan*, Tokyo 1953; Shinji Koike and Ryuichi Hamaguchi, *Japan's New Architecture*, Tokyo 1956; Udo Kultermann, *New Japanese Architecture*, London 1960.

SHINJI KOIKE

Jenney, William Le Baron, b. Fairhaven, Mass. 1832, d. Los Angeles 1907. Studied in Paris. He introduced the use of the steel frame in multi-storey buildings with his Home Insurance Building (Chicago, 1883–5; *p. 6); the lavish mouldings of his masonry show no aesthetic consequences of his innovation. First Leiter Building (1879), second Leiter Building (1889–90), both in Chicago.

Johansen, John MacL., b. New York 1916. Studied at Harvard University under Walter *Gropius and Marcel *Breuer and worked in the offices of Breuer and *Skidmore, Owings and Merrill. Johansen is keenly interested in structural experiments: designs for a holiday house with a *reinforced concrete shell and a 'streamlined house' with walls of sprayed reinforced concrete. His design for the US Embassy in Dublin, a rotunda with circular courtyard and a façade of prefabricated, reinforced concrete frames, is based on the Irish round-tower tradition.

Philip Johnson. Glass House. New Canaan, Conn., 1949

Johnson, Philip, b. Cleveland, Ohio 1906. Philip Johnson, the American architect, was the son of a prominent lawyer. In 1927, while studying classics at Harvard, he read an article on the modern movement in architecture by Henry-Russell Hitchcock which directed him towards his career: initially, in the thirties, as the first director of the pioneering architectural department of the Museum of Modern Art in New York; then, before the end of the forties, as a practitioner. During the period of his curatorship he distinguished himself as a propagandist and historian of the modern movement. In connection with the exhibition of modern architecture at the Museum in 1933, besides an influential catalogue, he wrote **The International Style* (1932) in collaboration with Hitchcock. It attempted an overall description of the aesthetic qualities of European modernism—and, incidentally, baptized the style with its generally accepted name (the suggestion of Alfred Barr, then Director of the Museum). Johnson's catalogue *Machine Art* (1934) was also influential, and the Museum's displays of industrial design under his aegis (while not exactly unprecedented in American museums) did much to stimulate museum interest in the exhibition of mass-produced objects. His catalogue for an exhibition of the work of *Mies van der Rohe (first edition, 1947; enlarged, 1953) was the first work on this architect.

Johnson's work as a propagandist for modern architecture whetted his appetite to become a practitioner. In the early forties, he left the Museum for Harvard, where he was strongly attracted by the teaching of Marcel *Breuer. But Mies, whom he had met in Europe in 1930, was his true mentor and he soon came to be known as Mies's most faithful disciple. His own 'Glass House' in New Canaan, Connecticut (1949) was derived from Mies's similar scheme for the Edith Farnsworth House in Fox River, Illinois (1950, but designed in 1946), and, more specifically, from the metal skeletal treatment of the buildings for the Illinois Institute of Technology. Despite these influences, the Glass House is a work of marked originality which instantly gained international recognition as among the masterpieces of the immediate post-war period. Unlike the austerely self-contained refinement of Mies's Farnsworth House, Johnson's Glass House possesses a romantic feeling for park-like landscape and a wealth of historical allusion (*Schinkel, *Suprematism, the diagram of the Acropolis from Choisy, for example). These qualities give an 18th-century quality of urbanity and wit to the play of the simple shapes on the terraced greensward: glass box, brick box and saucer pool diagonally opposed to one another around the axial vertical of Jacques Lipchitz's totemic *Figure*.

In a series of commissions for suburban houses Johnson elaborated the themes of the Glass House in various ways, and complicated them by the introduction of

Philip Johnson. Boissonas House. New Canaan, Conn., 1956

courts. Notable among these early houses are the Hodgson and Wiley Houses in New Canaan (1951 and 1953 respectively), the Davis House in Wyzata, Minnesota (1954), and the Rockefeller Guest House in New York (now the property of the Museum of Modern Art, 1950). Meanwhile, Johnson's appreciation of both the architectonic and landscape values of the court led to what may well be the finest urban space designed during the decade and a half following the Second World War, the garden of the Museum of Modern Art (1953).

With his Temple Kneses Tifereth Israel at Port Chester, New York (1954–5), Johnson began to throw off his spiritual apprenticeship to Mies for more personal statements, although he was to collaborate with Mies on the Seagram Building (1957–8), where his contributions are especially evident in the interior. In the Temple, the exposed Miesian metal skeleton is infilled with precast concrete slabs slotted with stained glass. The Ledoux-like ovoid entrance structure outside and the *Soane-like hung plaster vaulting within testify to his continued interest in bringing sophisticated historical allusions to bear on modern expression. Johnson's tentative use of precast concrete as a mural infilling in the Temple presages his increasing use of masonry in his recent buildings. In precast concrete or hand-carved masonry, he has reintroduced the classicist ideals of the portico and colonnade. His Sheldon Art Gallery for the University of Nebraska in Lincoln (under construction) and the New York State Theater for the Lincoln Center (completed in 1964) are major examples of this *neoclassicism. Curvatures introduced at the juncture of column and 'entablature' of the Nebraska building are, by his own admission, also influenced by Gothic architecture. In his *béton brut* chapel for the Benedictine Priory in Washington, D.C. (designed in 1961), the relative weight of this combined classical/neo-Gothic inspiration shifts. If buttresses and vault are obviously medieval in feeling, the columnar character of supports alternating with the buttressing, together with the contained simplicity of the overall mass, are less evidently classicist. On the other hand, the specific design of the members is unimaginable without reinforced concrete construction.

Among the most convinced (and convincing) of modern 'traditionalists' (as Johnson has sometimes termed himself), his eclectic evocation of past architecture in his own work is far-ranging. For example, the domical forms of a nuclear reactor building for Israel (1960) and a shrine at New Harmony, Indiana (1960)—the first a gently gored shape in poured concrete, the second a bent wood and plywood structure thatched in wooden shakes—recall similar undulating domes in such a late Imperial Roman work as Hadrian's Villa or in Borromini's Baroque churches. But there are subsidiary recollections of Egyptian temple complexes in the one, of Indian *stupas* and Norwegian stave churches in the other. Meanwhile, both recall the austere containment of Ledoux's massing. Johnson's early interest in the steel skeleton appears in his campus complex for the University of St Thomas in Houston, Texas (two sections completed in 1959). He based the complex on Thomas Jefferson's scheme at the University of Virginia for an arrangement of separate buildings around a rectangular green, all linked by a covered colonnade. This interweaving of elemental building masses and covered colonnades with landscape also appears in his pavilion buildings, where the basic pavilion (supports and a roof) is repeated in plan as an irregular checkerboard. The Boissonas House in New Canaan (1956) and a garden pavilion for the Glass House (designed in 1961) variously call up classical, Islamic, and possibly Japanese prototypes, without specific reference to any of these.

The catholicity of his historical allusion notwithstanding, certain qualities generally characterize Johnson's urbane architecture: severely elemental massing, meticulous detailing and finish, a formal elegance of planning which disciplines even the casual environment, and, finally, a sensitivity to landscape values ranging from the well-manicured park to the planted terrace. As a teacher and critic he has magnified the influence of his buildings.

Bibliography: John Jacobus, *Philip Johnson*, New York 1962; 'Glass House', *Architectural Forum*, *91*, New York November 1949; Henry-Russell Hitchcock, 'Philip Johnson', *Architectural Review*, *117*, London April 1955; Philip Johnson, 'The Seven Crutches of Modern Architecture', *Perspecta 3*, Yale Architectural Journal; William H. Jordy, 'The Mies-less Johnson', *Architectural Forum*, *111*, New York, September 1959; Ian McCallum, *Architecture USA*, London, New York 1959; Philip Johnson, *Perspecta 7*, pp. 3–8; Sibyl Moholy-Nagy, pp. 68–71; H.-R. Hitchcock, *Zodiac 8*, Milan 1961.

WILLIAM H. JORDY

Kahn, Albert, b. Rhaunen, Westphalia 1869, d. Detroit, Mich. 1942. Emigrated to America in 1881; 1928–32 in Russia (industrial building programme). Kahn's industrial buildings anticipated at an early date the precise and slender cubic shapes of the fifties (*Mies van der Rohe, Eero *Saarinen). Ohio Steel Foundry Company at Lima, Ohio (1939); automobile works in Detroit.

Philip Johnson. Theater of the Dance, Lincoln Center. New York. Project (first version)

Kahn, Louis I., b. Island of Osel, Estonia (Russia) 1901. Kahn came to the USA while young and received a traditional **Beaux-Arts* architectural education at the University of Pennsylvania, graduating in 1924. After various jobs and travel in Europe, he worked with an academic architect, Paul Cret, and during the depression did a project for the Philadelphia City Planning Commission. In 1941 he began an association with George *Howe, a pioneer in modern design in the USA who had created the earliest *International Style skyscraper outside Europe in the Philadelphia Savings Fund Society Building (with William *Lescaze) in 1932. Kahn's first work to attract any attention was the Carver Court War Housing Project, Coatesville, Pennsylvania (1942–4), in partnership with Howe and Oscar Stonorov. His independent practice dates from 1947. In 1950–1 he was resident architect of the American Academy in Rome, and subsequently became design critic at Yale. In 1955 he was named Professor of Architecture at the University of Pennsylvania.

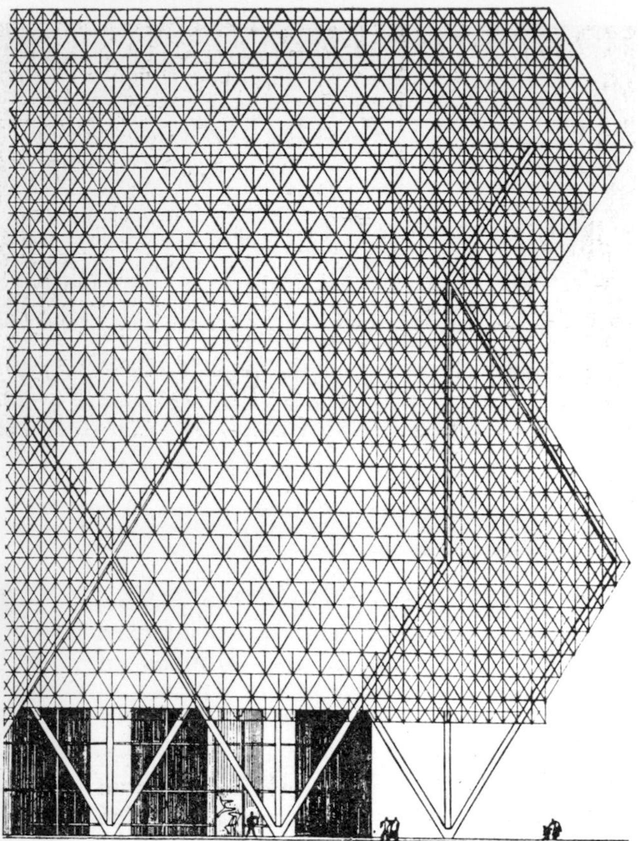

Louis I. Kahn. Building constructed from three-dimensional units. 1954. Project

Partly for lack of opportunity, partly because of an apparent reticence, Kahn did not emerge as a major creative figure until the mid 1950s. However, since that date he has been one of the most consistently discussed and admired of contemporary architects. Like all the undisputed masters of the 20th century, Kahn's mature style is the result of a dense fusion of many, sometimes contradictory, ideas and tendencies, all of which are brought together in a unique personal idiom. Unlike Philip *Johnson, Gordon *Bunshaft, and Eero *Saarinen, all of whom were drawing upon the industrial classicism of *Mies van der Rohe as a literal source for their designs of the early 1950s, Kahn, in his Yale Art Gallery, New Haven (1952–4), was already more self-reliant. The Miesian aspect of his first major building was not so much a matter of details and vocabulary as it was a question of creating large universal spaces for the gallery interiors (spaces which could be temporarily subdivided according to need) and a simple cubic mass for the exterior. As for the details, the concrete frame and the tetrahedrons of the ceiling structure were a vigorous formal statement coming at a time when elegance and polished perfection were the fashion. Even the exterior, though aggressively simple in its contrast of brick and glass, avoided the classicizing smoothness of the then-popular Miesian envelope.

When the mid-20th-century wave of *neo-classicism and academicism at last overtook Kahn's design in the 1956 Trenton Bath Houses, his taste had already departed from the refined norms of Americanized modernism. At Trenton, the regular cross-axial plan with five square spaces, all but the central one being covered by pyramidal hipped roofs, revealed Kahn's early formed attachment to the plan-types favoured by the *beaux-arts* tradition, a tradition which, around 1895, had helped to focus the early development of *Wright, and which slightly later performed the same service in the orientation of *Le Corbusier's very different style.

This academicism, which was a literal aspect of Kahn's modest yet monumental Trenton building, aided in the creation of the more personally expressive Richards Medical Research Building, University of Pennsylvania (1958–60). Widely heralded by critics and architects as an unusually new departure in an age largely given over to imitations of the recent past, chic variations of historical styles, or irresponsible personal adventures, Kahn's Towers are equally, perhaps even more important as a major reinterpretation of several of the canonical aspects of the modern movement. Indeed, familiarity with this cluster of concrete and brick forms only underscores Kahn's reflexive utilization of his immediate roots, a utilization which is in no sense eclectic or narrowly cerebral. Some critics have noted that Kahn's perceptible separation of 'served' and 'servant' spaces parallels specific theorems in Wright's early work, notably the Larkin Building, Buffalo (1904); others are struck by similar instances of abrupt formal juxtaposition (caused by functional differentiation) that occur in works by Le Corbusier; while perhaps the most penetrating observation of all is that Kahn has, in this picturesque, red-brick conglomeration, found a road back to mid-19th-century

Victorian design principles, without, at the same time, sacrificing the gains of the modern movement. On the basis of this single building, Kahn has obtained a unique place in the annals of contemporary architecture, one which will certainly grow in the light of new constructions which have already begun to issue from his office.

JOHN M. JACOBUS, JR

Kiesler, Frederick John, b. Vienna 1896, d. N.Y. 1965. Studied at Technische Hochschule; Academy of Fine Arts, Vienna. Member of De Stijl, 1925. Scenic designer, Juilliard School of Music, New York, 1933. Director of Architectural Laboratory at Columbia University, New York, 1936–42. One of the most prominent 'non-building' architects (designer rather than builder) in present-day America, Kiesler designed, in 1925, a City in Space that grew from bridge-building principles, and an Endless Theatre that developed into his Space House of 1934, and eventually into the well-known Endless House of 1959–60. Rejecting the post-and-lintel system, Kiesler conceived a more economical, freer use of space: a one-piece, irregular shell composed of highly sculptural egg shapes, mounted on service piers with a completely free-flowing floor plan. The house is created by applying a plastic substance over a sculptural mesh. In rejecting rectangular forms, Kiesler's theory recalls the 'eurhythmy' of Steiner's Goethaneum (*Expressionism) and the 'organic' flow of Hermann Finsterlin's fantasies.

Kiesler designed the Constructivistic Film Guild Cinema (1928) and, as a member of the firm of Kiesler and Bartos, the World House Galleries in New York. He designed the Sanctuary for the Dead Sea Scrolls in Jerusalem (1959). A model of the Endless House was exhibited at the Museum of Modern Art, N.Y., in 1959–60.

Author of: *Contemporary Art Applied to the Store and Display*, 1930; *Ten Years of American Opera Design at the Juilliard School*, 1941; numerous articles in *The Architectural Record*, *Architectural Forum*, *Art News*.

Frederick John Kiesler.
Model of The Endless House, 1959

Klerk, Michael de, b. Amsterdam 1884, d. Amsterdam 1923. Leading exponent of the generation of architects deriving from *Berlage, and centred round the journal **Wendingen* (*Netherlands). Residential buildings, especially in the suburbs of Amsterdam (*Expressionism; *p. 14)

Klint, Peter Vilhelm Jensen, b. near Skelskør 1853, d. 1930. Worked first as an engineer, then as a painter, and after 1896 as an architect. Best known is his Grundtvig Church in Copenhagen, *Denmark (1920–40), with its organ-shaped façade.

Kraemer, Friedrich Wilhelm, b. Halberstadt 1907. Studied at the Technical Colleges of Brunswick and Vienna. Private practice since 1935. Residential buildings, offices, schools, department stores, industrial buildings. Since 1946 he has been professor at Brunswick Technical College (Germany).

Labrouste, Henri, b. Paris 1801, d. Fontainebleau 1875. Trained at the *École des Beaux-Arts (Rome Scholar) which he later opposed with increasing vehemence. His epoch-making libraries employed steel frames encased in masonry. (Bibliothèque Ste Geneviève, Paris, 1843–50; Bibliothèque Nationale, Paris, 1858–68; *France)

Le Corbusier, b. La Chaux-de-Fonds, Switzerland 1887, d. 1965. Like few of his generation, Le Corbusier (Charles-Edouard Jeanneret, called LC) had the opportunity while still studying of familiarizing himself with all the endeavours that led to the emergence of the new style. At his art

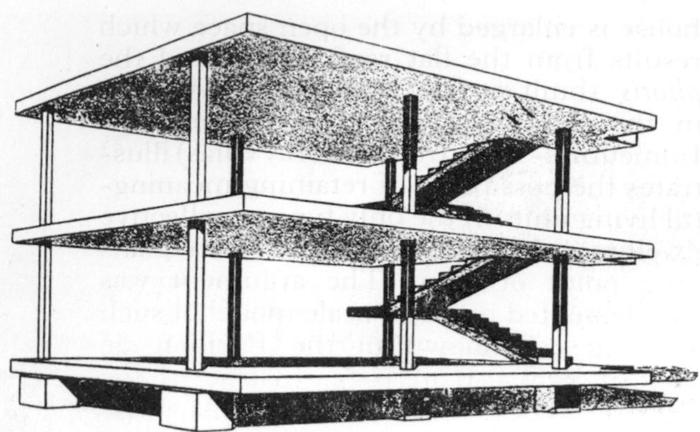

Le Corbusier. Dom-Ino system of construction. 1914

school in La Chaux-de-Fonds reverberations reached him of Art Nouveau (in particular from the École de Nancy) and its search for organic, ornamental forms. Then, in quick succession, he met nearly all the architects who had anything to give him: *Hoffmann in Vienna in 1907, *Garnier at Lyons and *Perret in Paris in 1908, and *Behrens in Berlin in 1910. He worked for a few months for both Perret and Behrens. In addition to his architectural and town planning studies, he was occupied from 1911 to 1912 with questions of mass-production and standardization in the circles of the *Deutscher Werkbund, which he had already been able to investigate under Perret, as far as they concerned the building trade. On extensive trips throughout Europe Le Corbusier, pencil in hand, analysed architectural shapes and settings from the Parthenon (*Neoclassicism) to a farmhouse, and from a Turkish summer house on the Bosphorus to Chartres Cathedral. After eventually settling down in Paris in 1917, he had his decisive encounter with Cubism. If we add that he was occupied already before 1920 with the industrialization of building not only theoretically but practically, and that he exhibited a complete mastery of his profession in at least one executed design (Villa at La Chaux-de-Fonds, 1916), we shall come to the conclusion that the so-called amateur disposed of a knowledge and experience which no university training could have given him.

His preoccupation with painting, which he has never given up, and the founding, with Ozenfant, of Purism (*Après le Cubisme*, 1918) are far more than a mere episode. In attempting to determine the position of creative thought in the light of Cubism, Le Corbusier developed a theory of aesthetics which he published in the journal *L'Esprit Nouveau* in the form of 'Warnings to Architects'. In these articles, which appeared in 1923 in book form under the title *Vers une architecture*, followed in 1925 by *L'Art décoratif d'aujourd'hui*, *Urbanisme*, Le Corbusier has given the pithiest account of his architectural ideas. He himself demonstrated what he meant, first by models and drawings (Citrohan houses, 1920–2; 'A contemporary city of three million inhabitants', 1922), then by a series of houses (for Ozenfant, Jeanneret, La Roche, Cook, the Bordeaux-Pessac housing estate, 1922–6; Pavillon de l'Esprit Nouveau, 1925; Maison Stein at Garches, two houses at the Weissenhof Exhibition, Stuttgart, Villa Savoye at Poissy, 1927–31). These buildings, projects and writings are of threefold importance (*International Style):

1. Every stylistic reminiscence is now rigorously removed from the vocabulary of

Le Corbusier

Le Corbusier. Immeuble-Villa. 1922. Project

form. In the uncompromising reduction of all buildings to the basic geometrical shapes of rectangle, plane surface, cube and cylinder may be recognized a transposition of purist pictorial composition. The architectural means employed are *pilotis* (free-standing columns at ground floor level), continuous strips of fenestration, glass walls, and flat roofs. The polychrome effects which Le Corbusier introduced at Pessac as a town-planning feature can also be traced back to insights gained when painting.

2. These distinctly provocative designs are meant to make clear the radically functional renovation of the house as an instrument of living; as is well known, Le Corbusier speaks of 'machines for living in'. After early studies of a more theoretical nature (Dom-Ino Houses, 1914; Monol Houses), Le Corbusier's investigations resulted in a prototype as early as 1922 (Second Citrohan House), which proved important for later developments. The living area available is newly distributed according to the way that domestic functions are grouped. The living-room runs through two storeys, and all parts of the dwelling are arranged *en suite*. The house is enlarged by the open space which results from the flat roof garden and the *pilotis* (built at Stuttgart, 1927). Already in the same year, 1922, his project for Immeubles-Villas (multi-storey villas) illustrates the possibility of retaining meaningful living units in the only type of collective dwelling acceptable from the town planning point of view. The argument was supplemented by a full-scale model of such a living cell shown in the Pavillon de l'Esprit Nouveau in 1925. Instead of the ordinary type of furniture, use was made partly of built-in units, partly of standard industrial products chosen for their purist shape.

3. The multi-storey villas belong to that class of novel town planning device by which the structure of present-day metropolitan areas might be adapted to the requirements of modern life. The plan for a 'contemporary city of three million inhabitants' certainly springs from Garnier's *Cité Industrielle* and is also in many ways reminiscent of *Sant'Elia's drawings for the *Città Nuova*, but in essential points differs from both of them. Garnier had thought of a town limited to 35,000 inhabitants, all engaged in industry; Sant' Elia had only sketched highly suggestive but isolated views of the town of tomorrow. Le Corbusier, however, from the outset steered towards the problem of the 'change-over town', as he called it later, a metropolis with diverse functions, which must be

Le Corbusier. Maison Stein. Garches, 1929

Le Corbusier. Maison Suisse. Cité Universitaire. Paris, 1930–2

disentangled. The Plan Voisin for Paris (1925) applies these theoretical studies to the particular case of Paris.
Le Corbusier is mainly concerned in the first instance to establish an orderly relationship between traffic lanes on the one hand and living and working zones on the other. Traffic must be classified, i.e. graded as to whether it is pedestrian or vehicular, through or delivery traffic. The tremendous loss of time occasioned by the incoherence of the present system may be reduced in this way. But 'traffic should not be allowed to develop'—the best way is to reduce distances to a minimum. If a metropolis is to be prevented from spreading out indefinitely, however, it must be built high: for residential areas multi-storey villas set in open parkland, instead of space-consuming, street-extending private houses; super-skyscrapers 1,300 feet apart, surrounded by gardens, for business districts. This is the only way to unravel the present-day mix-up of traffic, work and living functions and to reduce the metropolis to human dimensions.
Owing to the economic crisis of the thirties, commissions by rich patrons of the arts, who were the main clients of modern architecture in *France, were drastically reduced in number. Up to the outbreak of the Second World War, Le Corbusier devoted himself mainly to *town planning projects (for Algiers, Nemours (Algeria), Barcelona, Buenos Aires, Montevideo, São Paulo, Zlín, Hellocourt, 'Paris 1937', 'Paris Ilot insalubre no. 6') and to refining the methods which he had only roughly defined: classified traffic lanes (the '7V' system), living units (design for the International Exhibition of 1937) and 'Cartesian' skyscrapers (design for Algiers, 1938). From the start (1927) Le Corbusier took an active part in the work of *CIAM. The *Athens Charter is entirely his idea and was also drawn up by him. His research, limited at first to restoring the urban body to health, was extended to country planning from 1934 onwards. In particular he interested himself in the renewal of production centres, agricultural ('radiating farm' and collective village, 1934) and industrial ('green factory', 1939–40). The synthesis of these ideas he ultimately summarized in 1945 in *Les Trois Etablissements Humains*, a book whose influence is still growing.
In the thirties, Le Corbusier also worked on his projects for monumental, large-scale buildings; in these he demonstrates his mastery in the organization and three-dimensional design of complex building programmes: competition design for the League of Nations Palace, Geneva (*p. 16), 1927; plans for a museum with unlimited possibilities for extension (ultimately built in 1952–6 at Ahmedabad and Tokyo); the pensions office at Zurich; the Museum of Modern Art in Paris; a stadium and pageant arena for 100,000 spectators, etc. The only projects actually built were the Centrosoyus in Moscow, 1930; the Salvation Army Hostel and the Maison Suisse at the Cité Universitaire, Paris, 1931–2; and the Ministry of Education, Rio de Janeiro, *Brazil (with *Costa, *Niemeyer, *Reidy and others, 1936–45). The ascetic geometry of his vocabulary of form which typified his

Le Corbusier. Unité d'Habitation. Marseilles, 1947–52

early work is enriched by new elements in these buildings and projects. White stucco gives way to an untreated finish (concrete or even stone in the Villa at Les Mathes, 1935). The abstract planary nature of the outer walls is superseded by a sculptural treatment, whose characteristic element is the 'brise-soleil' screen shading the glass wall (Ministry at Rio). This change is also noticeable on the 1938 model of a skyscraper.

Le Corbusier suggested 'Housing and Homes' as a theme for the 1937 International Exhibition, and as the main exhibit a completely furnished living unit, which could be let at the end of the exhibition. The idea to which he had constantly recurred since his multi-storey villas of 1922 was now ready for execution. This was how, after the war, the Unités d'Habitation at Marseilles (1947–52), Nantes-Rezé (1952–7), Berlin (1957) and Briey-la-Forêt (1960) came into existence. Here Le Corbusier's philosophy of domestic architecture seems to have found its final expression: vertical garden cities, which afford every family a maximum of privacy and independence (but also of communal services) combined with the utmost exploitation of space. These monumental structures, subtly proportioned on Le Corbusier's *Modulor system, function impeccably as 'machines for living in' and belong, without any doubt, to the grandest architectural creations of the century. That they have found no imitator so far can only be explained, apart from the prejudice that still continues, by the unadmitted feeling that only Le Corbusier can play with such vast masses (350 flats in eight double-storeys) without being crushed. (*Brutalism; *Reinforced Concrete)

Le Corbusier. Supreme Court. Chandigarh, 1950–6

Le Corbusier. Project for Algiers Heights, 1942

The other main projects of the fifties are as monumental as the 'Unités' and as likely to discourage any possible imitators. The capitol of Chandigarh (from 1950) is an approximately lyrical enhancement for the new metropolis of the State of Punjab of the idea for a community centre which Le Corbusier had worked out for the small town of St Dié in 1945–6. The symbolic significance of the composition, stressed by the dramatic treatment of the individual buildings, has been combined with astonishing ease into a harmonious whole with the practical functions that the law courts and the ministries have to fulfil, while making use of whatever local building resources were available. In the development and circulation plans for the city itself, Le Corbusier was able for the first time to realize his theories on zoning and traffic separation, practically without restriction. The grid-type layout, which some critics beforehand had called inhuman, has in practice proved excellent.

The pilgrimage church of Notre-Dame du Haut at Ronchamp (1950–4) strikes one at first as a wilful piece of sculpture, as unsuitable for the fulfilment of any function as for instance F. L. *Wright's spiral shape for the Guggenheim Museum, built at roughly the same time. On closer examination, however, it proves to be an organism which (as previously with the living unit, the museum, the multi-storey offices, or even the farm) had been newly thought out in all its details and consequently completely altered in outward appearance. (*Glass; *p. 27) That the curved surfaces were not just an impulse to which Le Corbusier had succumbed when he was confronted for the first time with a religious theme, has been proved by the Dominican novitiate monastery of La Tourette, at Eveux near Lyons (1957). The rectangle to which Le Corbusier had dedicated the 'Poème de l'angle droit' in 1955, is now only reserved for what Le Corbusier calls 'phénomènes d'espace indicible', 'phenomena of ineffable space', which he regards as the highest perfection in architecture.

Such ideas, in which his work has always abounded, give even his secular buildings of the fifties an unforgettable, special note, whether they are 'Unités', museums, the

Le Corbusier. Maisons Jaoul. Neuilly, 1954–6

Le Corbusier. Notre-Dame du Haut. Ronchamp, 1950–4

Brazilian House at the Paris Cité Universitaire or smaller intimate buildings such as the Textile Industry Club, Shodhan House at Ahmedabad, and the Maisons Jaoul at Neuilly, or projects in which Le Corbusier's rich experience of architectural space has proved itself on difficult subjects such as the model for a multi-storey hotel at the Gare d'Orsay, Paris, or the design for a college building at Harvard (1961).

However diverse the shapes may be that Le Corbusier has employed—whether in the possibly most perfect example from his first creative period, the Villa Savoye at Poissy (*p. 19), or at Ronchamp or Chandigarh, his architectural work nevertheless displays an amazing unity. It can only be called 'classical', if this is taken to mean not a repertoire of forms and massing, but a sense of the right form. The traditional modules and orders represented a harmonious link between the human body and the dimensions of ancient buildings and articles of use. In our contemporary civilization, however, whose towns,

Le Corbusier. Monastery of La Tourette. Eveux, near Lyons, 1957

machines and equipment create completely new dimensions of space and time, they are no longer adequate. Their endless repetition is stifling, their extension emphatic and false. By a completely new, all-embracing system of measurement, by abandoning the scale imposed through dividing an elevation into storeys, but even more by an unprecedently sure instinct for proportion Le Corbusier has made his buildings examples of classical massing which contrasts sharply with the inhuman disorder of so many pseudo-modern buildings. Le Corbusier is the purest exponent of the French tradition in building, in whose noblest creations logic and lyric become one in the service of mankind.

Bibliography: Le Corbusier, *Oeuvre complète*, 1910–57, at present 6 volumes, Zurich 1929ff.; Le Corbusier, *Mon Oeuvre*, Paris 1960; Maximilien Gauthier, *Le Corbusier*, New York 1945; Stamo Papadaki, *Le Corbusier*, New York 1948; J. Alazard, *Le Corbusier*, Florence and Paris 1950; Anton Henze, *Le Corbusier*, Berlin 1957; Françoise Choay, *Le Corbusier*, New York 1958; Boesiger/Girsberger (editors), *Le Corbusier, 1910–60*, Zurich and Stuttgart 1960.

MAURICE BESSET

Lescaze, William, b. Geneva, Switzerland 1896. He was a pupil of Karl *Moser. Worked in France until 1920. Arrived in USA in 1920, worked in Cleveland for Hubbell and Benes. In 1923, returned to New York where he designed in a succession of styles, from the Collegiate Gothic of the Edgewood School (Greenwich, Conn.) to the 1925 Paris Modern of his interiors for the Macy's Exposition of 1928. In 1929, joined with George *Howe in the firm of Howe and Lescaze.

To Howe's maturity and experience, Lescaze brought an ability to handle newer modern forms. His own house in Manhattan (1934) was the first *International Style building of its kind in New York and may be profitably contrasted with Howe's Speizer House in Philadelphia (1935). The most significant product of this partnership was the highly interesting Philadelphia Savings Fund Society (PSFS) Building (1931–2). After the dissolution of the firm, Lescaze designed Unity House in the Pocono Mountains, Pa., and Williamsbridge Housing in Brooklyn, N.Y., an early modern housing development. His Longfellow Building in Washington, D.C., was the first International Style work in that city; it established a trend towards the exploitation of the cantilever that resulted in unrelieved piles of horizontal stripped windows. This now appears to have been a regression from the more sophisticated expression of the PSFS Building.

Since the Second World War, Lescaze has enjoyed tremendous success as a designer of commercial space in New York. His building at 711 Third Avenue is a restatement of the *parti* established at PSFS Building.

Author of: *Architecture for the New Theatre*, 1935; *The Intent of the Artist*, 1941; *On Being an Architect*, 1942.

Howe and Lescaze. Philadelphia Savings Fund Society Building. Philadelphia, 1931–2

Lewerentz, Sigurd, b. Bjärtrå near Sundsvall, Sweden 1885. After graduating from Göteborg Technical College (1908), he lived in Germany. Residential buildings and housing estates. Crematorium at Malmö (1943), church at Skarpnäck near Stockholm (1960). (*Sweden)

Lissitzky, Eliezer (El) Markovich, b. Polshinotz near Smolensk 1890, d. Moscow 1941. Lissitzky first studied at Darmstadt Technical College, 1909–14. Teacher at Moscow Academy, 1921. Emigrated to Germany and Switzerland, back in Russia 1928. Collaborated with the avant-garde of Central European architects (van *Doesburg, *Mies van der Rohe) and was a co-founder of *Constructivism. At the same time as *Tatlin's Memorial to the Third International, Lissitzky's office designed a speaker's platform (1920) in the form of a sloping steel structure of great expressiveness. In 1924, together with Mart Stam, he designed the 'Cloud Props' project, an extensively cantilevered office block on immense piers.

Lods, Marcel, b. Paris 1891. Collaborated with Eugène *Beaudouin. Designed buildings for the French Ministries of Education and War. Housing estate at Marly-le-Roi near Paris (with Honegger and Beuté), buildings in Guinea. (*France)

Loos, Adolf, b. Brno 1870, d. Vienna 1933. A keen admirer both of vernacular and Roman architecture, Adolf Loos was a great pioneer of the modern movement in Europe, and, at the beginning of the 20th century, one of the first architects to react against the decorative trends of *Art Nouveau.

Loos was the son of a stone-cutter. He attended classes at Reichenberg Polytechnic before studying architecture at Dresden technical college. On the conclusion of his studies he was anxious to broaden his outlook and in 1893 made a journey to the United States; he remained in America for three years, working by turn as a mason, a floor-layer and even as a dish-washer. During this time he was able to observe the innovations made by the young School of *Chicago: the expressive steel-frame structures Le Baron *Jenney introduced for office buildings, the austere blocks of *Burnham and *Root, and the uncompromising severity which *Sullivan was displaying in his famous Guaranty Building (Buffalo, 1894–5). Sullivan it was who, after providing American architecture with an original and personal style of floral surface decoration, wrote in 1892 in an article entitled 'Ornament in Architecture': 'It would be greatly for our esthetic good if we should refrain entirely from the use of ornament for a period of years, in order that our thought might concentrate acutely upon the production of buildings well formed and comely in the nude.'

This attitude was to provide Loos with a conception of major significance for his work. On his return to Europe in 1896, he settled in Vienna, a cosmopolitan centre with a culture typified by elegance of thought and sophisticated manners. In this milieu, Loos showed himself forthwith an ardent and aggressive doctrinarian. In a first series of articles published chiefly in the *Neue Freie Presse* between 1897 and 1898, he took up arms against the stylistic and aestheticizing tendencies preached by the painter Klimt and the architects *Olbrich and *Hoffmann to the Wiener Sezession, which they had founded in 1897. Basing himself partly on Sullivan's purist argument, and partly on the functionalist doctrine which Otto *Wagner had expounded to the Vienna Academy in 1894,

Adolf Loos. Kärntner Bar. Vienna, 1907

Loos set out to show that the type of ornament inculcated by Art Nouveau is unworthy of our culture; that a work divested of ornament is symbolic of pure and lucid thought and a high degree of civilization; that good form must find its beauty in the degree of usefulness it expresses, and in the indissoluble unity of its parts; and that consequently all ornamentation must be systematically rejected.

Loos was to resume and develop this thesis in a major essay published in 1908 entitled 'Ornament und Verbrechen' ('Ornament and Crime'). To spread his theories, he had founded a Free School of Architecture in 1906. His rationalist philosophy underlies his rare and very puritanical architectural works: the Villa Karma (Montreux, 1904); Steiner house (Vienna, 1910), one of the first private houses to be built in reinforced concrete, and a turning point in the history of modern architecture (reshaping of plan, new method of condensing and articulating internal space, purity of the straight line, flat roof, horizontal fenestration, dominance of solids, cubic style); the imposing Goldman commercial block on the Michaelerplatz (Vienna, 1910), where the arrangement of levels foretells the complete expression of the 'plan of volumes' achieved by the Rufer house (Vienna, 1922).

From 1920 to 1922 Loos was in charge of municipal housing in Vienna, where he drew up some bold development schemes, such as the Heuberg model estate. In 1923 he settled in Paris, where he established contact with the leading figures of the *Esprit Nouveau*. He frequented Dadaïst circles and built a house for Tristan Tzara (1926). Returning to Vienna in 1928, he built the Moller house at Pötzleinsdorf; the Khuner house at Payerbach (1930); and also in 1930, his finest work, the Müller house in Prague. (*p. 14; *Austria)

Bibliography: Adolf Loos, *Ins Leere gesprochen, 1897–1900*, Paris 1921; 2nd edition, Innsbruck 1932; Adolf Loos, *Trotzdem, 1900–1930*, Innsbruck 1931; Heinrich Kulka, *Adolf Loos*, Vienna 1931; Franz Glück, *Adolf Loos*, Paris 1931; Ludwig Münz, *Adolf Loos*, Milan 1956.

ROBERT L. DELEVOY

Luckhardt, Hans and Wassili. Wassili Luckhardt b. Berlin 1889. Hans Luckhardt b. Berlin 1890, d. Bad Wiessee 1954. Their first designs were in the Berlin *Expressionist style, characterized by the precision of their rectangles (Schorlemer Allee experimental estate, Berlin, 1927; private houses at Rupenhorn, Berlin, 1928) or dynamically curved blocks divided up by continuous strips of fenestration (projects for the new layout of the Alexanderplatz, Berlin, 1929). Berlin Pavilion at the Constructa Exhibition, Hanover (1951); Regional Government Offices, Munich (1957).

Adolf Loos. Maison Tristan Tzara. Paris, 1926

Bibliography: Udo Kultermann, *Wassili und Hans Luckhardt, Bauten und Entwürfe*, Tübingen 1958.

Lundy, Victor A., b. Los Angeles 1921. Studied at Harvard under *Gropius. Timber churches with large curved roofs (First Unitarian Church at Westport, Connecticut, 1961), Motel with reinforced concrete awnings at different heights (Warm Mineral Springs Inn at Venice, Fla., 1958). Exhibition pavilion of the US Atomic Energy Commission, a 'pneumatic' structure, Seattle (1962).

Lurçat, André, b. Paris 1892. His houses typify the style of the late twenties and

early thirties in *France (Villa Hefferlin at Ville D'Avray, 1931–2). School at Villejuif (1931–3).
Bibliography: André Lurçat, *Oeuvres Récentes I*, Paris 1961.

Lyons, Eric Alfred, b. 1912. Architect whose schemes have set a new standard for private-enterprise housing in *Great Britain, where he controls the planning and landscaping of entire estates. His layouts feature simple buildings that display an eye for textures, and the highly repetitive use of structural elements and equipment in dispositions which largely avoid streets by creating courtyards and varying patterns of 'external enclosures'; this he considers to be the secret of urbanity. Flats at Ham Common, near Richmond; at Blackheath; and West Hill, Highgate (for the Soviet Trade Delegation). Houses, flats and maisonettes at Cambridge; housing for old people at Bognor Regis, with certain shared accommodation.

Lyons, Israel and Ellis. Edward Douglas Lyons, Lawrence Israel, Thomas Bickerstaff Harper Ellis. Partnership that has developed a powerful and expressive style in reinforced concrete: Peckham Comprehensive School (reinforced concrete frame); Wolfson Institute, London University; theatre workshops for the Old Vic Company, with constant expression of function by exposed reinforced concrete frame, inside and out; Trescobeas Secondary Modern School, Falmouth; Finchley Town Hall.

Mackintosh, Charles Rennie, b. Glasgow 1868, d. London 1928. Mackintosh, a resolute adversary of historic revivalism, was one of the most brilliant precursors of 20th-century rationalist architecture. As leader of the *Art Nouveau movement in Great Britain this Scottish architect made, a contribution of fundamental importance in reappraising the rôle of function in building, expressed via a style based on ancient Celtic ornament and the cultural traditions of Japan.
When he was barely sixteen, Mackintosh entered John Hutchinson's office as an articled pupil; from 1885 he attended evening classes at the Glasgow School of Art. In 1889 he was engaged as a draughtsman in the building firm of J. Honeyman and Keppie, where he met the architect J. Herbert McNair, his future brother-in-law. He stayed with the firm until 1913, having become a partner in 1904. In 1890 he was awarded a scholarship which enabled him to make a study-tour in France and Italy. His first executed work, the corner tower of the Glasgow Herald Building (1894), reveals Mackintosh as about to emancipate himself from academic trammels. He participated (December 1895) in the opening exhibition of the Maison de l'Art Nouveau in Paris with a number of posters which already clearly displayed the linear symbolic style of the Glasgow School. In 1897, at the age of twenty-nine, he won the competition for an extension to the Glasgow School of Art. These buildings were erected between 1898 and 1909 and made a profound impression on the Continent at the time. In 1898 he drew up a bold scheme for a concert hall on a circular plan, covered by a parabolic dome, which was not however premiated at the Glasgow Exhibition of 1901.
At the same time Mackintosh was interested in the decorative arts and in furniture. The pieces he designed are notable for their character, which is at once exquisite and

Charles Rennie Mackintosh. Glasgow School of Art, 1898–1909

austere, slender and taut, based on the straight line and the right angle, and set off in light tones (ivory). The upswing of their slim parallels elongates their forms beyond any functional requirement, as Mackintosh's aesthetic fancy turns to mannerism. This is the style he adopted when commissioned in 1897 to design the interior decoration for Miss Cranston's chain of tea-rooms. The Buchanan Street Tea-room (1897–8) illustrates the curvilinear style of this first period (1894–1900) most completely: the walls are dominated by two-dimensional figures, tall and graceful, enclosed within a network of vertical lines and entwined by circular waves that evoke the manner of Klimt. This style first became known on the Continent through the illustrations published in 1897 by *The Studio*, followed the year after by the showing of a suite of furniture at Munich, and in particular by the contribution Mackintosh sent to the annual exhibition of the Wiener Sezession in 1900. The furniture and panels he showed at Vienna emphasize the close links between the Scottish trends and the Viennese School.

In the same year Mackintosh had married a former student of the Glasgow School of Art, Margaret Macdonald, an interior decorator and metalworker, whose sister Frances had married the architect Herbert McNair in 1899. These ties helped to knit together more closely a little group united since 1890 by similar professional and aesthetic interests, which had already won an international reputation under the name of The Four. It was as the leader of this group that Mackintosh entered a competition in 1901, organized under the auspices of the *Zeitschrift für Innendekoration* of Darmstadt by its editor, A. Koch. The subject was a house for a connoisseur, including its interior decoration. Mackintosh was awarded second prize. His scheme envisaged a revolutionary use of space, with an arrangement of large, simple volumes distinctly cubic in appearance, stripped, in elevation, of any kind of ornament or moulding, and marked by an asymmetrical predominance of solids over voids: it was a harbinger of the purist style of *Loos.

If the country houses Mackintosh built in the environs of Glasgow (Windy Hill at Kilmacolm, 1899–1901; Hill House at Helensburgh, 1902–3) still show external stylistic affinities with the Scottish baronial tradition (angle towers with conical caps, huge double-pitch roofs, massive chimneys), their internal layouts evince great boldness in the handling of space. The hall of Hill House (1903) is a masterpiece where light, colour, openwork partitions, cage-type lamps and light furniture combine in a spatio-dynamic composition that anticipates Russian *Constructivism and Dutch *Stijl.

The superb library which Mackintosh built as an addition to the Glasgow School of Art (1907–9) shows similar stylistic trends. The straight line reigns supreme, and the subtle arrangement of horizontal beams and rectangular pillars which support the galleries punctuate space in a manner hitherto unknown, raising architecture to the level of poetic abstraction. Similar principles are at work, with equal effect, in Mackintosh's last masterpiece, the Cranston Tea-room in Ingram Street (1907–11). Apart from this, in his short architectural career, the Scottish Pavilion at the Turin Exhibition of 1902 may be noted, which Mackintosh built and furnished.

He moved to London in 1913, where his activities were limited to designing furniture and printed fabrics. In 1920 he retired to Port-Vendres to devote himself exclusively to water-colour painting.

Bibliography: Hermann Muthesius, *Haus eines Kunstfreundes*, Darmstadt 1902; Nikolaus Pevsner, *Ch. R. Mackintosh*, Milan 1950; Thomas Howarth, *Charles Rennie Mackintosh and the Modern Movement*, London 1952.

ROBERT L. DELEVOY

Maekawa, Kunio, b. Niigata-shi, *Japan 1905. Studied at Tokyo University; worked for *Le Corbusier; on his own since 1935. Maekawa's investigations into the structural possibilities of reinforced concrete (stimulated by Pier Luigi *Nervi) led to buildings in a sculptural idiom: Town Hall at Fukushima (1958), Community Centre at Setagaya (1959). His Harumi flats in Tokyo (1957) carry over Japanese domestic traditions into the dimensions of a modern skyscraper. Maekawa has had a considerable influence on the younger Japanese architects; Kenzo *Tange joined him on finishing his studies.

Maillart, Robert, b. Berne 1872, d. Geneva 1940, After studying from 1890 to 1894 at Zurich Technical College (ETH), where he graduated as structural engineer, Maillart worked in various engineering offices until he became an independent partner in the building firm of Maillart and Co., Zurich, in 1902. In 1911 he was appointed a lecturer at Zurich Technical College. In 1912 he left Switzerland to build in Russia, whence he returned penniless after the Revolution. In 1919 he started an engineering office in Geneva followed in 1924 by others in Berne and Zurich.

Maillart has not only built bridges but has also designed the structural details for a large number of multi-storey buildings. The intrinsic character of his constructions shows up particularly clearly, however, in his bridges: these are the outcome of his ability to think through a problem in its entirety and to look for the specific solution to each specific instance, based on his own specially developed methods of construction. In 1901, Maillart built the first of his forty or so reinforced concrete bridges at Zuoz in the Engadine. It already displays some of the essential features of that concept of his which does away with the old principle of separation between the functions of bearing and loading. All parts of a bridge are integrated in their structural function; the roadway is no longer a load carried by the bridge vaults but is incorporated as a structure element. Economy of means, structural strength and harmonious balance make Maillart's bridges works of art to the extent that anything may be considered as art which is perfect of its kind.

Robert Maillart. Bridge over the river Thur at Felsegg, 1933

Maillart's most important bridges are those built according to the principle he developed of the triply articulated box girder; they include the Rhine bridge at Tavanasa (1905, destroyed 1927) and the Salginatobel bridge near Schiers (1929–30, 295 feet long), both in Graubünden; the Rossgraben bridge near Schwarzenburg in the Canton of Berne (1932, 269 feet long); the Arve bridge near Versey, Geneva (1936); and the overpass between Altendorf and Lachen, Canton Schwyz (1940), the last project personally supervised by Maillart. Another of his structural systems was the so-called stiffened bar arch which he used among others on the following: the Val Tschiel bridge (1925), and the curved Landquart railway bridge at Klosters (1930), both also in Graubünden; the Schwandbach bridge between Hinterfultigen and Schönentannen in the Canton of Berne (1933), also on a curve; and finally the Aire bridge at Lancy, Geneva, with an arch-span of 167 feet, designed in 1938 and built 1952–4. A number of his boldest bridge designs were never carried out.

Among the multi-storey buildings for whose architectural form Maillart's contribution was essentially responsible, the following may be mentioned: the entrance hall of a warehouse at Chiasso (1924–5) and the barrel-vaulted Cement Pavilion at the Swiss Provinces Exhibition, Zurich, 1939, a show building of the Swiss cement industry. His most important invention in the field of high structures was made in 1908 with mushroom slab construction, which he used for the first time on a large scale in 1910. In this method, columns, beams and floors are no longer treated as separate units as in timber or steel structures, but the column passes organically into the beamless floor slab. Here again, a structural system that is economical in the use of materials permits flexibility in application and helps to ensure a light and elegant appearance.

Bibliography: Max Bill, *Robert Maillart*, Zurich 1949; 3rd edition 1962.

MARGIT STABER

Malevich, Kasimir, b. Kiev 1878, d. Leningrad 1935. In his early days, he was strongly influenced by the paintings of the Post-Impressionists, the Fauves, and later the Cubists. Transition to geometric (*Suprematist) painting between 1913 and 1915. His 'suprematist architectures' are wooden sculptures (*Constructivism), in which he investigates the interrelationship of simple cubes. Visited the *Bauhaus (1927).

Mallet-Stevens, Robert, b. Paris 1886, d. 1945. Exponent of French avant-garde architecture in the late twenties and early thirties. His buildings, in particular private houses, are often characterized by over-emphasis of cubic form.

Markelius, Sven, b. Stockholm 1889. Graduated in 1913 from Stockholm Technical College and from the Academy of Fine Arts in 1915. Influenced by *Le Corbusier. Flats and offices, concert hall at Hälsingborg (1932). First won international recognition with his Swedish Pavilion at the World Fair in New York (1939). Responsible for the establishment of the satellite town of Vällingby near Stockholm (commenced 1953) in his capacity as head of the *town-planning department. (*Sweden)

Matthew, Robert Hogg, b. Edinburgh 1906. Studied at Edinburgh College of Art School of Architecture. From 1946 to 1953, he was architect to the London County Council, during which period his department emerged as one of the most progressive forces in the architecture of *Great Britain, and his Royal Festival Hall (1950) was acclaimed as the first modern building to achieve a feeling of monumentality. Appointed Professor of Architecture at Edinburgh University, 1953; in private practice with Stirrat Johnson-Marshall since 1957. University buildings for Dundee, Aberdeen and Edinburgh; Turnhouse Airport, Edinburgh, 1956; New Zealand House, Haymarket, London; seventeen-storey flats in the Gorbals, Glasgow; power station at Killin; Commonwealth Institute in Holland Park, London, with an ingeniously planned exhibition layout under a hyperbolic paraboloid roof. Far-reaching town- and country-planning proposals for the Government of Northern Ireland, 1963.

May, Ernst, b. Frankfurt 1886. Studied at Munich Technical College under Thiersch and *Fischer. Was City Architect at Frankfurt am Main between 1925 and 1930 (suburban development with extensive rationalization of building processes). In Russia (1930–4), later practised in East Africa. After the war served as town planner for several German towns.

Bibliography: J. Bueckschmitt, *Ernst May, Bauten und Planungen*, Stuttgart, in preparation.

Maybeck, Bernard Ralph, b. New York 1862, d. Berkeley, Calif. 1957. Studied at the École des Beaux-Arts in Paris. Was much impressed by the restoration work of *Viollet-le-Duc. Eclectic, especially Far Eastern motifs, which always played an important part on the west coast of America, were combined by him with structural experiments such as the employment of prefabricated units (Christian Science Church, Berkeley, 1910). Private houses, clubs. Fine Arts Building, San Francisco (1915) in neoclassic style with romantic trappings.

McKim, Mead and White. This New York architectural firm was founded by Charles Follen McKim, b. Chester County, Pa. 1847, d. 1909. He was joined by William Rutherford Mead, b. Brattleboro, Vt. 1846, d. 1928, in 1877, and by Stanford White, b. N.Y. 1853, d. 1906, in 1879. The firm is still in existence, and, as Steinmann, Cain and White, maintains an office on Park Avenue in New York. The most popular and successful firm of Victorian America, the founding architects combined an integrity and sensitivity which they owed partly to the influence of H. H. *Richardson, with an ultra-sophisticated and elegant use of Roman Renaissance forms. Now largely and unjustly unappreciated, the buildings produced by the firm were among the finest and most graceful of the period. McKim's energy and drive was nicely modified and complemented by White's suave mastery of design.

McKim's bolder hand may be seen in such projects in New York as Pennsylvania

Station (now demolished): its design was best known for having been modelled on the Baths of Caracalla, but it had perhaps more interest for its fine psychological effect on the spectator arriving in New York. Another of McKim's important works was the layout and design of the Columbia University campus on Morningside Heights (since outrageously vandalized by the addition of crude commercial buildings). His imaginative audacity can be seen in his early attempt to provide indirect lighting in Columbia's Low Library; a white wooden sphere was suspended beneath the deep blue dome to produce artificial moonlight, by reflecting the spotlight beams projected on it from the upper galleries. Still to be seen, the 'moon' now baffles most observers.

Stanford White's designs include the beautifully proportioned Washington Square Arch, perhaps the most refined and nicely conceived monument in Manhattan. White also built houses for Louis Comfort Tiffany, Charles Dana Gibson, and Joseph C. Pulitzer. His most ambitious plan was the famed old Madison Square Garden, with its 300-foot tower modelled after Seville's Giralda Tower and topped by the then scandalous nude *Diana* by Augustus Saint-Gaudens.

McKim, Meade and White. Pennsylvania Station. New York, 1906–10

Other major works in New York by the firm were the Pierpont Morgan Library, The College of the City of New York, New York University's Hall of Fame, the Metropolitan, University, Harvard and Century clubs, The New York Herald Building, the Knickerbocker Trust and National City banks, the Tiffany, Gorham and Municipal office buildings, Bellevue Hospital and the new Post Office. Works outside New York include additions to the University of Virginia, the Rhode Island State Capitol, Newport Casino, Walker Art Gallery at Bowdoin College, Maine, and the Agriculture and New York State buildings of the Columbian Exposition. In 1902, the firm was appointed by President Theodore Roosevelt to make additions to the White House in Washington, D.C.

The firm of McKim, Mead and White epitomized the gentlemanly elegance of turn-of-the-century America, and the taste and caprice of the '400'. As a major force in the nation's cultural development, the firm received world-wide acclaim and exerted enormous influence; it supplanted *Richardson Romanesque by imposing Imperial classicism on the 'White City' of the Columbian Exposition in 1893. There was a notorious scandal in 1906 when Stanford White was shot, ironically enough in his own Madison Square Garden, by Harry Kendall Thaw, following a romantic entanglement.

ARTHUR SPRAGUE

Mendelsohn, Erich, b. Allenstein, East Prussia 1887, d. San Francisco 1953. Among the architects of the 20th century who have used the new methods of construction made possible by steel and concrete with originality and imagination and have been successful in imparting to their buildings the quality of organic unity Erich Mendelsohn must hold a notable place. He received his architectural training at Berlin and Munich. In 1912 he started practice and for the first two years was engaged chiefly in stage designing, painting, and on projects for various buildings. During this period he became interested in the *Expressionist movement, and its influence can be seen in some of his early work. During the First World War he served in the German army, first on the Russian front and later on the Western front.

Erich Mendelsohn. Synagogue. Cleveland, Ohio, 1946–52. Project

Shortly after the war he held an exhibition in Berlin of architectural sketches which attracted considerable attention. They were designs of a wide variety of buildings: factories, grain elevators, observatories, religious buildings, in which steel and concrete were used expressively and in which the purpose of the building was suggested by the symbolism of its forms, thereby showing the influence of Expressionism.

One of his first buildings was the Einstein Observatory at Potsdam (1920) which caused a sensation. This was followed by a very large number of buildings that he designed during the twenties, including several departmental stores such as the Petersdorff Store at Breslau (1927), and the Schocken Stores at Stuttgart (1927) and Chemnitz (1928); a group of buildings adjoining Kurfürstendamm which included a cinema with a dramatic interior with horizontal emphasis (1928); and the Columbus House (1931), a large block of offices and shops in the Potsdamerplatz, which together with the Schocken Store at Chemnitz represent Mendelsohn's best work in Germany. The façades of both have long bands of fenestration alternating with opaque bands, and the whole effect is one of lightness combined with grandeur, the effect of lightness being achieved by a cantilevering of the walls beyond the structural supports.

Owing to the racial persecution which accompanied the rise to power of the

Erich Mendelsohn. Schocken Department Store. Stuttgart, 1927. Project

National Socialists, Mendelsohn left Germany in March 1933 and went to Brussels, and then to London, where he began practice in partnership with Serge Chermayeff in the summer of that year. For the next six years Mendelsohn divided his practice between England and Palestine. The principal work of the partnership with Chermayeff was the now famous De la Warr Pavilion, Bexhill, Sussex (1934). Mendelsohn's work in Palestine was more considerable and included two large hospitals, that at Haifa (1937) and the University Medical Centre on Mount Scopus, Jerusalem (1937–9); the Palestine Bank, Jerusalem (1938); several large houses, a college and library.

In 1941 Mendelsohn went to America, and after the war he started practice in 1945 in San Francisco. His principal work in America was the Maimonides Hospital in San Francisco (1946) and a series of large synagogues and community centres, some of which remained only projects. Those completed are at St Louis, Missouri (1946–50); Cleveland, Ohio (1946–52), which includes a large dome 100 feet in

Erich Mendelsohn. Schocken, later Merkur, Department Store. Stuttgart, 1927

Erich Mendelsohn. Columbus House. Berlin, 1931

Erich Mendelsohn and Serge Chermayeff. De la Warr Pavilion. Bexhill, 1934

Erich Mendelsohn. House on Pacific Heights. San Francisco, 1950–1

diameter; Grand Rapids, Michigan (1948–52); and St Paul, Minnesota (1950–4). Mendelsohn's work was characterized by a sympathetic and original use of materials, steel, concrete and glass, and by an expression of purpose through the forms of his building, seen in such works as the Observatory at Potsdam, the departmental stores in Germany, the Bexhill Pavilion, and the hospitals in Palestine. His designs were always actuated by the principles of organic unity, so that each part by its character denotes its relation to the whole, and each building is closely wedded to its site. The synagogue at Cleveland, where the forms of the building harmonize so well with the contours of the undulating site, is notable. (*Organic Architecture)

Bibliography: Mario Federico Roggero, *Il contributo di Mendelsohn alla evoluzione dell'architettura moderna*, Milan 1952; Bruno Zevi, 'Eric Mendelsohn', in *Metron*, Nos. 49–50, Rome 1954; Arnold Whittick, *Eric Mendelsohn*, London 1956, New York 1956, Bologna 1960.

ARNOLD WHITTICK

Messel, Alfred, b. Darmstadt 1853, d. Berlin 1909. Flats and commercial buildings, in particular department stores (Wertheim department store in Berlin, 1896), with extensive use of glass on façades and basically functional design.

Mexico. Mexico was the first of the Latin-American countries to come to terms with the claims of the *International Style. The revolt against the senseless imitation of inherited building forms in the mid-twenties, i.e. a decade before the building of the Ministry of Education at Rio de Janeiro, found expression first in the teaching of the architect José *Villagrán García and in his early works and those of his pupils Legorreta, *O'Gorman, de la Mora and Yáñez. The hospitals, houses and schools designed by this group took the Functionalism of *Le Corbusier's *Vers une architecture* literally, and thus presented the starkest contrast to the popular love of decoration. During the two subsequent decades, modern architecture made uninterrupted progress in Mexico. The economic advantages of the purism that went hand in hand with the new structural methods, account for only a part of its rapid success. In the main it was due to the fact that the

Enrique del Moral. 'La Merced' Market Hall. Mexico City, 1957

Pedro Ramírez Vázquez and Rafael Mijares. Ministry of Labour and Social Welfare. Mexico City, 1953

Juan O'Gorman, Gustavo Saavedra and Juan Martínez de Velasco. University Library. Mexico City, 1952

government held the modern style to be an adequate expression of its progressive administration and social building programme, and used it for numerous buildings, thus helping it to secure general approval. At the beginning of the fifties this development reached its peak in the building of the University City (to a layout by Mario Pani and Enrique del Moral) for 20,000 students, a number which has doubled in ten years. With the collaboration of approximately one hundred young architects and engineers, the extensive complex was finished in three years.
Mexico's building tradition, which in contrast to the *USA has strong roots in the centuries before and after its conquest by Europeans, has left its mark on the modern architecture of the country. In the University City this influence is immediately obvious in the extraordinary dimensions of its open spaces and in the ever-recurring passion for decoration. In the name of integrating art and architecture, the restraint of the last twenty years was abandoned and all available surfaces were covered with murals, mosaics and reliefs in an idiosyncratic social-realist style. In some cases, as for instance the main library (Juan O'Gorman) and the stadium (Diego Rivera), this kind of façade decoration may be considered successful. But its unfettered use, as for example on the Ministry of Transport building, has reduced this tendency to the absurd.
In the capital today, offices and hotels with *curtain walls reign supreme in the North American manner (architects: Alvarez, Marcos, Kaspé, Sordo Madaleno, Villagrán García and others). State-backed housing schemes are currently being promoted in increasing measure, and large, integrated complexes—whole districts even of apartment houses—are being built (architects: Felix Sánchez, Alejandro Prieto, Mario Pani). Private houses have a more distinctive personality, especially those in the new suburb of Pedregal, built on a foundation of lava in the southern part of Mexico City (architects: Barragán, Cetto, Greenham, Artigas, Attolini Lack, Rosen, Castañedo and others).
Mexico's contribution of the greatest significance to modern architecture lies in the most recent development of shell vaulting by *Candela. Often, in collaboration with other architects, he has built factories, warehouses, filling-stations, market halls, pavilions, restaurants and churches in free organic shapes, from which a new sculptural quality emerges. It was with similar intentions, based however not so much on structure as on a mannerist attempt to broaden the frontiers of architecture, that the sculptor Goeritz fashioned his 'emotional' casing for the Eco nightclub (1953) and the group of non-functional towers at the entrance to a satellite town under construction (1958). The painter-architect

Juan O'Gorman. O'Gorman House. San Angel, 1956

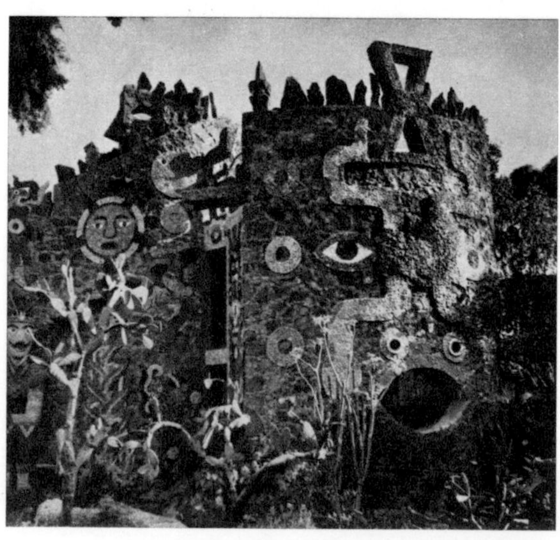

Juan O'Gorman peopled his fantastic dream cave inside and out with creations made of coloured stones and seashells. The school building programme of the present government, which will take till 1970 to complete, deserves the international regard which was given it at the XII Triennale at Milan. Its essential core is a school unit made up of prefabricated parts by the architect Ramírez Vázquez and his collaborators, which solves the urgent problem of Mexican village schools both economically and functionally.

Bibliography: I. E. Myers, *Mexico's Modern Architecture*, New York 1952; Henry-Russell Hitchcock, *Latin-American Architecture since 1945*, New York 1955; Max Cetto, *Moderne Architektur in Mexico*, Stuttgart 1960.

MAX CETTO

Meyer, Adolf, b. Mechernich, Eifel 1881, d. on the island of Baltrum, in the North Sea 1929. Trained as a cabinet-maker. Attended the Art School at Düsseldorf and worked as an architect with *Behrens and Bruno Paul. He taught at the *Bauhaus from 1919 to 1925 and worked as city architect in Frankfurt from 1926 to 1929. Meyer was a collaborator of *Gropius (Fagus Works at Alfeld, 1911, and Jena Municipal Theatre, 1925), then flats, schools, the planetarium of the Zeiss Works in Jena (1925–6), and municipal buildings in Frankfurt.

Meyer, Hannes, b. Basle 1889, d. Crocifisso di Savosa, Switzerland 1954. Appointed lecturer and studio master at the *Bauhaus, Dessau, and succeeded *Gropius as director (1928–30). Competed (with Hans Wittwer) for the League of Nations Building, Geneva (1927); German Trades Union School at Bernau (1928–30), a school laid out in separate blocks. Worked in the Soviet Union from 1930 to 1936, then in Switzerland; from 1939 to 1949 in Mexico. Meyer rejected architecture that depended on aesthetic principles of form: 'Architecture is not the individual, emotional activity of an artist. Building is a collective activity.'

Michelucci, Giovanni, b. Pistoia 1891. Took his architect's diploma at Florence in 1914. Joint architect of the S. Maria Novella Station at Florence (1933–6). Savings Bank, Florence (1953).

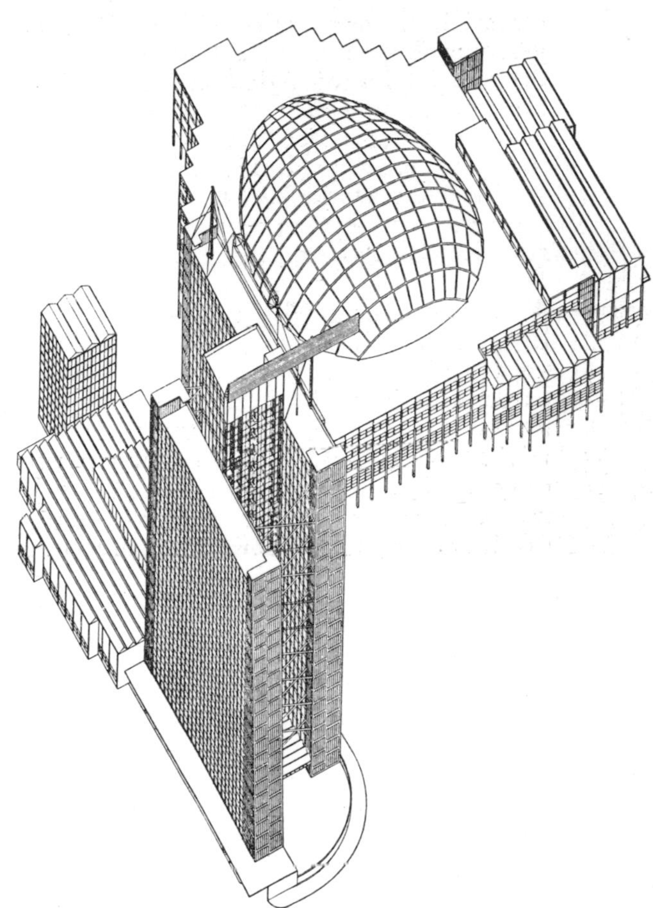

Hannes Meyer and Hans Wittwer. League of Nations Building, Geneva, 1927. Project

Mies van der Rohe, Ludwig, b. Aachen (Aix-la-Chapelle) 1886. Ludwig Mies van der Rohe, German-American architect, is generally acknowledged as one of the four most influential architects working during the first half of the 20th century—the others being Frank Lloyd *Wright, *Le Corbusier, and Walter *Gropius. He was born Ludwig Mies, later compounding his surname with that of his mother. Without formal training as an architect, his initiation into building and the superb craftsmanship for which his architecture is famous, came initially from his father, who was a master mason and the proprietor of a stone-cutting shop. Mies learned to draw as a designer for stucco decoration. In 1905 he went to Berlin where he worked briefly for a minor architect who specialized in wooden structures. Better to master this material, he apprenticed himself for two years to Bruno Paul, a leading furniture designer. In 1907 Mies set up briefly on his own as an architect, but the following year he joined Peter *Behrens, at the time the most creative architect in *Germany. While Mies worked in the office, Walter Gropius was among the chief designers, and Le Corbusier passed a few months there.

The three years which Mies spent with Behrens (until 1911) provided his most valuable training. In a sense Behrens's career anticipates Mies's. On the one hand, as the designer for the Allgemeine Elektricitäts Gesellschaft (AEG), Behrens not only designed the factory buildings of the German electrical combine but its products as well. More than any other architect of his generation, he therefore anticipated the ideal of the architect as a comprehensive designer for the modern industrial society. Behrens's product design in metal reinforced the training which Mies had received in cabinet making from Paul, while both contributed to Mies's achievement in furniture design. Moreover, Behrens's Turbine Factory in Berlin (1909), with its bold exposure of the metal structural frame infilled with glass, is astonishingly prophetic of Mies's much later development of an architecture austerely dependent on the naked metal skeleton. But Behrens's factory production represented one aspect only of his *œuvre*. He also brought the neoclassicism of Karl

Ludwig Mies van der Rohe

Mies van der Rohe. Kröller House. The Hague, 1912. Project

Mies van der Rohe. Glass skyscraper. 1920–1. Project

Friedrich *Schinkel to his architecture—especially to his monumental and domestic commissions, although Schinkelesque neoclassicism occasionally appears in the severe masonry piers and simplified pediments of some of his factories as well. To create a modern architecture with a neoclassical severity of means, purity of form, perfection of proportions, elegance of detail and dignity of expression is the underlying preoccupation of Mies's career. For this ideal he owed much to the imperfect synthesis of industrialism and neoclassicism in Behrens's work.

Initially, Mies was more overtly influenced by the neoclassical rather than by the industrial aspects of Behrens's work, in large part perhaps because he had served as the supervisor of construction for one of Behrens's most monumentally neoclassical edifices, the German Embassy in St Petersburg (1911–12). Leaving Behrens in 1911, Mies designed several houses in a neo-Schinkelesque style akin to Behrens's work. The most notable design of the group (and superior to the neoclassicism of his mentor) was a projected house and gallery for Mme H. E. L. J. Kröller (1912), the owner of the famed Kröller-Müller Collection. This went as far as a full-scale mock-up of the house in canvas and wood, built on the site at The Hague. For the Kröller commission, Mies went to Holland. There he came to know the work and philosophy of Hendrik Petrus *Berlage, who was the Dutch counterpart to Behrens. Where Behrens was primarily concerned with form, however, Berlage derived his architectural philosophy from the 19th-century moralistic theory of the 'honest' expression of structure and materials, which was Gothic rather than neoclassical in inspiration. Taken together, Behrens's emphasis on neoclassical form, Berlage's on revealed structure and materials, and their joint desire for a new architecture somehow expressive of modern conditions, might be said to stake out the territory which Mies would explore.

His romantic neoclassicism continued up to the war. After this interruption to his

Mies van der Rohe. Reinforced concrete office building. 1922. Project

career, there was, in 1919, one last post-war project in the Schinkelesque vein. Whereupon Mies's career in modern architecture was abruptly launched in a series of projects from 1919 to 1924 which are astonishingly varied and original. They reflect the sense of liberation in post-war Berlin which suddenly felt the impact of native *Expressionism, of De *Stijl from Holland, of *Constructivism and *Suprematism from Russia. Mies was active in this ferment, not only as a designer, but as a propagandist too. He was among the

Mies van der Rohe. Memorial to Karl Liebknecht and Rosa Luxemburg. Berlin, 1926

founders of the magazine *G* (for *Gestaltung*, or creative force) which was devoted to modern art. He joined the *Novembergruppe*. Founded in 1918, and named after the month of the Republican Revolution, this organization too publicized the modern movement. Mies directed the architectural section from 1921 until 1925. It was principally in the annual exhibitions of the *Novembergruppe* that his early modern projects appeared.

In two glass skyscrapers, the first (1919) of triangular forms, the second (1920–1) of curved free forms, Mies sought to dramatize the reflective qualities of glass in faceted shapes. In fact, the free form curvature of the second of these skyscrapers was specifically determined by the shape which produced the greatest play of light over the building. A project for a reinforced concrete office building (1922) was even more prophetic. Cantilevered slabs closed by a parapet permitted continuous inset window bands with the lightest of metal mullions. Although not widely known until much later, this project, among the first ribbon window designs, uses the ribbon motif so logically and purely that, as a consummate expression of what became a familiar element in modern architecture, it has remained unsurpassed. The initial series of projects is concluded by two houses. One, that of 1923 for a brick country house, uses De Stijl principles. Brick panels in slab, L and T shapes, infilled where necessary with floor-to-roof window panels, modulate a spatial continuity through their arrangement in a tense asymmetrical equilibrium in space. For the first time in architecture, the wall by its placement and shape actually generates the plan. Although the design is schematic only, it nevertheless represents the first truly architectural achievement employing De Stijl principles of composition, since earlier ventures had arbitrarily intermixed De Stijl with Cubist elements. The second project for a country house, this time for a concrete structure, is a spreading structure in a pinwheel composition around a multi-terraced site. Both the horizontality of the house and the determination of the irregular mass in accordance with the major elements of the plan run counter to the compact *prisme pur* enclosure of space which dominated the *International Style at the time. Mies's concrete country house in this respect looks rather ahead to later developments of the International Style after 1930. On the whole these five projects are among the most creative architectural conceptions of the early twenties, and remain among the least dated.

The latter half of the twenties finally sees a few (very few) executed buildings in Mies's modern style. Notable among them are the Monument to Karl Liebknecht and Rosa Luxemburg in Berlin (1926, and demolished by the Nazis). A textured brick slab, faceted with horizontal, box-like projecting and receding elements and

Mies van der Rohe. Wolf House. Guben, 1926

emblazoned at one end by the hammer and sickle with a flagstaff, it is among the few significant memorials erected in the 20th century. Two brick houses—the Wolf House in Guben (1926) and the Hermann Lange House in Krefeld (1928)—reveal how far Mies had come from his pre-war neo-Schinkelism, and how much his early neoclassicism continued to influence his work. Both possess a solidity and rootedness at variance with current practice in the International Style. Their elegance of detail and proportioning are such as Schinkel himself would have admired. The Wolf House is especially fine in the extension of the beautiful precision of the brick walls (a material which Mies had come to appreciate during his interlude in Holland) and in an abstract arrangement of brick terracing reminiscent of the Liebknecht-Luxemburg Monument. Meanwhile, during the late twenties, too, Mies continued to be interested in the glass office building, and he projected no less than four different schemes, none of which came to fruition. His early work in planning the exhibitions of the *Novembergruppe* prepared him to design several such exhibitions in which products are displayed with a restrained elegance that enhances their visual qualities.

His work at this time, however, is climaxed by two major works. One, the Weissenhof Project in Stuttgart (1927), was a large-scale outdoor exhibition of housing of various types with designs by most of the leading modern European architects. Sponsored by the *Deutscher Werkbund and directed by Mies, this outdoor exhibition contained no less than twenty-one permanent buildings, ranging from one-family villas to Mies's dominating apartment structure, together with an adjunct of temporary exhibits. The most comprehensive group endeavour of the International Style, it clearly revealed the unifying characteristics of European modernism, An even more impressive work qualitatively, and indeed among the masterpieces of modern architecture, was Mies's German Pavilion for the International Exhibition in Barcelona (1929). It continues the De Stijl experiment of Mies's project for a country house of 1922, but with a simplification of elements and a breadth of treatment far surpassing the complications of the earlier design. Over a portion of a

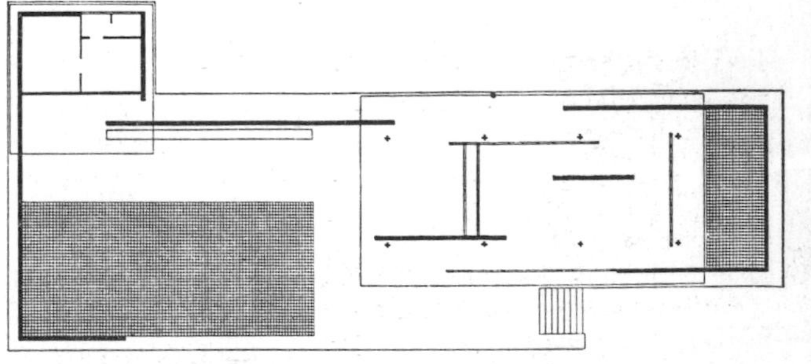

Mies van der Rohe. German Pavilion at the International Exhibition. Barcelona, 1929

raised podium, Mies lightly supported a reinforced concrete slab on cross-shaped, chrome-plated steel columns. He placed vertical slabs of travertine and panels of glass of various kinds well under the spreading slab of the roof. Partially enclosing the roofed area, and partially sliding from under it, these panels in their right-angled asymmetrical arrangement loosely, but firmly, ordered the space while preserving its continuity. Two pools completed the complex: the larger on the open terrace; the smaller at right angles to it at the opposite end of the podium. The smaller is enclosed in a semi-court created by the slide of the travertine panels from under the slab of the roof. The sculpture of a female figure by Georg Kolbe placed in the water serves as a tenuous point of destination within this scrupulously chaste pavilion, otherwise occupied (so far as the standard photographs tell us) only by some of Mies's furniture. It was in this pavilion that he displayed his famous 'Barcelona Chair'. Among the classics in modern furniture design, this was the culminating piece in a series of distinguished designs which Mies realized during the late twenties. Although relatively little noted during the summer of its existence, the photographic record of the modest structure—truly 'almost nothing' in Mies's own aphorism on his architecture—has made it among the most influential buildings of the 20th century.

Mies van der Rohe. Tugendhat House. Brno, 1930

Immediately after the Barcelona Pavilion, Mies designed the most important house of his European career, the concrete-surfaced Tugendhat House at Brno, Czechoslovakia (1930). Built on a gentle slope, the house presented a closed one-storey front to the street, with two storeys to the rear. The continuous space of the lower living floor with its chrome-plated columns and free-standing panels (one a semicircle of Macassar ebony) recalled the treatment of the Barcelona Pavilion. Here an even richer display of Mies's furniture completed an elegance, every detail of which (down to the curtain tracks) was meticulously custom-designed.

The Tugendhat House was Mies's last important executed building in Europe. Among the projects of the early and mid thirties the designs for houses within walled courts are the most interesting. Although the surrounding brick walls occasionally opened on to a distant view, for the most part these houses were wholly bounded by their rectangular frame, while in one instance several houses of various sizes, walled from one another, shared the same enframement. Inside the enclosure there was the usual Miesian spatial continuity interrupted here and there by carefully placed glass walls and solid panels, partially roofed (again slabs on metal supports), and partially open overhead. Indoors and out, ceiling and sky, solid and transparency are brought into intimate play with one another in these characteristically dynamic but serene spaces which are here adapted to a type of residence ideal for urban living.

On Gropius's recommendation Mies succeeded him as the Director of the *Bauhaus in 1930. Immediately thereafter, however, Nazi pressure forced Mies to move the school from Dessau to Berlin. There it had a tenuous existence, until Mies finally decided to close it in 1933. The hostile political environment made it increasingly impossible to work in Germany and, in the summer of 1937, when just past fifty, he emigrated to the *United States. There, in 1944, he became an American citizen.

Whereas Mies had built relatively little in Europe and his work was known to a discriminating few, his practice and influence grew rapidly in the United States. It

Mies van der Rohe. Farnsworth House, Fox River, Ill., 1946–50

was here, precisely a decade after his arrival, that Mies had his first large retrospective exhibition at the Museum of Modern Art in New York. For this exhibition his principal disciple, Philip *Johnson, published the first book on Mies's work—at a time when, as he notes in the preface, only two articles wholly devoted to Mies's work had appeared. This publicity and the importance of his American commissions established Mies's popular fame. In 1938 he had been called to teach at the Illinois Institute of Technology (then known as the Armour Institute) in Chicago, as Gropius had been somewhat earlier called to Harvard. His first major American commission, a campus plan (1940) and buildings (the first in 1942–3) for IIT, immediately established the central theme of his American work: the exposed metal frame as it reticulated neutral rectangular volumes. He viewed the cleared site, which consisted of a number of city blocks in a scrubby area of the Chicago South Side, as an idealized space, much like the podium of the Barcelona Pavilion. On this he arranged rectangular and slab-shaped blocks in accord with a modular grid for the entire project, such that semi-courts and corridors of space were created in a manner analogous to (but more formal than) his conditioning of interior space by slabs from the Barcelona Pavilion onward.

The revealed metal frame in his American buildings is rarely the structure itself, since fire regulations demand that most steel must be covered. Hence the visible 'structure' is more often symbolic of the reality beneath, much as pilasters symbolized columns in Renaissance buildings—except that Mies's pseudo-structure more convincingly resembles and more intimately relates to the real thing within. From the standard alphabet of the *steelmaker's catalogue (the I-shaped beams, the H's, L's, the plates, and channels), he welds mouldings as the metallurgical equivalent of the carved mouldings of the past. The careful proportioning of his frame, the gradation of components from heavy to light, the firm elegance of his profiling and the subtleties of transitions where corners occur or one material butts another: this intensity of effort and artistry expended on the image of the structure has been unexcelled and all but unmatched by his numerous followers, most of whom have taken his image as a mere convenience for prefabrication. (*pp. 21–22)

Even as the first buildings were going up on the IIT campus, Mies designed (1946, completed 1950) a glass and metal house for Dr Edith Farnsworth in Fox River, Illinois. Three floating slabs—a terrace slab, and behind it floor and roof slabs—are all lifted from the ground on metal I-beam supports. The welding of the supports to the sides of the slabs, as though magnetism kept the frame intact, enhances the floating quality of the spreading slabs. Smaller slabs, also seemingly floated, serve as stairs, from the ground to the terrace and from the terrace to the entrance porch of the rectangular glass-box living area. It is so apparently simple that the subtleties of this extraordinarily elegant frame are readily missed on casual inspection, as are the subtleties of a composition in which the evident asymmetry is countered by hidden symmetries.

In his American work especially Mies has repeatedly taken a basic building type—in this instance the open pavilion lightly supported around the perimeter—and worked variations on the theme. Thus he enlarged the pavilion theme of the Farnsworth House by suspending the roof slab from exposed girders in a series of projects which was eventually realized in Crown Hall for the School of Architecture and Design at IIT (1952). Again the floating stair slabs rise to the floating terrace, and more stairs rise to the floor slab, which is lifted a few feet above the ground much as that of the Farnsworth House. Despite appearances, however, the Crown Hall floor slab is conventionally supported from the basement beneath. Where the earlier glass box was completely open beneath its floor slab, this is glazed, so that Design can be crowded into the basement, while Architecture reigns in the all but uninterrupted space of the glass box above. Again, the openness of this space is enhanced by the suspended nature of the two slabs hanging or abutting (rather than resting) on their supports. In so far as Mies has been concerned with space at all in his American work, it has tended towards the universal box of Crown Hall and not towards the further development of the subtly modulated spaces of his European work after the Barcelona Pavilion.

Enlarged again, the pavilion becomes the project for a convention hall on the Chicago lake-front (1953). The roof slab of this unbuilt pavilion is a three-dimensional structure of interwoven trusses built on a cubic module of 30 feet in each direction and 30 feet deep. Mies designed this heroic structural slab to span 720 feet (or roughly two city blocks) so as to provide a column-free interior space with a height of 112 feet for a capacity audience of 50,000. Diagonal bracing extended from the outside edges of the three-dimensional ceiling trusses makes a two-dimensional truss of the exterior walls. This bracing brings the entire structure down on low reinforced concrete columns spaced 120 feet apart, with the area between available for entrances wherever needed. Finally, a pattern of triangles in light and dark metal panels not only dramatizes the triangulation of the structure, but also provides a compelling visual

Mies van der Rohe. Crown Hall, Illinois Institute of Technology. Chicago, 1952–6. Staircase

Page 197. Mies van der Rohe. Crown Hall, Illinois Institute of Technology. Chicago, 1952–6

entity for what Arthur Drexler in 1960 termed 'the most monumental image 20th-century architecture has yet produced'.

As the basic pavilion could be proliferated into a series of buildings, so could the skeletal skyscraper. Mies's two classic skyscrapers, Lake Shore Drive Apartments (1951) and the Seagram Building in New York (1958) are in a sense exactly the same building creating different experiences, much as the Greek Temple of Poseidon at Paestum and the Parthenon are at once the same building and different buildings. Relative to one another, the Paestum-like severity of Lake Shore contrasts with the Parthenaic refinement of the Seagram. In the Lake Shore Apartments, vertical blocks are set at right angles to one another across a narrow interval of space in such a manner that their static shapes are always in tension with one another. As we circle the complex, we find that it possesses neither a true 'front' nor a true 'back'. We always see the narrow side of one block against the broad side of the other in a constantly changing relationship. The I-beam projections from the walls appear to close over the windows seen obliquely and open over those seen head-on, while in moving so as to open those which closed we automatically close those which were open. The Seagram Building, on the other hand, reconciles the Lake Shore paradox of static elements in perpetual disequilibrium. The bronze building rises like a dense, dark cliff behind the absolute void of its entrance *plaza*. The axis of the *plaza* culminates in the formal grandeur of the entrance with its two-storey stilts each backed by the pylons of the elevator shafts. Where, in the window grid of the Lake Shore Apartments, horizontals constantly challenge the verticals, this tension too is reconciled in the Seagram by the clear affirmation of verticality. In the Lake Shore, then, a perpetual tension; in the Seagram, the reconciliation of tension in a formal climax. To cite Mies's famous axiom, 'Less is more.' As he has extracted architecture from the 'almost nothing' of the brick or the I-beam considered as ultimate 'things in themselves', so he has used elemental building types to squeeze different buildings from the same one. His approach is

Mies van der Rohe. Seagram Building. New York, 1958

Mies van der Rohe. Convention Hall. Chicago, 1953. Model

Mies van der Rohe. Lake Shore Drive Apartments. Chicago, 1951

narrow, and his austerity can lead to dryness where the problem has already been so substantially resolved that only refinement is left. But the narrowness of approach permits his passionate integrity and purifying artistry to come to focus. In his greatest works, the 'almost nothing' contains the paradoxical plentitude of an elemental demonstration.

Bibliography: Philip Johnson, *Mies van der Rohe*, 2nd edition, New York 1953; Ludwig Hilbersheimer, *Mies van der Rohe*, Chicago 1956; Arthur Drexler, *Mies van der Rohe*, New York 1960; Peter Blake, *Masters of Modern Architecture*, New York 1960; Ian McCallum, *Architecture USA*, London, New York 1959; 'Farnsworth House', *Architectural Forum*, *95*, October 1951; Arthur Drexler, 'Seagram Building', *Architectural Record*, *124*, July 1958; Lewis Mumford, 'Skyline: the Lesson of the Master', *New Yorker*, *33*, 13 September 1958; William H. Jordy, 'Seagram Assessed', *Architectural Review*, *124*, London December 1958; William H. Jordy, *Zodiac 8*, Milan 1960.

WILLIAM H. JORDY

Mills, Edward David, b. 1915. Studied at Polytechnic School of Architecture, London. In private practice since 1937; churches, schools, industrial buildings, research centres, flats and houses. Designed the British Industries Pavilion and the Britannia Inn at the Brussels International Exhibition, 1958.

Modular Coordination. It is, perhaps, unfortunate that the words 'module' and 'modular' were adopted by the pioneers of modular coordination and given a restricted sense after having been current in a wider meaning for several thousand years. 'Module' is the English, or French, form of the Latin *modulus*, which meant a small unit of measure, being the diminutive of *modus*. In classical architecture the modulus is half the diameter of the column at its base and is the unit for proportioning the classic order of column and entablature. Its actual size is not determined in advance, but prescribed for each particular design.

In modular coordination the module is not a unit of proportion, but a predetermined standard size used for coordinating the dimensions of components for building (doors, windows, panels, beams) with the dimensions of the spaces in a projected building into which they are intended to fit. The modular size (or basic size) of the component is expressed in the same whole number of modules as the size of its space in the building. The actual size of the component, the size found by measuring it, will be less than the modular size, by an allowance for the width of joint and for tolerances (manufacturing and positional).

The confusion between 'module' as a unit of standardization and its ancient use as one of architectural proportion persists, for example, in a misunderstanding of the use of Le Corbusier's 'Le Modulor'. This is, in fact, a method of applying the Golden Section proportion and has nothing to do with modular coordination. Modul*o*r has nothing in common with Modul*a*r.

The module in modular coordination is sometimes referred to as the 'Basic Module', to distinguish it from its multiples which are used as 'Planning Modules', 'Derived Modules', 'Design Modules' and so on. The best usage, however, is to confine the term 'module' to the Basic Module and to find other expressions, such as 'Planning Grid' for its multiples. This is because the size of the Basic Module has been fixed internationally as 10 centimetres for metric countries and 4 inches for countries using inches and feet, after a long process of debate and experiment. The logic behind the choice of this size as the Basic Module does not, by analogy, support the use of any other size, larger or smaller, repetitively as a module. In short, there is only one module (10 centimetres or 4 inches).

The international 10 centimetres/4 inches module is the resultant of two forces pulling against each other: the pull from manufacturers was to make it as large as possible in the interests of simplification and mass-production; that from architects was for it to be as small as possible for the greatest freedom of aesthetic and functional design. That this resultant should have been the same in all parts of the world, where the problem has been tackled, is a significant reassurance of its validity.

National standards have been published for modular coordination in the following countries, on the 10 centimetres module unless otherwise stated:

1942 France
1945 USA (4 in.)
1948 Belgium
1949 Italy
1951 Germany (10 cm. and 12.5 cm.)
1951 Norway
1951 Hungary
1952 Sweden
1953 Argentine
1954 USSR
1955 Chile
1955 Poland
1956 Portugal
1956 Roumania
1957 Austria
1958 Denmark
1958 India
1959 Canada (4 in.)

The promulgation of a national standard for modular coordination does not by itself achieve the savings in cost and in construction-time that are expected to derive from the use of the modular method. Much development work is required, by manufacturers in the choice of modular sizes for particular sets of components, and by architects in the application of the method to building design so as to incorporate standard modular components to the best advantage. In this process of development a vicious circle has constantly to be broken: manufacturers are reluctant to change their production to modular sizes until there is a clear demand for them from architects, whilst architects maintain that it is of no use to design modular buildings until ample ranges of modular components are available on the market. This vicious circle even appears in the 'planned economy' of Socialist countries, as is reported by a contributor from Poland to *The Modular Quarterly* (1963/1, p. 16).

In most of the countries named above, and in others, e.g. New Zealand and the Central American Republics, where modular coordination is under study but where a standard has not yet been issued, the development of modular method is entrusted to the Standards institutions or other agencies of government. In some, however, the initiative has been taken by private organizations.

In the USA there is the Modular Building Standards Association, Washington, D.C.; in Australia there is the Australian Modular Society, based at Sydney with branches in other states; and, in the United Kingdom, the Modular Society, London. Besides these three national societies (though the UK Modular Society has many overseas members) there is the International Modular Group, with its headquarters at the housing ministry in Copenhagen.

Finally, a few words on the situation in the United Kingdom at the time of writing (February 1963). It has not yet been possible to get the unanimous support from all sections of the building industry that is required for the issue of a British standard for modular coordination. Nevertheless, the Ministry of Public Building and Works has published a first statement on 'Dimensional Coordination for Industrialized Building', which in effect adopts the 4-inch module and the modular method for the whole of the government building programme, although for tactical reasons it adopts a somewhat off-beat terminology. This statement is expected to break the vicious circle and to create the demand from architects that will fill the *Modular Catalogue* of the Modular Society with ample ranges of modular components.

Bibliography: Modular Coordination—Second Report, EPA Project 174, OEEC., HMSO, London 1961; E. Corker and A. Diprose, 'The Modular Primer' in *Architects' Journal* 1.8.62 (reprinted by Modular Society); *Scandinavian Modular Coordination in Building*, Ministry of Housing, Copenhagen 1960; *The Modular Quarterly* (journal), London.

MARK HARTLAND THOMAS

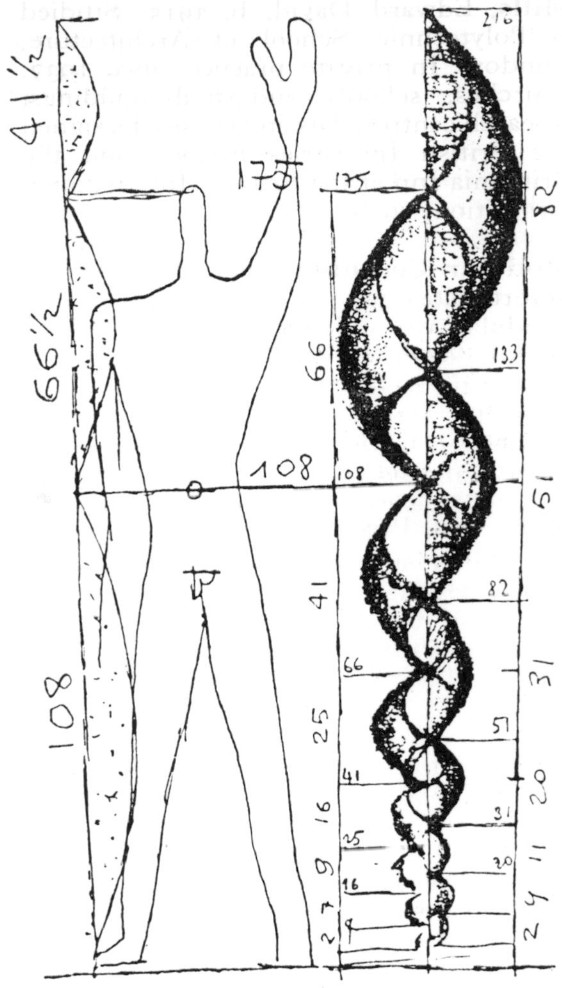

Modulor. A scale of proportions laid down by *Le Corbusier and his colleagues, 'which makes the bad difficult and the good easy' (Albert Einstein). The Modulor is based on two lines, arrived at via the Golden Section and related to the proportions of the human body. The initial dimension is 7 ft 5 in. (226 cm.) (an upright man with his hand raised) and half that, viz. 3 ft 9 in. (113 cm.). A man's height is taken as 6 ft (183 cm.).

Bibliography: Le Corbusier, *The Modulor: A harmonious measure to the human scale, universally applicable to architecture and mechanics*, London 1954. Continued in: Le Corbusier, *Modulor 2, 1955 (Let the user speak next)*, London 1958.

Morris, William, b. Walthamstow 1834, d. Kelmscott, Oxfordshire 1896. In 1861, together with artists from the Pre-Raphaelite Brotherhood, he founded the Morris Company whose products (furniture, textiles, metalwork, stained glass and wallpapers) sought to convey honesty and decency in the crafts. This attitude and the example set by the Red House at Bexley Heath, Kent, which Philip *Webb built for him, exerted a strong influence on the architecture of the times. Morris, who had trained under the architect G. E. Street, built nothing himself. (*Arts and Crafts)

Moser, Karl, b. Baden, Switzerland 1860, d. Zurich 1936. Studied at Zurich College of Technology and later at the École des Beaux-Arts, Paris; 1887–1915 architect at Karlsruhe, 1915–28 taught at Zurich. Moser, whose reinforced concrete Church of St Anthony, Basle (1926–7) was the counterpart to *Perret's Church at Le Raincy (1922–3), taught many modern Swiss architects. (*Switzerland)

Muthesius, Hermann, b. Gross-Neuhausen 1861, d. Berlin 1927. Studied at Berlin Technical College; worked in Wallot's office. Period in Japan; attaché at the German Embassy in London (1896–1903), with a brief to study English architecture and design. His book *Das englische Haus* (Berlin 1904–5) by spreading a knowledge of the works of *Voysey and his contemporaries stimulated a renaissance in domestic architecture on the Continent. Founder-member of the *Deutscher Werkbund.

Nash, John, b. London 1752, d. East Cowes 1835. After a varied career, he worked as an architect in London from 1796. Built partly in classic, partly in Gothic style. His friendship with the Prince of Wales, later King George IV, led to many important commissions: town planning, public buildings, landscaping, country estates, churches, buildings and designs for the Royal House, including the eccentric Brighton Pavilion (*p. 8).
Bibliography: Terence Davis, *The Architecture of John Nash*, London 1960.

Nelson, George, b. Hartford, Connecticut 1908. Designer (in particular furniture and advertising) and architect who faces the problems of modern industry in his architectural designs. Factories, private houses. The model of his experimental house (1957) incorporates a flexible arrangement of square room units.
Bibliography: George Nelson, *Problems of Design*, New York 1957.

Neoclassicism. In the German-speaking countries of Europe the new architecture of the 20th century was born under the sign of the Doric Column, which appears in *Behrens's Mannesmann Building, Düsseldorf, in *Mies van der Rohe's Perls House, Berlin, and in Adolf *Loos's 'Looshaus' in Vienna. At the same time, Loos, like Hermann *Muthesius and others, was acclaiming K. F. *Schinkel as 'the last great architect'. In the same years Julien Guadet, professor at the *École des Beaux-Arts in Paris, taught a system of architecture that had hardly changed from that taught eighty years earlier by J. N. L. Durand and contrived to impose its concepts even on students as radical as Auguste *Perret and Tony *Garnier. Thus, all the fathers of the modern movement in architecture were soundly grounded in neoclassicism, and—even while they protested their disgust at the academies—they took over into their own work the academic neoclassical apparatus of trabeated structure, the preference for simple geometrical forms and smooth surfaces, and the concept of 'elementary composition', i.e. design, as the assembly of a number of disparate volumes, each dedicated to a single identifiable function.
In this way a durable neoclassical tradition was built into modern architecture from the beginning and was the basis for most concepts of 'order' and 'discipline' current in the first thirty years of the century. Since technology was also seen as one of the enemies of disorder, the mechanistic enthusiasms of the Futurists were early assimilated to the neoclassical tradition—in the writings and designs of Antonio *Sant'Elia in 1914, the rhetoric of a Marinetti is allied to an architectural vision more classically pure than even that of Loos. In *Le Corbusier's *Vers une Architecture*, nine years later, parallels between machinery and classical architecture are openly drawn, and the author equates Phidias with the designer of modern sports cars.

Le Corbusier. The Parthenon. 1911. Sketch

By about 1930, however, a new generation of critics and historians who had attached themselves to modern architecture as its mouthpieces (e.g. Sigfried Giedion) began to offer an account of modern architecture that relied exclusively on a supposed *'Functionalist' origin, and by 1936 another historian, Nikolaus Pevsner, could offer an account of the rise of modern architecture in which the academic and neoclassical contributions were not discussed at all. Rapidly, and especially after the disastrous competition for the League of Nations headquarters in Geneva, classicism came to be regarded as the enemy of modern architecture. But this was classicism in the superficial and debased sense of 'ornamented with Greek and Roman detail', for the planning of Le Corbusier's unsuccessful entry in the competition was fully as academic and neoclassical as that of the preferred designs. Similarly one finds, in Italian modern architecture, *Terragni praised for his 'rationalism' and Piacentini damned for his classicism—though a comparison of the façade of Terragni's Casa del Fascio at Como reveals it to be fully as classicist as Piacentini's arcading at EUR42 (Terza Roma) which is fully as rational as Terragni's space-games.

This facile and purely stylistic opposition between modern and classical, this growing ignorance among modern architects of the origins of their own design techniques, was to lead to profound intellectual confusions in the years after the Second World War. On the one hand, Bruno Zevi was to point out, with justice, how neoclassicism was the outstanding weakness of much second-rate modern architecture, but at the same time many Anglo-Saxon critics failed to see that the supposed modernism

Mies van der Rohe. Perls House. Berlin. 1911

Mies van der Rohe. Crown Hall, Illinois Institute of Technology. Chicago, 1952–6

of the Italian buildings then in vogue was little more than a frank exhibition of a neoclassicism that they no longer recognized as their own, an error that left them entirely unprepared for the abandonment of the moral and functional imperatives of modern architecture by the *neo-Liberty faction in Northern Italy.

A similar confusion can be seen in the various valuations placed upon the architecture of Mies van der Rohe in the years after 1950. The English radical functionalist Llewelyn Davies read Mies's repetitive façades at the Illinois Institute of Technology as 'endless' and believed that their complex corners implied the continuation of the planes of the façades beyond the ends of the buildings. But a younger generation of English writers (e.g. Colin Rowe) rendered consciously classicist by the influential writings of Rudolf Wittkower (such as his book, *Architectural Principles in the Age of Humanism*) preferred to read the façades as closed, symmetrical compositions, and the complex corners as emphatic visual terminations, comparable to the doubling of pilasters at the corners of buildings, such as had been regular classical practice since the time of Bramante.

Among the intellectuals of Anglo-Saxon architecture the rediscovery of the roots of the classical tradition through the works of scholars like Wittkower had a profound influence and was seized upon as a welcome source of order in a modern architecture that, deprived of its classical origins, had lost its way in the formless currents of Functionalism. Under such names as neo-Palladianism or the New Formalism, it visibly affected the design of monuments as diverse as Marchwood II power station (England), designed by John Voelcker (of *Farmer and Dark), the Goodyear House in Connecticut, designed by John *Johansen, and even the first major building of the *Brutalist movement: Hunstanton School, by Alison and Peter *Smithson. But here the Anglo-Saxon stream of development divides; in *Great Britain the native preference for a functionalist solution, aided, no

Philip Johnson. Sheldon Art Gallery. Lincoln, Neb., under construction

Alison and Peter Smithson. Hunstanton School. Norfolk, 1954

doubt, by the example of the anti-classicism of Ronchamp and the absence of a strong *beaux-arts* tradition, produced a situation in which neoclassicism was absorbed back into a kind of rational functionalism, and became little more than a modular discipline for the design of structures (e.g. *CLASP schools).

But in the *USA neo-Palladianism rapidly struck root in a *beaux-arts* tradition that had been only thinly buried by the dominance of *Gropius, *Sert, *Breuer and Mies. Philip *Johnson progressed rapidly from the Miesian classicism of his own house at New Canaan to the revival of the vault-forms of Sir John *Soane in the adjoining guest-pavilion, and from there to the vaulting and axial planning of the Port Chester Synagogue, the clearest and most justifiable example of the neoclassical revival in the USA. A more subtle and guarded neoclassicism is seen in the work of Louis *Kahn: the concealed axiality of the Yale Art Gallery (1953); the use of elementary composition in the planning of the Philadelphia laboratories; the Laugier-esque primitivism of the Trenton bath-house (1955); and the pure *Prix-de-Rome* planning of the Torrey Pines Biological Institute.

This reawakening to the neoclassical roots of modern architecture coincided with a general relaxation of functionalist discipline, with rising standards of affluence and the retirement of Gropius from Harvard. The result, on the east coast at least, has been a slow recrudescence of *beaux-arts* academicism, with contrived symmetrical plans and even Doric columns such as could be seen in a number of designs that received awards from the magazine *Progressive Architecture* in 1962. In countries other than the USA, however, neoclassicism seems not to have proceeded any further than various forms of Miesian symmetry and rectangularity. But it does seem to be firmly entrenched as an essential part of the mental substructure of modern architectural design-practice, a geometrical discipline common to both classicizing formalists and prefabricating functionalists.

REYNER BANHAM

Louis I. Kahn. Baths. Trenton, N.J., 1956. Plan

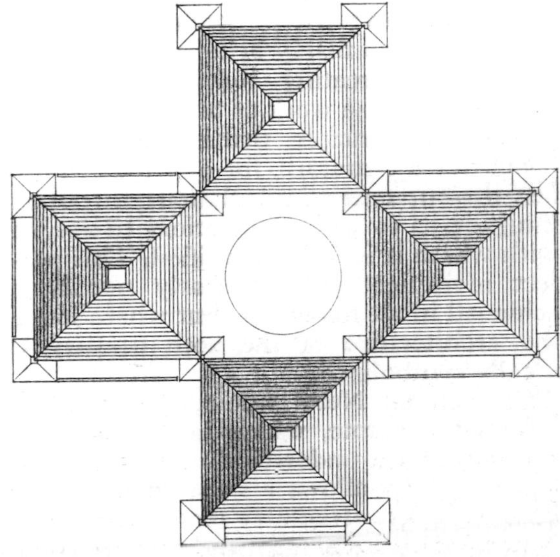

Neo-Liberty. Reversion of post-war Italian architects to *Art Nouveau (Italian: Stile Liberty) forms, in particular to its last geometrical phase, as practised in Vienna and Scotland. Attempts to justify this movement have sparked off heated controversies between English and Italian architectural writers.

Neoplasticism. Piet Mondrian's term for his own painting, developed from Cubist prototypes. The artists and architects of De *Stijl were the protagonists of neoplasticism's clear, geometric order and transferred its concepts to architecture.

Nervi, Pier Luigi, b. Sondrio, Lombardy 1891. Nervi graduated in engineering at Bologna in 1913. He lives in Rome and since 1946 has lectured on structural engineering in the Faculty of Architecture at Rome University. He was awarded an honorary degree by the University of Buenos Aires in 1950.
This great builder ranks with *Freyssinet and *Maillart in his prodigious ability to derive beauty from the results of calculations, and form from the nature of his materials and techniques, which he has made the instruments of his vision. He takes his place in the history of architecture above all for the absolute aesthetic value of some of his buildings, where technology and aesthetics combine to determine dimensions and proportions, based on the same structural rationale that presided at the birth of the pyramid and the column. He himself, on the other hand, has many times laid down the principle in his writings, which he firmly believes in, that the process of creating form is identical, whether it is the work of technicians or of artists: the principle, that is, whereby the beauty of a structure, for example, is not just the outcome of calculations, but of an intuition as to what calculations to use, or with which it is to be identified. This perfect identification has clearly not been achieved in all his works, but where it has the architecture of the 20th century is ideally symbolized.
The material Nervi has adopted is *reinforced concrete, which he moulds and works with an understanding of its possibilities which allows his imagination free rein. His first structures (for a theatre in Naples) date from 1927, the year in which

Pier Luigi Nervi. Communal Stadium. Florence, 1930–2

the *Movimento Italiano per l'Architettura Razionale* was founded, and the Weissenhof estate built at Stuttgart. The idea was gaining ground (the source of much subsequent misunderstanding) that 'form follows function', and it was this idea that brought the engineer Nervi into architecture forthwith. His first important work, the Communal Stadium at Florence (1930–2), consisting of nothing but exposed structural elements, was published straightaway in the most controversial journals as an example of modern architecture, which could be compared, in its dramatic exploitation of structure, with certain designs of *Le Corbusier and strikingly highlighted the expressive possibilities of the raw material, concrete.
Projects followed for viaducts, bridges, silos, tanks and even small revolving houses on a circular plan, which were never built. In 1935, however, Nervi designed a military hangar (of which versions were built, from 1936 to 1941, at Orvieto, Orbetello, and Torre del Lago) which started him on the study of roofs built up from a network of loadbearing joists. These were to prove the object of constant and

even deeper research on his part, in an infinite variety prompted by his taste for creation and experiment. In the hangars which he built (now destroyed) Nervi achieved a great step forward in the process of lightening his structures, at which he has been aiming all his life, for aesthetic as much as for technical reasons.

In the same period, around the year 1940, he brought to a successful conclusion the studies and experiments he had been carrying out to obtain 'strength through form' in buildings, i.e. strength in surfaces alone; this is at once the most technically interesting and the most aesthetically satisfying of his achievements. He went on to design a series of immense roofs for warehouses, factories, aircraft hangars, stations and pavilions of various kinds. In 1947 he built the swimming baths at Leghorn, and in 1948–9 the fantastic roof of the great hall of the Exhibition Building in Turin, which remains one of his masterpieces, although due to a misunderstanding on the part of those responsible for the actual erection an important internal detail was altered, thus depriving it of the perfection which Nervi's design had attained. The enormous building consists in effect of a single roof structure, made up of undulating prefabricated units; Kidder Smith has called it the finest exhibition building in Europe since *Paxton's Crystal Palace, and ranks it with Le Corbusier's Unité d'Habitation at Marseilles as the two most important buildings in post-war Europe.

A number of smaller buildings followed, based on the same principle of roofing in reinforced concrete which leaves the space below completely free; some are on a circular plan, such as the halls at Rome Lido and Chianciano Terme (1950–2). Sometimes Nervi works in conjunction with architects, but not always. In 1953 he planned a huge Sports Palace for Vienna on a circular plan, which carried his experience at Turin a stage further; it was not built, however, nor was a smaller, but equally impressive design for a hangar at Buenos Aires.

At the same time as the above works, Nervi was carrying out research on improved systems of reinforced concrete *prefabrication, using small ferroconcrete moulds for on-site manufacture, in conjunction with a movable type of staging patented by

Pier Luigi Nervi. Aircraft hangar. 1935

Pier Luigi Nervi. Exhibition hall. Turin, 1948–9

Pier Luigi Nervi. Main Railway Station. Naples, 1954. Project

himself, Bartoli and Angeli. This device permitted a great variety of designs based on a ribbed structure, making de *Baudot's boldest and most utopian designs now seem capable of realization. Another important invention of Nervi's in the technical field is his system for the hydraulic pre-stressing of reinforced concrete. But none of these researches is an end in itself. The ever greater liberty which these technical improvements bestow, by making work simpler and quicker, has led Pier Luigi Nervi to deeper researches of another kind, e.g. on rhythm as an element of beauty, as may be seen in his design for the concourse building of the new Main Railway Station in Naples (1954), in the Palazzetto dello Sport in Rome (1957), and above all in the conference hall of the Unesco Building in Paris (1953–7, jointly with Breuer and Zehrfuss). (*Italy; *Shell structures)

With its overtones of barbaric monumentality reminiscent of some ancient temple, combined with extreme technical and aesthetic modernity, the Unesco Building is one of Nervi's most interesting structures, one of the most interesting examples, in fact, of recent European architecture generally. The system of 'strength through form' has contributed to produce this splendid result. Strength was in fact achieved by corrugating the surfaces, and Nervi has studied the principle on the corrugated surfaces of shellfish, insects and flower calixes; the magical perfection of infinite smallness in nature seems to be transferred with the same qualities of strength and beauty to his own works.

In the construction of the Pirelli Skyscraper in Milan (1958, with Gio *Ponti and the architects of his office), the principle on which its strength is based is derived from nature too, viz. from the example of a tree. This is the prototype of the building's sectional development, with its four main stanchions growing ever more slender towards the top, as might have been seen more clearly if a lighter cladding had been used. Nervi's creative mastery of structure may also be seen in the most recent projects for which he has acted as the engineer: in the sail-like roof of the exhibition hall for the Centre National des Industries in Paris (1955), in the circular exhibition building in Caracas (1956), and in the enormous columns, shaped like palm trees, of the Palazzo del Lavoro at Turin (1961).

Bibliography: Pier Luigi Nervi, *Arte o scienza del construire?*, Rome 1954; Pier Luigi Nervi, *El lenguaje arquitectonico*, Buenos Aires 1950; Pier Luigi Nervi, *Costruire correttamente*, Milan 1954; G. C. Argan, *Pier Luigi Nervi*, Milan 1955;

Pier Luigi Nervi and Annibale Vitellozzi. Palazzetto dello Sport. Rome, 1956–7

Jürgen Joedicke, *The Works of Pier Luigi Nervi*, London 1957; Ada Louise Huxtable, *Pier Luigi Nervi*, New York 1960; Ravensburg 1961; Pier Luigi Nervi, *Neue Struckturen*, Stuttgart 1963.

GIULIA VERONESI

Netherlands. Modern architecture in the Netherlands undoubtedly begins with H. P. *Berlage, whose classic work is the Amsterdam Stock Exchange, completed in 1903. His immediate predecessor and contemporary was P. J. H. *Cuijpers, who as a follower of the romantic school was an enthusiastic adherent of *Viollet-le-Duc. His numerous works, including the Rijksmuseum (1885) and main railway station (1889) in Amsterdam, mark the close of eclecticism, and the neo-Gothic phase in particular, in the Netherlands. Despite his predilection for this style and the French neo-Renaissance, Cuijpers too, like Berlage, helped to promote the trend back to an architecture based on craft traditions. Nearly all the Dutch practitioners of arts and crafts around the year 1900 were graduates from Cuijpers's studio. From that time onwards, we can speak of a 'school of Berlage' also often referred to at the time as the Amsterdam School.

For the younger generation, Berlage was the leading personality of his time in the fields of art, architecture and handicrafts. His many lectures and articles exerted great influence. Breaking completely free from the eclecticism of the 19th century, he took as his starting point a consideration of the demands of reason and logic in the use of materials and in structure. As reinforced concrete was virtually unknown as an architectural medium at this time, he chose to work in brick. In his later works, however, he made an equally 'logical and honest' use of concrete.

Around 1910, a diametrically opposite movement began in Dutch architecture; its leading figure became Michael de *Klerk (1884–1923) together with P. L. Kramer and M. van der Mey. The best known example of this new *Amsterdam School is the Marine Terminus Building in Amsterdam (1914). This trend was basically anti-Berlage: individual artistic design was seen as the highest goal, and personal idiosyncrasies of detail were

P. J. H. Cuijpers. Rijksmuseum. Amsterdam, 1885

Hendrik Petrus Berlage. Stock Exchange. Amsterdam, 1897–1903

Michael de Klerk. Eigen Haard flats. Amsterdam, 1921

realized, where necessary, at the cost of logical construction and the right use of materials.

This period, which lasted from about 1912 to 1926, is characterized by a form of *Expressionism, comparable to that which was developing in *Germany; international interest was drawn to Dutch architecture, and to the new housing in Amsterdam in particular. A typical Expressionist façade-architecture developed at this time, which left the real problems of modern mass-housing untouched. The new estates in South

Willem Marinus Dudok. Town Hall. Hilversum, 1928–30

Amsterdam built in the years around 1922 all exhibit the influence of this romantic school, which has become identified today with the name of de Klerk, undoubtedly an architect of great gifts. The influence spread into the provinces, where it was long active, leaving its mark on numberless second- and third-rate buildings. Even Berlage was not wholly immune from it as his flats on the Mercatorplein in West Amsterdam show.

A new tendency emerged with the founding of De *Stijl, which set itself against both the unaffected outlook of Berlage and the romantic architecture of de Klerk and his circle. A violent struggle ensued, which led to the ultimate defeat of the romantic cause. In addition to J. J. P. *Oud, De Stijl attracted to its side such figures as Robert van't Hoff, Jan Wils and Gerrit Thomas *Rietveld. It was chiefly concerned with basic problems of space and colour. In principle, colour has no 'additional' decorative function, but acts rather as a space-moulding element. In practice, however, it turned out that spatial and decorative functions often overlapped.

After his break with van *Doesburg, Oud went his own way, while still adhering to De Stijl ideology, and became a leading figure in *Functionalism. His circle included J.B. van Loghem. J. A. Brinkman and L. C. van der *Vlugt, B. Bijvoet, J. *Duiker, Cor van *Eesteren, B. Merkelbach, Ch. J. F. Karsten, Rietveld, Mart Stam, J. G. Wiebinga, Jan Wils and B. Groenewegen. This powerful upsurge of functionalism again focused the attention of the architectural world on Holland, while simultaneously marking the end of the romantic Amsterdam School. The platform for functionalism was provided by the controversial journal *De 8 en Opbouw*, in whose pages the advanced spirits of Amsterdam and Rotterdam made common cause. It stood in opposition to the ethically and aesthetically orientated journal **Wendingen*. The fact that, since 1912, every new building in Holland required the official approval of a 'vetting' committee, explains why it took till 1930–2 for a pioneer building such as Duiker's open-air school in the Cliostraat, Amsterdam to get built, and then only in the face of numerous protests from the experts.

A completely independent part was played by Willem Marinus *Dudok. Though showing himself an admirer of Berlage in his early works, he gradually developed an extremely personal style, of which Hilversum Town Hall (1928–30) is a typical example. The 'Dudok Style' found many imitators in Holland up to about 1935, especially in the provinces.
Another turning point in Dutch architecture was reached in 1925, with the appointment of Professor G. M. Granpré Molière to Delft Technical College. His philosophy and system of aesthetics, based on the Roman Catholic religion, made a strong appeal to many students. The first building to appear which bore his stamp was the Town Hall at Enschede (1933) by his pupil G. Friedhoff; it also shows Scandinavian influence. With the professor from Delft, Dutch architecture became subject to ever more philosophical considerations. Granpré Molière was opposed to a so-called technical and materialistic outlook. He was against the undermining of religion, and against functionalism and humanism, which he considered the common denominator of everything Oud and his circle stood for. In the pre-war atmosphere of political unrest and increasing malaise towards the tendencies of modern culture and technology, the Delft theories fell upon fertile ground.
The School of Delft, which was historically orientated, especially in regard to church building and town planning, seemed to dominate Dutch architecture until about 1955. Architects and town planners from this group were entrusted with the reconstruction of bombed cities during and after the Second World War. Functionalism and De Stijl seemed to be played out. Granpré Molière exerted particular influence on the development of Dutch church architecture, and not only amongst his fellow-Catholics, but on Protestant architects, too. The character of the Delft School was chiefly determined by the real or supposed tradition of Dutch building, and the maintenance and romantic perpetuation of craftwork in the manner of Berlage. This led to the evocation of great interest in comparable architectural trends in the Scandinavian countries and Germany (Tessenow, *Muthesius). Four years of German occupation also naturally left their mark.

Johannes Andreas Brinkman and L.C. van der Vlugt. Van Nelle tobacco factory. Rotterdam, 1928–9

J. H. van den Broek and Jacob B. Bakema. Lijnbaan pedestrian precinct. Rotterdam, 1953

The situation changed around 1950. It was in particular the badly damaged city of Rotterdam that led the way. The traditional type of reconstruction scheme that had been originally planned was abandoned and a new one adopted. Rotterdam became a centre of architectural and town-planning activity, thanks chiefly to the work of van den *Broek and *Bakema. The former was appointed professor at Delft Technical College in 1948. He and Bakema challenged the concepts of the Delft School, and in this they were supported by Oud and a small group of fellow spirits. Functionalism began to develop again, but it was of a clearly different type from that which had flourished from 1925 to 1935. In Amsterdam itself however, few buildings of note have been erected, save for the large town extension schemes in West Amsterdam. A scheme for a new town hall by the architects Berghoef and Vegter encountered stiff opposition both from the profession and the public. The two architects were convinced disciples of Granpré Molière.

Aldo van Eijck. Municipal Orphanage. Amsterdam, 1955

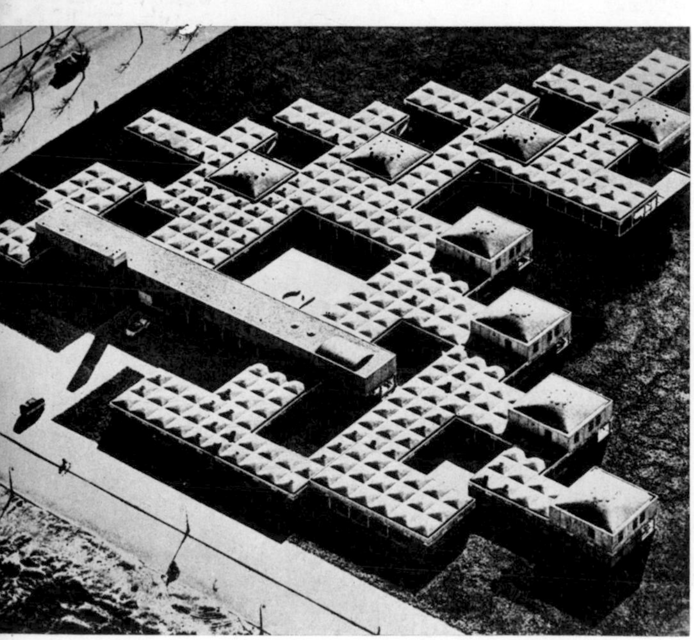

The general impression made by Dutch architecture a few years after the Second World War was chiefly one of diversity and vigour. The works of architects in Sweden, Italy and North and South America (*Breuer, *Gropius, *Mies van der Rohe) were making their influence felt, as was the ever-increasing number of publications. The *CIAM idea was revived, and its meaning for our time was critically reassessed. The desperate housing shortage focused particular interest on this sphere of building. The well-nigh impregnable bastion of the romantic Delft School was being progressively undermined in practice. After *c.* 1955 even its most zealous adherents became converted—some hesitantly, others out and out—to a new and in many respects modern form of functionalism. A comparison of the highly ornate Provincial Authority Headquarters at Arnhem (1955) with the Town Hall at Groningen (1961), both by J. J. M. Vegter, illustrates this change. Delft School concepts held out longest in the sphere of Catholic church building, especially in the predominantly Catholic provinces of North Brabant and Limburg, in the south, where the so-called 'Hertogenbosch School' clung on to the North Italian type of Early Christian basilica. But here too, in Catholic, lay, and architectural circles, loud protests have been voiced against this trend, and attempts are being made to exploit new methods, as in Protestant church architecture, where reinforced concrete is no longer rejected out of hand as an ignoble material.

By the side of good contemporary design, a vast amount of building has gone up in what is no more or less than bread-and-butter modern. This is especially the case with housing. The few notable figures include van den Broek, Bakema and later, Aldo van *Eijck; Rietveld's work is greatly admired by most of the younger generation. Dissatisfaction with CIAM's doctrinaire outlook led to the setting up of Team X, whose views have been appearing in the Dutch press since 1959, especially in the journal *Forum*, and have given rise to sharp controversy. 'Architecture is the three-dimensional expression of human behaviour' (Bakema).

An attempt to carry some new ideas into effect may be seen in the Municipal Orphanage, Amsterdam (1955), by Aldo van Eijck. The transitions from exterior to interior, and the spatial relationships of this building make it one of the most important of its time. Van Eijck and his circle have been able to realize their theories to a certain extent in planning for the village of Nagele, in the south-east Polder. Van den Broek and Bakema's proposals for the Kennemerland region of Noord-Holland also herald some new developments in the field of town planning. The same architects' design for a civic centre at Marl, currently under construction, will no doubt give ample expression to the new theories of the *Forum* group.

Bibliography: J. P. Mieras and F. R. Yerbury, *Dutch Architecture in the 20th Century*, London 1926; J. J. Vriend, *Nieuwere Architectuur* Amsterdam 1957; J. J. Vriend, *Reflexen*, Amsterdam 1958; J. J. Vriend, *Algemeen Overzicht Architectuur van deze eeuw*, Amsterdam 1959; G. M. Granpré Molière, *Woorden en Werken*, 1949; H. L. C. Jaffé, *De Stijl 1917–31. The Dutch Contribution to Modern Art*, Armsterdam 1956; R. Blijstra, *Netherlands Architecture since 1900*, Amsterdam 1960.

J. J. VRIEND

Neutra, Richard Joseph, b. Vienna 1892. Neutra was trained at the Technische Hochschule, Vienna, receiving his diploma in 1917. He met Adolf *Loos in 1910 and was influenced by the elder architect's work (e.g. the Steiner House, 1910), by his strictures against the use of ornament in architecture and by his admiration for American design (which Loos knew at first hand from a stay in the USA in 1893–6). Neutra was also impressed with the novel character of Otto *Wagner's Vienna subway entrances, dating from before 1900.

Richard Neutra. Lovell House. Los Angeles, 1927–9

Richard Neutra. Sidney Kahn House. San Francisco, 1940

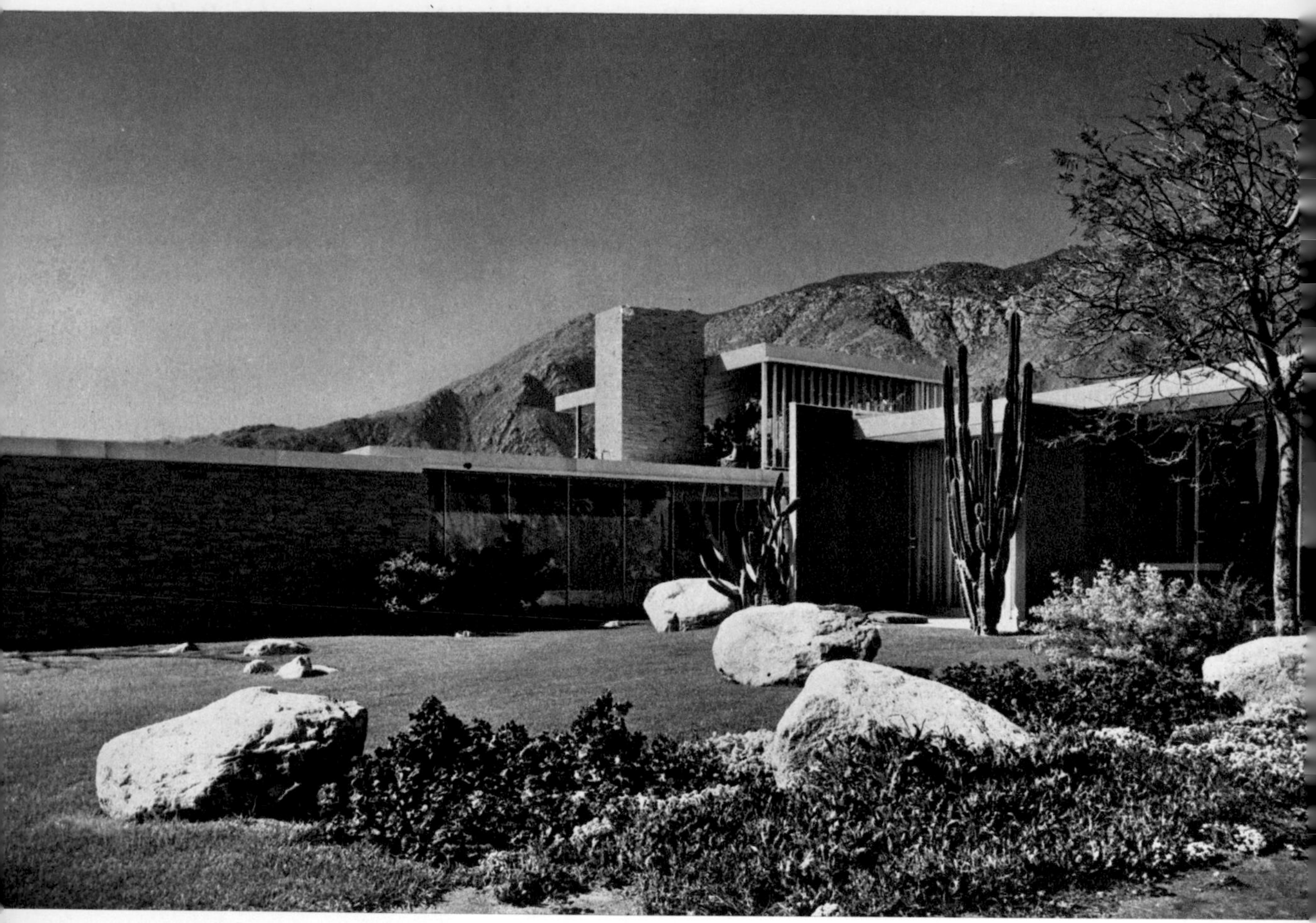

Richard Neutra. Kaufmann Desert House. Palm Springs, Cal., 1946–7

In 1911 his interest in American architecture was broadened through the discovery of the work of Frank Lloyd *Wright which had just been extensively published in Europe. Many of the motifs that dominate Neutra's architecture today, a half-century later, can be traced to this familiar and influential source.

Immediately after the First World War Neutra worked in Switzerland, gaining experience in the fields of landscape and city planning. Employed in the Municipal Building Office, Lukenwalde, Germany, in 1921, he subsequently became associated with Erich *Mendelsohn in 1922. The following year Mendelsohn and Neutra were awarded a First Prize for a Business Centre in Haifa. Neutra moved to the USA in 1923, and for the next few years he worked alternately in Chicago, with the large commercial firm of *Holabird and Roche, and at Taliesin, Spring Green, Wisconsin, with Frank Lloyd Wright. In 1926 he settled in Los Angeles, beginning his practice in the office of another Vienna-born architect, Rudolph *Schindler.

Schindler had been an assistant of Wright in the construction of several houses in Los Angeles in the early 1920s, and in 1926 was building the concrete-framed Lovell House, Newport Beach, in a striking, liberated style reflecting his origins, both in the proto-*International Style of Central Europe and in the more romantic architecture of Wright. In 1927 Schindler and Neutra collaborated in a project for the League of Nations competition.

Under these several influences Neutra's personal style rapidly came into focus in the late 1920s. The key work in his early maturity was the rambling, quasi-picturesque Lovell House (1927–9) built for Schindler's former client on a steep, challenging Los Angeles hillside site. A contemporary (albeit geographically isolated) of *Le Corbusier's noted Villa Stein, Garches, France, and *Mies van der Rohe's Barcelona Pavilion, Neutra's steel-framed Lovell House, with its slabs and balconies supported from above by steel cables, differs in certain structural details from these European masterworks, but is stylistically identical in terms of its thin, weightless forms which only partly enclose a series of fluidly juxtaposed interior spaces. Neutra developed and expanded this International Style into a more pronounced personal idiom throughout the 1930s in such houses as the one built for Josef von Sternberg, San Fernando Valley (1936), and these simple forms were often realized in novel or unusual materials. Always interested in large-scale planning, with implications of social welfare, Neutra found a wartime opportunity in the Channel Heights Housing Project, San Pedro, California (1942–4), where out of necessity redwood was substituted for the more familiar materials of the machine age. At the same time he worked on numerous projects for schools and health centres in Puerto Rico.

The apogee of Neutra's career occurs in the immediate post-war era with the construction of the Kaufmann Desert House, Palm Springs (1946–7), and the Tremaine House, Santa Barbara (1947–8). Here the elegant restatements of the by now traditional International Style themes reach a degree of elegance and precision that is not present in the earlier work, and these features are further enhanced by sensitive siting and landscaping. In 1949, with an expanding practice, he formed a partnership with Robert E. Alexander. Since that time domestic work has had to vie with more sizeable projects in Neutra's *œuvre*. While his houses of the 1950s have almost invariably maintained the suavity of those of the 1940s, the designs have tended towards the rhetorical in their repetition of earlier motifs. In general, in the most recent phase of his career, Neutra's customarily sensitive works have appeared to have less and less relevance with the constantly changing direction and interest that is to be found in the main stream of building design in the late 1950s and early 1960s.

Bibliography: Richard Neutra, *Survival through Design*, New York 1954; W. Boesiger, *Richard Neutra, 1950–60, Buildings and Projects*, Zurich 1959; Esther McCoy, *Richard Neutra*, Ravensburg 1962.

JOHN M. JACOBUS, JR

Niemeyer, Oscar, b. Rio de Janeiro 1907. The leading exponent of modern architecture in *Brazil, by virtue of the extent, the scope and the character of his work, Oscar Niemeyer Soares Filho, as his name is written in full, has had a rich and varied career. He graduated in 1934 from the National School of Fine Arts, Rio, and a few years later stepped into a position of effective leadership when he succeeded Lúcio *Costa as the head of the design team for the new building of the Ministry of Education and Health. Since then he has always been in the front line of architectural development in Brazil, setting trends and opening up new avenues of plastic expression, as well as influencing students and fellow architects to a very noticeable degree.

Niemeyer himself was decisively influenced by *Le Corbusier, with whom he worked on the design for the Ministry of Education and Health during the master's short stay in Brazil, in 1936. He began by applying Le Corbusier's basic ideas, as in the Day Nursery, Rio de Janeiro (1937). Very soon, however, he branched out in a personal direction, adding to such ideas an element of adaptation to local conditions, an imaginative and creative exuberance, and a typical lightness of touch, which to this day distinguishes all his work, even when it is apparently massive or heavier than usual.

Disregarding the tenets of orthodox *Functionalism whenever they seemed to him to run counter to the ideal of architecture as a great art of expression and of social purport, Niemeyer has consistently striven for beauty and harmony, grace and elegance in an enriched formal vocabulary as the legitimate goals of architectural creation in opposition to merely technical and functional refinements. Unafraid of the curved line, for which he found good precedent in Brazilian Baroque architecture, Niemeyer has used it with an instinctive lyrical touch and an uninhibited spontaneity throughout his career—free-flowing and seemingly arbitrary in the earlier phases, subtly distilled and sophisticated in his later work, where conciseness of expression is equally

Oscar Niemeyer. Yacht Club. Pampulha, 1943

stressed in the straight and in the curved lines of the composition. This use of the curved line, however, is but one aspect of Niemeyer's most characteristic contribution to modern architecture, his genuine inventiveness, always blossoming in beautifully expressive new forms, or in the revitalized use of consecrated ones. In this connection, his collaboration with numerous structural designers must be mentioned, starting with Emilio Baumgart in the early days and reaching supreme fulfilment with Joaquim Cardoso, from Pampulha to Brasilia.

Oscar Niemeyer, Zenon Lotufo, Helio Uchôa and Eduardo Kneese de Mello. Palace of Industry, Ibirapuéra Park, São Paulo, 1951–4

The extent and variety of Niemeyer's significant work, both the executed jobs and the relatively fewer unrealized projects, defeat any attempt to shorten their list. If four larger ones may be thought to highlight Niemeyer's career—Pampulha (1942), São José dos Campos (1947), Ibirapuéra (1950–4), and Brasilia (1956–61)—a great many others have to be taken into account in the intermediate periods. Prior to Pampulha, besides the Brazilian Pavilion at the New York World's Fair in 1939, with Lúcio Costa, three others must be noted: the Hotel Ouro Preto (1940); the architect's own house in Rio (1942); and his competition design for the National Stadium (1941); the first for its fusion of old and new in the traditional setting of the colonial town, the second for its open interior plan, on three levels, and its pioneering use of an inside ramp, the third as a first example of large-scale planning.

The Pampulha group of buildings, famous for its display of new forms, different yet kindred, its gay interplay of light and shade and its deliberate integration of architecture with painting and sculpture—the Casino with the ovoid prism well joined to the crisply rectangular block, the circular Dance Hall with its freely flowing marquee, the Yacht Club with its inverted double slope roof, and the St Francis Chapel with its several parabolic domes—also marks the beginning of the close collaboration between Niemeyer and Juscelino

Kubitschek, then Mayor of the City, later Governor of the State, of Minas Gerais, and finally, as President of the Republic, the creator of Brasilia.

The period from 1942 to 1947, to which belong the Boavista Bank, Rio (1946), distinguished by its unassuming openness and its light undulating glass-brick wall in the main banking hall, the Municipal Theatre in Belo Horizonte and the Cataguazes Academy for Boys (1946), as well as the Peixoto residence (1943), is important because of a number of projects which, though never carried out, led Niemeyer into an intensive study of residential architecture. He discovered new possibilities in the interplay of volumes, planes and levels, and better relationships with the site and the view. These conceptions were realized in the Staff Housing units for the São José dos Campos Aeronautical Technical Centre (1947), built as part of an overall scheme which had won first prize in a competition. Later in 1947 Niemeyer joined the international team entrusted with the design of the United Nations' Headquarters in New York, strongly influencing the final scheme, derived from Le Corbusier's and Niemeyer's proposed solutions.

Oscar Niemeyer. Sul America Hospital. Rio de Janeiro, 1953

Then follow a series of projects exploring the use of reinforced concrete in the development of complex curved surfaces, such as the twin-theatre Annexe for the Ministry of Education and Health esplanade (1948), the proposed shell-like dome for a monument to Rui Barbosa (1949), or

Oscar Niemeyer. President's Palace, Brasilia, completed 1959

the Duchen Factory (1950, with Helio Uchôa), a 300-metre-long block dramatized by a row of double-span curved rigid frames, spaced 10 metres apart, carrying a roof slab designed to improve the distribution of light; and several equally important jobs emphasizing the possibilities of long straight lines, in wide overhangs or in variously designed sloping supports, as in both the Club and the School at Diamantina (1951), or in the Governor Kubitschek Building in Belo Horizonte (1951), a huge apartment unit complex of two tall simple towers contrasting with the flowing lines of the supporting single storey, which covers almost two city blocks.

All this led to the Parque Ibirapuéra exhibition buildings for the Fourth Centennial of the City of São Paulo, a rare instance of integrated planning of a group of permanent fair buildings over a wide area. Niemeyer unified the scheme by the spreading irregular marquee which links the various blocks to each other; two low ones, 140 metres long, Palace of Nations and Palace of States, with their tilted concrete brackets; the three-storey Palace of Industry, 250 metres long, with its various interior levels capriciously silhouetted by the outline of the mezzanine slab; and the dome-like Palace of the Arts, with its spectacular and almost surrealist interior. All these were designed in 1951 (with Zenon Lotufo, Helio Uchôa and Eduardo Kneese de Mello as associate architects, Gauss Estellita and Carlos Lemos as collaborators).

The sweep and imaginativeness of the Ibirapuéra job, dramatizing and stressing the simplicity of the scheme and of the general concept, in contrast to the hodgepodge usually found in exhibition grounds, seems an appropriate stepping-stone for Niemeyer's crowning achievement, the design of the main public buildings of Brasilia (1950–60). In the intervening

Oscar Niemeyer. Museum with Congress Building in the background. Brasilia, completed 1960

period he is working on the Sul America Hospital (1953); his own house at Gavea (1953), a leaf-like slab inserted in a gorgeous sub-tropical site; the High School at Belo Horizonte (1954), with its striking eye-like auditorium; a project for a museum at Caracas in the form of an inverted pyramid (1954); and an apartment building in the Hansa district of Berlin (1955).
In Brasilia, however, where he was given the task of designing all the main public buildings, Niemeyer was able not only to express the symbolic content of each job and of the whole, implicit in Lúcio Costa's sophisticated general plan, but also to achieve it within a restrained vocabulary, in which poetic flights of imagination, severely disciplined, only highlight, where the artist considers necessary, the particular significance of one or another element in the general context: for example, the beautiful colonnade of the Palace of Dawn, an original theme whose variations may be found in the Supreme Court Building or in the Highland Palace; the startling flower-like design for the Cathedral; the concave and convex dome of the Congress Building in contrast to the soaring twin towers and the horizontal expanse of the base block; farther away, the truncated pyramid of the Opera House; all of them unforgettable accents underlining, against the backdrop of Brasilia's wide horizon, the essential quietness, the coherent simplicity and dignity of all the other architectural elements.
Bibliography: Oscar Niemeyer, *Minha Experiencia em Brasilia*, Rio de Janeiro 1961; Stamo Papadaki, *The Work of Oscar Niemeyer*, New York 1950; Stamo Papadaki, *Oscar Niemeyer—Works in Progress*, New York 1956; Stamo Papadaki, *Oscar Niemeyer*, Ravensburg 1962. Also most of the issues of *Modulo*, which document Niemeyer's later work, especially with regard to Brasilia.

HENRIQUE E. MINDLIN

Nizzoli, Marcello, b. Boretto, Reggio Emilia 1895. Architect, painter and designer. Housing at Ivrea (together with Annibale *Fiocchi and Mario Oliveri), Palazzo Olivetti in Milan (together with Gian Antonio Bernasconi and Annibale Fiocchi, 1954). (*Curtain Wall; *Italy)

Nowicki, Matthew, b. 1910, d. 1949 in a plane crash on the way from India to the United States. He was the architect of the arena at Raleigh, N.C. (completed 1952–3), together with *Deitrick and Severud. Together with Albert Mayer, he produced the first town plan for the new capital of the Punjab, Chandigarh, but this was not executed. (*Suspended Roofs)

Noyes, Eliot, b. Boston 1910. Architect and designer. Studied at Harvard Graduate School of Architecture, latterly under *Gropius and *Breuer. Sometime director of the Department of International Design at the Museum of Modern Art. His balloon house at Hobe Sound, Florida, was made by spraying concrete on an immense inflated balloon, to produce a hemispherical shell.

O'Gorman, Juan, b. Coyoacán, Mexico 1905. Pupil of José *Villagrán García. His private houses at San Angel (1929–30) are amongst *Mexico's first buildings in the *International Style. Mosaics on the University Library, Mexico, 1952. O'Gorman's own house, a fantastic dream castle in a mannered style, takes advantage of a natural grotto in the rocks.

Olbrich, Joseph Maria, b. Troppau 1867, d. Düsseldorf 1908. Architecture, arts and crafts, book design. Pupil of Otto *Wagner,

Joseph Maria Olbrich. Hochzeitsturm. Darmstadt, 1907

co-founder of the Vienna Sezession, whose exhibition building he designed in 1898–9. Olbrich was the architect of nearly all the buildings for the exhibitions on the Mathildenhöhe in Darmstadt. His Hochzeitsturm ('Wedding Tower') at Darmstadt (1907) is one of the most distinguished pieces of civic adornment in modern architecture. (*p. 12)

Organic Architecture. That architecture should in its appearance have a character similar to a natural organism and give the same impression of unity has actuated the work of some of the most important architects of the age, of whom Henry van de *Velde and Erich *Mendelsohn are notable examples in Europe and Louis *Sullivan and Frank Lloyd *Wright in America.

Different theories of organic architecture have been advanced and there is some confused thinking on the subject. It is therefore important to try to dispel this confusion. Some writers have confused the idea of organic architecture with functional building according to social needs, so that if a house is designed in stages according to changing needs, rooms being added as the family grows, that is regarded as organic. It might be regarded as organic building for social needs, but it is too simple and elemental an idea to cover the meaning of organic architecture as conceived by the famous architects mentioned and by others who have been influenced by the idea.

The theory derives from ancient Greek and Roman architecture, and was further developed during the Renaissance. The Greeks based the proportions that should determine the design of temples on the proportions of the human figure. This is recorded and developed by Vitruvius, and many artists of the Renaissance inevitably adopted the theory. Vasari remarked that architecture must appear organic like the body, and Michelangelo held that a knowledge of the human figure led to a comprehension of architecture. Later writers have

Alvar Aalto. Aalto House. Helsinki, 1935–6

Erich Mendelsohn. Synagogue. Cleveland, O., 1946–1952. Model

Frank Lloyd Wright. Jacobs House. Middleton, Wis., 1948

seen in the theory of *Einfühlung*, whereby bodily feelings are projected into the forms of a building, the basis of a modern theory of organic architecture. Although there is a kinship between the two they are not identical. One is the recognition that our bodily existence and bodily feelings must be the measure of the world around us, the other is the application of the principles of that organic life to design.

The nature of organic structure indicates these principles. We find in all natural organisms a certain harmony of parts in relation to the whole which appears to be conditioned by the work the organism is designed to perform, and we find in nature that the plan of an organism influences the character of the subordinate organisms. Transferred to a building this means the integration of the parts with the whole, so that the design of the whole controls the design of the subordinate parts. In addition it would appear to mean that the forms of a building integrated into an harmonious whole shall express a purpose similar to the conditioning of the forms of an organism by the work it is created to perform. This purpose may be to express the structure, such as emphasis on the lines of stress, of thrust and support, and in this there is again the link with *Einfühlung*. The application could not legitimately be extended further to include the social purpose of the building, for this enters the realms of symbolism and departs from the physical context of organic architecture.

We find the theory controlling the work of many modern architects. It was a consistent aim with van de Velde and Mendelsohn, and the latter was pleased when Einstein remarked of his Observatory building at Potsdam that it was Organic. Most architects who are guided by the theory of organic unity do not limit it to the building but insist that the building should be a unity with its surroundings, especially with the site, with the earth on which it stands. Frank Lloyd Wright was especially insistent on this, and he said that a building should not be *on* a hill, but *of* a hill, that it should appear to grow out of the earth. With domestic architecture he said that house and garden should be one, and that it should be difficult to discern where the house ends and the garden begins, a characteristic found in much Japanese architecture. Mendelsohn in many of his buildings let the contours of the ground control the design of his buildings. In brief, organic architecture is not only the complete harmony of the parts of a building with the whole but an integration of the building with its site and surroundings. In a theory of organic architecture, building and town planning should conform to the unity, to the integration of parts, found in the natural world.

Bibliography: Walter Curt Behrendt, *Modern Building*, London 1937; Frank Lloyd Wright, *An Organic Architecture—The Architecture of Democracy*, London 1939; Bruno Zevi, *Towards an Organic Architecture*, London 1950.

ARNOLD WHITTICK

Otto, Frei, b. Siegmar near Chemnitz 1925. Designs for suspended roofs and inflated plastic structures. Marquees at the Federal Flower Shows in Kassel (1955) and Cologne (1957).

Bibliography: Frei Otto, *Über zugbeanspruchte Konstruktionen*, Berlin 1962.

Oud, Jacobus Johannes Pieter, b. Purmerend 1890, d. 1963. Oud received his education at the Quellinus School, the State School of Draughtsmanship in Amsterdam, and Delft Technical College, which awarded him an honorary doctorate after the Second World War. He worked for the architects Jan Stuijt and Theodor *Fischer in Munich for a time, and

Jacobus Johannes Pieter Oud. Workers' housing estate. Hook of Holland, 1924

Jacobus Johannes Pieter Oud. Shell Building. The Hague, 1938

became City Architect of Rotterdam in 1918, where he was responsible for the Spangen and Tussendijken housing estates (1920). Oud played a leading part in the development of *Functionalism in Western Europe, from the stage of *Neue Sachlichkeit* to the emergence of the *International Style (*p. 14).

Round about the year 1916, Oud came into contact with Theo van *Doesburg, and was an active participant in the new De *Stijl movement. Like most of his generation, Oud was a great admirer of *Berlage, as his early works clearly show. Berlage's honest handling of materials and structure was to influence Oud's functionalist architecture strongly, despite its complete difference of form. Oud was faced with the difficult task of translating De Stijl's often all too theoretical ideas into practical building terms. Examples of his De-Stijl-type architecture include the Café de Unie in Rotterdam (1924–5, destroyed 1940), a project for terraced housing on the promenade at Scheveningen (1917), and a design for a factory at Purmerend (1919). After a few years, Oud broke with van Doesburg, who laid too much stress on the rôle of abstract painting in modern architecture. The housing schemes at Oud-Mathenesse (1922), Hook of Holland (1924–7) and Kiefhoek, Rotterdam (1925–7) demonstrate the transition to *Neue Sachlichkeit*. From about 1935 onwards, Oud renounced the strictly functionalist style (Shell Building, The Hague, 1938, and several post-war office blocks in Rotterdam). This defection drew on him some sharp criticism, which still affects the estimation of his *oeuvre*. His competition design for the South Holland Local Government offices at the Hague (1952, not premiated), and more recent buildings such as the Bio-Children's Convalescent Home near Arnhem (1952–60), demonstrate, however, that the Shell Building belongs to a transitional period influenced by the general tension in Europe on the eve of the Second World War. The same malaise in orthodox Functionalism, albeit differently manifested, is clearly implied in the developments of the last ten years (*CIAM, Otterlo, 1959).

In his book *Mijn Weg in De Stijl* (1961) Oud wrote: 'The desire for abstraction requires melody. Pure abstraction is like religion without humanity. Humanity means living in the flowing continuum of daily existence. The flow and rhythm of daily existence demand melody from architecture.'

Bibliography: J. J. P. Oud, *Holländische Architektur* (Bauhausbücher 10), Munich 1926; J. J. Pieter Oud, *Mijn Weg in De Stijl*, Rotterdam 1961; Henry-Russell Hitchcock, *J. J. P. Oud*, Paris 1931; Giulia Veronesi, *J. J. Pieter Oud*, Milan 1953.

J. J. VRIEND

Jacobus Johannes Pieter Oud. Bio-Children's Convalescent Home near Arnhem, 1952–60

Paxton, Joseph, b. Milton-Bryant, Bedfordshire 1803, d. Sydenham 1865. A farmer's son, Paxton was trained as a gardener and became head gardener to the Sixth Duke of Devonshire at Chatsworth, Derbyshire, in 1826. Subsequently he became the Duke's land-agent, business adviser and friend. Paxton had no training as an engineer or architect, but had a gift for shrewd observation and deduction; he proceeded empirically in all his ventures, which stemmed from his own knowledge of natural phenomena.

Paxton had started experimenting with horticultural building at Chatsworth in 1828, and in 1831 hit upon the idea of the 'ridge and furrow' roof. This was refined in detail to become a sloping glass roof without rafters, with very light sash-bars and with the Paxton gutter, which collected both internal and external moisture as well as being a structural member. This roofing was entirely of wood and glass, the wooden parts being produced by machinery which Paxton himself had designed. Hollow cast-iron columns were introduced to support longer spans, serving also for drainage of the roofs. This principle was followed in the curvilinear Great Conservatory at Chatsworth (1836–40), the curved members being of laminated wood, the house being 277 feet long, 123 feet wide and 67 feet high. From curved roofs Paxton moved to a flat roofing system, still with ridges and furrows, for the Lily House of 1849. This was essentially the same system—except for a necessarily larger iron framework—as that used by Paxton in his design for the Great Exhibition Building of 1851, erected in concert with the contractors, Fox and Henderson, and the glass-maker R. L. Chance. This, the largest building ever erected up to that date, was a completely *prefabricated structure of standardized, mass-produced parts, based on a module of 24 feet, covering a ground area of over 770,000 square feet. The materials were used afterwards in the erection of the Crystal Palace at Sydenham (1852–4, destroyed by fire 1936), a more elaborate design with three arched transepts and a vaulted nave. Amongst other designs by Paxton for glass buildings were the projects for Crystal Palaces in New York and Paris, the latter being as long as the 1851 building but with three great circular domes in front (*p. 5).

Joseph Paxton, Crystal Palace. London, 1851

At the same time as he was developing his glass structures, Paxton was building conventional masonry houses in accepted styles, including the mansions of Mentmore, Buckinghamshire; Ferrières, near Paris; and Lismore Castle in Ireland. As a landscape architect he designed the grounds of the Crystal Palace, modified the gardens at Chatsworth and laid out a number of public parks, notably that at Birkenhead. He experimented successfully with hydraulic engineering, constructing the highest fountain jet in the world at Chatsworth,

Joseph Paxton. Crystal Palace. Sydenham, 1852–4

and in heating and ventilating. His interests as a railway promoter, contractor and Member of Parliament led him to advocate important town-planning schemes, of which the most important were the Thames Embankment (1864–70) and his project for the Great Victorian Way (1855). The latter was to be an eleven-mile-long 'girdle' around central London, to solve its traffic problems, combining a glass-roofed road lined by houses, shops and public buildings with railways on upper tiers.
Bibliography: Violet Markham, *Paxton and the Bachelor Duke*, London 1935; G. F. Chadwick, *The Works of Sir Joseph Paxton*, Architectural Press, London 1961.

G. F. CHADWICK

Pei, Ioh Ming, b. Canton, China 1917. Studied at the Massachusetts Institute of Technology and at Harvard. Office blocks, department stores, town planning projects. The Mile High Center at Denver, Col. (1956) has an attractive façade design featuring two intersecting systems: columns and beams with dark cast-aluminium cladding; the air conditioning ducts are sited behind strips of bright enamelling. Has worked on the development plans of Washington, Chicago and Philadelphia.

Auguste Perret. Apartment Block, Rue Franklin. Paris, 1903

Perret, Auguste, b. Brussels 1874, d. Paris 1954. Perret had his first architectural training at the Paris *École des Beaux-Arts, which he left, however, before sitting his finals. He entered his family's building firm, which had early specialized in reinforced concrete construction; the first building he himself designed dates already from the year 1890.
Perret is frequently reproached with having, on the one hand, applied reinforced concrete methods that were still in their infancy at the time of his first sensational buildings (apartment house in the Rue Franklin, Paris, 1903; Garage Ponthieu, Paris, 1906; Théâtre des Champs-Elysées, Paris, 1910–13) to a system of columns and beams taken over from carpentry, hence depriving architecture for decades to come of freedom in employing the new material. On the other hand it is said that in his old ago he grafted neoclassic features onto this monolithic material which were in no ways a logical outcome of its use (Mobilier National, Paris, 1931; Musée des Travaux Publics, 1937; atomic research station, Saclay, 1947; reconstruction of Le Havre). The reproach of neo-Academic formalism is justified as regards Perret's late work. His talent for structurally lucid design peters out into empty trifling. It can hardly be claimed, however, that Perret's early intervention in the history of reinforced concrete construction has had negative consequences. Not only did Perret make it possible to use *reinforced concrete in architecture, which none of his contemporaries succeeded in doing to the same extent, he was also the only one among the pioneers of modern architecture who did not simply preach 'honest building' but practised it as well. His system of columns and beams, the essence of the whole method of framed structures, accords exactly with the demand for economy of formwork. The fruit of his mature years displays a perfection of craftsmanship which is only to be encountered elsewhere in *Mies van der Rohe, who, incidentally, has not a little in common with Perret.
But Perret was not just a consummate structural designer who paved the way to architecture for reinforced concrete. His

consistent use of the material resulted in a number of buildings still considered exemplary today, among them that masterpiece of 20th-century architecture, the Church of Notre-Dame at Le Raincy (1922–23). There the neoclassicist Perret has paradoxically been successful—uniquely in his time—in reviving the Gothic church lunette. His numerous villas and studio-houses of the next decade are characterized by precision and delicacy of proportion and detailing. The sharp distinction made between framework and infill is raised to the point of dogma and leads to a new conception of form reminiscent of the purest creations of a Gabriel or *Schinkel. Thus both traditions of French rationalism are perpetuated in Perret's reinforced concrete style, that of the neo-Gothic, as significantly formulated by *Viollet-le-Duc, and that represented by the classicism of Perret's teacher Guadet.

The freest expression of Perret's structural genius is to be found in his industrial commissions where he is relieved of the frustrating task of achieving monumentality (warehouses at Casablanca, 1915; clothes factory and scene painting studio, Paris, 1919; workshops for steel or aluminium rolling mills at Montataire, 1920 and Issoire, 1939; watch factory at Besançon, 1939; aircraft hangar at Marseilles, 1950). Unhampered by decorative details, these purely functional buildings however lack those amazing effects achieved by *Maillart, *Nervi, or *Freyssinet through the use of novel structural shapes. And yet they have an elegance and dignity, attained by their unparalleled lucidity of construction and harmony of rhythm and proportion. Perret's industrial buildings, from the Garage Ponthieu to the marine laboratories on the Boulevard Victor, Paris (1928), like those by Saarinen and Mies, rank amongst the most important architectural efforts to stress the 'nobility of the industrial age'.

Finally, Perret's research into the standardization and industrialization of building components should be mentioned, which apart from anything else was not without influence on his sometime pupil *Le Corbusier.

Auguste Perret. Notre-Dame. Le Raincy, 1922–3

Bibliography: Auguste Perret, *Contribution à une Théorie de l'Architecture*, Paris 1952; P. Jamot, *A. et G. Perret et l'Architecture du Béton Armé*, Paris and Brussels 1927; Ernesto N. Rogers, *Auguste Perret*, Milan 1955; Bernard Champigneulle, *Auguste Perret*, Paris 1959; Peter Collins, *Concrete—The Vision of a New Architecture*, London 1959.

MAURICE BESSET

Auguste Perret. Place de l'Hôtel de Ville. Le Havre, commenced 1947

Hans Poelzig. Grosses Schauspielhaus. Berlin, 1919

Gio Ponti. Pirelli Building. Milan, 1958

Poelzig, Hans, b. Berlin 1869, d. Berlin 1936. Poelzig exerted great influence in Germany both as an architect and as a teacher (Professor at the Charlottenburg Technical College). His office building, Breslau 1911, anticipates the favourite motive of the twenties, fenestration in horizontal strips. Industrial buildings such as the Luban chemical factory near Posen (1911–12) and the water tower at Posen (1911) are the forerunners of Poelzig's Expressionist phase. His designs just after the First World War (Project for the Salzburg Festival Theatre, 1920–1) are of visionary imagination. The rebuilding of the Schumann Circus into Max Reinhardt's Grosses Schauspielhaus was based on these designs (Berlin 1919): a 'space-cave' masked by stalactite-shapes, which made acting on an arena stage feasible. Towards the end of the twenties, Poelzig went over to buildings of a monumental straightforwardness. (Administrative block for IG-Farben, Frankfort on the Main, 1928–31). (*Expressionism; *Steel)
Bibliography: Theodor Heuss, *Hans Poelzig, Lebensbild eines deutschen Baumeisters*, Tübingen 1955.

Polk, Willis Jefferson, b. near Frankfort, Kentucky 1867, d. San Mateo, Calif. 1924. Pupil of *Maybeck. The Hallidie Building (San Francisco, 1918) by Polk and Co. is one of the first buildings with a fully glazed, non-loadbearing outer wall (*curtain wall).

Pollini, Gino, b. Rovereto, Trentino 1903. Graduated Milan 1927. Founder-member of **gruppo* 7. Works in collaboration with Luigi *Figini. (*Italy)

Ponti, Gio, b. Milan 1891. Ponti is the best known Italian architect today. He graduated in Milan in 1921, and already had some professional experience when the foundation of the *Movimento Italiano per l'Architettura Razionale* in 1927 presented Italian architects with radically new problems and new responsibilities, at a period when the *Novecento Italiano's* neoclassic revivalism was triumphant.
In this current, which saw the end of *Futurism, Gio Ponti practised an elegant 'modernism', derived partly from the Viennese style of the time, mixed with neoclassic motifs and rationalist lucidity. In

Gio Ponti. Italian Institute. Stockholm, 1959

contrast to the other architects of his generation, who relied on the classical effects of arches and columns and took no account of the new developments in building technology, Ponti adhered in general to the tenets of the rationalist and functionalist school; but he stayed clear of the controversies, perilously conducted by Persico and Pagano, nor did he join the revolt of the younger architects (banded together as **gruppo* 7) against revivalism, the historic styles and the abuse of decoration.

Ponti founded the journal *Domus* in 1928. Now the most widely read publication in the field of interior decoration, it proved a very effective instrument at the time in improving the taste of the Italian middle classes. In 1933, before he had discarded his neoclassicist leanings, Ponti was appointed to the executive committee of the V Milan Triennale, then known as 'Ponti's Triennale'. Its great merit was that it opened the doors of this famous international exhibition to the young 'rationalists' of the Milanese avant-garde, who had now become the most representative architects of the modern movement. During these years Ponti did a good deal of work in the field of industrial design, to new criteria; built flats, churches and factories; and wrote articles and books (e.g. *La casa all'Italiana*, 1933) in which he put forward the viewpoint that architecture must always preserve some national characteristics.

Ponti's long series of buildings began in 1923. In 1934 he designed the Institute of Mathematics for the University of Rome; but it was only in 1936, with his scheme for the Catholic Press Exhibition in Vatican City, one of his happiest creations, that he gave up the strict symmetry and conventions of neoclassicism. Again in 1936 he designed the first office block for the Montecatini Company in Milan (the second dates from 1951), in which he combined *Novecento* elements (e.g. maximum plastic evidence of volumes) with others of the rationalist system of aesthetics. This imposing building remains one of his most important and lasting works. After a series of projects carried out in every part of the world save in Italy, from São Paulo to Caracas, and from Paris to Stockholm, he achieved his masterpiece in 1958 with the Pirelli Skyscraper in Milan (with *Nervi as structural engineer), whose outline is now universally familiar. This building, with its hexagonal plan and its sides tapered like a ship's bows, has affected the town planning layout of the whole surrounding zone, itself partly designed by the same architect.

Among the buildings he has currently under construction may be mentioned a new hospital for Milan, with an interesting surface treatment; two churches; offices for the Bagdad Planning Board; and eight ministry buildings for Islamabad, the new capital of Pakistan. Since 1936 Gio Ponti has lectured in the faculty of architecture at Milan Polytechnic, and has held courses in the Universities of São Paulo, Paris, Delft, Istanbul, Barcelona, Caracas, Zurich, Stockholm, Madrid and Gothenburg. He was the first president of the International Museum of Modern Architecture, founded in Milan in 1961.

Bibliography: Gio Ponti, *Amate l'Architettura*, Milan 1957; Edoardo Persico, 'Giovanni Ponti', in *L'Italia Letteraria 29*, April 1934; James S. Plaut, *Espressione di Gio Ponti*, Milan 1954.

GIULIA VERONESI

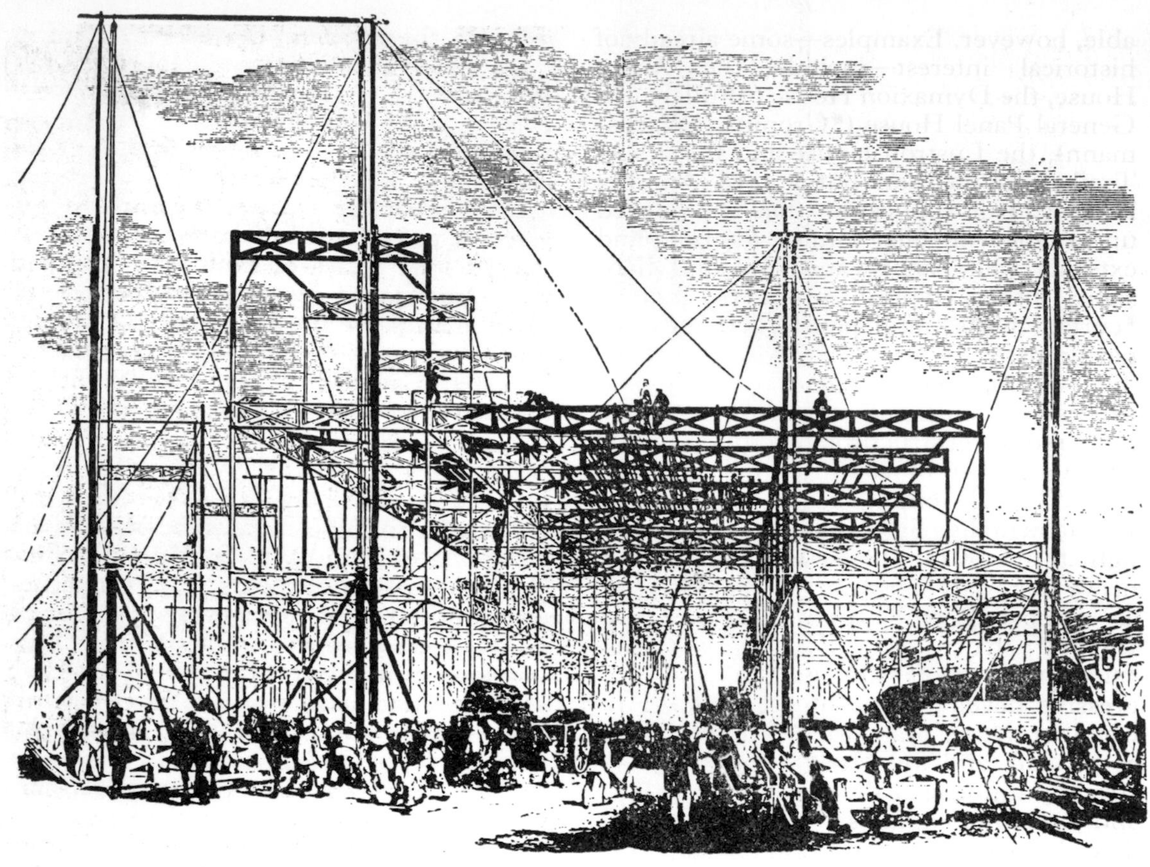

Joseph Paxton. Crystal Palace. London, 1851. Assembling prefabricated units

Powell and Moya. Philip Powell and John Hidalgo Moya. Studied at the Architectural Association School of Architecture, London, and founded their partnership in 1946, two years after graduating, to carry out the Pimlico Housing Scheme, London, which they had won in competition against sixty-four entrants with a design that proved a significant landmark in the attempt to establish a post-war vernacular. Vertical feature ('Skylon') at the South Bank Exhibition, London, 1951; Mayfield Comprehensive School, Putney, 1956, 'subtle, elegant, humane' (Ian Nairn); Princess Margaret Hospital, Swindon; undergraduates' rooms at Brasenose College, Oxford; hexagonal theatre with an arena stage, Chichester, 1962.

Prefabrication. Prefabrication is the attempt of modern building technology to increase building productivity. Many variations of this idea and its realization are feasible and are already being developed today. Even traditional building consists of a large number of parts previously fabricated in factories, but they rarely exhibit common principles of design, structure or manufacture. Besides raising productivity by the use of rationalization on the building site, the logical aim of prefabrication must be the factory-made building, turned out by industrial production techniques. The method still in use today of craft prefabrication is imperfect and must be supplemented by the complete interposition of industrial manufacturing processes. Entire dispensation with site work, however, is only possible in the case of smaller private houses (prefabricated houses). That is why the greatest efforts are being concentrated on turning out this type of building in factories.

These attempts to produce a prefabricated or even an industrially manufactured house have so far not evinced any conclusive results. Many prototypes and some production models of certain series are available, however. Examples—some already of historical interest—include the Acorn House, the Dymaxion House (*Fuller), the General Panel House (*Gropius, *Wachsmann), the Lustron House and the TVA-Trailer, to mention but a few. Another large field of application that has opened up is that of filler units, internal and external wall panels, and roof and floor slabs; other typical products include *curtain walls, infill panels and movable partitions.

The various materials and the industrial processes connected with them have rendered novel structural methods possible and a number of countries have already turned out some excellent products. Fundamentally light structural systems, light forms of building with light or even heavy materials show the greatest progress as compared with traditional building. Integral structures, *space frames and *suspended roofs are particularly progressive developments of this method of building. Other branches of industry, such as aircraft and vehicle production, have strongly influenced the ideas of architects and structural engineers.

The hazards of prefabrication and the industrial manufacture of buildings lie on the sociological plane. Heavy structural systems are particularly unsuitable as they lack adaptability to the multifarious natural patterns of population and their ways of living. That is why adaptability in building

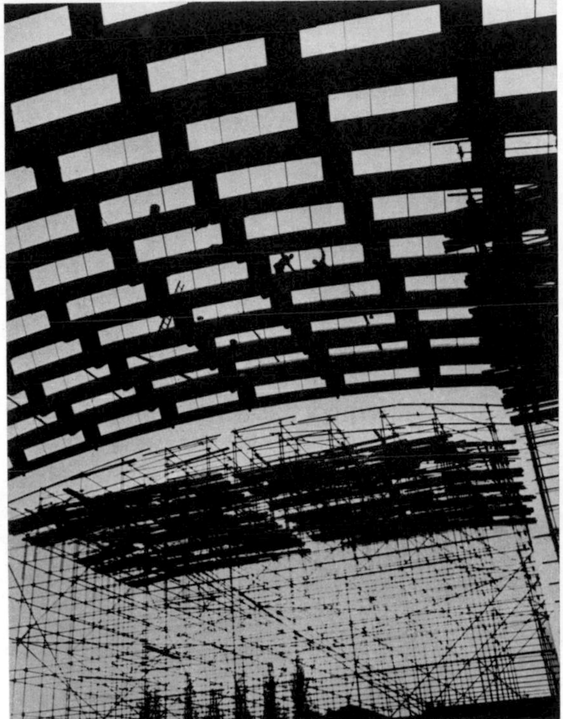

Pier Luigi Nervi. Exhibition hall, Turin, 1948–9. Erecting prefabricated reinforced concrete units from a mobile staging

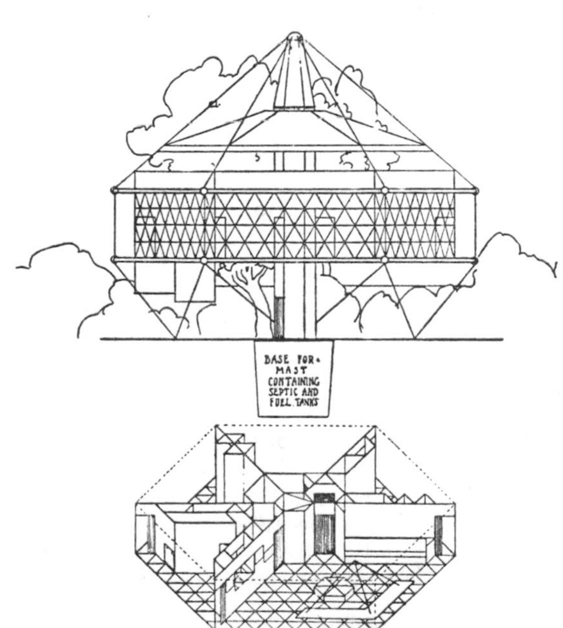

Below left. Richard Buckminster Fuller. Dymaxion House, 1927. Elevation and isometric view

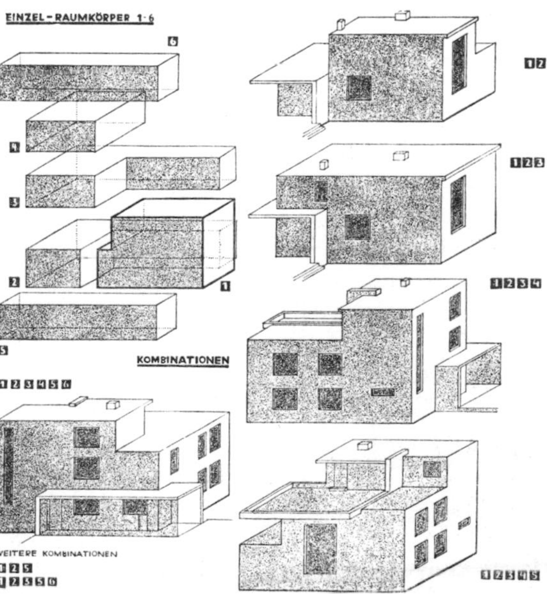

Walter Gropius. Type series house, with various methods of combining the individual components. 1923. Project

is given special consideration when prefabricated structures and components are designed: hence the emergence of 'building block' systems that can be combined to meet different circumstances, together with the reduction of the total number of building types, effected by standardization. Modular coordination, which has long been recognized as a prerequisite for rational manufacture and planning, has been introduced in many countries and is proving an indispensable rule in the design of these new building products.

The achievements of individual countries have been helped by the conscious co-operation of industry, government departments and large planning and construction teams. In the *United States, the mass-production of family houses has made great headway, while *curtain walling in particular has been developed for multi-storey buildings. In *Great Britain, after the Second World War, a systematic development of various methods of light prefabricated construction for school buildings has taken place, which have not only quickly solved a technological problem but have also made an indirect contribution to education for free and contemporary living. In *France, Scandinavia and the USSR likewise since the Second World War numerous prefabricated heavy structural systems, based on concrete units, have been devised for multi-storey blocks of flats. Examples, however, which are functional and economic in their countries of origin are not necessarily suitable for export elsewhere without modification. Another interesting development towards complete prefabrication has taken place, again in the United States. In 1960, for example, twice as many trailers, i.e. mobile houses, have been manufactured as prefabricated stationary houses. Thus for the first time we have a building completely prefabricated in the factory, from raw material to final assembly.

Kaija and Heikki Siren. Terraced housing on the Tapiola estate, 1954–5. Erecting a prefabricated façade unit

With the introduction of prefabrication and the aim of industrial manufacture the demands on architects, planners and engineers have risen. The traditional methods of architectural design are no longer sufficient. These new requirements and the increased responsibility that goes with them make it essential today to transfer the methods of applied science and industrial engineering to architecture. Architecture is thus becoming more and more of an applied science.

Bibliography: Buckminster Fuller, *Brief Building Construction*; Robert W. Marks, *The Dymaxion World of R. Buckminster Fuller*, New York 1960; Konrad Wachsmann, *Wendepunkt im Bauen*, Wiesbaden 1959.

HERBERT OHL

Prouvé, Jean, b. Nancy 1901. What Jean Prouvé, constructor in light metal, has in common with the great ironwork engineers of the 19th century, apart from a sure feeling for his material and a wealth of technical and design ideas, is a dynamic conception of the interplay of the different components and functions of a structure, regardless of whether he is designing a prefabricated façade element, a living unit, a school or a desk. Jean Prouvé is a son of the painter Victor Prouvé, who played a leading part in the École de Nancy, one of the most important centres of Art Nouveau. A trained art-metalworker, Prouvé tackles the formal problems of construction in the 'organic' spirit of this school. For him, form can develop only from a synthesis of all structural and functional components, which in their turn must be considered as parts of a unique constellation. At the same time he is fully aware that the road to the architecture of the future inevitably leads via the thoroughgoing industrialization of building methods, and that industrialization without sweeping standardization of forms is unthinkable.

Prouvé escapes this dilemma by an empirical attitude which abolishes all formalism. As early as 1934 he developed *curtain walling, which he employed in 1936 for a club house at Buc airport and in 1937–9 at the Maison du Peuple at Clichy (architects *Beaudouin and *Lods). But while this type of structure often becomes a purely graphic pattern, Prouvé has created a number of variants that constitute a series of very acceptable formal innovations, conceived from a need to achieve the best possible adaptation to particular technical and functional requirements: Building Industry Association Headquarters, Paris, 1950 (with Lopez); Exhibition Hall, Lille (with Herbé); CNIT Exhibition Hall, Paris (with *Zehrfuss, Camelot and de Mailly) and the French Pavilion at Brussels (with Gillet), 1958; block of flats, Paris, 1954 (with Mirabaud); hall for the *100 Years of Aluminium* exhibition in Paris, 1954; Technical College, Lyons (INSA with Perrin-Fayolle); Central Research Institute of Grenoble University, 1959. Prouvé considers that all building components, from roof slabs to built-in cupboards, and from the columns to the essential services (kitchen, bath, w.c.) can be factory-made, ready for assembly in the same way as façade units, and put into service structurally as well as functionally at the same time. As a result of decades of research, which led to the extensive redesigning of all these elements, Prouvé began to mass-produce prefabricated buildings of all types (houses, schools, offices, canteens, workshops, laboratories, holiday camps), among which the shell type houses (estate at Meudon, 1949), the Abbé Pierre House, the isothermal living quarters for Sahara conditions and the schools deserve special mention.

Jean and Henri Prouvé, André Sive. Experimental houses. Meudon, 1954

Despite the extreme economy of their method of production and their standardization, these buildings possess an almost luxurious character and retain a high degree of individuality. This is in contrast to the usual dreary monotony found in prefabricated buildings and recalls instead the affluent architecture of *Mies van der Rohe.

Jean Prouvé and Maurice Novarina. Refreshment room. Evian, completed 1957

Jean Prouvé, Belmont and Silvy. Point block of flats for lecturers, Cité Universitaire. Nancy. Project

The reason is not so much the precise finish and the carefully planned equipment but the feeling of freedom bestowed by the elegance of proportions and forms and the generous distribution of space. In some buildings (villas at Nancy and on the Côte d'Azur, school at Villejuif, refreshment room at Evian) Prouvé's artistry in structure reaches a point of perfection, where the building seems to be weightless. Although the shell of such buildings is exclusively of glass, they do not appear to be mere glass boxes. Tensile stresses which infuse the structural forms with a lively excitement, hinged stanchions with asymmetrically cantilevered arms, intersections which are not rectangular but acute or quite gradual, even with curved transitions, and finally a spatial flow which is never unnecessarily interrupted, all these combine to lend his buildings a clear, gay character which is unique in the architecture of today. These designs, which originated in the laboratory and the factory, have nothing artificial or schematic about them; on the contrary, they are alive and unfold with a surprising spontaneity, like organisms friendly to man.

Bibliography: Special issue of the journal *Architecture*, Nos. 11/12, Brussels 1954; Françoise Choay, 'Jean Prouvé' in *L'Oeil*, Vol. X, No. 46, Paris 1958; G. Gassiot-Talabot, 'Jean Prouvé' in *Cimaise*, Vols. VII-VIII, No. 54, Paris 1961.

MAURICE BESSET

Rainer, Roland, b. Klagenfurt 1910. Trained at the Vienna Technical College. Began teaching 1953; professor at the Vienna Academy of Fine Arts (1956). Since 1958 town planner at Vienna. Schools, housing (prefabricated housing estate for Vienna XIII, together with Auböck, 1954), municipal halls for Vienna (1954–8), and Bremen (under construction). (*Austria)

Reidy, Affonso Eduardo, b. Paris 1909. Reidy graduated at the Escola Nacional de Belas Artes, Rio, in 1930. Before joining the design team of the Ministry of Education Building, he had already produced a significant straightforward job in the 'Home of Good Will', a charitable institution for old people (1931–2), and when Lúcio *Costa appointed *Warchavchik Professor of Architectural Design at the School of Fine Arts (1931) had served as his assistant. Subsequently, his work developed in a subtly personal manner, characterized not only by the apparent casualness with which he embarked upon the most daring formal or structural scheme but also by a pioneering research into new architectural and technical solutions, noticeable, to a greater or lesser degree, in all his projects and finished work. Among others, in the designs for the City Transport Service

Affonso Eduardo Reidy. Pedregulho Estate. Rio de Janeiro, commenced 1947

Offices and Workshops, Rio (1939), with double saw-tooth roofs over the workshops area; for a pumping station in Rio (1949), a service installation transformed into an attractive spot in a park by the sculptural integration of all the elements of the programme; the design for a Museum of Visual Arts, São Paulo (1951), a clean-cut triangular prism sitting on an expressive base structure, on a highly irregular site; or for a Student Theatre, Rio (1955), with the structural supports of the auditorium roof almost floating in mid-air, cantilevered from the massive stage block. And again, in such finished work as the 'Pedregulho' Housing Development, Rio (begun in 1947), with its 260-metre-long apartment block, following the winding contour of the hillside, and its imaginatively designed school, gymnasium, clinic, laundry and

Affonso Eduardo Reidy. Museum of Modern Art. Rio de Janeiro, commenced 1954. Sketch

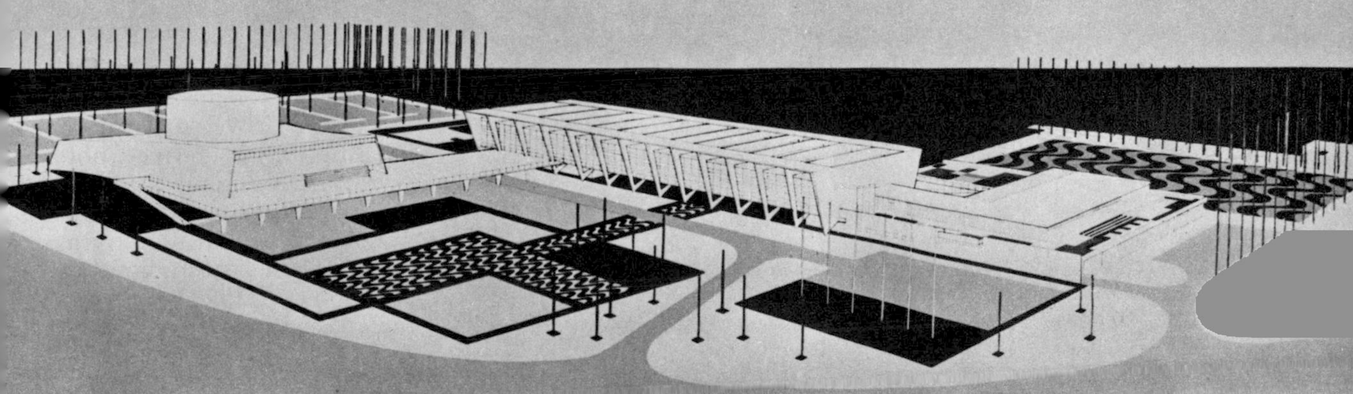

market; or the Marechal Hermes Community Theatre, Rio (1950), a precise and pleasant application of the inverted double slope roof; or the private houses built for Miss Carmen Portinho (1952–4) or Dr Couto e Silva (1955) as well as his latest country house near Petropolis. These same qualities find expression in several important projects still under construction: the 'Gavea' Housing Development, in Rio (1954–), an extension of the principles first applied in the 'Pedregulho' project; the Experimental School in Asuncion, Paraguay (1953–), and the Museum of Modern Art of Rio de Janeiro (1954–), two limpid groupings of various different volumes, underlined by serene rows of concrete ribs enclosing and supporting roof and floor slab, and characterized by freely flowing wide spaces as well as by the novel ways in which natural daylight is combined with artificial lighting; the headquarters for the Rio City Employees Insurance Fund (1957–), with its striking *brise-soleil* façade arrangement. (*Brazil)

Reidy's superb plan for the development of Santo Antônio Hill, in the centre of Rio (1948), still under way, has unfortunately suffered the impact of bureaucratic antagonism in many important respects.

Bibliography: K. Franck, *The Works of Affonso Eduardo Reidy*, London 1960.

HENRIQUE E. MINDLIN

Reinforced Concrete. In 1895, François Hennebique completed the Charles VI Mill at Tourcoing. Its loadbearing structure in reinforced concrete was clearly expressed in the elevations; designed without any straining after decorative effects, it fulfilled the functional and technical requirements of its industrial programme admirably, achieving a formal equilibrium and a new vocabulary of style without recourse to traditional solutions. Two years later, Anatole de *Baudot, with the technical collaboration of Contamin, finished building the Church of St Jean-de-Montmartre, Paris—the first conscious exploitation of the new material for architectural and compositional ends as compared with purely technical ones.

It was in this way, at the end of the 19th century, that the design possibilities of a new material were demonstrated in the first buildings to use it, though it had been discovered, experimented with and its basic technical properties established over the course of the previous fifty years. Reinforced concrete is an artificial monolithic material, derived from the union of steel and concrete, when the latter hardens after the mix has been poured in a fluid state into specially prepared shuttering. The concrete itself is obtained from mixing cement, water and aggregate (sand and gravel) in proportions that vary with the technical results required. The steel reinforcement consists of a cage of steel bars, normally round, though other special sections are sometimes used to increase the degree to which the reinforcement is anchored in the concrete. The size and disposition of the bars is determined in accordance with the particular static and technical requirements involved. The shuttering which holds the mix in its liquid state until it has set, determines the shape of the concrete. Shuttering, or form-work as it is sometimes called, is made up of timber boards, metal panels or units of other material; structural, economic, architectural and decorative factors influence the choice. The two components of reinforced concrete perform the static functions appropriate to their respective properties: basically, the concrete takes up the compressive stresses, and the steel absorbs those of tension.

The idea of assigning different but complementary stress-resistant functions to different materials within the same static system, was first developed and applied many centuries ago; examples may be found in the use of chains for tying in vaults in Byzantine, Islamic, Italian Gothic, Renaissance and Baroque architecture, for which iron, and more anciently wood, was employed. Working to different formal standards, static systems were also evolved, especially after the Late Renaissance, in which the device for resisting tensile stress (chain or hoop) was masked. In Paris, from the 17th century onwards, stressed reinforcements were incorporated and interposed between single elements of the same masonry structure (colonnade at the Louvre by Claude Perrault, 1665–80; portico of the Church of Ste Geneviève (later the Panthéon) by Germain Soufflot, 1757–90). At the Panthéon in particular, the iron ribs, disposed in a more complex manner than hitherto, specifically absorb the forces of tension and shear, thus achieving empirically the typical layout of the bars in reinforced concrete and anticipating intuitively the results that were to be reached a hundred years later by the processes of scientific calculation.

The first instances of the employment of iron in conjunction with concrete, however, only go back to the first half of the 19th century: these consist of wrought-iron I-section floors with thin curved metal plates running between the girders, filled in on top with concrete; the engineer William Fairbairn built an eight-storey refinery at Manchester in 1845 using such a system, patented in 1844. A number of basic experiments were carried out between 1849 and 1878: in 1849–50 the French gardener Joseph Monier made some concrete tubs for orange-trees in which he embedded a mesh of iron rods; J. L. Lambot exhibited a boat in concrete on a frame of iron flats at the 1855 Paris Exposition; in 1861, the French builder François Coignet improved the strength of his concrete structures by inserting a metal mesh in them; a British immigrant to America, Thaddeus Hyatt, outlined the theory of reinforced concrete in 1877 on the basis of tests with beams, made for him at a laboratory in London. Between 1867 and 1878 Monier took out a series of patents for various applications, showing a clear appreciation of the different stress-resistant properties of iron and concrete respectively. Theoretical and experimental research carried out chiefly by Wayss, Bauschinger, Contamin, Bordenave, Hennebique, E. Coignet and De Tedesco succeeded between 1880 and 1900 in fully establishing the main characteristics and the static behaviour of the new material, and the theoretical bases for calculating structures in it. The use of reinforced concrete began to spread at the beginning of the 20th century in projects of ever-increasing importance; official standards and codes of practice were called for, and these were published in various countries in the first decades of the century.

The young French architect Tony *Garnier in his scheme for a *Cité Industrielle* (1901–4) made sytematic use of reinforced concrete and other modern materials, adopting the unadorned grid system even for housing and offices, which Hennebique had employed for the first time in 1895 for the Charles VI Mill. He thus anticipated by almost twenty years an architectural idiom that was first to become widespread only in the period of the *International Style.

At the same epoch, Auguste *Perret, at the beginning of his career as an architect and builder, erected a house in the Rue Franklin,

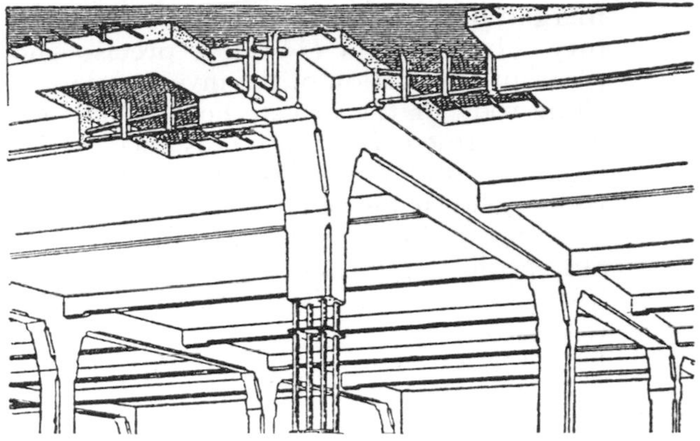

Hennebique's reinforced concrete system, 1892

Anatole de Baudot and Contamin. Church of St Jean-de-Montmartre. Paris, 1894–7

Tony Garnier. Town Hall. Cité Industrielle. 1901–4. Project

Paris, in which he exploited the technical possibilities of a reinforced concrete-framed structure (smaller size of stanchions and greater freedom of manoeuvre with them) to resolve a difficult planning problem, basing the architectural treatment of the façade on the contrast between the loadbearing frame and the infill panels. Meanwhile, in the villa he built himself at Bourg-la-Reine in 1904, Hennebique demonstrated the static possibilities of reinforced concrete in controversial fashion with such structural novelties as an octagonal tower carried on 13-foot cantilevers. The architectural idiom employed is still traditional and eclectic, but Hennebique, perhaps unconsciously, opened up new prospects of three-dimensional design.

The first, almost contemporary, works of the Swiss engineer Robert *Maillart, on the other hand, are the result of a far-reaching attempt to achieve absolute stylistic purity by deliberately aiming at unity of form and static behaviour in his structures. In his bridge over the Rhine at Tavanasa (1905) carriageway and structural framework are intimately fused to produce a structural and plastic unity. The first example of mushroom slab construction occurs in a warehouse he built in 1910 at Zurich, where beams are eliminated and the floor slab itself is designed in such a way as to take over their static functions.

The problem of large-span roofs, hitherto dealt with by using steel-frame structures, was now finally tackled and solved in reinforced concrete. In his Centenary Hall at Breslau (1912–13), Max *Berg roofed the central area of the assembly hall with a dome made up of huge concrete ribs 213 feet in diameter. Eugène *Freyssinet covered his two airship hangars at Orly (1916–24) with a barrel vault consisting of a thin membrane of reinforced concrete, pleated to give the necessary rigidity, and parabolic in overall section to reduce tensile stresses to a minimum.

The employment of reinforced concrete for large industrial complexes became a regular practice. In 1915, the engineer Matté Trucco began building the Fiat-Lingotto works at Turin, with an area of over a hundred acres. He adopted reinforced concrete for every type of structure, solving technical problems of great difficulty in the automobile testing track he sited on the roof of a five-storey factory, and the access ramp that leads up to it.

It was during these years, too, that *Le Corbusier, not yet thirty, was working out the premises of his architectural manner. Reinforced concrete seemed to him to be the most appropriate medium for realizing them in. With his project for the Dom-Ino houses (1914), based on a modular grid in reinforced concrete, he set forth the theoretical preconditions for designing a free plan. America, too, whose architecture had developed during the 19th century via the habitual adoption of the steel frame, began to accept the use of reinforced concrete (albeit not without controversy), especially for large-scale industrial buildings (warehouse for Montgomery, Ward & Co., Chicago, by Schmidt, Garden and Martin, 1908; silos at Fort William, Ont., *c.* 1900). *Gropius published these buildings in 1913 in the Annual of the *Deutscher Werkbund, acknowledging them as creations of modern architecture.

The commission to design the Einstein Observatory Tower at Potsdam in 1920 gave Erich *Mendelsohn his first opportunity of bringing to actual realization the architectural vision which had been maturing in his sketches from 1914 to 1919

Max Berg. Centenary Hall. Breslau, 1912–13

Auguste Perret. Garage Ponthieu. Paris, 1906

(*Expressionism). Reinforced concrete is the material theoretically best adapted for modelling a form that has to be rendered as a fluid, homogeneous and continuous mass, and for creative works of architecture freed from the traditional schematism of horizontal and vertical lines. It was impossible to make use of the new material, however, because no curved shuttering was available: the tower had to be built in brick and rendered over. The full exploitation of the plastic possibilities of concrete was achieved shortly afterwards, in the German Expressionist manner, with the War Memorial at Weimar by Gropius (1921) and the Goetheanum at Dornach by Rudolf Steiner (1925–8).

Inspired by the climate of research and experiment of the early post-war years, *Mies van der Rohe prepared a scheme for the *Novembergruppe* Exhibition in 1922 for a reinforced concrete office block in which the stanchions are set back from the façades and support the floors, which project out all round, by a cantilever arrangement. The external walls assume the character of a series of horizontal strips, one on top of the other. In the years that followed, this architectural idiom became the common property of the rationalist movement, and may be met with in the works of many architects before the Second World War, modified to accord with personal styles (Boots' Factory at Beeston, by Sir E. Owen *Williams, 1932; Open-Air School, Amsterdam, by J. *Duiker, 1930–2; tobacco factory at Linz, by P. *Behrens, 1930–5).

Perret, meanwhile, had carried his architectural use of reinforced concrete further. In the Church of Notre-Dame, Le Raincy (1922–3), a limited budget favoured the elimination of many of the frills usual in ecclesiastical work. The reinforced concrete frame supports a system of vaults and forms the bell-tower. The walls are perforated concrete panels set with coloured glass. The decorative result is indubitably rich, despite the poverty of materials and the rough appearance of the concrete left completely exposed. Karl *Moser's Church of St Antony, Basle (1926–7) is an organic structure in frankly exposed reinforced concrete which derives its inspiration from the contemporary works of Perret.

Walter Gropius adopted reinforced concrete construction in 1925–6 for all the buildings of the Bauhaus. The individual character of the various structural elements, however, was not stressed by underlining their physical consistency and technical properties, but static and formal design was rigorously conditioned by architectural and functional requirements. Henceforth reinforced concrete became a structural element of great versatility, capable of responding to all the demands made on it by the compositional freedom of modern architecture, without having to assume major status as a source of expression. In Le Corbusier's Pavillon Suisse (1930–2) the reinforced concrete substructure, consisting of six huge piers over which the steel frame of the upper storeys is cantilevered, provides an airy and welcoming portico that is imposing in appearance while effecting a happy transition between the external surroundings and the inside of the building. The surface of the concrete is left in the state it was when the shuttering was struck, the irregular impressions made by the timber creating a kind of decorative effect.

Le Corbusier. Unité d'Habitation. Nantes-Rezé, 1952–7

Thus began a long series of works in which Le Corbusier was to interpret with extraordinary freedom the technical, architectural and decorative possibilities of reinforced concrete, thereby setting a trend that found many followers amongst the practitioners of modern architecture in Europe and beyond (Ministry of Education, Rio de Janeiro, by *Costa, *Niemeyer, *Reidy and Vasconcellos, 1936–43; consultant architect: Le Corbusier). In the Unité d'Habitation at Marseilles (1947–52), reinforced concrete is systematically employed for the main framework of the building, cladding on the façades and 'interior roads', sun-breaks and emergency stairs. In the Church of Notre-Dame du Haut, at Ronchamp (1950–4), the inventive plan for Chandigarh (1950 onwards) and the Dominican Convent of La Tourette (1957) Le Corbusier has finally freed himself of rigid geometrical schemes, relying on reinforced concrete for a type of three-dimensional creation that is not limited to single elements but comprises the total scope of the architectural organism.

Frank Lloyd *Wright, too, has employed a strongly personal and at times unprecedented style in the projection of bold, if

Page 239. Pier Luigi Nervi. Exhibition Hall. Turin, 1948–9

Viljo Revell and Keijo Petäjä. Teollisuuskeskus Hotel and offices. Helsinki, 1952

not always strictly pertinent, structural schemes in the field of residential and commercial building. Notable examples of his use of reinforced concrete include the Imperial Hotel, Tokyo (1916–22), an earthquake-proof design with projecting floor slabs; 'Falling Water' House at Bear Run, Pa. (1937–9) with its cantilevered balconies; the Johnson Wax Building, at Racine, Wis. (1936–9), featuring umbrella-type columns; the laboratory tower at the same site (1949), where the upper floors are cantilevered out from a central core; the Guggenheim Museum, New York (1956–9), based on a spiral ramp; and the Price Tower at Bartlesville, Okla. (1955).

The reconstruction of Le Havre (1947–54) gave Perret the opportunity at last for a great experiment in the employment of reinforced concrete on an urban scale, making extensive use of heavy *prefabrication. Methods like these had been successfully tried out in the inter-war period (Le Corbusier, at the Pavillon Suisse; *Beaudouin and *Lods at La Muette, 1933); they have since been developed further in *France and many other European countries, including the Soviet Union.

Besides these experiments in coordination aimed at industrializing the building trade in the service of vast housing projects, further refinements of technique were worked out and gained currency in the field of multi-storey structures. Pier Luigi *Nervi employed undulating prefabricated reinforced concrete units on a vast scale in his Exhibition Hall at Turin (1948–9), considerably reducing the self-weight of the structure while greatly increasing its elasticity and tensile strength. In the Unesco Building, Paris (1953–7, with *Breuer and *Zehrfuss), he stresses the correspondence between the way the structure is modelled and the development of bending moments by varying the depth and profile of the undulations in the roof of the Conference Hall.

Nervi's vaults; Maillart's bridges, and his barrel-vaulted pavilion for the cement industry at the Swiss Provinces Exhibition in Zurich (1939); the structures of Eduardo *Torroja and the recent emergence of *shell structures (*Candela), all show the current tendency in engineering to transcend the orthogonal system of beams and girders in order to attain a structural unity in the whole building. For their arena at Raleigh, N.C. (1952–3), *Deitrick, *Novicki and Severud adopted reinforced concrete for the anchorage structure of the tension cables of the *suspended roof. Opportunities for using reinforced concrete have been multiplied still further by the introduction of pre- and post-stressing, in which the steel reinforcement is placed in stress either before or after the concrete is poured.

Reinforced concrete is now being used for tower blocks of flats or offices, achieving parity of esteem in a sector which for many decades had been the exclusive prerogative of steel. In Mies van der Rohe's design for the Promontory Apartments, Chicago (1949) and *BBPR's scheme for the Torre Velasca, Milan (1957), two structural solutions were drawn up and compared, one using reinforced concrete, and the other steel. The choice fell in both cases to reinforced concrete, Mies keeping to the strict grid system he had envisaged for either solution, and BBPR, on the other hand, opting for a more continuous and unitary scheme which the choice allowed. The Pirelli Building by Gio *Ponti and others (1958) and the Torre Galfa by M. Bega (1959), both at Milan, make use of great reinforced concrete piers, sited orthogonally, as the bases of their support structures. In their departure from the usual grid pattern they open up new possibilities for attaining variety and freedom in design.

Bibliography: C. Cestelli-Guidi, *Cemento armato precompresso*, Milan 1960; R. Gabetti, *Origini del calcestruzzo armato*, Turin 1955; R. Morandi, *Strutture di cemento armato e di calcestruzzo precompresso*, Rome 1954; P. Collins, *Concrete: The Vision of a New Architecture*, London 1959.

GIUSEPPE VARALDO
GIAN PIO ZUCCOTTI

Viljo Revell. Toronto City Hall. 1958. Model

Revell, Viljo, b. Vaasa, Finland 1910. Revell studied at a time when Functionalism had its first flowering in *Finland. His studies, during which he also worked as an assistant to Alvar *Aalto, were completed in 1937. Already before then he had built the so-called 'Glass Palace' with two colleagues, Kokko and Riihimäki, a department store which introduced a bold piece of modern architecture into the then very conservative scene at Helsinki. For his diploma design, Revell characteristically chose a real subject: a building for a small manufacturer; and he dealt with the problem in a logical way, as a rationalist would. An eye for the practical solution, a propensity for systematic thought and a talent for organization fitted him for the directorship of the Reconstruction Office, founded by the Association of Finnish Architects during the war, and later for the chairmanship of the Finnish Standards Committee.

Revell's first important design was for an office block with a hotel, Teollisuuskeskus at Helsinki (1952, in collaboration with Keijo Petäjä). His studio had meanwhile become a kind of headquarters for the new Rationalism in Finland, and the way up for many of today's leading young architects led through Revell's office. Revell often confined himself to critical advice when training his assistants, who were allowed much freedom. An impressive number of competition prizes and completed buildings are the visible achievement of this constantly rejuvenated team (Meilahti Primary School, Helsinki, 1953, together with Osmo Sipari; experimental housing at Tapiola; luxurious private villas, terraced houses).

The clear layout, the externally simple but effective shape and the precise planning of the Kudeneule Textile Works at Hanko (1955) are immediately obvious. Revell does not stress the repetition of secondary elements but presents a unified formal theme. He prefers to work with large structures and wide spans. This conception is also apparent in some of his unbuilt competition

designs (Sininen Nauha housing estate, planned for Helsinki, 1954; Tasa, planned for Tampere, 1953) in which Revell's ideal becomes obvious: wide open spaces, whose only boundary is the horizon.
Together with H. Castrén, B. Lundsten and S. Valjus, Revell won the competition for Toronto City Hall in 1958. The design arose out of an attempt to emphasize the significance of this public building by giving it a shape that would mark its difference from the commercial skyscrapers. At the same time, the building is an expression of Revell's striving after free form, which has also been apparent in other rationalists towards the end of the fifties. Revell's generalizing, international and industrially orientated outlook is in contrast with the rest of Finnish architecture, which mostly shows a preference for individual building on a small scale and in a style that tends to betray a craft approach. But it is exactly because contrasts are conducive to development that Revell's influence is so fruitful.

KYÖSTI ÅLANDER

Richardson, Henry Hobson, b. St James Parish, La. 1838, d. Boston 1886. Richardson was the second American architect (the first was Richard Morris Hunt, 1827–95) to study at the École des Beaux-Arts in Paris. A change in the family's fortune due to the American Civil War forced him to seek employment in Paris, with the office of Henri *Labrouste. He returned to Boston in 1865, and set up practice the following year. His early works were of high quality, still reflecting the eclectic anarchy then prevalent in the *USA. In the eighties, he developed a bold, personal use of forms and materials recalling the Romanesque, typical features being heavy, rough stone courses, round arches and towers. He was responsible for making the window an integral part of interior design, with its size and placement determined by internal need rather than external regularity. He made a trip to England in 1882. Richardson was a forceful and energetic architect with a highly individualistic approach to his profession, and his influence on his contemporaries was enormous. Among those associated with him were C. F. *McKim and Stanford White, the painter John LaFarge and the sculptor Augustus Saint-Gaudens. In a series of commissions during the eighties, Richardson transformed the typical New England cottage into a rambling, spacious house by combining a free-flowing, asymmetrical plan with a keen appreciation of the colours and textures of local materials; this had the effect of bringing the house into harmony with its environment, a development which had considerable effect on the young Frank Lloyd *Wright. Richardson was the first American architect to take an interest in functional buildings such as railroad stations and libraries, which had previously been designed by engineers. He altered the image of the architect in American society by interesting himself in designing buildings for public service, rather than restricting his craft to commissions from the financial aristocracy, as Hunt had done.

In commercial architecture the Richardson Romanesque, as it has come to be called, was influential in Cincinnati, St Louis, Cleveland and, most significantly, in Chicago, where his monumental Marshall Field Wholesale Store was a key monument in the evolution of the *Chicago School. Other major works by Richardson are the Albany Cathedral, New Brattle Square Church in Boston, the Courthouse and Jail in Pittsburgh, the M. F. Stoughton House in Cambridge, Mass., and the Walter Charing House, Brookline, Mass.

Henry Hobson Richardson. Marshall Field Wholesale Store. Chicago, 1885–7

Richardson's dynamic use of materials, especially the rough, massive stone-and-masonry surfaces of his buildings, were a powerful expression of the Romantic tradition. Although his ideas and ideals were long influential, his style, as such, was superseded by the Imperial classicism of *Burnham and McKim's 'White City', the Columbian Exposition of 1893 in Chicago.

Riemerschmid, Richard, b. Munich 1868, d. Munich 1957. Architect and designer. Riemerschmid, like many artists of the *Art Nouveau, progressed from painting to the applied arts. In 1897 he was a founder-member of the United Workshops for Art in Craft; 1901, interior decoration of the Munich Theatre; 1910, factories at Hellerau.

Gerrit Thomas Rietveld. Schröder House. **Utrecht, 1924**

Rietveld, Gerrit Thomas, b. Utrecht 1888. Rietveld worked as an apprentice from 1899 to 1906 in his father's joinery shop, and then ran his own cabinet-making business in Utrecht (1911–19). His first architectural studies were carried out under the architect P. J. C. Klaarhamer in Utrecht (1911–15); Rietveld was also an admirer of *Berlage. In 1918, chiefly through the agency of Robert van't Hoff, he came into contact with the founders of the *Stijl movement, of which he remained a member till 1931. His early furniture designs (from 1918) were primarily three-dimensional compositions. In 1921 he began collaborating with the interior decorator Tr. Schröder-Schräder (Rietveld-Schröder House, Utrecht, 1924). Work with van *Doesburg and van *Eesteren followed in 1923. Rietveld was one of the founders of *CIAM at La Sarraz in 1928. From then on he worked as an architect in the Netherlands (terraced housing, Utrecht, 1931–4; Vreeburg Cinema, Utrecht, 1936), Germany, Austria, Italy (Venice Biennale, 1953), Curaçao, France and Belgium.
After his difficult start, which brought him, however, international fame, the number of Rietveld's commissions began to dwindle (shops for the Wessels company, Utrecht 1923, now altered). From 1931 onwards, when *De Stijl* ceased publication and the group broke up, modern architecture passed through a difficult period in the *Netherlands, having to sustain a running battle with the historicizing 'national' style. This trend received a particular fillip in the years 1945–55, and its practitioners considered Rietveld's work to be completely superseded. His reputation began to revive with the new interest shown in America, and later Europe, in the work of Mondrian and De Stijl. Since then Rietveld has received an increasing number of important commissions, and achieved complete recognition by the younger generation of architects (country houses; Soonsbeek Pavilion, near Arnhem, 1954, since demolished; De Ploeg Textile Works, Bergeijck, 1956; housing development, Hoograven, 1954–6, with other architects).
One of the main characteristics of Rietveld's work is his three-dimensional handling of space, which has developed from De Stijl practice without ever becoming fixed in rigid attitudes. This also explains his consistent interest in interior decoration and furniture design. Rietveld has always been receptive to anything new, whether in materials or methods, while making no concessions to the merely fashionable. His use of the primary colours red, blue and yellow still testifies to his close allegiance to De Stijl. But the natural colours of his materials have gained the upper hand, and together with a restrained palette of

Gerrit Thomas Rietveld. House. Ilpendam, 1959

white, grey and black, help to set off the ever-cubistic forms of his architecture.
Bibliography: Th. M. Brown, *The Work of G. Th. Rietveld*, Utrecht 1958.

J. J. VRIEND

Ring, Der. Berlin architects' association founded in 1925. Among its members were such eminent German architects as *Bartning, *Behrens, Döcker, *Gropius, *Häring, Haesler, *Hilberseimer, the brothers *Luckhardt, *May, *Mendelsohn, *Mies van der Rohe, *Poelzig, *Scharoun, and the brothers *Taut.

Rogers, Ernesto N., b. Trieste 1909. Graduated Milan 1932. Belongs to the architectural team *BBPR. Publisher of the architectural journal *Domus*, then (since 1954) of the architectural journal *Casabella Continuità*.
Bibliography: Ernesto N. Rogers, *Esperienza dell'Architettura*, Turin 1958.

Root, John W., b. Lumpkin, Ga. *c.* 1850, d. Chicago 1891. Partner of Daniel Hudson *Burnham. (*Chicago School)

Rotterdam, School of. *Stijl, De.

Rudolph, Paul, b. Elkton, Ky. 1918. Studied at Harvard University under Gropius. Since 1958 Chairman of the Department of Architecture at Yale University, New Haven, Conn. Rudolph developed an astonishingly wide range of design features ('new freedom') in his search for an individuality appropriate to the function of each building: Jewett Arts Center with resemblance to the neighbouring neo-Gothic buildings of Wellesley College, Mass. (1955–9); schools at Sarasota, Fla.; a scheme featuring closely interlocking blocks for a motel at Waverly, N.Y., and students' quarters at Yale University, New Haven (both started in 1960); an elegant cantilevered concrete structure for a multi-storey garage at New Haven (started 1959); a building radiating in many directions as a chapel at Tuskegee, Ala. (started in 1960). (*USA)

Russia. The development of Russian architecture in the 19th and 20th centuries has been as contradictory and seemingly inconsistent as the Russian character itself. Dependent always on the personal whims of her rulers, Russia's style of building has altered with each change of rule. In St Petersburg, the first quarter of the 19th century was dominated by the classicism of the reign of Alexander I (1801–25); the architecture was worthy of the enlightened age which produced Speransky, Karamzin, Pushkin, and Lermontov. The Alexandrine period is best summarized by the work of Karl Ivanovich Rossi (1775–1849), a Russian whose family was of Italian origin. With the advent of Rossi, the use of Greek forms—which had closely paralleled similar developments in the USA—gave way to Roman classical forms used on a fantastic scale, in a deliberate attempt to rival Rome itself. Rossi's Glavnyi Shtab (General Staff) complex of 1818–29, facing the Winter Palace, focusses attention on that masterpiece by Rastrelli while asserting itself across the Palace Square in a colossal curving bastion accented by a magnificent divided triumphal arch at the centre. Rossi here boldly defined what is probably the grandest plaza ever conceived—a fitting stage for the drama played out a century later, in 1917, when the Bolsheviks stormed the Winter Palace.

The succession of Nicholas I (1825–55) to the throne was as disastrous for the continuation of fine building as it was for the other liberal arts. The affinity in the court for German examples brought on a spate of tasteless, dull variations on Romanesque Style, and such bizarre revivalisms as Menelaw's Egyptian Gate. However, if interest waned in the capital, there were currents stirring in Moscow by mid-century which gave rise to older national forms.

August Augustovich Monferrand's (1786–1858) ponderous Cathedral of St Isaac in St Petersburg (1820–57) has been characterized as the last building of 19th-century Russian classicism. It was nearly contemporaneous with the Church of the Redeemer by Konstantin Andreevich Ton (1794–1881) which may be considered the first step toward the formulation of the lozhno-russki stil, the 'Pseudo Russian Style', better known here as the Slavic Revival. The Slavic-European controversy touched off increased interest in Russian cultural history and produced a national 'Renaissance', one long-range by-product being the Ballets Russes and the circle of Mir Iskusstva (World of Art). The folk operas by Rimski-Korsakov, the fairy-tale paintings by Vasnetsov and Bilibin and increasing scholarly research in Russian history were all characteristic of this movement.

The more extensive works of architecture in the Slavic Revival Style in Moscow, such as V. O. Sherwood's (1832–97) Historical Museum and A. H. Pomerantsev's Torgovye Riady (now GUM Department Store), on Red Square, were ponderous and heavy-handed, often mere repetitions of the intricate mouldings and fanciful forms of the Kremlin Towers and such monuments as the 16th-century Cathedral of Vasilii Blazhennyi (St Basil). But many more intimate buildings, such as Pozdeev's Igumnov House and Friedenburg's Shchukin House, give a lighthearted and refreshingly playful impression by using those forms with more intelligence and wit. A conscious effort was made to revive lost building crafts, a movement not unrelated to that of William Morris in England; many Slavic Revival buildings are adorned with ceramic tile in characteristically Russian combinations of brilliant colour.

At the turn of the century, there was no clear division in Russia between the Slavic Revival and *Art Nouveau. The two styles rather merged to form a distinctive variant on Art Nouveau; as Stil Moderne, this style was frequently imbued with Slavic forms and colour combinations, and almost always retains a unique Russian flavour. A. V. Shchussev's Kazan Railway Station in Moscow is a fairy-tale palace in Slavic Revival terms, but across the street O. Shekhtel's more interesting Yaroslavl Station combines Slavic Revival colour and exoticism with the liquid movement and the 'buggy' detail of Art Nouveau.

The Soviet Revolution brought with it the birth of abstract and non-objective painting and, in architecture, *Constructivism. While the repercussions in Western Europe of this vital and unprecedented development have been fairly well documented, it is less well known that the native Russian movement persisted down to 1934, producing remarkable projects and buildings whose contribution to architecture has yet to be assessed. After *Tatlin's Monument of the Third International, the determining project was the Vesnin brothers' Labor Palace of 1923—a vast, revolutionary plan in which the architects attempted to apply the more practical and aesthetically valuable elements of Constructivism of Tatlin, *Lissitzky, *et al.*, to rational Socialist building. Under the leadership of Moisei Ginzburg, an outstanding architect in his own right, the later Constructivists grappled with problems of Socialist building and planning that were on the scale of Rossi's St Petersburg. Notable projects were I. I. Leonidov's incredible Lenin Library, a huge glass sphere resembling a gargantuan light bulb, Barchin's elegant Izvestia Building (1928), and later, Ginzburg and the Vesnin brothers' Project for the Ministry of Heavy Industry (1934, prefiguring the Pan Am Building in New York). During the 1920s a considerable influence on Soviet architecture was exerted by the USA, especially in the field of industrial building through the firm of Albert *Kahn.

Moscow State University. Moscow, 1949

The Kremlin Palace of Congresses. Moscow, 1959–60

The *International Style, without its bourgeois accoutrements, crashed into prominence in the USSR in 1928 with *Le Corbusier's Tsentrosoyuz. By the early thirties the Russian problem came to world-wide attention in the great competitions for the Palace of the Soviets. Never built, the foundation for this mighty project has become, under Khrushchev, an outdoor swimming pool.

By 1934, all independent architectural activity had been banned and the various organizations were squeezed into the new Soviet Academy of Architecture, thus ending all experimentation.

Stalinist architecture, often thought to be the product of a totalitarian régime, was, oddly enough, largely a continuation of 19th-century Neoclassicism under the direction of Tsarist-trained academicians. A. V. Shchussev, author of the aforementioned Kazan Railway Station and, in 1924, of Lenin's Mausoleum in Moscow (the original design was a flagrant imitation of an archaeological reconstruction of 1896, of the Mausoleum at Halicarnassus), the academicians Rerberg (Kiev Station, 1914), Shchouko, Fomin and Zholtovski—all returned from the obscurity they had endured during the bright years of Constructivism to burden the countryside with the familiar 'official' Graeco-Roman forms of the thirties.

After the Second World War the country set about repairing the devastation wrought by the fascist hordes, and whole cities were rebuilt from the ground up. In Moscow the official style, sometimes referred to as 'Stalin Gothic', took the form of inflated spire-buildings in an unconsidered Neoclassic mode, often with eccentric, even humourous variations—bundled wheat 'Corinthian' capitals, and a Baroque heraldry of hammers, sickles, shields and stars.

The most grandiose and offensive of these buildings is the inhumanly scaled and shoddily constructed Moscow State

University, built in 1949. The highest building in Europe, it serves as a symbol of the oppressive and anaesthetizing weight of the dogma of Stalin's rule on the very mind of the nation. Now thoroughly despised by the Russians themselves, the spire-buildings serve only as painful reminders of the waste and excesses of the Stalin years.

With the process of 'de-Stalinization' since the denunciation of the 'cult of personality' by Khrushchev, in 1956, the stirrings of a trend toward ideological coexistence have prompted Russian architects, especially those of the younger generation, to reach back into their own heritage and to knit together the break in their great architectural tradition. As the colourful and lighthearted Slavic Revival appeared after the grim years of Nicholas I, so may a new movement spring forth in the second half of the 20th century.

Glimmers of hope are to be seen in the Kremlin Palace of Congresses of 1959–60, an adequate if somewhat ostentatious step (particularly in the interior) into the idiom of the International Style, and out of the chaotic 'classicism' of the years before 1953. A most promising development has been the well-planned and disarmingly pleasant Palace of Pioneers in Moscow, of 1959–62. This charming complex combines a typically Russian play of grand free spaces with the colour and fantasy of brightly decorative wall surfaces, accented by a row of banners of the sixteen republics of the USSR. A dramatic triangular pylon dominates the layout, reminiscent of earlier Constructivist vertical accents.

Bibliography: Circle, London 1937; George H. Hamilton, *The Art and Architecture of Russia*, Baltimore 1954; El Lissitzky, *Russland. Die Rekonstruktion der Architektur in der Sowjet-union*, Vienna 1930.

ARTHUR SPRAGUE

Saarinen, Eero, b. Kirkkonummi, Finland 1910, d. Birmingham, Mich. 1961. Eero Saarinen was the son of the architect Eliel *Saarinen. He came to the USA with his family in 1923, and received his degree from Yale University in 1934. He travelled in Europe in 1934–6, and subsequently entered into partnership with his father at Cranbrook. Although Eero's influence is certainly to be seen in his father's work from the late 1930s onward, it was the winning of the Jefferson Memorial Competition, St Louis, 1949 (which he had entered by himself), that established the younger man as a separate personality.

Eero Saarinen. Kresge Auditorium, Massachusetts Institute of Technology. Cambridge, Mass., completed 1955

His first major work, the General Motors Technical Center, Warren, Michigan, completed in 1955, was for a client who had originally engaged his father for the task. Eero Saarinen and his associates responded to the demands of this remarkable challenge with considerable distinction. The numerous buildings of simple, cubic shape are spaced irregularly around a central lagoon in a manner reminiscent of the master plan of *Mies van der Rohe for the Illinois Institute of Technology, Chicago (1940). However, the shapes of the Saarinen buildings are more individualized in scale and surface modulation, and are more varied in colour than is the case with Mies's inveterately regularized 'industrial classicism'. Together with the contemporary works of Philip *Johnson and of *Skidmore, Owings and Merrill, Saarinen's General Motors designs determined the trends that would dominate American architecture until the late 1950s.

In the light of his subsequent development, and of the evolution of architecture that has taken place since then, this General Motors 'style' already seems at least superficially antiquated. Two 'central plan' edifices for the Massachusetts Institute of Technology, Cambridge, Mass., finished in 1955, the shell-domed Kresge Auditorium and the Chapel, indicate a multiple heritage as well as a diverse future for

Eero Saarinen. Yale Hockey Rink. Yale University, New Haven, Conn., completed 1958

Saarinen's architecture. The simple domical form enclosed a complexly shaped auditorium with a single, sweeping curve in a way that provoked much criticism, especially from those who felt that the arbitrary-seeming form of the exterior was not suited to the varied requirements of the interior space. There is indeed a paradox in the outer forms and the interior workings of the Kresge Auditorium, and it tends to underscore one of the most challenging problems in recent architecture. The difficulty comes about from the recurring effort to reconcile a style appropriate to the exact programme of the building and the technological nature of modern construction with the desire to use forms of a pure, simplified character, indeed forms with pronounced classicizing overtones. In their late styles, both Mies van der Rohe and *Le Corbusier have found eminently successful personal means of reconciling the paradoxical demands of the machine age with their latent predilections for inventing shapes whose ancestry lies in classic or pre-classic Mediterranean architecture. (*p. 24; *International Style) Saarinen's difficulty—and, for that matter, the difficulty encountered by many of his contemporaries—is that his reconciliation seems tentative and insecure. It is made to seem even more unconvincing in the Kresge Auditorium with the presence near by of the more romantic, subjective form of the Chapel, a work which seems to be a devout evocation of his father's stylistic conceptions. The lack of *rapport* between these two MIT structures, which, in itself, is thought-provoking, sounds a warning as to the shifting nature of Eero's later development until his untimely death in 1961. Subsequent designs for large interior spaces, such as the Ingalls Hockey Rink, Yale University, the TWA Terminal, Kennedy Airport, N.Y., and the Dulles Airport, Washington, D.C., show a more comprehensible relationship between interior space and exterior form. However, while the spaces themselves seem to indicate a common spirit of dynamic coordination, the forms are heterogeneous. The spaces may be expressive or appropriate in a dramatic way, yet one wonders whether there is a justifiable relation between these inventions and the material demands of the programme and of structural technology.
Only the future will be in a position to bear out the validity of these designs, as well as such 'neo-academic' designs for government structures as the American Embassies in London and in Oslo, buildings which represent other efforts at creating distinctive and unique-seeming forms at the expense of allowing a more personal, idiomatic style to evolve. The London Embassy was intended to harmonize with the vernacular architecture of London, but failed to accomplish this aim. The residential colleges at Yale are yet another effort to harmonize with tradition, or, more

exactly in this case, with the neo-traditionalism of 'collegiate Gothic', while at the same time maintaining the imprint of modernism. We cannot be sure that Eero Saarinen developed a new method for the design of contemporary buildings; indeed, it can almost be said that he did not produce an individual, consistent style. None the less, he produced a sequence of influential if not organically related buildings that have been much discussed, and which surely illuminate the direction taken by modernist architecture in the 1950s.

JOHN M. JACOBUS, JR

Saarinen, Eliel, b. Rantasalmi, Finland 1873, d. Michigan 1950. Saarinen studied painting at the University and architecture at the Polyteknisk Institut, Helsinki (1893–7). In 1896 he formed a partnership with Herman Gesellius and Armas Lindgren, and in 1899–1900 they received international recognition with the Finnish Pavilion at the Paris Exposition. Significantly, their somewhat neo-medieval design indicates a possible influence from American architects such as H. H. *Richardson and Louis *Sullivan, and at the same time reveals the spirit of the *Art Nouveau in certain decorative touches.

In 1902 Gesellius, Lindgren and Saarinen began work on a joint residence and studio, Hvitträsk, in the wooded countryside outside Helsinki. Certainly one of the most important examples of domestic architecture at the turn of the century, and, in spite of its somewhat indigenous appearance, worthy of comparison with contemporary houses in various parts of the world by *Wright, *Voysey, *Mackintosh and *Hoffmann, Hvitträsk also demonstrates that its architects were familiar with the new spirit in interior design that was then centred in Vienna and Glasgow. Equally, this studio-house reveals an awareness of the progressive domestic designs of such late-19th-century masters as Philip *Webb, Richard Norman *Shaw and Richardson. A similar awareness is to be found in the Saarinen design for the Helsinki Railway

Eliel Saarinen. Cranbrook School for Boys. Bloomfield Hills, Mich., 1925

Eliel and Eero Saarinen. Christ Lutheran Church, Minneapolis, Minn., 1949–50

Station of 1904, constructed from 1910 to 1914. A typical eclectic monument of the period, its boldly articulated and simply detailed masonry masses sum up a variety of academic, romantic and rational influences that were common at the time. More important, however, is the individual character which Saarinen has wrought from these multiple inheritances of the early modern tradition, and the personal infusion which makes this design unique in the railway architecture of the period. Its creative spirit is equalled only in the more severe romanticism of *Bonatz's nearly contemporary Stuttgart Station.

The scope of Saarinen's architectural practice continued to expand during this decade with his involvement in a number of city planning schemes, one of which was a project for Canberra, Australia. His participation in the competition for the Chicago Tribune Tower, 1922 (for which he received a second prize), led to further work in the USA, to which he moved permanently in 1923. In 1925 he began work on what was destined to become a group of schools at Cranbrook, Michigan. In 1928 he built his own house in Cranbrook, a simple pale brick structure which seems closer in appearance to the bland 'collegiate Gothic' of 20th-century American architecture than to the more pronounced modelling and incisive detail of Saarinen's earlier and more overtly romantic style. Other features at Cranbrook are distantly suggestive of Wright's characteristic use of horizontals, with sheltered loggias, etc. By way of contrast the Cranbrook Academy design of 1940 possesses a dry, neoclassic solemnity, and although its plans and elevations are not perfunctory they are similar in appearance to the simplified, modernized academic traditionalism that was a feature of monumental architecture throughout the world in the 1930s. Comparison of the Cranbrook buildings of the 1920s and 1930s with the earlier Helsinki Station reveals little or no intensification or development of a personal style, but instead only an overall simplification or generalization of forms that are ultimately derivative.

In 1937 Eliel Saarinen formed a partnership with his son, Eero *Saarinen, and many of his last works must be considered as fundamentally collaborative designs. The Kleinhans Music Hall, Buffalo, New York (1938), clearly indicates an awareness of the new European architecture of the 1920s and early 1930s, which had blossomed after Saarinen's departure from Finland. Here and in a series of churches culminating in Christ Lutheran, Minneapolis, Minn. (1949–50), there is an effective blend of the half-century-old romantic, craftsman-like approach in both decoration and constructive elements, along with a new spirit of design that is more decisive in its geometric simplicity, bolder in the abstract handling of spatial and lighting elements, and even outwardly functional in the sense of the word as then understood. The first Saarinen projects for the General Motors Technical Center were done in 1945, but the definitive designs were not completed until after his death in 1950. The final result was a group of buildings in a severe, industrial, *Mies van der Rohe style that in certain ways is foreign to the more genteel, occasionally unobtrusive personal manner of Eliel Saarinen.

Bibliography: Eliel Saarinen, *Search for Form*, New York 1949; Albert Christ-Janer, *Eliel Saarinen*, Chicago 1949.

JOHN M. JACOBUS, JR

Sant'Elia, Antonio, b. Como 1880, d. Monfalcone 1916. Sant'Elia studied architecture at Milan and later at Bologna, where he graduated at the age of twenty-four. He then began to work for other architects, and to design for himself in the manner of Otto *Wagner's Vienna School. He was greatly attracted by many features of North American civilization, not those realistic and rational aspects of it which had impressed Adolf *Loos, but the romantic aspects of its technical development and the progressive expansion of an industrial metropolis. The new city, the city of the future, thus appeared to him a reality that could be achieved in Italy too, but an Italy shaken from her long sleep and aroused to life once more. He set himself to work out a grandiose project for a *Città Nüova*, both in general and in detail, which was shown in 1914 at the first exhibition in Milan by the *Nuove Tendenze* group, of which he was a member. Designs for 'Structures of a modern metropolis' were displayed at the same exhibition by Sant'Elia's fellow student, the architect Mario *Chiattone, who shared his ideals.

Antonio Sant'Elia. Città Nuova. 1914. Project

In the catalogue to this exhibition Sant' Elia published a diffuse manifesto on the need for breaking with the past in order to create in Italy too, where 'everything had to be revolutionized', a new architecture, as new as 'the state of mind' of the younger generation; this alone could give valid form to the city of men freed from the bonds of traditions and conventions. Thus, for Sant'Elia, it was eminently a case of historical necessity.

His text was published again a few months afterwards by Marinetti, who had modified it on a number of points. Henceforth one speaks of *Futurist architecture, and Sant' Elia himself is referred to as a Futurist. In reality Sant'Elia was a Socialist, who had joined Marinetti's movement without enthusiasm, for it was of an outspokenly nationalist character and ended up a few years later by going along with Fascism completely. Sant'Elia, however, did not have much time to think out his position as an architect vis-à-vis Marinetti, for he was called up in 1915 on Italy's entry into the war and was killed a year later leading an assault.

Sant'Elia's architecture had very little affinity with the beginnings of the modern movement that was currently stirring in *Germany and *Austria; it remains an isolated phenomenon in Europe, although it introduced a number of motifs to Italian culture and a stylistic formula that had much in common with Russian *Constructivism. Its main influence was on the architecture of the great international exhibitions and their pavilions. But it is due to him that Italian culture, shaken by his words, looked for the first time at the problem of the new architecture as a problem, albeit a limited one, of a new life and new customs, in an age that witnessed the triumph of the petit-bourgeois mentality.

Antonio Sant'Elia. Skyscraper. 1914. Project

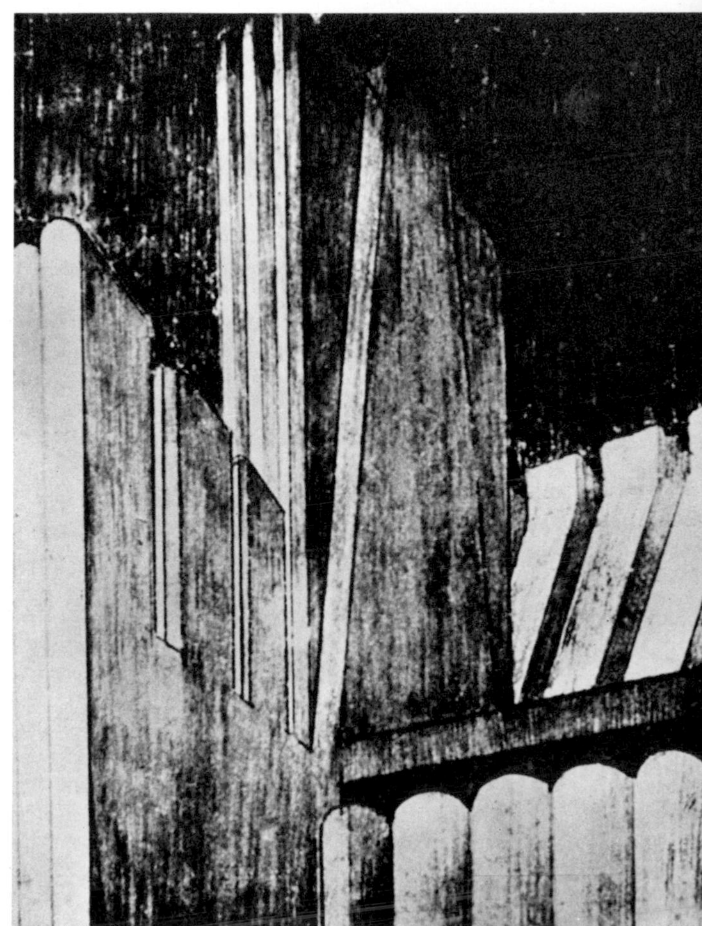

Hundreds of Sant'Elia's designs have come down to us; one of them was actually built posthumously at Como, although altered in too many details. A recurrent theme in them is the architecture of a metropolis, derived from a mechanical and industrialized civilization: towering buildings with external elevators, multi-level road bridges, enormous stations, and imaginary factories: monuments of the city of the future, seen through the vision of Sant'Elia, and raised by their unreal dimensions and perspectives to the level of symbols. A permanent exhibition of Sant'Elia's works has been opened at the Villa Olmo near Como.

Bibliography: Giulio C. Argan, 'Il pensiero critico di Antonio Sant'Elia', in *L'arte*, Rome September 1930; Alberto Sartoris, *Antonio Sant'Elia*, Milan 1930; Gherardo Dottori, *Sant'Elia e la nuova architettura*, Rome 1933; Francesco Tentori, 'Le origini liberty di Antonio Sant'Elia' in *L'architettura*, Rome July/August 1955 and January/February 1956; Umbro Apollonio, *Antonio Sant'Elia*, Milan 1958.

GIULIA VERONESI

Scarpa, Carlo, b. Venice 1906. Pavilions for the Biennales at Venice, new fittings and extensions of museums in Florence, Palermo, Possagno, Venice, Verona. Organic architecture in the manner of Frank Lloyd *Wright.

Scharoun, Hans, b. Bremen 1893. Scharoun grew up in Bremerhaven until he took his school certificate; he studied from 1912 to 1914 at Berlin Technical College, and during his military service worked as an architect on reconstruction in East Prussia, whence he established contact with Bruno *Taut and the circle of young architects round him in Berlin. In 1925 Scharoun accepted an appointment through Oskar Moll at Breslau Academy of Art and Crafts. Here he met Rading and they collaborated on schemes in Breslau and Berlin. For the WUWA (Home and Work Exhibition, Breslau, 1928) he built an apartment block with set-back floors, roof gardens and communal services on the ground floor; and a private house in 1927 on the Weissenhof estate of the *Deutscher Werkbund at Stuttgart, co-ordinated by *Mies van der Rohe. (*Expressionism)

As a member of the Berlin architectural association *Der *Ring*, Scharoun designed the layout of the large Siemensstadt estate. There in 1930 he built a number of blocks of flats, standing set back from the street, with living-rooms extending the entire depth of the block from wall to wall. In the twenties in Berlin, Scharoun participated in numerous town planning schemes and competitions under the leadership of Martin *Wagner. He built blocks of flats at the Kaiserdamm, Hohenzollerndamm and Flinsberger Platz in an attempt to keep the business of renting flats an economic proposition for private enterprise by carefully thought-out planning.

For the exhibition '*Sun, air and houses for all*' at the Berlin Funkturm in 1932, Scharoun built a 'growing house'. His design is based on the grid system to give the builders a precise synopsis of costs during the whole process of erection, together with the necessary extensions. In the same year, he built a house for an industrialist by the name of Schminke at Löbau in Saxony, a steel-frame structure that seems to be freely suspended amidst the scenery.

Under the Nazis, Scharoun was cut off entirely from all chance of executing major schemes. He was merely allowed to build private houses in and around Berlin. In these years of enforced inactivity, he worked on numerous drawings and designs whose ideas he drew on in later work. After the end of the war in 1945, he was appointed by Berlin Corporation head of the Department for Building and Housing. He prevented the complete demolition of many factories and offices in the shattered city and set up the planning group called the 'Berliner Kollektiv', which presented a revolutionary plan for the rebuilding of Berlin in 1946. This plan was an application and development of theoretical work by Miljutin and Soraja y Matyas, and a realization and continuation of Martin Mächler's theories: 'not a land-use plan but a dynamics plan' His work on the centre of Berlin was continued in 1958 in the *Metropolis Berlin* competition, 'the first design that deserves to be taken seriously in the rebuilding of the city centre'. While working on detailed plan analyses for the Havel area (Spandau, Potsdam) in his capacity as head of the Building Institute at the German Academy of Sciences from 1947 to 1950, he was also (until 1960) lecturer in town planning at Berlin Technical

University, of which he was one of the re-founders in 1946.

In this post-war period, he carried out many important competition designs: the rebuilding of the island of Heligoland, the Liederhalle in Stuttgart, the American Memorial Library and an old-people's home in Berlin. Prize-winning and world famous designs such as the theatre at Kassel and the National Theatre at Mannheim were never built; they were based on a far-reaching analysis of theatrical problems. An analysis of the principles affecting the spatial problems of school buildings led to a design for a primary school at Darmstadt on the occasion of his Darmstadt lecture on 'Man and Space' in 1951. Scharoun's design marks an important advance in his work as well as in the development of modern architecture. In 1955 he was commissioned to build the Geschwister Scholl High School at Lünen, Westphalia, completed in 1962. The classrooms in this girls' school have been arranged as a 'flat', in order to humanize the division between school and home in modern education. 'Scharoun is the guarantor of a continuity between post-1918 and post-1945 *Germany.' (*L'Architettura*).

This continuity is expressed particularly in his residential buildings. In 1947 Scharoun designed a suburb south of the Stalinallee, as it later became, his first attempt to combine some ideas of Ludwig *Hilberseimer's with the experience he had gained on the Siemensstadt scheme in the 1930s, and to create a design team. In 1954 he submitted plans and models for the rebuilding of the Hansa district, which he was commissioned to do by the revived *Ring*. He also built 'homesteads' in Charlottenburg-Nord (1955–61), a further development from linear building in its social aspect, as evaluated by the most recent research. At Stuttgart, Scharoun built Romeo and Juliet point blocks in collaboration with Wilhelm Frank, whose penthouses and studios must be understood as the completion of a design which had hitherto featured only low buildings. These blocks show a connection with the idea that underlies the Breslau Exhibition flats of 1928. They may similarly be associated with the concept of *townscape, as are the 'Salute' block at Stuttgart and the concert hall for the Berlin Philharmonic

Hans Scharoun. Apartment house at the Home and Work Exhibition. Breslau, 1928

Hans Scharoun. Schminke House. Löbau, 1932

Hans Scharoun. Charlottenburg-Nord housing estate. Berlin, 1955–61

Orchestra, both of which have recently been constructed.

Scharoun was awarded the commission for building the new Berlin Philharmonic Concert Hall as a result of a prize-winning competition design which condenses the unity of music and space into three-dimensional form.

Bibliography: Margit Staber, 'Hans Scharoun. Ein Beitrag zum organischen Bauen', in *Zodiac 10*, Milan 1962.

KLAUS-JAKOB THIELE

Hans Scharoun. Concert Hall for the Berlin Philharmonic Orchestra. Berlin, under construction. Section

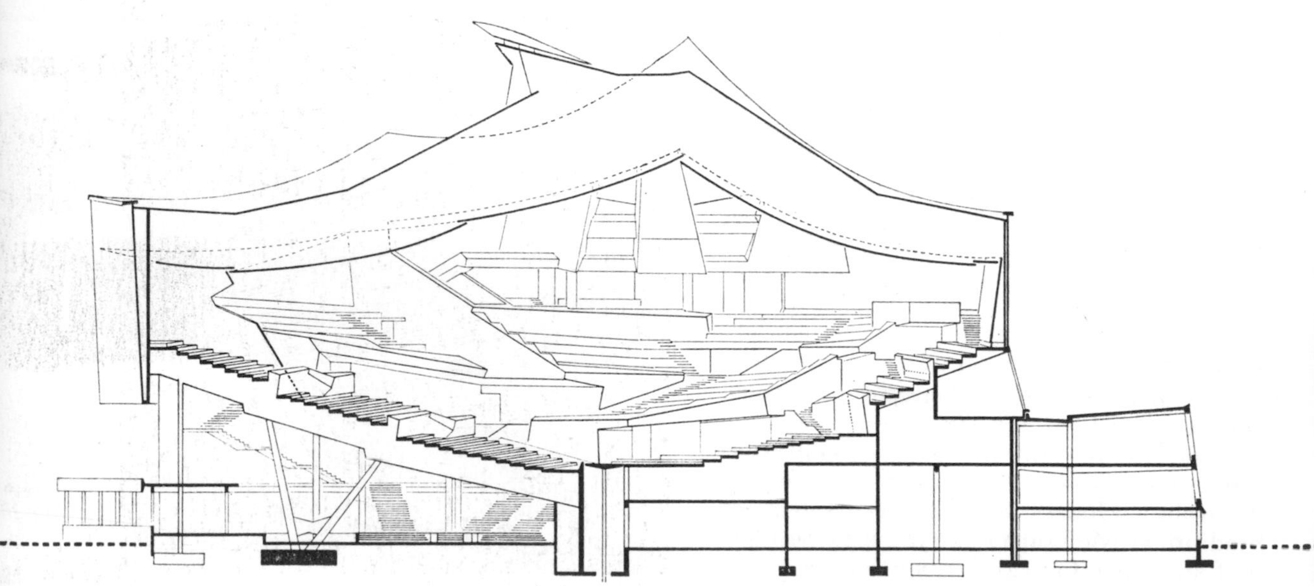

Schindler, Rudolph M., b. Vienna 1887, d. Los Angeles 1953. Studied at the Vienna Academy of Art, strongly influenced by Otto *Wagner; 1913 emigrated to Chicago; 1916–21 worked in Frank Lloyd *Wright's office. In Schindler's buildings the relationship of horizontal and vertical, solid and void appear as an American parallel to De *Stijl (Lovell Beach House, Newport Beach, 1926).

Schinkel, Karl Friedrich, b. Neuruppin 1781, d. Berlin 1841. Architect and painter. Pupil of David and Friedrich Gilly. Extensive journeys in Italy and France; worked

in Berlin. Schinkel combined classical forms with a romantic spirit in his dignified designs: New Guard House, Unter den Linden (1815–16), Theatre (1818–31), Old Museum (1823–8), all at Berlin. Early Gothic Revival work in his Memorial to Queen Louise (1810) and his Werdersche Church in Berlin (1824–30). Schinkel influenced *Mies van der Rohe and through him 20th-century architecture with his designs for a shop (1829) whose façades consist of glass areas divided by masonry piers, and with his country-house projects. *Bibliography:* Paul Ortwin Rave, *Karl Friedrich Schinkel, Das Lebenswerk*, 1942–56. (*Germany)

Schwarz, Rudolf, b. Strasbourg 1897, d. Cologne 1961. Pupil of *Poelzig. His ecclesiastical buildings form an important contribution to modern Catholic church design. Schwarz sought to create with them 'high inhabitable pictures like life-size parables'. Fronleichnam Church, Aachen (in collaboration with Hans Schwippert, 1928), St Anne, Düren (1951–6), St Michael, Frankfurt (1953–4). (*Germany) *Bibliography:* Rudolf Schwarz, *Kirchenbau*, Heidelberg 1960.

Seidler, Harry, b. Vienna 1923. Studied at Harvard University, Cambridge, Massachusetts, and Manitoba, Canada. Collaborated with *Breuer and *Niemeyer. Since 1942 independent practice in Sydney, Australia. Houses and offices; Olympic Stadium at Melbourne (1956), a suspended roof structure for 125,000 spectators. *Bibliography:* Harry Seidler, *Houses, Interiors and Projects,* Sydney 1954.

Harry Seidler. Lend Lease House, Sydney

Semper, Gottfried, b. Hamburg 1803, d. Rome 1879. From 1834 in Dresden which he left for political reasons in 1849. Stayed in Paris and London. In Zurich (1855), Vienna (1871). His work is removed from the romantic classicism of *Schinkel, who was a friend of his. His adaptations of Romanesque, Gothic and Renaissance features are typical examples of 19th-century historicism. Semper's originality lies in his massing, where the building's function stands out sharply. (The projecting curvature of the auditorium in the Dresden Opera House, 1837–41, rebuilt in 1878 following the fire of 1871). Dresden Art Gallery (started 1847); Burgtheater in Vienna (rebuilt differently, 1874–88). His theoretical writings stress the influence of structure on style and recommend the use of colour in architecture. (*p. 9)
Bibliography: Gottfried Semper, *Der Stil in den technischen und tektonischen Künsten*, Frankfurt 1860–3.

Sert, José Luis, b. Barcelona 1902. Studied at the Escuela Superior de Arquitectura in Barcelona; 1929–30 worked for *Le Corbusier and Pierre Jeanneret in Paris. Emigrated to the United States in 1939; 1947–56 President of *CIAM at whose instance he published among other writings *Can our Cities Survive?* (3rd edition, Cambridge, Mass. 1947). Since 1958 Dean of the Harvard Graduate School of Design. US Embassy, Bagdad (commenced 1955); Harvard University Health Center, Cambridge, Mass. (1957–61); Maeght Museum, St Paul-de-Vence (work still in progress). Extensive town-planning projects.

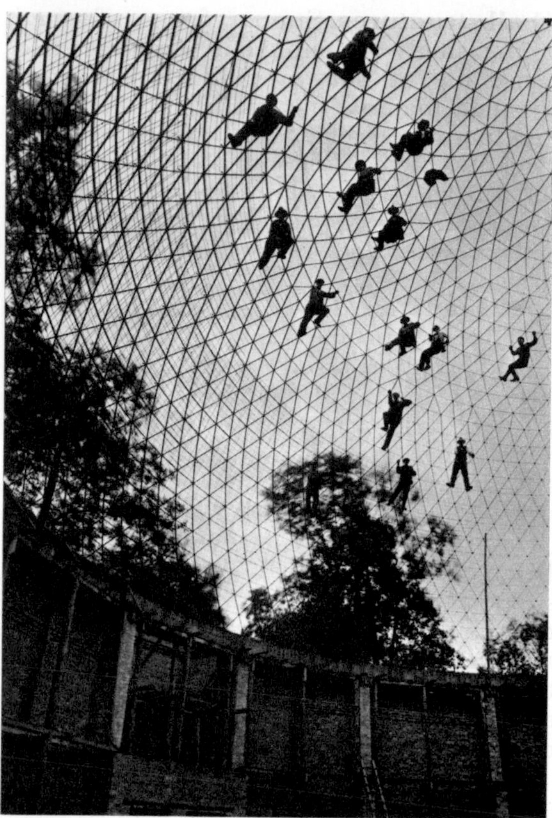

Walter Bauersfeld, Grid for the shell dome of the Planetarium in the Zoological Gardens. Berlin, 1926

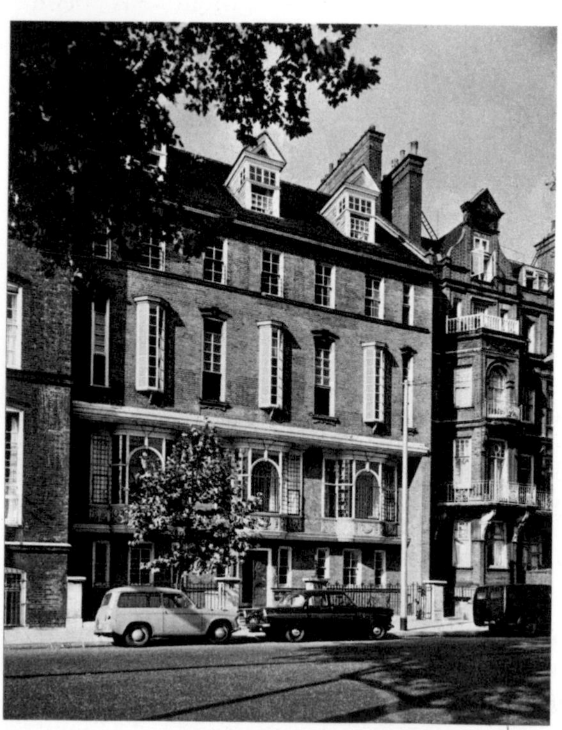

Richard Norman Shaw. Old Swan House. London, 1876

Shaw, Richard Norman, b. Edinburgh 1831, d. Hampstead 1912. Studied at the Royal Academy, London. Shaw, who synthesized numerous influences and styles in his own work, exercised a strong influence on his contemporaries with his churches, offices and in particular with his tasteful private houses. Among the latter, the Old Swan House, London, is especially distinguished by its delicate and slightly mannered proportions.

Shell structures. Support features formed from a singly or doubly curved surface and consisting of tension- and compression-resistant material (i.e. material resistant to bending) are called shell structures; the thickness of the shell is slight in relation to its surface area. The most important properties of a shell are that it is not straight but curved, and it is thin. Hence the designer also calls the shell a plane support structure. A girder on the other hand is called a beam-type support structure. In a plane support structure, two dimensions (length and width) are considerably greater than the third (thickness); in a beam-type support structure, however, two dimensions (depth and width of section) are decidedly smaller than the third (length).

Beam-type support structures and plane support structures are different with regard to their stresses. A girder which is loaded at right angles to its axis is acted on by bending moments and sheer stress, whereas an ideal shell has neither bending moments nor sheer stress, only normal stresses uniformly distributed over its thickness. A girder resists loading by its strength, a shell by its shape. A simple test will explain the structural properties of a shell. A piece of paper, spread out flat and held along its two edges, will bend. It cannot even carry its own weight, let alone additional loads. But if the same piece of paper is curved and held along its edges, it develops a surprising rigidity. In nature we find many forms comparable to our new shell structures. We may mention diatoms, single-cell creatures consisting of siliceous algae; eggs, sea-shells and snails. These shapes are built on the principle that a firm casing may be formed from the minimum of material. Their rigidity does not depend on the firmness of the material or its thickness, but on the casing's curved shape.

The engineers Walter Bauersfeld and Franz Dischinger deserve the credit for having established the theoretical and practical advantages of shell construction. It is true that early attempts to calculate similar structures can be found in the literature of the end of the 19th century and the beginning of the 20th, but no practical use was made of this theory. Bauersfeld and Dischinger in the early twenties were the first to tackle the problem both in theory and in practice and thus laid the foundations

Eduardo Torroja. Grandstand. Zarzuela race course, near Madrid, 1935

for one of the most interesting developments in the field of structural engineering. Since that time development has been rapid and constant. In the twenties the first barrel and dome shells were constructed by the Zeiss-Dywidag process, invented by Bauersfeld and Dischinger, (Dome shells: experimental structure near Jena, 1922; factory for Schott and Gen., 1923–4; Jena Planetarium, 1925. Barrel shells: roof of the exhibition halls at the GESOLEI, Düsseldorf, 1926; market hall, Frankfort on the Main, 1926–7. Intersecting barrel shells in the shape of cross-arched vaults: market hall, Leipzig, 1927–9; market hall, Basle, 1929). *Freyssinet built the market hall at Rheims in the shape of a barrel vault (1928–9) and the repair work-shop at Bagneux as a conoidal one (1928–9). As early as 1934 G. Baroni built the first shell in Milan in the shape of a hyperbolic paraboloid (iron foundry at Milan) and in 1938 the first shell in the shape of an upturned umbrella (warehouse at Ferrara). Bernard Lafaille has been working with shell structures since 1929. Between 1931 and 1933 different types of hall structures

Pier Luigi Nervi and Annibale Vitellozzi. Palazzetto dello Sport. Rome, 1956–7

were put up on a grid system, where the shell thickness for spans between 98 and 164 feet was a mere 2 to $2\frac{3}{4}$ inches. A little later, Konrad Hruban worked on similar structural shapes. After 1940 his shells developed in the form of hyperbolic paraboloids began to be used and are employed in many ways for industrial buildings. Eduardo *Torroja designed the roof of the market hall at Algeciras (1934), the racecourse at Zarzuela (1935) and the ball-games hall, Madrid (1935). Dischinger constructed a number of large-span aircraft hangars in the thirties (Bug/Rügen hangar 1936–7). *Maillart's Cement Hall for the Swiss Provinces Exhibition, Zurich, 1938–9, may be called a model instance of the structural and sculptural possibilities of shell construction.

It is at first amazing that up to the present time the knowledge of these structures and their application has remained confined to a small circle of architects. Neither *Le Corbusier, nor *Gropius, not *Breuer concerned themselves during the twenties or thirties with shell structures. It is only now, in a changing architectural world, that architects regard shell construction as a suitable means for realizing their ideas. Frequently, however, they restrict themselves to accepting shapes designed by structural engineers. The task that lies before architects of employing this form of construction as an architectural medium is only being achieved step by step.

The application of shell construction is now reaching every type of architecture. Among the most important examples are the airport reception buildings at St Louis, Mo. by Hellmuth, Leinweber and *Yamasaki, engineers Roberts and Schaefer Co. (1953–5); exhibition hall of the Centre National des Industries et Techniques at Paris by Camelot, de Mailly and *Zehrfuss, engineer Esquillan (1957–8); Palazzetto dello Sport, Rome, by A. Vitellozzi, engineer *Nervi (1956–7); Palazzo dello Sport, Rome, by Piacentini, engineer Nervi (1958–60); TWA reception building at Kennedy Airport, New York, by Eero *Saarinen and Associates (1961–2); Windward City Shopping Centre at Kaneohe, Hawaii by Wimberley and Cook, engineer Bradshaw (1957); buildings by Félix *Candela; market hall at Royan by Simon, Morisseau, engineer René Sarger (1955).

Bibliography: Jürgen Joedicke, *Schalenbau* (= Dokumente der Modernen Architektur 2), Stuttgart 1962.

JÜRGEN JOEDICKE

Sheppard, Richard Herbert, b. 1910. Studied at the Architectural Association School of Architecture, London; in private practice since 1938, latterly with Geoffrey Robson and other partners. Wide range of buildings, especially educational ones; awarded RIBA Bronze Medal for Harrowfield Boys' School, Harold Hill, Essex (1954). Winner of the limited competition for Churchill College, Cambridge (1959) with a design featuring twenty courts grouped informally round a library and

Page 259. George Francis Hellmuth, Joseph William Leinweber and Minoru Yamasaki. Airport reception building. St Louis, Mo., 1953–5

INFORMATION

clerestory-lit reading room in the centre. Students' hall of residence, Imperial College, London; pithead bath, Dudley Colliery, Northumberland.

Siren, Heikki and Kaija. Heikki Siren, b. Helsinki 1918, Kaija Siren, b. Kotka 1920. Studied at Helsinki Technical College. Since 1946 this married couple have had an office of their own. Schools, housing (in part *prefabricated), office blocks, Small auditorium of the Finnish National Theatre, Helsinki (1954); Chapel, Otaniemi Technical College (1957). (*Finland)

Skidmore, Owings and Merrill (SOM) (Louis Skidmore, b. 1897, Nathaniel A. Owings, b. 1903, and John O. Merrill, b. 1896).

Skidmore, Owings and Merrill. Lever House. New York, 1952

Skidmore, Owings and Merrill. Connecticut General Life Insurance Building, Hartford, Conn., 1957

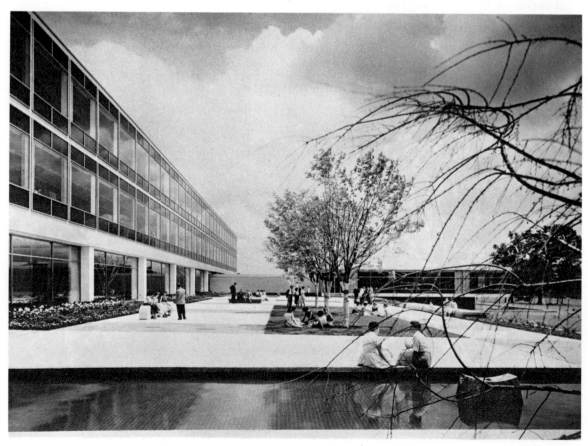

This American architectural firm was founded by Messrs Skidmore and Owings in 1935 and the partnership was expanded to include Mr Merrill in 1936. Although the two founders had been associated with the 'modernistic' designs of the Chicago 'Century of Progress' Exposition (1933), the impact of the firm upon the course of recent architecture was not significant until after the Second World War. Its leadership dates from the completion of the Lever Building, Park Avenue, New York City (1952), the design of Gordon *Bunshaft, a partner in the firm who has been largely responsible for the establishment and direction of the SOM style. The Lever design was one of the very first successful commercializations of the *Mies van der Rohe geometry of metal and glass; so successful that by the end of the 1950s imitations of this specific office block could be found in London, Copenhagen, Caracas and elsewhere. (*p. 23; *Steel)

Since that date SOM, with offices in Chicago, San Francisco and Portland, Oregon, as well as in New York, has proceeded to refine the original model in a series of increasingly simple yet elegant glass towers, notably those for Inland Steel, Chicago (1954), Pepsi Cola (1959), Union Carbide (1960), and Chase Manhattan Bank (1957–61), the last three in New York City. Their style has been imitated at one time or another, albeit usually in a coarsened form, by almost every large American architectural firm, irrespective of location or previous taste. This largely SOM-created image of expensive efficiency became, by the end of the 1950s, the most universally admired quality in large-scale architectural schemes. Their abstractly classicizing contemporary idiom, with all of its carefully proportioned urban restraint, was even applied in large-scale offices constructed in artfully landscaped rural sites, notably in the entirely glazed three-storey blocks of the Connecticut General Life Insurance Company, near Hartford, Conn. (1957). Similar elements were utilized on a vaster scale and in a more dramatic, mountainous setting in the Air Academy, Colorado Springs, Colo., finished 1959. This huge complex heralded the momentary establishment of the SOM modernist idiom as the semi-official architectural style of the day.

However, at the exact moment of the greatest success of this mirror-like purist style, which was the ultimate and most academic manifestation of the taste established by the masters of the *International Style of the 1920s, new tendencies were to be discerned in other SOM projects and realizations. The John Hancock Building, San Francisco (1960), rather self-consciously rejected the glass *curtain wall in favour of a bay system of separate windows and load-bearing external walls. A vigorous, structurally expressive touch was provided by the flaring concrete piers which formed the Expressionistic 'order' of the ground floor and mezzanine. In other projects, such as the Banque Lambert, Brussels (1958), or in the Rare Book Library, Yale University, New Haven, Conn., still other design innovations appear, all of which represent divergences from the established orthodox modernism of the glass box. In the Yale design the rectangular cubic form of the building is carried upon a huge Vierendeel truss which is supported by four concrete pylons at the corners. Hence while the bulky mass is dramatically elevated from the ground, it

Skidmore, Owings and Merrill. John Hancock Building. San Francisco, 1960

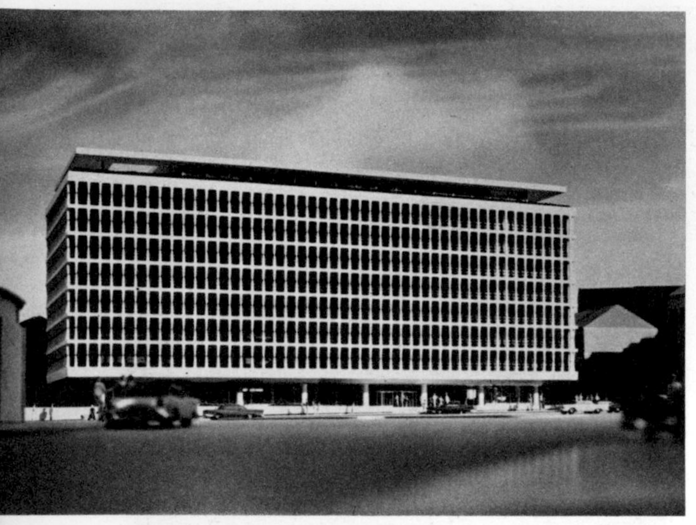

Skidmore, Owings and Merrill. Banque Lambert. Brussels, 1958. Model

does not float gracefully or hover above the site in the characteristically contemporary fashion of the Lever Building, nor are its forms sheathed in the seemingly weightless glass surfaces first employed by the International Style. Instead the external surfaces are divided into emphatic grid patterns by precast concrete elements of a marble aggregate.
SOM is not the largest of American architectural firms; neither is it truly typical of the building design industry in the USA, if only because of its superior taste and understanding of the stylistic requirements of contemporary commercial and monumental architecture. However, its finest work does represent in a particularly elevated fashion the aspirations of a major segment of today's architectural profession.
Bibliography: Ernst Danz, *SOM: Architecture of Skidmore, Owings and Merrill 1950–1962*, London 1963.

JOHN M. JACOBUS, JR

Smithson, Alison and Peter. Alison Smithson, b. Sheffield 1928. Peter Smithson, b. Stockton-on-Tees 1923. The Hunstanton School, Norfolk (1954), ranks as the first example of *Brutalism. Their design for the Berlin City competition (third prize) provides for a closed pedestrian precinct on a second level. Economist Bldg., London (begun 1962; *Neoclassicism).

Soane, Sir John, b. Goring-on-Thames 1753, d. London 1837. Appointed architect to the Bank of England in 1788, for which he carried out alterations and new additions from 1788 to 1833. Numerous government commissions; from 1806 professor at the Royal Academy. Churches, private houses, villas. His composition with abstract shapes reminiscent of the French revolutionary architects, the broad disposition of his volumes and masses, as well as the exposed cast-iron construction of his cupolas have earned Soane the reputation among modern architects of being contemporary in feeling.
Bibliography: J. N. Summerson, *Sir John Soane*, London 1952; Dorothy Stroud, *The Architecture of Sir John Soane*, London 1961.

Soleri, Paolo, b. Italy 1920. Since 1947 in the United States. Influenced by Frank Lloyd *Wright for whom he worked. Admirer of Antoni *Gaudí. Advanced designs such as the tubular bridge (1947) and the project for a 'town on a table mountain' with two million inhabitants (since 1959). Among his few executed designs is the House in the Desert (Cave Creek, Ariz., 1951, together with Mark Mills) which is roofed by two movable hemispheres, and a ceramics factory at Vietri sul Mare near Salerno (1954), a five-storey hall with spiral ramps.

Sommaruga, Giuseppe, b. Milan 1867, d. Milan 1917. Studied architecture at the Brera, Milan. He was the main exponent of Italian *Art Nouveau, together with D' *Aronco and *Basile. Sommaruga employed floral Art Nouveau details, particularly in his decorative friezes, which contrast with the bare masonry. Palazzo Castiglioni, Milan (1900–3), Mausoleum Faccanoni, Sarnico (1907).

Space Frames. The development of space frames is a challenging task for engineers and architects. The traditional concept of a linear progression of stresses in structures has been extended by a system involving the spatial dissolution of the stresses, with all the load-bearing members working together. Thus structures could be devised that are remarkable for stability and load-bearing capacity despite their low weight. A wealth of possibilities for the dissolution of tensile and compressive stresses in space grids has already been examined.
The different systems are principally distinguished by the geometric form of the

Paolo Soleri and Mark Mills. House in the Desert. Cave Creek, Ariz., 1951

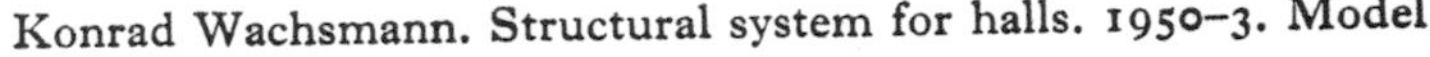

Konrad Wachsmann. Structural system for halls. 1950–3. Model

grid module they use, which often already constitutes a stable element. Further distinctions result from the uniform use of tension and compression members or surfaces, or by a clear differentiation between tension and compression members. The most extreme, efficient and fascinating structures are undoubtedly the continuous tension-compression systems made up of cables and struts by Buckminster *Fuller.

The natural requirement that buildings should afford protection from the elements leads to the development of closed surfaces. These surfaces are integrated into the space frame as tension or compression components and become an effective part of the structure. This method of construction affords further important advantages in that even plastics can be employed as structural building materials. In this instance, the low modulus of elasticity of these materials is of no effect due to the extraordinarily advantageous spatial distribution of stresses and the geometrical stability of the structure as a whole.

Space frames are particularly suitable for prefabrication, due to their multitude of modular components. That is why all space frame structures so far known are made of standardized prefabricated building components which can be quickly erected by simple methods such as the Unistrut, Mero and Space-Deck systems. Outstanding schemes made possible by this development include: the aircraft hangar built as early as 1946 by *Wachsmann and the different types of geodesic domes by *Fuller. Makowski and Le Ricolais have made further important advances towards a full theoretical and practical understanding of the distribution of stresses in these systems.

These structures will become ever more important in the future, as their current applications already indicate. The freedom of uninterrupted space and spans which they afford, even of the largest dimensions, and their almost unlimited adaptability to changing and diverse requirements, permit functional solutions of a completely new type.

The architectural expression of these structures is leading to a new aesthetic dimension. In a way that compares with the composition of matter itself, they provide direct spatial models of their theoretical content in their dematerialized multiformity.

Richard Buckminster Fuller. Geodesic Dome. 1954. Individual units of cardboard

Bibliography: Buckminster Fuller, *Brief Building Construction*; Z. S. Makowski, *Space Structures*; Konrad Wachsmann, *Wendepunkt im Bauen*, Wiesbaden 1959; Robert W. Marks, *The Dymaxion World of Buckminster Fuller*, New York 1960.

HERBERT OHL

Spence, Sir Basil, b. India 1907. Studied at the Schools of Architecture of London and Edinburgh Universities. Assisted Lutyens on the Viceroy's House, New Delhi. In private practice since 1930. Won the competition for Coventry Cathedral (1951); Sea and Ships Pavilion, at the South Bank Exhibition, *Festival of Britain; university buildings at Durham, Exeter, Liverpool, Newcastle, Nottingham and Southampton. His design for Sussex University is a Piranesian fantasy of flat arches and barrel vaults. Housing estates at Dunbar, Selkirk and a premiated

Page 265. Basil Spence. Coventry Cathedral. 1954–62

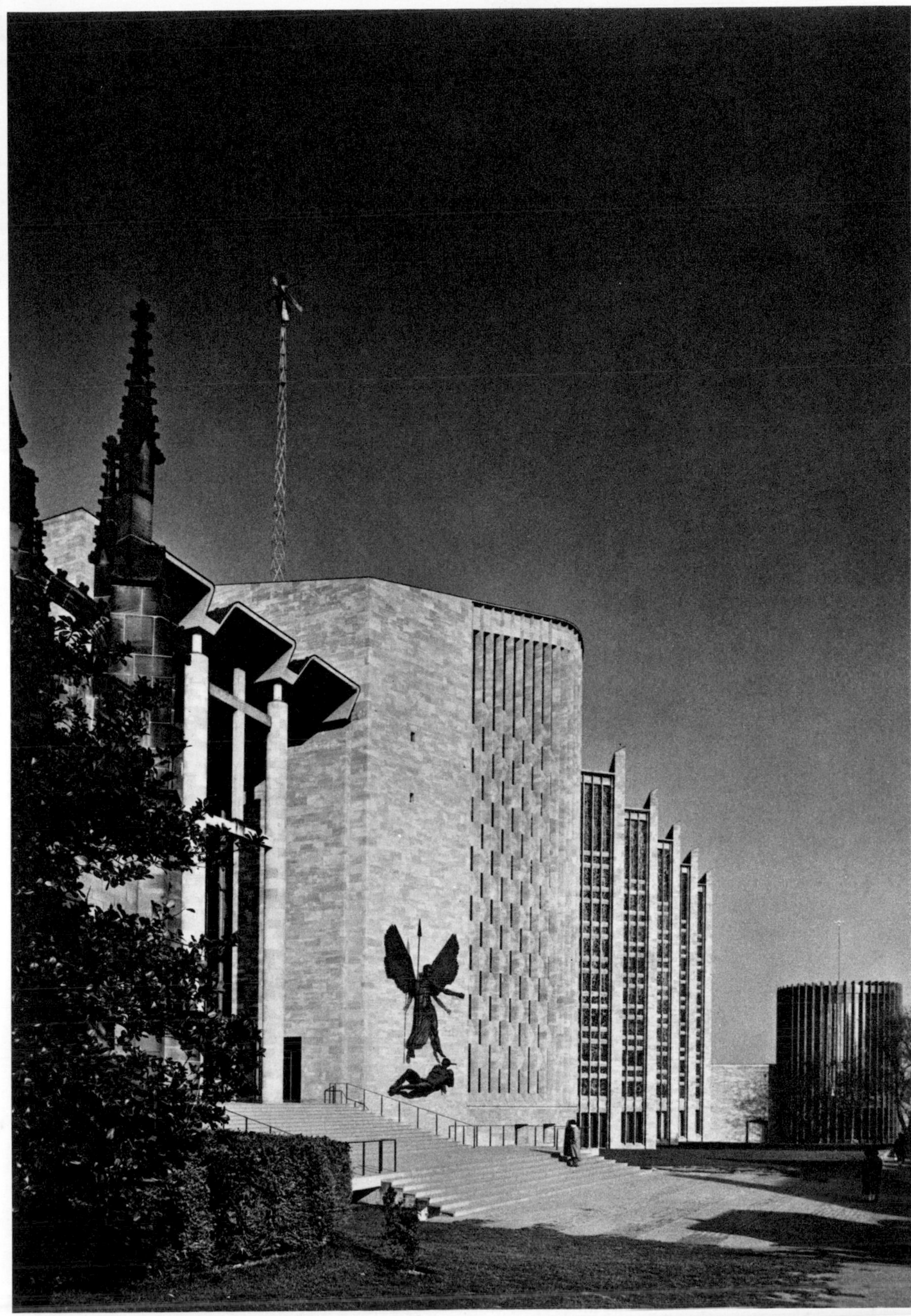

scheme at Sunbury-on-Thames (1951); tall blocks of flats in the Gorbals, Glasgow and Basildon Town Centre. Churches, theatres, factories and office buildings, including Thorn House, St Martin's Lane, London (1959). His most celebrated design, that for Coventry Cathedral (1954–62), represents an attempt to express a traditional layout in a contemporary idiom. As such it may be considered to have achieved a fair measure of success, though it does not display any radical re-thinking from the point of view of the liturgical movement, or the modern movement in architecture. *Bibliography:* B. Spence, *Coventry Phoenix*, London 1962.

HAROLD MEEK

Eugène Emmanuèle Viollet-le-Duc. Assembly Hall. 1863–72. Project

Steel. In the second half of the 18th century the first steps were taken in England which opened up the way for the industrial manufacture of iron products at Abraham Darby's Coalbrookdale foundry: coke was used in 1747 for smelting iron ore instead of charcoal, and by 1750 they were able to produce malleable pig-iron in bars. Up to then iron had only been worked by the elementary methods of artisan production, and was used for two main purposes in building: for structural members, mostly in tensile stress (tie-rods, chains, tie-bars for arches and vaults), and for wrought-iron.

The first of the new manufactured products used in building construction were cast-iron girders, beams and columns. The first known use of cast-iron columns in England is in St Anne's Church, Liverpool, by a certain Dodd (1770–2). Matthew Boulton and James Watt built a seven-storey cotton mill in Salford (1801) with an internal framework of cast-iron columns and inverted T-section beams with external walls of solid masonry. In the following decades this type of construction was frequently adopted for factories and warehouses (mills in Derbyshire and Lancashire; warehouses at St Katherine's Docks, London, by Thomas Telford, 1824–8 and at Liverpool Docks by J. Hartley, 1824–45). In an eight-storey refinery built in 1845, William Fairbairn adopted an analogous system, but for cast-iron beams substituted wrought-iron I-sections, and instead of the shallow brick arches running between girders employed in the previous factories he used thin curved metal plates, filled in with concrete. Meanwhile John Cragg had built three churches at Liverpool, St

Matthew Boulton and James Watt. Cotton Mill. Salford, 1801

George's, St Michael's and St Philip's (1813–16) to designs by Thomas Rickman, using cast-iron frames throughout.

Taking advantage of the ease with which different types of section could be obtained in cast-iron, Humphrey Repton designed a pheasant-house for the Royal Pavilion at Brighton in 1808, fanciful in its general lines and decorative details. The Pavilion itself was built by John Nash in 1818 in the 'Indian Style', and made use of cast-iron on a grand scale for the first time in a prestige building (columns, girders, dome structure, decorative elements).

In France, the roof of the Théâtre Français, Paris, was built on an iron frame to the designs of Victor Louis (1786), and Bélanger and Brunet rebuilt the dome of the Halles au Blé, destroyed by fire, in iron and copper (1811). This rapid and widespread recourse to iron is due to its properties of adaptability to complex profiles by means of casting, its fire-resistance, ease of use and ability to span large areas with slender members at distant centres.

Works involving particular technical difficulties were faced from the outset and solved. The earliest cast-iron bridge was built over the Severn at Coalbrookdale between 1775 and 1779. It spans 100 feet and consists of five ribs subdivided into two series of half-arches, each cast in a single piece by the Darby Foundry. An experiment of great boldness was completed in 1796 with the Sunderland Bridge, spanning 236 feet, erected by Rowland Bourdon over the Wear to a design of Tom Paine's. This structure was built up from ribs consisting of openwork cast-iron voussoirs and wrought-iron straps, laid upon timber centering. The same technique, derived from masonry construction, was proposed by Telford in 1801 for a bridge across the Thames with a span of 600 feet, which was never realized, however, due to difficulties in acquiring the land on either bank for the abutments. In France, too, iron was used in 1801–3 for a bridge that still exists and is in use: the Pont des Arts, Paris, a multiple arch structure by de Cessart and Dillon.

The technique of constructing suspension bridges had been developed from the end of the 18th century, firstly with chains and later with wire ropes (Conway Castle Bridge, by Telford, 1822–6; Rhône Bridge, by Séguin, 1824). In 1836, I. K. Brunel

James Bogardus. Cast-iron foundry. New York, 1848–9

commenced building the Clifton Suspension Bridge over the river Avon, at Bristol, which with its span of 700 feet is one of the masterpieces of 19th-century engineering. Brunel, a naval architect, pursued the experiments begun around the year 1825 on the application of iron to shipbuilding. In 1843, he launched the first screw steamer to cross the Atlantic; it had an iron hull, and initiated the technique of self-supporting riveted shell structures. Similar techniques were adopted for other major engineering projects, as instanced by Robert Stephenson's Britannia Bridge over the Menai Straits (1846–50) which features pairs of huge rectangular wrought-iron tubes which run between massive masonry towers.

Simultaneously with these developments improvements were being made in the technology of iron manufacture. The production of puddle iron entered the industrial stage in 1840; steel production with Bessemer converters began in 1856, followed by the open-hearth process in 1864 and the basic converter process in 1878. The *glass industry had made great strides, too, from the second half of the 18th century onwards, and the combination of glass and iron opened up new possibilities in architecture: galleries, conservatories, exhibition buildings such as Joseph *Paxton's Crystal Palace in London and

Gustave Eiffel and L. A. Boileau. Bon Marché Department Store. Paris, 1876

buildings at the various Paris Exhibitions, culminating in Dutert and Contamin's Machinery Hall (1889), whose nave is roofed via a series of three-hinge portals with a span of *c.* 380 feet.

An important rôle in the gradual perfecting of structural methods and components was played by Gustave *Eiffel; the designer of many bridges, viaducts and the Eiffel Tower, he pursued an architectural ideal that sought to make the essential lines of a structure correspond with its static functions. The architect Henri *Labrouste, who founded a private school of architecture in Paris with the aim of teaching strict adherence to the demands of function and structure, designed the Bibliothèque Ste Geneviève (1843) and the Bibliothèque Impériale (1855) using a system of cast-iron columns and arches to give greater space, though retaining eclectic or traditionally academic forms for the walls that formed the outer shell and for the decoration. In his Bibliothèque Nationale (1858–68), while employing the same structural and decorative schemes as in the Bibliothèque Impériale for the reading room, he adopted a system of stanchions, girders and floor grilles for the book stacks that allowed the daylight, coming in from above, to filter down to the lower floors; the structural elements are exposed to view without any decorative trimmings, and conspire to produce novel spatial effects of a high order. Another important contribution to the handling of internal spaces was made by the Bon Marché department store in Paris (1876), by Boileau and Eiffel, who achieved their effects by an airy system of foot-bridges, supported by slender columns and lit by the large glazed roof.

The years around the middle of the 19th century saw the beginnings of framed construction as we know it now. A decisive step in this direction was the replacement of solid external walls by columns and beams or arches in cast-iron. The first evidence of the new technique may be seen in the work of James *Bogardus, who is considered the inventor of this method of construction, on the basis of his designs (New York World's Fair, 1853) and executed projects (five-storey factory, New York, 1848; Harper and Brothers Building, New York, 1854). The system underwent notable developments, including those in quality, in the United States (riverfront buildings at St Louis) and England (commercial buildings in Liverpool). All the formal elements of these cast-iron façade structures, however, were taken from the traditional repertory of 19th-century historicism.

One of the first buildings to use a framed construction throughout was the Chocolat Menier factory built at Noisiel-sur-Marne, near Paris by Jules Saulnier in 1871–2. The iron frame, with diagonal struts clearly showing on the façade rests on four hollow iron girders supported by four masonry

Page 269. Ferdinand Dutert and Contamin. Machinery Hall at the International Exhibition. Paris, 1889

piers built up on the bed of the Marne. The reconstruction of Chicago, growing rapidly after the fire of 1871, provided the impulse for exploiting the possibilities of frame construction (hitherto only used for industrial buildings) in multi-storey commercial blocks, with their need for fireproofing and broad areas of glass. William Le Baron *Jenney, having used the by now usual internal structure with iron columns in his first Leiter Building (1879), employed a complete metal framework for the Home Insurance Building (1883–5), though the surrounding masonry wall shared part of its loadbearing functions. With the second Leiter, Manhattan and Fair Buildings, he refined his structural system, reducing the façades to a form of light cladding carried on a uniform metal frame, thus achieving the prototype of the modern office block. In the spirit of Le Baron Jenney, the architects of the *Chicago School perfected the system, and in the Loop district defined the original architectural physiognomy of the first centre of the modern movement. Having passed through a phase of attempting to interpret the new structures by adapting traditional stylistic details, they began to derive their forms logically from the framed structure, and abandoned superimposed decoration (Marquette Building by *Holabird and Roche, 1894; Reliance Building by *Burnham and *Root, 1890–5; Carson, Pirie and Scott Building by *Sullivan, 1899). After the 1893 Columbian Exposition in Chicago, American architecture underwent a period of stylistic eclipse with the return of eclecticism and academicism. Meanwhile however, steel frame techniques for skyscrapers were making progress—sometimes sensationally so—throughout America (Woolworth Building [58 storeys] 1912; Empire State Building [85 storeys] 1931, both in New York).

The main exponents of progressive architecture in Europe at the turn of the century approached the use of steel without any preconceptions, and employed it freely in their schemes in conformity with their own styles and the possibilities they saw for applying it. Victor *Horta in the Hôtel

Victor Horta. Hôtel Aubecq, Brussels, 1900. Dome over the stair well

Hans Poelzig. Water tower. Posen, 1911

Otto Bartning. Steel Church. Cologne, 1928

Tassel (1893) and the Maison du Peuple (1896–9) in Brussels achieved a perfect unity between structure and decoration. H. P. *Berlage obtained unusual effects in his Amsterdam Stock Exchange (1897–1903) by exposing the structural elements. Otto *Wagner in the hall of the Post Office Savings Bank in Vienna (1904–6) aimed at unity of composition by reducing the individual structural elements to their simplest formal expression. Peter *Behrens in his AEG Works, Berlin (1908–9) revealed that steel, too, had a secret form of expression that lay within the material itself. Hans *Poelzig infused a unitary character into the variegated structures that went to make up his water tower at Posen (1911), derived from his *Expressionist type of sensibility.

The modern movement, in the period after the First World War, took the steel-frame structure for granted, as an indispensable instrument for achieving freedom and rationality in design. In the Weissenhof Estate at Stuttgart (1927) and in other more or less contemporary works, the masters of the modern movement (*Neutra, *Le Corbusier, *Mies van der Rohe, *Mendelsohn) presented a substantially unified panorama to the public, in which a joint purpose and a broad measure of agreement were more in evidence than any personal differences. A common denominator was the principle of the pure expression of function by structural elements. Around 1930, modern architecture began to gain ground in America, and the *International Style was applied uncompromisingly to the skyscrapers, too, where the severity of the modern method brought a notable measure of lucidity to the traditional treatment (Philadelphia Savings Fund Society Building by *Howe and *Lescaze, 1932).

The outburst of building activity after the Second World War helped to perfect and spread the methods of steel frame construction to the most diverse of building types. The need to make savings in time, cost and upkeep led the industry to prefabricate various versions of *curtain walling, which afford numerous possibilities for architectural expression. Outstanding contributions in these fields of research have been made by Mies van der Rohe, whose theoretical studies go back to the year 1919.

Parallel to the work of perfecting the steel frame construction, other forms of structural technique have been studied and applied: *suspended roofs, hung from stressed steel cables; *shell structures in welded plate (water tower at General

Skidmore, Owings and Merrill. Manufacturers Trust Company. New York, 1953–4

Ludwig Mies van der Rohe. Crown Hall, Illinois Institute of Technology. Chicago, 1952–6. Steelwork in course of erection

Motors Technical Center, Detroit, by Eero *Saarinen, 1955); wide span cantilever roofs of ribbed flats on reinforced concrete piers (hangar at San Francisco airport, by Goldsmith, 1959; Palazzo del Lavoro, Turin, by *Nervi, 1961); reticulated *space frames of prefabricated modular units (geodesic domes by Buckminster *Fuller and studies by K. *Wachsmann). These new techniques, which provide the opportunity and means for bold architectural experiments, may be considered the bases for developing new forms of expression and design.

Bibliography: John Gloag and Derek Bridgwater, *A History of Cast Iron in Architecture*, London 1948; O. Johannsen, *Geschichte des Eisens*, Düsseldorf 1953; *Construire en acier, Bauen in Stahl*, Zurich 1956; V. Zignoli, *Costruzioni metalliche*, Turin 1956–7; *Ponti stradali in acciaio*, Milan 1958; Konrad Wachsmann, *Wendepunkt im Bauen*, Wiesbaden 1959; H. R. Hitchcock, *Early Victorian Architecture in Britain*, London 1954; T. K. Derry and T. I. Williams, *A Short History of Technology*, Oxford 1960.

GIUSEPPE VARALDO
GIAN PIO ZUCCOTTI

Stijl, De. A group of artists and architects, formed in Leiden in 1917, which published a journal of the same name; its members included Vilmos Huszar, Antonie Kok, Piet Mondrian, Jacobus Johannes *Oud and Theo van *Doesburg. They were subsequently joined by the architects Robert van't Hoff, and Gerrit Thomas *Rietveld, the painter Bart van der Leck and the sculptor and painter Georges Vantongerloo.
The type of design associated with De Stijl was very much determined by the neoplasticism of the painters Piet Mondrian and Theo van Doesburg; it implied, in every respect, a break with tradition. Like neoplasticist painting, De Stijl architecture was influenced by Cubism, too. Right angles and smooth walls were almost exclusively the order of the day; the demand for unmistakably spotless surfaces excluded the use of bricks, which

Theo van Doesburg and Cor van Eesteren. Studies for a private house. 1923

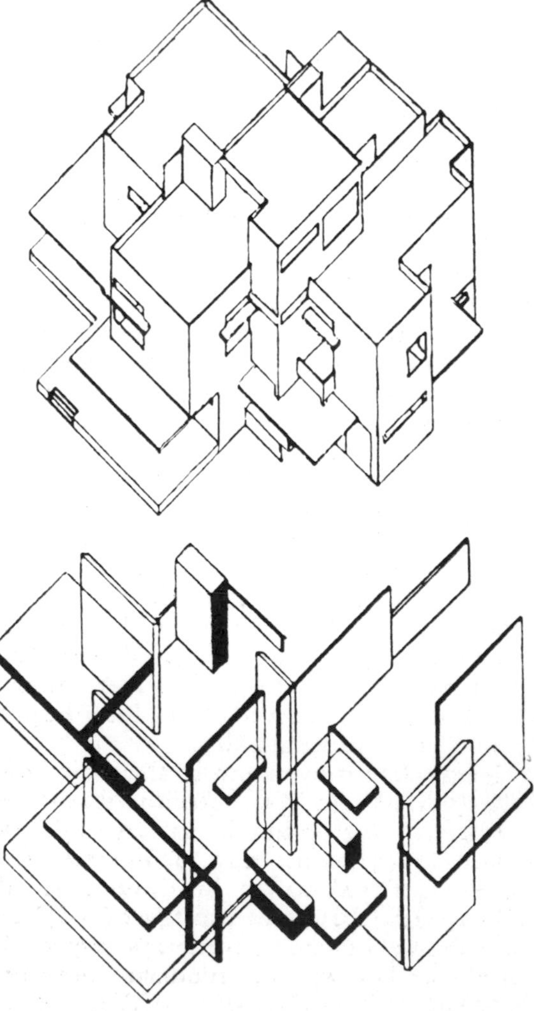

gave too graduated and imprecise a colour-effect. The cube or parallelopiped served as the point of departure, but the cubic shape, as an elementary expression of space, was not felt as something static, but as part of an infinite environment, into which the internal walls continued. Hence every circumscribed definition of a building by front, side or rear elevations was rejected. The designed space, i.e. the room, opened out on all sides into the universal space, conceived of as a crystal.

New attitudes emerged with regard to the use of colour, both as regards external surfaces and interior decoration. Colour no longer served as an element of decoration, but helped to define space. Following Mondrian's example, the primary colours, red, blue and yellow, were used exclusively; white, black and grey were admitted as contrasting tones. All other colours were regarded as impure, in stark contrast to the picturesque brown tones that had prevailed in late-19th-century interiors. Typical examples include Rietveld's Schröder House in Utrecht (1924) and the Café de Unie in Rotterdam by Oud (1924–5, destroyed in the 1940 blitz).

Its cubistic design, simplicity and austerity of line are the reasons why the architecture of De Stijl is often confused with the concept of 'Neue Sachlichkeit', a term that was applied to German painting around 1925. De Stijl architecture certainly exerted great influence, and set the type for developments in the later twenties (*Functionalism, *International Style) with its new attitude to space.

Robert van't Hoff. Huis ter Heide. Utrecht, 1916

But despite the contrary asseverations of its supporters, De Stijl was to a great extent an aesthetic theory. In this respect it differed from later developments, since Functionalism and the International Style rejected all fixed notions of aesthetics, believing in the unity of form and function.

The translation of De Stijl's theories into architectural practice was not accomplished without a measure of conflict. After an initial period of collaboration, the partnership between Oud and van Doesburg broke up, since Oud's solid expertise in architecture was confronted by the brilliant dilettantism of a painter and theoretician, who, as an architect, was self-taught. Oud developed his

J. J. P Oud. Factory at Purmerend. 1919. Project

architecture from the tentative essays of De Stijl, and went on to exert a leading influence on Functionalism in W. Europe. Reminiscences of De Stijl features are still discernible in Rietveld's buildings, especially in the décor; his work, and with it the significance of De Stijl, were rediscovered by the younger generation of architects after 1945.

Bibliography: De Stijl, Internationaal Maandblad voor de Nieuwe Kunst, Wetenschap en Kultuur, Leiden 1917–31; *De Stijl*, Catalogue 81 of the Stedelijk Museum, Amsterdam 1951; Bruno Zevi, *Poetica dell'architettura neoplastica*, Milan 1953; H. L. C. Jaffé, *De Stijl 1917–1931, The Dutch Contribution to Modern Art*, Amsterdam 1956.

J. J. VRIEND

Stillman and Eastwick-Field. John Cecil Stillman and John Charles Eastwick-Field. Miscellaneous practice including houses, hospitals and farm buildings. Point block of flats at Hide Place, Westminster, for the local authority, with extensive use of pre-cast concrete techniques. Authors of a valuable study on joinery practice.

Stirling and Gowan. James Stirling and James Gowan. Partnership producing work of distinctive plastic effect. Housing at Ham Common (1958) with imaginative use of untreated concrete detailing to give rich sculptural quality; rehousing scheme at Preston with powerful visual patterns of fenestration evoking *Constructivist imagery.

Hugh Stubbins. Congress Hall. Berlin, 1957

Stone, Edward Durell, b. Fayetteville, Ark. 1902. Stone, who was called 'a young man with a brilliant future' by Frank Lloyd *Wright, first built clearly defined square blocks with smooth white surfaces, punctuated by strips of fenestration (Mandel House at Mount Kisco, New York, 1930; Museum of Modern Art, New York, 1939, together with Philip L. Goodwin). Commissions abroad, especially in tropical and sub-tropical countries, may have led to his now characteristic screen walls, non-loadbearing partitions in front of or behind the real structural members. These pierced walls of tiles, profilated bricks or metal grilles, which provide shade and ventilation, and which Stone employs in all buildings, appear as huge, carpet-like patterned areas and often go together with classically symmetrical plans and façades: Medical Centre at Palo Alto, Calif. (1957–60); US Embassy at New Delhi (1958). Stone used them also for the circular US pavilion at the Brussels Exhibition of 1958, where the roof structure rested on a compression ring more than 328 ft in diameter. (*p. 23; *USA)

Stubbins, Hugh, b. Powderly, Ala. 1912. Became Walter *Gropius's assistant at Harvard Graduate School of Design in 1939. Private houses, schools, office blocks, churches. The stage of the Loeb Theatre at Harvard (1957–60) can be changed from a proscenium type to an arena. The Congress Hall in Berlin, which was erected for the Interbau Exhibition, comprises auditorium, conference rooms, exhibition hall and theatre. Its saddle-shaped roof, whose weight is partly carried by walls and internal columns, partly by two anchors, is a bold feat of engineering.

Subtopia. Term coined by Ian Nairn to connote 'the world of universal low density mess . . . an even spread of abandoned aerodromes and fake rusticity, wire fences, traffic roundabouts, gratuitous notice-boards, car-parks and Things in Fields' extending out from suburbia to the country 'and back into the devitalized hearts of towns, so that the most sublime backgrounds, urban or rural, English or foreign, are now to be seen only over a foreground of casual and unconsidered equipment, litter and lettered admonition. . . . Within the town the agents of Subtopia are demolition and decay, buildings replaced by bijou gardens, car-parks and underscale structures, reduction of density where it should be increased (and the) reduction of vitality by false genteelism, of which Municipal Rustic is the prime agent.'

Bibliography: Ian Nairn, *Outrage*, London 1955; Ian Nairn, *Counter-attack against Subtopia*, London 1957.

Sullivan, Louis H., b. Boston 1856, d. Chicago 1924. Sullivan's fame is based upon the refinements that he introduced in the design of large metal-framed commercial buildings, and upon the development of an organic theory of architecture. In 1873 he attended architectural classes at the Massachusetts Institute of Technology and subsequently worked for the Philadelphia architect, Frank *Furness. Afterwards he spent a few months at the *École des Beaux-Arts, Paris (1874), and in 1876 went to Chicago to seek employment. After several routine positions, he joined the staff of Dankmar *Adler and rapidly displayed

Adler and Sullivan. Auditorium Building. Chicago, 1886–9

his talents as a designer. Two years later, in 1881, the partnership of Adler and Sullivan was formed, Adler devoting his energies to technical and business problems while Sullivan carried the burden of responsibilities with respect to design. The early work of this partnership is outwardly utilitarian, though its style remains somewhat tentative. It is only with the design of the Auditorium Building, Chicago (1886–9) that Sullivan's talent comes into focus. The monumental, round-arched vocabulary which dominates the exterior sheath of the Auditorium Building (which was an hotel and office building as well as a theatre) derives from the example of *Richardson, notably his Marshall Field Warehouse, Chicago (1885–7). On the other hand, the interior, and notably the proscenium of the auditorium, is one of the most original instances of planning and decoration in American architecture (*USA).

Louis H. Sullivan. Wainwright Building. St Louis, 1890–1

Office buildings—skyscrapers—were the stock-in-trade of the Chicago architectural profession, and Sullivan accommodated himself to such programmatic limitations during a decade (the 1890s) of extremely successful commercial design before a combination of personal and business problems deprived him of major commissions. After 1900, and the nominal close of the earlier portion of his career, most of his works were modest-sized edifices for clients in small mid-western farming communities.

Sullivan's Chicago skyscrapers of the 1890s reflect his sensitivity with respect to the adjustment of external detail to the rhythms and proportions of the building's structural core, the steel frame. Contrary to the implications of his oft-quoted epithet, 'Form follows function', Sullivan used the building's material and structural requirements as a point of departure for his creation, rather than conceiving of functional expression as a fixed, limited goal. The Wainwright Building, St Louis (1890–91) and the Guaranty Building, Buffalo (1894–5), represent the maturing of this attitude, which is well expressed by the title of an article by Sullivan of 1896, 'The Tall Office Building Artistically Considered'.

After the termination of Sullivan's partnership with Adler, he was sometimes engaged to design the façades of commercial buildings that were built by other architects, as in the Bayard Building, New York (1897–8), and the Gage Building, Chicago (1898–9). The adjustments of proportion and the expressive clarity of detailing in the cornices and vertical members of these two façades are not equalled by their general shape, over which Sullivan had no control; it is regrettable that he did not have an opportunity in this period to build the kind of free-standing skyscraper that is so common today. Not even the corner site of his Carson, Pirie & Scott Store, Chicago (1899), his last major commercial building, suggests what he would have done on an

Page 277. Adler and Sullivan. Auditorium Building. Chicago, 1886–9. Stair well

Louis H. Sullivan. Carson, Pirie and Scott. Chicago, 1899

open site, since the client insisted upon the round corner element and the mass of the building was subsequently extended by D. H. *Burnham, albeit using Sullivan's elevation. Thus his genius is apparent here only in the adjustment of detail to the bay system imposed by the steel frame.

Under the circumstances it is understandable that Sullivan's gift for inventive ornament, ultimately of a quasi-Art Nouveau, organic quality, developed to such a remarkable extent. This interest almost dominates his formal, monumental work, notably the Wainwright Tomb, St Louis (1892), and the Transportation Building at the Chicago World's Columbian Exposition of 1893. This latent urge towards the fusion of elaborate ornament with rhetorical, monumental forms is developed in his late, post-1900 work, notably in the National Farmers Bank, Owatonna, Minn. (1907–8), and in the Farmers and Merchants Union Bank, Columbus, Wis. (1919). Critical appraisal of these buildings has tended towards condescension as they are supposed to represent a falling off of creative force and functional cogency. However, an objective consideration of these small but major designs amply demonstrates Sullivan's continued development and creative maturity, albeit in a direction that is not immediately related to the more revolutionary strains of contemporary architecture.

In contrast to these almost traditional buildings, Sullivan's writings, notably *Kindergarten Chats* (1901) and *The Autobiography of an Idea* (1922–3), contain flashes of wisdom and insight into the evolution of contemporary architecture. However, these thoughts, occasionally beautifully expressed, are buried in texts which are turgid and unnecessarily repetitious. Contrary to accepted opinion, the very best of Sullivan's late work is to be found consistently in his buildings, and only occasionally in his writings.

Bibliography: Hugh Morrison, *Louis Sullivan, Prophet of Modern Architecture*, New York 1952; Willard Connely, *Louis Sullivan as he lived*, New York 1960.

JOHN M. JACOBUS, JR

Suprematism. A term invented by Kasimir *Malevich for purely abstract art, of the kind he first exhibited in 1915. Suprematism meant for Malevich the 'Supremacy of pure sensation in the fine arts'. The simple elements of form in his paintings are also applied to abstract architectonic compositions.

Suspended Roofs. Suspended roofs originated from the discovery that a structure consisting of tensile members involves little self-weight yet is capable of supporting relatively great loads. Tents and suspension bridges are early examples. As distinguished from these is an essentially new principle which consists in providing complete rigidity of form by the use of saddle-shaped surfaces (especially hyperbolic paraboloidal planes or lattices). Any deformation of shape such as buckling, oscillation or vibration caused by wind force or by self-weight can thus be avoided.

The hall at Raleigh by *Deitrick and *Nowicki (1952–3) is one of the first known

Matthew Nowicki, William H. Deitrick and Fred Severud. Arena. Raleigh, N.C., 1952–3

examples of this type of construction and the new kind of architecture to which it has given rise. It served as a pointer to the future of the new building method; apart from its logical use of stressed cable lattices, it also employs extremely light-weight prefabricated slab units for cladding purposes. Simultaneously with the new saddle-shaped suspended roofs, cable lattices or *shell vaults, methods of supporting compressive stresses via optimum stress arcs or modified thrust collars were developed. New shapes for roofs and halls and in particular a methodical system of foundations were developed by Le Ricolais, in theory and experimentally, as an extension of these principles. Inspired by the possibilities of traditional tent shapes and the new knowledge about suspended roofs, Frei *Otto has produced a wealth of forms in which he has used the roofing material itself as a structural component.

Suspended roof systems have introduced new possibilities to modern architecture, which question the whole principle of the use of rectangular shapes, while considerably enriching the contemporary idiom at the same time.

Bibliography: Frei Otto, *Über Zugbeanspruchte Konstruktionen*, Berlin 1962.

HERBERT OHL

Sweden. Industrialism came rather late to Sweden. In the late 19th century the economy of the country was still mainly based on agriculture, mining and forestry. Architecture followed the general European development on rather a moderate scale. The tendency of the 1880s was a combination of stylistic eclecticism and realistic treatment of the materials. In the following decade a German-influenced neo-Baroque played an important part. This was the background for the rise of modern Swedish architecture.

Its key figure was Ferdinand Boberg (1860–1946). Under the influence of the American H. H. *Richardson he began about 1890 to design a series of buildings such as the fire station at Gävle and the old Stockholm electricity works, which are characterized by a functionalist grouping of massive, block-like volumes. In his subsequent work the cubic heaviness is developed, but set off against concentrated elegant ornaments, in which the inspiration of *Sullivan is evident.

Towards the turn of the century the influence of *Art Nouveau was beginning to be felt in Sweden. It was, however, of rather a well-balanced and moderate character. An important part was played by the painter Carl Larsson, whose blond interiors from his own home greatly influenced interior architecture. In the bank buildings of Gustaf Wickman (1858–1916) neo-Baroque and Art Nouveau are skilfully mingled in sculpturally expressive forms. The desire to discard historical forms is especially evident in an interesting group

Carl Bergsten. Liljevalch Gallery. Stockholm, completed 1916

of office buildings in Stockholm designed by different architects. The façades all show a pronounced vertical treatment, often with very big glass areas between narrow pillars. Internally skeleton construction is used. Outstanding are a couple of buildings created by Ernst Stenhammar (1859–1927) and Erik Josephson (1864–1929).

Most important of the architects who tried to get away from the old forms were Carl Bergsten (1879–1935) and Georg A. Nilsson (1871–1949). The radical ideas of Bergsten reflect the influence of the Vienna Sezessionists, but in his tendency to regard the building as made up of geometrical planes he is also strongly reminiscent of *Berlage and Frank Lloyd *Wright. This is shown in his remarkable competition project for the Stockholm City Hall of 1905. The Norrköping Exhibition of the following year and the Hjorthagen Church in Stockholm gave him opportunities to realize his ideas. Nilsson's production as a whole is much more moderate, but some of his works show an evident affinity with the Anglo-Saxon modernists. His finest work is the iron-skeleton office building in Stockholm, Regeringsgatan 9, the final culmination of this modern school.

Other tendencies had by then become dominant. A group of architects had taken up Boberg's cubic forms and combined them with a new interest in materials of a rich, living texture, such as red brick or traditional Swedish timber. This 'national realism' derived partly from *Morris and his successors in England and the Nyrop circle in Denmark, but old Swedish architecture came to be of increasing importance as a source of inspiration. Nevertheless the character of the movement was not reactionary. The stress on traditional techniques and constructions was rather natural in a country where industrialism had not yet advanced very far. But what was modern was the social awareness of the leading architects. For perhaps the first time low-cost housing was seen as a task worthy of first-rate architectural treatment. The building which is generally regarded as the first work of this school is the one completed for the Medical Society in Stockholm in 1905 by Carl Westman (1866–1936). He used the traditional forms

Page 281. Erik Gunnar Asplund. Stockholm Exhibition. 1930

SVENSKA SLOJDFORENINGE
KOMMISSARIAT
INFORMATION
KORTBYRÅ
EXPEDITION

Sven Markelius. Concert Hall. Hälsingborg, 1932

in a realistic and rational way, as is shown expecially in his Stockholm Law Courts Building ten years later. The functional ideals of the period were even more stressed in the work of Erik Hahr (1869–1944), for many years city architect of Västerås, where he carefully preserved the old character of the town but also added industrial buildings and workmen's houses; these are remarkably advanced for their day, but nevertheless clearly show the links with tradition. Hahr's work also illustrates a very important feature of the architecture of this time, namely the strong feeling of relationship between buildings and town planning.

The artistic possibilities of this architecture of volumes and materials were exploited to the full by Ragnar Östberg (1866–1945), the supreme artist of the period. His greatest work, the Stockholm City Hall, was a source of inspiration to others during the long history of its design and erection, but by the time it was completed in 1923 other ideas had taken the lead. Romantic in a way, similar to Östberg's buildings, but more freely modern in its details, was the Engelbrekt Church in Stockholm by Lars Israel Wahlman (1870–1952). Quite different is Wickman's great wooden church at Kiruna, a remarkably powerful synthesis of form and structure. These are the two most important works in the religious architecture of the period.

About 1910 the school of national realism had become dominant in Swedish architecture. But at the same time the first signs of a reaction began to appear among the younger architects. They started to look for geometrical precision, for the nuances of lines and shadows and for materials of a more abstract character. Instead of heavy blocks they wanted to create a lighter impression. It was natural that their interest began to turn towards classicism. The first of the leading architects to develop these tendencies was Ivar Tengbom (b. 1878), who had been one of the foremost theorists among the national realists. Gradually he introduced a more restrained way of handling the materials and a simplification of forms—a typical example of the progressive, in no way revolutionary development towards a completely new architecture that has characterized so many Swedish architects.

But the greatest of the modernists, Carl Bergsten, saw clearly that classicism was only a stage in the search for pure new forms. In his Liljevalch Art Gallery in Stockholm, completed in 1916, he had covered quite a good bit of the way. The block character is gone, exterior and interior have been put in close relation to one another. One of the central ideas behind 20th-century architecture, the continuity of space, is appearing.

In the development of modern architecture as we see it today no generation has played a greater part than those born about the middle 1880s, the generation of *Gropius, *Le Corbusier, and *Mies van der Rohe. Three very important Swedish names belong to this group: Osvald *Almqvist, Gunnar *Asplund and Sigurd *Lewerentz. They started within the bounds of national realism. When Lewerentz designed a group of holiday houses in the Stockholm archipelago in 1914, he used the forms of Swedish tradition, but in such a timelessly functional way that these little houses are extremely difficult to date. Through Kay *Fisker they came to exercise a considerable influence on Danish architecture. A couple of years later Almqvist created the 'Bergslagsbyn', a village for the workmen and employees of the Domnarvet iron works, where the red wooden houses and the carefully studied town plan make up a model housing scheme which must be counted as one of the best Swedish examples from this century. Asplund at the same time was developing a feeling for space which was fundamentally related to modern international tendencies, only that he worked with more traditional forms. But it became increasingly clear that his classicism was only a superficial, artistic game and that his real development lay deeper.

With the 1920s industrial architecture came to be of real importance. On the merits of his water-power stations Almqvist must be counted one of the great pioneers in the field, judged from an international point of view. The mighty Forshuvudforsen of 1921 still remains in the functional tradition, but with Hammarforsen and Krångforsen, both designed and built in 1925–8, he had cut all ties with the past. These buildings, extremely pure and simple, have nevertheless a very strong dynamic expression, conveying something of the idea of water-power. Chenderoh in Malaya, completed in 1930, is perhaps even finer in its bright, calm clarity.

Almqvist had developed into 'the first Swedish functionalist' practically independently of all influences from abroad. At about the same time, however, Le Corbusier's theories got an intelligent and far-seeing interpreter in the person of Uno Åhrén (b. 1897). Of first-rate importance also was the founding in 1925 of the Co-operative Society's architects' office, with Eskil Sundahl (b. 1890) as chief architect. The factories, shops and other works sponsored by this office came to be known for a purist quality with strong social, and one might even say moral, aspects, which became of decisive importance for the whole Swedish architecture of the 1930s.

In 1930 Asplund was finally ready to discard the cloak of formalism under which he had been carrying out his studies of space problems and room relations during the whole of the 1920s. In the Stockholm Exhibition he exploited to the full the artistic possibilities of the 'new architecture' with a refinement and an elegance probably unsurpassed to this day. Within a very short time functionalism then became generally accepted in Sweden. The ground had been well prepared. The progressive political atmosphere favoured the social consciousness which had for so

Sven Backström and Leif Reinius. Gröndal Estate. Stockholm, 1944–5

Sigurd Lewerentz. Björkhagen Church. Skarpnäck near Stockholm, 1960

Sven Backström and Leif Reinius. Town centre with cinema and assembly rooms in background. Satellite town of Vällingby, near Stockholm, commenced 1953

long been part of the architectural programme; on the formal side, the more abstract line in the classicism of the 1920s had been gradually leading up to pure *Functionalism. Of course there were differences of opinion and heated debates, but hardly worth mentioning if we compare the situation in most other countries where the new ideas had to fight hard against official resistance. In this way Sweden became the 'model country' of modern architecture in the 1930s. But to a considerable extent the real strength lay on the side of the social programme. Much of what was built seems in retrospect rather dry and schematic. This concerns especially the town plans with their parallel blocks, where a correct orientation was valued higher than the creation of outdoor rooms between buildings.

Nevertheless there were many buildings of high artistic value. The leading name was Asplund, who was now softening the abstract character of the pioneer works by his exquisite feeling for different materials. The Gothenburg Concert Hall by Nils Einar Eriksson (b. 1899) shows similar qualities. Le Corbusier's influence is evident in the works of Sven *Markelius, especially in his private houses. But the strongest personal note is to be seen in the very limited production of Lewerentz, who shows a deep feeling for all the technical and aesthetic aspects of building, accepting no ready-made solution but working until the problems are mastered. Thus, while Lewerentz's buildings are always technically right, as independent works of art they also stand on a level above most contemporary architecture and show a continuous personal development. In 1937 he built a remarkable private house at Falsterbo; the landscaping of the Stockholm Forest Cemetery round Asplund's crematorium is chiefly his work, and in 1943 he completed his own crematorium in Malmö in the cemetery which he had begun to plan already in 1920.

In the 1940s a reaction started against international Functionalism. This was partly caused by the war, which cut off contacts with other countries and also restricted the use of certain building materials. Swedish architecture turned provincial. The clarity of the 1930s gave way to a superficial play with forms and materials. This romanticism could, however, sometimes lead to fine results, as in the Karlskoga Town Hall and Hotel by Sune Lindström (b. 1906), where it was combined with strongly disciplined volumes. A new tradition in brick building was formed. A really positive contribution of the decade was the abandoning of the stereotyped housing schemes in favour of differentiated plans, where the architects sought to create more 'home-like' surroundings and the plans of the houses themselves were very thoroughly studied. The partners Sven Backström (b. 1903) and Leif Reinius (b. 1907) are the most important architects of such projects.

With the 1950s a new wave of international influences swept over Sweden. This time, however, it was less surely handled than in the 1930s. There was no artist of Asplund's calibre to take the lead. Perhaps the general level might be called quite good, but there were no highlights. The really important things still happened on the programme side, above all in civic planning, where such projects as the Vällingby scheme, with its much-studied social and commercial centre, saw the light. The rebuilding of the central parts of Stockholm is another gigantic project which has attracted much interest. But here again uncertainty in the treatment of volumes, materials and details has often been manifest.

A new reaction began to appear at the end of the 1950s. Interest in the truly three-dimensional aspects of architecture has awakened again, but it has not taken the form of any wild experimentation. The liking for the simple cube is coming back, combined with a tendency to strong individualization. Not seldom colourful materials such as bricks are used. There are certain parallels to the tendencies of about 1910. These ideas have come to light most vigorously in church architecture. The works of Peter Celsing (b. 1920) offer a good field for study. But most remarkable is Lewerentz's church at Skarpnäck near Stockholm, a group of low brick volumes that seem to be in some way naturally grown on their site. There is nothing radically new in such a way of building, but it has here been given the timeless quality of a great work of art. And continued progress has always been more popular than revolution in Sweden.

Bibliography: G. E. Kidder Smith, *Sweden Builds*, 2nd edition, New York 1957; *New Swedish Architecture*, Stockholm 1939; *Swedish Housing of the 'Forties*, Stockholm 1950; *New Architecture in Sweden*, Stockholm 1961 (all published by SAR, the National Association of Swedish Architects).

BJÖRN LINN

Switzerland. Long before the term modern architecture could be used with regard to Switzerland, Robert *Maillart (from 1901 onwards) constructed his reinforced concrete bridges which were as technically audacious as they were aesthetically perfect. Karl *Moser, whose Church of St Anthony at Basle (1926–7) was the first ecclesiastical building in Switzerland built entirely of reinforced concrete, taught the next generation of architects while he was professor (1915–28) at Zurich Technical College (ETH). At the same time, Hans Bernoulli by his writings awakened their

Karl Moser. Church of St Anthony. Basle, 1926–7

Paul Artaria, Hans Schmidt, Max E. Haefeli, Carl Hubacher, Rudolf Steiger, Werner M. Moser and Emil Roth. Neubühl Estate. Zurich, 1930–2

sense of responsibility for civic design and town planning; he, too, was a professor at the ETH (Chair of Civic Design, 1919–39). The younger generation gave their point of view in the journal *ABC* (1924, Hans Schmidt and Mart Stam). Karl Moser's successors to the professorship were O. R. Salvisberg and Hans Hofmann.

Above all, *Le Corbusier's ideas exerted great influence. The Weissenhof houses at Stuttgart (1927) and the developments in Holland were studied. The *Bauhaus, directed in 1928–9 by the Swiss architect Hannes *Meyer, after Gropius's resignation, made its effects felt in Switzerland, too. Meyer's Trade Union School at Bernau (1928) was one of the first examples of a purely functional building; his design for the League of Nations Building at Geneva (1927), awarded the third prize, was the antithesis to Le Corbusier's scheme, which came first. *CIAM was founded at La Sarraz in 1928 and the *élite* of the world's architects joined it. In the ideological struggle against 'vernacular style', the new buildings erected between 1930 and 1940 achieved the homogeneity of functional thought: precise, objective and unpretentious, adapted to the rich local tradition of burgher and peasant culture and to the variety yet compression of the landscape within the framework of a federally constituted democracy. A high standard of housing was achieved, backed by perfection of structure and workmanship. Switzerland built excellent housing estates, hospitals and schools; her theoretical contributions, publications and exhibitions were influential. Paul Artaria, Ernst F. Burckhardt, Karl Egender, Max Ernst Haefeli, Werner M. Moser, Emil and Alfred Roth, Hans Schmidt, Otto Senn and Rudolf Steiger began to work at this time; Max *Bill and Hans Fischli came from the Bauhaus.

The National Provinces Exhibition at Zurich in 1939 (chief architect Hans Hofmann) aimed at showing a cross section of all that had been built since 1914. One of its positive results was the foundation of the Swiss Town and Country Planning Association (1943). The next National Provinces Exhibition to be held in Lausanne in 1964 will itself be an example of modern planning, and will make a fundamental attempt to tackle the planning problems of our time (chief architect: A. Camenzind; divisional architects: Max Bill, Zurich; Fréderic Brugger, Lausanne; Tita Carloni, Lugano; Jean Duret, Geneva; Marc-J. Saugey, Geneva; Florian Fischer, Basle; Jakob Zweifel, Zurich).

The Neubühl estate by the Werkbund at Zurich (1930–2) became a prototype of its kind: it featured differentiation of living requirements, standardization of units, and provision of open spaces by arranging the blocks at angles to each other (Artaria and

Hermann Baur. School on the Bruderholz. Basle, 1938–9

Max Bill. College of Design (Hochschule für Gestaltung). Ulm, 1953–5

Schmidt; M. E. Haefeli; C. Hubacher; R. Steiger, W. M. Moser and E. Roth). The housing scheme for Prilly near Lausanne went even further (1947; M. E. Haefeli, W. M. Moser, R. Steiger, M. Hottinger—not built) in envisaging a mixed development, including point blocks. The Gellert district at Basle (general layout by H. Baur, 1956) adopted the same principle but different means of execution. The estate at Halen near Berne (1957; Atelier 5, Berne, and Niklaus Morgenthaler) is a group of detached houses set close together in the manner of a village and rationalized by the use of prefabricated concrete units.

Hospital and school buildings were freed from schematism. At the cantonal hospital, Zurich (started 1942; M. E. Haefeli, R. Steiger, W. M. Moser, H. Weideli, J. Schütz, H. Fietz) spatial unity has been achieved in accommodating the most modern therapeutic knowledge, with its facilities in a constant state of renewal and extension. The current level of this development may be seen in Zurich Dental Institute, by the same architects. The school on the Bruderholz at Basle by Hermann Baur (1938–9) gave the lead to this type of district school, freely laid out amidst greenery. There is a large number of excellent examples of this kind today everywhere in Switzerland. The school building programme of Zurich in particular is remarkable for its far-sighted planning for anticipated requirements under the direction of progressive architects. Larger schools are best represented by the technical colleges: Zurich, Karl Egender, (1926–32); Berne, Hans Brechbühler, (1937–9); and Basle, H. and H. P. Baur, F. Bräuning and A. Dürig (1956–61). As an example of the organization of a complex group of buildings in a natural setting, on the basis of uniform elements, the College of Design (Hochschule für Gestaltung) at Ulm by Max Bill may be cited (1953–55). A similar problem arose at Zurich, where the Freudenberg cantonal school by Jacques Schader (1958–61) had to combine two types of schools on a limited site.

Rudolf and Peter Steiger. 'Cern' Laboratory. Geneva, 1954–60

Max E. Haefeli, Werner M. Moser, Rudolf Steiger, O. Caretta and André Studer. Multi-storey office block 'zur Palme'. Zurich, under construction. Model

Since 1945, new buildings in Switzerland have assumed a multitude of shapes. Typical examples include the churches that followed Le Corbusier's experiment at Ronchamp. The multi-storey office building 'zur Palme' in Zurich by M. E. Haefeli, W. M. Moser, R. Steiger, O. Caretta and A. Studer (under construction) attempts a form of three-dimensional modelling inspired by Frank Lloyd *Wright. The terraced layouts at Zug by F. Stucky and R. Meuli (1957–60) and at Zurich-Witikon by C. Paillard and Peter Leemann (1959–60), with flats stacked above each other in self-contained living zones, are all distinguished by the utmost economy in the exploitation of the site. Large blocks of flats with a high standard of comfort have appeared, particularly in Geneva (Denis Honegger, Arthur Lozeron, Marc-J. Saugey). The construction of the 'Cern' Research Centre near Geneva by R. and P. Steiger (1954–60) successfully coped with spatial requirements of a hitherto unknown category for nuclear research. In French Switzerland modern architecture has made a late start, although the famous Swiss architect Le Corbusier, who has been living in Paris since 1917, came from this region. The Italian part of Switzerland has started even later to let modern architecture in; but there Italian influence is unmistakable.

Bibliography: Max Bill, *Moderne Schweizer Architektur 1925–1949*, Basle 1949; G. E. Kidder Smith, *Switzerland builds*, London and New York 1950; Hans Volkart, *Schweizer Architektur*, Ravensburg 1951.

MARGIT STABER

TAC (The Architects Collaborative), founded in 1946, an architectural association in which Walter *Gropius joined with architects of the younger generation (Norman Fletcher, John Harkness, Robert McMillan, Louis McMillen, and Benjamin Thompson). Gropius here realized his conception of 'teamwork by individualists' in such large TAC schemes as the Harvard Graduate Center (1949–50), the US Embassy in Athens (1961), and the project for Bagdad University.

Tange, Kenzo, b. Imabari City in Shikoku 1913. Tange spent his high school days at Hiroshima. Imabari and Hiroshima are both located facing the Inland Sea, which is said to be the Mediterranean Sea in *Japan. Being fascinated since early days by *Le Corbusier, whose works are based on Mediterranean traditions in Europe, Tange entered the Tokyo Imperial University and took architectural courses in the Department of Engineering from 1935 to 1938. Immediately after his graduation, he entered Kunio *Maekawa's architectural office, and later with Maekawa he joined the Japanese Werkbund. While he was working there, he was almost entirely responsible for the planning of the Kishi Memorial Gymnasium. Later, in 1941, he re-entered the Tokyo University and took a post-graduate course. In 1942 he was awarded first prize in a competition for the design of a Far East memorial building sponsored by the Japanese Architectural Institute. A year later he won a prize for the plan of a Japan-Thai cultural centre to be built in Bangkok. However, none of these projects were realized. His first building to be erected was a Pavilion of Local Products for the Kobe Industry and Trade Fair (1950), which was removed after the fair was over.

Page 289 Kenzo Tange. Town Hall of the Kagawa Prefecture, 1958

Kenzo Tange. Peace Centre. Hiroshima, 1955–6

From that time Tange's creative talent rapidly increased. He designed the Ehime Convention Hall and his own house in 1954 as well as the Shimizu Town Hall. The Kurayoshi Town Hall was built in 1956, and the Tokyo Metropolitan Government Office was completed in 1957. Other important buildings were the Peace Centre in Hiroshima, a library for children which reveals his originality in space vision, and the small but carefully planned Tsuda College Library in Tokyo.
Tange's aim has always been to integrate Japan's architectural traditions with the needs of modern society, and he sought an answer to this problem through the planning of a series of buildings for local communities; he reached a successful solution in the Kagawa Prefectural Office completed in 1958. The realization of the project owed a great deal to the influential

Kenzo Tange. Town Hall. Shimizu, 1954

governor, Kaneko, who appreciates Tange's work. The building marks a peak in his career. Versatility and creative power have characterized Tange's work from the time he participated in the prize competition up to the present with his design for the Sogetsu Hall in 1960. If he succeeds in establishing his architectural philosophy on a firmer foundation, he should be one of the leading architects of the future.
He has written an essay on the 'Relation between Regional Planning and Architectural Design in Big Cities', and received his doctor's degree. At present, he is a professor at the Tokyo University and gives lectures on City Planning in the Engineering Department.
Bibliography: Robin Boyd, *Kenzo Tange*, New York 1962.

SHINJI KOIKE

Tatlin, Vladimir E., b. Moscow 1885, d. 1952. Graduated 1910 from the Academy. First Constructivist type of work 1913–15. His design for a memorial to the Third International (1920) was a leaning spiral made of steel and wire and anticipates the buildings and designs of *Constructivism; Tatlin imagined the memorial as a 1,300-ft-high structure with large rooms.

Taut, Bruno, b. Königsberg 1880, d. Ankara 1938. Pupil of Theodor *Fischer. Erected a 'Monument of Steel' at the Leipzig Building Exhibition of 1913, and a glass pavilion at the 1914 Cologne Exhibition, which demonstrated in a most imaginative way the potentialities of *glass as a building material. During the First World War produced designs for Utopian *Alpine Architecture* (published Hagen 1919). Worked as City Architect at Magdeburg. Housing estates in Berlin in the *International Style. Taut went to Moscow in 1932, to Japan in 1933, and to Istanbul in 1936.
Bibliography: Bruno Taut, *Die neue Baukunst*, Berlin 1929.

Taut, Max, b. Königsberg 1884. Private practice since 1911. Schools, housing and office buildings (in particular for trade unions; headquarters for the German Printers' Union, Berlin, 1928); 1945–53 Professor at the Berlin College of Fine Arts.

Tecton. Architectural team founded by Berthold Lubetkin, to which Anthony Chitty, Lindsey Drake, Michael Dugdale, Val Harding and Denys Lasdun belonged. Highpoint Flats, Highgate (1933), Finsbury Health Centre, London (1938–9). The work of this group received popular recognition with their buildings for the London Zoo; *reinforced concrete was used imaginatively. (*Great Britain)

Telford, Thomas, b. Westerkirk, Dumfriesshire 1757, d. London 1834. Scottish architect and engineer. Stone buildings with large areas punctuated by projecting planes, not by ornaments, with Romanesque touches (St Catharine's Dock, 1824–8). Bold designs for bridges making use of cast iron (design for a Thames bridge, London, 1801; Conway Castle Bridge, 1822–6). (*p. 6)

Terragni, Giuseppe, b. Meda near Milan 1904, d. Como 1942. Terragni is one of the most complex and at the same time most consistent figures of the early modern movement in Italy. His work covers a period of only thirteen years, from his graduation in Milan in 1926 to the time of his call-up in 1939. He fought on the Greek and Russian fronts, was repatriated to Italy, and died of the after-effects of exhaustion in January 1942. In this short span he was responsible for some of the most significant buildings produced during the period, beset with so many difficulties and reverses, that brought Italian architecture from its neoclassical and eclectic backwaters to join the mainstream of the modern European style.

Terragni originally adhered to the *Novecento Italiano* group, which set out on a rationalist basis to restore plastic values and a sense of volume to modern architecture, in opposition to the new *International Style, which depended for effect on the manipulation of surfaces. In 1926 he helped to found the *Movimento Italiano per l'Architettura Razionale,* which unleashed the whole weight of the academic opposition against the young members of **gruppo* 7 (Terragni, *Figini, *Pollini, Frette, Larco, Rava and Libera); he kept up the lively controversy which ensued to the very end of his life, writing his last article from the Russian front. The debate was a difficult and bitter one, since the protagonists on both sides were Fascists, and in consequence the movement's ideology ended in a hopeless impasse of opinions, tastes and interests.

Terragni's best arguments were his buildings, however. His first design to be carried out was a block of flats at Como (1927), called Novecomum, a typically 'novecentist' design which caused a considerable stir. A series of shops and interior decoration schemes followed, with various contributions to the Monza Biennali and the 1933 Milan Triennale. In 1932 he designed a hall for the Exhibition of the Fascist Revolution in Rome. In the same year he drew up plans for the Casa del Fascio at Como (completed in 1936), which remains the purest and most interesting monument of the *Novecento Italiano,* standing as it does on the verge of *Functionalism. The building is a cube devoid of any movement or ornament, in which solids and voids, by virtue of the violent contrasts they afford of light and shade, create a dramatically punctuated architectural dialogue. This austere and interesting building is the only

Giuseppe Terragni. Novecomum, Como, 1927

Giuseppe Terragni. Casa del Fascio. Como, 1936

one to have conferred a European validity on that typically Italian phenomenon, the *Novecento*. It was denounced however by Giuseppe Pagano in the pages of *Casabella* as an example of '17th-century affectation applied to Functionalism', since he feared that the younger generation of Italian architects might be diverted by it from their true objectives.

In his next work, however, a kindergarten at Como (1937), Terragni abandoned the *Novecento* line to create, within the framework of European Functionalism, the most elegant and lucid of his projects. Three houses dating from the same year (Villa Bianca at Seveso, Villa Bianchi at Rebbio and the Casa Pedraglio at Como) restate the problem in strictly geometrical terms, while pointing somehow to a specifically 'spatial' type of solution. With his last important work, the Casa Frigerio at Como (1939), the volumetric cube is broken up, although a freely articulated plan is not achieved. Among his other works may be mentioned four houses in Milan (1935–6, in collaboration with Pietro Lingeri) and the Casa del Fascio at Lissone (1939, with Carminati).

Terragni left behind him a large number of architectural and town-planning schemes; also a collection of controversial writings which reveal that intellectual honesty and sensitivity which led him, on the eve of his death, to renounce his great political error in despair.

Bibliography: Giuseppe Pagano, 'Tre anni di architettura in Italia', in *Casabella*, February 1937; Mario Labò, *Giuseppe Terragni*, Milan 1947; Attilio Podestà, 'Omaggio a Terragni' in *Emporium*, Vol. CVII, No. 640, April 1948; Giulia Veronesi, *Difficoltà politiche dell'architettura in Italia, 1920–1940*, Milan 1953.

GIULIA VERONESI

Torroja, Eduardo, b. Madrid 1899, d. 1961. Studied civil engineering in Madrid. He was director of the Instituto Técnico de la Construcción y del Cemento, and an honorary doctor of numerous universities.

Torroja belongs to the great creators of architectural form in the 20th century. As his many works built in Europe, Africa and America strikingly demonstrate, he possessed great imaginative powers, capable of stating surprising problems and devising

unexpected solutions for them, together with an immense technical capacity for solving these problems and actually carrying out the solutions. His views may be found in essence in his book *Philosophy of Structures*, where we see how different he is from the usual mathematical type of engineer when he asserts from the outset the rights of the imagination and declares that calculations only serve to show whether what has been imagined will stand.
According to Torroja, there are three classes of structure: those which serve to contain a volume, those which carry loads and those which resist thrusts. The architectural problem centres round his system of four equations with four unknowns. The equations are those of ultimate purpose, static function, aesthetic qualities and economic conditions. The unknowns are the materials, the structural types, the critical shapes and sizes and the actual building process. In determining structural types, Torroja started by considering the conditions of stress. The networks set up by the systems of stress, namely the lines of tension and compression, allowed him to emphasize the way each form works. As regards materials, recognizing the truth of *Wright's assertion that each one of them speaks its own language, he concentrated on exploiting the great properties of reinforced and pre-stressed concrete, which was his favourite means of expression.
In considering the question of aesthetic expression, Torroja believed that truth alone was not enough and that a psychological factor in the material supervened which might lead to the possibility of structural jests, surprising absurdities and a gratuitous playfulness. Notwithstanding this, he considered simplicity a virtue. In regard to the architectural forms of his times, he used to speak with a certain sadness about materialism, and about those who disclaim nature on anti-romantic grounds while assigning excessive value to rhythm. He accepted an essentially baroque principle in maintaining the idea that the eye is deceptive, and in preferring psychological phenomena to material reality. Although regular geometrical forms exist

Eduardo Torroja. Grandstand at Zarzuela race track, near Madrid, 1935

Eduardo Torroja. Church of the Ascension. Xerralló, 1952. Sketch

in some of his works, such as the twelve-sided concrete coal bunker he built for the Instituto Técnico de la Construcción y del Cemento (Madrid, 1951), most of his designs employ folded, undulating or warped shapes.

In 1928, *Freyssinet took out the first patent for pre-stressed concrete. A year later, Torroja was using it for the Tempul bridge, where the longitudinal girders were pre-stressed. His ribless roof for Algeciras Market Hall (1933) was Torroja's response to the ribwork of Basle Market Hall (1929). For the Zarzuela race track near Madrid in 1935 he designed a system of fluted grand-stand roofs with a very extensive cantilever, counterbalanced by vertical tie rods behind the stanchions. In the same year he built the shell roof of the Frontón Recoletos, whose form derives from the penetration of two barrel vaults of different dimensions running parallel to each other. The hyperboloid form of a reservoir for Madrid (1936) was the forerunner of the great hyperboloid dome of the water tower at Fedala, Morocco (1956). (*Shell structures)

Torroja's Aldoz aqueduct (1939), with X-shaped pipeline supports, broke new ground in this type of structure. His Martín Gil bridge over the Esla (1940) with its 623-foot span, broke the world record for a single arch. It is currently (1963) the third largest in the world in absolute span, and the second largest railway bridge. The Torrejón de Ardoz hangars, with their structural panache, were completed in 1942; in the following year, the great roof over the entrance to the Campo de Les Corts in Barcelona, with its sinuous outline, is the first of Torroja's major works to feature organic asymmetry; its final flowering is to be seen at the Táchira Club at Caracas (1957).

Torroja's churches at Xerralló, Sant Esperit and Pont de Suert (1952) are the first examples of modern religious art to be found south of the Pyrenees since the Civil War.

Bibliography: Eduardo Torroja, *Philosophy of Structures*, California 1958; Eduardo Torroja, *The Structures of Eduardo Torroja*, New York 1958; Fernando Cassinello, 'Eduardo Torroja' in *Cuadernos de Arquitectura*, Barcelona 1961; Eduardo Torroja, *Logik der Form*, Munich 1961.

ALEXANDRE CIRICI-PELLICER

Town planning is the preconcerted disposition of urban living-space. Already in the tight society in the years prior to 1800, consideration was given to the building of cities in a manner which could be termed planning. The planned layout of a town, however, was such a self-evident part of government that any special discipline concerned with the technical or economic questions of town layout or planning was simply not referred to.

Even the distinction between towns that have grown and those that have been planned was only invented by art historians of the last century, attempting to demonstrate, for some of the historical towns at least, an ideal conception of their time, 'growth from the free interplay of forces'. Ungeometrical towns were said to have 'grown', in contrast to those with geometrical shapes. Today, however, we know that towns of both basic shapes, regular and irregular, have been planned at some time or other, and that an act of foundation preceded the existence of each town. Most town extensions, too, were planned or comprised in an overall scheme. The common interest of all citizens in effective defence by a system of fortifications made it necessary to conform to a plan.

For a long time the irregularly shaped town was thought to represent an earlier stage of development, the regular shape a later one. No single form, however, has exclusively prevailed at any time. Aristotle, who summarized the whole scientific knowledge of antiquity and remained a supreme authority throughout the Middle Ages, declared that both methods had their advantages and disadvantages, and both might be used according to local conditions. The irregular shape is said to be the more economical one. The necessity for defence and the prevalence of emotional tendencies certainly led to a predominance of ungeometric shapes in the early periods of town development, while the rational and economic tendencies of later epochs displayed a preference for geometric formations. Changes in society have also played their part in the differentiation of town shapes.

After 1800, the last effective possibility of controlling town growth in Central Europe was lost. With the removal of fortifications and quick growth due to increased prosperity as a consequence of industrialization, cities spread rapidly along their main arteries, beyond their former limits. Property speculators provided hastily erected tenement houses, badly lighted and cramped, for the mass of people streaming into the towns from the country. Building by-laws which permitted a shameless exploitation of people and sites left their mark on the appearance of these districts. The grid-type layouts of the surveyors, the unvaried street widths and heights, and the squares dotted here and there without rhyme or reason, were meant to be neutral, so as to avoid obstructing the action of economic forces. The fate of the town was thus left to chance and speculation, and it grew in unconnected single phases.

Around the year 1900, movements for social reform attempted to remedy the poor living conditions of the towns (E. *Howard, H. George, Damaschke, Fritsch, Eberstadt and others). The science of town planning was gradually developed; with the foundation of town planning associations the recognition emerged that town and country must complement each other and be subjected to a common plan (Unwin, Schumacher). Traffic considerations came first, closely followed by economic factors. For a time, living conditions occupied the focus of attention, then politico-sociological aspects of the town and finally the demand for green belts and landscaping. Only a team consisting of every kind of specialist (mining engineers, surveyors, architects, economists, sociologists, doctors, lawyers

Georges-Eugène Haussmann. Boulevard Richard-Lenoir. Paris, 1861–3. Remedial measures are confined to cutting new streets through

and landscape architects) is in a position to grasp such a complex problem as the town of today, and to work out a plan that does justice to all these aspects of development. Academies and associations such as *CIAM (with its *Athens Charter) drew up minimum requirements and optimum conditions for the renewal or reconstruction of cities. A recognition of the basic needs a town has to provide for (work, living, traffic, leisure) and their correct co-ordination with each other was a start. Minimum health requirements for sunshine, daylight, dust and noise abatement, green belts and open spaces, were formulated. The subdivision of the town into organic units with service centres featuring schools, churches, cultural buildings and shops, separated from other such units by belts of parkland, became a further instrument of urban design. In this conjunction the problem arose of how to ensure the best use of city sites. City centres needed thinning out, while denser development was called for on the peripheries; hence internationally valid specifications for optimum land use were involved.

The 'floorspace index' represents the ratio of the total floor area of a building to the area of its site, and may vary from 2.0 to approximately 0.2 in areas with main services (highest in business areas; City of London currently 6.3!). These rules have become necessary not only to ensure sufficient ventilation, sunshine, daylight and parkland; they are an essential consequence of the ever-increasing density of traffic. For volume of building and volume of traffic are interrelated: by reducing the volume of building, a reduction of traffic density can be achieved. A floor-space index of 1.0, which may be regarded as the upper limit for purely residential areas, corresponds to a population density of 200 inhabitants per net acre, and a building density of about 60 dwelling units per acre, while the cities of Central Europe have maximum population densities of 400 an acre.

In urban residential districts supplied with main services, FSI 0.2 should not be exceeded (giving a plot area of about 360 square yards) as otherwise the town spreads out uneconomically. No type of development is more expensive than the type of 'suburban sprawl' generally encountered today, with detached private houses on 1,200 square yard plots. While it is essential to thin out the unsanitary and overcrowded tenements that often survive in central zones, a denser development of the outlying suburbs is currently aimed at by planners. By adjusting both extremes, towns with an average FSI of 0.4 would not have to extend beyond the present boundaries of their built-up areas. In Berlin, the most densely populated district of Kreuzberg has 480 dwelling units per acre, while that of Zehlendorf has only 5. If the regulations for distances between buildings and the restrictions on density are adhered to, the problem of correct orientation for blocks of flats or rows of houses is no longer a difficult one. The most favourable disposition in the British Isles is without doubt a south-west aspect, but others are also possible and have advantages for certain occupations or members of the family. One thing must however be avoided, living-rooms facing north!

The type of building presents another problem, whether multi-storey, medium-high or low. Where no specific housing tradition prevails, as it does in countries such as England, the United States and Holland where low structures are the general rule, the type of building to be erected is determined by considerations of profitability to the landlord and ease of running. Sociological and biological factors

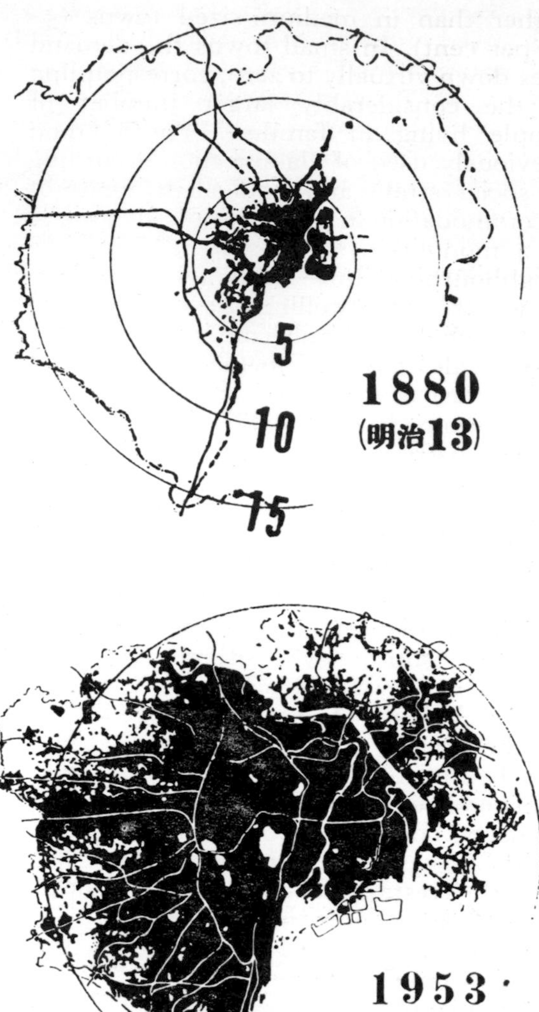

Area of Tokio in 1880 and 1953. An increase in radius from 5 to over 15 km.

should, however, be the criterion. Low buildings are usually better for people with children and dependents who feel united as a family. Multi-storey blocks of flats are more suitable for childless couples, unmarried people and families whose jobs require them to move about. The medium-high building has become almost meaningless, and simply serves to make the supply of accommodation of various types appear the more diverse. In cities and metropolitan areas, the number of people requiring flats in multi-storey blocks may be estimated at 20–30 per cent, naturally higher than in medium-sized towns (5–20 per cent). In small towns the demand goes down virtually to zero, corresponding to the considerably larger number of people living in families. The method previously used of classification according to social strata and equivalent types of accommodation has all the disadvantages of a monolithic social system. Within a neighbourhood unit—preferably in a group of about 100 dwellings—every type of professional and family combination on the social scale should be included.

In the last century, industries were sited in the immediate neighbourhood of residential districts, as had been the custom of the old craft manufactories. It was not due to the resultant inconvenience but to the lack of space for extension that factories were moved to the outskirts and into industrial districts. With the introduction of electrical power, dust-extraction plants, and the sub-division of industry into smaller factory units, partial decentralization of industry becomes possible: either in the shape of small industrial plants attached to the neighbourhood units or by transference to the country. Only heavy industry, complex processes and offensive trades are tied to actual industrial districts. For the rest, industry can become the most flexible unit in the town, as its buildings usually have to be replaced after ten to twenty years.

Town planning measures are most easily realized nowadays in matters of traffic engineering, which everybody can understand. In the last thirty years enormous sums have been spent in the United States on the provision of highway facilities, but without remarkable success. The lesson to be learnt from this by European town planners is the need to avoid excess traffic by advance planning, thinning out congested areas and redirecting traffic sources and their destinations. Journeys to and from work make up 60–70 per cent of all the traffic in a town. Consideration of how living and working zones might be related to each other, and how change of workplace and removal from home could be coupled, is of such significance that it cannot be rejected by references to individual liberty. Shopping, school and leisure

J. H. van den Broek and Jacob B. Bakema. The Lijnbaan pedestrian street. Rotterdam, 1953

journeys can be reduced by planning (gardens surrounding houses, parks accessible on foot, shopping centres, schools and cultural facilities within the district). What essential traffic remains should be directed via differentiated lanes (motorway to residential street) so that its main stream makes contact with the town according to its nature. The town itself should be divided into traffic-free precincts, in which only pedestrians, cyclists and emergency traffic (doctors, police) are permitted. On the edge of the pedestrian precincts there should be adequate parking facilities.

Parks as recreational areas in the centre of a town have only been called for in our own times. It is the town planner's task today to link up incidental open spaces such as parks, cemeteries, the areas between buildings, allotments, sports grounds, and rivers and lakes with their banks into an interconnected green network. Like the traffic network, the green network should pass through each district so that each part of a town, and the countryside also, may be reached on foot via one of these links. These green belts should contain all secondary schools, sports facilities and baths, and any woodland in the town. Apart from them there are the green areas inside the individual districts, which accommodate playgrounds, primary schools and nursery schools. These constitute the actual centre of the district.

The vast extension in the size of towns means that the city centre forfeits its vitality. Hence the city must be decentralized, i.e., on the one hand it must be afforded increased ground space to accommodate ever-growing public and private services; on the other hand, all functions which have no definite central character can be moved into the suburbs. Satellites or New Towns are built to relieve the city's burden.

In Great Britain the New Town Act of 1946 provided for the development of a series of townships, each with populations of between 30,000 and 50,000. Apart from the usual apparatus of civic amenities, each town was designed to attract its own

Stockholm City Planning Office; Chief Architect: Sven Markelius. Satellite town of Vällingby, near Stockholm, commenced 1953. Site plan

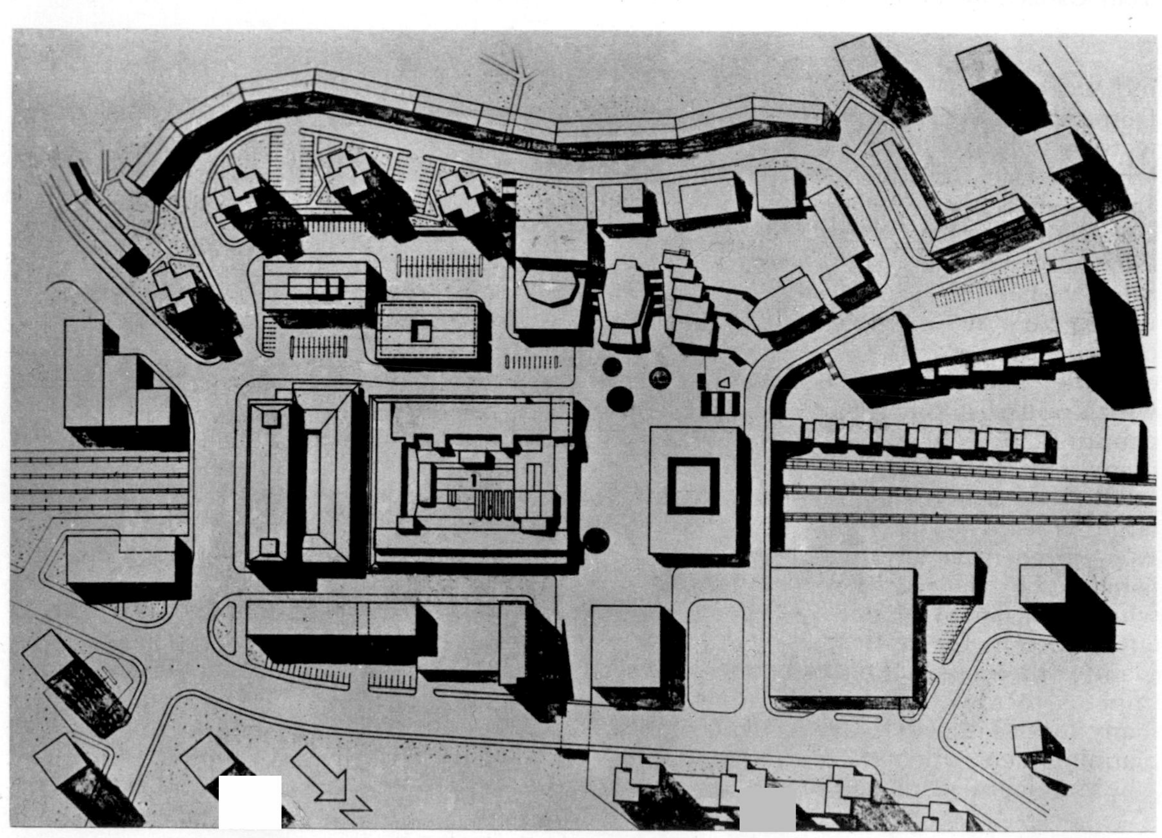

Tony Garnier. Residential district. Cité Industrielle. 1901–4. Project

industries of various types, to prevent it from lapsing into a mere dormitory. Projects include Basildon, Stevenage, Harlow (chief planner: F. Gibberd), Hatfield (L. Brett), Peterlee, Newton Aycliffe and Corby in England; East Kilbride and Glenrothes in Scotland; and Cwmbran in South Wales. The standard of achievement varies, but the more successful express considerable urban distinction. Their example, and the progressive legislation which underlies them, have inspired other countries, Scandinavia in particular. Germany, too, has recently built a number of satellite towns in the neighbourhood of the larger cities.

A comprehensive advance in planning law is marked by the 1947 Town Planning Act, which lays an obligation on all planning authorities in Great Britain to produce a plan for their areas. This has given a great impetus to town planning practice, since many local authorities have had to set up planning departments for the first time. The development plans they are expected to work out, are based on a simple form of comprehensive survey, showing the future policy of land use in each area, and indicating where development or re-development is expected to take place; these plans are reviewed at five-yearly intervals. In addition, the 1947 Act provides for the safeguarding of trees and woodlands and the protection of buildings of historic interest, which it requires to be listed; it also embodies powers for the control of outdoor advertising.

Subsequent legislation includes the 1951 New Streets Act, which ensures that private developers do not leave their highways unadopted, and the 1952 Town Development Act, designed to facilitate the planned expansion of towns chosen to receive overspill populations.

Many schemes for the comprehensive re-development of central areas have been drawn up in recent years, frequently in collaboration with property companies.

Bibliography: Lewis Mumford, *The Culture of Cities*, New York 1938; Roland

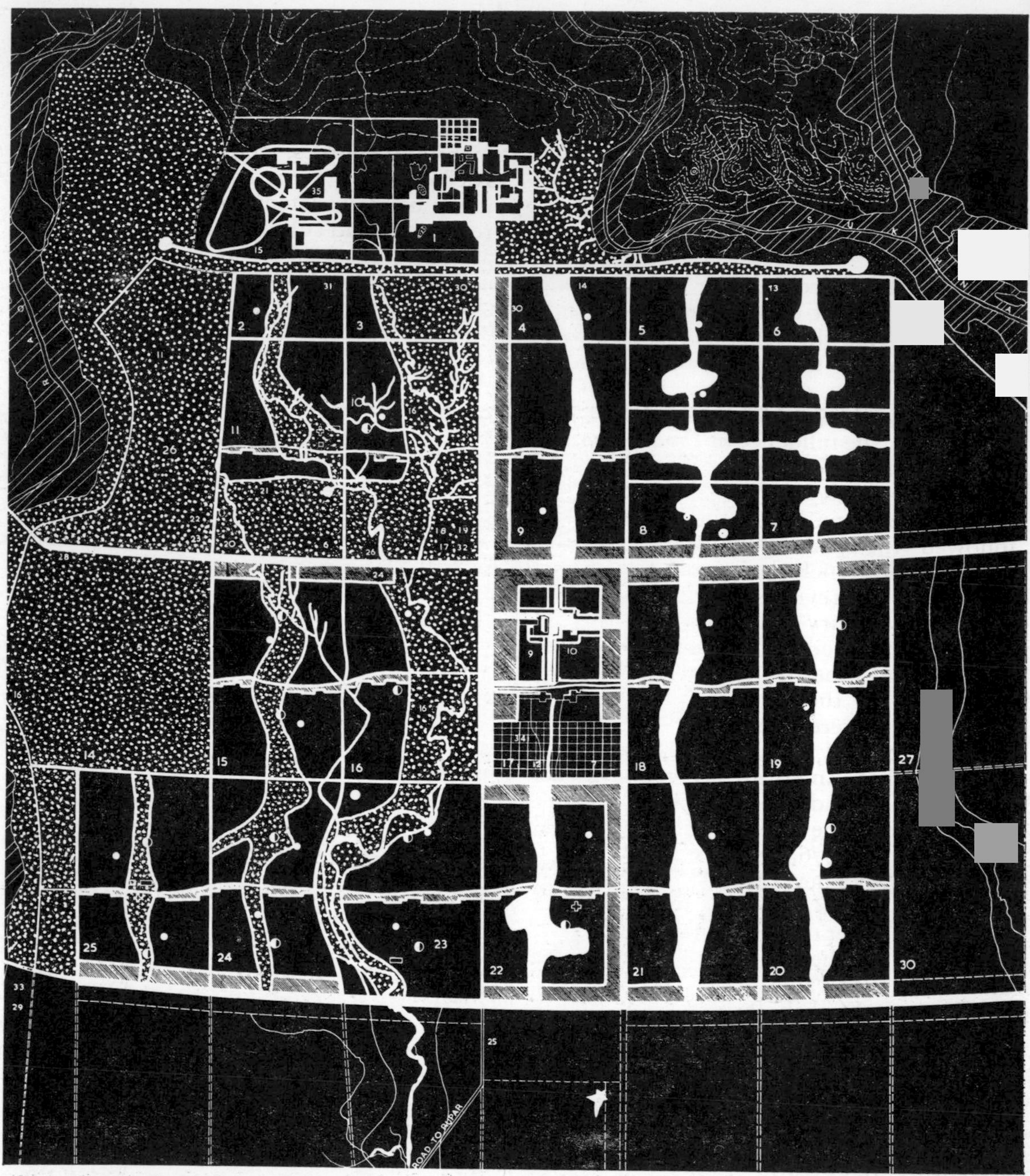

Le Corbusier. Chandigarh, commenced 1950. Site plan

Rainer, *Städtebau und Wohnkultur*, Tübingen 1948; Frederick Gibberd, *Town Design*, London 1953; 4th edition 1962; Hans Bernhard Reichow, *Die autogerechte Stadt*, Ravensburg 1959; Fritz Jaspert, *Vom Städtebau der Welt*, Berlin 1961; Gordon Cullen, *Townscape*, London 1962.

HUBERT HOFFMANN

Townscape. Concept evolved in the late forties by analysing examples of consciously or unconsciously successful town design in terms of the progressive revelation of space and function to the moving spectator; influenced in part by the theories of English 18th-century landscape architects, which are transferred to an urban setting.

Invaluable discipline for the appreciation of historic towns, and the application of the lessons so learnt to the design of new ones.

Bibliography: Gordon Cullen, *Townscape*. London 1961.

HAROLD MEEK

Urbanism. *Town Planning.

USA. American architecture was for a long period an outpost of the European mainstream. During the colonial era (17th and 18th centuries) the styles were scarcely more than echoes of British practice at the same moment. With the coming of the Revolution, the influence of France became momentarily predominant. Then, for the first three-quarters of the 19th century, building developments in the United States followed the pace established both by British and French designers. The classical and Gothic revivals were succeeded by those mid-century Victorian fashions that were championed by Ruskin, Eastlake, *Morris and other writers, while Parisian influences in the guise of the Second Empire style were equally pervasive.

While it would be an exaggeration to maintain that American architecture had attained independence as well as maturity by the time of the Philadelphia Centennial Exposition of 1876, the date can be taken as symbolic of a new turn. At this juncture, American artists became aware of the unique character of their own colonial past, and, while in the process of making this discovery, they came under the influence of the new English taste for vernacular post-medieval styles, a revival movement that is generally if not especially accurately referred to as the Queen Anne. These two phenomena, in effect complementary manifestations of the same late 19th-century eclectic development, were present in varying degrees in the work of the three major American architects of the period, Henry Hobson *Richardson, Louis *Sullivan, and Frank Lloyd *Wright. Wright not only played a major creative rôle in the domestic architecture of the 1890s, but continued in both a creative and patriarchal capacity to mould and influence architecture in America and in Europe well past the middle of the 20th century.

It is conceivable that Richardson was the first architect of the post-Renaissance period to whom the word 'genius' is not inappropriate. In his ponderous, taciturn style were united the moralistic, revivalistic and rational principles of diverse earlier tendencies. However, above and beyond its manifold sources, the personal style of Richardson is remarkably fused, and the inner conflicts latent in its origins are so reconciled and submerged that it is eclectic and revivalistic only in methodology. In actuality these robust masonry or wood shingle forms are among the most disciplined and unified creations of the last century. It was the example of Richardson that helped to clarify the somewhat less certain taste of Louis Sullivan, who had been at first inspired by a Victorian architect of almost grotesque power, Frank *Furness, and only subsequently by the new technology of the steel-framed tall office building, which was invented and popularized in Chicago in the 1880s, a rational type of design that is identified by the sobriquet *'Chicago School'. Sullivan's most striking accomplishments of the 1890s in commercial architecture were echoed in the perceptive if less elegant skyscraper designs of Daniel H. *Burnham and John W. *Root, whether in the dense masonry structure of the Monadnock Building (1891) or in the expressive steel-framed Reliance Building (1890–4), a glazed thirteen-storey shaft. In contrast to these striking manifestations of commercial efficiency in a materialistic era, the early tall office buildings in New York were less boldly simplified in aspect, though their greater attention to variety of detail, as in Richard Morris Hunt's Tribune Building, New York (1873–5), was more original than is generally realized.

Frank Lloyd Wright is the third and most spectacular of this triumvirate in American architecture. An assistant of Louis Sullivan until he established his own practice in 1893, Wright subsequently devoted most of his efforts to domestic architecture, and if his position long went largely unrecognized in the USA—although his work always earned a degree of respect and admiration, if usually qualified in tone—the brilliant spatial inventions of his suburban Chicago houses of the period 1893–1909, culminating in the Robie House of 1909, were of immeasurable influence in Europe. These works were published and exhibited in Germany in 1910–11, and to

Frank Furness. Pennsylvania Academy of Fine Arts. Philadelphia, 1872–6

Louis H. Sullivan. Auditorium Building. Chicago, 1886–9

judge from the works of the masters of the *International Style, together with their subsequent testimony, they had a tremendous impact. Wright's domestic architecture of 1900 was complemented by the work of others in his immediate circle, and his principles were echoed on the west coast in the domestic work of Charles and Henry *Greene, notably the Gamble House, Pasadena (1908–9), in which seemingly exotic oriental elements are successfully blended with an indigenous offshoot of the Queen Anne known as the 'Shingle Style', a mode originally popularized by Richardson. A similar independence was manifested by Bernard R. *Maybeck in his Christian Science Church, Berkeley (1910), in which a concrete structure is enriched by provocative medievalizing timber details. Equally picturesque effects, but in an academic, indeed, Imperial Roman garb, were produced by Maybeck in his Fine Arts Building for the 1915 San Francisco Exhibition, a temporary structure in pink stucco that still stands, albeit in a ruinous state.

Louis H. Sullivan, Getty Tomb. Chicago, 1890

The taste which stands behind the general style if not the personal feeling expressed in Maybeck's Fine Arts Building had earlier been crystallized at the World's Columbian Exposition, Chicago (1893), where a group of architects led by the fashionable academic firm of McKim, Mead and White (who had begun as disciples of Richardson) produced the famous 'White City' of Imperial Classicism in plaster and lath. Largely if not completely divorced from this *beaux-arts* design discipline was Sullivan's Transportation Building, with its intricately detailed round-arched portal which was admired by European if not by American visitors.

With this unmistakable 'revolution' in favour of the classical modes, which in a decade spread across the country, Sullivan and other independent-minded architects gradually lost contact with what seemed at the time to be the main stream of modern architectural design, a main stream which produced buildings such as the Pennsylvania Station, New York (1906–10), by McKim, Mead and White, which was not only stylistically neoclassical but went so far as to seek identity with a distant past through the imitation of certain portions of a typical Roman bath. Such accomplishments almost totally eclipsed for the moment the works of Sullivan's old age, such as the National Farmers Bank, Owatonna, Minnesota (1907–8). Here the block-like design cut with a massive round arch bears analogies not so much to the current academic fashion, as to the earlier idiom of Richardson. Sullivan's work of this period is in effect a vital, organic outgrowth of the late-19th-century traditions, whereas that of McKim, Mead and White is a largely sterile, even if scholarly, product of the same tradition.

If Wright, the Greene brothers, Maybeck and a few others clearly belong to an independent movement in architecture around 1900, along with Sullivan, the same

Charles and Henry Greene. Gamble House, Pasadena, 1908–9

cannot be said for a host of other interesting architects active during the first two or three decades of the 20th century in the USA. Among the domestic specialists of the period, few seem in retrospect to have been so able and craftsmanlike as the Philadelphia firm of Mellor, Meigs and Howe. Their abilities to produce a bland if arcane eclecticism are amply illustrated in the house of 1914 at Chestnut Hill, Pennsylvania, built for George *Howe, the junior member of the firm, who was later to reject this tentative style for a more forthright modernism.

Monumental architecture at this epoch is represented by Cass Gilbert's (1859–1934) Gothic skyscraper, the Woolworth Building, New York (1913); Bertram Grosvenor Goodhue's (1869–1924) tentatively 'modernistic' Nebraska State Capitol and Los Angeles Public Library of the 1920s, in which the departing spirit of 19th-century eclecticism makes one last effort to survive in a provocative compromise form; or in James Gamble Rodgers's (1867–1947) numerous designs for Yale University, beginning in 1917, which depend for their sense of medieval authenticity upon a particularly luxuriant texture and carefully studied detailing. The classical tradition was maintained by Henry Bacon's (1866–1924) Lincoln Memorial, Washington (1914–22), and by John Russell Pope's (1874–1937) National Gallery of Art, Washington (1937), both extraordinarily pure revisions of the academic formula. Most of these able designers were nearly exact contemporaries of Wright, and it is therefore all the more interesting to compare the latter's idiosyncratically monumental Hollyhock House, Los Angeles (1920), with the more customary monumentalism of the others. Another contemporary of Wright, Albert *Kahn, had a rather different contribution to make to the growth of recent American architecture. From the first decade of the century his vast organization specialized in large-scale industrial work, and continued the process of developing the large office which had been inaugurated by the academically inclined firms of the 1880s and 1890s. However, the work of the 1920s in the USA, curious and interesting as it is, completely lacks the forthright intensity of the new architecture that was then emerging in Europe. Indeed, the work of Wright at this time, even when viewed in the context of the more traditionally oriented buildings of the day, was less acutely creative than at an early or at a later period. But already there were signs that this era of somnolence was not destined to last. In 1923 the Finnish architect, Eliel *Saarinen, settled in America, representing the vanguard of a coming wave of distinguished European *émigrés*. While his work never quite fulfilled the promise of his earliest endeavours in Finland, and instead appears tentative in style if forthright in its programmatic solutions, a rather different and more unmistakable contemporaneity was to be found in the designs of Rudolph *Schindler and Richard *Neutra, two architects of Viennese origin whose particular dispositions were influenced by such disparate stimuli as Otto *Wagner, Adolf *Loos, and Frank Lloyd Wright. The houses built first by Schindler and, subsequently, by Neutra in and around Los Angeles, were the very earliest manifestations in the USA of the technique and taste that were later identified as the *International Style. The clear, unmistakably pure character of their works demonstrated that the tentative modernism of a Goodhue or an Eliel Saarinen would become outmoded along with the more literal sort of historicism as soon as the new architecture had spread.

The speed with which the new ideas and motifs took hold can be illustrated in the transformation of Raymond *Hood's widely admired skyscraper designs, which changed from a neo-Gothic mode in the Chicago Tribune Tower (1923, with J. M. Howells, b. 1868), to a simplified abstract mode which is, albeit superficially, both functional and futurist, in the New York Daily News Buildings (1930). A much more profound essay in 'Skyscraper International' was the tower of the Philadelphia Savings Fund Society by George Howe and William *Lescaze of 1932, whose expression of vertical structural members on one side is set in contrast to the horizontal expression of cantilevers on

Henry Bacon. Lincoln Memorial. Washington, D.C., 1914–22

Raymond M. Hood and J.M. Howells. Daily News Building. New York, 1930

William Lescaze and George Howe. Philadelphia Savings Fund Society Building. Philadelphia, 1932

another. Such integral relationships between the frame of the building and its surface is analogous to the practice of the earlier Chicago School, although the formal vocabulary conforms with the new European fashion. This unusually frank design is in distinct contrast with the tallest of all tall office buildings, the Empire State Building, New York, by Shreve, Lamb and Harmon (1930–2), which manages to be 'traditional' without being recognizably revivalistic in style.

The 1930s were marked by two events which had the dual effect of releasing contemporary American architecture from the predominantly tentative statements of modernism, and of forming the basis from which the post-Second World War leadership of the USA in the development of world architecture would suddenly grow. The first of these was the renaissance of Frank Lloyd Wright (no other word will suffice), which reached an initial climax in the Kaufmann House, 'Falling Water' (1936), a building in which the organic, naturalistic features inherent in Wright's design philosophy were reconciled with the machine-like clarity characteristic of the European modern movement. Seconding this noteworthy achievement in the re-integration and development of 20th-century American architecture was the arrival in the USA of several of the chief mentors of the International Style itself: Walter *Gropius and *Mies van der Rohe were joined by others of more Expressionist leanings like Erich *Mendelsohn or by their younger disciples such as Marcel *Breuer. Gropius continued his rôle as an educator which he had begun in the *Bauhaus by taking charge of the Architectural School at Harvard, while Mies assumed a similar rôle at the Illinois Institute of Technology, Chicago. Both contributed to the development of American modernism at this juncture with distinctive and influential buildings. Mies's master plan for the new campus of IIT, perfected in 1940, did not exert a great influence for perhaps a decade, and then, suddenly, its cool, pristine, stately geometry became the paragon of new architecture in the 1950s. More immediately influential were a series of houses designed by Gropius in collaboration with Breuer in the neighbourhood of Boston, Mass. in the late 1930s and early 1940s, houses in which the severe geometry of the International Style was tempered and transformed by the native wood-frame traditions of New England domestic architecture.

This transplanted style quickly evolved in the direction of something more organic and romantic in the post-1945 houses of Breuer, and was in fact anticipated in the domestic architecture of the Western States, generally known as the Bay Region Style. The restrained manner of William W. *Wurster and the more personal styles of Harwell Hamilton Harris and John Yeon represented, throughout the 1940s, one of the most vigorous schools of domestic architecture; it remains far more memorable than the much publicized Scandinavian 'New Empiricism' of the same epoch. However, few works of this group were quite so remarkable as developments of the fluent, interlocking spatial

Frank Lloyd Wright. Kaufmann House, 'Falling Water'. Bear Run, Pa., 1936

schemes of the International Style as were the southern California villas of Richard Neutra that date from the late 1940s. At the same period there are other more novel developments in domestic architecture that are due to Frank Lloyd Wright, whose second house for Herbert Jacobs, Middleton, Wis. (1948), is, in its fortress-like, primitive character, an extraordinary reaction against the openness and sophisticated modernism of Neutra's contemporary dwellings. Indeed, in many of his more monumental designs of the 1940s and 1950s Wright seems to be continuing and reinterpreting the massive and closed 19th-century forms of Richardson and Sullivan, giving them a new contemporary relevance rather than merely 'reviving' them.

Other characteristics of this varied and formative period can be seen in two academic buildings in Cambridge, Mass.: Alvar *Aalto's Baker House at the Massachusetts Institute of Technology (1948) and Walter Gropius's Harvard Graduate Center of 1950. The former, a tawny brick serpentine slab, represents the continued growth of the romantic, empirical strain (as opposed to the more provocative personal mode of Wright) in American architecture. On the other hand, the layout and elevations of the Harvard Graduate Center are dependent upon the tradition of purged and simplified geometry that was earlier realized in the Bauhaus itself, but with one important difference: the contrasts between the shapes and locations of the various elements are less harsh and bold. Each of these buildings illustrates in its own way an aspect of 20th-century modernism that was on the wane in the late 1940s.

The immediate future was destined to be predicated upon two much more simple and intellectual domestic designs of the period: Mies van der Rohe's Farnsworth House, Fox River, Ill. (1946–51); *Johnson's Glass House, New Canaan, Conn. (1947–9). In many respects the spatial and planning techniques of these two highly specialized dwellings are dependent upon a half-century of the machine aesthetic, and as such are outgrowths, if not ultimate manifestations, of the International Style. However, the reduction and simplicity of the cubic form, and the crystalline uniformity of the enclosing glass introduces a degree of regularity in both houses that is in contrast to the more diverse and irregular shaping and surfacing of the 'functional' architecture of the 1920s. The new architecture of the 1950s was to learn much from this carefully stated neoclassicization of the machine aesthetic. Equally, the precision with which these and other works by Mies and Johnson were rendered was an external and easy-to-imitate element that was swiftly turned into a popular fashion in the commercial architecture of the period. The firm of *Skidmore, Owings and Merrill—in effect a latter day successor to both the academicism of McKim, Mead and White and the utilitarianism of Albert Kahn—dominated this side of American architecture, especially through the quality of its commercial designs, and it continued to be acutely sensitive to shifts of taste when, in the late 1950s, its manner edged away from the glass box to more solid-seeming forms.

The early 1950s also witnessed the emergence of Eero *Saarinen, son of the pioneer Finnish architect. His General Motors Technical Center, Warren, Michigan, has a superficial Miesian character, but the varied proportions indicate a certain freedom of stylistic disposition which would lead to a pronounced design eclecticism in the late 1950s. This direction is amply documented in his new residential colleges for Yale University (1962) in which an abstract and empirical design is made to blend subtly with the elegant historicism of James Gamble Rodgers's collegiate Gothic of a generation before. A similar testing of various modernist idioms, together with a tentative eclecticism, is revealed in the designs of Paul *Rudolph, who had achieved considerable success as a designer of houses about 1950, and who, in the subsequent decade, has made interesting contributions to the expansion of the contemporary idiom in larger buildings. In particular, Rudolph has

Alvar Aalto. Everett Moore Baker House, Massachusetts Institute of Technology. Cambridge, Mass., 1948

Ludwig Mies van der Rohe. Lake Shore Drive Apartments. Chicago, 1950–1

recently made an effort to transpose the vigorous late style of Le Corbusier in designs for religious, educational and commercial buildings.

The most fashionable of recent architects have tended towards a certain decorative elaboration in the composition of façades. Perhaps the most successful of these designers a few years ago was Edward D. *Stone, whose American Embassy in New Delhi, India (1958), was the first of a series of endeavours to create an officially endorsed modernism. A more recent example is Saarinen's Embassy in London (1960). However, the opulent yet brittle mannerisms of Minoru *Yamasaki, with façades protected by metal grilles and thinly disguised historical motifs, is perhaps an even more potent fashion in the early 1960s. In spite of these somewhat frigid, superficial efforts to create a revisionist movement in contemporary architecture, the older practitioners have tended to hold fast to the creative basis if not to the external appearances of their previous work. In his ultimate works, Wright created a dazzling array of forms, but they were invariably imagined upon the basis of previous designs. Mies's latest projects have been for buildings abroad, notably in Mexico and Germany, and thus his tenacity in holding to the style he perfected twenty years ago, especially in the face of change reflected both in the ephemeral work of the 1960s, and of normal development in the work of direct followers such as Johnson, and Skidmore, Owings and Merrill, is particularly noteworthy.

As if to compensate for Mies's relative inactivity recently in the USA, *Le Corbusier, the most distinguished of the veteran modernists remaining in Europe, was invited to design a new Art Center at Harvard in 1960. The characterful forms of this new building will thus form a challenging comparison with the other significant contemporary works of the last decade in Cambridge, Mass., those of Gropius, Aalto and Eero Saarinen. However, to the dynamic inflections of a sculptural sort that are now being introduced into American architecture by way of Le Corbusier, there is another, equally rugged, manner that is to be seen almost exclusively in the new work of Louis I. *Kahn. Hardly known a decade ago, except to a loyal band of young students, by the

Paul Rudolph. Jewett Arts Centre, Wellesley College, Mass., 1955–9

Edward Durell Stone. US Pavilion at the International Exhibition. Brussels, 1958

late 1950s his fame was already assured. Kahn's forthright concrete frame structures possess the semblance of a design philosophy relevant for their period and a final outward appearance which appeals both to a taste for contrasts of form and for certain kinds of justifiably accidental effects. Consequently, Kahn's few executed buildings may well turn out to be the most historically important if least typical designs of the early 1960s. Indeed, the nature of his style is such that it suggests the fulfilment of a century of American architecture, subsuming some of the profoundest lessons of Wright, Sullivan, and Richardson, and reaching so far back as to make relevant once again the century-old Victorian 'realism' of Sullivan's early mentor, Frank Furness.

The other side of the current picture is also traditionalist, but, it would seem, takes its cue from the alternate, academic current of the American development. The handsome, tasteful designs for Lincoln Center, New York, the work of several architects, including Wallace *Harrison, Max *Abramovitz, Philip Johnson, Skidmore, Owings and Merrill, and the late Eero Saarinen, seem to represent a blend of the challenging modernist discipline of a quarter-century ago with the half-century-old security of academicism as earlier represented by McKim, Mead and White. Of all the buildings at Lincoln Center, only Johnson's N.Y. State Theater seems to be the outcome of anything more than the most superficial decorative approach.

Under these confusing and rather inconsistent circumstances it is not easy succinctly to characterize the American scene in the 1960s. However, it is clear that an epoch of assimilation is past and the modern movement, brought to a climax in Europe in the 1920s and 1930s, has been incorporated into the evolving tradition of American architecture. The latter has, thereby, achieved new responsibilities through a generally recognized world-wide leadership which places new demands as well as a new dignity upon its subsequent development.

Bibliography: E. B. Mock, *Built in USA 1932–1944*, New York 1944; Henry-Russell Hitchcock and Arthur Drexler, *Built in USA: Post-war Architecture*, New York 1952; Lewis Mumford, *Roots of Contemporary American Architecture*, New York and London 1952; Ian McCallum, *Architecture USA*, London 1959; Wayne Andrews, *Architecture in America*, New York 1960; Esther McCoy, *Five California Architects*, New York 1960; 'America', *Zodiac 8* (special number), Milan 1961; John Burchard and Albert Bush-Brown, *The Architecture of America*, Boston and Toronto 1961; C. W. Condit, *American Building Art*, Vol. I, The 19th century; Vol. II, The 20th century, New York and London, 1960 and 1961.

JOHN M. JACOBUS, JR

Utzon, Jørn, b. Copenhagen 1918. Utzon is the most original talent in modern Danish architecture. From the earliest years of his career he was possessed by an organic sense of architecture which was inspired by Frank Lloyd *Wright and Alvar *Aalto and strengthened by a period of study in the USA and six months' work in Aalto's Helsinki drawing office (1946). For the young Utzon the functionalism of the thirties had ended in formalism, and the traditionalism of the forties, a consequence of the isolation and restrictions caused by the war, was totally lacking in relevance to the technical and scientific developments of the times. He considered that a progressive architecture could be learned from the laws of nature, and that new materials should be used in accordance with their own properties. He was himself able to live up to these very ambitious demands thanks to his originality, imagination and professional skill.

Utzon completed his secondary education in 1937 and entered the architectural school of the Academy of Arts, where he was taught by Kay *Fisker and Steen Ejler Rasmussen. He qualified in 1942 and then worked for three years in Stockholm, where his encounter with Gunnar *Asplund's architecture in particular influenced his development. In the following year he received prizes in a series of competitions for projects worked out in collaboration with Tobias Faber and submitted a design for the Crystal Palace in London together with Faber and Mogens

Jorn Utzon. House. Holte, 1952–3

Irming. Also important at this time was his friendship and collaboration with the Norwegian architect, Arne Korsmo.

In 1952 he built his own house in Hellebæk on a southward facing slope at the edge of a wood; the spaciousness and open groundplan were quite new to Denmark at that time. A little later, 1952–3, he built a house in Holte, whose inspiration was more Japanese. Its concrete frame holds the otherwise timber-clad house a storey above the ground. During the first half of the fifties he received prizes in several Swedish competitions, including a plan for the Elineberg housing estate, which was subsequently realized (in collaboration with E. and H. Andersson).

Jorn Utzon. Opera House. Sydney, Australia, 1956. Model

In 1956 Utzon received first prize for a highly original plan in the international competition for a new Sydney Opera House, to be placed on a mole in the middle of the city's harbour. The opera house, concert hall and foyers are to lie under shells 200 feet in height on an extensive stepped platform. This platform will serve as the cover for a lower level with experimental theatre, access for vehicles, extra space, etc. The shells are planned according to a bold and original scheme developed in collaboration with Ove Arup in London. The project was hailed by Harry *Seidler as 'pure poetry', but the detailed planning shows the presence of a logical and realistic architect, able to turn his visions into reality. In a number of projects from 1958 to 1960 Utzon varied the idea of raised platforms or bastions, with vehicular access below and the building proper above (Højstrup Workers' High School, 1958; a row of buildings in Frederiksberg, near the centre of Copenhagen, 1959; International Exhibition in Copenhagen, 1960). Smaller, but no less characteristic, is the plan for the Melli Bank in Teheran (1958).

While Utzon was working on these dynamic and imaginative projects, two housing estates in northern Zealand were erected—Kingohusene near Helsingør (1957–60) and the Danish Co-operative Building in Fredensborg. Both are chains of houses with courtyards or gardens, staggered to fit the topography. Each house and garden is enclosed by yellow brick walls of various heights. The houses are small and inexpensive and remind one of a North African village.

TOBIAS FABER

Vago, Pierre, b. Budapest 1910. Came to Paris at eighteen years of age to study under Auguste *Perret at the École Spéciale d'Architecture. While still a student, in 1932, he became editor-in-chief of the journal *L'architecture d'aujourd'hui*. In 1934 designed a prefabricated all-metal house. Town planning, schools, housing (in Berlin 1957, with flat-units one and a half storeys high), churches (Basilica of Pius X at Lourdes, commenced 1954, with *Freyssinet as engineer).

Van de Velde, Henry, b. Antwerp 1863, d. Zurich 1957. Henry van de Velde was the apostle in theory and practice of functional aesthetics and 'pure form'; between 1900 and 1925 he exerted a decisive influence on architecture and the applied arts, particularly in Germany. Born of a middle-class Flemish family, van de Velde was attracted to music, literature and painting before turning to architecture. He was a student at the Académie des Beaux-Arts at Antwerp in 1881, where he attended the painting classes; he continued with Carolus Duran in Paris from 1884 to 1885. He made contact with the Impressionist painters and Symbolist poets, and was particularly impressed by Seurat, whose pointilliste technique seemed to embody a spatial concept capable of opening up new prospects in architecture. Returning to Antwerp, van de Velde took part (1886) in founding the cultural circle named *Als ik Kan* (after Van Eyck's motto), and a year later, *L'art indépendant*, an association of young neo-Impressionist painters. From 1889 onwards he took part in the international activities of the famous avant-gardist Brussels group known as *Les XX*, where he discovered the synthetical art and flowing hand of Gauguin, the English *Arts and Crafts Movement, and the socially orientated work of William *Morris. Towards 1890 he became associated with the journal *Van Nu en Straks*, for which he devised a revolutionary layout, new typography and woodcut ornaments in a style derived from Gauguin. This undertaking, which played an important rôle in the renaissance of Belgian book production, started van de Velde on the road to the craft side of art. Henceforth, following the example of William Morris, he gave up painting (1893) and concentrated on illustration. He designed a mural tapestry, 'The Angels' Vigil' (1891, Zurich, Kunstgewerbemuseum), and went on to three-dimensional work with the creation of his first pieces of furniture (1894), the last stage before entering, shortly after his marriage, on the royal road of architecture proper.

In 1895 (two years after *Horta's Hôtel Tassel) van de Velde built his own home, 'Bloemenwerf' at Uccle near Brussels. It is designed as an organic whole and completely fitted out (joinery, hardware, furniture, carpets, curtains, dinner service, glasses, silver) in a uniform style of English inspiration, thus conforming with the theories which he set out in his own

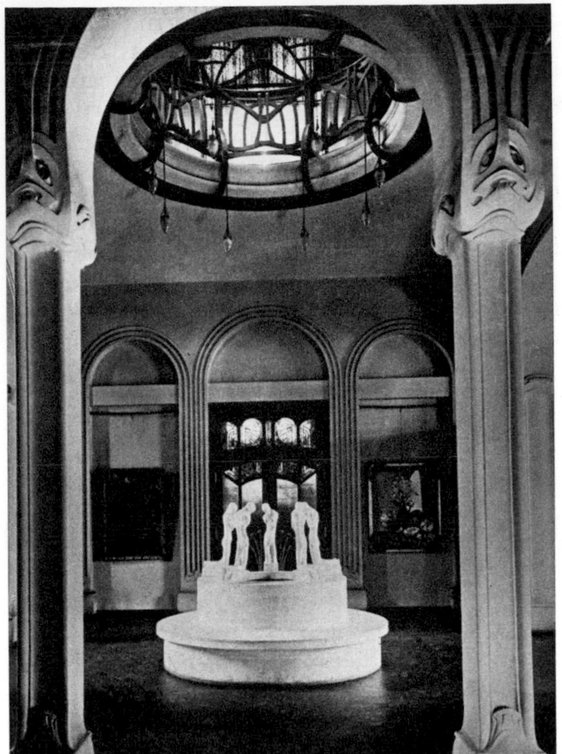

Henry van de Velde. Karl-Ernst Osthaus Museum. Hagen, 1900–2

publications (*Déblaiement d'art*, *L'art futur*, *Aperçu en vue d'une Synthèse d'art*). Noteworthy features include a return to a rational style that 'frankly and proudly' displays the processes of manufacture in all fields, an uncompromising logic in the use of materials, and a rejection of all ornament inspired by nature and all historic detailing. But van de Velde's renewed awareness of structural function, his desire to cast off dead tradition and his basic rationalism still retained sentimental overtones. His thought was instilled with German romanticism. 'Whether it was a matter of the works of German, Austrian or Dutch artists', he wrote later, 'we were all more attached than we thought to a kind of romanticism which would not allow us to consider form "without ornament", we were too much painters, too much wedded to literature, to glimpse the necessity of abandoning ornament and decoration . . . the temptations and subconscious insinuations of romanticism prompted us to bend and twist our structural schemes and present them as ornaments acting as structural elements, or as structures imbued with the rhythm of a linear ornament. This failing that characterizes my first works has nothing to do with the rise of Art Nouveau, which certain writers have fathered on me, and which enshrined an amalgam of the type of ornamentation I was using around 1894 and the kind of floral ornament associated with the drawings of long-haired women that Otto Eckmann was turning out in Berlin at the same period, and which he had borrowed from the English Pre-Raphaelites.'

The fact remains that van de Velde's cult of linear ornament, of the undulating line, was strengthened by his enthusiastic adherence to the neo-romantic theory of empathy, formulated by Lipps in 1903. The originality of his designs soon caught the attention of the art historian Julius Meier-Graefe and the art dealer S. Bing, who helped to ensure their international popularity. In 1896 Bing invited van de Velde to fit out four rooms of a shop he was opening in Paris under the name of *L'Art Nouveau*. His robust and curvilinear furniture, in a style very like that introduced by the young Liége-born designer Georges Serrurier-Bovy in 1894, aroused much

Henry van de Velde. Art School. Weimar, 1906

Henry van de Velde. Werkbund Theatre. Cologne, 1914

enthusiasm at the Dresden Exhibition of Applied Arts in 1897.

Henceforth, van de Velde's path was clear: he would make his career in Germany. Before he left Belgium (1899), Meier-Graefe commissioned him to do the interior decoration of the *Maison Moderne* he had founded in Paris, and introduced him to the *Pan* group in Berlin, where he also won many commissions (Hohenzollern Craftwork Shop, 1899; Haby's barber shop, 1901; premises for the Habana Tobacco Co., 1900; Esche House, Chemnitz, 1902). During the winter of 1900–1, he undertook a lecture tour in Germany, during which he explained his artistic principles (published in 1902 under the title of *Kunstgewerbliche Laienpredigten*). At the instance of K. E. Osthaus, he undertook the interior decoration of the erstwhile Folkwang Museum at Hagen (1900–2; exhibition rooms, glass cases, stairs, handrails, decorative glazing, mouldings, furniture, etc). The strong modelling and curved ornamentation of this building are typically Art Nouveau, and mark the culminating point of the first phase of van de Velde's career, which closes with the rest room he designed for the Dresden Exhibition of Applied Arts in 1906.

The second phase, from 1906 to 1914, is opened by the foundation and building of the Weimar School of Applied Arts, thanks to van de Velde's influence with the Grand Duke of Saxe-Weimar, to whose court he had been attached since 1901 as artistic counsellor, charged with raising the level of design in local industry. Here he found an ideal field for exercising his vocation as a teacher. He introduced a new system of instruction based on the development of spontaneous feeling and a constant recourse to the student's powers of invention, avoiding the use of models from the past and the study of historic styles. These methods gave rise to new forms, which German industry was not slow to adopt. 'We shall be obliged to recognize one day,' van de Velde subsequently observed, 'that these objects with their rational shapes prepared the way for the advance of a rational type of architecture, and largely contributed to its general diffusion. Their principles are the same as those that modern architecture was based on afterwards.'

The design of the Weimar school buildings clearly expresses in itself the development of van de Velde's architectural thought. Although traditional building methods are employed, a surer sense of space and volume is evinced. The straight line returns, ornament is purified and stress laid on plastic expression, as in the Werkbund Theatre. This celebrated building, now destroyed, was built for the Werkbund Exhibition of 1914, in Cologne. Laid out on a symmetrical plan, with a heavy traditional shell, albeit of original appearance, it embodied numerous innovations that provided a brilliant answer to the requirements of the dramatic art of its day: auditorium in the shape of an amphitheatre, independent proscenium, circular horizon, and, in particular, tripartite stage. Van de Velde, who was friendly with Gordon Craig and Max Reinhardt, had already in 1911 drawn up the first plans for the Théâtre des Champs-Élysées, Paris.

The outbreak of the First World War marks the commencement of the third and final phase of van de Velde's career (1914–57). He moved to Switzerland in 1917, where he became intimate with Romain Rolland and E. L. Kirchner. In 1921 he transferred to Holland, where he was commissioned by the Kröller-Müller family to design a museum, which he ultimately built, to a modified plan, at Otterlo (1937–54). This building is a work of great simplicity and harmony, free of all rhetorical efforts; it is perfectly adapted to its site and function

(one level throughout, main and secondary circulation, top lighting, etc.).
Van de Velde returned to Belgium in 1925. With the support of the Minister C. Huysmans, he was given the opportunity once more of carrying out the experiments he had conducted at Weimar: in 1926 he founded the Institut des Arts Décoratifs de la Cambre, which later became the École Nationale Supérieure d'Architecture et des Arts Décoratifs. He was the principal of this school until 1935; in addition, he occupied the chair of architecture at the University of Ghent from 1926 to 1936. He settled at Oberägeri in Switzerland in 1947, where he began writing his memoirs.
Van de Velde's work is dominated by his controversial and acute writings. His thought is condensed in the *Formules de la Beauté architectonique moderne* (Weimar 1917), revised and re-issued as *Formules d'une Esthétique moderne* (Brussels 1923), which stands to early-20th-century architecture as do Maurice Denis's *Théories* (1890) to the painting of his time. Among van de Velde's most important collaborators and pupils may be mentioned Victor *Bourgeois, J. J. Eggerick, R. Verwilghen, and L. Stynen.
Bibliography: Henry van de Velde, *Déblaiement d'art*, Brussels 1894; Henry van de Velde, *L'art futur*, Brussels 1895; Henry van de Velde, *Aperçu en vue d'une Synthèse d'art*, Brussels 1895; Henry van de Velde, *Geschichte meines Lebens*, Munich 1962; Karl Ernst Osthaus, *Henry van de Velde. Leben und Schaffen des Künstlers*, Hagen 1920; J. Mesnil, *Henry van de Velde et le Théâtre des Champs-Elysées*, Brussels; O. J. Maurice Casteels, *Henry van de Velde*, Brussels 1932; 'Henry van de Velde', Special Issue of *La Cité*, Brussels 1933, No. 5–6; Herman Teirlinck, *Henry van de Velde*, Brussels 1959.

ROBERT L. DELEVOY

Viganò, Vittoriano, b. Milan 1919; graduated there 1944. Residential and sports buildings. His Istituto Marchiondi (Milan 1957) with its dramatically accentuated structure, heavy massing and untreated, exposed concrete is regarded as the Italian variation of *Brutalism.

Villagran Garcia, José, b. Mexico City 1901. Studied architecture at Mexico University. Teacher of most modern Mexican architects and pioneer of modern architecture in *Mexico. Numerous schools, public and welfare buildings.

Villanueva, Carlos Raúl, b. Croydon, England 1900. More than any other individual architect Villanueva has been responsible for the impressive development of modern architecture in Venezuela. He studied at the *École des Beaux-Arts in Paris. In a way typical of his generation throughout Latin America, his early work was an attempt to renew, with discriminating connoisseurship, the traditions of local colonial architecture. Quite soon, however, he came to a deep understanding of the new ways of thought in architecture and devoted himself with a missionary ardour to the spread of modern architecture in his own land.
To the inspiration received from the great masters of his time Villanueva adds characteristic personal elements: a dynamic and spontaneous quality in structural design, forcefully expressed in exposed concrete; a catholicity of taste reflected in extensive collaboration with many painters and sculptors as well as in a daring use of polychromy; and a feeling for large-scale composition which enables him to cope with the enormous building programme resulting from the rapid development of the country. Villanueva's impact is also felt in the fine architectural tradition established by the housing authority, the *Banco Obrero*, whose gigantic operations on a consistently high level have enabled many younger architects to start promising careers. Among Villanueva's most important work the buildings for the University City in Caracas obviously come first. The Olympic Stadium (1950–1), with its daringly cantilevered marquees, built in shell concrete, with exposed ribs, and the Auditorium and the Covered Plaza (Aula Magna and Plaza Cubierta, 1952–3) are the best known. The Aula Magna, one of the most beautiful assembly rooms in the world, has a clean white curved ceiling against which float a large number of variously coloured and shaped panels, designed by Alexander Calder (with R. Newman as acoustics specialist). The austerity of the exterior, emphatically expressing the structural framework, is compensated by the gaiety and airiness of the Plaza Cubierta, the large semi-enclosed

Carlos Raúl Villanueva. Olympic Stadium. Caracas, 1950–1

foyer, displaying works of art by Arp, Léger, Vasarely, and others. In all the other buildings, such as the library, the hospital, the various schools, an individual theme is carried through, the result of special research into each particular programme, boldly expressed in a framework of exposed concrete, often filled in with variously coloured panels covered with mosaic.

Of Villanueva's huge housing projects, called for by the rapid growth of Caracas (163,000 inhabitants in 1936, 359,000 in 1941, 718,000 in 1951, and 1,300,000 today) at least two, located in this city, must be mentioned as examples: the 'Dos de Diciembre' Housing Estate, with 2,366 dwellings for 12,744 people—400 persons per hectare—designed in collaboration with José Manuel Mijares, José Hoffman and Carlos Branco; and the 'El Paraiso', a smaller estate, with duplex units in a four-storey and a sixteen-storey building, (the density only 200 people per hectare), designed in collaboration with Carlos Celis and José Manuel Mijares. In both, the provision of ancillary facilities, social and commercial, is typical of the architect's humanistic approach. The extremely frank expression of the structure distinguishes these buildings, like most of Villanueva's, from the work of other Venezuelan architects such as Bernardez, Vegas and Galia, or Guinand and Benacerraf, which

seems closer to an international idiom. But it is precisely this distinction that lends to Villanueva's work its characteristic pioneering and dynamic spirit. (*p. 26)
Bibliography: Henry-Russell Hitchcock, *Latin-American Architecture since 1945*, New York 1955.

HENRIQUE E. MINDLIN

Viollet-le-Duc, Eugène Emmanuèle, b. Paris 1814, d. Lausanne 1879. In 1840 began a series of important restorations of medieval buildings, of doubtful quality, however, by current standards of conservation; these include Vézelay, Carcassonne, Amiens, Pierrefonds, Notre-Dame de Paris. He had controversies with the *École des Beaux-Arts, to which he was appointed in 1863. His influential writings (*Dictionnaire de l'Architecture*, 1854f., *Entretiens sur l'Architecture*, 1863–72), although supporting the tendencies to stylistic copyism of the times, went far beyond Viollet-le-Duc's own work in their demand for rationality of structure. (*Steel)

Vlugt, L. C. van der, b. Rotterdam 1894, d. Rotterdam 1936. Housing and schools. 1925 in partnership with J.A. *Brinkman. (*Netherlands)

Voysey, Charles Annesley, b. Hessle, Yorkshire, 1857, d. Winchester 1941. Architect and designer of great influence on English and Continental *Art Nouveau. His private houses, mostly small, go back to the tradition of the English country house and are examples of building 'from the inside out' in functional design. (*p. 11)

Wachsmann, Konrad, b. Frankfort on the Oder 1901. Wachsmann has been a pioneer of industrialized building in theory, practice and teaching. He has always advocated that the scientific and technical resources of mass production should be applied to the processes of building, and he holds a corresponding structural and aesthetic conception of architecture. He came straight from building in timber to the problems of prefabrication. Trained as joiner and carpenter, Wachsmann was a student at the Arts and Crafts Schools of Berlin and Dresden (under Heinrich Tessenow) and at Berlin Academy of Art, where he was a star pupil of Hans *Poelzig's. From 1926 to 1929 he worked as chief architect for the firm of Christoph and Unmack who were the largest manufacturers of timber buildings in Europe at the time. In 1932 he was awarded the Rome Prize by the German Academy in Rome. In the years following, which he spent in Rome, he was occupied with building blocks of flats in reinforced concrete. Emigrating to the United States, he founded a partnership with Walter

Carlos Raúl Villanueva, Carlos Celis and José Manuel Mijares. El Paraiso Flats. Caracas

Carlos Raúl Villanueva. Building for the Faculty of Architecture and Town Planning of the University. Caracas, 1957. Large Hall.

Konrad Wachsmann. Structural system for halls. 1950–3. Model

*Gropius from 1941 to 1948, from which emerged the General Panel Corporation, the first fully automated factory for the production of prefabricated building components. In 1950 Wachsmann, who has been an American citizen since 1946 and who lives partly in America and partly in Europe, was appointed professor at the Illinois Institute of Technology at Chicago and director of the Department of Advanced Building Research. Since then, with the support of the American Government, he has directed architectural seminars at universities and colleges in Japan, Israel, Austria and Germany. In recent years he has conducted research on town and country planning in the United States, and on multi-storey building in Europe.

Konrad Wachsmann. Perspective of a structural unit. 1953

Wachsmann's research has concentrated on the basic character of universal elements in building construction which can be mass produced. His starting point is '*modular coordination', which governs the relationship of the various building components to each other. These components should be as simple as possible and capable of as many different combinations as possible. A 'universal module', identical with the 'planning module', comprises all the modular categories (material, performance, construction, installation, etc.). The resulting abstract data are carried over into the concrete conception of a standard form.

Wachsmann's research has found a practical application above all in the General Panel System, which is made up of prefabricated timber units. In the forties, he was commissioned by the US Air Force to develop the 'Mobilar Structure', a system for the construction of aircraft hangars to any required size by the addition of steel struts, whose tubular diameter possesses extremely favourable static properties. He made a special study of the nature of the connections and joints of cellular structures such as Buckminster *Fuller's geodesic domes or Le Ricolais's space structures, built up from similar elements. In 1951, he worked out a classification system for modular coordination for the Federal Housing Agency in Washington as an example of the rational planning of vast building programmes.

Wachsmann carried out part of his research in the form of team-work with his students in the course of his teaching activities. On the rôle of the architect within the industrialized building process he says: 'It will be the task of the universal planner to combine the requisite technological components by a creative act into a complete whole. The universal planner becomes part of the creative team, combining prefabricated parts and planning with them in the widest sense.' He has anticipated the future time and again with his apparently utopian projects, and has stimulated discussion, beyond the limits of architecture, on the problem of the spirit in a technical civilization. (*Space Frames)

Bibliography: Konrad Wachsmann, *The Turning Point of Building*, New York 1961; Konrad Wachsmann, *Aspekte*, Wiesbaden 1961.

MARGIT STABER

Wagner, Martin, b. Königsberg 1885, d. Cambridge, Mass. 1957; 1926–33 City Architect of Berlin, where he was closely associated with *Gropius, *Häring, *Mies van der Rohe, *Poelzig, *Scharoun. Emigrated to the United States. Lecturer at Harvard University (1936–50).

Wagner, Otto, b. Penzing, near Vienna 1841, d. Vienna 1918. A precursor of 20th-century architecture and town planning, Wagner was the founder of the Vienna School, which rose to fame through its most brilliant disciples: Adolf *Loos, Josef *Hoffmann and Joseph Maria *Olbrich. He was the spiritual heir of *Viollet-le-Duc, and played a part in *Austria equivalent to that of *Sullivan in the United States, van de *Velde in Belgium and *Berlage in the Netherlands. His work is based fundamentally on a renewed awareness of the plan, adapted to the requirements of social progress and current advances in technology; it expresses an unerring renewal of architectural thought and symbolizes the great changes in taste that were taking place at the turn of the 19th and 20th centuries.

Wagner began his studies in 1857 at the Vienna Technical College. He spent some time in 1860 at the Berlin Academy of Building, and completed his training at the school of architecture of the Vienna Academy from 1861 to 1863. The first phase of his career is marked by a historical outlook. He adopted a form of classicism derived from the Tuscan and Florentine High Renaissance: closed plans that were lucid, logical and very severely geometrical. His work earned him such a reputation that he was commissioned in 1890 to draw up a scheme for completely remodelling the city of Vienna. Of this, the only item to be carried out was the construction (1894–7) of the Stadtbahn, or metropolitan railway network, intended to provide rapid communication with the suburbs and to thin out city traffic.

In 1894 he was appointed head of a special class in architecture at the Vienna Academy. This year also marked the opening of a second phase in the development of his work (1894–1901), characterized firstly by his assumption of a definite theoretical standpoint and next by his adherence to the system of aesthetics proclaimed at Brussels, Paris and Munich by the adepts of *Art Nouveau. While van de Velde was

Otto Wagner. Majolika-Haus. Vienna, *c.* 1898

Otto Wagner. Post Office Savings Bank. Vienna, 1904–6

opening his famous campaign in Brussels to purify the language of architecture (*Déblaiement d'art*, 1894), Wagner put forward in his inaugural lecture at Vienna Academy (1894) a doctrine that has become famous under the title of *Moderne Architektur*. In his view, the new architecture must take the requirements of modern life as its point of departure, and find adequate forms to express them. Two years after Sullivan's plea (*Ornament in Architecture*, 1892), and three years before the first statements of Loos, Wagner was extolling horizontal lines, flat roofs, and a stripped-down style that would draw its powers of expression from a striking affirmation of structural principles and the loyal use of materials, with steel in particular affording solutions that were new and bold.

The Stadtbahn station in the Karlsplatz (1899–1901) may serve to illustrate this transitional period. The use of a steel frame, in accordance with current French practice at the time, requires all archaeological reminiscences to be dispensed with; but by combining the straight line and the curve in floral ornamentation, a compromise is struck between doctrinal rigour and the inflections made fashionable by Art Nouveau.

Wagner went on to adopt a more radical attitude in full conformity with the principles he defended. The Post Office Savings Bank in Vienna (1904–6) dominates the third and last phase of his career; the economy of its trapezoidal plan, developing harmoniously around a central hall, the feeling for monumentality, the flexible handling of space, the complete eschewal of ornament and the perfect integration of steel and glass all go to make this building an unmistakable landmark in the history of contemporary architecture.

Bibliography: Otto Wagner, *Moderne Architektur*, Vienna 1896; 4th Edition: *Die Baukunst unserer Zeit*, Vienna 1914; Joseph August Lux, *Otto Wagner*, Munich 1914; Hans Tietze, *Otto Wagner*, Vienna 1922.

ROBERT L. DELEVOY

Warchavchik, Gregori, b. Odessa 1896. Trained in Rome. Warchavchik, who published a 'Manifesto of Functional Architecture' in 1925, built private houses in Brazil in the *International Style in the late twenties.

Webb, Philip, b. Oxford 1831, d. Worth, Sussex 1915. Assistant of G. E. Street, in whose office he met William *Morris. Associate in the Morris Company (*Arts and Crafts). Built houses in which he employs late-medieval building methods to create unconventional designs without resorting to historical copyism. The Red House near Bexley Heath, Kent (1859).

Weese, Harry, b. Chicago 1915. Trained at Massachusetts Institute of Technology and at Harvard University, Cambridge, Mass. Collaborated with Gordon *Bunshaft (*Skidmore, Owings and Merrill). Houses, schools, project for US Embassy at Accra (Ghana).

Wendingen. Dutch architectural journal (until 1936) which served as the focus for a group of architects in *Amsterdam.

Werkbund. *Deutscher Werkbund.

Williams, Sir E. Owen, b. Tottenham, London 1890. Reinforced concrete structures important in the development of modern English architecture. Boots' factory at Beeston near Nottingham (1932), Empire Swimming Pool, Wembley (1934), Peckham Health Centre (1936), aircraft hangars in London (1955). (*Great Britain)

Wright, Frank Lloyd, b. Richland Center, Wis. 1867 or 1869, d. Taliesin West, Ariz. 1959.

After Frank Lloyd Wright's death at the end of an architectural career that had continued for more than seventy years, he was very generally considered the greatest American architect and one of the three or four greatest architects of the 20th century. Yet recurrently, and to the end, his work had been the subject of controversies and it is unlikely that in the future all those controversies will be resolved in his favour —nor perhaps would he have wished it to be so. Even the date of his birth is disputed —he believed he was born in 1869, but evidence in the family records indicates 1867. Of English origin on his father's side and Welsh on his mother's, it was the Celtic strain in his temperament that dominated; at the same time he considered himself the most American of Americans, or as he was inclined to put it, Usonians.

His remarkably long career not unnaturally

Frank Lloyd Wright

divides into a succession of phases, from his education in the 1870s and 1880s in which his exposure to the Froebel kindergarten system and his reading of such architectural writers as *Ruskin and *Viollet-le-Duc seem to have played as great a part as the two years he spent studying engineering at the University of Wisconsin, to the final florescence of the 1950s. Nor, on the testimony of his remarkable autobiography can the ambience of his grandfather's farm near Spring Green, Wisconsin, be ignored in the early formation of his agrarian preferences and his special attitude towards nature and the nature of materials.

After a very brief initial period of work in the office of the minor 'Shingle Style' architect J. L. Silsbee in Chicago, he entered in 1888 the employ of Louis *Sullivan, the greatest American architect of the day, always to Wright the *Lieber Meister*. In that office he was early entrusted with the domestic commissions, notably the Charnley House in Chicago of 1892. But in his personal work, which began with the construction of his own house in Oak Park, Illinois, in 1889 and which naturally increased in volume after his break with Sullivan in 1893, many influences other than Sullivan's are evident, notably from such architects of the eastern seaboard as *Richardson, Bruce Price, and *McKim, Mead and White. Following on the apprentice work of the nineties, in which his own studio in Oak Park (1895), the windmill for his aunts at Spring Green (1896), and the River Forest Golf Club (1898) may be cited as especially significant, he came to maturity almost precisely in 1900.

In that year the Bradley and Hickox Houses in Kankakee, Ill. and the design for 'A Home in a Prairie Town' (published in the *Ladies Home Journal* in February 1901) initiated the series of his Prairie Houses, his earliest major contribution to modern architecture. In the Prairie Houses, of which the most notable were perhaps the Willitts House in Highland Park, Ill. and the Heurtley House in Oak Park (1902), the Martin House in Buffalo, New York (1904), the Glasner House in Glencoe, Ill. (1905), the Coonley House in Riverside, Ill. and the Isobel Roberts House in River Forest, Ill. (1908), and above all the Robie House in Chicago and Mrs Thomas Gale's House in Oak Park (1909), the American house was revolutionized with results that later affected house-design internationally. Characteristically the plans of these houses were articulated in X, L, and T shapes, with free spatial flow between the principal living areas. Externally they were low and horizontal, with windows arranged in continuous bands under the wide-spreading eaves of low hipped or gabled roofs which also subsumed porches within the carefully ordered compositions. Except for leaded-glass windows with delicate geometrical patterns, there was usually no ornament whatsoever and, except for occasional bold cantilevering of the roofs, no real modification of standard American building methods.

Already in 1901, however, he had published in *The Brickbuilder* a project for a cast-concrete bank and in non-domestic work was soon exploiting *reinforced concrete structure. When his work was brought to the attention of European architects by the Wasmuth publications of 1910 and 1911, the Larkin office building in Buffalo, New York (1904), the Unity Church in Oak Park (1906) and even the

small hotel in Mason City, Iowa (1909) were perhaps more influential than the domestic work. Their complex cubic forms, spatial development in three dimensions, and expressive exploitation of new building materials and methods appealed strongly to younger architects abroad, and this influence played some part in the adumbration of the *International Style in Europe in the following fifteen years.

For various reasons personal and general the next decade was less productive for Wright. But to these years, often considered his 'Baroque' period, belong the destroyed Midway Gardens in Chicago (1913), in which the sculptured and painted decoration paralleled and even prefigured aspects of post-Cubist art in Europe, and the big Imperial Hotel (1916–22) in Tokyo.

With his return to America in the early 1920s came a group of concrete-block houses in California, the most notable the Millard House in Pasadena (1923). Here a new setting and a new material induced a total revolution in his house design, with crisper forms, all-over patterned surfaces and invisible flat roofs. His own house, Taliesin, near Spring Green, Wisconsin, first built in 1911 and rebuilt after fires in 1914 and 1925, was more in the line of the earlier Prairie Houses, but characteristically adapted to a hillside and making expressive use of the local limestone.

In the mid and late 1920s Wright's career seemed for some years to have come to an end and he was already considered an 'old master', left behind by the new developments in architecture of that decade. Projects, however, notably that for the Noble apartment house in Los Angeles of 1929, indicated his will to rival, if not to imitate, the new architecture that he scorned as mere 'boxes on stilts'; and when the curve of his production turned up once more in the mid 1930s two extraordinary works, 'Falling Water', the Kaufmann house outside Pittsburgh (1936) and the S. C. Johnson & Son administration building in Racine, Wis. (1936–9) indicated in

Frank Lloyd Wright. Robie House. Chicago, 1909

Frank Lloyd Wright. Unity Church. Oak Park, 1906

Frank Lloyd Wright. Millard House. Pasadena, 1923

their totally different ways—extravagant exploitation of cantilevering; utilization of free-standing mushroom columns—the assurance with which he was now ready to handle reinforced concrete. In their almost total avoidance of ornament, in the subtle handling of a wide gamut of materials—from the Taliesin-like stonework of the core of 'Falling Water' to the metallic slickness of the glass-tube fenestration of the Johnson Building—these works displayed his ever-increasing sensitivity to materials old and new. (*pp. 12, 19–20; *Glass) Also to the late 1930s belong his 'Usonian' houses with walls of wooden-sandwiches and flat roofs of crossed wooden scantlings, modest dwellings built at surprisingly low cost in which his planning reached its extreme of openness with the substitution of clerestory-lighted 'work-spaces' attached to the main living areas for conventional kitchens. The range and size of his commissions was already widening. But more significant perhaps for the final florescence of his last twenty years than the large project of 1938 for a new campus for Florida Southern College in Lakeland, Fla., where construction started in 1940 and continued into the 1950s, was the variety of response evoked by the opportunity to work in sharply contrasted natural settings: the desert of Arizona, where he began his own winter establishment 'Taliesin West' at Scottsdale in 1938 and the exemplary Pauson House of 1940 at Phoenix, making use of 'desert concrete' in which large rough blocks of local stone were laid up loosely in forms with a minimum of cement binding; the hills of Los Angeles, where the Sturgis House (1939), a 'box without stilts', although visibly of brick and redwood, was cantilevered by hidden stall beams even more boldly than the terraces of 'Falling Water'; not to speak of Florida, where the warm climate and the lush foliage encouraged a return to the patterned block-work of the earlier California years. (*USA)

Parallel to this was an extraordinary increase in the range of geometrical and structural themes which he was to continue to develop to the end of his life. In addition to the rectangular forms characteristic of his work in the first quarter of the century, he now became fascinated with plan-patterns based on 60°–30° angles, on circles, and even on spirals. Early instances

Frank Lloyd Wright. Kaufmann House, 'Falling Water'. Bear Run, Pa., 1936

of these new approaches can be found in the projects of his fallow 1920s, but their full exploitation came only with the years after the Second World War. The 60°–30° angles appeared first in the San Marcos project for a resort in Chandler, Ariz. in 1927 and were first carried to execution in the Hanna House in Palo Alto, Calif., in 1937. The circle and the helix were the theme of the Strong Automobile project for Maryland (1925), but came to ultimate realization in the Guggenheim Museum, designed 1943–6 and built 1956–9.

Frank Lloyd Wright. Taliesin West. Scottsdale, near Phoenix, Ariz., 1938

The remarkably prolific and varied production of Wright's last decade of activity, including several major works such as the County Buildings for Marin County, California, which are still in construction, has not yet been sorted out and published in dated sequence.

In the vast variety of his plans, which included fantastic urban projects for Bagdad as well as for Pittsburgh and Madison, Wis., not to speak of a Mile High Skyscraper, it is difficult to see what were the main lines along which he was moving. Responsive, perhaps, to the new international architectural climate of the 1950s, as he had once before been to the climate of the late 1920s and early 1930s, he seemed ready to initiate a new style with each major project. Yet more careful study of the drawings of his earlier periods of activity often reveal that what seemed to be wholly new developments of his later decades were in fact the realizations of ideas long nurtured; thus the design of the Price Tower at Bartlesville, Okla. (1955) can be traced back through several intervening versions to the St Mark's Tower project for New York (1929).

In conclusion it should be noted that Wright was not a silent creator. Difficult as it may be sometimes to see precisely how, in detail, his ambitions for a universal

Frank Lloyd Wright. Price Tower. Bartlesville Okla., 1955

Frank Lloyd Wright. Beth Sholom Synagogue. Elkins Park, Pa., 1959

'*organic architecture' of the 20th century reached the particular expression that they did in his own works, his career owed much to what he said and wrote. Posterity will have more material concerning Wright than can be readily digested for a long time in a tremendous *œuvre*, a vast volume of intrinsically fascinating drawings, and a written gospel, on which to base a later judgement on this great architect, who was also perhaps the greatest American of his generation.

Bibliography: Frank Lloyd Wright on Architecture, ed. Frederick Gutheim, New York 1941; Henry-Russell Hitchcock, *In the Nature of Materials, 1887–1941, The Buildings of Frank Lloyd Wright*, New York 1942; Frank Lloyd Wright, *Auto-*

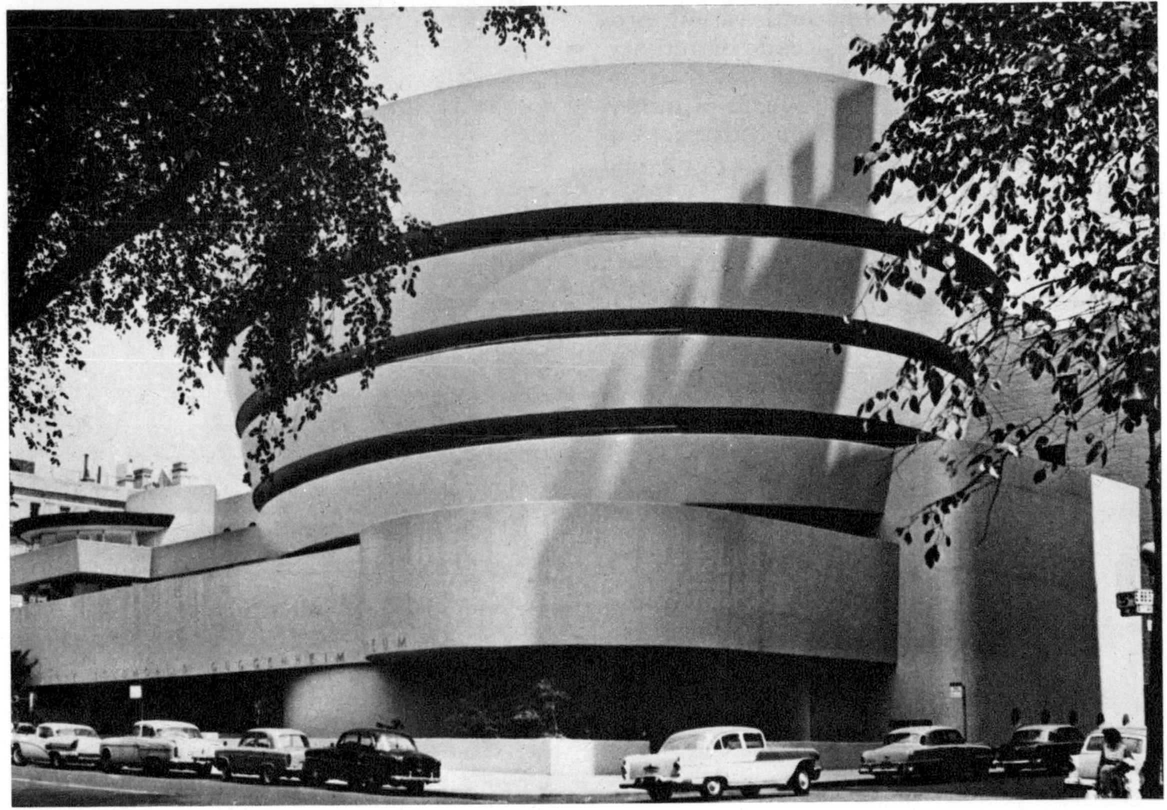

Frank Lloyd Wright. Guggenheim Museum. New York. Designed 1943–6, built 1956–9

biography, New York 1943; Frank Lloyd Wright, *Testament*, New York 1957; *Drawings, Frank Lloyd Wright*, New York 1959; *The Drawings of Frank Lloyd Wright*, ed. Arthur Drexler, New York 1962; Vincent J. Scully, Jr, *Frank Lloyd Wright*, New York 1960, Ravensburg 1961.

HENRY-RUSSELL HITCHCOCK

Wurster, William Wilson, b. Stockton, Calif. 1895. Studied at the University of California. Independent practice from 1926; since 1945 in partnership with Bernardi and Emmons. Wurster, who was influenced by *Maybeck, is an exponent of the 'Bay Region Style', the Californian variant of modern American architecture. He became known through his town and country houses which are distinguished by their modesty, adaptation to environment and consideration of locally prevailing social, economic and climatic conditions. Wurster, who thinks of *Aalto as a like-minded person, talks of an 'every-day-architecture' which is more concerned with function than form.

Yamasaki, Minoru, b. Seattle 1912. Studied at the Universities of Washington and New York. Worked in the offices of the Empire State Building architects Shreve, Lamb and Harmon; with *Harrison, Fouilhoux and *Abramovitz; and with Raymond Loewy Associates. He achieved international notice together with Hellmuth and Leinweber, his partners at the time, for the airport at St Louis (1953–5) whose reception halls consist of a series of intersecting barrel vaults. (*Shell structures)

Yamasaki is an admirer of *Mies van der Rohe, although he aims increasingly at a 'richness' which 'would make Mies frown' (Yamasaki). A characteristic feature of his style is the dissolution of the wall into an apparently textile-like fabric, which veils the structural members: umbrella walls made of profilated blocks at the Society of Arts and Crafts and at the American Concrete Institute (1958) at Detroit; metal grilles in the Reynolds Metals Office in Detroit (1959). Axial plans, silhouettes enlivened by turrets or top lighting visible from the exterior, and exuberant layouts

Minoru Yamasaki. Century 21 Exposition. Seattle, 1962. Model

Yorke, Rosenberg and Mardall. London (Gatwick) Airport, Stage 1. 1958. Terminal Building and Central Pier

with gardens and pools contribute to the impression of contrived elegance which is typical of Yamasaki's later designs. Canopied structures for the American pavilion at the New Delhi Fair (1960) and the Exposition at Seattle (1962). (*p. 25)

Yorke, Francis Reginald Stevens, b. 1906, d. 1962. Studied at Birmingham University School of Architecture. Founder member of MARS (British section of *CIAM) and pioneer of modern architecture in *Great Britain, with his reinforced concrete houses at Gidea Park, Essex (1933, with W. *Holford, G. Stephenson and A. Adam) and house at Nast Hyde, Hatfield (1935). In partnership with Marcel *Breuer, 1935–37, and from 1944 with Eugene Rosenberg and Cyril Mardall, in the firm of Yorke, Rosenberg and Mardall, which has been responsible for many important projects, including schools at Stevenage (1947–9), Oldbury, and Pool Hill, Salop. (1955–7, with extensive use of timber cladding), academic buildings in London, Merthyr Tydfil and Leeds; housing at Stevenage, Harlow and the Hansa district of Berlin; hospitals at Londonderry, Crawley and Hull; a department store at Sheffield, and Gatwick Airport, Sussex. The firm's own office in London, a restrained but finely proportioned and detailed building, was awarded the RIBA Bronze Medal for 1962. Yorke was the editor of the annual volume *Specification* from 1935 to the time of his death, and was the author of standard works on modern houses and (with Frederick *Gibberd) modern flats.

HAROLD MEEK

Zanuso, Marco, b. Milan 1916; graduated there 1939. Olivetti factory at São Paulo (1956–8), a scheme consisting of honeycomb cells, roofed with thin shell vaults. Also worked as a journalist.

Zehrfuss, Bernard, b. Angers 1911. Studied at the École des Beaux-Arts, Paris. Awarded the Rome prize of the French Academy in 1939. Unesco building, Paris (1953–7, in collaboration with *Breuer and *Nervi). Exhibition building of the Centre National des Industries et Techniques, Paris (1958, in collaboration with Camelot and De Mailly). Industrial buildings (Renault Works at Flins, 1953; Mame Printing Works at Tours).

Selected bibliography on the history of modern architecture

See also the bibliographies at the end of individual articles

Banham, Reyner, *Theory and Design in the First Machine Age*, London 1959.

Banham, Reyner, *Guide to Modern Architecture*, London 1962.

Behrendt, Walter Curt, *Modern Building. Its nature, problems and forms*, New York 1937.

Benevolo, Leonardo, *Storia dell'architettura moderna*, 2 volumes, Bari 1960.

Blake, Peter, *The Master Builders*, New York 1961.

Conrads, Ulrich and Hans G. Sperlich, *Phantastische Architektur*, Stuttgart 1960.

Darmstaedter, Robert, *Künstlerlexikon. Maler-Bildhauer-Architekten*, Berne and Munich 1961.

Dorgelo, A., *Modern European Architecture*, Amsterdam 1959.

Enciclopedia Universale dell'Arte. Encyclopaedia of World Art. Venice, Rome, New York, Toronto, London 1959 ff.

Francastel, Pierre (editor), *Les Architectes Célèbres*, 2 volumes, Paris 1959.

Giedion, S., *A Decade of New Architecture —Dix Ans d'Architecture Contemporaine*, Zurich 1954, 1st edition 1951.

Giedion, S., *Space, Time and Architecture*, Cambridge, Mass. 1956, 1st edition 1941.

Gropius, Walter, *Internationale Architektur*, Munich 1925.

Handbuch moderner Architektur, Berlin 1957.

Hilberseimer, Ludwig, *Internationale Neue Baukunst*, Stuttgart 1926.

Hilberseimer, Ludwig, *Grossstadt-Architektur*, Stuttgart 1927.

Hitchcock, Henry-Russell, *Modern Architecture, Romanticism and Reintegration*, New York 1929.

Hitchcock, Henry-Russell, *Architecture: Nineteenth and Twentieth Centuries*, Harmondsworth 1958.

Hitchcock, Henry-Russell and Philip Johnson, *The International Style. Architecture Since 1922*, New York 1932.

Joedicke, Jürgen, *A History of Modern Architecture*, London 1959.

Jones, Cranston, *Architecture Today and Tomorrow*, New York 1961.

Kultermann, Udo, *Baukunst der Gegenwart*, Tübingen 1958.

Pevsner, Nikolaus, *Pioneers of Modern Design. From William Morris to Walter Gropius*, London 1936.

Platz, Gustaf Adolf, *Die Baukunst der neuesten Zeit*, Berlin 1927.

Richards, J. M., *An Introduction to Modern Architecture*, London, Baltimore 1953.

Roth, Alfred, *La Nouvelle Architecture—Die neue Architektur—The New Architecture*, 4th edition, Zurich 1948.

Sartoris, Alberto, *Gli elementi dell'architettura funzionale*, 3rd edition, Milan 1941.

Sartoris, Alberto, *Encyclopédie de l'architecture nouvelle*, 3 volumes, Milan 1954–57.

Sartoris, Alberto, *Introduzione alla architettura moderne*, 3rd edition, Milan 1948.

Scully, Vincent, *Modern Architecture*, New York 1961.

Siegel, Curt, *Strukturformen der modernen Architektur*, Munich 1960.

Smith, G. E. Kidder, *The New Architecture of Europe*, London 1961.

Taut, Bruno, *Die neue Baukunst in Europa und Amerika*, Stuttgart 1929.

Thieme, Ulrich and Felix Becker (editors), *Allgemeines Lexikon der Bildenden Künstler von der Antike bis zur Gegenwart*, 37 volumes, Leipzig 1907–50.

Wasmuths Lexikon der Baukunst, 5 volumes, Berlin 1929–37.

Whittick, Arnold, *European Architecture in the Twentieth Century*, First Vol.: *1800–1924*. Second Vol.: *1924–1933*, London 1950–53.

Zevi, Bruno, *Architecture as Space*, New York 1957.

Zevi, Bruno, *Storia dell'architettura moderna*, 3rd edition, Turin 1955.

Photograph sources

The publishers are indebted to all individuals and institutions listed below who have kindly supplied photographs for publication in this book and especially to the Rijksvoorlichtingsdienst, The Hague; the Suomen Rakennustaiteen Museo, Helsinki; and to Mr Edgar Kaufmann jr., New York.

A.C.L., Brussels; Agtmaal, van, Hilversum; Aistrup, Wedboek; Annan, Glasgow; Apollo, Helsinki; Architectural Photographing Company, Chicago; Architectural Review, London; Beider, Basel; Ben Schnall, New York; Bentham-Moxon Trustees, London; Beratungsstelle für Stahlverwendung, Düsseldorf; Bildarchiv Foto, Marburg; Bladh, Bromma; Borremans, Cachan; British Features, Bonn; Bulloz, Paris; Casali, Milan; Cellard, Bron; Cetto, Mexico City; Checkman, Jersey City; Chevojon, Paris; Deutsche Presse-Agentur, Frankfurt; Diederichs, Berlin-Lankwitz; Dino, Milan; Doeser, Laren; Dotreville, Brussels; Dumont, Royan; Dupain, Sydney; Dyckerhoff und Widmann, Munich; Faigle, Stuttgart; Farbwerke, Hoechst; Finsler, Zurich; Fortunati, Milan; Fotogramma, Milan; Friedrich, Berlin-Lichterfelde; Futagawa, Tokyo; García Moya, Madrid; Gasparini, Caracas; Gautherot, Rio de Janeiro; Georges, New York; Gerlach, Vienna; Giraudon, Paris; Gmelin, Dornach; Grünert, Zurich; Guerrero, New York; Hanley; Havas, Helsinki; Hedrich-Blessing, Chicago; Heidersberger, Braunschweig; Held, Weimar; Helmer-Petersen, Copenhagen; Hervé, Paris; Høm, Copenhagen; Hubmann, Vienna; Ingervo, Helsinki; Jacobs, Berlin-Lichterfelde; Joedicke, Stuttgart; Jonals, Copenhagen; Josuweck, Cologne; Kersting, London; Kidder Smith, New York; KLM Aerocarto, Amsterdam; Köster, Berlin-Lichterfelde; Korab, Birmingham, Alabama; Kunstgewerbemuseum, Zurich; Laboratorio Fotografico, Rome; Landesbildstelle, Hamburg; Larson, Stockholm; Lazi, Stuttgart; Lens Craft, New York; Library of Congress, Washington; Luckhaus, New York; Madenskey, Vienna; Mäkinen, Helsinki; Maltby, London; Manchete, Rio de Janeiro; Mango, Naples; Maré, London; Mari, Rome; Martin, Paris; MAS, Barcelona; Michel, Rio de Janeiro; Møller, Århus; Moisio, Turin; Molitor, Ossining; Moosbrugger, Basel; Moncalvo, Turin; Moscardi, São Paulo; M.R.L., Strassburg; Müller, Alfred, Rio de Janeiro; Murasawa, Tokyo; Museum of Modern Art, New York; National Buildings Record, London; New York Daily News; Nilsson, Stockholm; Ojen, van, The Hague; Österr. Nationalbibliothek, Vienna; Pennsylvania Railroad, New York; Pfau, Mannheim; Pietinen, Helsinki; Pfriem, Paris; Publicam, Hilversum; Reens, New York; Renes, Amsterdam; Roos, Helsinki; Roubier, Paris; Ryan, Minneapolis; Schiller, Mill Valley; Schwab, Stuttgart; Science Museum, London; Shokokusha, Tokyo; Shulman, Los Angeles; Sibbelee, Amsterdam; Smith, Wilton; Sörvik, Göteborg; Souza, Rio de Janeiro; Spaziani, Rome; Spreng, Basel; Steiger, Stuttgart; Steuer, Chicago; Stillman, Litchfield, Connecticut; Stoedtner, Düsseldorf; Stoller, Rye; Strüwing, Copenhagen; Sturtevant, San Francisco; Sundahl, Stockholm; Syndicat d'Initiative, Évian; Szarkowski, Ashland, Wisc.; TASS Agency, Moscow; Urbschat-Fischer, Berlin-Charlottenburg; USIS, Bad Godesberg; Vasari, Rome; Velin, Helsinki; Versnel, Amsterdam; Victoria and Albert Museum, London; Villani, Bologna; Viollet, Paris; Volkart, Stuttgart; Vriend, Amsterdam; Vrijhof, Rotterdam; Wåhlén, Stockholm; Wahlström, Helsinki; Wasastjerna, Helsinki; Wayne Andrews, New York; Whittick, Crawley; Wickberg, Helsinki; Winkler, Stuttgart; Wölfl, Vienna; Wrubel, Düsseldorf; Zerkowitz, Barcelona; Zumstein, Berne.

Index of names

Architects whose names appear in italic have individual entries. Figures in roman type indicate text references; those in bold type refer to the illustrations.

A CREATIVE LEGACY

A History of **THE NATIONAL ENDOWME**

Visual Artists' Fellowship Program 1966 – 1995

A CREATIVE LEGACY

A History of **THE NATIONAL ENDOWMENT FOR THE ARTS**

Visual Artists' Fellowship Program 1966 – 1995

Introduction by BILL IVEY

Essay by NANCY PRINCENTHAL

Essay by JENNIFER DOWLEY

Harry N. Abrams, Inc., Publishers

in association with

NATIONAL
ENDOWMENT
FOR THE ARTS

3/02

Editor: Adele Westbrook

Art Director: Eric Baker

Designer: Pooja Bakri, Eric Baker Design Associates

Library of Congress Cataloging-in-Publication Data

Princenthal, Nancy.
A creative legacy: a history of the National Endowment for the Arts Visual Artists' Fellowship Program/introduction by William Ivey; essay by Nancy Princenthal, essay by Jennifer Dowley.
p. cm.
ISBN 0–8109–4170–8
1. National Endowment for the Arts. Visual Artists' Fellowship Program–History. 2. Art–Scholarships, fellowships, etc.–United States. 3. Government aid to the arts–United States. I. Dowley, Jennifer. II. Title.
N8838.P75 2001
707' .9'73–dc21
2001001355

Published in 2001 by Harry N. Abrams, Incorporated, New York

Printed and bound in Japan
10 9 8 7 6 5 4 3 2 1

Harry N. Abrams, Inc.
100 Fifth Avenue
New York, N.Y. 10011
www.abramsbooks.com

Contents

Acknowledgments

Work on this book began in 1996 after the U.S. Congress terminated Visual Artists Fellowships. With the approval of the National Council on the Arts, we began the long process of assembling all the materials to create this document. In selecting the artists whose work was to be included in this book, a review process that mirrored the Endowment's grant review process took place. I sent out the complete list of 4,500 national fellowship recipients to fourteen museum curators/directors around the country and asked them to select one hundred artists whose work was significant in the development of American art. We are most grateful to them for accepting this challenge. They are: Amada Cruz (Bard College), Jim Demetrion (Hirshhorn Museum and Sculpture Garden), Suzanne Ghez (Renaissance Society), Thelma Golden (Norton Family Foundation), Stephen Gong (University Art Museum, Berkeley), Kathy Halbreich (Walker Art Center), John Hanhardt (Guggenheim Museum), Peter Hassrick (independent), Karin Higa (Japanese American Historical Museum), Ruth Kohler (Kohler Art Center), Andrea Miller-Keller (independent), Kenneth Trapp (Renwick Gallery), Adam Weinberg (Addison Gallery), and Debra Willis-Kennedy (Smithsonian). Their nominations were in turn reviewed and narrowed further by: Arthur Danto (arts writer), Hugh Davies (Museum of Contemporary Art, San Diego), Merry Forresta (National Museum of American Art), and Ned Rifkin (The Menil Collection). We found this process of narrowing to be extremely difficult. This was a case of the quality of the whole being far greater than the individual examples we were able to accommodate in our publication. Fortunately, the National Museum of American Art's archive, which we commissioned as a companion project to this one, is able to carry far more information than can be contained in this book.

There are a number of people whose encouragement and support were critical in the implementation of this publication. First, there is Paul Gottlieb, former President, Publisher, and Editor-in-Chief, of Harry N. Abrams, Inc. He believed in this project as an important contribution to American cultural life and out of his respect for the work of the Visual Artists' Fellowship Program undertook its publication. Two of Abrams' editors worked with me in sequence over the years to see that the book was shaped properly: Margaret Kaplan and Adele Westbrook. At the Arts Endowment, several people saw to it that this project evolved thoughtfully and with full support. Susan Clampitt, former Deputy Chairman for Programs at the Arts Endowment, first recognized the significance of this effort and gave it its initial boost. Jane Alexander, our Chairman at the time of its initiation, was fully committed to its undertaking. In subsequent years, Scott Shanklin-Peterson, Senior Deputy Chairman and Karen Christensen, Deputy Chairman for Grants and Awards, provided me with the time and encouragement to see it through. Bill Ivey, NEA Chairman at the time of publication, supported the project through it's completion. Michael Faubion, Council Coordinator, was invaluable in researching the history of the program and assembling much of the data for this project. He had been with the Visual Arts Program since 1977 and participated in implementing the Fellowship Program in later years. Each Director of the Visual Arts Program (Henry Geldzahler, Brian O'Doherty, James Melchert, Benny Andrews, Richard Andrews, Susan Talbot, and Rosalyn Alter) is to be commended for his or her stewardship of the Fellowships through many turbulent moments. Each maintained the priority of the fellowships within the Arts Endowment's overall agenda. Arts Resources International, under the able direction of Don Russell, performed heroically in assembling much of the material for this book. Don's dedication to the details of this project stems from his extraordinary understanding of and commitment to contemporary artists. My thanks go to Michael Brenson for developing an essay for this book that was subsequently expanded and published separately as a book entitled *Visionaries and Outcasts: The NEA, Congress, and the Place of the Artist in America.* His thoughtfulness and integrity inspired my own commitment to this project long after I left the Arts Endowment. Nancy Princenthal has written a most intelligent and fair minded essay that provides a coherent and lucid reading of the many-layered art world represented by the Fellowships Program context in the development of American art within which the Visual Artists, Fellows sit. Finally, I am grateful to M. Stroud for providing me with time in a beautiful environment where I was able to think, write, and assemble much of this project.

Jennifer Dowley
Director, Museums and Visual Arts
National Endowment for the Arts
September 1994–June 1999
March 2001

Introduction

By Bill Ivey

In September of 1965, as President Lyndon Johnson signed legislation creating the National Endowment for the Arts, his prepared remarks indicated that the new agency "will support our symphony orchestras," and "bring more great artists to our schools." Johnson also predicted a National Theater, National Opera, and "a National Ballet Company." Over time, grants to orchestras and school residencies for artists have become mainstays of NEA's work; national performing arts bodies never materialized under the Endowment's umbrella.

That President Johnson's vision was less than fully premonitory should not diminish our regard for the men and women who helped create the framework for an agency that was to have "an unprecedented effect on the arts." Rather, the President's statement is a reminder that, at its birth in the mid-1960s, the character of the National Endowment for the Arts was almost entirely unformed.

It was left to those who first took on the task of directing the agency's affairs to define the Endowment's precise function and its manner of working. These early leaders faced a daunting task. The NEA had virtually no programming budget, and there existed only the slenderest of infrastructures linking up the tiny world of America's not-for-profit arts.

Further, the Rose Garden signing ceremony did not completely resolve the debate that had swirled about the possible creation of a federal arts agency. Some critics and observers had argued that a centralized arts authority would establish an "official" art, that it would be exclusionary or elitist, or that it would squander limited resources on work of no lasting merit. It was left to the new agency to sort these issues out; to provide the NEA with a set of programs and a method of working that would over time alleviate skepticism about a centralized entity overseeing government funding for the arts.

The Endowment's Visual Artists' Fellowships, celebrated in this volume, did much to define the NEA. In both the substance and process of the NEA's work, fellowships to visual artists became models for connecting federal dollars with working artists.

First, by embracing living American artists, the full range of their working processes, and their occasionally challenging output the agency placed itself squarely within the great tradition of enlightened patronage and won the respect of visual arts professionals in the academic community as well as the museum and gallery worlds.

Second, in implementing its Visual Artists' Fellowship Program, the NEA engaged working artists in the process of selecting fellowship recipients, and gradually developed procedures that would enable the federal arts agency to conduct a fair, national process of adjudication based upon the close scrutiny of work samples. This system offered an alternative to the usual selection structures that were most often in the hands of curators, critics or scholars. Artists selecting artists provided the program an authority it could otherwise not have claimed.

The Visual Artists' Fellowship Program evolved through its thirty-year history. The geographical reach, composition of panels, and size of awards were all adjusted as the Endowment responded to advice from its panels. And, the impact of the fellowships was remarkable. Through grants or participation in panels, the NEA's program reached many of the most influential and critically acclaimed artists of the 1960s, 1970s, and 1980s. Not infrequently, fellowships were awarded early in a career, providing a boost of cash and recognition at a key moment in the evolution of an artist's work. The nearly 300 works reproduced here, and the impressive list of Visual Arts Fellows Artists' Fellowship recipients honored over the years, are testimony to the importance of the Arts Endowment to the visual arts in the United States in the second half of the 20th century.

Ultimately, this engagement between our federal arts agency and contemporary visual art could not survive a shift in the winds of political fortune. In the mid-1990's, faced with a conservative Congressional leadership and deprived of the Cold-War argument which viewed artists as valued symbols of America's free spirit, legislation forced the elimination of most of the NEA's fellowships.

Although they were one of many strategies adopted by the Arts Endowment over the years, the Visual Artists' Fellowships helped establish the NEA's credentials as an agency committed to creativity and to the makers of art. The program also connected the Endowment to the contemporary American art world defined by museums, galleries, universities and publications.

Most importantly, the NEA Visual Artists' Fellowships linked the agency with working artists. And, in making that connection, the NEA discovered its core commitment to the human dimension of art and art making: the well-being of artists; the vitality and longevity of their careers; the regard with which artists are viewed by the society at large. The Endowment's commitment to artists remains strong, fueling the NEA's continuing efforts to find ways to nurture, through direct support, the work of America's art makers.

BILL IVEY
Chairman
National Endowment for the Arts
March 2001

ARTISTS' ARTISTS:
The NEA Visual Artists' Fellowship Program

By Nancy Princenthal

One of the most powerful of honorifics, in the visual arts, is "artists' artist." It is a term for the painter or sculptor or performance artist who is perhaps not (yet) widely recognized by the public at large, or by those who buy and sell art, or even necessarily by the critics, but is admired with special fervor by those practicing in the same discipline. Over the course of its nearly thirty-year history, the Artists' Fellowship Program of the National Endowment for the Arts established a monumental record of artists' artists, of professionals chosen by panels comprised overwhelmingly of their peers (though administrators, historians, and critics also participated). The panelists looked not for evidence of popular acclaim, but for those who deserved it; without setting themselves the goal of predicting success, their decisions were often premonitory.

Neither the work that was supported, nor the fellowship program itself, can be summarily characterized. If they could–if the Endowment's legacy in this field could be accommodated within a single framework, or ideology, or even a coherent set of descriptive terms–the program would have been an abject failure. The record of recipients does, however, tell a story. It is vivid and engrossing, but it is not easy to decipher, since it's written in several dialects. And perhaps that is its main plot: how over the lifespan of the fellowship program, the language of visual art has divided, multiplied, interwoven–and, as a result, thrived.

This essay is organized around 100 fellowship recipients whose work is illustrated in the color-plate section of the book. They were selected, from among the thousands of artists who received individual artists' grants over the twenty-eight-year life of the program, in much the same way that the awards were first made: a panel of arts professionals from around the country was asked to submit nominations, and a second panel made the final selections. (During most of the run of the fellowship program, applications were received, ultimately in the thousands, on an open basis; but for the first three years, before it was widely known, the program relied on the nominations of panelists.) The panelists who selected artists for this book represent the national scope, and the conceptual and stylistic breadth, of the fellowship program itself. Inevitably, the panel's choices reflect the interests of administrators and writers working in the field today; the artists they have chosen are, mainly, those whose work remains vital to the art production of our time. But every effort was made to reflect, as well, the changing nature of the program as it evolved, and thus this sampling permits the reconstruction of an essential passage in American visual art.

The Sixties

Representing the sixty artists who were awarded fellowships in the first round (1967) are Mark di Suvero, Dan Flavin, Sam Gilliam, Donald Judd, Agnes Martin, Robert Morris, Edward Ruscha, Tony Smith, and H. C. Westermann. Nominated by the program's first panelists, these artists were more established and widely acclaimed at the time they received support than most who would receive grants subsequently. The early awards signaled the prestige of the NEA program, and also its prescience, since these artists remain among the leading figures of their generation. Their work at the time tended to be big, clean, and bold; in keeping with prevailing tendencies, it was largely (though not exclusively) abstract. Much of it articulated a distinctly American position for visual art, and a strong relationship with unmistakably American kinds of mass media, in a period of deep interest in national cultures. All could be labeled with ease as either painting or sculpture. (At the outset, there was only one category for grant applications–"artist." Separate grants in the categories "painting" and "sculpture" were not made until 1981, though photography, crafts, printmaking, conceptual/performance art, and video were all introduced as application categories in the interim.) Most of the early recipients were white men, an inequity that would soon be redressed.

But these were hardly safe choices. A solid core of this first-round work–that by Flavin, Judd, Martin, Morris, and Smith–is Minimalist, recognizable as such by its sleek, dispassionate geometry. (Represented by black-and-white illustrations in this book are several other Minimalists of this generation who received NEA fellowships, including Carl Andre, Ronald Bladen, Sol LeWitt, Robert Mangold, David Rabinowitch, and Fred

Sandback.) Minimalism's provocation is today hard to recapture, largely because the simple clear forms associated with it (and with conceptually distinct earlier European experiments in reductive abstraction) have long since become part of the commercial design vernacular. But if the work is examined on its own terms (and several of these artists were active writers and polemicists) its radicalism is hard to miss. Rejecting standard compositional technique-focal points and hierarchically ordered areas of subsidiary interest, for one; the visible record of the artist's expressive touch, for another–the Minimalists not only abjured figuration, they also defied established assumptions within abstract art.

A primary commitment was to presentation, at the expense of representation; not just mimesis, but all kinds of metaphor were rejected outright. The new work celebrated the art object in itself, as a material presence, as a document of the labor invested in it by the artist, and as the occasion for a physical and/or perceptual experience for the viewer. But among Minimalism's many challenges, one was of a different order: it was launched against traditions governing category distinctions in the arts, as, for instance, those separating sculpture and functional object, or painting, or theatrical prop. Such challenges to conventional definitions of the arts were not new to the '60s generation (they can be seen in aspects of Modernism going back to the early twentieth century) but they are firmly identified with these artists–and, indeed, with the Endowment's Visual Artists' Fellowship Program itself. If anything can be said to have constituted an ongoing preoccupation for the program, it is support of the ever-increasing diversity of methods and media in visual art, whether such support meant helping to articulate new disciplines, or, more often, condoning–and facilitating–the fluid exchanges between them.

A certain amount of pressure is exerted, in the art market, by the simple demand for traditionally defined objects: paintings and works on paper that can be hung in a domestic interior and, with somewhat more difficulty, sculptures that can be installed there. This is hardly the only factor determining the commercial, much less the critical, viability of art. Certainly the degree of influence exerted by the market on art is debatable, and clearly museums and other public exhibiting institutions have become crucially important as sources of financial support for the arts. However, just as clearly, the government can play a critical role in freeing artists from the need to comply with the preferences and constraints of private collectors.

To be sure, for many artists awarded fellowships in the late '60s, and later, "circumvention of the commercial sector" (a term in wide circulation at the time) was, at most, a secondary concern.[1] When Judd, for instance, opened his influential article "Specific Objects," by claiming that "Half or more of the best new work in the last few years has been neither painting nor sculpture,"[2] he was describing the work's challenges to historical art, and not, primarily, to that art's market. The same is true of Mark di Suvero's work, which managed to be both painterly and sculptural, bringing the bravado of big-gesture brushwork to the construction of assembled and welded sculpture. Tony Smith, an architect by training, applied the modularity and functional imperatives of his design practice to his sculpture, though he kept the two disciplines discrete. (Judd, by contrast, ultimately became very interested in integrating fine and applied art as the Bauhaus and De Stijl masters of the early twentieth century had advocated, a goal he achieved at the residential, studio, and exhibition spaces at the Chinati Foundation in Marfa, Texas, illustrated here.) Dan Flavin, working throughout his career with simple configurations of colored fluorescent light bulbs, illuminated (in more ways than one) the relationship between sculpture and useful design, though his work had no direct functional application.

But for all the Minimalists, including those who, like Robert Morris, explored very different issues in later work, the rejection of a metaphorical in favor of a plainly declarative visual language also implied a repositioning of art with respect to ordinary life. Sculptures and paintings were not transcendent objects; it was precisely their ordinariness, their quiddity, that merited enhanced attention. Making art did not involve sublimation into a realm of rarefied sensibility, it was work, pure and simple. Knocked off its pedestal, both symbolically and literally, art was to be created by laborers, in industrial spaces, using commercial materials.

Of course, this thinking (and its rhetoric) caught in its net many artists whose motivation was quite different. For instance, the painter Agnes Martin, associated by age with the Abstract Expressionists (she was born in 1912), is affiliated by style with the Minimalist artists, especially in her use of the Cartesian grid. But her meditative work reflects, in its colors and the tenor of its hand-penciled lines, an acute sympathy for the conditions of light and atmosphere in the natural world. "It is not what is seen, it is what is known forever in the mind,"[3] Martin has said in response to questions about her work's relationship to the landscape of the Southwest, where she moved from lower Manhattan in 1967, the same year the NEA awarded her a fellowship. Ed Ruscha, of the same generation as the largely East-Coast Minimalists, is a Los Angeles-based artist whose sharp, funny paintings combined elements of consumer-happy Pop and archly cerebral Conceptualism with a distinctly Southern California focus on car culture, and a driver's-eye perspective on the West Coast landscape. Sam Gilliam, a painter based in Washington D.C., was associated there with the Color Field painters who took up the legacy of Abstract Expressionism. Staining raw canvas with freely poured pigments, the Color Field artists caused paint to literally become part of the support surface, making image and object inseparable in a manner only one step removed from what the Minimalists were doing in sculpture at the same time. One of the best-known African-American artists of his time, Gilliam, born in 1933 in Tupelo, Mississippi, remains an active and widely admired abstractionist, whose paintings (as illustrated here) have increasingly involved constructed three-dimensional elements.

H.C. Westermann, a renegade prankster of the highest order, was initially based in Chicago, and became a mentor there to younger artists establishing an acidly comic regional painting idiom determinedly independent of New York. A masterful carpenter, Westermann fashioned his sculpture from wood, hardware, and miscellaneous commercial objects, investing them with significance both emotionally gripping and impenetrably ironic. *The Walnut Death Ship* illustrated here, one of a series of such vessels (they derive from an aircraft carrier attack that Westermann survived during service in World War II), combines comedy and tragic mortality in equal measure, its fastidious construction no security against its terrible, laughable fate.

In short, the artists of the first round include both clear favorites and long shots, artists already or soon to be successful in the major centers of contemporary art, and others whose work was less well-known outside a group of local, ardent admirers. Several of the artists awarded fellowships in the first years would later receive support in other fellowship categories, from Painting to New Genres. And in the next few years, the NEA program's embrace of artists working in new disciplines greatly increased. Recipients in the next two years included a quartet of diverse artists whose (loosely defined) common purpose was the investigation of perception, as shaped both physiologically and culturally. Richard Tuttle, a fellowship recipient in 1969, is a visual poet who works at the very brink of immateriality, making objects consisting of nothing more (in the most attenuated examples) than bent wire and its shadow. A deeply reflective and disciplined artist, Tuttle trains his sight on visual incidents of such frailty and precision, realized in such eminently disposable materials (they have included bubble wrap, Styrofoam, and tin foil), that his work is easily overlooked—or, paradoxically, condemned for being too precious. But the exacting standards he sets for his audience, calling for appreciation of surpassingly subtle variations in texture, light, contour, and weight, have had a broad impact on the expectations and habits of art viewers.

James Turrell, a 1968 recipient, is as committed as Tuttle to an art of light, shadow, and their most carefully calibrated perturbations. But Turrell manipulates these elements with work that ranges from the room-sized (walk-in installations composed of controlled volumes of colored light, such as the rich, tart *Key Lime* illustrated here) to the colossal: for many years, he has been working at Roden Crater, an extinct volcano in Arizona, subtly transforming it into a vast optical instrument with ramps and apertures placed to frame particular events in the solar and celestial calendar. Though not yet fully available to the public, Turrell's Roden Crater project has already exerted considerable influence on art's physical and conceptual limits.

But in terms of shaping patterns of expectation and understanding for art, few artists who emerged in the late sixties have been as influential as Bruce Nauman, a 1968 fellow. Sensitive from the beginning to the manifold paradoxes involved in laying claim to perceptual experience, Nauman has devised a seemingly endless variety of exercises for examining the relative privileges of authorship, response (both perceptual and emotional), and consumption. The materials he uses have included steel mesh fencing, taxidermists' plastic molds, and neon signage; landmark works have ranged from an ironically spectacular enlargement of his own signature (extended vertically fourteen times, in neon) to videotaped performance—staged pratfalls, in slow motion; screaming heads, in real time—that make extreme physical and psychological states seem abstract. Greatly interested in wordplay, Nauman gravitates toward its limits: "I think the point where language starts to break down as a useful tool for communication is the same edge where poetry or art occurs," he said in a 1989 interview.[4]

These artists' work, concerned above all with sensory experience rather than material value ("This is not minimalism and it is not conceptual work, it is perceptual work," Turrell has said),[5] stretched the art market's tolerance. Not that it lacked commercial and institutional support. Nauman had his first solo exhibition, at the Nicholas Wilder Gallery in Los Angeles, when he was just twenty-four; he had a one-person show at Leo Castelli in New York two years later, and his first museum survey by the time he was thirty, in 1972 (the NEA grant came when he was twenty-seven); Tuttle's work, which also won early acclaim, was the subject of a 1975 exhibition at the Whitney Museum of American Art. Still, these artists' work was hardly free of controversy, and the ambivalence toward the commercial market it reflected is visible in other decisions they have made. Tuttle, Nauman, and Turrell have all, independently, chosen to live in the rural Southwest, far from major centers of contemporary art production. And, however much success it has garnered, it is hard to imagine any of this work being developed with the commercial market as its sole support, since rethinking every aspect of the relationship between artists and viewers—as perceivers, respondents, and, not least, consumers—is critical to its meaning. Indeed the reconfiguration of the public, understood both in the aggregate and as disparate communities and individuals, with vastly different predispositions, expectations, and interests, is one of this work's most important impulses.

The Seventies: Three-DImensional Work

By 1973, the circle of visual arts fellowship recipients had again widened exponentially. Robert Irwin, a California-based artist, was deeply interested, like his colleague Turrell, in shaping perceptual experience through subtle manipulations of light. Beginning with paint on canvas, but soon moving to theatrical scrim (as in the later work illustrated here), Irwin created light-controlled conditions for optical responses that hovered just short of flat-out illusion. Irwin's interest in shaping experience has since found expression in designs for public spaces, from the gardens that flank the J. Paul Getty Museum in Los Angeles to the atrium of the Old Post Office building in Washington,D.C, where the National Endowment for the Arts has its headquarters. With his public projects, Irwin became a leading figure in developing a kind of public art conceived in response to the conditions of its site. In a treatise called *Being and Circumstance: Notes toward a Conditional Art*, he promoted a "phenomenal, conditional, responsive art" that is "site conditioned/determined. Here the sculptural response draws all of its cues (reasons for being) from its surroundings. This requires the process to begin with an intimate, hands-on reading of the site."[6]

Richard Artschwager, like H.C. Westermann, is a skilled carpenter. Although he was a student in New York of the French Modernist Amedée Ozenfant for two years after World War II, Artschwager initially spurned this training, opening a small furniture factory before devoting himself full time to art. Combining the rigors of fine cabinet-making with the insouciance of Pop, Artschwager entered into an investigation of the meaning of integrity—of "honesty to materials" and to the forms demanded by function—as it applies both to objects generally deemed "useful" (tables and chairs, for instance), and to art. The resulting hybrids have included unusable furniture, Formica-surfaced sculpture, and, ultimately, photo-based images executed in acrylic on textured plastic surfaces.

Well into the seventies, a great deal of work recognized by the Endowment continued to engage ideas related to Minimalism. Barry Le Va's sculpture, really a variant of Post-Minimalism rather than Minimalism proper, was based on the random dispersal of common materials, a compositional strategy meant in part to express the physical world's inexorable progress toward chaos. (The "Post" in Post-Minimalism is misleading, since distinguishing the two chronologically is difficult, though it does separate a more lenient, process-oriented approach from a more rigorously rectilinear and machined one.) Scattering strips of felt, shattered glass, powder, and ball bearings at random on the floor, Le Va (who received a fellowship in 1976) created ephemeral landscapes determined by the chance confluence of the particulars of a given space, set of materials, and gestures. (In the years since, Le Va's work has grown increasingly rule-determined, as in the work illustrated here, while remaining unyieldingly abstract.)

On the other hand, Joel Shapiro (a 1975 recipient) redirected the language of Minimalism toward the figure, producing highly simplified geometric forms that by the middle seventies had organized themselves into diminutive houses. Oddly positioned, placed at the end of shelves extending from the wall or atop tables stood on the floor, these toy-sized structures each established a kind of perceptual quarantine; the spatial environments they produced in their own immediate vicinity seemed unnervingly discontinuous with the bigger, more shapeless and ambiguous world to which the viewer was, by default, relegated. (Shapiro's recent work includes over-life-size human figures, though its forms remain simple and sticklike, and are still, always, off balance, as can be seen in the public sculpture illustrated here.) Nancy Graves (a 1973 recipient) was a realist of a different persuasion who first gained recognition for sculptures of camels, a subject matter sufficiently odd, realized with a fidelity sufficiently exacting, that the very tradition invoked—figurative sculpture—seemed unequal to the results. In subsequent work, Graves used a great variety of found material, most strikingly fruits, vegetables, and other flora cast in metal, welded together in freely associative compositions, and painted with equal license. Unquestionably a species of objective figuration, Graves's sculpture threw both parts of the term into question, transforming the most familiar of objects into characters in a language of unrestricted and highly expressive abstraction.

As can be seen in Graves's work, the mid-seventies was a period in which influences from outside mainstream Modernist traditions were strongly felt, often expressed through craft techniques—an interest pursued, in part, because of late Minimalism's emphasis on process rather than product. For instance Martin Puryear, a 1977 recipient, studied woodworking and other craft techniques in both Africa and Scandinavia, and brought these disparate experiences to bear in his eccentric abstractions, which often weave subtle historical references into technique, as well as subject matter. Puryear has worked with a very wide range of materials, from rawhide and wood (using furniture-making techniques) to tarred wire mesh (from shipbuilding) to, in recent work, cast metal; his work's references range from tribal artifacts to futurist shelters. Significantly, Puryear, who is black, sought not "primitivism" but skill in Africa; writing about his work in 1989, curator Robert Storr compared it to Westermann's and Artschwager's, and noted that "of late . . . the concept of mastery has fallen into almost total disrespect, becoming little more than an epithet for the ostentatious display of facility . . . [but] to speak of mastery does not suppose an innate capacity nor assert a suspect claim to 'genius.' It simply names the culmination of a prolonged and utterly practical education."[7] Similarly, Jackie Winsor (who received three fellowships, the first in 1974), chose methods and materials—including, early in her career, wound twine—that reflected a similar interest in traditional techniques, and in ensuring that the creative process is clearly manifest in the finished object.

The sculpture of Puryear and Winsor resides comfortably within the precincts of contemporary art; the work of ceramists Robert Arneson, Michael Lucero, and Peter Voulkos, on the other hand, lives an edgy life between art and craft. All were awarded grants as "artists," Arneson in 1973, Voulkos in 1976, and Lucero in 1979; Voulkos and Lucero would subsequently receive fellowships in the Crafts category, a field in which they maintain distinguished careers without in any way relinquishing the attention of the art world. Arneson, who later received support as a sculptor, was a figurative artist of great ebullience and reckless humor. Crossing wires between cool, Pop-related figuration and dangerously hot-headed political satire, he demonstrated unrivaled virtuosity in his medium, while also using techniques (gluing together elements broken in firing, for instance, or applying both glazes and paint to fired clay) considered taboo in the field. Voulkos, a mentor to a generation of American artists and craftspeople who use fired clay, was himself inspired by the gestural freedom of the Abstract Expressionists, with whom he is roughly contemporary (he was born in 1924), and also by the Zen embrace of chance and accident in design. His free-form compositions in clay, which dispense with conventional requirements regarding both function and technique, are poles apart from the work of the younger Michael Lucero, who has flouted a different set of rules. Lucero mixes messages with abandon in his work, which often takes the form of usable vessels, though its language is of the most exuberant figurative painting.

Of course, the artists emerging at this time were not the first to trounce boundaries between disciplines, or to bring foreign objects into the practice of art (in both cases, Picasso and Duchamp are generally considered to have gotten there first, at roughly the same time, in the second decade of the twentieth century). John Chamberlain, who received a fellowship in 1974, was like Voulkos an immediate heir to Abstract Expressionism and its painterly license (Chamberlain was born in 1927),[8] and he too interpreted this legacy in a surprising material: crushed automobile-body parts, paint and rust intact. His first use of such "colored steel" was a sculpture made of the fender from a friend's old car, in 1957; it was quickly followed by others incorporating materials scrounged from old benches, signs, buckets, lunch boxes—anything made of painted metal. Soon, though, Chamberlain restricted himself to scrapped cars, taking advantage of visual accidents caused by age, neglect, and physical injury, and eventually simulating such effects with great abandon.

The younger sculptor Judy Pfaff (who received her first NEA fellowship in 1979) is connected to the same painterly tradition, though the more direct link in her work is with such experiments in chance composition and the expression of natural entropy as were found in the Post-Minimalist work of, for instance,

Barry Le Va. Using everything from mylar and lucite (in her early installations) to uprooted trees and metal cable (more recently), Pfaff constructs paintings in space, their high-velocity contours soaring from wall to wall and ceiling to floor. Nancy Rubins (whose first grant came in 1977) works with even more varied materials and in a more anarchic spirit; she has used everything from mattresses and frosted cakes (as illustrated here) to, literally, the kitchen sink, submerging major home appliances and other domestic flotsam in towering explosions of concrete, in early work, or, subsequently, stringing her eccentric materials up on wire cable. But for the sheer abandon with which he mixes up disciplines, historical styles, and narrative traditions, few artists can rival Terry Allen, who received the first of three fellowships in 1973. A composer and lyricist, performer, and sculptor of assemblages, he draws upon his Texan background, and the love of storytelling for which Texas is renowned, in fashioning multimedia work that includes songs, sets, players, and dramatic material both live and taped, remembered, invented, and freshly seen.

The Seventies: Two-Dimensional Work

In painting as in three-dimensional work, there existed considerable interest during the 1970s in negotiating a balance between the tight-lipped, stripped-down geometric abstraction of the mid-sixties and the prolix, polyglot work that would characterize the following decade. Like the sculptor Joel Shapiro, the painter Jennifer Bartlett (a 1976 recipient) was finding ways to loosen the strictures of Minimalism without sacrificing its visual logic and conceptual motivation. In Bartlett's work, the grid became the organizing principle for vast, serialized narratives, the components of which, both figurative and abstract, were painted on square, baked-enamel-on-metal panels. Hung like tiles in regular rows, the panels were systematic and at the same time wildly spontaneous. Some of the panels were self-contained pictorial elements, while in other cases imagery spilled across several adjacent tiles. Redirecting the lessons of Minimalism with both respect and humor, Bartlett's work at this time also drew upon comic strips, so important to the development of Pop art, and film, which is similarly composed of sequential frames, and which likewise relies on montage and elision.

The same sources influenced Susan Rothenberg, a painter who emerged around the same time (and received a fellowship in 1979). Included, as was Bartlett, in a 1978 Whitney Museum exhibition called *New Image Painting* (the label "New Imagist" was soon applied to Shapiro as well; among other NEA recipients included in this group are Robert Moskowitz and Joan Brown, whose work is illustrated in black-and-white), Rothenberg first gained attention for a series of paintings of horses, a subject she had arrived at intuitively after experimenting with a range of media and practices, including performance and process-oriented abstract painting. The animals were shown in profile and at rest, their contours painted across two adjacent canvas panels, the imagery freehand but schematic, psychological associations clearly present but held in check by the static regularity of the composition and its repetition. Describing the "perversity" of her goals at this time, Rothenberg said, "I like tension. To take something that had implied motion and not use it in that way; to have something that was volumetric and not use it that way."[9] Rothenberg's work would soon become considerably freer, with deeper and darker depicted space, and more richly allusive subject matter. But it has retained the self-questioning aspect—the querulous contours, ambiguous subjects, and brushstrokes that tend to assert their independence from mere description—of work that does not take figuration as a self-evident justification for painting.

Standing in equally close, though similarly covert, relationship to Minimalism are Chuck Close's super-scaled photo-based portrait paintings of friends and colleagues and, as illustrated here, of himself. These endlessly engrossing paintings are now as widely popular as they are critically acclaimed. But in 1973, when Close received a fellowship, his audience was restricted by the painting's identification with groundbreaking, and admittedly difficult, Conceptualist explorations of the relationship between photography and painting, and their relative reliability as objective registers of visual truth. Gridding his canvases with the same meticulous regularity as Agnes Martin—a procedure he continues to follow, even as his paintings have exploded with color and digressive linear pattern—Close plotted his pictures like topographical maps, filling in the details of facial features as if they were just so much quantifiable data.

Alice Neel was, like Close, primarily a portrait painter, but was otherwise *sui generis*, a rogue realist who followed no stylistic trend or ideological inclination, and treated her subjects with heedless candor. Neel was seventy-three when she was awarded a fellowship in 1973, and though she was ardently admired by some, she was hardly well-known. "I developed my own way. I'm an intellectual also. I know all the theory of everything, but when I paint I don't think of anything except the subject and me,"[10] she told an interviewer, with typical frankness, in 1983, the year before her death (and seventeen years before her first major museum exhibition). The legacy of Expressionism, latent in Neel's portraiture and approached circuitously in Rothenberg's paintings, was engaged more directly in the work of some of their contemporaries. It is reflected, for instance, in the dense, lush landscape paintings, freely brushed and richly colored, of Gregory Amenoff (a 1980 recipient). In recent years, Amenoff's imagery, while still organic, has grown increasingly abstract. But it remains sufficiently Expressionist in both metaphorical reach and technical execution that one critic has hailed its "allegorical psychodrama."[11]

Other painting supported in the middle 1970s was based even more explicitly in narrative, from the most eccentric and insular to the equally plainspoken and social. Jim Nutt, whose first fellowship was awarded in 1974, is a Chicago-based artist and was associated there with a short-lived but influential group called the Hairy Who. Taking up H. C. Westermann's challenge, they developed a visual language as appealing and funny as the Sunday comics, and as unsettling as any newspaper's most disturbing headlines. As is true of the Surrealist tradition on which he draws, the provocation of Nutt's paintings, with their promiscuous mingling of mismatched human features, tends to be sexual.

In Nancy Spero's work, on the other hand, the challenge is to the blunted sensibilities of an endemically violent society. Also at one time a Chicago-based artist (educated at the School of the Art Institute of Chicago, and also the Ecole des Beaux-Arts in Paris, she has lived in New York City since 1964), Spero addressed herself from the start to topical issues. Early drawings took the war in Vietnam as subject matter, suggesting its brutality allusively, in frail, bloody traces of injured bodies. Spero's subsequent work addressed violence against women—and also represented women triumphant. Drawing freely from ancient Egyptian, Greek, and Celtic imagery, as well as prehistoric artifacts, Spero forged a language that, in her own description, expresses both the joyous, even ribald sexuality and the violent oppression, that have historically been the poles of women's experience. Often, she works on long paper scrolls, and, as illustrated here, in even more ephemeral techniques and media including imagery handprinted directly on the wall.

Difficult by design, Spero's work was long neglected; she was fifty-one when she received an NEA fellowship, in 1977.

Betye Saar, awarded her first NEA fellowship in 1974 (when she was forty-eight), borrows, as does Spero, from a wide range of commercial and handcrafted, secular and religious artifacts from American, African, and other cultures. Her richly textured assemblages invoke the spiritual value attributed to talismanic objects in traditional religious practice, but also draw upon such Modernist sources as Joseph Cornell's Surrealist boxes and collages. The work of Faith Ringgold (whose first NEA grant came in 1979) also often hovers between image and object, and, like Saar, she has been a pioneer in bringing African-American subjects and traditions to mainstream Modernism. An activist since the sixties on behalf of women in the arts, and black women in particular, Ringgold has worked in a variety of media, including painting and sculpture. But she is best known for her wall hangings made of painted, tie-dyed, and pieced fabric that literally stitch together complex narrative cycles and textile traditions. In addition to telling stories of great complexity and wit, Ringgold's wall hangings helped gain critical recognition for handiwork historically associated with women. (Miriam Schapiro, whose work is illustrated in black-and-white, was another pioneer in the integration of "women's work"—stitched fabric, in particular—to the language of mainstream contemporary art.) Robert Colescott, first awarded a fellowship in 1976, was trained in French Modernism (he spent a year studying in the studio of Fernand Léger, in Paris). But he has long been responsible for some of the most outspoken, and scathingly funny, critiques of racism undertaken in paint on canvas. Mixing black, white, Old Master, and vernacular subjects, with a preference for the most hallowed of art-historical and pop-cultural icons, he creates epic paintings that are as formally irreverent as they are politically freewheeling.

The Seventies: Hybrid Forms

One striking characteristic of much sculpture of the seventies—including that of Irwin, Turrell, Pfaff, and Rubins (and of younger artists such as Jessica Stockholder, represented here by a black-and-white illustration)—is that it is not freestanding, but is instead often made on site for temporary exhibition, and is impelled, at least in part, by that site's particular conditions. It represents one aspect of the widespread inclination to reorient art's focus toward the context of its reception. In other such work, the emphasis is placed on art's practical utility and social use. The manifold defining characteristics of a given site, ranging from its size and shape, adjacent structures and natural features, to its function, cultural character, and historical background, become central considerations. While rewarding informed, practiced, and perceptive viewers, such work appeals even to those who don't know they're encountering art. In supporting it, the NEA strengthened a crucial link in the chain of mutual interests and responsibilities that unites artists and the public, even–perhaps especially–those who don't consider themselves among contemporary art's audience.

Mary Miss and Scott Burton both took leading roles in this reorientation, and both have worked collaboratively with architects and landscape architects to realize ambitious permanent designs for substantial public spaces. Burton first gained attention for performance work, but is best known for his functional chairs and benches, tables and lighting fixtures, designed for both interior spaces (from corporate lobbies to private residences) and outside plazas and parks. (When he received his first fellowship in 1975, it was for the early performance and installation work; a 1986 grant came when the functional work was well underway.) Burton's work is erudite and often subtly humorous, though its materials and proportions–he favored solid polished stone, as well as various metals–suggest perfect sobriety. While his furniture reflected his study of both vernacular American and European Modernist models, it offers abundant visual and practical satisfactions to viewers (or, users) without such information. Similarly, Miss (a grant recipient in 1974, 1975, and 1984) makes outdoor, permanent work that involves seating and lighting, as well as landscape design. Often (as is illustrated here), Miss incorporates water into the work's design. Where possible, walkways skirt rivers and lakes and sometimes even sink below them (in landlocked sites, they occasionally slide below grade), reminding viewers of the permeability to nature of even the most built-up urban areas.

Though it advanced physical experience–negotiating a public place, sitting comfortably, enjoying well-designed light and shade–into a primary position in visual art, the work of Burton, Miss and their peers (including Siah Armajani, who worked collaboratively on one occasion with Burton, and whose work is illustrated in black-and-white) did so with considerable tact and decorum. On the other hand, the impetus for the early work, executed in the first years of the 1970s, of Chris Burden and other like-minded artists was a much more disturbing kind of physical engagement. As was true of several artists of this time (including, for instance, Dennis Oppenheim, whose work is illustrated in black-and-white), Burden soon moved on to freestanding sculpture (as illustrated here). But the most widely discussed work he had done at the time the NEA awarded him a fellowship, in 1974, involved using his own body as a sculptural medium. Burden submitted himself to a series of punishing exercises, including confining himself to a 2 x 2 x 3' gym locker for five days in 1971, while he was still a student, and having himself crucified on the roof of his own car, in 1974. (Somewhat less dramatically, Oppenheim used his body to demonstrate basic physical principles: in *Parallel Stress,* he stretched himself between two mounds of dirt, parodying Minimalist expressions of the effects of gravity on mass; in *Reading Position for a Second Degree Burn,* he sunbathed with an open book on his chest, which turned his skin into a kind of photographic surface). A great deal of twentieth-century art to this point had been made in materials not traditionally associated with fine art, and certainly the effort to engage the audience viscerally as well as intellectually is not new to our time. But the work of Burden, Oppenheim, and others in this period raised the stakes considerably, reflecting the tenor of a violent period in the nation's history with work that was sometimes angry and often emotionally aggressive, even if it placed the highest demands on the artists themselves. The rigors of this work brought farce and pain into close proximity, putting the audience in a position scarcely more comfortable than the ones the artists designed for themselves.

As is indicated by the pattern of NEA awards, performance art in the early and mid-seventies was an area in which the balance of power tipped, for the first time, towards women. Laurie Anderson (a grant recipient in 1974), Hannah Wilke (1976), and Carolee Schneemann (1974), all received crucial support at this time (all three would receive subsequent support under the category Conceptual/Performance/New Genres). The strong presence of women in the development of performance art can be explained in several ways. First and most importantly, the emphasis on explicit representations of the body was closely tied to a growing awareness of the many ways women had been excluded in art. A longstanding bias against expressing the lived experience of women, in practical, emotional, physical, and intellectual terms, was disclosed by an emerging feminist movement in art (only to reveal, somewhat belatedly, that the life of the body for men had also long been suppressed). Hardly less important was the simple recognition that professional opportunities for women in the arts remained very limited; by introducing a new range of material, and a format in which to broadcast it, women were taking their careers into their own hands in more ways than one.

The most provocative subject such performers addressed, of course, was sexuality. For both Wilke and Schneemann, this meant baring themselves literally as well as figuratively, in assaults against propriety that were instrumental in unblocking avenues of discussion about the mutual effects of power and gender. By taking responsibility for representations that in some ways mimicked—even exceeded—the objectifying, and demeaning, depictions of women in historical art and contemporary commercial imagery, Schneemann and Wilke redirected the animus of such exposure. (The later work of both women is more elegiac, as is illustrated here in Schneemann's *Mortal Coils,* memorializing friends and colleagues, and Wilke's excruciating late self-portraits, which document an ultimately losing struggle with cancer.) Anderson's more broadly focused work began with casual solo performances, including one in which she played a violin while wearing ice skates whose blades were frozen into blocks of ice; the performance ended when the ice melted. Subsequent work grew much more technically ambitious, generally involving the electronic manipulation of sound and light to spectacular effect, while continuing to explore interactions between historical themes, popular culture, and deeply personal perceptions.

The importance of these interdisciplinary modes—installation, public art, and performance art—for reshaping contemporary visual culture can hardly be overestimated. And they emerged in a period, the latter half of the 1970s, during which the NEA achieved its full stride. Some work funded at this time is still controversial enough to remain a weapon in the fight against government involvement in the arts; some has become so well and widely appreciated that it is, by contrast, thought too commercial to have warranted public funding. On the other hand, the material success of fellowship recipients can be cited to argue that the peer panel process did not simply prop up work that lacked popular appeal. There is really no secure position in this ongoing debate. Caution should be used, for example, in promoting the "seed money" effect, since it is neither a necessary or sufficient justification for government support of unfamiliar, challenging artwork. Ultimate commercial success is only one gauge, and an especially fallible one, of art's merit; the qualities that the marketplace endorses, and the relatively small number of dealers and collectors who so heavily influence what is seen and sold in galleries (and who all too often influence, in turn, museum exhibitions and purchases as well) simply cannot reflect the breadth of artwork being made at any given time. What does seem essential is that at a critical and confusing moment—at a time when self-descriptions of the art scene first began to regularly feature the term "pluralism"—the Endowment helped support tremendously important and difficult work that otherwise might not have survived.

Moreover, in these newest disciplines the fellowship program complemented funding the Endowment was increasingly providing to experimental arts organizations, many of them run by artists. NEA policy decisions at this time, making support for such work routine by reorganizing the application process, could thus be said to have had a particularly far-reaching impact. But while it responded with laudable sensitivity to the conditions under which art was made and shown, the Endowment never—and this is an important distinction—determined the art's content; to do so would be radically inconsistent with a democratic cultural agency and, no less, with the way lasting art is conceived.

Diversifying Fellowship Categories: The Later Years

The first years of the 1980s saw a major expansion of the NEA's budget, and of the number of artists who turned to it for support. The high-water mark of individual applicants to the visual arts program was reached in 1981, when more than ten thousand fellowship requests were submitted. Funding peaked the next year, when nearly three and a half million dollars was awarded to 337 artists in seven categories. These numbers, and the threat of severe funding cuts to the NEA, pushed the Endowment to reorganize the granting process. In the event, the Endowment was pared down less during the early 1980s than had been feared. But the impetus to reformulate the application process was sustained, not only by budgetary restrictions but, more importantly, by the increasing diversity of artwork submitted for review. The biggest change was the introduction of new application categories. In the initial years—1967, 1968, and 1969—there had been a single category: "Artist." No grants were awarded in 1970; in 1971, the first subcategory was established, for photography. There were no grants again in 1972. In 1973, a second subcategory was established for crafts; printmaking followed the next year. (Printmaking was returned to the unrestricted "Artist" category in 1978, but became independent again in 1982, this time broadened to include drawing and artists' books.) Video was introduced in 1975, and "Conceptual and Performance" in 1976. In 1982, this category was expanded to include "New Genres," the name to which the category would be simplified in 1985, when it first included video. (In 1983, as a result of funding cutbacks, applications began to be reviewed on an alternate-year basis, with half the categories considered each year.) Strikingly, the general rubric "Artist" wasn't dropped until 1982, making "Painting" and "Sculpture" the last two categories to appear on the list of application options.

These repeated revisions to the application process confirmed the NEA's commitment to a very wide range of work—a range matched in the spectrum of regions, ages, and backgrounds represented by artists who received fellowships. But the ongoing redefinition of categories was much more than a bureaucratic response to shifting demographics. The peer review process itself brought artists and panelists alike to the very heart of visual art's most pressing issues. Not incidentally, panel participants, who gained unparalleled access to the widest possible spectrum of contemporary artists' work, as well as to each other's experience and insight, returned from these unique forums with a deeply enriched understanding of current American art.

Photography

It is in the nature of contemporary art that even those disciplines defined soonest in the life of the Fellowship Program, and with the greatest apparent clarity, began to break down over time. When photography, for instance, was first offered (in 1971) as a category under which to apply, the distinction between it and other media was perfectly clear. Prominent among the recipients of support during the early and middle 1970s were such revered masters of the medium as Harry Callahan (who was born in 1912) and Aaron Siskind (born 1903). Though Callahan moved into color photography toward the end of his career, he was best known for spare black-and-white images of urban and rural landscapes, and for brooding portraits, especially the many haunting images of his wife. Siskind, who was affiliated in the 1930s with the Film and Photo League, shared the League's emphasis on photography's social responsibilities. He remained throughout his career a principled documentarian of urban life, while sustaining also a formal affinity with the Abstract Expressionist painters. Helen Levitt's deeply sympathetic but unsparing images of New York City street life were not as widely celebrated in 1976, when she received a grant, as they would later become.

Robert Adams, Lee Friedlander, and Joel Meyerowitz, photographers of the next generation (all were born in the 1930s), brought attention to aspects of the natural and social landscape that were also of interest, in the 1960s, to the Pop artists. (In fact, Friedlander collaborated on an important series of images with the Pop painter Jim Dine.) Adams did so in dispassionate views of technology's fitful incursions into vast stretches of the rural West, Friedlander with detached images of the urban East, and Meyerowitz, a pioneer in the use of color photography, in the peculiarly American landscapes that lie between city and country. The American South, indelibly documented by Walker Evans in the 1930s, is the subject of the great majority of photographs, most of them in color, by William Christenberry (born 1936, in Tuscaloosa) and William Eggleston (born 1939 in Memphis). Working in the tradition of Evans, who was a mentor and friend, Christenberry has assembled a record of the rural South that includes sculpture and installation work as well as the photographs that are his primary medium. Both Christenberry and Eggleston find in the rural South, most often shown devoid of people, a connection to the land and to history that is often tinged with melancholy and not infrequently with menace (especially in Christenberry's documents of Ku Klux Klan paraphernalia). Their work is equally colored by a regionally distinctive sense of calm and sometimes, especially as in Eggleston's examinations of decidedly domestic environments (including, as here, the inside of a rather neglected freezer), a decidedly mordant sense of humor. Frank Gohlke, like Meyerowitz and Adams, is a sharp observer of the indifferent landscapes of the semi-industrialized Midwest, including its grain elevators and tornado-swept prairies; Gohlke (a fellowship recipient in 1978 and 1986) has also worked extensively in the American South, and he too cites Evans as his "first teacher."[12]

Hiroshi Sugimoto (who received funding in 1982) finds images in both the manmade and natural world of near-perfect abstraction: seascapes in which a glassy ocean, evenly illuminated by an unseen sun or moon, shares the frame with a similarly uninflected sky—or, in remarkably similar compositions, huge movie screens, dominating empty picture palaces, provide expanses of mysterious illumination as boundless as an open sea. It is to this solid tradition, of photography used as a tool to examine unexplored aspects of American culture, that such controversial artists as Robert Mapplethorpe (a 1994 recipient) and Nan Goldin (1990) belong. Like Larry Clark, recognized by the Endowment in 1973 for his ground-breaking photographs of the cast-off tough kids of Tulsa, Oklahoma, Goldin and Mapplethorpe have pointed the camera in places it hadn't been before. Whether boldly documenting non-mainstream sexual and social behavior, or representing objects and settings that relate to the human body only metaphorically (if at all), their work is as recklessly provocative in its subject matter as it is painstakingly self-conscious, even conservative, in its technical execution.

But from fairly early on, the fellowship program also extended support to photographers who muddied the waters, blurring boundaries with conceptual art, and wreaking particular havoc with the idea that photography represented any kind of reliable record of objective experience. John Baldessari, who received a fellowship as an artist in 1974 and as a photographer in 1982, was among the most influential of such meddlers. One especially resonant innovation was the use of existing photography; promotional black-and-white stills from Hollywood movies, for example, were cropped and composed to form cryptic narratives, twice or more removed from reality. The younger artist Richard Prince, who received a fellowship in photography in 1984, worked at that time primarily with advertising imagery, "appropriating" it, as Baldessari had done. But in Prince's work the emphasis shifted slightly, from the construction of rebus-like fictions to a self-examination of the mechanisms of representation. In particular, Prince and his colleagues were interested in the saturation of contemporary culture with commercial imagery, which, they suggested, was undermining the perhaps misguided pursuit of visual novelty. (As is evident in the work illustrated here, Prince has gone on to assimilate other existing bodies of work into his own, including a parodied version of organic abstraction, and verbal jokes lifted from mainstream media.)

The recycling of existing imagery was not the only strategy used to challenge the documentary value of photography. Another approach has involved creating staged tableaux for the camera to record, the scenes often every bit as elaborate as those for theater or film. Duane Michals (a 1976 recipient) is a forerunner in this field, having long made photoportraits in series that liberally employ costumes and props to suggest the psychological attributes of their subjects, which are often further explored in handwritten captions. Robert Cumming, who like Baldessari was awarded fellowships both as an artist (in 1974) and as a photographer (in 1973), was one of the first to experiment with truth-dodging techniques on both sides of the camera's lens. Starting in the early 1970s, Cumming constructed elaborate tableaux and then photographed them, creating images that are both objective records of a specific physical reality and utterly fictive; since then, he has further expanded the medium's frontiers in work that brings together drawing, printmaking, and color photography. (Also prominent in developing this genre is Sandy Skoglund, whose work is illustrated in black-and-white.) Carrie Mae Weems (a recipient in 1991 and 1994) has also staged sequential photonarratives, in which she uses autobiographical and historical material to examine devilishly complicated issues of race and class. Drawing progressively tighter connections in her work between history, wishful thinking, mischievous tinkering, and outright fiction, Weems reflects on the more or less innocent kinds of forgetfulness that shape expression of social experience.

Perhaps most familiar to the general public, in the genre of staged photography, are the color portraits William Wegman (a photography fellowship recipient in 1982) has made of his dogs. His several generations of Weimaraners have been dressed up and down and induced to perform an endless variety of mournful, goofy antics, which he documents with utterly straight-faced aplomb.

Crafts

In the work of these and other photographers, and in the way it is discussed, exhibited, and marketed, the medium's definition has grown progressively blurred, the clarity of its boundaries declining in direct proportion to the growth of its influence on other disciplines. To some extent, this has also been true for crafts, the other category introduced early in the NEA's Fellowship program (1973). Among the first recipients in this field were several artists who also received support in other categories, including Peter Voulkos and Michael Lucero, and they are hardly the only craftspeople recognized by the fellowship program whose work also falls within the purview of sculpture and/or painting. Viola Frey (a crafts fellowship recipient in 1978) and Betty Woodman (1980 and 1986) are, like Lucero, both artists who use fired and glazed clay, but to call them ceramists is to scant the painterly quality of their work, and its commanding figurative scope. John Cederquist, who received a crafts fellowship in 1975, makes trompe l'oeil furniture, a genre he invented more or less single-handedly. The painted wooden surfaces of his chairs, chests, beds, and tables are indebted to illusionistic painting and printmaking both Western and, particularly, Japanese. And glassmaker Dale Chihuly (a fellowship recipient in 1975 and 1979) has been immensely influential in bringing handmade glass into the material repertory of hundreds of sculptors who do not consider themselves craftspeople—a term that, indeed, fits Chihuly himself imperfectly.

Judith Schaechter (who received fellowships in 1986 and 1988) creates intricate stained glass, radically updating the symbolic program associated with the medium while hewing to its demanding technique. John McQueen (a four-time recipient, in 1977, 1979, 1986, and 1992) began making functional baskets as an extension of his sculptural practice in 1975. Hollowed logs and bird nests, cardboard boxes and origami have served as starting points for bent, stitched, and woven containers made from the branches and bark of ash, elm, and birch; he first incorporated words into his work in 1979, thereby thickening the net of references to the human body and its intentions. Joyce Scott (who received a fellowship in 1988) avails herself of a wide range of materials and process, including jewelry, weaving, papermaking, performance art, and mixed-media installations. Angry, elegant, and often funny, Scott's work examines such oppressive stereotypes of African-American women as Aunt Jemima and other commercialized mammy figures, often through the use of traditional craftwork, as in the intricate beadwork illustrated here.

Printmaking, Drawing, and Artists' Books

Printmaking was the next category introduced, in 1974; drawing was included starting the next year. Here, too fellowships were awarded to artists who had been (or would be) recognized in other categories, including Terry Allen and Robert Cumming. In this case, though, crossing disciplines is only to be expected, as it is a long-established practice for painters and sculptors (among others) to elaborate their ideas on paper both before and after realization in other media. Some artists, however, do consider paper their primary medium. Enrique Chagoya (a recipient in 1992 and 1993) mixes found and original imagery in work that addresses the legacy of colonialism through the layering of different cultures' icons. Susan Crile (who received support in this category in 1989, and for painting in 1982) bases her abstract imagery in natural references, to which the shape and texture of the paper she uses is sometimes a link. Many artists awarded grants in this category were attracted by the relative ease with which works on paper, particularly those printed in multiple, can be disseminated (that is, they are generally more portable, and affordable, than most unique works). This preference was reflected in the emergence, in the early and mid-seventies, of a new generation of artists' books (defined, roughly, as original art in book form). Guillermo Gomez-Pena uses a very wide variety of media, and his impassioned, politically activist work could hardly be more different in sensibility from Lawrence Weiner's laconic, highly abstract use of words to reconfigure space. But both artists turned to offset publications in order to make their ideas available to a wider public (Gomez-Pena received support in this category in 1987, Weiner in 1985). And in doing so, both have supported the admittedly challenging notion that visual art can be read between the covers of a book. Indeed, the NEA's recognition of artists' books at this time represents, once again, its support for media that leap across barriers separating contemporary art from the general public, as both are conventionally defined.

Video

An independent category was established for video in 1975. The Endowment's early recognition of artists working with the young medium is remarkable, and surely among the Visual Artists' Fellowship Program's most praiseworthy—and prescient—decisions. Again, a quarter of a century's hindsight clouds the courage in such support, since video is now so thoroughly integrated into the contemporary artist's repertory of expressive tools that it is hard to recapture its radical nature. The artists awarded fellowships early on included a great many who went on to achieve resounding acclaim, even if, in most cases, such recognition came after decades of relative obscurity, including Gary Hill, Mary Lucier, Tony Oursler, Nam June Paik, and Bill Viola. A handful experimented with video only briefly, if productively: Vito Acconci, originally a poet, has availed himself of nearly every medium in a kaleidoscopic career; after receiving support for video, in 1976 and 1978, he received two fellowships in the Conceptual/Performance/New Genres category (in 1983 and 1993); William Wegman, too, of dog-portrait fame, won support early on (in 1975) for experimentation with video. Joan Jonas was an intrepid explorer of several disciplines nascent in the 1970s, including installation and live performance as well as the video work; she was awarded five fellowships (more than any other artist in the program's history) between 1975 and 1991.

Perhaps most widely acclaimed among the first generation of video artists, all of whom made critical contributions to the technical and expressive development of the medium, is Nam June Paik (a grant recipient in 1977). Born in Korea in 1932, trained in Western music in Japan, and introduced to Zen

Buddhism by the American composer John Cage while studying composition in Germany, Paik heralded—or warned of—the globalism of TV in all its deeply questionable splendor. (The video maps, one of which is illustrated here, are among its most explicit illustrations.) Paik had begun exploring the formal possibilities of television by the early 1960s, first using portable video equipment in 1965 (when Sony introduced it). He describes himself as bringing the same degree of abstraction to TV as the Impressionists had to painting. Emptiness—freedom from self-reflection, from critical thought, from consciousness itself—can be, as in Zen, a spiritual goal; as a description of art (and of commercial television programming) it can also be a withering condemnation. In much of his work, Paik placed these alternatives in mutually contemplative positions, as with *TV Buddha,* in which a small statue of Buddha contemplates its reflection in a live-feedback monitor.

Some of these themes still motivate the work of younger video artists, though the medium's capabilities have of course grown exponentially. Gary Hill (who received four fellowships, the first in 1979) uses video to probe the terrain between textual and visual self-representation, and between bodies as experienced internally and as seen from without. Bill Viola (also a four-time recipient) has made breathtaking spectacles of natural elements, as in floor-to-ceiling cascades of water and fire that literally consume, by the strength of visual seductiveness, the human subjects shown contending with them. Mary Lucier (a fellowship recipient in 1978, 1980, and 1981) creates complex installations that often concern memory, both personal and social, as it is evoked in particularly resonant places. In the enormously engaging work of Tony Oursler (who was awarded fellowships in 1978, 1983, and 1989), tightly framed video images of talking heads—and weeping, laughing, muttering, haranguing, and silent ones—are projected onto a variety of faceless three-dimensional objects, animating them with TV-trapped personas.

New Genres

The connection seems clear between video and the assortment of work grouped under the category Conceptual/Performance/New Genres, in which it was subsumed in 1985 (when the category name was simplified to New Genres). Video (like film) is of course a time-based medium, and as such shares a kinship to other performing arts. Yet the appearance of Conceptual art in this category reveals that its aegis served, above all, to name the perennially unclassifiable. Here the art forms that are more or less homeless by design, that in their very conception resist categorization and the customary constraints of presenting organizations, got a fair hearing.

George Maciunas, who received a grant in 1977, was a chief figure in the anarchic movement called Fluxus, in which an international group of artists joined ranks to contest the very notion of organized art movements, challenging every barricade still standing between art and life. Their work—spontaneous and planned events, offset-printed and handmade publications, assemblages of found (and sometimes perishable) objects—was often ephemeral and always surpassingly irreverent, and their affiliation (strongest in the late 1960s) was brief. But the influence of Fluxus has only grown in importance since then. Meredith Monk, who received a fellowship in 1987, is an artist whose career also reaches back to the late sixties. When she presented her first performance, in 1969, she was already a veteran participant in earlier Happenings and other avant-garde experiments in theater and dance. The many autobiographical operas Monk has developed since combine lush, largely vocal music with live and projected imagery in changing tableaux, their episodic narratives ranging across history and extending into the future.

Some of the work supported in the New Genres category approaches politics and social issues head on, making it a lightning rod for controversy; it is in fact the deeply held belief of those involved with such work that fostering heated debate, and arousing an increasingly apathetic body politic, are the most valuable things an artist can do. Hans Haacke, for example, who was awarded a fellowship in 1978, has long been one of visual art's most incisive social analysts, focusing attention on the intersection between commerce, politics, and art in work that is both passionate and openly encouraging to dissent. Adrian Piper, trained in philosophy and practiced in Conceptual art, focuses attention on issues of race and class, targeting in particular those areas—and those viewers—that seem most comfortably resolved (Piper received fellowships in 1979 and 1982). Fred Wilson (a 1993 recipient) also contests the assumption that major cultural institutions have successfully addressed racism and its legacy; on the contrary, as Wilson reveals with scorching tact in his installations, racial biases are so deeply rooted, and so commonplace, that their all too durable effects have become extremely difficult to isolate and recognize. (In the work illustrated here, the point was made by re-positioning objects in the Maryland Historical Society's own collection, so that slave shackles, for instance, were placed alongside Colonial silver in a vitrine containing American metalwork.)

Dara Birnbaum (who received a grant in 1991) is a veteran video artist with an acute eye for the visual language of the mass media, and especially of network news. The mingled histories of Spanish and American politics over the course of the twentieth century, particularly as they are played out in the sphere of commercial culture, are some of the themes of Francesc Torres's mixed-media installations (he was a fellowship recipient in 1980, 1982, and 1983). Bruce and Norman Yonemoto are brothers who have collaborated since the mid-1970s on film, installation work, and video. The prevailing influences on a California upbringing in the 1950s—popular movies and TV, primarily—are layered with references to Japanese culture in their work, for which they were awarded fellowships in 1983, 1985, and 1989. The installations of Inigo Manglano-Ovalle (a recipient in 1995) often involve video, and generally address an intersection between formal and social issues. One recent installation examined the aesthetics of surveillance, from simple snooping to meteorological monitoring to watching and analyzing the flow of financial data; other work (including that illustrated here) explores medical technology, in particular new forms of genetic imaging and identification.

Mike Kelley is a widely influential California-based artist who has made sculpture, installations, drawings, and artist's books, and early in his career was particularly involved with performance (for which he was awarded a fellowship in 1985). His acknowledged influences range from contemporaries Julia Heyward and Matt Mullican, to Gertrude Stein and William Burroughs, of whose writing Kelley has said, in a description that serves his own performance work as well, "It's all scrambled and turned into a quite private thing—really morose and at the same time howlingly funny. It doesn't have those elements of teary-eyed expressionism. That quality is there, but it's intelligent."[13] Charles Ray, like Kelley a California-based artist, was also funded by the NEA in 1985 for work in the New Genres category; Ray's early experimentation with a Conceptualist kind of performance (enacted mostly without audiences, it is known through photographs) was critical to the development of his later work, most of it in sculpture and installation (for which he received NEA support in 1988). Exploring, with the barest minimum of props, the ways that bodies respond to elementary physical forces, he gently parodied similar investigations by the Minimalist artists of a previous generation. At the same time, he began a distinctive exploration of the area between routine physical phenomena and utterly confounding perceptual experience, often (as in the sculpture illustrated here) using incongruities of scale, weight, or motion.

Ida Applebroog (a fellowship recipient in 1980, 1985, and 1991) has been an artist of uncompromising individuality throughout her career, helping to develop new genres and mixing existing ones almost from the start. Applebroog first gained recognition with a laconic, often bitingly funny series of offset booklets, many of them about familiar emotional predicaments and in particular those that occur within couples; these informal publications were sent, free of charge, to a few hundred colleagues and friends. The paintings that came afterward were ambitious both formally and conceptually, but they retained the sequential narrative structure of the booklets, and continued to reflect Appelbroog's angry and astute sensibility. Alexis Smith (a recipient in 1976 and 1987) is also a narrative artist at heart. Having begun by making intricate two-dimensional work, followed by installations, she went on to permanent, public art. It sustains a theme Smith describes as "paradise lost," with figurative imagery that mixes historical and contemporary references.

Felix Gonzalez-Torres (who received fellowships in 1989 and 1993) is best known for the offset reproductions—his subjects range from nearly empty skies and beaches to a single week's victims of gun violence in the United States—that he presented in stacks and distributed for free at museums and galleries. With this work, Gonzalez-Torres took fairly breathtaking leaps across traditional barriers between public and private exhibition, ownership, and emotional exchange. Equally unflinching, if allusively expressed, was his work's confrontation with mortality, which for Gonzales-Torres (who died of AIDS in 1996) was an inescapable theme. The designed disappearance of his cheap, stacked prints, like the inevitable dimming of the ordinary commercial light bulbs in the curtain of light illustrated here, are indelible images of an essential poise between physical decay and spiritual endurance. No less audacious, and just as deceptively quiet, are the installations of Ann Hamilton (a 1993 recipient). Her keen sense of history, and equally acute sensitivity to the poetry of tactile and visual experience, motivates work that is also impelled by the character of the place in which it is realized and seen.

The necessity of developing a category as broadly framed as Conceptual/Performance/New Genres seems clearly mandated by multi-media, interdisciplinary work as patently resistant to classification as Felix Gonzalez-Torres', or Ann Hamilton's. Perhaps more surprising—and instructive—is the funding, in this category, of work that at first glance seems easily classifiable as photography (for which dedicated funding had existed since 1971). Cindy Sherman (a fellowship recipient in 1977 and 1979) makes photographs that generally highlight stereotypical roles for women, often using herself as subject; the first for which she won acclaim were simulations of black-and-white promotional stills for noir-ish Hollywood movies. Later (as illustrated here), her work grew increasingly lavish, its references ranging across source materials both sublime and grotesque. Sarah Charlesworth (awarded grants in 1976, 1980, and 1983) has reworked photographs borrowed from the news and advertising industries. Even more provocatively, Sherrie Levine (a 1985 recipient) gained widespread attention for photographs of well-known work by master photographers, her images being visually indistinguishable from the originals. Levine's more recent work has continued to probe issues of authenticity, often in three-dimensional works whose points of reference grow increasingly complex.

The work of Sherman, Charlesworth, and Levine is not exclusively, or even primarily, concerned with immediate, intuitive visual response. It is meant instead for second thoughts and double takes. Sometimes condemned for relying on "insider knowledge" (though such knowledge is merely informed interest, freely available to all), this kind of work is simply a form of introspection—an example, for which there is extensive historical precedent in painting and sculpture, of reflection on some of art's basic questions. Is it originality that matters most? Financial value? Evidence of the artist's skill and "touch"? What are the visual codes in circulation at a given historical moment, and how do the mass media shape and exploit them? Far from being self-indulgent, as this kind of work is also sometimes called, it is really rather self-sacrificing, since its timeliness and topicality make it particularly vulnerable to obsolescence. And, at the same time, it is especially valuable to the culture, offering a forum for debate, for reviewing unexamined assumptions and discarding those that no longer serve. Here, too, support from outside the commercial sector, even if it is not sustaining, is critical. Often (as with Charlesworth and Levine), the market ultimately underwrites even that which most directly opposes it—and in so doing, not coincidentally, radically changes its meaning. But the climate for undertaking such self-critical work, essential to the vitality of the arts, is immeasurably enhanced by the presence of alternate, public forms of both professional validation and practical assistance.

It is deeply ironic but perhaps inevitable that the last two independent categories established for applicants to the NEA's individual Artists' Fellowship Program, in 1981, were for painting and sculpture (beginning in 1982, fellowships in these, and all other, categories were awarded in alternate years). Moreover, many of the artists awarded grants in painting and sculpture could have (and often had) applied for support in other disciplines. Thus Robert Arneson and Viola Frey were recognized as sculptors after having received fellowships in the Crafts category; Charles Ray and Fred Wilson, also recipients of fellowships in sculpture, had received support in the Conceptual/Performance/New Genres category. And, like many sculpture fellowship recipients who had previously received grants simply as "Artists" (including Scott Burton, Mary Miss, Dennis Oppenheim, Judy Pfaff, and Nancy Rubins), many younger artists who applied as sculptors concentrated on public art that crossed paths with architecture. Maya Lin received a grant as a sculptor in 1985, three years after completing her widely acclaimed Vietnam Veterans' Memorial in Washington, D.C. (which she had designed while still an undergraduate at Yale, a commission awarded by a separate program of the NEA). Mel Chin, who was awarded a grant for sculpture in 1988, works across a range of media and formats, from altered objects (for example, a baseball bat refashioned into the blades of a ceiling fan, inscribed with a text recalling a racist murder committed with a bat) to full-scale installations. Of primary importance to Chin are public works, including the ongoing project *Revival Field* (illustrated here). Developed in collaboration with a professional agronomist, it involves planting "hyper-accumulating" vegetation that absorbs toxins from contaminated soil. Similarly, many artists who received fellowships in painting had been supported as conceptual/performance artists (Ida Applebroog, for instance), or worked with media that could have been welcome in the Crafts category (such as the painter, childrens' book illustrator and quilt-maker Faith Ringgold).

Epilogue

It is impossible to summarize the work of these 100 artists, and no easier to say how their careers would have differed without government support—or, in turn, how the course of the visual arts over the past thirty-five years would have been altered by the absence of the fellowship program. Clearly, there is no single kind of art associated with NEA support. Nor was the Endowment ever able (even if the will had been there) to wrest control of visual art's development away from the other forces that affect it. Surely some wonderful artists would have turned away from the field without the psychological and material boost that a fellowship represents; just as surely, many others would have flourished without it. No data analyst in the world could describe the game being played given these players and their strategies; there are simply too many variables. It is, in fact, nearly impossible to know where the playing field begins and ends—an ambiguity that only increased over the three decades during which the fellowship program existed.

And yet, some conclusions can be drawn. Without such fellowships, and the direct link they represent between individual creators and their Federal government, there is far less incentive to engage in explorations of the mutual commitments shared by artists and the public—including, especially, those who don't count themselves among contemporary art's most sympathetic audience. The termination of the fellowship program entailed the loss of this sense of reciprocity, and with it a crucial inducement for artists to consider the dynamics of art's public reception, a willingness that led, during these years, to ceaseless experimentation with media and modes of presentation. And, equally important, the general tax-paying public lost a crucial stake (however symbolic it may have been, given the NEA's always extremely modest budget) in the creation of the nation's visual culture. Without the NEA fellowship program, the general public has that much less reason to pay attention to artwork outside the compass of the known and familiar.

The loss of individual fellowships, in short, brings the visual arts one step closer to the kind of insularity of which the NEA's detractors have always—falsely—accused it. A small, closed art world governed by an elite is much more likely to result from reliance on the marketplace—on galleries, and collectors, as first judges of new talent—than from soliciting the advice of a regionally and professionally diverse, and constantly changing, group of artists and arts professionals. The elimination of the fellowship program is a grave disservice to artists. But its termination does just as great an injustice to the public at large, because all of our country's constituents deserve to be addressed by the most ambitious, inventive, and respected artists working today.

1
Christopher Wilmarth, a grant recipient in 1969, 1977, and 1980 (his work is illustrated here in black-and-white), was among the few artists who actively campaigned against the gallery system, renouncing SoHo in the middle 1980s and opening his own gallery, called The Studio for the First Amendment.

2
Donald Judd, "Specific Objects," *Arts Yearbook 8*, New York, 1965, p. 74.

3
Quoted in Marja Bloem, "An Awareness of Perfection," *Agnes Martin: Paintings and Drawings* (exhibition catalogue), Amsterdam, Stedelijk Museum, 1991, p. 39.

4
Quoted in Robert Storr, "Beyond Words," *Bruce Nauman* (exhibition catalogue), Walker Art Center, Minneapolis, and Hirshhorn Museum and Scultpure Garden, Washington, D.C., 1994, p. 55.

5
Quoted in Josef Helfenstein, "First Light and Catso White," *James Turrell: First Light* (exhibition catalogue), Kunstmuseum, Bern, 1991, p. 11. Reprinted in Jonathan Fineberg, *Art Since 1940: Strategies of Being,* Harry N. Abrams, Inc., New York, 1995, p. 308.

6
Robert Irwin, *Being and Circumstance: Notes Toward a Conditional Art,* Lapis Press, Larkspur and Pace Gallery, New York, 1985, p. 27.

7
Robert Storr, "The Thing Shines, Not the Maker': The Sculpture of Martin Puryear," in Neal Benezra, *Martin Puryear,* Thames and Hudson, New York and Art Institute of Chicago, 1991, p. 133

8
"I'm sure that Abstract Expressionism is where I was intuitively, whether or not I was conscious at the time of what the influence was," Chamberlain told Julie Sylvester. In Julie Sylvester, *John Chamberlain: A Catalogue Raisonné of the Sculpture 1954-1985,* Hudson Hills Press, New York and The Museum of Contemporary Art, Los Angeles, 1986, p. 14.

9
In Joan Simon, *Susan Rothenberg,* Harry N. Abrams, Inc. New York, 1991, p. 47.

10
Interview with Frederick Ted Castle, *Artforum,* October 1983, reprinted in *Alice Neel: Paintings Since 1970,* Pennsylvania Academy of the Arts, Philadelphia, 1985, no pagination.

11
Donald Kuspit, "Gregory Amenoff, Hirschl and Adler Modern," *Artforum* vol. 31. No. 10 (Summer 1993), p. 106.

12
In *Aperture* no. 126, Fall 1992, page 53.

13
Kelley interviewed by John Miller, in *Mike Kelley,* A.R.T. Press/Art Resources Transfer, 1992, p. 9.

COLOR PLATES

Acconci Studio
(Vito Acconci, Luis Vera, Celia Imrey, Dario Nunez, Jenny Schrider, Charles Doherty, and Saija Singer)

Flying Floors for Ticketing Pavilion
1998

Painted steel, terrazzo, carpet, plantings, light, 26 x 36 x 45'
Terminal B/C, Philadelphia Airport

Robert Adams

On Signal Hill, Overlooking Long Beach, California
1983

Gelatin-silver print

Terry Allen

The Perfect Ship
(from 'A Simple Story (Juarez)')
1992

Multimedia installation with sound, neon and video, 20 x 20 x 60'
Wexner Center for the Visual Arts, Columbus, Ohio

Courtesy L.A. Louver, Venice, California, Gallery Paule Anglim, San Francisco, California and Betty Moody Gallery, Houston, Texas

PHOTOGRAPHER: Fredrik Marsh

Gregory Amenoff
March
1998

Oil on canvas, 76 x 66"

Courtesy Nielsen Gallery, Boston

PHOTOGRAPHER: Steve Bates

Laurie Anderson
Stories From The Nerve Bible
1992

Premiered at Expo, Seville

Ida Applebroog
Noble Fields
1987

Oil on canvas, 86 x 132"
Guggenheim Museum Collection

PHOTOGRAPHER: Jennifer Kotter

Robert Arneson

Chemo 1

1992

Bronze, 47 x 21 x 19"

Courtesy George Adams Gallery, New York, Brian Gross Fine Art, San Francisco

Richard Artschwager

Untitled

1997

Formica, aluminum, and acrylic on wood board, 89 x 40 1/2 x 1" (left), 66 1/2 x 58 1/2 x 1" (right)

Private collection, Geneva, Switzerland

John Baldessari

Goya Series: AND

Ink jet print, hand lettering on canvas, 75 x 60"

Museum of Modern Art, New York

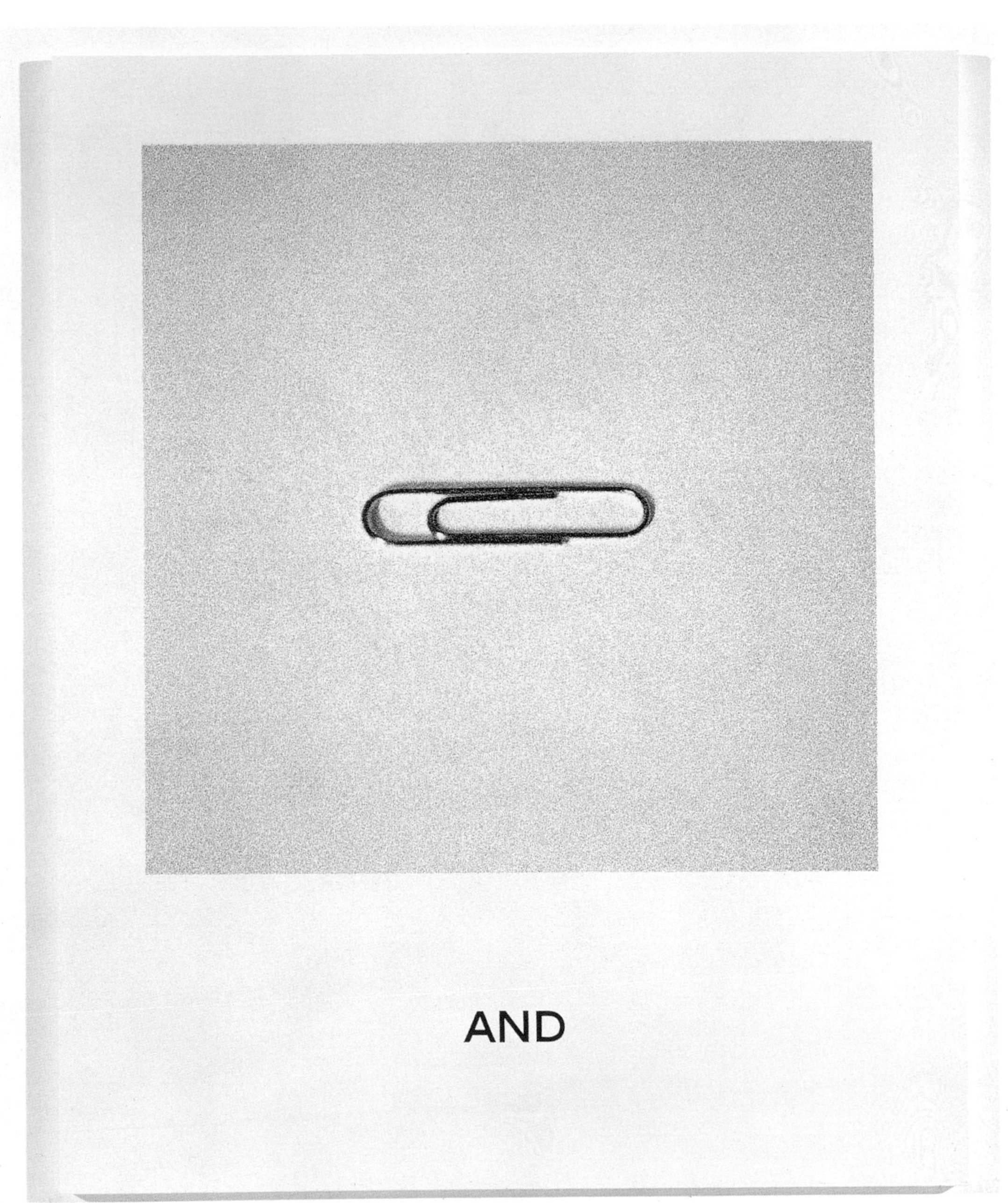

Jennifer Bartlett
Small House, Big House
1998

Oil on canvas, 40 x 80"

Private collection

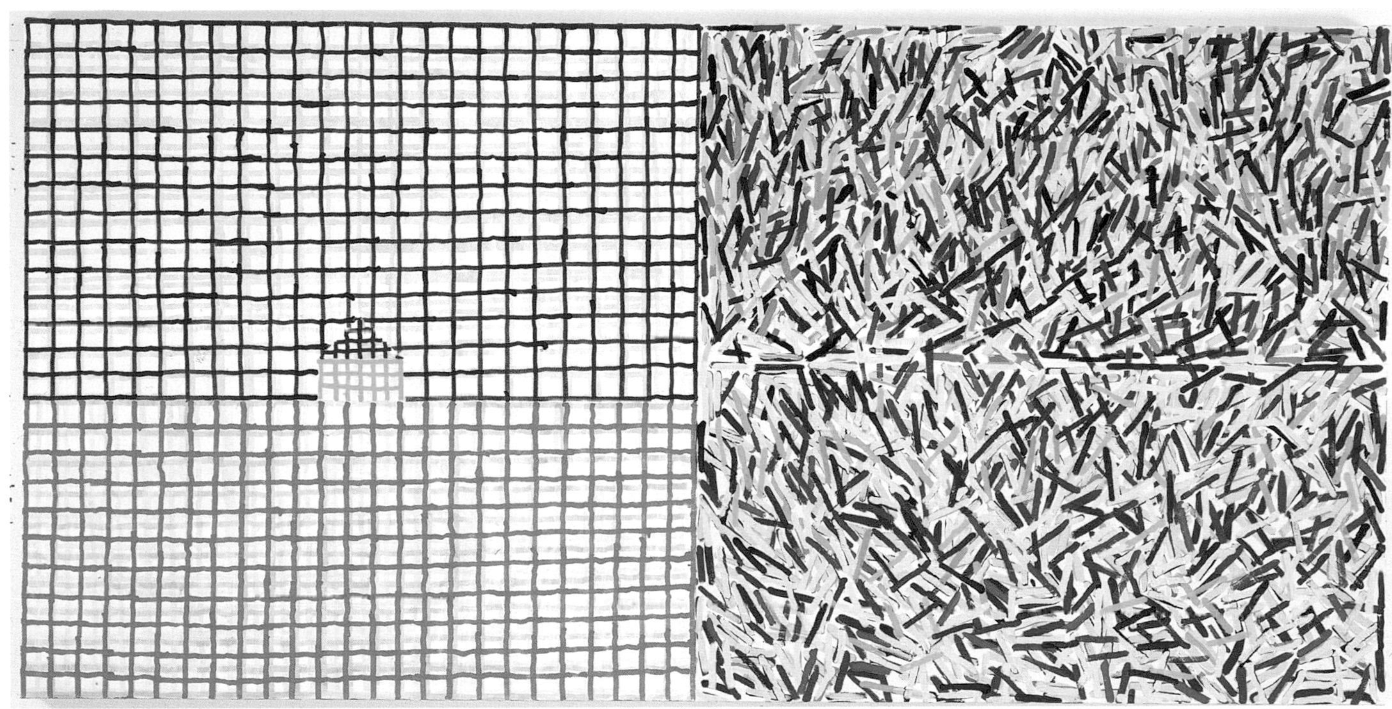

Dara Birnbaum
Hostage
1994

6-channel color video, 10-channel audio, steel suspension system, Plexiglas shields with painted targets, interactive laser beam and receiver

Paula Cooper Gallery, New York

PHOTOGRAPHER: Geoffrey Clements

Chris Burden
The Flying Steamroller
1996

1968 Huber road grader, steel, concrete, 56' 6" x 56' 6" x 21'

PHOTOGRAPHER: Gerald Zugmann/MAK-Austrian Museum of Applied Arts

Scott Burton

Two Part Bench: A Pair

1988

Porto Beige Limestone, 41 x 52 x 23 1/2"

Courtesy Max Protetch Gallery, New York

Harry Callahan
Ireland
1979

Dye transfer print, image 9 1/2 x 14 3/8", paper 17 5/8 x 22 3/8"

Courtesy PaceWildensteinMacGill, New York

John Cederquist

Tubular

1990

Baltic birch plywood, Sitka spruce, maple, epoxy resin inlay, aniline dye, litho inks, metal hardware, 84 x 48 x 16"

Greenhil Collection

Courtesy Franklin Parrasch Gallery

PHOTOGRAPHER: Mike Sasso

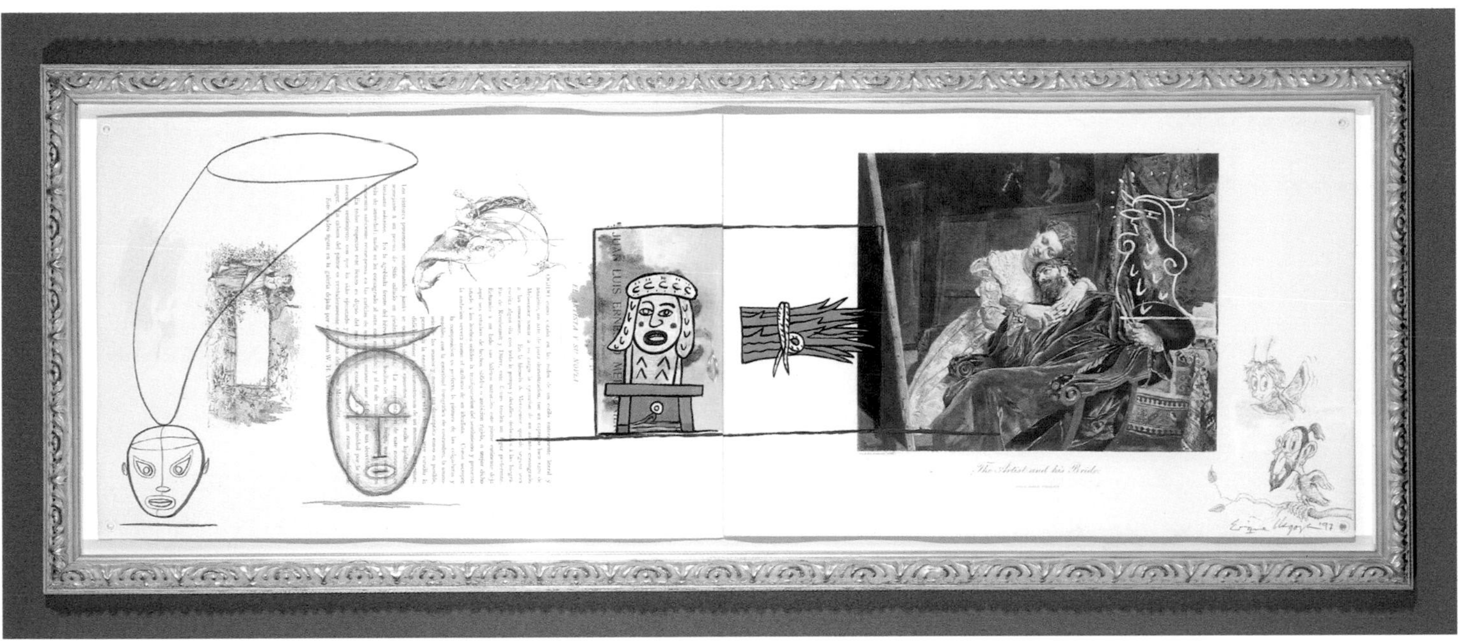

Enrique Chagoya
The Artist and His Bride
1997

Acrylic, oil, ball point pen, graphite on 19th century original etching, 11 x 32"

PHOTOGRAPHER: Eugenio Castro

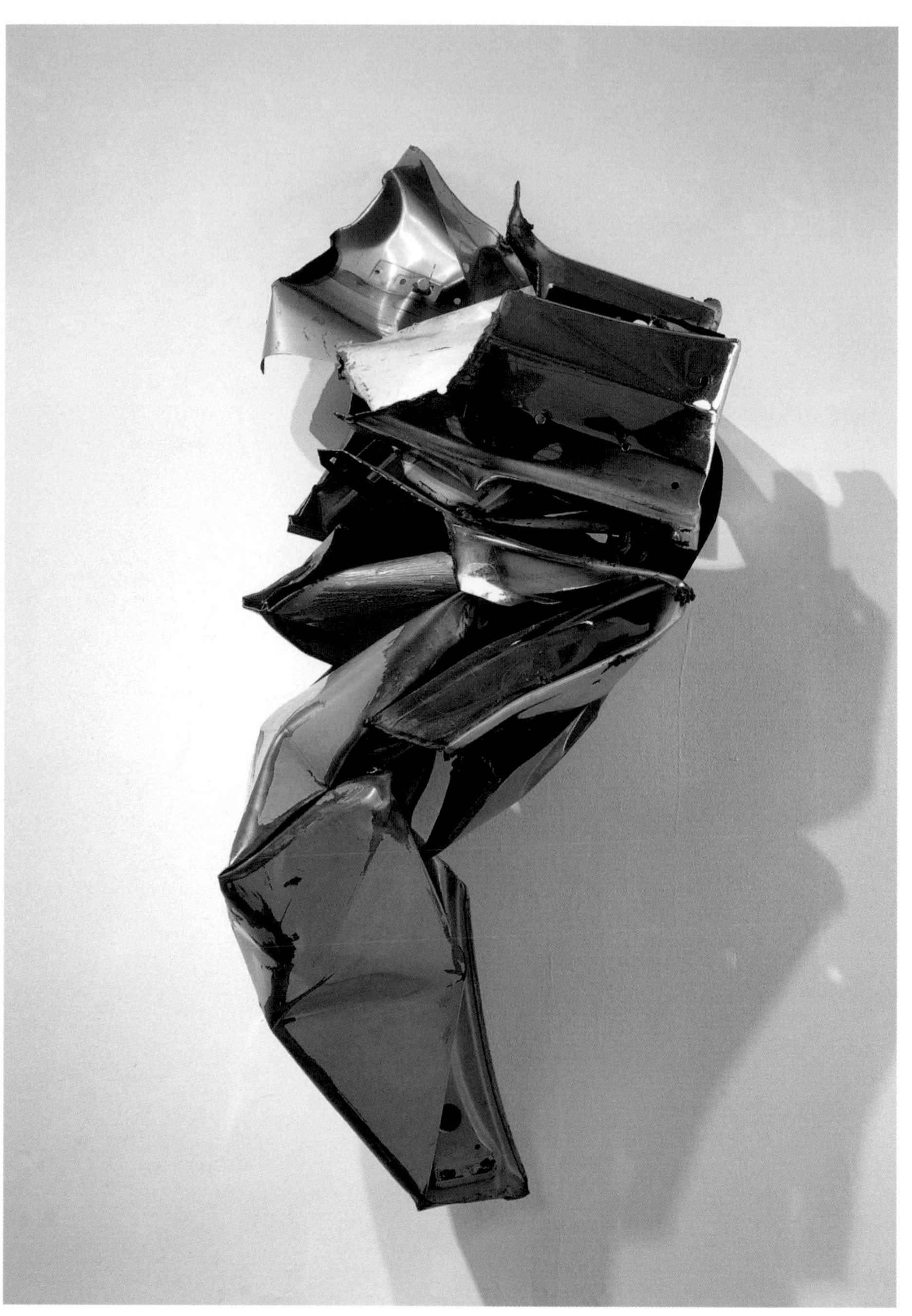

John Chamberlain
Decker and Dicker
1975

Enamel on painted steel, 65 x 26 1/2 x 26"
(165 x 67.5 x 66 cm)

Courtesy PaceWildenstein, New York

PHOTOGRAPHER: Gordon Riley Christmas

Sarah Charlesworth

Control & Abandon

(from Natural Magic series)

1992–93

Laminated cibachrome with laquered wood frame, 41 1/4 x 33 1/2"

Dale Chihuly

Prussian Blue Seaform Set with Chinese Red Lip Wraps

1994

Blown glass, 18 x 35 x 22"

PHOTOGRAPHER: Claire Garoutte

Mel Chin
Revival Field
1990–ongoing

Plants, industrial fencing on a hazardous waste landfill, 9 x 60 x 60'

PHOTOGRAPH: Walker Art Center, Minneapolis

William Christenberry
Windows of Palmist Building, Havana Junction, Alabama
1981

EK 74 Photograph, 8 x 10"

Larry Clark
Sketches for Tulsa Movie Coming Soon
1996

Portfolio of 12 C-prints, 18 x 12"

Courtesy Luhring Augustine, New York

Chuck Close

Self-Portrait

1997

Oil on canvas, 8' 6" x 7' (259.1 x 213.4 cm)

Private collection, New York

Courtesy PaceWildenstein, New York

PHOTOGRAPHER: Ellen Page Wilson

Robert Colescott
Ode to Joy (European Anthem)
1997

Acrylic on canvas, 90 x 114"

Courtesy Phyllis Kind Gallery, New York

Susan Crile

Conflagration: Oil & Fire

1992–93

Oil and pumice on canvas, 92 x 168"

Collection Julia and Waring Partridge

PHOTOGRAPHER: Ellen Page Wilson

Robert Cumming
Beehive/Books
1992

Granite, 6 1/2'

Private collection, Nantucket, Massachusetts

Mark di Suvero
Pyramidian
1987–95

Steel, 60 x 60'

Courtesy of Storm King Art Center, Mountainville, New York. Gift of the Ralph E. Ogden Foundation

PHOTOGRAPHER: Jerry L. Thompson

William Eggleston
Troubled Waters
1980

Dye-transfer print, 16 x 20"

Dan Flavin
Untitled
1996

Pink, yellow, green, blue, and filtered U.V. flourescent light, approximately 125 x 30'
Installation of four-foot fixtures in two opposing bands for the east and west interior walls of Richmond Hall

The Menil Collection, Houston

PHOTOGRAPHER: Hickey-Robertson

Viola Frey
The Argument
1995

Ceramic, 31 x 35 x 13"

Private collection

Courtesy Rena Bransten Gallery, San Francisco

PHOTOGRAPHER: Sue Tallon

Lee Friedlander

Las Vegas

1997

Black-and-white photograph, 10 x 10"

Sam Gilliam
Hood
1999

Acrylic on wood, 34 x 27 x 10"

PHOTOGRAPHER: Mark Gulezian

Frank Gohlke

Port of Cleveland–Cleveland, Ohio

1997

Courtesy Bonni Benrubi Gallery, New York

Nan Goldin
Pavel on the Beach, Positano, Italy
1996

Color photograph, 30 x 40"

Courtesy Matthew Marks Gallery, New York

Guillermo Gomez-Pena

The Mexterminator Project

1997–99 (ongoing)

Performance with Roberto Sinfuentes

PHOTOGRAPHER: Clarissa Horowitz

Felix Gonzalez-Torres

Untitled (Foreground)
1993

15 watt light bulbs, porcelain light sockets and extension cords, dimesions vary with installation. Installed at The Solomon R. Guggenheim Museum, New York

Untitled (Background)
1993

Paint on wall, dimensions vary with installation. Installed at The Solomon R. Guggenheim Museum, New York

Courtesy Andrea Rosen Gallery, New York

PHOTOGRAPHER: David Heald

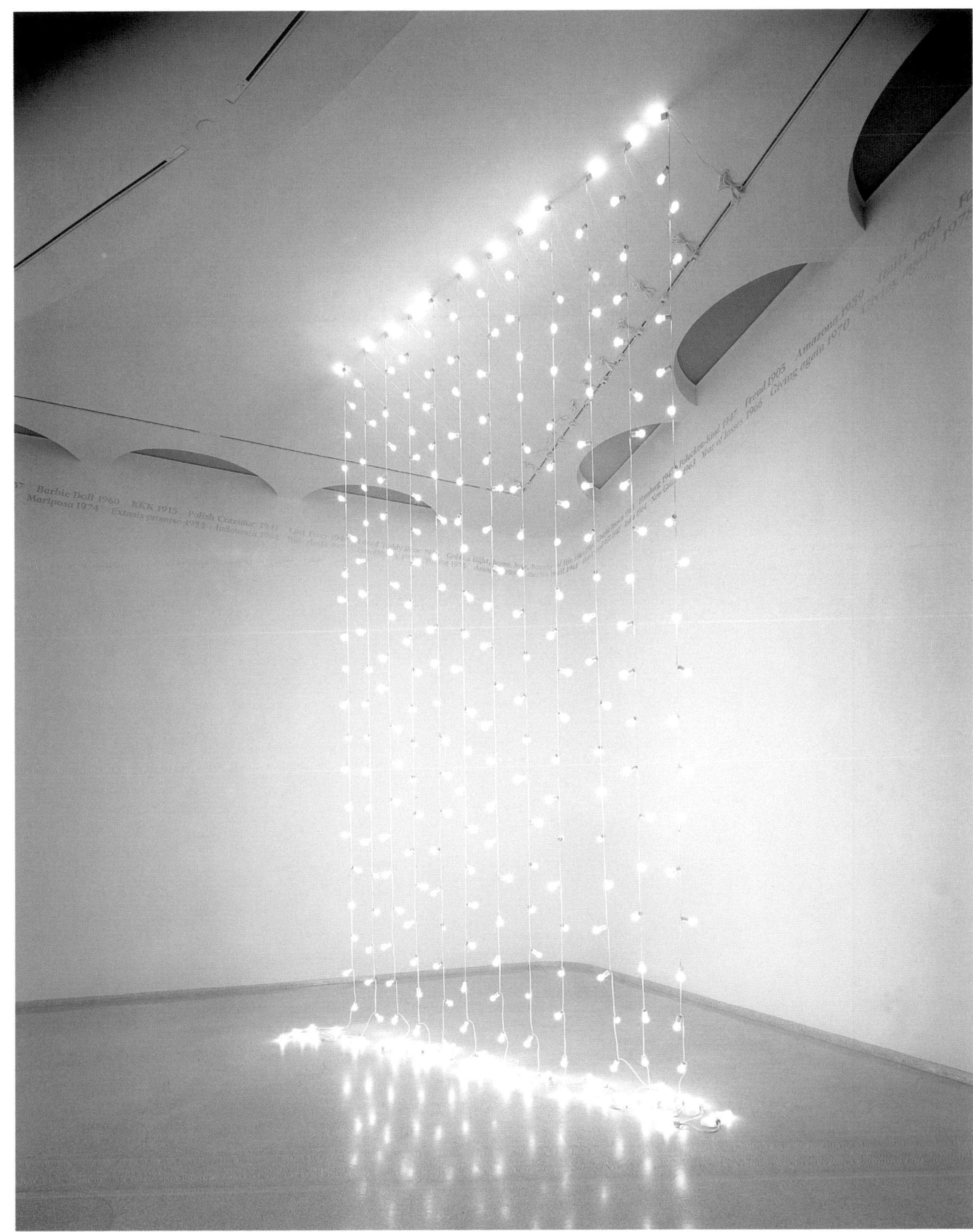

Nancy Graves

Metaphor and Melanomy

1995

Bronze, Polychrome patina naz-dar ink over incralac, 8' 6" x 8' 11" x 6' 1"

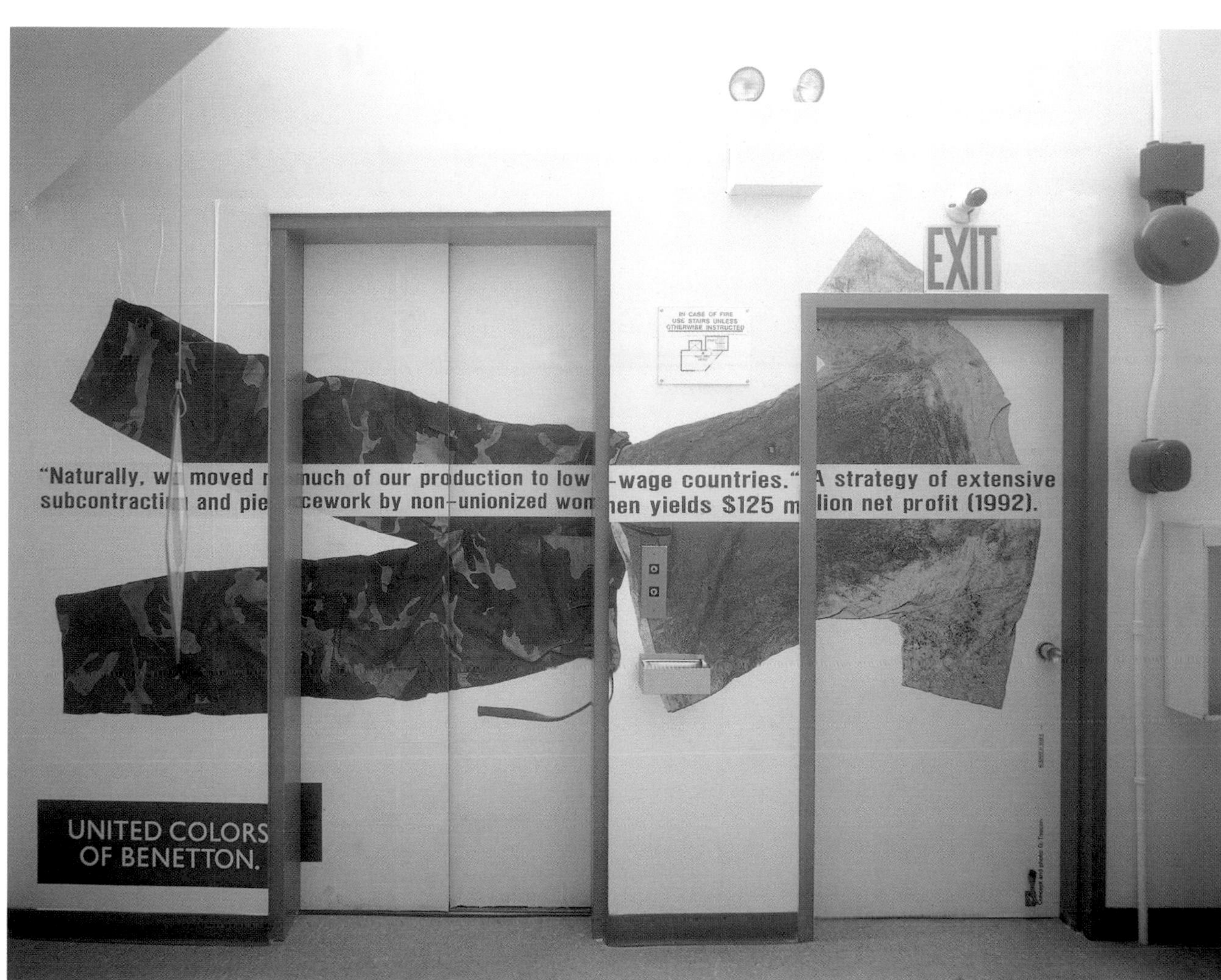

Hans Haacke
Dyeing for Benetton
1994

Temporary installation

PHOTOGRAPHER: Fred Scruton

Ann Hamilton

mantle

1998

Shortwave radio with voices in various languages, table mounded with 60,000 cut flowers, seated figure stitching the seams of wool coats. Miami Art Museum, Miami, Florida

Photograph courtesy Sean Kelly, New York

PHOTOGRAPHER: Thibault Jeanson

Gary Hill
Hand Heard
1995–96

Five-channel video installation with five color projections

Courtesy Donald Young Gallery, Chicago

Robert Irwin

1°2°3°4°

1992

Three voile tergal (scrim) walls, violet, green, and orange, five floating frames painted with black acrylic lacquer, front to back, 14 x 38' each, three walls 10 x 26' each, five frames

Courtesy PaceWildenstein, New York

PHOTOGRAPHER: Bill Jacobson

Joan Jonas
Volcano Saga
1987

Performance at Performing Garage, New York

Courtesy Pat Hearn Gallery, New York

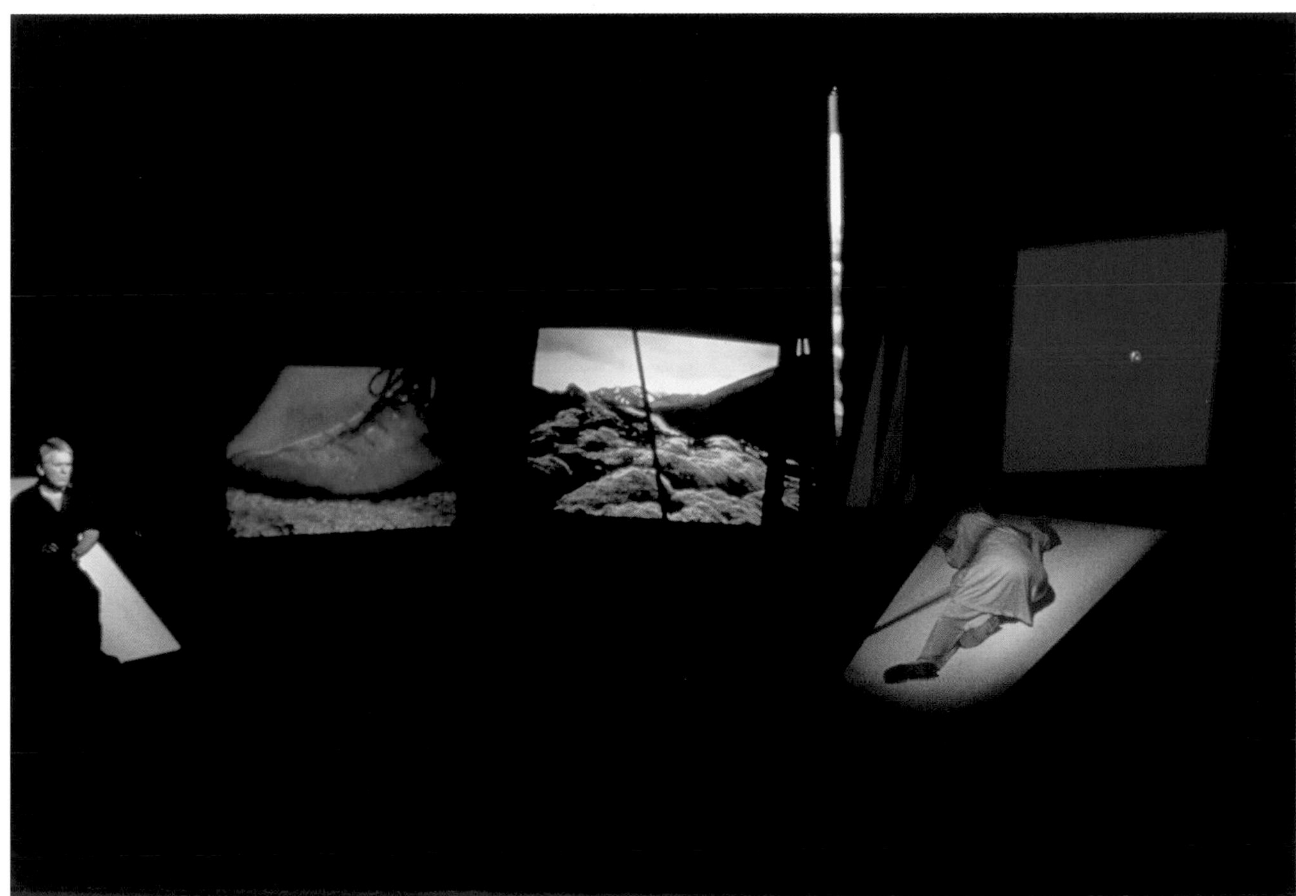

Donald Judd

Group of One Hundred Untitled Works in Mill Aluminum (detail)
1982–86

Mill aluminum, each unit 41 x 51 x 72"
Permanent installation in two buildings at the Chinati Foundation

Courtesy The Chinati Foundation, Marfa, Texas

Mike Kelley

Catholic Tastes

1994

Installation view

PHOTOGRAPHER: Douglas M. Parker Studio

Barry Le Va

Diagram for Two Separate Installations

1982

Mixed media collage, 48 x 48"

Courtesy Nolan/Eckman Gallery, New York

Sherrie Levine
Black-and-White Bottles
1992

Cast glass, sandblasted, 13 x 3" each

Courtesy Margo Leavin Gallery, Los Angeles

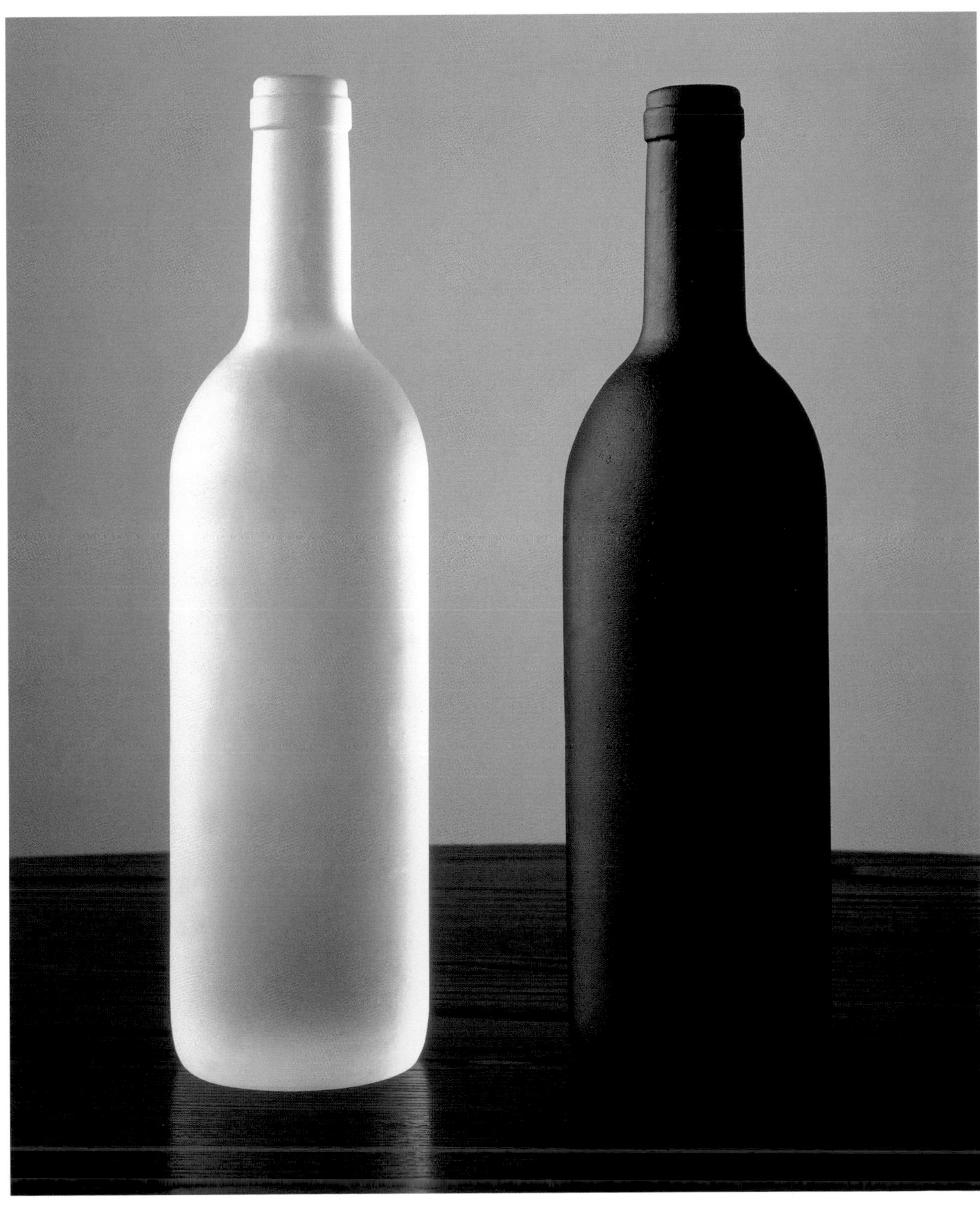

Helen Levitt

New York

1985

Gelatin silver print, 11 x 14"

Courtesy Laurence Miller Gallery, New York

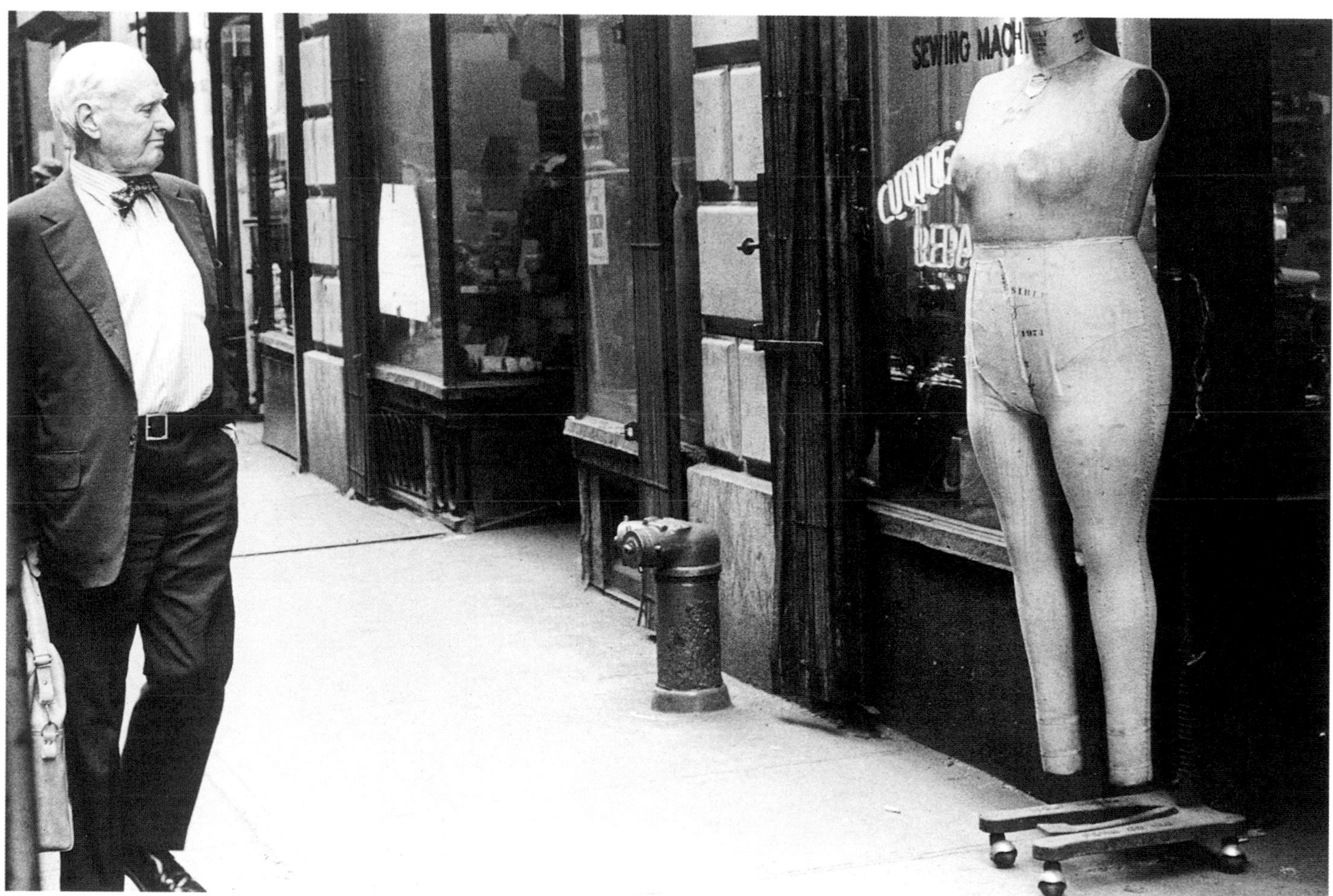

Maya Lin
Untitled
1997

Topographic landscape, foreground particle board, 16' x 18' x 18"; Avalanche, 14 tons broken glass

Sponsored by Southeastern Center for Contemporary Art, Winston-Salem

Michael Lucero

Flora (Reclamation Series)

1997

Clay with glazes, 92 x 30 x 19"

Courtesy Fay Gold Gallery, Atlanta

Mary Lucier
Noah's Raven
1993

Mixed-media, video, and sound

Collection, ZKM Museum of Contemporary Art, Karlsruhe, Germany

PHOTOGRAPHER: Tim Thayer

George Maciunas

Excreta Fluxorum, Fluxus Editions

1972–77

Wood, plastic, paper, and manures from various animals and insects

Courtesy of The Gilbert and Lila Silverman Fluxus Collection Foundation

PHOTOGRAPHER: Brad Iverson

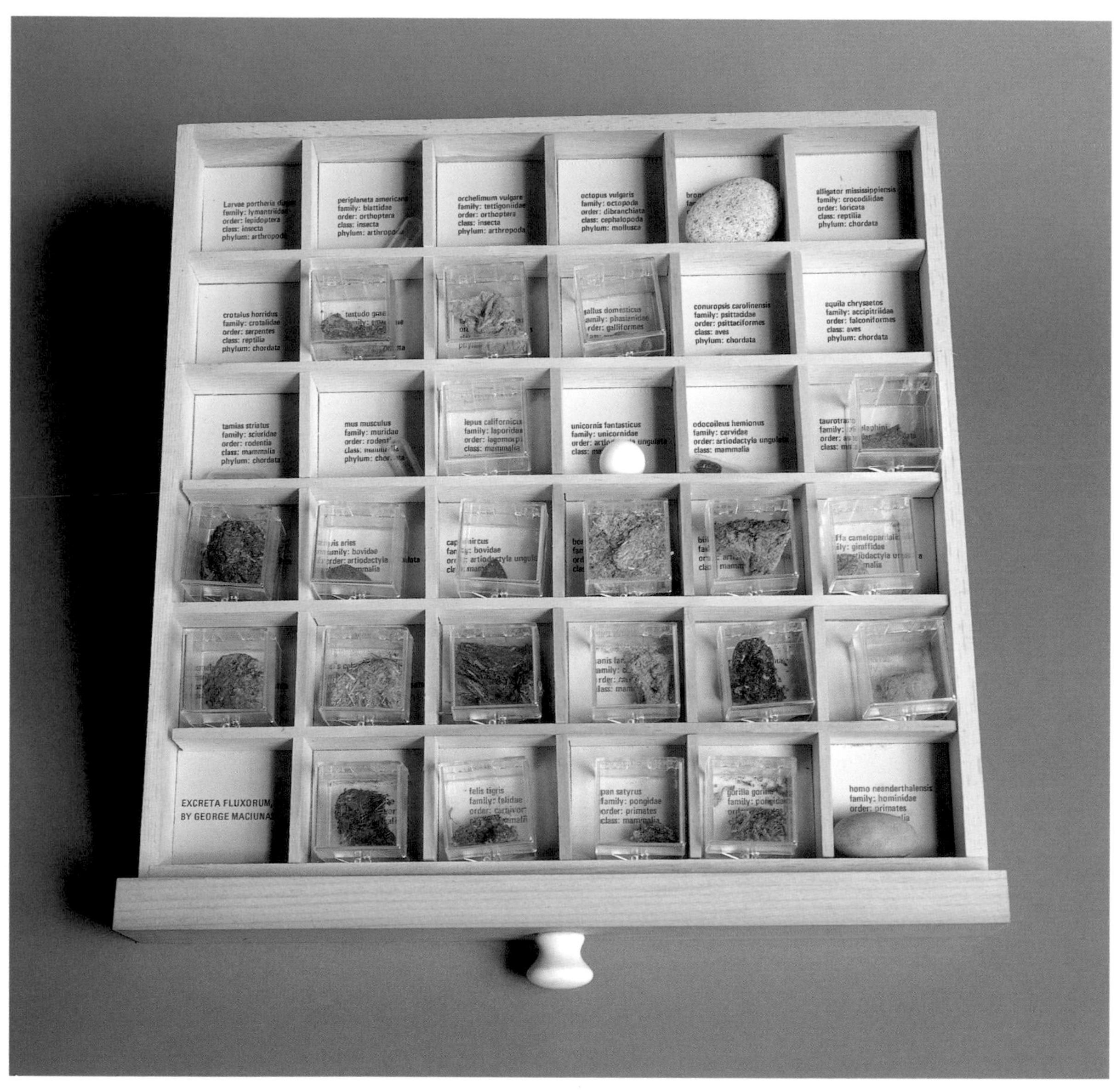

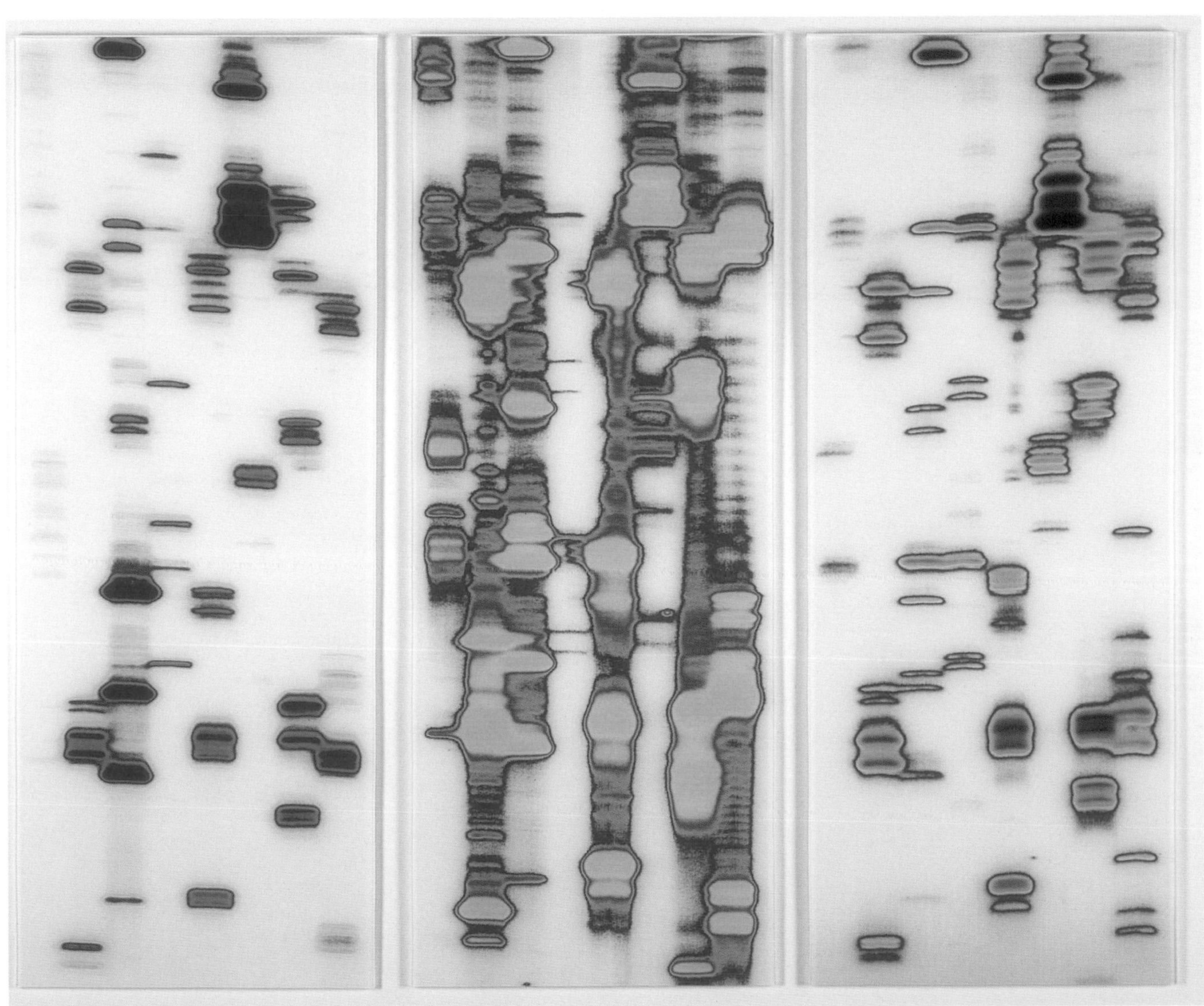

Inigo Manglano-Ovalle
Doug, Joe, and Genevieve
(from Garden of Delights)
1998

C Print of DNA Analyses, 60 x 69"

Courtesy Max Protetch Gallery, New York

Robert Mapplethorpe
Calla Lily
1988

Agnes Martin
Untitled #12
1997

Acrylic and graphite on canvas,
60 x 60" (152.4 x 152.4 cm)

Courtesy PaceWildenstein, New York

PHOTOGRAPHER: Ellen Page Wilson

John McQueen

The Other Side of the Moon

1993

Tulip, poplar maple bark, blackberry vines, 33 x 17"

Courtesy Garth Clark Gallery, New York

PHOTOGRAPHER: Karen Bell

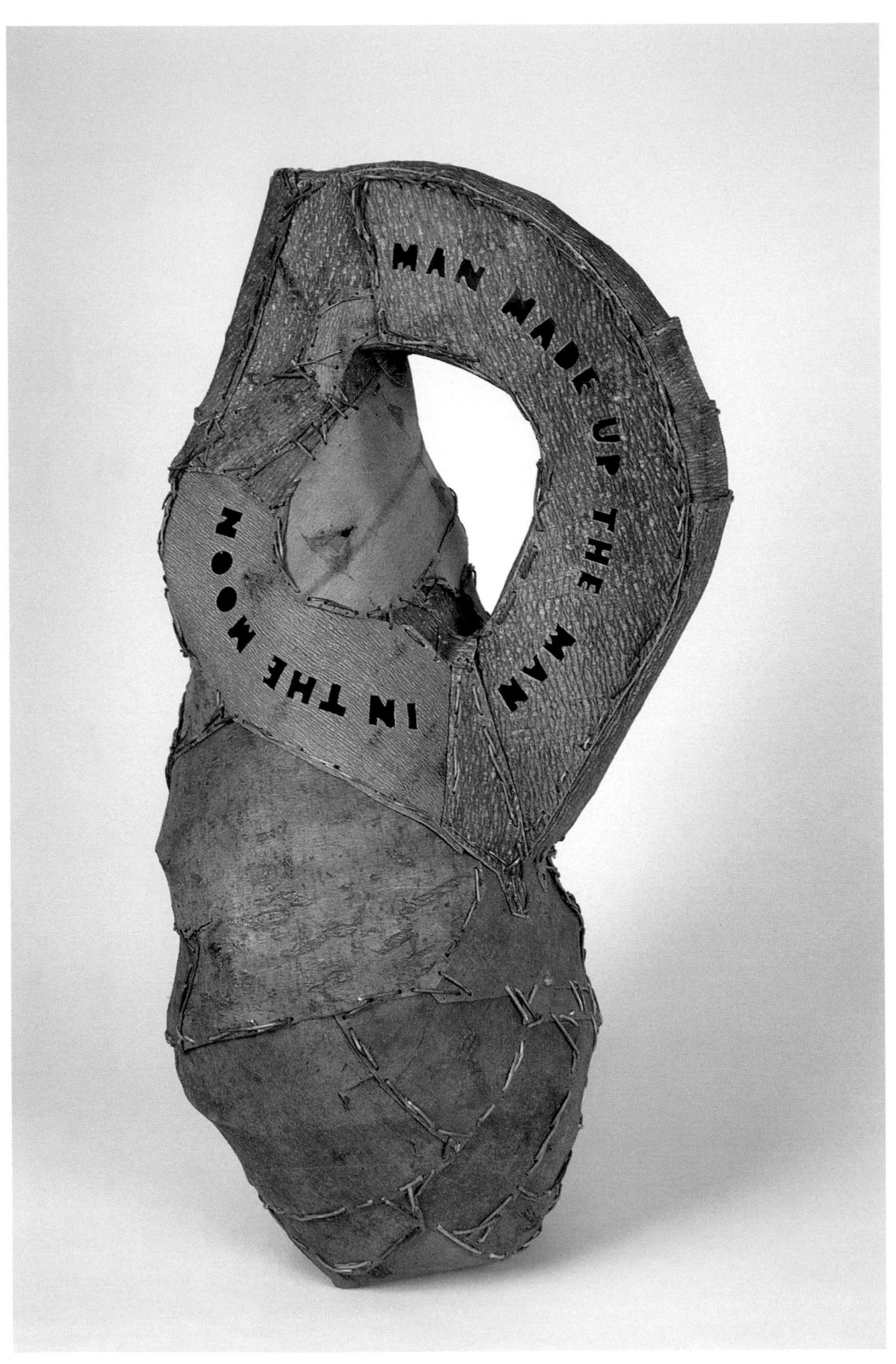

Joel Meyerowitz
Hartwig House, Truro
1976

Ektacolor RC print, 8 x 10"

Duane Michals

The Sight of Sound

1985

Black-and-white photograph, 5 x 7"

Courtesy PaceWildensteinMacGill, New York

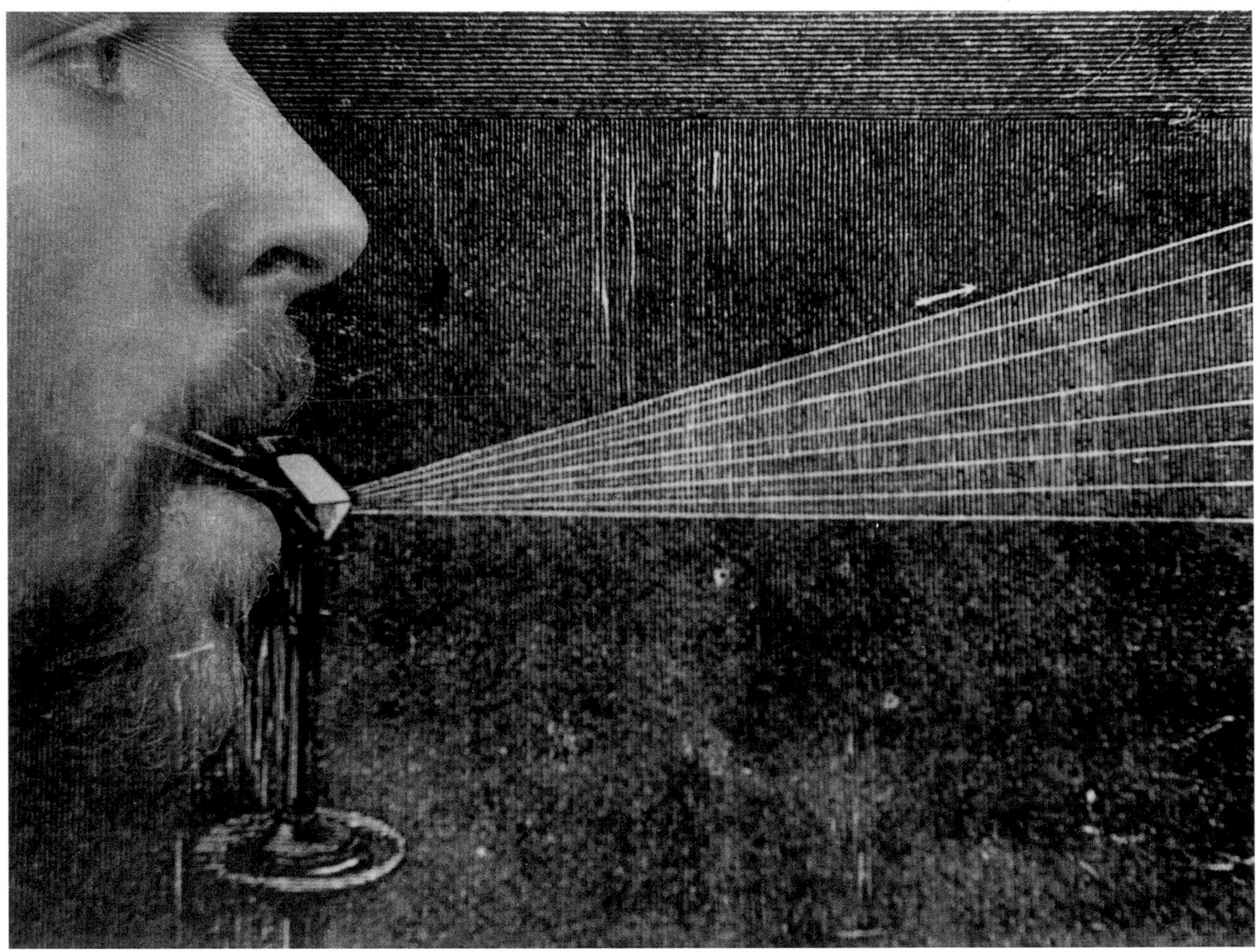

Richard Misrach
Diving Board, Salton Sea
1983

Dye coupler photograph, 40 x 50"

Mary Miss

Greenwood Pond: Double Site

1989–96

6.5 acre site

Des Moines Art Center, Des Moines, Iowa

Meredith Monk
16 Millimeter Earrings Installation (detail)
1998

Part of the exhibit *Art Performs Life: Merce Cunningham, Meredith Monk, Bill T. Jones*, Walker Art Center, Minneapolis

PHOTOGRAPHER: Dan Dennehy

Robert Morris

Disappearing Places (TYSZOWEE)

1988

Lead and steel, 36 x 46 3/8 x 1 3/4"

Courtesy Sonnabend Gallery, New York

Bruce Nauman

Carousel (Stainless Steel Version)
1988

Stainless steel, cast aluminum, polyurethane foam, wire, 7 x 18'

Collection Ydessa Hendeles Art Foundation, Toronto

Courtesy Sperone Westwater, New York

Alice Neel

Geoffrey Hendricks and Brian

1979

Oil on canvas, 44 x 34" (111.7 x 86.3 cm)

Photograph Courtesy Robert Miller Gallery, New York

James Nutt
Twinge
1998

Acrylic on canvas, 13 x 13"

Collection Hirshhorn Museum and Sculpture Garden, Smithsonian Institution, Washington, D.C., partial gift of anonymous donor

PHOTOGRAPHER: Michael Tropea

Tony Oursler

Bottom

1996

Video projector, videocassette recorder, tripod, videotape, wood, Plexiglas, ceramic, and water, 53 x 11 x 11"
Performer, David West

Courtesy the artist and Metro Pictures

Nam June Paik
Electronic Superhighway
1995

Continental U.S.: 313 televisions, Alaska: 24 televisions, Hawaii: 1 television per Hawaiian island, laser disc players, laser discs, approximately. 60 video distribution amps, approximately 20 fans, video camera, approx. 7 units scaffolding, 200-watt audio system, "state borders" fabricated steel, neon, Continental U.S.: 15 x 32 x 4', Alaska: 5 x 7' x 20", Hawaii: 6 x 6' x 15"

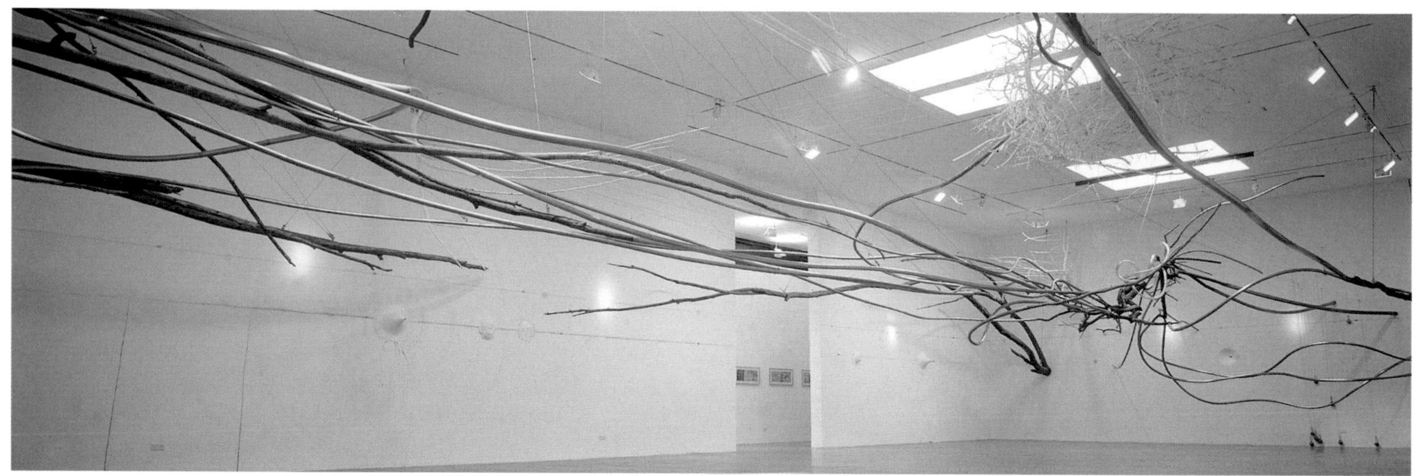

Judy Pfaff

Ear To Ear

1995

Mixed-media installation at Williamson Gallery, Art Center School of Design, Pasadena, California

PHOTOGRAPHER: Steve Heller

Adrian Piper
Out of the Corner
1990

Video, monitors, chairs, table, black-and-white photographs, 18 videotapes

Collection Whitney Museum of American Art, New York

Richard Prince

Ten or Eleven

1996

Acrylic, silkscreen, and charcoal on canvas, 61 1/2 x 48" (156.2 x 121.9 cm)

Courtesy Barbara Gladstone, New York

Martin Puryear
Untitled
1997

Wire mesh and tar, 66 x 76 1/2 x 37 1/4"

Collection Detroit Institute of Art, Detroit

Courtesy Donald Young Gallery, Chicago

Charles Ray

Fall '91

1991

Mixed-media, 96" tall

Photograph courtesy Feature Inc., New York

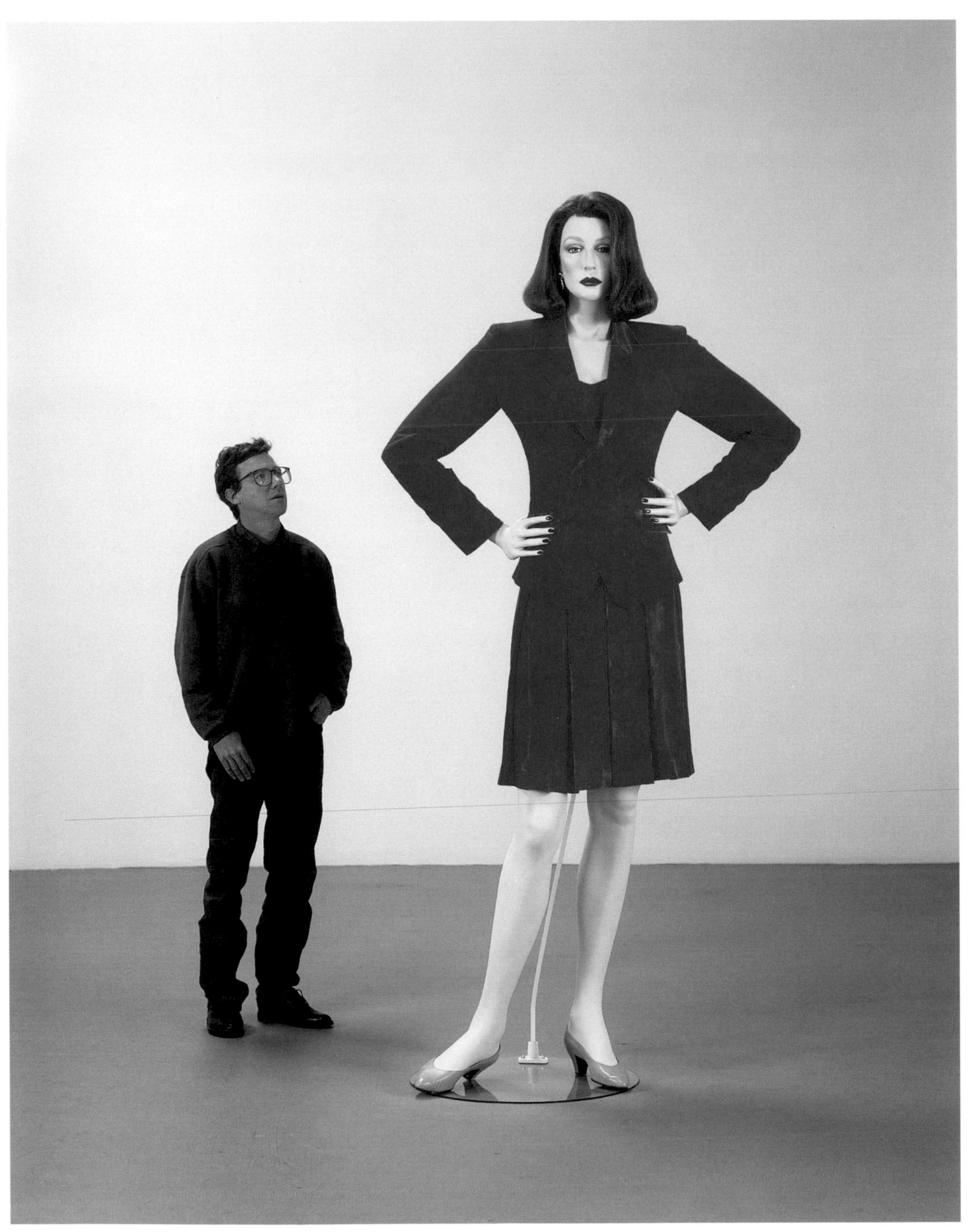

Faith Ringgold
Born in a Cotton Field
(The American Collection #3)
1997

73 1/2 x 79 1/2"

Private Collection

Susan Rothenberg

Canadian Geese

1996–97

Oil on canvas, 84 x 113" (213.4 x 287 cm)

Private collection

Courtesy Sperone Westwater, New York

Nancy Rubins
Mattresses & Cakes
1993

Mattresses and cakes, 21' high

Courtesy Paul Kasmin Gallery, New York

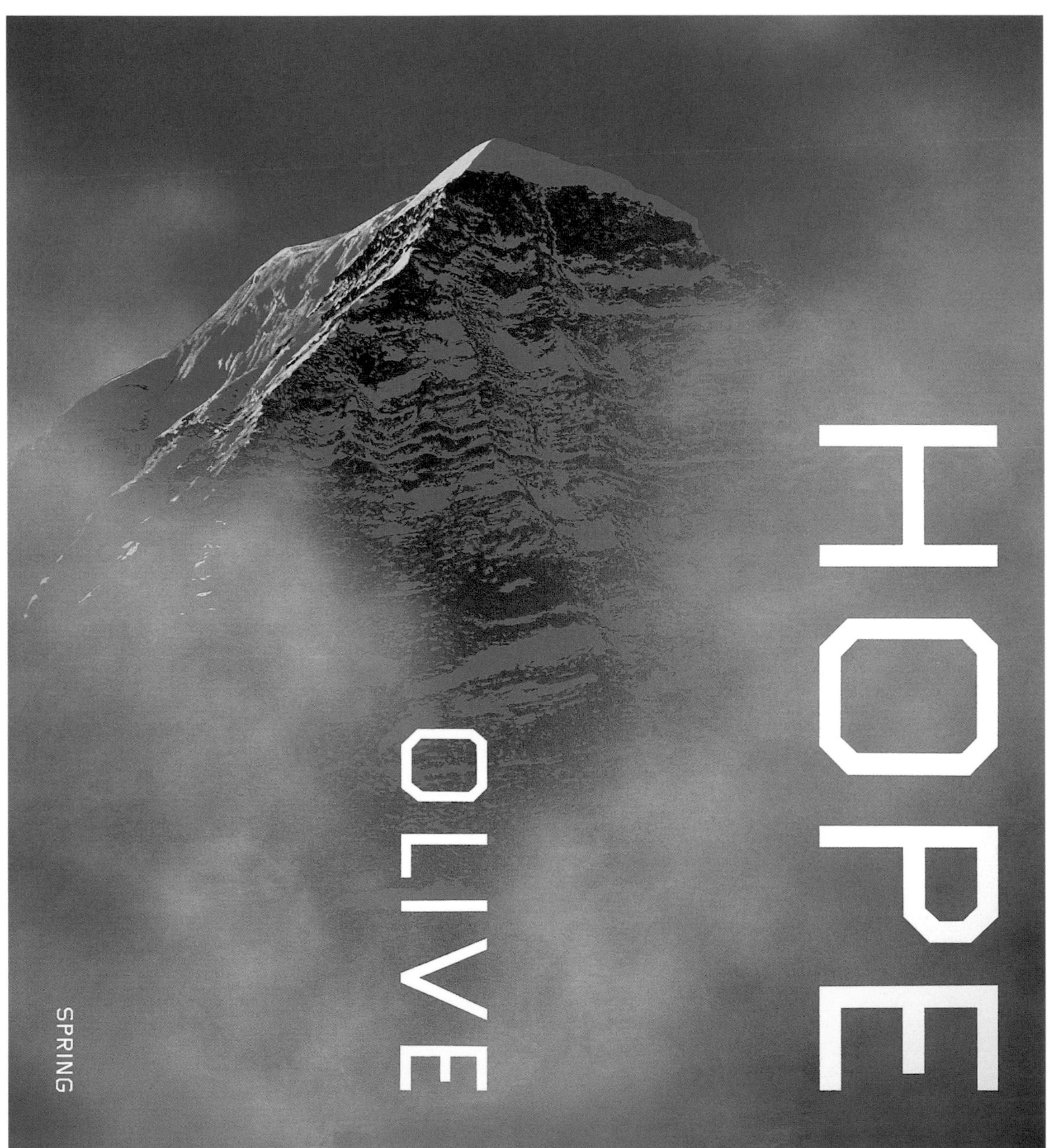

Edward Ruscha

Hope, Olive, Spring

1999

Acrylic on canvas, 72 x 64" (83 x 162 cm)

Courtesy the artist and Gagosian Gallery

PHOTOGRAPHER: Paul Ruscha

Betye Saar
Our Lady of the Shadows
1989

Mixed-media wall assemblage, 14 x 11 x 1"

PHOTOGRAPHER: William Nettles

Judith Schaechter

Girl vs. Mess

1997

Stained glass, 23 x 30"

Collection Marc Connelly

Carolee Schneemann
Mortal Coils
1994–95

Installation view
Slide projectors, motorized mirror systems, motorized manila ropes

Joyce Scott

P-Melon #1

1996

Blown glass and beads, 11 x 14 x 8"

Collection of the artist

PHOTOGRAPHER: Kanui Takeno

Joel Shapiro
Untitled
1998–99

Aluminum and stainless steel,
13' 10" x 14' 5" x 15' 8"
Piazza Barberini, Rome

PHOTOGRAPHER: Mimmo Capone

Cindy Sherman

Untitled

1996

Cibachrome, 58 x 39"

Courtesy the artist and Metro Pictures

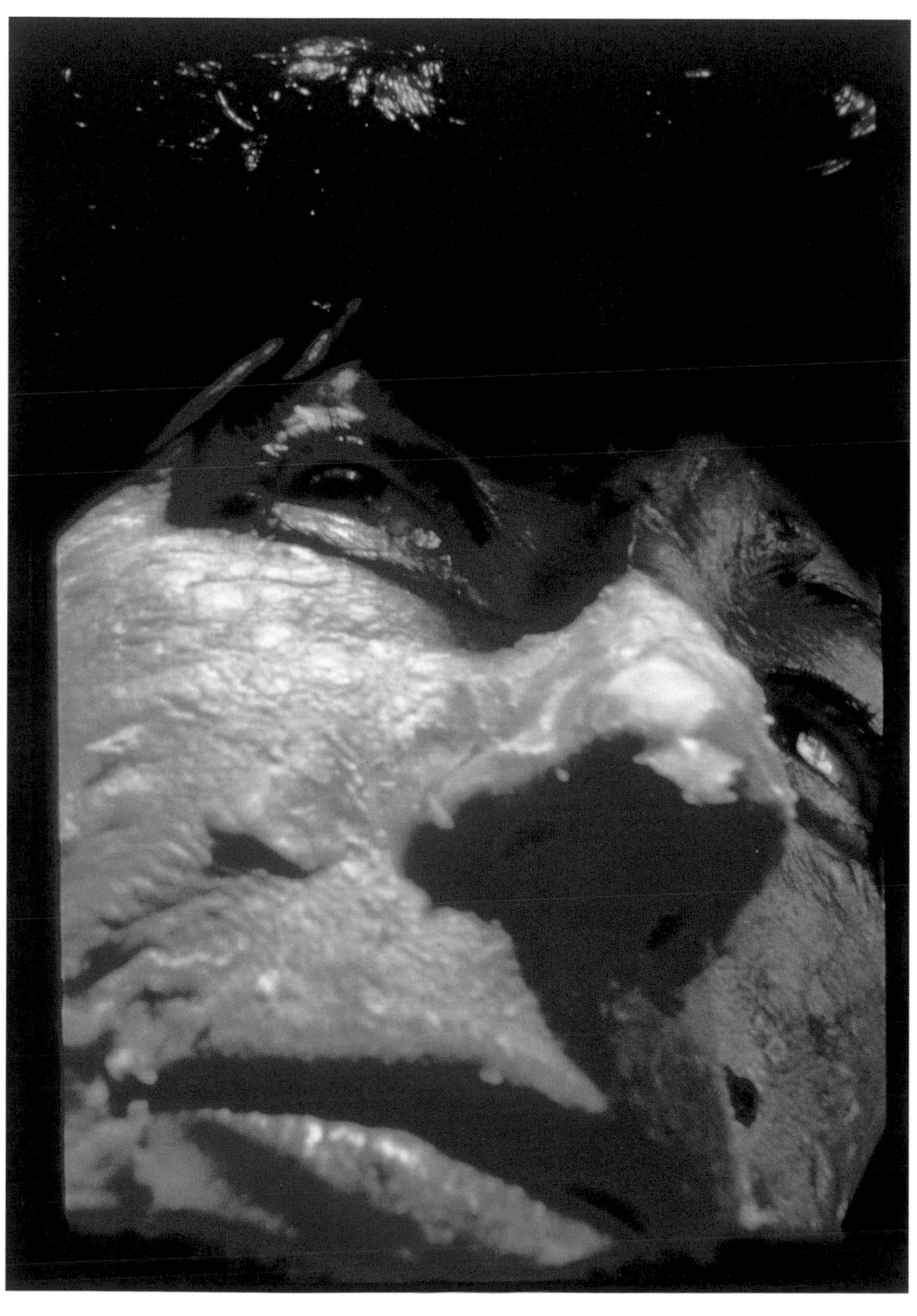

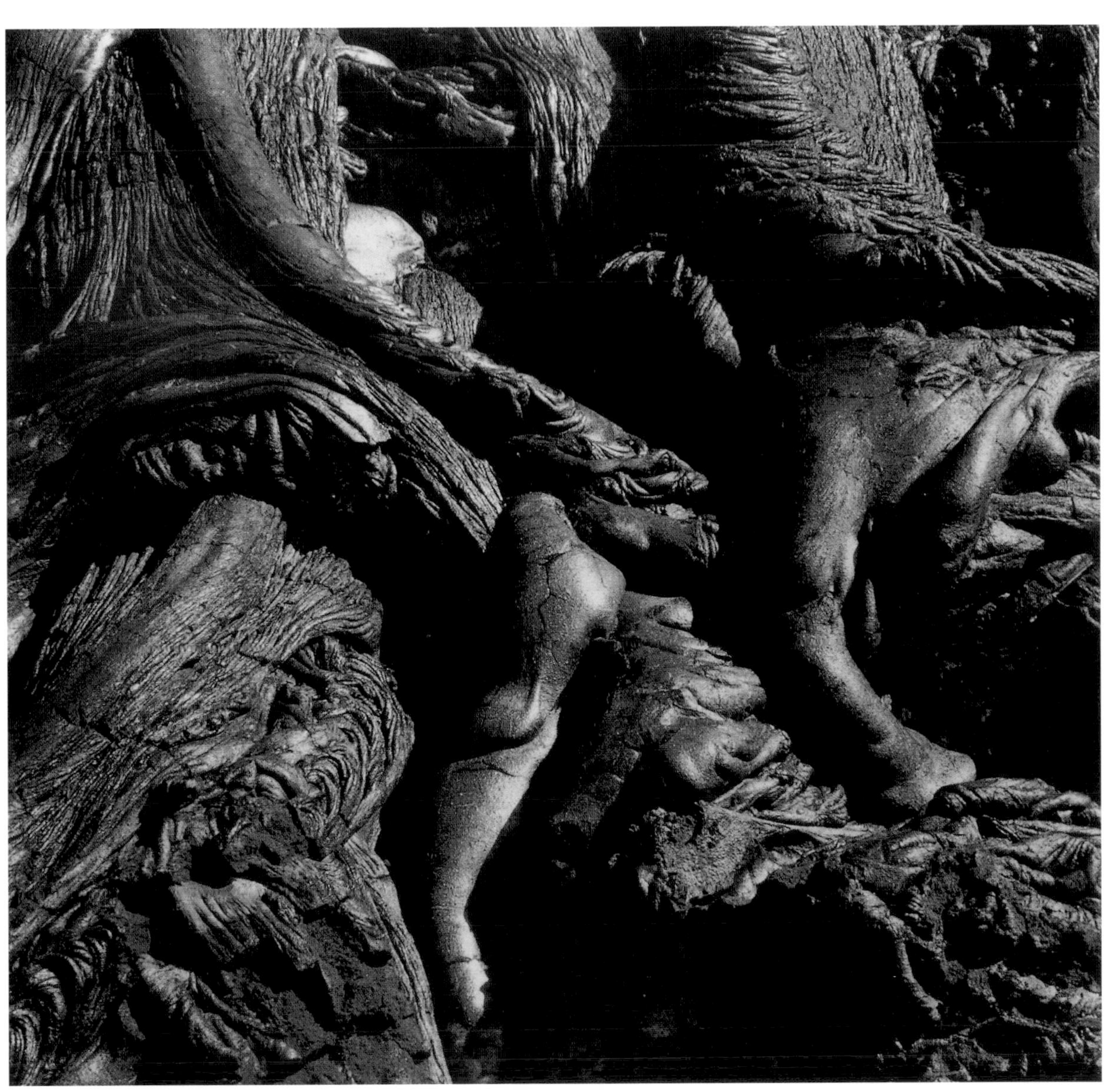

Aaron Siskind
Volcano 69
1980

Gelatin silver print
7 1/4 x 7 1/4"

Courtesy The Center for Creative Photography, The University of Arizona

Alexis Smith

Snake Path

1992

Slate and concrete path,
granite book and bench

Stuart Collection, University of California, San Diego

PHOTOGRAPHER: P. S. Rittermann

Tony Smith
Ten Elements
1975–79

Aluminum, paint, each element approximately 4' high

PHOTOGRAPHER: Geoffrey Clements

Nancy Spero

Ballad von der Judenhure Marie Sanders III (Brecht)
1998

Installation with handprinting on walls
(interior view). Festpielhaus Hellerau, Dresden

PHOTOGRAPHER: Lothar Sprenger

Hiroshi Sugimoto
N. Atlantic Ocean, Cape Breton Island
1996

Black-and-white photograph, 20 x 24"

Courtesy Sonnabend Gallery, New York

Francesc Torres
Primal Pilots
1995

Multimedia installation
Fundacio Antoni Tapies, Barcelona, Spain

James Turrell
Key Lime π
1998

Flourescent light

PHOTOGRAPH: Gerald Zugman

Richard Tuttle

New Mexico, New York, B, #5

1998

Acrylic on fir plywood, 23 1/4 x 24"
(59 x 61 cm)

Courtesy Sperone Westwater, New York

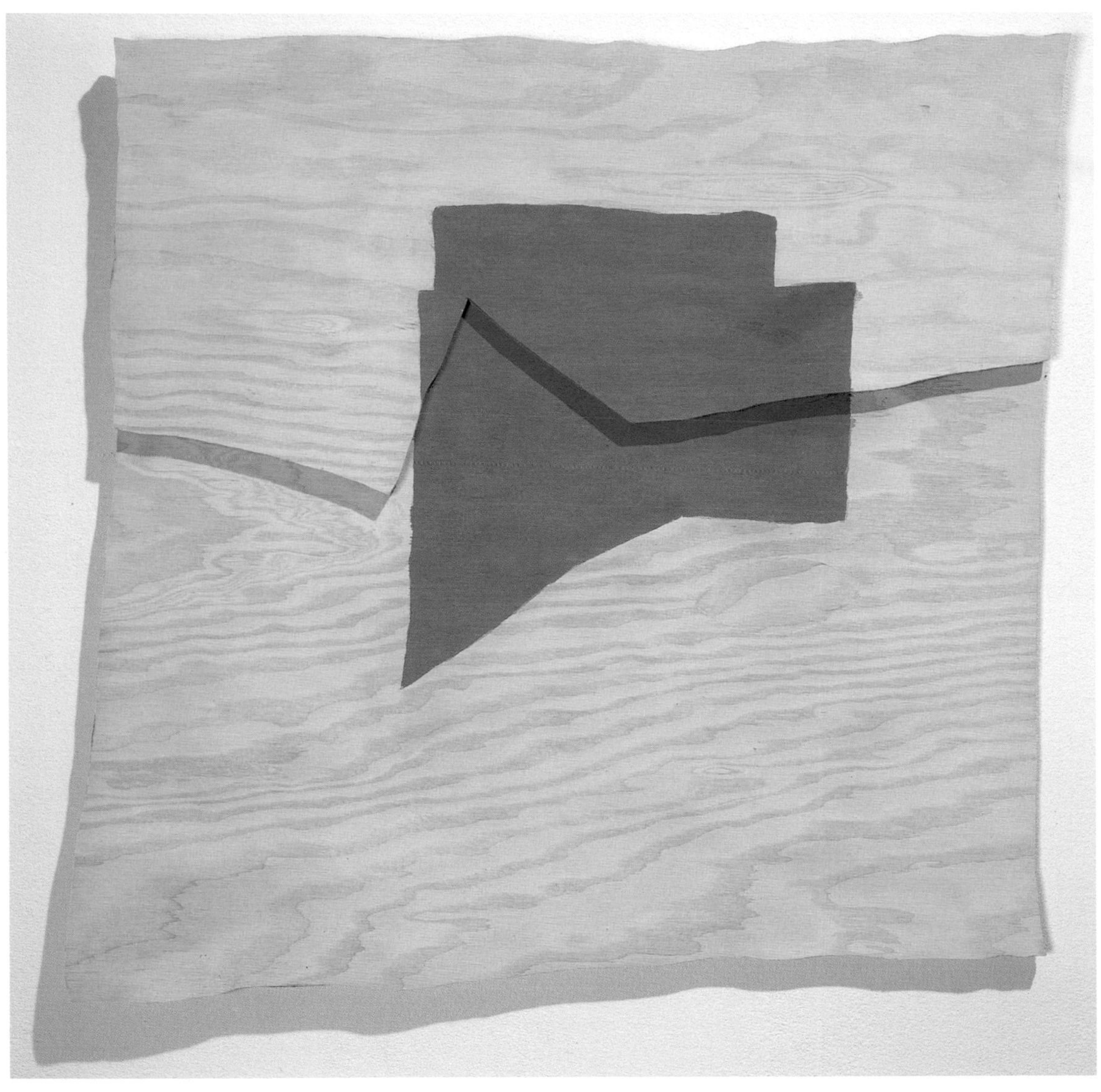

Bill Viola
Room for St. John of the Cross
1983

Video/sound installation, 14 x 24 x 30'

Collection The Museum of Contemporary Art, Los Angeles; The El Paso Natural Gas Company Fund for California Art

PHOTOGRAPHER: Kira Perov

Peter Voulkos

Nemo

1997

Wood-fired stoneware, 43 1/2 x 24" diameter

Private collection

PHOTOGRAPHER: Schopplein Studio

Carrie Mae Weems
Ritual and Revolution
1998

Multimedia installation with sound and 15 digital prints on sheer cloth, various sizes

William Wegman

Hitch

1998

Color Polaroid, 20 x 24"

Lawrence Weiner

Many Colored Objects Placed Side By Side To Form A Row Of Many Colored Objects

1976

Installation Ghent, Belgium

H. C. Westermann

Walnut Death Ship In A Chestnut Box

1974

Copper, chestnut, ebony, walnut, zebrawood,
18 x 25 x 8 1/4"

Collection Joanna Beall Westermann

Courtesy Lennon, Weinberg, Inc., New York

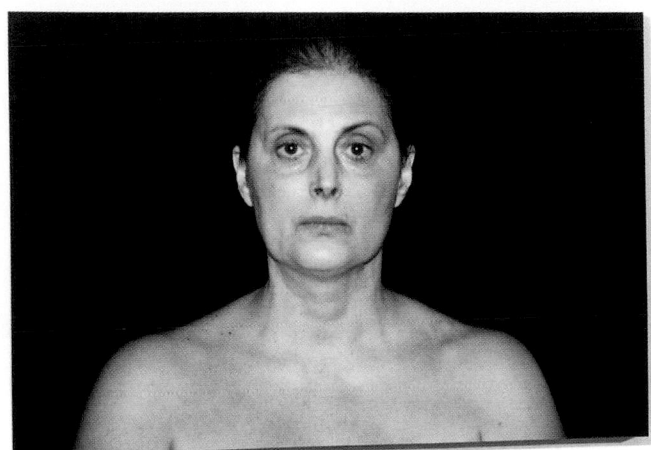

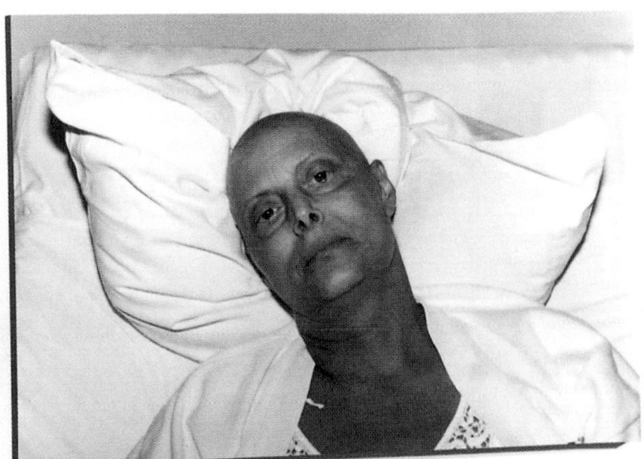

Hannah Wilke
February 20, 1992/August 18, 1992, #7,
from Intra-Venus
1992–93

Chromagenic supergloss prints, 2 panels
47 1/2 x 71 1/2" each

Courtesy Estate of Hannah Wilke and Ronald Feldman Fine Arts, New York

PHOTOGRAPHER: Dennis Cowley

Fred Wilson

Truth Trophy and Pedestals

1992

Detail from Mining the Museum exhibition, the Contemporary Museum, Baltimore

PHOTOGRAPHERS: Marg Connor and Anna Sobaski

Jackie Winsor

Pink and Blue Piece

1985

Mirror, wood, paint, cheesecloth,
31 x 31 x 31"

Courtesy Paula Cooper Gallery, New York

Betty Woodman

Balustrade Vase 97–5

1997

Glazed earthenware, 62 x 58 x 9"

Courtesy of the artist and Max Protetch Gallery, New York

PHOTOGRAPHER: Dennis Cowley

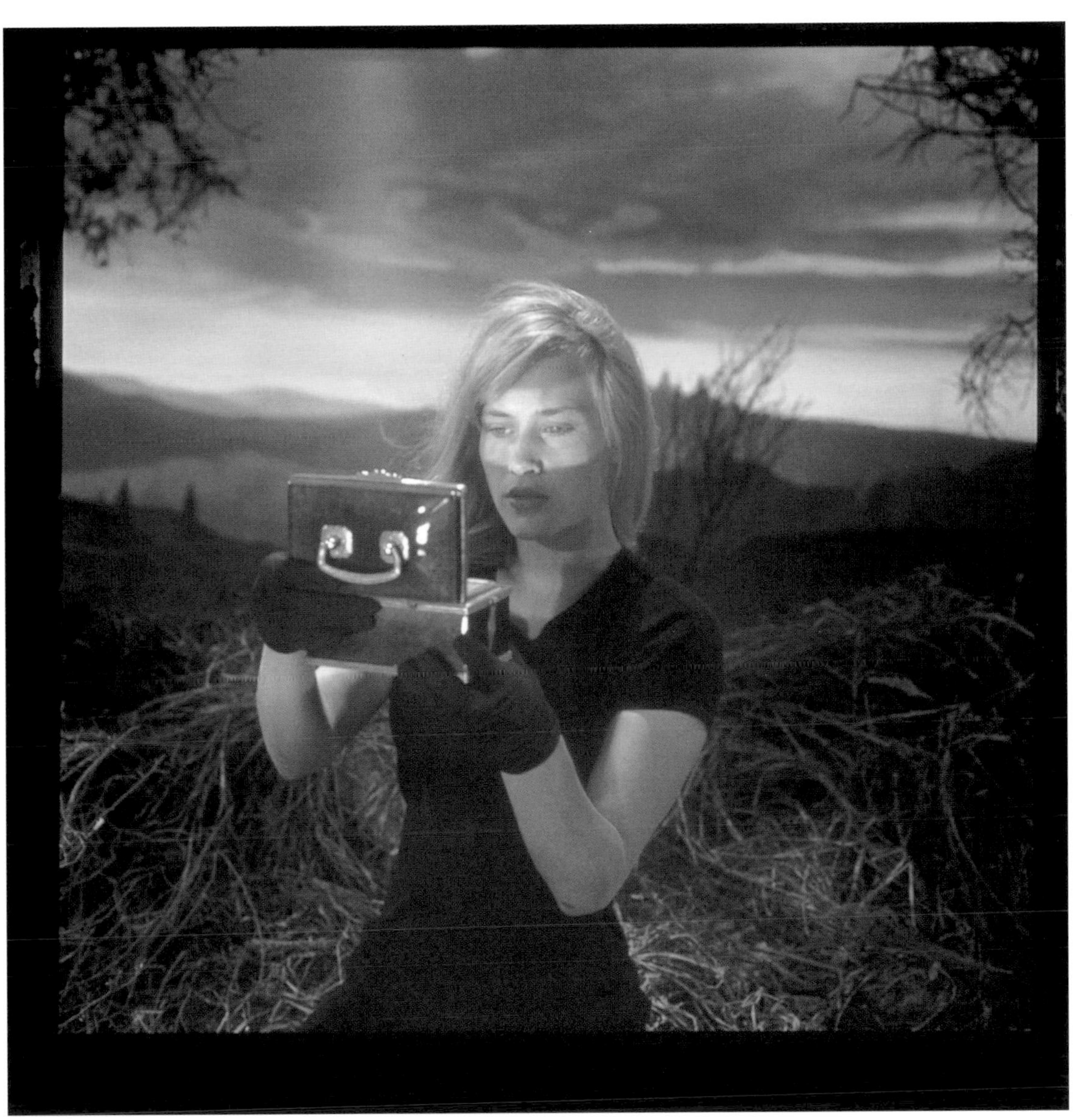

Bruce and Norman Yonemoto
Made In Hollywood
1990

Single-channel video, dimensions variable

Visual Artists' Fellowships

By Jennifer Dowley

Program History

This book is a monument to a nearly thirty-year investment by the United States government in fostering the creative work of thousands of American visual artists. It is a record of the National Endowment for the Arts' Visual Artists' Fellowship Program, which began in 1966, shortly after the Endowment was formed and continued until 1995, when Congress included strictures in the Endowment's appropriations bill prohibiting the awarding of fellowships to visual artists.[1] While the book is a compilation of the history of the Fellowship Program, it is also a portrait of the federal government's commitment to nourishing American culture at its very roots. It documents the policy of the National Endowment for the Arts to foster a strong and diverse cultural legacy by investing in artists so that they might spend time making art. The result, thirty years later, is an extraordinarily diverse and rich portfolio that reveals not only the major art movements of the latter part of the twentieth century but also a tremendously eclectic range of work being created by artists in every corner of the country. This investment in literal terms amounted to $52 million awarded through 6,500 fellowships to about 5,000 artists in the disciplines of painting, sculpture, crafts, works on paper, photography, printmaking, video, performance art, installation work, artists' books, and other visual arts forms.

The intention of this effort to chronicle the Arts Endowment's support of artists is not only to make visible for the first time, in one place, the names of all the fellowship recipients, but also to elucidate the processes that evolved over the decades to select those artists. This book makes available the information needed for more extended public conversations about the overall impact and value of such an investment of public dollars. Specifically, this book contains a listing of all the artists who received a fellowship directly from the National Endowment for the Arts and through the Arts Endowment's Regional Fellowship Program instituted in the early 1980s. It also includes a listing of the panelists who selected the national Visual Artists' Fellowships, and factual information on the numbers of applications, fellowships, and award categories. This compilation not only documents the nature of a major national cultural endeavor, but makes visible and available for analysis what, for many, was a symbol of enlightened support for artists over several decades.

A companion project to this publication is being administered by the National Museum of American Art (NMAA). The Arts Endowment engaged NMAA to make the fellowship recipients' slides originally submitted to the Endowment (Visual Artists' Fellowship Program) for review available on the Internet. Approximately half the artists who received fellowships gave permission for their work to be included. This archive will be maintained and updated by NMAA and may be reached through the Arts Endowment's Internet site: www.arts.gov.

The Concept of Fellowships

While no government can call a great artist or scholar into existence, it is necessary and appropriate for the Federal Government to help create and sustain not only a climate encouraging freedom of thought, imagination and inquiry but also the material conditions facilitating the release of this creative talent." The National Foundation on the Arts and Humanities Act of 1965, Section 951, (7)

From its earliest days, the National Endowment for the Arts made the decision to grant support directly to individual visual artists while committing itself to the support of institutions such as museums, visual artists' working facilities, and art schools. The nature of this direct support to artists was important. These were grants that artists could use in whatever way they saw fit to further their work. These were not grants to support specifically described projects. They were investments in the future work of an artist. Benny Andrews, an artist and Director of the Visual Arts Program (1982–1984) said that "fellowships are as close as you can get to supporting imagination." Fellowships were forward-looking grants based on the potential the artist applicant could demonstrate from work accomplished to date, as evidenced by slides or video and a résumé. This material was reviewed under the lens of "artistic excellence" by ever-changing panels of artists and curators. The selection processes shifted as the years went by, responding to the increase in the numbers of applicants and an ongoing effort to improve the process, but remained essentially the same at the core:

a peer panel review. The Visual Arts Program staff's goal was to create and implement a process that was fair and democratic. While by nature a human and therefore imperfect process, this goal to be fair and democratic inspired modifications to perfect the process over the years.

How It Worked

The fellowships began under the direction of Henry Geldzahler, the first Director of the Visual Arts Program. To select the fellowship recipients, he assembled groups of artists and curators that met in different regions of the country. The panelists brought lists of artists' names to the meeting and the recipients were nominated and selected from these lists. This nomination process was used only for the first three years. Under the subsequent leadership of Brian O'Doherty, the first guidelines were developed and widely distributed in 1973. The program evolved from using nominations to favoring an application process, open to any artist who was a U. S. citizen or permanent resident and who was not a student. As the Chronology following this Essay reveals, the number of applicants steadily increased, reaching a high of more than ten thousand per year in 1981. Between 1973 and 1981, new categories were created to accommodate the kind of work that artists were submitting to the program. "Printmaking" was created in 1974 and then eliminated as an independent category in 1978, only to re-emerge again in 1982 as "Printmaking/Drawing/Artists Books" and to change to "Works on Paper" in 1991. "Conceptual/Performance" was added in 1976 and became "Conceptual/Performance/New Genres" in 1982, evolving in 1989 to "New Genres," and "Other Genres" in 1993.

During the program's earliest days, there were no separate categories for different art forms—the fellowships were known simply as "Artists' Fellowships." It is interesting to note that the first specific discipline categories to be established were for photography in 1971 and crafts two years later. This designation signaled the Endowment's commitment to embracing all disciplines in the visual arts, not just painting and sculpture, which always attracted the largest number of applicants. Neither of these categories (photography or crafts) was renamed over the subsequent years of the Program. It must not go unnoticed that photography and crafts, art forms that evoked controversy in and of themselves in the world of the visual arts, were recognized as categories of their own early on, and by 1983 they had achieved a financial weight in fellowship size equal to that of painting and sculpture.

"Video" emerged in 1975 as a genre that was welcomed to the "Artists' Fellowship" category. In 1980, Video became a distinct category that was co-funded by the Endowment's Media Arts Program, and it awarded fifty-one fellowships: sixteen at $10,000 and thirty-five at $3,000. It maintained its own category through 1983, after which it was subsumed into "Conceptual/Performance /New Genres" in 1985.

1982 was an important year in the development of the Fellowship Program. That year saw the reorganization of the applications into the six disciplines that were to define the program for the rest of its existence: Painting, Sculpture, Printmaking/Drawing/Artists Books, Photography, Crafts, and Conceptual/Performance/New Genres. While Video retained its status as a separate category for another two years before merging with Conceptual/Performance/New Genres, these six categories defined the structure of the program for the next thirteen years. Because of impending budget cutbacks, a two-year cycle was instituted: Painting, Printmaking/Drawing/Artists Books, and Conceptual/Performance/New Genres were reviewed one year, and Sculpture, Photography, and Crafts the next, alternating until the program's end. There were approximately five thousand applications per year after 1982. The program was managed by two full-time staff members, augmented during panel season by several interns, as well as five or six people from the permanent staff of the Visual Arts Program. The size of the award was increased to $20,000 in 1991 under Director Susan Lubosky Talbot, and remained at that level for the remainder of the program.

The Regional Programs

The Regional Fellowship Program was initiated in 1983 by Leonard Hunter, Assistant Director, (1980–83), and then championed by Benny Andrews, Director of the Visual Arts Program (1982–84). The intention of this program was to extend support for visual artists throughout the country via a regionally-based mechanism that would inevitably reach more artists than a Washington-based federal system ever could. The result over the years was the development of a two-tiered structure for visual artists in which a painter, for example, could apply one year for a national fellowship and the next year for a regional fellowship. The regional fellowships were administered by the regional arts agencies established during the mid-1970s with large annual grants from the Visual Arts Program at the Arts Endowment.[2] It took until 1990 for all six regions to join the effort, and until 1992 for all six to offer all the categories in alternating years. By then artists living anywhere in the country, working in any medium, could apply every year for a fellowship, either at the national or regional level. The program had two grant levels, one awarded nationally in Washington at $20,000, and one at the regional level at $5,000. This structure was seen by the NEA and by the various policy panels that advised the program over the years as the appropriate culmination of several decades of effort to implement what the Arts Endowment's original legislation called for: creating "the material conditions facilitating the release of . . . creative talent" in the visual arts. This two-tiered structure continued for three years until the fellowship program was terminated.

Decision Making

How the fellowship decisions were made has been the subject of much speculation. I had the honor of assembling and chairing three Fellowship panels during the spring of 1995 before the program ended. We spent a great deal of time assembling the panels. We worked with a complex matrix, bringing aesthetic, cultural, ethnic, and geographic diversity to the process. By the time I arrived at the Endowment, a tradition had been in place to form panels that would include several artists, usually former fellowship recipients, one curator, and one layperson (someone who did not make his or her living from the arts). Since the early 1980s, an effort was made to engage a panelist only once,[3] thereby constantly circulating the decision-making process so that it was freshly constituted at its core every year. The autonomy and integrity of this citizens' panel review was essential. It was equally essential that the panel change in composition every year to maintain a lively and democratic currency that reflected the changing notions of aesthetic quality with which the art world was wrestling.

Jim Melchert and Leonard Hunter, respectively Director (1977–81) and Assistant Director of the Visual Arts Program (1980–83), were key players in devising a voting system that brought a high degree of integrity to the review process and made manageable an undertaking fraught with the potential for chaos. By the time they came to the Endowment, the number of annual applications was enormous in some categories: three thousand in painting, and two thousand in sculpture. The sheer quantity of slides (at ten per applicant from 1981 onward) was daunting. The process they established in 1980 remained intact for fifteen years until the end of the program, with constant adjustments being made to fine-tune the process and respond to panelists' suggestions for improvements.

Applications were received at the Arts Endowment several months before the panel meetings, thus permitting the staff to process paperwork and organize slides from between five thousand to ten thousand applications. The panelists arrived to spend five days in a darkened room, working by the light of five projectors shooting images onto a large horizontal screen. After a brief orientation by the staff outlining the review criteria and the voting process, the work began.

During Round One, the initial review, staff announced the applicant's name and then projected two sets of five slides on the screen for a total of fifteen to twenty seconds for all ten slides. There was no conversation among the panelists, just quiet, intense looking and the marking of ballots. The panelists had been instructed that the sole criterion for their decision making was "artistic excellence and artistic merit." They scored their ballots and as their patterns of voting became evident, staff ascertained a logical cut-off point. About fifty percent of the artists were eliminated in this first round.

The staff worked into the evenings re-loading slide trays for the remaining artists to be reviewed during Round Two. Slides were projected again for the panel's review. Again there was no discussion, and voting continued in silence. This time, however, staff read information about one of the slides on the screen, including the artist's name, the date, size, and medium of the image. Another substantial number of artists was eliminated at this stage.

Round Three began on the fourth day. Slides of artists still contending were reloaded and shown yet again. This time there was discussion among the panelists focusing not only on "excellence" but also on the applicant's "record of professional activity and achievement." A staff member gave a brief summary of an artist's biographical highlights as his or her slides were shown, and read the artist's statement from the application, but voting continued individually and in silence.

Round Four began on the fifth and final day with the staff presenting the list of remaining artists in ranked order according to the panelists' votes. The panel went over the list three or four times, raising hands to vote for an artist to receive a fellowship, with a majority carrying the decision. These final rounds elicited intense conversation among the panelists. This was also when the third criterion came into full play: "whether the applicant's work reflects a serious continued investigation of important or significant aesthetic concerns and a potential for further artistic development during the proposed fellowship period."

The panelists' understanding of what was at stake for the artists under consideration was acute, making the final moments all the more charged. Richard Andrews, Director (1985–87) put it well: "So few fellowships could be awarded (about two percent of the total number of applicants) that there was always much anguish on the part of panelists, as the final recommendations were tallied. Part of the concern stemmed from the feeling that the process, no matter how well administered, was inherently imperfect, as the panelists' understanding of an artist's work rested on the ability of photographic slides to convey image, scale, and material, to say nothing of light, performance, or new technologies. But the bulk of the distress arose from a very genuine concern for the artists' struggle to create and the belief that, somehow, the vitality of artmaking so evident in the slides would be nourished and encouraged by fellowship support."

For the record, it should be noted that it was the job of the Visual Arts Director and all other staff to facilitate the discussion and not to proffer opinions. To my knowledge, that neutral stance was upheld throughout the decades. In fact, in one case, the Director would actually leave the room so as to be entirely removed when the final decisions were made by the panelists. This hands-off stance by the staff was important. Our energy was invested in researching and appointing the panel, as well as in encouraging applications. After that, the process took over and we became stewards of what had been created. The Director's job was to facilitate the panelists' discussion so that it focused on the review criteria and stayed true to the highest level of debate. The Director was also responsible for creating a forum within which all views could be expressed. It was out of this lively, intense, and frequently highly creative environment that fellowship decisions were made. The final step in the decision making process was review by the National Council on the Arts, a presidentially by appointed body, and by the Chairman of the Arts Endowment.

One interesting aspect of the program was that there was no firm number of fellowships or budget allocation given to any panel. The focus of the panel was entirely qualitative, and not influenced by the funds available. There was a total budget for all three fellowship panels each year: for example, $2 million in 1994 for one hundred fellowships at $20,000 each, but they could be spread over the three categories in any way the panelists decided. Curiously, this rather mysterious financial allocation process worked unerringly with no problem for many years.

Application Forms

Years of advice from panels resulted in revised application forms so that only the most critical information was presented with the least burden possible put on the artist. Application forms were designed to meet the minimum requirements placed on any government agency, and the panelists' need for enough information to adequately evaluate the requests for support. This included basic biographical information, educational background, and brief exhibition histories, all contained on a simple one-page form. The most important part of the application was the slides and these were accompanied by a list giving date, title, medium, and dimensions, as well as a short statement describing the work. Project descriptions were not requested, since the nature of a fellowship was an open-ended investment in an artist's ongoing creative work. During the last five years of the program, however, the form included a question that asked how the applicant would see his or her "work being advanced by this fellowship." This request was added as a result of increased scrutiny from Congress as to the tangible results of fellowship support for individual artists. Panelists, however, tended to retain their focus on the slides as the measure for final decisions.

Grant Amounts

Grant amounts fluctuated during the course of the Fellowship Program, increasing every few years, mainly to keep pace with inflation. The principal grant amount ranged from $5,000 in 1967, to $20,000 in 1995. Tiered grant amounts were introduced in 1974, intended to reflect stages of artists' careers, variously characterized as emerging, mid-career, and established. With the institution of the two-year application cycle in 1983–84, a three-level grant amount system was introduced, with the highest, $25,000, reserved for a very limited number of established artists who had long careers and had made substantial contributions to the visual arts field as a whole. This exercise was abandoned after three application cycles. It was felt that this hierarchy of achievement was not easily ascertained for the large pool of artists under consideration. Beginning with the 1991-92 cycle, as described earlier, national fellowships were awarded at a single level of $20,000, while regional fellowships were awarded at $5,000.

Policy Issues

All of the changes in categories, the shifts in grant amounts, the nuances in language and changes in the application form came about after significant consultation with the field. Staff were constantly traveling both to promote and explain the program to constituents, and to listen to their comments. The panelists played a key role in advising staff on improving its practices. Major decisions were undertaken after consultation with Policy Panels (later known as Overview Panels), comprised of professionals from the visual arts field. Participants had to have served on selection panels in the year or two immediately prior. These were intense two-day meetings where the pros and cons of various issues were thrashed out. Panelists' input was taken seriously by the staff, giving them the momentum and justification to carry ideas forward into more formal policy decisions and practices. One of the axioms of the Arts Endowment was to be open to the voice of practice, the reality of life in the studio, gallery, and museum. Staff saw themselves as conveners and collectors of information on an ongoing basis, drawing directly from the places where the real cultural work was being created. This information and advice was the oxygen that breathed life into policy. For decades, the priority of the Visual Arts Program was artists' fellowships, and this priority was affirmed year after year by Policy panelists, staff, and the National Council on the Arts.

The End

In July 1995 the decision was made by Congress to eliminate the fellowship funding not only for visual artists but for choreographers, playwrights, museum professionals, composers, and solo performance artists. The only funding remaining after 1995 for individuals was for Literature Fellowships and awards for lifetime achievements: Heritage Fellowships in the Folk and Traditional Arts and American Jazz Masters Fellowships. The impact of the loss of the fellowships to visual artists has been far-reaching and yet to be really understood. Symbolically, the loss of the federal government's interest in its own creative citizens struck hard at artists' morale, particularly among the younger generation. In real terms, the lack of Arts Endowment money stimulating the creation of new work that was not dependent on the market place has literally meant that many artists have not had the resources to develop new work. Curators have not had access to new work for exhibitions and in some cases have had to forego an intended project, or in other cases, have raised funds privately to provide the artist with the means to create the work. Another consequence of the loss of fellowships is the inability of the Arts Endowment to target quality work being created outside the mainstream art market place, which is confined to the major American cities. The fellowship program was a kind of antidote against the art market's inevitable geographic myopia—looking out for the broader national cultural interests.

The Arts Endowment is now on the cusp of new growth and expansion. It is to be hoped that this growth will bring a newly considered and strengthened role for direct federal support of visual artists. Perhaps this documentation of the thirty-year accomplishment of the Visual Artists' Fellowships will provide fertile ground for thinking about the government's impact on the lives and work of artists and its potential to create an environment that is conducive to the best in imaginative thinking among America's visual artists. As the new century unfolds and distance from the cultural turbulence of the past ten years is gained, a clearer understanding of the important role artists play in maintaining a healthy democracy and in cultivating what it means to be an American will surely be possible.

[1] Section 328 (1) of Public Law 104-134, April 26, 1996 reads: "The Chairperson shall only award a grant to an individual if such grant is awarded to such individual for a literature fellowship, national Heritage Fellowship or American Jazz Masters Fellowship."

[2] The Regional Arts Organizations were established by cooperating state arts agencies and by the Arts Endowment. They are: Arts Midwest in Minneapolis, Mid-Atlantic Arts Foundation in Baltimore, Mid-America Arts Alliance in Kansas City, New England Foundation for the Arts in Boston, Southern Arts Federation in Atlanta, and Western States Arts Federation, located at the time in Santa Fe.

[3] Out of a total of 521 fellowship panelists, forty (seven percent) served more than once. Of those, thirty-one served twice, six served three times, and three served four times. After 1980, no one was appointed as a fellowship panelist if he or she had served in that capacity before.

Chronology

The National Endowment for the Arts

Visual Artists' Fellowships

Note: The original fellowship category "Artists" encompassed all visual art media. Over time, sub-categories were implemented, in order to enhance peer panel expertise. Sub-categories often evolved into separate categories and, in some cases, there was fluctuation back and forth between category and sub-category status. Categories for new art forms were often grouped together. Finally, names given to certain categories changed over time, such as when Printmaking/Drawing/Artists' Books became Works on Paper or Conceptual/Performance/Video became New Genres and finally Other Genres.

1967

Artists Fellowships	60
Grant Amount	$5,000
Total funds awarded	$300,000

Applications by nomination only

FELLOWSHIP SELECTION PANELISTS John Denman, collector, Seattle WA.; Martin Friedman, curator/director, Walker Art Center, Minneapolis, MN.; Edward Henning, curator, Cleveland Art Museum, Cleveland, OH.; Walter Hopps, curator/director, Pasadena Art Museum, Pasadena, CA.; John Humphrey, curator, Museum of Modern Art, San Francisco, CA.; Richard Hunt, artist, Chicago, IL.; Robert Motherwell, artist, New York, NY.; Barbara Rose, critic, New York, NY.; George Segal, artist, New Brunswick, NJ.

1968

Artists Fellowships	29
Grant Amount	$5,000
Total funds awarded	$145,000

Applications by nomination only

FELLOWSHIP SELECTION PANELISTS Edward Bryant, teacher, University of Kentucky, Lexington, KY.; James Byrnes, curator/director, Delgado Museum, New Orleans, LA.; James Camp, teacher, University of South Florida, Tampa, FL.; Van Deren Coke, curator, University of New Mexico, Albuquerque, NM.; Donald Goodall, teacher, University of Texas, Austin, TX.; Benjamin Williams, curator, North Carolina Museum, Raleigh, NC.

1969

Artists Fellowships	30
Grant Amount	$5,000
Total funds awarded	$150,000

Applications by nomination only

FELLOWSHIP SELECTION PANELISTS Richard Bellamy, curator, Goldowsky Gallery, New York, NY.; Henry Hopkins, curator/director, Los Angeles County Museum of Art, Los Angeles, CA.; Hilton Kramer, critic, New York, NY.; Frank Stella, artist, New York, NY.; Virginia Wright, collector, Seattle, WA.

1970

No fellowships awarded

1971

Artists Fellowships	20
Photography Fellowships	23
Fellowships awarded	43
Grant Amount, Artists	$7,500
Grant Amount, Photography	$750–4,000
Total funds awarded	$197,000

Open applications and by nomination

FELLOWSHIP SELECTION PANELISTS, ARTISTS James Camp, teacher, University of South Florida, Tampa, FL.; Sam Gilliam, artist, Washington, DC.; James Melchert, artist, University of California, Berkeley, CA.; William Seitz, curator/director, Rose Museum, Brandeis University, Waltham, MA.; James Speyer, curator/director, Art Institute of Chicago, Chicago, IL.

FELLOWSHIP SELECTION PANELISTS, PHOTOGRAPHY Van Deren Coke, curator, University of New Mexico, Albuquerque, NM.; Alan Fern, curator, Library of Congress, Washington, DC.; John Szarkowski, curator, Museum of Modern Art, New York, NY.

1972

No fellowships awarded

1973

Artists Fellowships	45
Crafts Fellowships	34
Photography Fellowships	60
Fellowships awarded	139
Grant amount, Artists	$7,500
Grant amount, Crafts	$3,000
Grant amount, Photography	$1,200–5,000
Total funds awarded	$657,200
Open applications	

FELLOWSHIP SELECTION PANELISTS, ARTISTS Van Deren Coke, curator, University of New Mexico, Albuquerque, NM.; James Demetrion, curator/director, Des Moines Art Center, Des Moines, IA.; Mel Edwards, artist, New York, NY.; Ted Potter, curator/director, Southeastern Center for Contemporary Art, Winston-Salem, NC.; Stephen Prokopoff, curator/director, Museum of Contemporary Art, Chicago, IL.; Wayne Thiebaud, artist, San Francisco, CA.

FELLOWSHIP SELECTION PANELISTS, CRAFTS James Melchert, artist, University of California, Berkeley, CA.; Rose Slivka, critic/curator, American Crafts Council, New York, NY.; Peter Voulkos, artist, San Francisco, CA.

FELLOWSHIP SELECTION PANELISTS, PHOTOGRAPHY Peter Bunnell, curator/director, Princeton Museum, Princeton, NJ.; Alan Fern, curator, Library of Congress, Washington, DC.; Michael Hoffman, editor, Aperture, New York, NY.; Aaron Siskind, artist, Providence, RI.; John Szarkowski, curator, Museum of Modern Art, New York, NY.

1974

Artists Fellowships	144 from 2,627 applicants
Crafts Fellowships	50 from 649 applicants
Prints Fellowships	30 from 299 applicants
Fellowships awarded	224 from 3,575 applicants
Grant amount, Artists	$1,000, $3,000, $7,500
Grant amount, Crafts	$3,000
Grant amount, Prints	$3,000
Total funds awarded	$920,000
Open applications	

FELLOWSHIP SELECTION PANELISTS, ARTISTS Fred Barzyk, curator/director, WGBH, Boston, MA.; Mel Edwards, artist, New York, NY.; Barbara Haskell, curator, Pasadena Art Museum, Pasadena, CA.; Henry Hopkins, curator/director, Museum of Modern Art, San Francisco, CA.; Richard Hunt, artist, Chicago, IL.; Peter Plagens, artist/critic, Los Angeles, CA.; Ted Potter, curator/director, Southeast Center for Contemporary Art, Winston-Salem, NC.; George Segal, artist, New Brunswick, NJ.; Diane Waldman, curator, Guggenheim Museum, New York, NY.

FELLOWSHIP SELECTION PANELISTS, CRAFTS William Brown, curator/director, Penland School, Penland, NC.; Lois Moran, editor, American Craft Council, New York, NY. Ronald Pearson, artist, Haystack Mountain School of Crafts, Deer Isle, ME.

FELLOWSHIP SELECTION PANELISTS, PRINTS Alan Fern, curator, Library of Congress, Washington, DC.; Una Johnson, curator/critic, New York, NY.; Louise Nevelson, artist, New York, NY.

1975

Artists Fellowships (including sub-category for Video)	135 from 1,865 applicants
Crafts Fellowships	47 from 759 applicants
Photography Fellowships	50 from 1,616 applicants
Prints Fellowships	25 from 270 applicants
Fellowships awarded	257 from 4,510 applicants
Grant amount, Artists	$2,000, $3,000, $4,000, $8,000
Grant amount, Crafts	$5,000
Grant amount, Photography	$5,000
Grant amount, Prints	$3,000
Total funds awarded	$1,155,000
Open applications	

FELLOWSHIP SELECTION PANELISTS, ARTISTS Richard Hunt, artist, Chicago, IL.; Robert Irwin, artist, Venice, CA.; Robert Murdock, curator, Dallas Museum, Dallas, TX.; Richard Kevorkian, artist/teacher, Virginia Commonwealth University, Richmond, VA.; Richard Koshalek, curator/director, Fort Worth Art Museum, Fort Worth, TX.; Robert Morris, artist, New York, NY.; Marcia Tucker, curator, Whitney Museum of American Art, New York, NY.

FELLOWSHIP SELECTION PANELISTS, VIDEO Russell Connor, curator/director, Cable Arts Foundation, New York, NY.; Joseph Kosuth, artist, New York, NY.; David Ross, curator, Long Beach Museum of Art, Long Beach, CA.; Stan Vanderbeek, artist/teacher, University of South Florida, Tampa, FL.

FELLOWSHIP SELECTION PANELISTS, CRAFTS Hazel Bray, curator, Oakland Museum, Oakland, CA.; Nilda Getty, artist, Fort Collins, CO, Francis Merritt, curator, Haystack Mountain School of Crafts, Deer Isle, ME.

FELLOWSHIP SELECTION PANELISTS, PHOTOGTAPHY Robert Adams, artist, Longmont, CO.; Peter Bunnell, curator/director, Princeton Museum, Princeton, NJ.; Judy Dater, artist, San Anselmo, CA.; Fred Parker, curator, Friends of Photography, Carmel, CA.; John Szarkowski, curator, Museum of Modern Art, New York, NY.

FELLOWSHIP SELECTION PANELISTS, PRINTS Alan Fern, curator, Library of Congress, Washington, DC.; Vincent Longo, artist, New York, NY.; Elke Solomon, curator, Whitney Museum of American Art, New York, NY.

1976

Artists Fellowships *(including sub-categories for Conceptual/ Performance and Video*	152 from 3,308 applicants
Crafts Fellowships	60 from 1,626 applicants
Photography Fellowships	41 from 1,545 applicants
Prints Fellowships	8 from 499 applicants
Fellowships awarded	261 from 6,978 applicants
Grant amount, Artists	$2,000, $5,000, $10,000
Grant amount, Crafts	$5,000
Grant amount, Photography	$7,500
Grant amount, Prints	$3,000
Total funds awarded	$1,202,500

Open applications

FELLOWSHIP SELECTION PANELISTS, ARTISTS Robert Ellis, artist, Albuquerque, NM, Robert Irwin, artist, Venice, CA.; John Neff, curator, Detroit Institute of Arts, Detroit, MI, Philip Pearlstein, artist, New York, NY.; Dorothea Rockburne, artist, New York, NY.; Gudmund Vigtel, curator/ director, High Museum of Art, Atlanta, GA.

FELLOWSHIP SELECTION PANELISTS, CONCEPTUAL/PERFORMANCE Eleanor Antin, artist, Solana Beach, CA.; Joseph Kosuth, artist, New York, NY.; Jane Livingston, curator, Corcoran Gallery, Washington, DC.; Kynaston McShine, curator, Museum of Modern Art, New York, NY.

FELLOWSHIP SELECTION PANELISTS, VIDEO Fred Barzyk, curator/director, WGBH, Boston, MA.; Jack Boulton, curator/director, Contemporary Arts Center, Cincinnati, OH, Ed Emshwiller, artist, Wantaugh, NY.; David Ross, curator, Long Beach Museum of Art, Long Beach, CA.

FELLOWSHIP SELECTION PANELISTS,CRAFTS Robert Hart, administrator, Bureau of Indian Affairs, Washington, DC.; David Hanks, curator,Philadelphia Museum of Art, Philadelphia, PA.; Wilhelmina Godfrey, artist, Buffalo, NY.; Ruth Kohler, curator, Kohler Art Center, Sheboygan, WI, Harrison McIntosh, artist, Claremont, CA.

FELLOWSHIP SELECTION PANELISTS, PHOTOGRAPHY Thomas Garver, curator, Fine Arts Museums, San Francisco, CA.; Jonathan Green, artist/teacher, MIT, Aperture, New York, NY.; Kenneth Josephson, artist/teacher,Art Institute of Chicago, Chicago, IL.; Anne Noggle, artist/curator, Fine Arts Museums, San Francisco, CA.; John Szarkowski, curator, Museum of Modern Art, New York, NY.

FELLOWSHIP SELECTION PANELISTS, PRINTS Robert Johnson, curator, Fine Arts Museums, San Francisco, CA.; William Lieberman, curator,Museum of Modern Art, New York, NY.; Vincent Longo, artist, New York, NY.

1977

Artists Fellowships *(including sub-categories for Conceptual/ Performance, Prints, and Video)*	110 from 3,000 applicants
Crafts Fellowships	58 from 1,192 applicants
Photography Fellowships	40 from 1,356 applicants
Fellowships awarded	208 from 5,548 applicants
Grant amount, Artists	$3,000, $7,500, $10,000
Grant amount, Crafts	$5,000
Grant amount, Photography	$7,500
Total funds awarded	$1,313,500

Open applications

FELLOWSHIP SELECTION PANELISTS, ARTISTS Jackie Ferrara, artist, New York, NY.; Robert Murdock, curator, Dallas Museum of Art, Dallas, TX, John Neff, curator, Detroit Institute of Arts, Detroit, MI, Jim Roche, artist, Tallahassee, FL, Joan Snyder, artist, New York, NY.; William Wiley, artist, Forest Knolls, CA.

FELLOWSHIP SELECTION PANELISTS, CONCEPTUAL/PERFORMANCE Scott Burton, artist, New York, NY.; Robert Cumming, artist, Orange, CA.; Jane Livingston, curator, Corcoran Gallery, Washington, DC, Prints, Robert Johnson, curator, Fine Arts Museums, San Francisco, CA.; William Lieberman, curator, Museum of Modern Art, New York, NY.; Vincent Longo, artist, New York, NY.; Robert Rauschenberg, artist, New York, NY.

FELLOWSHIP SELECTION PANELISTS, PRINTS Robert Johnson, curator, Fine Arts Museum, San Francisco, CA.; William Lieberman, curator, Museum of Modern Art, New York, NY.; Vincent Longo, artist, New York, NY.; Robert Rauschenberg, artist, New York, NY

FELLOWSHIP SELECTION PANELISTS, VIDEO Jack Boulton, curator, International Exhibitions/AFA, Washington, DC, Howard Fried, artist, San Francisco, CA.; David Loxton, curator/director, WNET, New York, NY.; Olivia Tappan, curator, WGBH, Boston, MA

FELLOWSHIP SELECTION PANELISTS, CRAFTS John Cederquist, artist, Capistrano, CA.; Marion Heard, administrator, Arrowmont School, Gatlinburg, TN, Stanley Lechtzin, artist/teacher, Tyler School of Art, Philadelphia, PA, Warren MacKenzie, artist, Stillwater, MN.; Scott O'Dell, curator, Smithsonian Institution, Washington, DC.; Alice Parrot, artist, Santa Fe, NM

FELLOWSHIP SELECTION PANELISTS, PHOTOGRAPHY John Bullard, curator/director, New Orleans Museum of Art, New Orleans, LA, Carroll Hartwell, curator, Minneapolis Institute of Arts, Minneapolis, MN, Nathan Lyons, artist/admin., Visual Studies Workshop, Rochester, NY.; Margery Mann, artist/critic, Davis, CA.; Garry Winogrand, artist, Austin, TX.

1978

Artists Fellowships	
Fellowships (including sub-categories for Conceptual/Performance, Prints, and Video)	127 from 3,683 applicants
Crafts Fellowships	41 from 1,421 applicants
Photography Fellowships	39 from 1,701 applicants
Fellowships awarded	207 from 6,805 applicants
Grant amount, Artists	$3,000, $7,500, $10,000
Grant amount, Crafts	$7,500
Grant amount, Photography	$7,500
Total funds awarded	$1,364,000
Open applications	

FELLOWSHIP SELECTION PANELISTS, ARTISTS Roger Brown, artist, Chicago, IL.; Rafael Ferrer, artist, Philadelphia, PA.; Nancy Graves, artist, New York, NY.; Bruce Nauman, artist, Pasadena, CA.; Brenda Richardson, curator, Baltimore Museum of Art, Baltimore, MD.; Paul Sarkisian, artist, Cerillos, NM.

FELLOWSHIP SELECTION PANELISTS, CONCEPTUAL/PERFORMANCE Roselee Goldberg, curator, The Kitchen, New York, NY.; Robert Irwin, artist, Los Angeles, CA.; Robert Watts, artist, Bangor, PA

FELLOWSHIP SELECTION PANELISTS, PRINTS Kathan Brown, curator/director, Crown Point Press, Berkeley, CA.; John Dowell, artist, Philadelphia, PA.; Roland Ginzel, artist, Chicago, IL.

FELLOWSHIP SELECTION PANELISTS, VIDEO George Bolling, artist, Berkeley, CA.; Peter Campus, artist, New York, NY.; Anne Focke, administrator, and/or service, Seattle, WA.; Barbara London, curator, Museum of Modern Art, New York, NY.

FELLOWSHIP SELECTION PANELISTS, CRAFTS Dale Chihuly, artist/teacher, RISD, Providence, RI.; Ken Ferguson, artist, Kansas City, MO.; Arline Fisch, artist, San Diego, CA.; Ruth Kohler, curator/director, Kohler Art Center, Sheboygan, WI.; Claire Zeisler, artist, Chicago, IL.

FELLOWSHIP SELECTION PANELISTS, PHOTOGRAPHY Lewis Baltz, artist, Sausalito, CA.; Van Deren Coke, curator, University of New Mexico, Albuquerque, NM.; Linda Connor, artist/teacher, San Francisco Art Institute, San Francisco, CA.; Evelyn Hofer, artist, New York, NY.; William Jenkins, curator, International Museum of Photography/Eastman House, Rochester, NY.

1979

Artists Fellowships *(including sub-categories for Conceptual/Performance, Prints, and Video)*	160 from 4,063 applicants
Crafts Fellowships	48 from 1,368 applicants
Photography Fellowships	56 from 1,844 applicants
Fellowships awarded	264 from 7,275 applicants
Grant amount, Artists	$3,000, $10,000
Grant amount, Crafts	$3,000, $10,000
Grant amount, Photography	$3,000, $10,000
Total funds awarded	$1,891,000
Open applications	

FELLOWSHIP SELECTION PANELISTS, ARTISTS Linda Cathcart, curator, Albright-Knox Gallery, Buffalo, NY.; Anne d'Harnoncourt, curator, Philadelphia Museum, Philadelphia, PA.; Luis Jimenez, artist, Roswell, NM.; Sol LeWitt, artist, New York, NY.; Mary Miss, artist, New York, NY.; Ray Saunders, artist/teacher, California State University, Hayward, CA.

FELLOWSHIP SELECTION PANELISTS CONCEPTUAL/PERFORMANCE Claire Copley, curator, New York, NY.; Peter Frank, critic, New York, NY.; Barry LeVa, artist, New York, NY

FELLOWSHIP SELECTION PANELISTS, PRINTS Wendy Calman, artist/teacher, University of Indiana, Bloomington, IN.; Nathan Oliveira, artist/teacher, Stanford University, Stanford, CA.; Bill Walmsey, artist/teacher, Florida State University, Tallahassee, FL.

FELLOWSHIP SELECTION PANELISTS, VIDEO Stephen Beck, artist, Berkeley, CA.; Juan Downey, artist, New York, NY.; Nancy Drew, curator, Long Beach Museum, Long Beach, CA.; Robert Stearns, curator, Contemporary Arts Center, Cincinnati, OH.

FELLOWSHIP SELECTION PANELISTS, CRAFTS Paul DuFour, artist/teacher, Louisiana State University, Baton Rouge, LA.; Gary Griffin, artist/teacher, Rochester Institute of Technology, Rochester, NY.; Janet Kummerlein, artist, Kansas City, MO.; Jacqueline Rice, artist/teacher, RISD, Providence, RI.; Josine Starrels, curator, Municipal Gallery, Los Angeles, CA.

FELLOWSHIP SELECTION PANELISTS, PHOTOGRAPHY Thomas Barrow, artist/teacher, University of New Mexico, Albuquerque, NM.; Harry Callahan, artist, Providence, RI.; Patricia Fuller, administrator, Art in Public Places, Seattle, WA.; Robert Heineken, artist/teacher, University of California, Los Angeles, CA.; Anthony Hernandez, artist, Los Angeles, CA.; Anne Tucker, curator, Museum of Fine Arts, Houston, TX.

1980

Artists Fellowships *(including sub-categories for Conceptual/ Performance, and Prints)*	262 from 4,808 applicants
Crafts Fellowships	71 from 1,348 applicants
Photography Fellowships	98 from 2,233 applicants
Video Fellowships	51 from 195 applicants
Fellowships awarded	482 from 8,584 applicants
Grant amount, Artists	$3,000, $10,000
Grant amount, Crafts	$3,000, $10,000
Grant amount, Photography	$3,000, $10,000
Grant amount, Video	$3,000, $10,000
Total funds awarded	$1,891,000
Open applications	

FELLOWSHIP SELECTION PANELISTS, ARTISTS Thomas Garver, curator, Newport Harbor Museum, Newport Beach, CA.; Nancy Holt, artist, New York, NY.; Alex Katz, artist, New York, NY.; Nilda Peraza, curator, Museum of Contemporary Hispanic Art, New York, NY.; Katherine Porter, artist, Lincolnville, ME.; Martin Puryear, artist, Chicago, IL.

FELLOWSHIP SELECTION PANELISTS, CONCEPTUAL/PERFORMANCE Vito Acconci, artist, New York, NY.; Alexis Smith, artist, Los Angeles, CA.; William Wegman, artist, New York, NY.

FELLOWSHIP SELECTION PANELISTS, PRINTS Anna Bliss, artist, Salt Lake City, UT.; Mike Kanemitzu, artist, Los Angeles, CA.; Howardena Pindell, artist, New York, NY.

FELLOWSHIP SELECTION PANELISTS, CRAFTS Art Carpenter, artist, Bolinas, CA.; Jamie Carpenter, artist, New York, NY.; Marlene Gabel, curator, Contemporary Crafts Gallery, Portland, OR.; Aleksandra Kasuba, artist, New York, NY.; Gerhard Knodel, artist/teacher, Cranbrook Academy, Bloomfield Hills, MI.; David McDonald, artist/teacher, Syracuse University, Syracuse, NY.

FELLOWSHIP SELECTION PANELISTS, PHOTOGRAPHY Carole Kismaric, editor, Aperture, New York, NY.; Bart Parker, artist/teacher, Rhode Island School of Design, Providence, RI.; Leland Rice, artist, Inglewood, CA.; Eve Sonneman, artist, New York, NY.; Evon Streetman, artist/teacher, University of Florida, Gainesville, FL.

FELLOWSHIP SELECTION PANELISTS, VIDEO Jaime Davidovich, artist, New York, NY.; Gayla Jamison, curator, Image, Film, & Video, Atlanta, GA.; David Ross, curator, University Art Museum, Berkeley, CA.; Ira Schneider, artist, New York, NY.

1981

Artists Fellowships *(including sub-categories for Conceptual/Performance.; Painting, Prints, Sculpture, and Video):*	168 from 6,313 applicants
Crafts Fellowships	48 from 1,783 applicants
Photography Fellowships	51 from 2,066 applicants
Fellowships awarded	267 from 10,162 applicants
Grant amount, Artists	$2,000, $4,000, $6,250, $12,500
Grant amount, Crafts	$4,000, $12,500
Grant amount, Photography	$4,000, $12,500
Total funds awarded	$2,544,500
Open applications	

FELLOWSHIP SELECTION PANELISTS, CONCEPTUAL/PERFORMANCE Rafael Ortiz, artist/teacher, Rutgers University, New Brunswick, NJ.; Nigel Redden, curator, Walker Art Center, Minneapolis, MN.; Moira Roth, critic/teacher, University of California, San Diego, CA.

FELLOWSHIP SELECTION PANELISTS, PAINTING Pat Adams, artist/teacher, Bennington College, Bennington, VT.; Robert Ryman, artist, New York, NY.; Wayne Thiebaud, artist/teacher, University of California, Davis, CA.; Diane Vanderlip, curator, Denver Art Museum, Denver, CO.

FELLOWSHIP SELECTION PANELISTS, PRINTS Bob Blackburn, administrator, Printmaking Workshop, New York, NY.; Sam Gilliam, artist, Washington, DC.; Marcia Isaacson, artist/teacher, University of Florida, Gainesville, FL.; Joan Lyons, artist/curator, Visual Studies Workshop, Rochester, NY.

FELLOWSHIP SELECTION PANELISTS, SCULPTURE Larry Bell, artist, Taos, NM.; Jackie Ferrara, artist, New York, NY.; Ira Licht, curator, Lowe Art Museum, Coral Gables, FL.; Lisa Lyons, curator, Walker Art Center, Minneapolis, MN.; Manuel Neri, artist, University of California, Davis, CA.

FELLOWSHIP SELECTION PANELISTS, VIDEO Kathy Huffman, curator, Long Beach Museum, Long Beach, CA.; John Hanhart, curator, Whitney Museum of American Art, New York, NY.; Shigeko Kubota, artist/curator, Anthology Film Archive, New York, NY.

FELLOWSHIP SELECTION PANELISTS, CRAFTS Joyce Bacerra, artist, Pasadena, CA.; Imelda de Graw, curator, Denver Art Museum, Denver, CO.; Ray King, artist, Philadelphia, PA.; Judy McKie, artist, Cambridge, MA.; John Paul Miller, artist/teacher, Cleveland, OH.

FELLOWSHIP SELECTION PANELISTS, PHOTOGRAPHY Anthony Barboza, artist, New York, NY.; Robert Cumming, artist, West Suffield, CT.; Robert Jones, artist/teacher, University of Arizona, Tucson, AZ.; Ellen Manchester, administrator, Sun Valley Center, Sun Valley, ID.; Joyce Neimanas, artist/teacher, Chicago Art Insitute, Chicago, IL.

1982

Conceptual/Performance/ New Genres Fellowships	13 from 164 applicants
Crafts Fellowships	59 from 1,071 applicants
Painting Fellowships	82 from 1,566 applicants
Photography Fellowships	82 from 1,455 applicants
Printmaking/Drawing/Artists' Books Fellowships	27 from 496 applicants
Sculpture Fellowships	62 from 839 applicants
Video Fellowships	12 from 156 applicants
Fellowships awarded	337 from 5,747 applicants
Grant amounts, Conceptual/Performance/ New Genres, Crafts, Painting, Photography, Sculpture, Video	$5,000; $25,000
Grant amount, Printmaking/Drawing/Artists' Books	$5,000; $25,000
Total funds awarded	$3,425,000

Open applications

FELLOWSHIP SELECTION PANELISTS, CONCEPTUAL/PERFORMANCE/NEW GENRES Joan Jonas, artist, New York, NY.; Hans Haacke, artist, New York, NY.; Barbara Smith, artist, Los Angeles, CA.

FELLOWSHIP SELECTION PANELISTS, CRAFTS Jamie Carpenter, artist, New York, NY.; Diane Itter, artist, Bloomfield Hills, MI.; Jun Kaneko, artist/teacher, Cranbrook Academy, Bloomfield Hills, MI.; Marcia Lewis, artist/teacher, Long Beach College, Vista, CA.; Robert Strini, artist, Superior, MT.

FELLOWSHIP SELECTION PANELISTS, PAINTING Elmer Bischoff, artist, San Francisco, CA.; Linda Cathcart, curator/director, Contemporary Arts Museum, Houston, TX.; Chuck Close, artist, New York, NY.; Robert Colescott, artist, San Francisco, CA.; Robert Mangold, artist, New York, NY .

FELLOWSHIP SELECTION PANELISTS, PHOTOGRAPHY Carl Chiarenza, artist/teacher, Boston, MA.; Roy DeCarava, artist, Brooklyn, NY.; Robert Fichter, artist/teacher, University of Florida, Tallahassee, FL.; Susan Rankaitis, artist, Inglewood, CA.; Martha Rosler, artist/critic, Rutgers University, New Brunswick, NJ.

FELLOWSHIP SELECTION PANELISTS, PRINTMAKING/DRAWING/ARTISTS' BOOKS Benny Andrews, artist, New York, NY.; Ed Ruscha, artist, Los Angeles, CA.; Esther Sparks, curator, Chicago Art Institute, Chicago, IL.

FELLOWSHIP SELECTION PANELISTS, SCULPTURE Terry Allen, artist, Fresno, CA.; Deborah Butterfield, artist, Bozeman, MT.; Martin Puryear, artist, Chicago, IL.; Marcia Tucker, curator/director, The New Museum, New York, NY.

FELLOWSHIP SELECTION PANELISTS, VIDEO Ilene Segalove, artist, Venice, CA.; Arthur Tsuchiya, artist, Hoboken, NJ.; Steina Vasulka, artist, Santa Fe, NM.

1983 *Note: Beginning this year, funding categories shifted to alternate year cycles. Regional Arts Agencies gradually phased in categories not offered in a given year by the NEA. Regional Arts Agencies are noted in parentheses following the categories they offered. In order to target emerging artists, previous NEA recipients were not eligible to receive regional fellowships. The number of applicants to Regional Arts Agencies and the names of panelists are not included because the information was incomplete or not available.*

Conceptual/Performance/New Genres Fellowships	46 from 243 applicants
Painting Fellowships	107 from 2,503 applicants
Photography Fellowships (Mid-America Arts Alliance)	20
Printmaking/Drawing/Artists' Books Fellowships	45 from 997 applicants
Video Fellowships	20 from 158 applicants
Fellowships awarded	238 from 3,901 applicants
All NEA categories	$5,000; $15,000; $25,000
Grant amounts for Regional Art Agency grants	$3,500
Total funds awarded	$2,390,000

Selections based on applications

FELLOWSHIP SELECTION PANELISTS, CONCEPTUAL/PERFORMANCE/NEW GENRES
Bill Buchen, artist, New York, NY.; Suzanne Lacy, artist/teacher, Los Angeles, CA.; Adrian Piper, artist/critic, Ann Arbor, MI.; Jock Reynolds, artist/teacher, San Francisco State University, San Francisco, CA.; Robert Stearns, curator, Walker Art Center, Minneapolis, MN.; William Wegman, artist, New York, NY.

FELLOWSHIP SELECTION PANELISTS, PAINTING Andrew Keating, artist, Seattle, WA.; Gabriel Laderman, artist, New York, NY.; Margit Omar, artist, Los Angeles, CA.; Peter Plagens, artist/critic, University of North Carolina, Chapel Hill, NC.; Joan Semmel, artist, New York, NY.; Lowery Sims, curator, Metropolitan Museum, New York, NY .

FELLOWSHIP SELECTION PANELISTS, PRINTMAKING/DRAWING/ARTISTS' BOOKS
Garo Antreasian, artist/teacher, University of New Mexico, Albuquerque, NM.; Bill Jensen, artist, New York, NY.; Donald Kuspit, critic/teacher, State University of New York, Stony Brook, NY.; Andrea Miller-Keller, curator, Wadsworth Atheneum, Hartford, CT.; Bill Schade, artist, Albany, NY.

FELLOWSHIP SELECTION PANELISTS, VIDEO John Baldessari, artist/teacher, California Institute for the Arts, Los Angeles, CA.; Willie Longshore, artist/teacher, Ohio State University, Columbus, OH.; Carrie Rickey, critic, New York, NY.; Norie Sato, artist, Seattle, WA.; Warner Wada, artist, New York, NY.

1984

Crafts Fellowships	76 from 1,569 applicants
Photography Fellowships	74 from 1,737 applicants
Printmaking/Drawing/Artists' Books Fellowships (Mid-America Arts Alliance)	20
Fellowships awarded	290 from 5,022 applicants
All NEA categories	$5,000;$15,000; $25,000
Regional Art Agency grant amount	$3,500
Total funds awarded	$2,800,000

Open applications

FELLOWSHIP SELECTION PANELISTS, CRAFTS Frederico Armijo, artist, Albuquerque, NM.; Jonathan Fairbanks, curator, Museum of Fine Arts, Boston, MA.; Harvey Littleton, artist, Spruce Pine, NC.; Mineo Mizuno, artist, Los Angeles, CA.; Eleanor Moty, artist/teacher, University of Wisconsin, Madison, WI.; Cynthia Schira, artist/teacher, University of Kansas, Lawrence, KS.

FELLOWSHIP SELECTION PANELISTS, PHOTOGRAPHY Paul Berger, artist/teacher, University of Washington, Seattle, WA.; Roland Freeman, artist, Washington, DC.; Vida Freeman, artist/teacher, California State University, Northridge, CA.; Elaine Mayes, artist/teacher, Bard College, New York, NY.; Carol Squiers, curator/critic, New York, NY.; Jeff Weiss, artist, Chicago, IL.

FELLOWSHIP SELECTION PANELISTS, SCULPTURE David Ireland, artist, San Francisco, CA.; Mary Jane Jacob, curator, Museum of Contemporary Art, Chicago, IL.; Judy Pfaff, artist, New York, NY.; Italo Scanga, artist/teacher, University of California, San Diego, CA.; Ursula Von Rydingsvard,artist/teacher, Yale University, New York, NY.; Chester Williams, artist/teacher, Florida A&M University, Tallahassee, FL .

1985

Conceptual/Performance/ New Genres	56 from 494 applicants
Crafts Fellowships (Arts Midwest, Mid-America Arts Alliance, Southern Arts Federation)	29
Painting Fellowships	131 from 3,516 applicants
Photography Fellowships (Arts Midwest)	10
Printmaking/Drawing/Artists' Books Fellowships	70 from 1,594 applicants
Fellowships awarded	296 from 5,604 applicants
Grant amounts, NEA	$5,000;$15,000; $25,000
Regional Art Agencies grant amount	$3,500
Total funds awarded	$2,866,500

Open applications

FELLOWSHIP SELECTION PANELISTS, CONCEPTUAL/PERFORMANCE/NEW GENRES
Douglas Huebler, artist, Los Angeles, CA.; Mary McArthur Griffin, curator, New York, NY.; Tony Labat, artist, New York, NY.; James Pomeroy, artist, San Francisco, CA.; Robert Stearns, curator, Walker Art Center, Minneapolis, MN.; John White, artist, Venice, CA.

FELLOWSHIP SELECTION PANELISTS, PAINTING Joan Brown, artist, San Francisco, CA.; Audrey Flack, artist, New York, NY.; Marvin Harden, artist, Chatsworth, CA.; Richard Loving, artist, Chicago, IL.; Peter Morrin, curator, High Museum, Atlanta, GA.; Pat Steir, artist, New York, NY .

FELLOWSHIP SELECTION PANELISTS, PRINTMAKING/DRAWING/ARTISTS' BOOKS
Martha Beck, curator/director, Drawing Center, New York, NY.; Kathan Brown, curator/director, Crown Point Press, Oakland, CA.; Cheryl Goldsleger, artist/teacher, University of Georgia, Athens, GA.; Ellen Lanyon, artist, Chicago, IL.; Roger Shimomura, artist/teacher, University of Kansas, Lawrence, KS.; Paul Zelevansky, artist, New York, NY .

1986

Crafts Fellowship	86 from 1,619
Painting Fellowships (Arts Midwest, Mid-America Arts Alliance, Southern Arts Federation)	53
Photography Fellowships	51 from 1,754
Printmaking/Drawing/Artists' Books Fellowships (Southern Arts Federation)	7
Sculpture Fellowships	94 from 1,921
Fellowships awarded	291 from 5,294
NEA grant amounts	$5,000, $15,000 $25,000
Regional Art Agencies grant amount	$3,500
Total funds awarded	$2,480,000

Open applications

FELLOWSHIP SELECTION PANELISTS, CRAFTS Wayne Higby, artist/teacher, Alfred University, Alfred, NY.; Michael Peed, artist, Bozeman, MT.; Helen Shirk, artist, San Diego, CA.; Susan Stinsmuehlen, artist, Austin, TX.; Kenneth Trapp, curator, Oakland Museum, Oakland, CA.; Anne Wilson, artist/teacher, Chicago Art Institute, Chicago, IL.

FELLOWSHIP SELECTION PANELISTS, PHOTOGRAPHY Ricardo Block, artist, St. Paul, MN.; Richard Misrach, artist, Emeryville, CA.; Julio Mitchel, artist, New York, NY.; Barbara Norfleet, artist/curator, Harvard University, Cambridge, MA.; Kenneth Shorr, artist/teacher, University of Arizona, Tucson, AZ.; Robert Sobieszek, curator, International Museum of Photography/George Eastman House, Rochester, NY.

FELLOWSHIP SELECTION PANELISTS, SCULPTURE Michael Brewster, artist, Los Angeles, CA.; Sue Graze, curator, Dallas Museum, Dallas, TX.; Betye Saar, artist, Los Angeles, CA.; Michael Steiner, artist, New York, NY.; Margaret Wharton, artist, Chicago, IL.; Jackie Winsor, artist, New York, NY.

1987

Conceptual/Performance/New Genres Fellowships:	39 from 501 applicants
Crafts Fellowships (Arts Midwest)	10
Painting Fellowships	176 from 3,356 applicants
Photography Fellowships (Arts Midwest, Mid-America Arts Alliance, Southern Arts Federation)	35
Printmaking/Drawing/Artists' Books Fellowships	26 from 1,409 applicants
Sculpture Fellowships (Southern Arts Federation)	10
Fellowships awarded	296 from 5,266 applicants
NEA grant amounts	$5,000;$15,000; $25,000
Regional Art Agencies grant amount	$3,500
Total funds awarded	$2,507,500

Open applications

FELLOWSHIP SELECTION PANELISTS, CONCEPTUAL/PERFORMANCE/NEW GENRES
Ping Chong, artist, New York, NY.; Dorit Cypis, artist, Minneapolis, MN.; Roselee Goldberg, curator/critic, New York, NY.; Mike Kelley, artist, Los Angeles, CA.; Paul Kos, artist, San Francisco, CA.; Mary Lucier, artist, New York, NY.

FELLOWSHIP SELECTION PANELISTS, PAINTING Ross Bleckner, artist, New York, NY.; Susan Crile, artist, New York, NY.; Charles Garabedian, artist, Santa Monica, CA.; Kathy Halbreich, curator/director, List Visual Arts Center, Cambridge, MA.; Michiko Itatani, artist, Chicago, IL.; Merrill Mahaffey, artist, Boulder, CO.

FELLOWSHIP SELECTION PANELISTS, PRINTMAKING/DRAWING/ARTISTS' BOOKS
Phyllis Bramson, artist, Glenview, IL.; Vernon Fisher, artist, Denton, TX.; Margo Humphrey, artist, Oakland, CA.; Michael Hurson, artist, New York, NY.; Jane Kessler, curator, Mint Museum, Charlotte, NC.; Michelle Stuart, artist, New York, NY.

1988

Crafts Fellowships	103 from 1,847 applicants
Painting Fellowships (Arts Midwest, Mid-America Arts Alliance, Southern Arts Federation)	47
Photography Fellowships	60 from 1,721 applicants
Sculpture Fellowships	89 from 1,746 applicants
Printmaking/Drawing/Artists' Books Fellowships (Arts Midwest, Mid-America Arts Alliance, Mid Atlantic Arts Foundation, Southern Arts Federation, Western States Arts Foundation)	48
Painting Fellowships (Arts Midwest, Mid-America Arts Alliance, Southern Arts Federation)	47
Fellowships awarded	347 from 5,314 applicants
NEA grant amounts	$5,000;$15,000; $25,000
Regional Art Agencies grant amounts	$3,500
Total funds awarded	$2,502,500

Open applications

FELLOWSHIP SELECTION PANELISTS, CRAFTS Margie Hughto, artist/curator, Syracuse, NY.; Richard Marquis, artist, Seattle, WA.; Wendy Maruyama, artist, Oakland, CA.; Robin Quigley, artist, Providence, RI.; Jane Sauer, artist, St. Louis, MO.; John Stephenson, artist, Ann Arbor, MI .

FELLOWSHIP SELECTION PANELISTS, PHOTOGRAPHY
William Christenberry, artist, Washington, DC.; Eileen Cowin, artist, Culver City, CA.; Tony Mendoza, artist, New York, NY.; Terence Pitts, curator, Center for Creative Photography, Tucson, AZ.; Linn Underhill, artist, Lisle, NY.; Wendy Watriss, artist/curator, Foto Fest, Houston, TX

FELLOWSHIP SELECTION PANELISTS, SCULPTURE John Buck, artist, Bozeman, MT.; Amalia Mesa-Bains, artist/curator, San Francisco, CA.; Joel Shapiro, artist, New York, NY.; Linda Shearer, curator, Museum of Modern Art, New York, NY.; Peter Shelton, artist, Los Angeles, CA.; Mary Stoppert, artist, Chicago, IL

1989

Crafts Fellowships (Arts Midwest, Mid-America Arts Alliance, Mid Atlantic Arts Foundation, Southern Arts Federation, Western States Arts Foundation)	65
Painting Fellowships	169 from 3,483 applicants
New Genres Fellowships	59 from 404 applicants
Photography Fellowships (Arts Midwest)	10
Printmaking/Drawing/Artists' Books Fellowships	70 from 1,864 applicants
Sculpture Fellowships (Arts Midwest, Mid-America Arts Alliance, Southern Arts Federation)	30
Fellowships awarded	403 from 5,751 applicants
NEA grant amounts	$5,000; $15,000
Regional Art Agencies grant amount	$5,000
Total funds awarded	$3,185,000

Open applications

FELLOWSHIP SELECTION PANELISTS, NEW GENRES She Lea Cheang, artist, New York, NY.; Ann Hamilton, artist, Santa Barbara, CA.; Carole Ann Klonarides, curator, New York, NY.; Julie Lazar, curator, Museum of Contemporary Art, Los Angeles, CA.; Allan McCollum, artist, New York, NY.; Allen Ruppersberg, artist, New York, NY.

FELLOWSHIP SELECTION PANELISTS, PAINTING Mel Bochner, artist, New York, NY.; Patricia Gonzalez, artist, Houston, TX.; Henry Hopkins, curator, Weisman Foundation, Los Angeles, CA.; Alex Katz, artist, New York, NY.; Elizabeth Murray, artist, New York, NY.; Patricia Paterson, artist, Leucadia, CA.

FELLOWSHIP SELECTION PANELISTS, PRINTMAKING/DRAWING/ARTISTS' BOOKS Elizabeth Armstrong, curator, Walker Art Center, Minneapolis, MN.; Eric Fischl, artist, New York, NY.; Valerie Jaudon, artist, New York, NY.; Roberto Juarez, artist, Miami, FL.; Gael Stack, artist, Houston, TX.; Garner Tullis, artist/curator, Tullis Workshop, Santa Barbara, CA.

1990

Crafts Fellowships	64 from 1,646 applicants
Painting Fellowships (Arts Midwest, Mid Atlantic Arts Foundation, Western States Arts Foundation)	55
Painting/Works on Paper Fellowships (Mid-America Arts Alliance, Southern Arts Federation)	40
Photography Fellowships	53 from 1,712 applicants
Sculpture Fellowships	60 from 1,995 applicants
Works on Paper Fellowships (Arts Midwest, New England Arts Foundation)	25
Fellowships awarded	297 from 5,751 applicants
NEA grant amounts	$5,000; $20,000
Regional Art Agencies grant amount	$5,000
Total funds awarded	$2,730,000

Open applications

FELLOWSHIP SELECTION PANELISTS, CRAFTS Robert Brady, artist, California State University, Sacramento, CA.; Karen Karnes, artist, Morgan, VT.; Marcia Manhart, curator, Philbrook Art Center, Tulsa, OK.; John Prip, artist, Rehoboth, MA.; Joyce Scott, artist, Baltimore, MD.; Dick Weiss, artist, Seattle, WA.

FELLOWSHIP SELECTION PANELISTS, PHOTOGRAPHY Tina Barney, artist, Watch Hill, RI.; Joe Deal, artist/teacher, Washington University, St. Louis, MO.; Merry Foresta, curator, National Museum of American Art, Washington, DC.; George Krause, artist/teacher, University of Houston, Houston, TX.; Mike Mandel, artist/teacher, Cabrillo College, Santa Cruz, CA.; Clarissa Sligh, artist, New York, NY.

FELLOWSHIP SELECTION PANELISTS, SCULPTURE Maria Brito, artist/teacher, Miami-Dade College, Miami, FL.; Holliday Day, curator, Indianapolis Museum, Indianapolis, IN.; Jene Highstein, artist, New York, NY.; Douglas Hollis, artist, San Francisco, CA.; Ken Little, artist/teacher, University of Texas, San Antonio, TX.; Judith Shea, artist, New York, NY.

1991

Crafts Fellowships (Arts Midwest, New England Arts Foundation)	20
New Genres Fellowships	22 from 348 applicants
Painting Fellowships	65 from 3,116 applicants
Photography Fellowships (Arts Midwest, Mid-America Arts Alliance, Mid Atlantic Arts Foundation, New England Arts Foundation, Southern Arts Federation, Western States Arts Foundation)	65
Works on Paper Fellowships	18 from 1,694 applicants
Sculpture Fellowships (Arts Midwest, Mid Atlantic Arts Foundation, Southern Arts Federation, Western States Arts Foundation)	40
Fellowships awarded	230 from 5,158 applicants
NEA grant amounts	$20,000
Regional Art Agencies grant amounts	$5,000
Total funds awarded	$2,725,000

Open applications

FELLOWSHIP SELECTION PANELISTS, NEW GENRES Lawrence Andrews, artist, San Francisco, CA.; Michael Auping, curator, Albright-Knox Gallery, Buffalo, NY.; Bonnie Clearwater, layperson, Grassfield Press, Miami Beach, FL.; Cecelia Condit, artist/teacher, University of Wisconsin, Milwaukee, WI.; Annette Lemieux, artist, Brookline, MA.; Pat Oleszko, artist, New York, NY.; Stephen Prina, artist, Los Angeles, CA.

FELLOWSHIP SELECTION PANELISTS, PAINTING Graham Beal, curator, Joslyn Art Museum, Omaha, NE.; Janet Fish, artist, Rutland, VT.; Tressa Miller, layperson, Security Pacific, Los Angeles, CA.; Robert Moskowitz, artist, New York, NY.; Gladys Nilsson, artist, Wilmette, IL.; Andrew Spence, artist, New York, NY.; Masami Teraoka, artist, Waimanalo, HI.

FELLOWSHIP SELECTION PANELISTS, WORKS ON PAPER David Bates, artist, Dallas, TX.; Ruth Fine, curator, National Gallery of Art, Washington, DC.; Manuel Gonzalez, layperson, Chase Manhattan Bank, New York, NY.; Jack Lemon, teacher/curator, Landfall Press, Chicago, IL.; Winifred Lutz, artist/teacher, Tyler School of Art, Philadelphia, PA.; Sabina Ott, artist, Los Angeles, CA.; David True, artist/teacher, Cooper Union, New York, NY.

1992

Crafts Fellowships	33 from 1,664 applicants
Painting Fellowships (Arts Midwest, Mid Atlantic Arts Foundation, New England Arts Foundation, Western States Arts Foundation)	42
Painting/Works on Paper Fellowships (Mid-America Arts Alliance, Southern Arts Federation)	40
Photography Fellowships	38 from 1,708 applicants
Sculpture Fellowships	0 from 1,868 applicants because panel resigned in protest
Works on Paper Fellowships (Arts Midwest, Mid Atlantic Arts Foundation, New England Arts Foundation, Western States Arts Foundation)	40
Fellowships awarded	193 from 5,240 applicants
NEA grant amounts	$20,000
Regional Art Agencies grant amounts	$5,000
Total funds awarded	$2,030,000

Open applications

FELLOWSHIP SELECTION PANELISTS, CRAFTS William Daley, artist/teacher, University of the Arts, Philadelphia, PA.; Glen Kaufman, artist/teacher, University of Georgia, Athens, GA.; Thomas Loeser, artist/teacher, University of Wisconsin, Madison, WI.; Hiroko Pijanowski, artist/teacher, University of Michigan, Ann Arbor, MI.; Judith Schaecter, artist, Philadelphia, PA.; Davira Taragin, curator, Toledo Museum, Toledo, OH.; Laila Twigg-Smith, layperson, collector/patron, Honolulu, HI.

FELLOWSHIP SELECTION PANELISTS, PHOTOGRAPHY Jim Casebere, artist/teacher, Rockland Community College, New York, NY.; Robert Dawson, artist/teacher, City College, San Francisco, CA.; Barbara Hitchcock, layperson, Polaroid Corporation, Cambridge, MA.; Maria Martinez-Canas, artist, Miami, FL.; Ray Metzker, artist, Philadelphia, PA.; Lorna Simpson, artist, Brooklyn, NY.; David Travis, curator, Art Institute of Chicago, Chicago, IL.

FELLOWSHIP SELECTION PANELISTS, SCULPTURE Richard Fleischner, artist, Providence, RI.; Ronald Jones, artist/teacher, Yale University, New Haven, CT.; Susan Krane, curator, High Museum, Atlanta, GA.; Daniel Martinez, artist/teacher, University of California, Irvine, CA.; Mia Westerlund Roosen, artist, New York, NY.; James Surls, artist, Cleveland, TX.; Virginia Wright, layperson, collector, Seattle, WA.

1993

Crafts Fellowships (Arts Midwest, Mid-America Arts Alliance, Mid Atlantic Arts Foundation, New England Arts Foundation, Southern Arts Federation, Western States Arts Foundation)	60
Other Genres Fellowships	34 from 413 applicants
Painting Fellowships	57 from 2,397 applicants
Photography Fellowships (Arts Midwest, Mid-America Arts Alliance, New England Arts Foundation, Southern Arts Federation, Western States Arts Foundation)	50
Sculpture Fellowships (Arts Midwest, Mid-America Arts Alliance, Mid Atlantic Arts Foundation, New England Arts Foundation, Southern Arts Federation, Western States Arts Foundation)	60
Works on Paper Fellowships	19 from 1,716 applicants
Fellowships awarded	280 from 4,526 applicants
NEA grant amounts	$20,000
Regional Art Agencies grant amount	$5,000
Total funds awarded	$3,050,000

Open applications

FELLOWSHIP SELECTION PANELISTS, OTHER GENRES Jerri Allyn, artist/teacher, New School, New York, NY.; Marilyn Gladstone, layperson, consultant, Washington, DC.; Carlos Gutierrez-Solana, artist/curator, Artists' Space, New York, NY.; Andrea Miller-Keller, curator, Wadsworth Atheneum, Hartford, CT.; Celia Munoz, artist, Arlington, TX.; Robert Peters, artist/teacher, University of Chicago, Lake Forest, IL.; Bruce Yonemoto, artist/teacher, Art Center College, Pasadena, CA.

FELLOWSHIP SELECTION PANELISTS, PAINTING Susanne Ghez, curator, Renaissance Society, Chicago, IL.; Roger Herman, artist/teacher, University of California, Los Angeles, CA.; Lester Loo, layperson, collector, Colorado Springs, CO.; Melissa Miller, artist, Austin, TX.; Catherine Murphy, artist, Poughkeepsie, NY.; Robert Reed, artist/teacher, Yale University, New Haven, CT.; Dan Ramirez, artist/teacher, University of Wisconsin, Madison, WI.

FELLOWSHIP SELECTION PANELISTS, WORKS ON PAPER Gregory Amenoff, artist, New York, NY.; Jane Bickerton, layperson, Atlanta College Art, Atlanta, GA.; Suzanne Delehanty, curator, Contemporary Arts Museum, Houston, TX.; James Drake, artist, El Paso, TX.; Nancy Friese, artist/teacher, Rhode Island School of Design, Providence, RI.; Glenn Ligon, artist, New York, NY.; Ray Yoshida, artist/teacher, Art Institute of Chicago, Chicago, IL.

1994

Crafts Fellowships	28 from 1,325 applicants
Painting Fellowships (Arts Midwest, Mid-Atlantic Arts Foundation, New England Arts Foundation, Western States Arts Foundation)	80
Painting/Works on Paper Fellowships (Mid-America Arts Alliance, Southern Arts Federation)	60
Photography Fellowships	28 from 1,773 applicants
of which three were rejected by National Council on the Arts	
Sculpture Fellowships	32 from 2,070 applicants
Works on Paper Fellowships(Arts Midwest, Mid-Atlantic Arts Foundation, New England Arts Foundation, Western States Arts Foundation)	40
Fellowships awarded	268 from 5,168 applicants
NEA grant amounts	$20,000
Regional Art Agencies grant amounts	$5,000
Total funds awarded	$2,660,000

Open applications

FELLOWSHIP SELECTION PANELISTS, CRAFTS Linda Bills, artist, Baltimore, MD.; Eddie Dominguez, artist, Tucumcari, NM.; Deborah Groover, artist/teacher, Penland School, Penland, NC.; Lorna Higuchi, layperson, collector, Anaheim, CA.; Mary Lee Hu, artist/teacher, University of Washington, Seattle, WA.; John Perrault, curator/critic, NY Experimental Glass Workshop, New York, NY.; Stephen Whittlesey, artist/teacher, University of Massachusetts, West Barnstable, MA .

FELLOWSHIP SELECTION PANELISTS, PHOTOGRAPHY Ellen Brooks, artist/teacher, New York University, New York, NY.; Mary Frey, artist/teacher, University of Hartford, Springfield, MA.; Andy Grundberg, curator/critic, Friends of Photography, San Francisco, CA.; William Larson, artist/teacher, Maryland Institute College of Art, Collegeville, PA.; Martina Lopez, artist/teacher, University of Notre Dame, Chicago, IL.; David Madson, layperson, University of Minnesota, Minneapolis, MN.; Patrick Nagatani, artist/teacher, University of New Mexico, Albuquerque, NM.

FELLOWSHIP SELECTION PANELISTS, SCULPTURE Thomasine Bradford, artist, Atlanta, GA.; Houston Conwill, artist, New York, NY.; Mineko Grimmer, artist, Los Angeles, CA.; Bob Haozous, artist, Santa Fe, NM.; John Newman, artist/teacher, Yale University, New Haven, CT.; Deborah Emont Scott, curator, Nelson-Atkins Museum, Kansas City, MO.; Bernadine T. Speers, layperson, Banc One Indiana, Indianapolis, IN.

1995		
	Crafts Fellowships (Arts Midwest, Mid-America Arts Alliance, Mid Atlantic Arts Foundation, New England Arts Foundation, Southern Arts Federation, Western States Arts Foundation)	60
	Other Genres Fellowships	18 from 375 applicants
	of which six were rejected by National Council on the Arts	
	Painting Fellowships	21 from 2,577 applicants
	Photography Fellowships (Arts Midwest, Mid-America Arts Alliance, Mid Atlantic Arts Foundation, New England Arts Foundation, Southern Arts Federation, Western States Arts Foundation)	60
	Sculpture Fellowships (Arts Midwest, Mid-America Arts Alliance, Mid Atlantic Arts Foundation, New England Arts Foundation, Southern Arts Federation, Western States Arts Foundation)	60
	Works on Paper Fellowships	19 from 1,833 applicants
	Fellowships awarded	238 from 4,785 applicants
	NEA grant amounts	$20,000
	Regional Art Agencies grant amount	$5,000
	Total funds awarded	$2,060,000
	Open applications	

FELLOWSHIP SELECTION PANELISTS, OTHER GENRES Suzanne Bloom, artist/teacher, University of Houston, Houston, TX.; Edgar Heap of Birds, artist/teacher, University of Oklahoma, Norman, OK.; Heidi Kumao, artist/teacher, Syracuse University, Syracuse, NY.; Jill Medvedow, curator, Gardner Museum, Boston, MA.; Walter Parsons, layperson, KCTS-TV, Seattle, WA.; Scott Rankin, artist/teacher, Illinois State University, Chicago, IL.

FELLOWSHIP SELECTION PANELISTS, PAINTING Julie Auger, layperson, collector, Aspen, CO.; Rodney Carswell, artist/teacher, University of Illinois, Oak Park, IL.; David Diao, artist/teacher, Whitney Museum of American Art, New York, NY.; Denzil Hurley, artist/teacher, University of Washington, Seattle, WA.; Hung Lui, artist/teacher, Mills College, Oakland, CA.; Sylvia Plimack Mangold, artist, Washingtonville, NY.; Terry Sultan, curator, Corcoran Gallery of Art, Washington, DC

FELLOWSHIP SELECTION PANELISTS, WORKS ON PAPER Rupert Garcia, artist/teacher, San Jose State University, Oakland, CA.; Eddie Granderson, artist/curator, City Gallery, Atlanta, GA.; Susan King, artist/curator, Paradise Press, Los Angeles, CA.; Richard Shack, layperson, collector, Miami, FL.; Patricia Watkinson, curator, Washington State University Museum, Pullman, WA.

Visual Arts Policy/Overview Panelists

Note: The Visual Arts Program convened policy overview panels from 1977 through 1995 when the agency was reorganized. After 1983, this panel (like others throughout the Arts Endowment) was renamed the "Overview Panel." These panels, comprised of individuals who had recently served on one of many other visual arts panels, reviewed program priorities and made recommendations on such issues as fellowship amounts or changes in review criteria. Their recommendations were reviewed for approval by the National Council on the Arts and then implemented by staff through guidelines and new initiatives.

1977

Benny Andrews, artist, New York, NY.
Anne d'Harnoncourt, curator, Philadelphia Museum of Art, Philadelphia, PA.
Carole Kismaric, editor, Aperture, New York, NY.
George Lakoff, teacher, University of California, Berkeley, CA.
Ed Levine, artist/teacher, Minneapolis College, Minneapolis, MN.
Nathan Lyons, artist/teacher, Visual Studies Workshop, Rochester, NY.
Warren MacKenzie, artist, Stillwater, MN.
Eudorah Moore, curator, California Design, Pasadena, CA.

1978

Benny Andrews, artist, New York, NY.
Anne d'Harnoncourt, curator, Philadelphia Museum of Art, Philadelphia, PA.
Newton Harrison, artist, San Diego, CA.
James Haseltine, director, Washington State Arts Commission, Olympia, WA.
Carole Kismaric, editor, *Aperture*, New York, NY.
George Lakoff, teacher, University of California, Berkeley, CA.
Ed Levine, artist/teacher, Minneapolis College, Minneapolis, MN.
Warren MacKenzie, artist, Stillwater, MN.

1979

Panel Chair: **Ed Levine,** artist/teacher, Minneapolis College, Minneapolis, MN.
Robert Adams, artist, Longmont, CO.
Benny Andrews, artist, New York, NY.
Anne d'Harnoncourt, curator, Philadelphia Museum of Art, Philadelphia, PA.
Anne Focke, administrator, and/or service, Seattle, WA.
Janet Harris, director, Indiana Arts Commission, Indianapolis, IN.
Luis Jimenez, artist, El Paso, TX.
Ruth Kohler, curator/director, Kohler Arts Center, Sheboygan, WI.
Nathan Lyons, artist/teacher, Visual Studies Workshop, Rochester, NY.
Warren MacKenzie, artist, Stillwater, MN.
George Segal, artist, New Brunswick, NJ.

1980

Panel Chair: **Ed Levine,** artist/teacher, Minneapolis College, Minneapolis, MN.
Robert Adams, artist, Longmont, CO.
Benny Andrews, artist, New York, NY.
Richard Artschwager, artist, New York, NY.
Anne d'Harnoncourt, curator, Philadelphia Museum of Art, Philadelphia, PA.
Anne Focke, administrator, and/or service, Seattle, WA.
Janet Harris, director, Indiana Arts Commission, Indianapolis, IN.
Luis Jimenez, artist, El Paso, TX.
Ruth Kohler, curator/director, Kohler Arts Center, Sheboygan, WI.
Nathan Lyons, artist/teacher, Visual Studies Workshop, Rochester, NY.
Warren MacKenzie, artist, Stillwater, MN.

1981

Panel Chair: **Anne Focke,** administrator, and/or service, Seattle, WA.
Richard Artschwager, artist, New York, NY.
Douglas Davis, artist/critic, New York, NY.
Robert Irwin, artist, Los Angeles, CA.
Bernard Kester, artist/teacher, Los Angeles, CA.
Ruth Kohler, curator/director, Kohler Arts Center, Sheboygan, WI.
Rosalind Krauss, critic, *October* Magazine, New York, NY.
Bart Parker, artist, Providence, RI.
Carlos Solana, staff, New York State Council on the Arts, New York, NY.
Anne Tucker, curator, Museum of Fine Arts, Houston, TX.

1982

Panel Chair: **Anne Focke,** administrator, and/or service, Seattle, WA.
Richard Artschwager, artist, New York, NY.
Dale Chihuly, artist, Cranston, RI.
Douglas Davis, artist/critic, New York, NY.
David Driskell, critic/teacher, University of Maryland, Hyattsville, MD.
Robert Irwin, artist, Los Angeles, CA.
Bernard Kester, artist/teacher, University of California, Los Angeles, CA.
Rosalind Krauss, critic, *October* Magazine, New York, NY.
Bart Parker, artist, Providence, RI.
Carlos Solana, staff, New York State Council on the Arts, New York, NY.
Anne Tucker, curator, Museum of Fine Arts, Houston, TX.
Martha Wilson, curator/director, Franklin Furnace, New York, NY.

1983

Panel Chair: **Irving Sandler,** critic/teacher, New York, NY.
Richard Andrews, LAA staff, public arts program, Seattle, WA.
Dale Chihuly, artist, Pilchuck School, Seattle, WA.
Chuck Close, artist, New York, NY.
Bing Davis, artist, Dayton, OH.
Douglas Davis, artist/critic, New York, NY.
Ronald Feldman, dealer, commercial gallery, New York, NY.
John Giancola, staff, New York State Council on the Arts, New York, NY.
Rosalind Krauss, critic, *October* Magazine, New York, NY.
Donald Kuspit, critic, State University of New York, Stony Brook, NY.
Al Nodal, curator/director, Otis Parsons Gallery, Los Angeles, CA.
Adrian Piper, artist/critic, Ann Arbor, MI.
Susan Rankaitis, artist, Inglewood, CA.
Jock Reynolds, artist/director, Washington Project for the Arts, Washington, DC.
Marcia Tucker, curator/director, The New Museum, New York, NY.

1984

Panel Chair: **Irving Sandler,** critic/teacher, New York, NY.
Richard Andrews, LAA staff, public arts program, Seattle, WA.
Alan Bunce, critic, *Christian Science Monitor,* Boston, MA.
Garth Clark, dealer, commercial gallery, Los Angeles, CA.
Chuck Close, artist, New York, NY.
Anita Contini, curator/director, Creative Time, New York, NY.
Bing Davis, artist, Dayton, OH.
Jackie Ferrara, artist, New York, NY.
Henry Geldzahler, curator/critic, New York, NY.
Kathy Halbreich, curator, Massachusetts Institute of Technology, Cambridge, MA.
Nancy Lurie, dealer, commercial gallery, Chicago, IL.
Sarah Lutman, administrator, Fleishhacker Foundation, San Francisco, CA.
Henry Moran, director, Mid-American Arts Alliance, Kansas City, MO.
Susan Rankaitis, artist, Inglewood, CA.
Jock Reynolds, artist/director, Washington Project for the Arts, Washington, DC.

1985

Panel Chair: **Henry Geldzahler,** curator/critic, New York, NY.
Anita Contini, curator/director, Creative Time, New York, NY.
Helen Drutt English, dealer, commercial gallery, Philadelphia, PA.
David Fraher, director, Arts Midwest, Minneapolis, MN.
Kathy Halbreich, curator, Massachusetts Institute of Technology, Cambridge, MA.
David Jacobs, artist/critic, University of Arizona, Tucson, AZ.
Luis Jimenez, artist, Hondo, NM.
Mark Lere, artist, Los Angeles, CA.
Richard Loving, artist, Chicago, IL.
Jim Pomeroy, artist, San Francisco, CA.
Irving Sandler, critic/teacher, New York, NY.
Gary Super, artist/administrator, Atlanta, GA.

1986

Panel Chair: **Anita Contini,** curator/director, Creative Time, New York, NY.
Ricardo Block, artist, St. Paul, MN.
Jack Boulton, curator, Chase Manhattan Bank, New York, NY.
Luis Jimenez, artist, Hondo, NM.
Christoper Knight, critic, *Herald Examiner,* Los Angeles, CA.
Richard Loving, artist, Chicago, IL.
Sarah Lutman, administrator, Fleishhacker Foundation, San Francisco, CA.
Marc Pally, artist/administrator, Community Redevelopment Agency, Los Angeles, CA.
Lisa Phillips, curator, Whitney Museum of American Art, New York, NY.
Jim Pomeroy, artist, San Francisco, CA.
Rita Starpattern, staff, Texas Commission on the Arts, Austin, TX.
Susan Stinsmuehlen, artist, Austin, TX.

1987

Panel Chair: **David Fraher,** director, Arts Midwest, Minneapolis, MN.
Mary Beebe, curator, Stuart Collection/University of California at San Diego, La Jolla, CA.
Susan Crile, artist, New York, NY
Jennifer Dowley, director, Headlands Art Center, Sausalito, CA.
Vernon Fisher, artist, Denton, TX.
Jeff Hoone, artist/director, Light Work, Syracuse, NY.
Judith Kirshner, curator, Terra Museum, Chicago, IL.
Carole Kismaric, editor, *Aperture,* New York, NY.
Susan Stinsmuehlen, artist, Austin, TX.
Philip Yenawine, curator, Museum of Modern Art, New York, NY.

1988

Panel Chair: **David Fraher,** director, Arts Midwest, Minneapolis, MN.
David Avalos, artist, San Diego, CA.
Gary Garrels, curator, Dia Art Foundation, New York, NY.
Olivia Georgia, curator/director, Maryland Art Place, Baltimore, MD.
Jeff Hoone, artist/director, Light Work, Syracuse, NY.
Judith Kirshner, curator/teacher, Chicago, IL.
Inverna Lockpez, artist/director, INTAR/International Arts Relations, New York, NY.
Wendy Maruyama, artist, Oakland, CA.
Amalia Mesa-Bains, artist/curator, San Francisco, CA.
Martha Schwartz, artist/architect, San Francisco, CA.
Philip Yenawine, curator, Museum of Modern Art, New York, NY.
Zenia Zed, artist/critic, Atlanta, GA.

1989

Panel Chair: **David Fraher,** director, Arts Midwest, Minneapolis, MN.
Liz Armstrong, curator, Walker Art Center, Minneapolis, MN.
Deborah Butterfield, artist, Bozeman, MT.
Houston Conwill, artist, New York, NY.
Eileen Cowin, artist, Culver City, CA.
Jennifer Dowley, director, Headlands Art Center, Sausalito, CA.
Robert Gaylor, artist/director, Center for Contemporary Arts of Santa Fe, Santa Fe, NM.
Wayne Higby, artist/teacher, Alfred University, Alfred, NY.
Janet Kardon, curator/director, American Craft Museum, New York, NY.
Peter Taub, artist/director, Randolph Street Gallery, Chicago, IL.
Cesar Trasobares, LAA staff, public art program, Miami, FL.
Diane Vanderlip, curator, Denver Art Museum, Denver, CO.

1990

Panel Chair: **Jennifer Dowley,** director, Headlands Art Center, Sausalito, CA.
Joe Deal, artist/teacher, Washington University, St. Louis, MO.
Suzanne Delehanty, curator/director, Contemporary Art Museum, Houston, TX.
Richard Fleischner, artist, Providence, RI.
Merry Foresta, curator, National Museum of American Art, Washington, DC.
Wayne Higby, artist/teacher, Alfred University, Alfred, NY.
Jean McLaughlin, staff, North Carolina Arts Council, Raleigh, NC.
Claire Peeps, editor/administrator, Los Angeles Festival, Los Angeles, CA.
Judith Shea, artist, New York, NY.
Joyce Scott, artist, Baltimore, MD.
Cesar Trasobares, artist/consultant, public art program, Miami, FL.
Ella King Torrey, layperson, Pew Charitable Trusts, Philadelphia, PA.

1991

Panel Chair: **Jennifer Dowley,** director, Headlands Art Center, Sausalito, CA.
Graham Beal, curator/director, Joslyn Art Museum, Omaha, NE.
Joe Deal, artist/teacher, Washington University, St. Louis, MO.
Susan Dickson, staff, Ohio Arts Council, Columbus, OH.
Glenn Harper, editor, *Art Papers,* Atlanta, GA.
Al F. Harris, artist/curator, CRCA/ University of Texas, Arlington, TX.
Andrew Leicester, artist, Minneapolis, MN.
Susana Leval, curator, El Museo del Barrio, New York, NY.
Stephen Prina, artist, Los Angeles, CA.
Emily Pulitzer, layperson, collector, St. Louis, MO.
Amy Sandback, editor, *P.P. Rindge,* Rindge, NH.
Judith Shea, artist, Housatonic, MA.
Fred Wilson, artist/director, Longwood Arts Project, New York, NY.

1992

Panel Chair: **Joe Deal,** artist/teacher, Washington University, St. Louis, MO.
Graham Beal, curator/director, Joslyn Art Museum, Omaha, NE.
Susan Dickson, staff, Ohio Arts Council, Columbus, OH.
Jennifer Dowley, curator/director, Headlands Art Center, Sausalito, CA.
Glenn Harper, editor, *Art Papers*, Atlanta, GA.
Al F. Harris, artist/curator, CRCA/ University of Texas, Arlington, TX.
Andrew Leicester, artist, Minneapolis, MN.
Susana Leval, curator, El Museo del Barrio, New York, NY.
Stephen Prina, artist, Los Angeles, CA.
Emily Pulitzer, layperson, collector, St. Louis, MO.
Amy Sandback, editor, *P.P. Rindge,* Rindge, NH.
Judith Shea, artist, Housatonic, MA.
Fred Wilson, artist/director, Longwood Arts Project, New York, NY.

1993

Panel Chair: **Joe Deal,** artist/teacher, Washington University, St. Louis, MO.
Deborah Bright, artist/teacher, Rhode Island School of Design, Providence, RI.
Jacqueline Crist, staff, Idaho Commission on the Arts, Boise, ID.
Judith Kirshner, curator/critic, University of Illinois, Chicago, IL.
Kyong Park, artist/director, Storefront for Art & Architecture, New York, NY.
Stephen Prina, artist, Los Angeles, CA.
Renny Pritikin, curator/critic, Yerba Buena Center, San Francisco, CA.
Cesar Trasobares, artist/consultant, public art program, Miami, FL.
Fred Wilson, artist/director, Longwood Arts Project, New York, NY.
Virginia Wright, layperson, collector, Seattle, WA.

1994

Panel Chair: **Michael Moore,** staff, New England Foundation for the Arts, Cambridge, MA
Jerri Allyn, artist/teacher, New School, New York, NY.
Suzanne Delehanty, curator/director, Contemporary Art Museum, Houston, TX.
Susanne Ghez, curator/director, Renaissance Society, Chicago, IL.
Marilynn Gladstone, layperson, trustee, Washington, DC.
Allan Millar, administrator, Yerba Buena Center, San Francisco, CA.
Robert Peters, artist/teacher, University of Chicago, Chicago, IL.
Robert Reed, artist/teacher, Yale University, New Haven, CT.
Pablo Schugurensky, staff, Washington State Arts Commission, Olympia, WA.
John Scott, artist/teacher, Xavier University, New Orleans, LA.

1994

Panel Chair: **David Fraher,** director, Arts Midwest, Minneapolis, MN.
Chris Bruce, curator, Henry Art Gallery, Seattle, WA.
Mary Jane Jacob, curator, Chicago, IL.
William Larson, artist/teacher, Maryland Institute, Collegeville, PA
Stella MacGregor, administrator, public art program, Lexington, MA.
Judy Moran, artist/consultant, San Francisco, CA.
Kyong Park, artist/director, Storefront for Art & Architecture, New York, NY.
Michael Peranteau, curator/director, DiverseWorks, Houston, TX.
Lari Pittman, artist, Los Angeles, CA.
Bernandine Speers, layperson, BancOne, Indianapolis, IN.

1995

Panel Chair: **Anne Focke,** consultant, Seattle, WA.
Gregory Amenoff, artist, New York, NY.
Nayland Blake, artist, San Francisco, CA.
Tom Borrup, administrator, Intermedia Arts, Minneapolis, MN.
Glenn Harper, editor, *Art Papers,* Atlanta, GA.
Judith Kirshner, curator/critic, University of Illinois, Chicago, IL.
William Larson, artist/teacher, Maryland Institute, Collegeville, PA.
Ree Schonlau, administrator, Bemis Center for Contemporary Art, Omaha, NE.
Cesar Trasobares, consultant, Miami, FL.
Nadine Francis West, layperson, mayoral assistant, Hartford, CT.

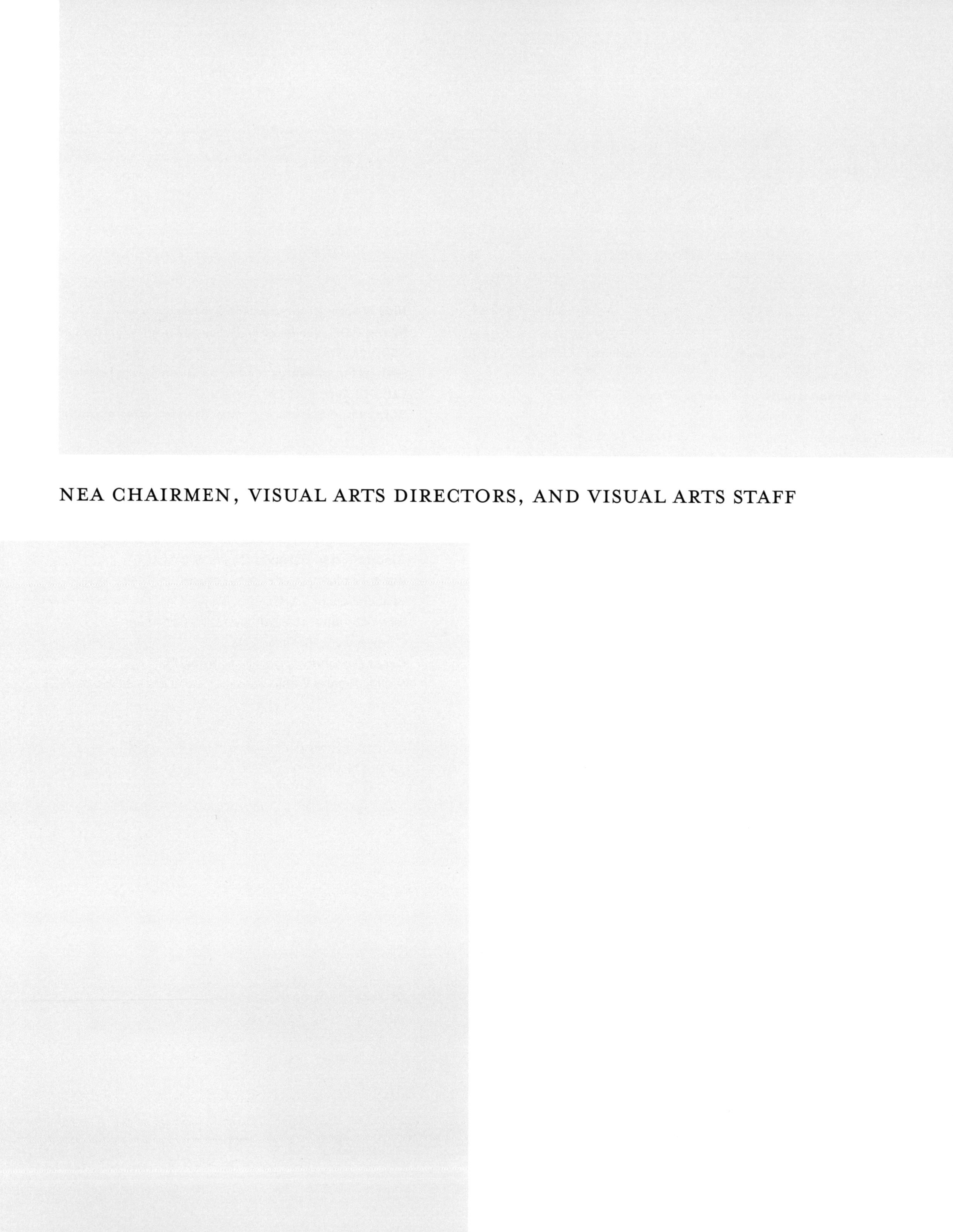

NEA CHAIRMEN, VISUAL ARTS DIRECTORS, AND VISUAL ARTS STAFF

NEA Chairmen

Roger L. Stevens, Chairman	*1965–1969*
Nancy Hanks, Chairman	*1969–1977*
Livingston L. Biddle, Jr., Chairman	*1977–1981*
Frank Hodsoll, Chairman	*1981–1989*
John E. Frohnmayer, Chairman	*1989–1992*
Jane Alexander, Chairman	*1993–1997*
Bill Ivey, Chairman	*1998–2001*

Visual Arts Directors

Henry Geldzahler, Director	*1966–1969*
Brian O'Doherty, Director	*1969–1976*
James Melchert, Director	*1977–1981*
Benny Andrews, Director	*1982–1984*
Richard Andrews, Director	*1985–1987*
Susan Lubowsky, Director	*1989–1992*
Rosalyn Alter, Director	*1992–1994*
Jennifer Dowley, Director	*1994–1999*

Visual Arts Staff, 1965–1999

Eva Antoniou, Secretary
David Bancroft, Administrator Specialist
Charles Bish, Assistant/Fellowships
Ruth Bond, Assistant/Fellowships
Roger Bruce, Coordinator/Photography
Elena Canavier, Coordinator/Crafts
Richard Carey, Assistant/Fellowships
Paul Carlson, Administrator/Specialist/Photography
Sue Coliton, Specialist/Visual Arts
Laura Coyle, Assistant/Fellowships
Renato Danese, Assistant Director
Annette Davis, Assistant
James Dean, Assistant/Fellowships
Nancy Drew, Coordinator/Visual Arts
Jean Efron, Assistant
Mary Fahey, Assistant
Michael Faubion, Assistant Director, Acting Director, Coordinator, Specialist,Assistant/Fellowships
Vicki Fern, Assistant
Ramiro Fernandez, Specialist/Fellowships, Assistant/Fellowships
Patrick Fisher, Specialist/Crafts
Laura Friesen, Assistant/Fellowships
Patricia Fuller, Coordinator/Public Art
Kathy Gauss, Specialist/Photography
Kerrie Gillis, Assistant/Fellowships
Diane Gingold, Specialist/Public Art
Michael Giza, Specialist/Crafts
Rodney Goldstein, Specialist/Photography
Elise Goldstein, Assistant
Maria Goodwin, Specialist/Public Art
Beth Hameleinen, Assistant/Fellowships
Jackie Harmon, Secretary
Leonard Hunter, Assistant Director, Acting Director
Melanie Kersey, Assistant/Fellowships
Richard Koshalek, Assistant Director
Bert Kubli, Specialist/Public Art
Gretchen Lapp, Assistant/Fellowships
Camille Larsen, Specialist/Visual Arts
Lisa Levine, Specialist/Visual Arts
Ira Licht, Coordinator/Public Art
Silvio Lim, Specialist/Fellowships, Assistant
Maria Los, Assistant/Fellowships
John Maggiotto, Specialist/Visual Arts
John McLean, Specialist/Crafts
Starke Meyer, Assistant
Melanie Modlin, Assistant
Julia Moore, Administrator
Eudorah Moore, Coordinator/Crafts
Jennifer Neimur, Specialist/Fellowships, Assistant/Fellowships
Stacy Paleologos, Specialist/Public Art, Specialist/Fellowships, Assistant/Fellowships
Sue Pitler, Assistant/Fellowships
John Prince, Assistant
Lorie Rotenberg, Assistant/Fellowships
Dana Rust, Specialist/Visual Arts
Malcolm Ryder, Specialist/Fellowships
Jack Seely, Assistant
Jamela Simpson, Assistant
Mary Smith, Assistant
David Steinberg, Specialist/Fellowships, Assistant/Fellowships
Saul Straussman, Assistant
Katherine Suttles, Administrator
Jack Weiland, Assistant/Fellowships
Glenn Yokley, Secretary
Sandra Zimmerman, Coordinator/Crafts

BLACK-AND-WHITE PLATES

Dennis Adams
The Archive
1990

Ink jet color print, fluorescent light, Plexiglas and Duratrans, 238 x 282 x 427". Pedestrian tunnel, Hirshhorn Museum and Sculpture Garden, Washington, D.C.

PHOTOGRAPHER: James Cohrssen

Jo Harvey Allen
Counter Angel
1982

Solo performance, written and performed by Jo Harvey Allen

PHOTOGRAPHER: Tom Vinetz

Nicholas Africano
Actor
1986

Cast bronze, cast glass, cloth, wood, marble base, 22 x 22 x 8"

Carlos Alfonzo
Trail
1985

Acrylic on canvas, 103 x 112"

Private collection.
Courtesy McMurtrey Gallery, Houston

Carl Andre
Stone Field Sculpture
1977

Thirty-six glacial boulders. Hartford, Connecticut

Courtesy Paula Cooper Gallery

Benny Andrews
Migrants (Langston Hughes Series)
1996

Oil and collage on paper, 27 3/4 x 39 1/4"

Courtesy ACA Galleries, New York

PHOTOGRAPHER: Michael Korol

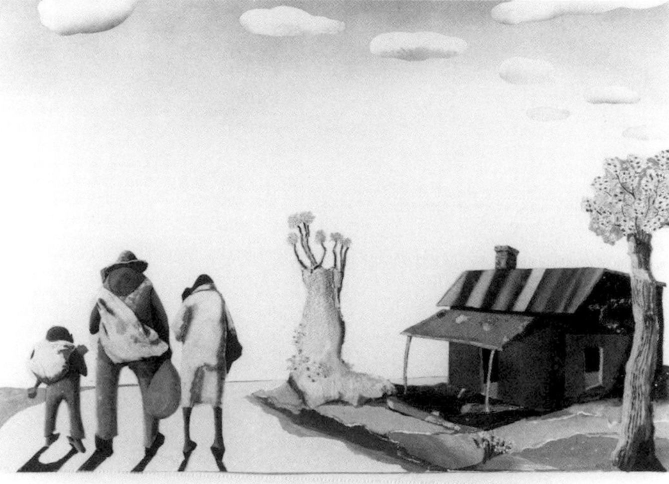

Lawrence Andrews
Vrischikasana-Tardieu Spots
(from *Wounded Series)*
1998

Digital photographs

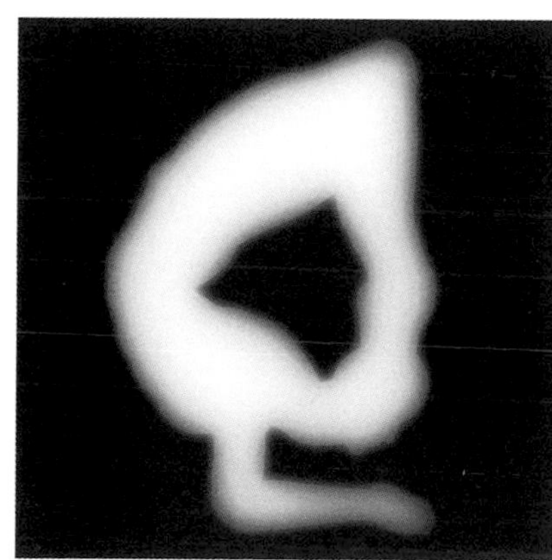

Eleanor Antin
Eleanora Antinova In "Pocahontas"
(from *Recollections Of My Life With Diaghilev)*
1979–80

Silver print, 11 x 14"

Courtesy Ronald Feldman Gallery, New York

Siah Armajani
Lighthouse and Bridge
1996

Lighthouse 60 x 60' steel reflected arch pedestrian bridge (adjacent to the Ferry Landing at Staten Island) connecting the plaza to the Ferry Terminal. Staten Island, New York.

Courtesy Max Protetch Gallery, New York

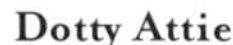

Dotty Attie
An Eminent Painter
1989

Oil on canvas, 20 panels 6 x 6", 16 panels 4 x 6"

Courtesy P. P. O. W Fine Arts, New York

PHOTOGRAPHER: Adam Reich

Rudy Autio
Gifthorse
1994

Stoneware ceramic, 38 1/2 x 31 x 20"

PHOTOGRAPHER: Chris Autio

Alice Aycock
.c. Functional and Fantasy Stair and Cyclone Fragment
1996

Spiral Stair and Cone, aluminum and structural steel with painted steel sheathing, Suspended Cyclone Fragment, aluminum with structural steel pole, Cone 24 x 22', Spiral Stairs 28', Cyclone Fragment 32 x 20'

San Francisco Main Library, California

Lewis Baltz
Element #12 (from New Industrial Parks near Irvine, California)
1974

Black-and-white gelatin silver print, 6.38 x 9 1/2"

Courtesy Luisotti Gallery, Santa Monica

Judith Barry
Maelstrom: May Laughs
1989

Video installation, dimensions variable

Photograph courtesy Whitney Museum of American Art, New York

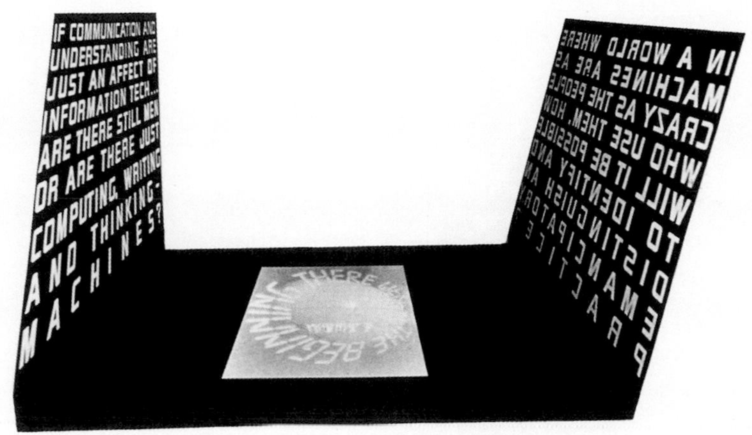

Larry Bell
6x6x4 ABCD
1999

4 glass panels coated with Inconel, 72 x 72" each panel. Installation, Wood Street Galleries, Pittsburgh

PHOTOGRAPHER: Bill Wade

Howard Ben Tre'
Double Wrapped Form
1994

Cast glass, lead, patina, 57 x 18 1/2 x 18 1/2"

PHOTOGRAPHER: Ric Murray

Lynda Benglis
Tossana
1995-96

Stainless steel wire mesh, zinc, aluminum, silicone bronze, 49 x 63 x 14"

PHOTOGRAPHER: Douglas M. Parker

Garry Bennett
Chest Bench #2
1991

Painted wood and leather, 28 x 77 1/4 x 19"

Courtesy Leo Kaplan Modern, New York

PHOTOGRAPHER: M. Lee Fatherree

Willie Birch
Knowing Our History
1992

m/m papier mâché, 80 x 88 x 17"

Courtesy Arthur Roger Gallery, New Orleans

Ronald Bladen
X
1967

Painted wood, 22 x 26 x 14'.
Exhibition photograph, Corcoran Gallery of Art, Washington, D. C.

Courtesy Ronald Bladen

Ross Bleckner
Fallen Object
1987

Oil and linen, 48 x 40"

Courtesy Mary Boone Gallery, New York

PHOTOGRAPHER: Zindman/Fremont

Mel Bochner
Remarks On Color
1999

Oil on canvas, 36 x 48"

Jonathan Borofsky
Hammering Man at 3,007,624
1990–91

Steel, 70'

Commission: Messe Turm, Frankfurt, Germany

Courtesy Paula Cooper Gallery, New York

Gandy Brodie
Stravinsky
1975

Oil on canvas, 25 x 19 1/4"

Courtesy Gandy Brodie

PHOTOGRAPHERS: Robert E. Mates and Susan Lazarus

Christopher Brown
Swimming in China
1985

Oil on canvas, 72 x 144"

Courtesy Campbell-Thiebaud Gallery, San Francisco

PHOTOGRAPHER: Ira Schrank

Joan Brown
The Bicentennial Champion
1976

Enamel on canvas, 96 x 78"

Joan Brown, Collection Michael Hebel and Noel Neri
Courtesy George Adams Gallery, New York

PHOTOGRAPHER: eeva inkeri

Beverly Buchanan
Restored Shack
1993–94

Wood, tar paper, mixed-media, 20 x 26 x 16"

Courtesy Steinbaum Krauss Gallery, New York

PHOTOGRAPHER: Adam Reich

Deborah Butterfield
Argus (PJ)
1997

Cast bronze, 81 x 104 x 40"

Denver Museum of Art Collection

James Lee Byars
The Perfect Death
1977

Venetian glass, silk paper, gold ink, 19 x 19 x 2" (48 x 48 x 5 cm)

Courtesy Galerie Michael Werner, Cologne and New York

Jo Ann Callis
Untitled (Angel)
1992-94

C-Print, 40 x 30"

Paul Caponigro
Callanish Stone Circle, Isle of Lewis, Hebrides, Scotland
1972

Silver chlorobromide print, 9 1/4 x 131/4"

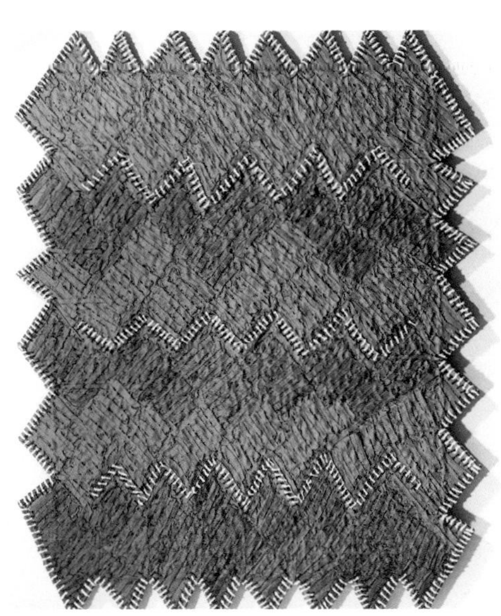

Cynthia Carlson
Katzenjammer
1976

Acrylic paint on canvas and wood, 57 x 70 1/2"

PHOTOGRAPHER: Bruce C. Jones

Wendell Castle
Voyage
1995

PC wood, walnut, mahogany, 44 x 39 x 19"

PHOTOGRAPHER: David Mohney

Vija Celmins
To fix the image in memory (detail)
1977-82

Stones and painted bronzes

PHOTOGRAPHER: Vija Celmins

Theresa Cha
Other Things Seen, Other Things Heard
1978

Black-and-white film of performance,
9 1/4 x 1 1/2"

Gift of the Theresa Hak Kyung Cha Memorial Foundation, Berkeley Art Museum and Pacific Film Archive

PHOTOGRAPHER: Ben Blackwell

Albert Chong
The Cowrie Necklace
1993

Gelatin silver print, 30 x 40"

Ping Chong
In the Absence of Memory
1989

Mixed-media, site specific installation

Y. David Chung
Luxorview Dusk
1993

Mixed-media, 52 x 192"

Linda Connor
Crocodile, Valley of the Kings, Egypt
1989

Photograph, 8 x 10"

Sue Coe
Exxon
1990

Gouache, watercolor, and graphite on board, 23 1/8 x 29" (59 x 73.6 cm)

Courtesy Galerie St. Etienne, New York

Houston Conwill
The New Ring Shout
1992–95

Collaborative Team: Houston Conwill, sculptor; Joseph De Pace, architect, graphic artist; Estella Conwill Majozo, poet. Interior floor installation over the site of The African Burial Ground, Federal Office Building, New York. 38' x 10" diameter terrazzo and brass cosmogram and accompanying design of Rotunda ceiling and lighting.

Lia Cook

Presence/Absence: Soft Touch

1997

Cotton, rayon, handwoven Jacquard, 48 x 40"

Private collection

John Coplans

Self Portrait (Back With Arms Above)

1984

Silver gelatin print, 42 x 32"

Courtesy Andrea Rosen Gallery, New York

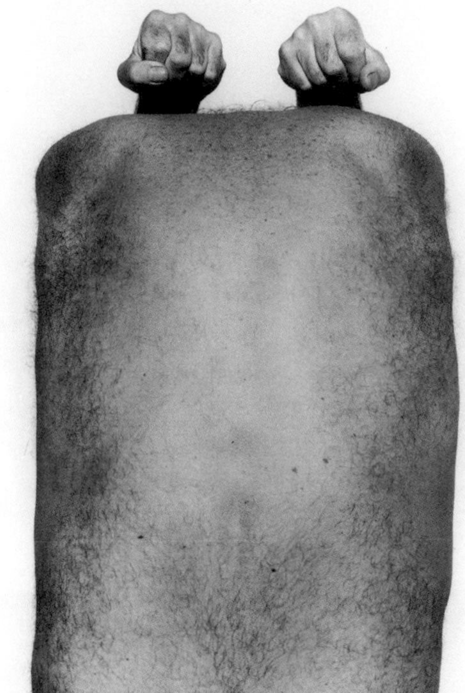

Dorit Cypis

Framing Memories I Never Had

1998

Mixed-media, slide dissolve projection with projection equipment and cloth

Collection of the artist

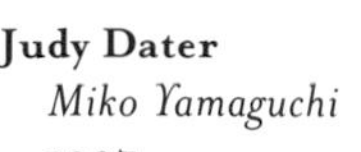

Judy Dater

Miko Yamaguchi

1997

Gelatin silver print, 20 x 16"

Gene Davis
Raspberry Icicle
1967

Acrylic on canvas, 116 x 219 5/8"
(294.6 x 558.4 cm)

National Museum of American Art,
Smithsonian Institution Collection

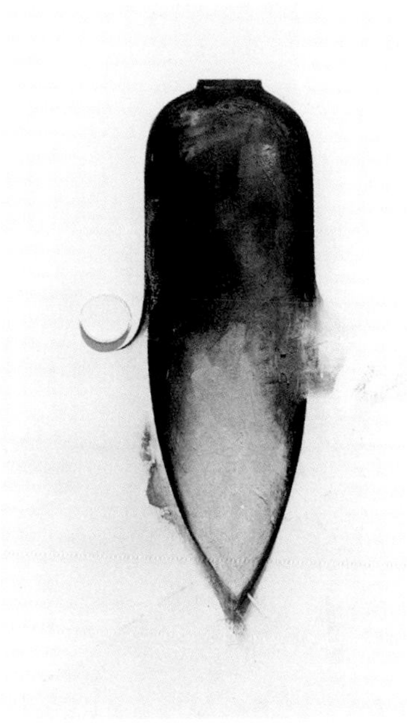

Jay DeFeo
Lotus Eater No. 1
1974

Acrylic and assemblage on masonite,
72 1/2 x 48 1/2"

PHOTOGRAPHER: M. Lee Fatherree

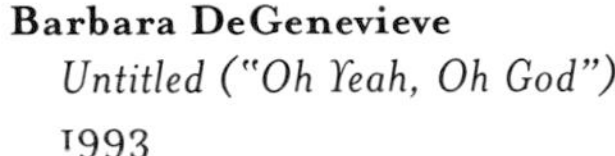

Barbara DeGenevieve
Untitled ("Oh Yeah, Oh God")
1993

Photograph, stretched fabric, paint, macaroni,
56 x 174 x 1"

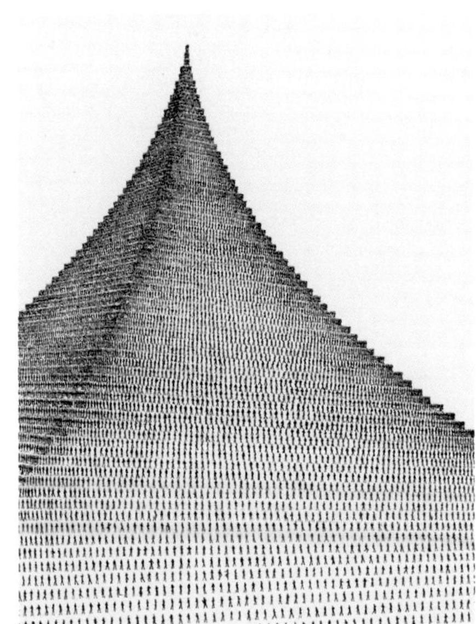

Agnes Denes
Pascal's Perfect Probability Pyramid & The People Paradox— The Predicament (detail)
1980

India ink on silk vellum, 32 x 43"

Donna Dennis
Deep Station
1981–85

Wood, glass, electrical fixtures, acrylic and enamel paint, metal, cellulose compound, rubber, plastic, 135 x 240 x 288" (detail view)

Courtesy Holly Solomon Gallery, New York

PHOTOGRAPHER: Peter Mauss Esto

Lewis DeSoto
Ship
1998

Steel, computerized guidance system, motors, fog machine, 22 x 70 x 12"

Photograph courtesy Bill Maynes Gallery, New York

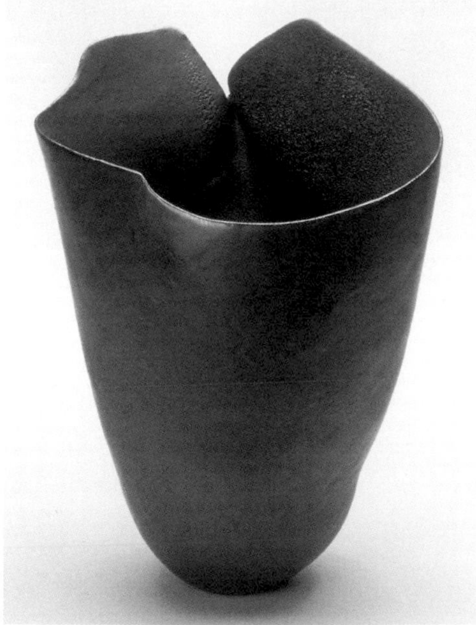

Richard DeVore
#851
1998

Ceramic, 18 x 12 1/2 x 11"

Courtesy Max Protetch Gallery, New York

PHOTOGRAPHER: Vanderbuff

Ellen Driscoll
The Loophole of Retreat
1991

Wood, metal, motor, cloth, plaster, glass, light, lenses, One 8 x 8 x 13' camera obscura, One 10' diameter ceiling-mounted wheel with 1 rpm motor, 12 objects, One 22" x 22' accordion book, Seven 5' x 7" diameter wooden columns suspended with hidden light source, glass lens.

PHOTOGRAPHER: George Hirose

Melvin Edwards
Premonition
1990

Welded steel, 18 x 11 x 11"

Courtesy CDS Gallery, New York

Richard Estes
The Plaza
1991

Oil on canvas, 36 x 66" (91.44 x 167.64 cm)

Courtesy Marlborough Gallery, New York

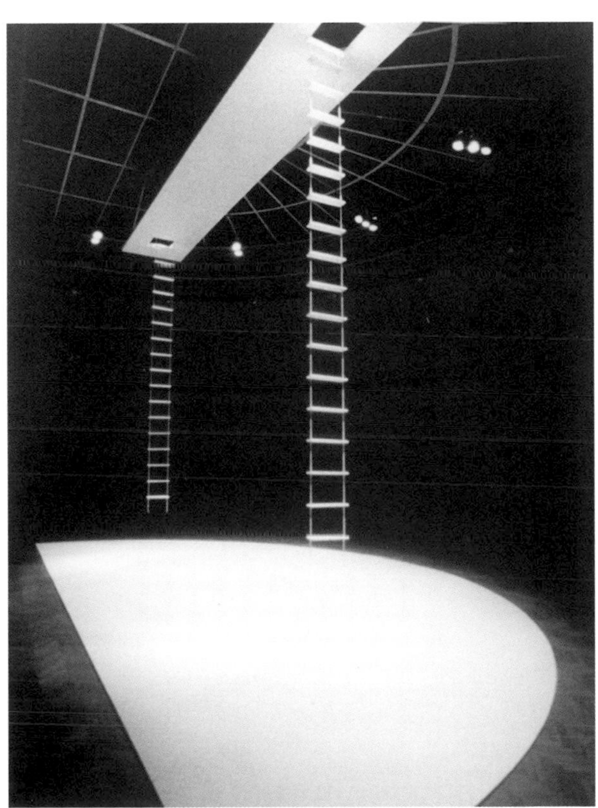

Wendy Ewald
F for Fruta (from *The Alphabet Project*)
1997-98

Silver print, 8 x 10" detail from 78 x 84" pyramid of 30 photographs. Wendy Ewald and the English as a Second Language students at Bethesda Elementary School, North Carolina

Teresita Fernández
Untitled (Crawlspace)
1997

Wood, cast plaster, rope, pencil drawing, 18 x 36 x 18'. Installation at The Corcoran Gallery of Art, Washington, D.C.

Courtesy Deitch Projects, New York

PHOTOGRAPHER: Peter Harholdt

Howard Finster

The Devil's Vice

1984

Enamel, wood, 18 x 16"

Courtesy Phyllis Kind Gallery, New York

Mary Fish

Image from Lahgo Náhodeesdzá
(Time Called For A Better Way of Being)

1995

Photo emulsion on earth-rubbed paper, 22 1/4 x 30 1/4"

PHOTOGRAPHER: Mary Fish

Vernon Fisher

Variations on an Ending

1999

Acrylic on canvas, 46 1/2 x 52 1/2"

Courtesy Charles Cowles Gallery, New York

Louise Fishman

Tossed As It Is Untroubled

1997

Oil on canvas, 30 1/4 x 20 1/4" (76.8 x 51.4 cm)

Courtesy Cheim & Read Gallery, New York

Jane Freilicher
Flower Against a Blue Window
1997
Oil on canvas, 24 x 20"
Courtesy Tibor de Nagy Gallery, New York
PHOTOGRAPHER: Adam Reich

Rupert Garcia
Hello, Good-bye, Hello
1992
Oil on paper, 72 x 120"
PHOTOGRAPHER: M. Lee Fatherree

Jim Goldberg
Untitled from *"Spit"* (detail)
1999
Diazo print, 30 x 40"
Courtesy PaceWildensteinMacGill, New York

Carmen Garza
Empanadas (turnovers)
1991
Gouache painting, 20 x 28"
Collection Romeo Montalvo, MD., Brownsville, Texas
PHOTOGRAPHER: Judy Reed

Peter Gourfain
A Last Supper
1993
Terra-cotta, 36 x 36 x 10"
PHOTOGRAPHER: Kevin Noble

Doug Hall
The Terrible Uncertainty of the Thing Described (detail)
1987
Four-channel video installation with sculptural and electronic components
PHOTOGRAPHER: Hansen/Mayer

Maren Hassinger
On Dangerous Ground
1981
Wire rope, 21 bushes, each approximately 4 x 3 x 3'. Installation at the Los Angeles County Museum of Art
PHOTOGRAPHER: Adam Avila

Connie Hatch
Some Americans Forced to Disappear (from *A Display of Visual Inequity* series)
1990
Transparencies with shadows, text, panels, each portrait 10 x 8 x 12"
PHOTOGRAPHER: C. Hatch

Robert Heinecken
Barbara Campaign Fund Raising in Middle America
1992

Collage on existing cardboard figures,
72 1/4 x 47 3/4"

Al Held
Requiem III
1996

Acrylic on canvas, (triptych, right section)
180 x 216" (450 x 540 cm)

Photograph Courtesy Robert Miller Gallery, New York

George Herms
Scientific American
1973

Assemblage, 40 x 20 x 8"

Courtesy Nicholas Wilder Gallery, Los Angeles

PHOTOGRAPHER: Frank J. Thomas

Jene Highstein
Flame
1996

Reinforced black concrete, 10 x 6 x 5'

Collection of the artist

Roni Horn

Untitled (Gun)

1994

Solid aluminum and plastic, 26 units, each 5 x 5" x variable length, stacked height 10' 8", edition 2/3

Courtesy Matthew Marks Gallery, New York

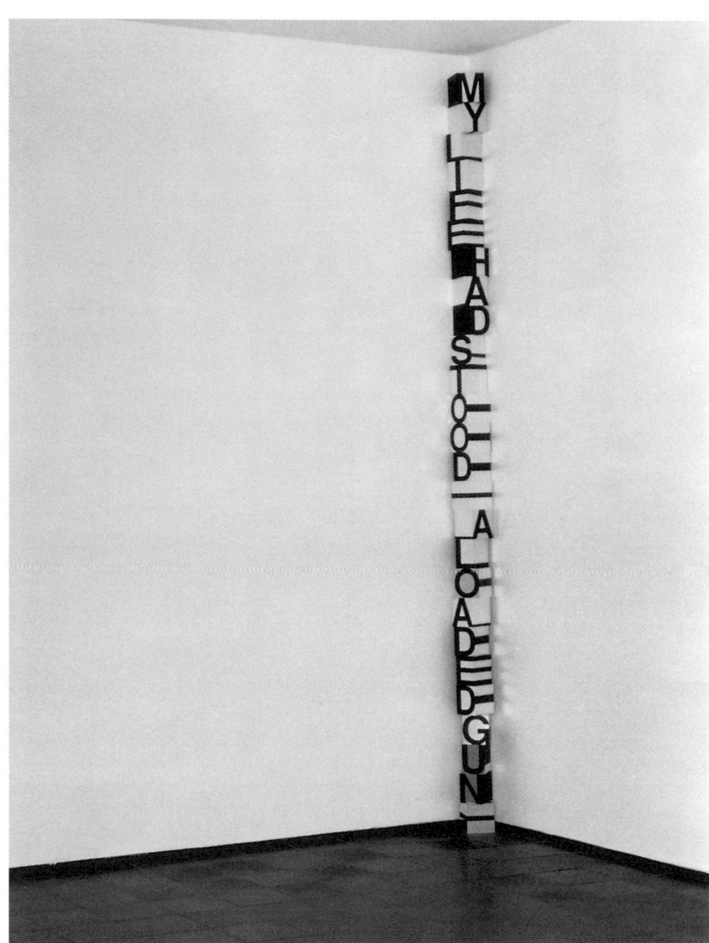

Mildred Howard

Last Train From Caney Creek to 16th and Wood

1994

Mixed-media installation, 80 x 40'

PHOTOGRAPHER: Ben Blackwell

John Hull

Aftermath

1994

Acrylic on canvas, 72 x 84"

Denver Art Museum Collection

PHOTOGRAPHER: Joseph Szaszfai

Peter Hujar

David Wojnarowicz with a Snake

1981

Silver print, 20 x 16"

Courtesy James Danziger Gallery, New York

David Ireland
Dumbball Action On Going Process Work
1992

Concrete, 4" diameter

PHOTOGRAPHER: D. Ireland

Alfredo Jaar
The Eyes Of Gutete Emerita
1996

Quad vision light boxes with black-and-white and color transparencies; each box: 26 x 23 x 6"; time cycle: 45', 30', 15' and 1/5 seconds; overall dimensions: 26 x 48 x 6"

Bill Jensen
Hunger
1984-85

Oil on linen, 16 x 20"

Private collection
Courtesy Mary Boone Gallery, New York

PHOTOGRAPHER: Steven Sloman

Luis Jimenez.
Musteño
1998

Fiberglass, 8'2" high

Kristin Jones/Andrew Ginzel
Interim, after the end and before the beginning
1995

30 x 88 x 22'. Brooklyn Academy of Music, Next Wave Festival, Artists in Action: presented at the Queens Museum of Art, New York

PHOTOGRAPHER: T. Charles Erickson

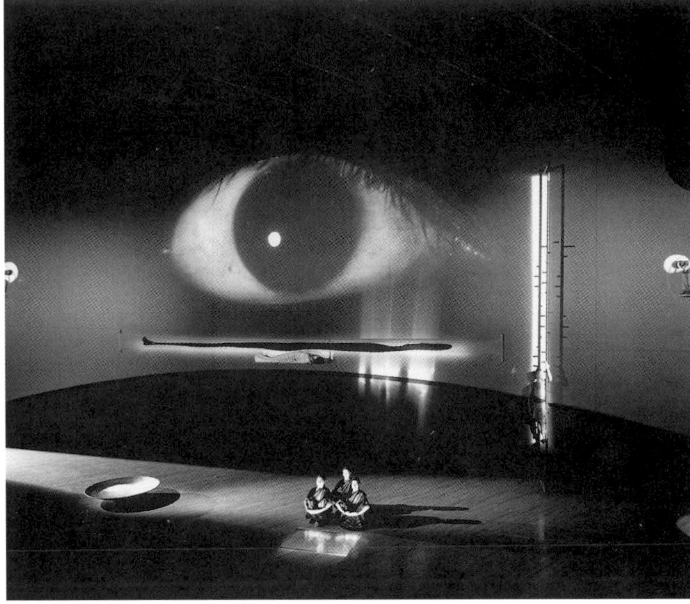

Raymond Jonson
Polymer No. 6
1976

Polymer, 30 x 27"

Bequest of Raymond Jonson, Collection of the Jonson Gallery of the University of New Mexico Art Museums, Albuquerque

Jun Kaneko
Installation, Gallery Takagi, Japan
1991

Glazed ceramics and painted floor

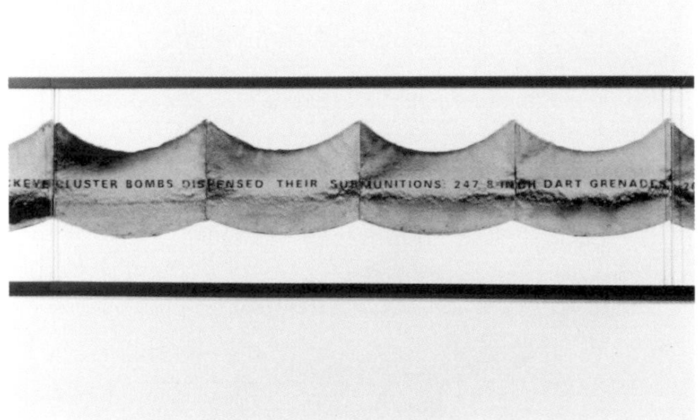

Mary Kelly
Mea Culpa
1999

Lint, detail: 4 of 19 units, overall: 17 x 235 x 2"

Courtesy Postmasters Gallery, New York

Byron Kim

1984 Dodge Wagon

1994

Oil and wax on linen and panel, 44 x 90"

Collection Peter and Eileen Broido
Courtesy Max Protetch Gallery, New York

PHOTOGRAPHER: Dennis Cowley

Mark Klett

Contemplating the View at Muley Point, Utah

1994

Silver gelatin photograph, 16 x 20"

Jin Soo Kim

Untitled Environment

1988

Mixed media, 156 x 504 x 384"

Courtesy Walker Art Center, Minneapolis

PHOTOGRAPHER: Glenn Halvorson

Gerhardt Knodel

16 Provinces of Natur

1996

Fiberglass, stained glass, stainless steel and carpet, 14 x 28 x 14'

Collection American Center, Southfield, Michigan. Courtesy Sybaris Gallery, Michigan

PHOTOGRAPHER: G. Knodel

Komar and Melamid

George, Vladimir, Isadora and Marcel

1996–97

Tempera and oil on canvas, 66 x 98"

Courtesy the artists and Ronald Feldman Fine Arts, New York

PHOTOGRAPHER: Zindman/Freemont

Paul Kos

Study Model for the Galvanized Bell

1988

Galvanized garbage cans and washtubs,
3 x 6 x 6' for a projected scale of 35 x 30 x 30'

Courtesy of Gallery Paule Anglim, San Francisco

PHOTOGRAPHER: Ken Miller

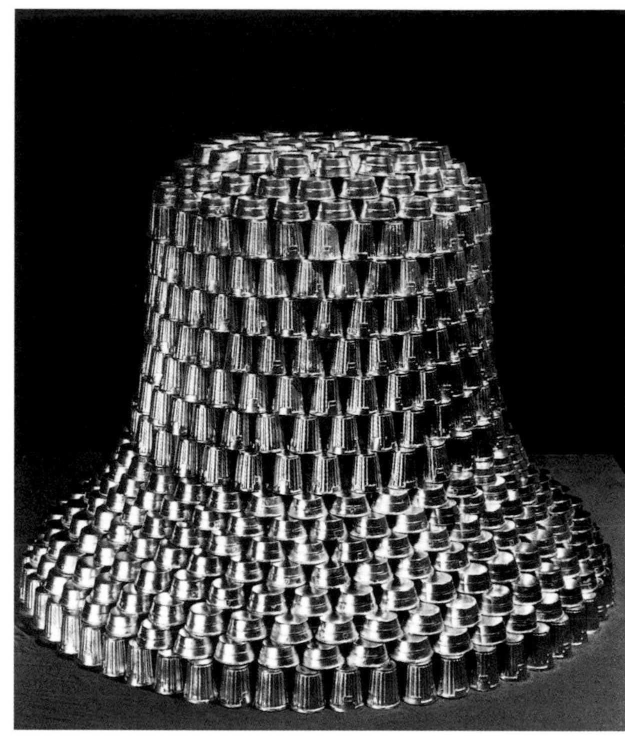

Howard Kottler

Face Vase

1985

Ceramic, glaze, luster, 14 x 10 x 3"

PHOTOGRAPHER: Roger Schreiber

Barbara Kruger

Bus Shelter Image

1991

New York Public Art Fund

Louise Lawler
She Wasn't Always A Statue (A)
1996–97

Black-and-white photograph, 17 3/4 x 18 1/2"

Courtesy Metro Pictures, New York

Shigeko Kubota
Jogging Lady
1993

Video monitors, metal, 43 x 80 x 34"

PHOTOGRAPHER: Peter Moore

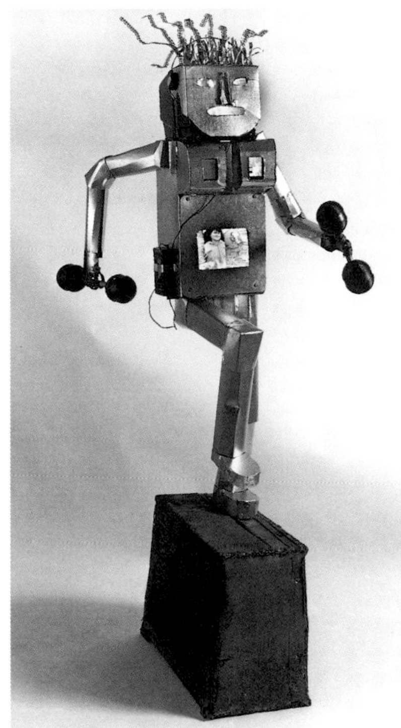

Annette Lemieux
The Ingestion and Excretion of the One By the Other
1991

Latex on canvas with 50 wax objects, 79 x 120 x 96"

Private collection
Courtesy McKee Gallery, New York

David Levinthal
Untitled (from the series *Barbie*)
1998

Polaroid Polacolor ER print, 24 x 20"

Collection of the artist

Norman Lewis
Players Four
1966

Oil on canvas, 76 x 50"

Collection of Tarrin M. Fuller

PHOTOGRAPHER: Henry Lau

Sol LeWitt
X with Columns
1996

Cinder block and concrete, 14 x 26 x 26'

Collection Walker Art Center, Minneapolis
Partial gift of the artist with funds provided by the Judy and Kenneth Dayton Garden Fund and materials provided by Anchor Block Company

Glenn Ligon
Red Portfolio
1993

Black-and-white silver print, 8 x 8"

Courtesy of the artist

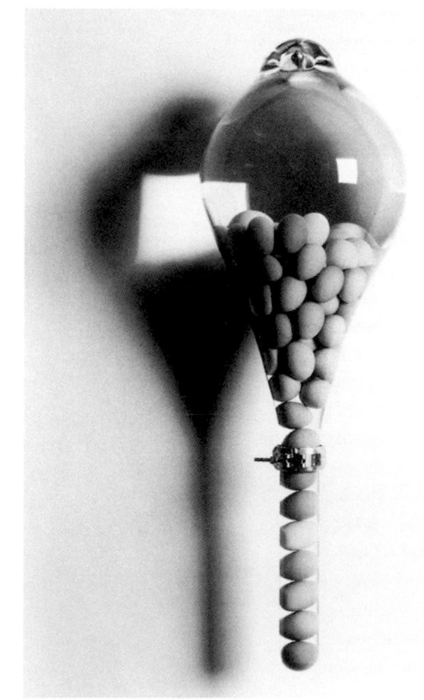

Donald Lipski
Poxabogue Pond No. 29
1995

Glass, eggs, preservative solution, 36 x 12 x 12"
Hot glass formed by Michael Scheiner

Courtesy Galerie Lelong, New York

PHOTOGRAPHER: Tim Lee

Ken Little
Monitor
1982

Shoes, clothes, paint on wood and paper armature, 46 x 90 x 24"

Collection of Jack Blanton Museum of Art

Hung Liu
Chinese Profile III
1998

Oil on canvas, 80 x 80"

Private collection
Courtesy Steinbaum Krauss Gallery, New York

PHOTOGRAPHER: Ben Blackwell

Robert Lobe
Zone
1998

Hammered steel, 76 1/2 x 81 x 25"

Collection of the artist.

Courtesy Senior and Shopmaker Gallery

Danny Lyon
Road to Ocasinga, Chiapas, Where 750 Zapatistas Died
1995

Black-and-white photograph

© Danny Lyon
Courtesy Edwynn Houk Gallery, New York

Nathan Lyons
Elvis
1998

Silver gelatin photograph, 4 1/2 x 6 3/4"

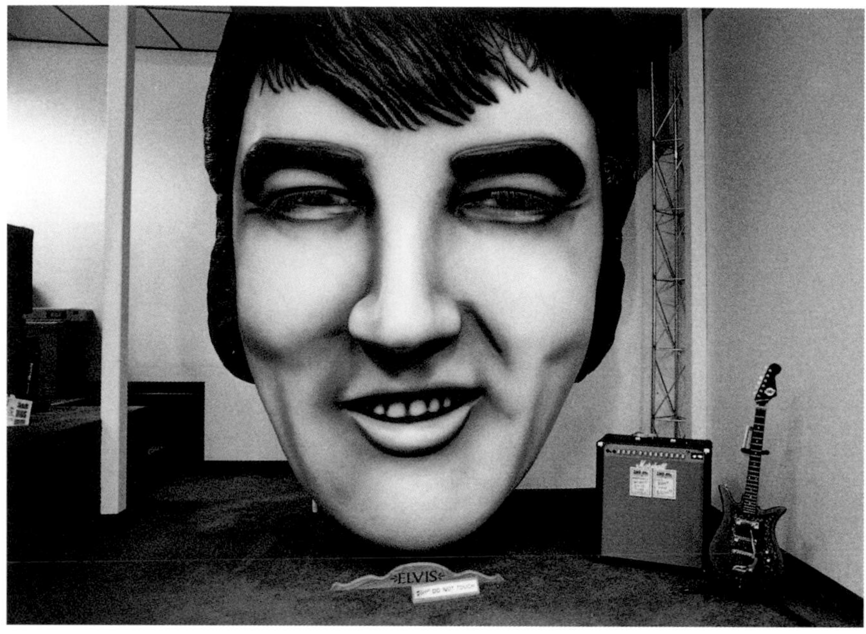

Sylvia Mangold
The Locust Trees with Maple
1989

Oil on linen, 24 x 20"

Courtesy Alexander and Bonin, New York

PHOTOGRAPHER: D. James Dee

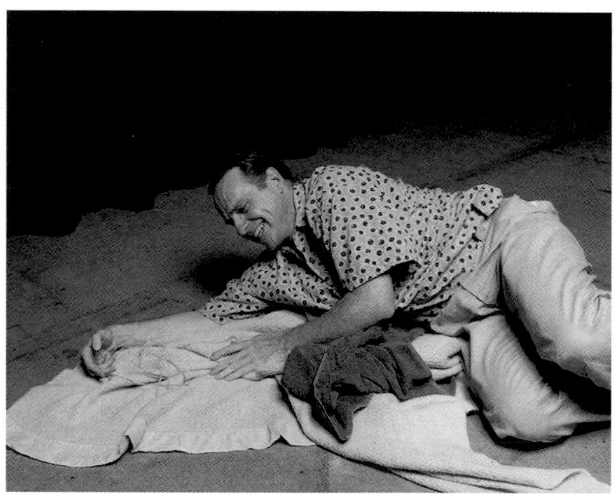

John Malpede
Bronx Train
1995

Performance

PHOTOGRAPHER: Martin Cox

Robert Mangold
Green/Black Zone Painting VIII
1997

Acrylic and black pencil on canvas,
90 x 198 1/4"
(228.6 x 503.6 cm)

Collection Museum Wiesbaden, Wiesbaden, Germany

Courtesy PaceWildenstein, New York

PHOTOGRAPHER: Ellen Page Wilson

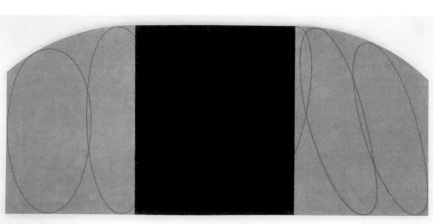

Christian Marclay
Guitar Neck
1992

Collage, record covers, 73 x 19"

Collection Eileen and Peter Norton, Santa Monica

PHOTOGRAPHER: Douglas M. Parker Studio

Tom Marioni
Wednesday
1989

Shadow box, mixed-media, 36 x 24 x 4"

Collection Twig Smith

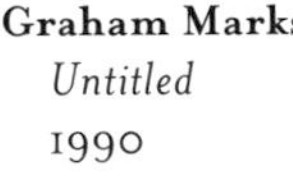

Graham Marks
Untitled
1990

Earthenware clay, 32 x 32 x 35"

Kerry Marshall
Souvenir I
1997

Acrylic and glitter on unstretched canvas banner, 9 x 13'

Collection Museum of Contemporary Art, Chicago
Courtesy Jack Shainman Gallery, New York

Daniel Martinez
Museum Tags: Second Movement (Overture), or Ouverture con Claque (Overture with Hired Audience Members)
1993
3 x 6"
Whitney Biennial, Whitney Museum of American Art, New York

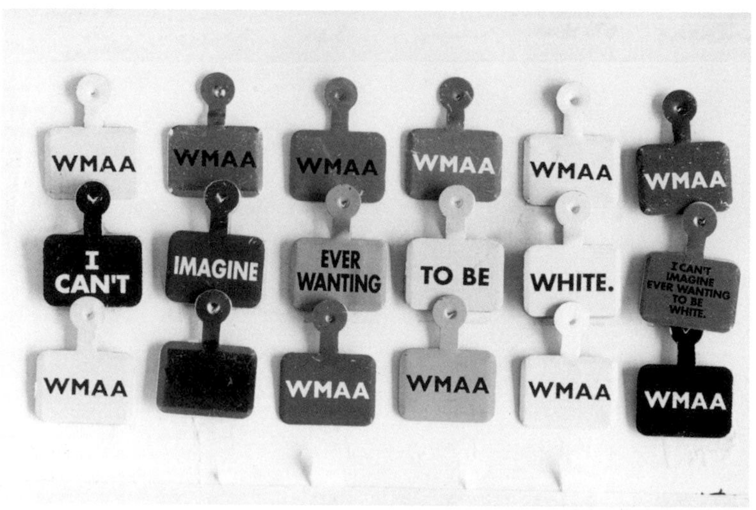

Wendy Maruyama
Ooh-La-La Vanity
1994
Polychromed mahogany, mirror, silk, 28 x 50 x 30"
Collection Wendy Joseph
PHOTOGRAPHER: C. Okazaki Studios

Paul McCarthy
Hollywood Halloween, 2 of 5
1977
Black-and-white photograph

Allan McCollum
Plaster Surrogates
1982-83
Enamel on solid-cast hydrostone, installation view
Marian Goodman Gallery, New York

John McLaughlin
Untitled #22
1974

Acrylic on canvas, 60 x 48"

Courtesy Tobey C. Moss Gallery, Los Angeles

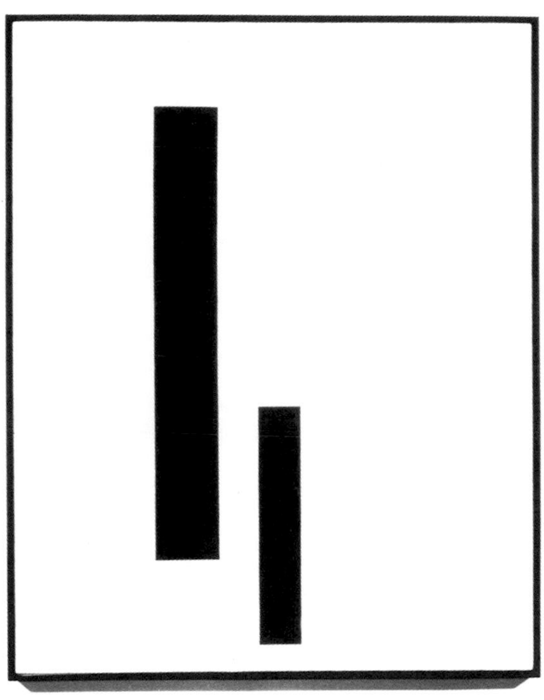

James Melchert
Messages
1992

Glazed earthenware and copper filament, 17 1/2 x 17 1/2 x 3/4"

Courtesy Revolution Gallery, Detroit and New York

PHOTOGRAPHER: Lee Fatheree

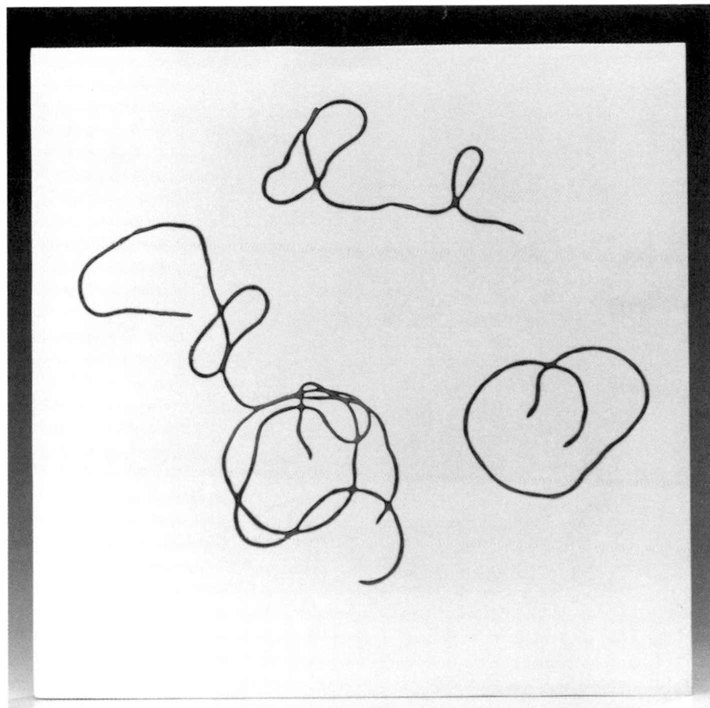

Ana Mendieta
Untitled (from the *Silueta Series*)
1980

Black-and-white photograph, 8 x 10"

Photograph of carved earth with root, Montana de San Felipe, Mexico
Courtesy of Ana Mendieta and Galerie Lelong, New York

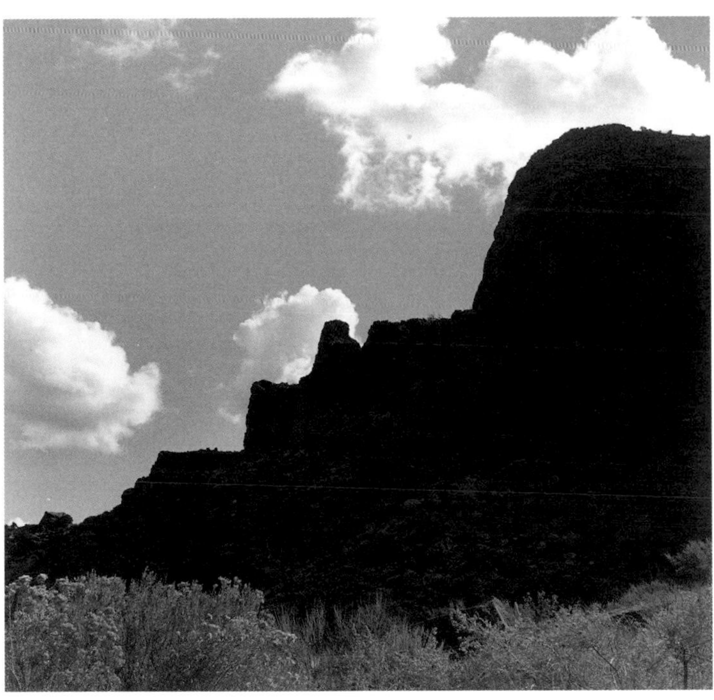

Ray Metzker
Untitled, Utah
1998

13 1/2 x 13 1/2

Courtesy Laurence Miller Gallery, New York

Melissa Miller
Graze
1998

Oil on canvas, 24 x 24"

PHOTOGRAPHER: Bill Kennedy

Robert Moskowitz
Iceberg
1984

Oil and latex on canvas, 56 x 157 3/8"

The Corcoran Gallery of Art Collection, Washington, D. C.
Gift of the Friends of the Corcoran

Matt Mullican
Untitled (Glass ball with ink)
1998

Photogram, 8 x 10"

Antonio Muntadas
The Board Room
1987

Installation, 30 x 51'

Collection of the National Gallery, Ottawa, Canada

Catherine Murphy
Curtained Window
1994

Oil on canvas, 48 x 73 1/2"

Collection, Museum of Fine Arts, Boston
Courtesy of Lennon, Weinberg, Inc., New York

Ron Nagle
Bruised Boy Cup
1995

Mixed-media, 12 x 12 x 12"

Courtesy Garth Clark Gallery, New York

PHOTOGRAPHER: Don Tuttle

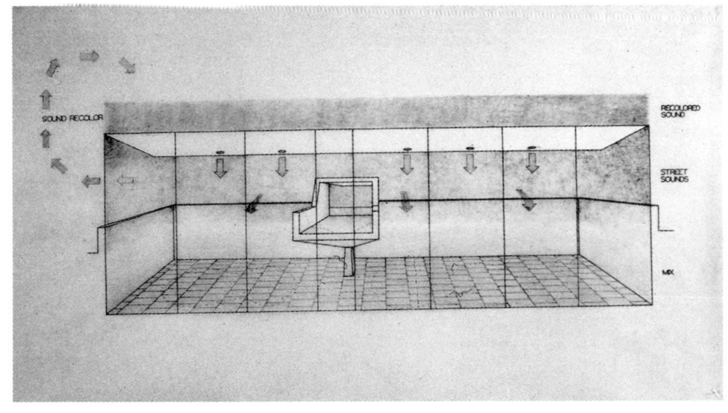

Max Neuhaus
Time Piece Archetype
1983

Colored pencil on paper, 82.5 x 151 cm. Sound Work References: Exhibition: Whitney Biennial, Sculpture Court, Whitney Museum of American Art, New York, 10 x 30 meters

Anne Noggle
Myself As A Pilot
1982

Photograph, 16 x 20"

Courtesy Andrew Smith Gallery, Santa Fe

Nathan Oliveira

Wild Dog Seeking Its Shadow

1997

Oil and alkyd on canvas, 90 x 78"

Courtesy John Berggruen Gallery, San Francisco

Dennis Oppenheim

Stage Set for a Film

1998

Painted steel, acrylic, galvanized steel, vinyl siding, asphalt shingles, industrial lights, concrete foundations, 420 x 300 x 300"

Collection of the City of Valladolid, Spain

PHOTOGRAPHER: Rose Rongac

Pepon Osorio

En la barberia no se llora

1994

Mixed-media and barber chair

Courtesy the artist and Ronald Feldman Fine Arts, New York

PHOTOGRAPHER: Dennis Cowley

Tom Otterness

Law of Nature

1997

Bronze, dimensions of Jury: 55 x 63 x 24 1/2", dimensions of Judge/Defendant: 73 1/2 x 41 x 19" Detail (Trial Scene) from larger installation at Mark O. Hatfield Federal Courthouse, Portland, Oregon

Courtesy Marlborough Gallery, New York

PHOTOGRAPHER: Laurie Black

John Outterbridge
John Ivery's Truck: Hauling Away the Traps and Saving the Yams
1993–94

Wood, rag and metal, 18 1/2 x 20 1/2 x 50"

Courtesy of the artist

PHOTOGRAPHER: Sammy Davis

Philip Pearlstein
Nude With Mummy Balloon
1997

Watercolor on paper, 40 1/2 x 60"

Courtesy Robert Miller Gallery, New York

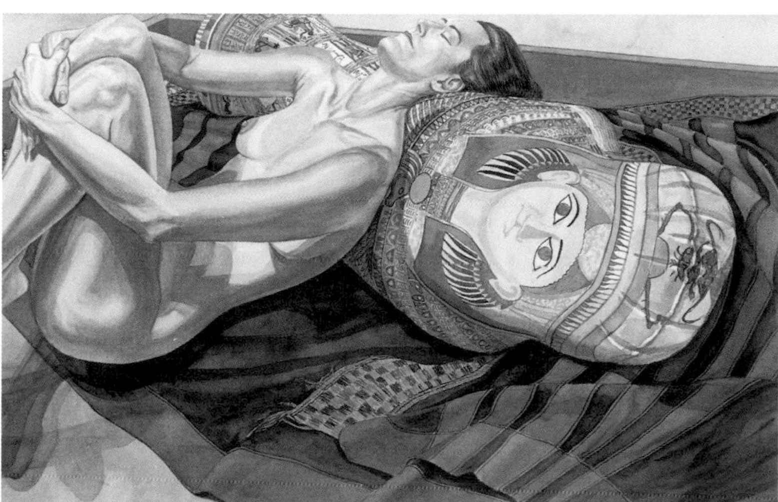

Howardena Pindell
Scapegoat
1990

Acrylic, tempera, oil stick, polymer transfer on canvas, 72 x 141"

Collection Studio Museum in Harlem, New York

PHOTOGRAPHER: James Dee

Jim Pomeroy
Berthold Brecht. n.d.

Computer-generated print. 8 x 10"
Center for Creative Photography,
The University of Arizona

David Rabinowitch

Metal Constructions in 13 Masses and 4 Scales, I

1989

Hot rolled steel, 200 x 184 x 5"

Collection the artist and Akira Ikeda Gallery, New York/Tokyo

PHOTOGRAPHER: Adam Rzepka

David Reed

Judy's Bedroom

1992

Variable painting featured: #328, bed, bedding, headboard, lamp, videotape: Two Bedrooms in San Francisco, Judy's Bedroom, 1994 featuring painting #328 inserted into Alfred Hitchcock's film Vertigo, Universal Pictures, 1958. Installed at the Museum of Contemporary Art, San Diego

PHOTOGRAPHER: P.S. Rittermannu

Yvonne Rainer

Film About a Woman Who . . .

1974

16mm, black and white, 105 minutes, frame enlargement 5 x 7"

Courtesy Zeitgeist Films, New York

Dorothea Rockburne

Tacoma Bridge Resonance

1997

Caran-Dache Neocolor II on Indigo Pigment 90% cotton 5% abaca 5% line paper and translucent abaca paper, 33 x 29 1/2"

Collection of the artist

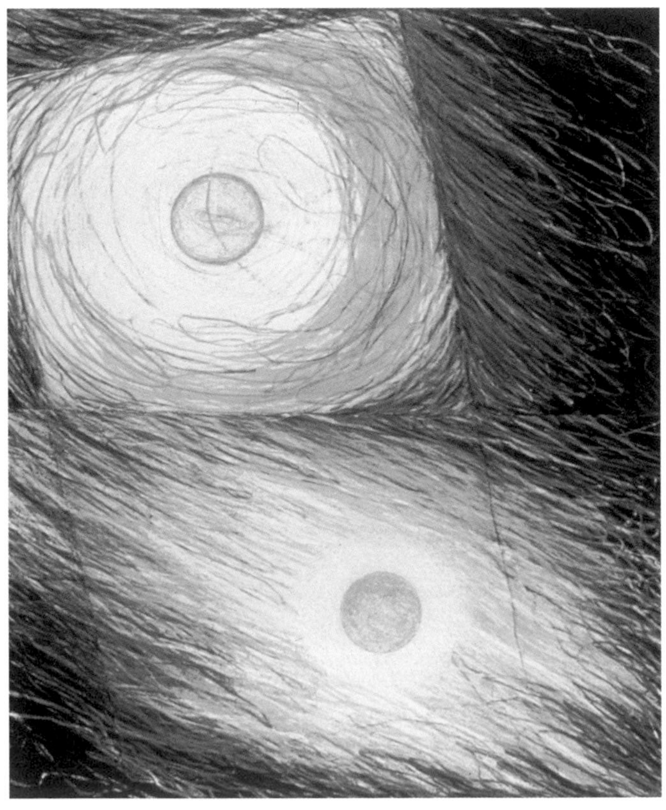

Tim Rollins

Study for Amerika XIII

1991

Watercolor/paper, linen, 60 x 48"

Courtesy Mary Boone Gallery, New York

PHOTOGRAPHER: Oren Slor

Rachel Rosenthal

Pangaean Dreams: A Shamanic Journey

1990–95

Performance
Premiered at the Santa Monica Museum of Art, 1990

Courtesy The Rachel Rosenthal Company

PHOTOGRAPHER: Jan Deen

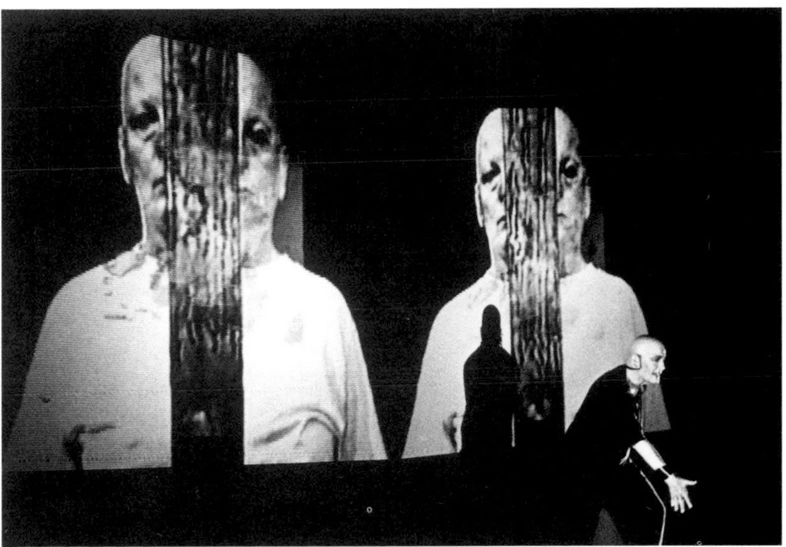

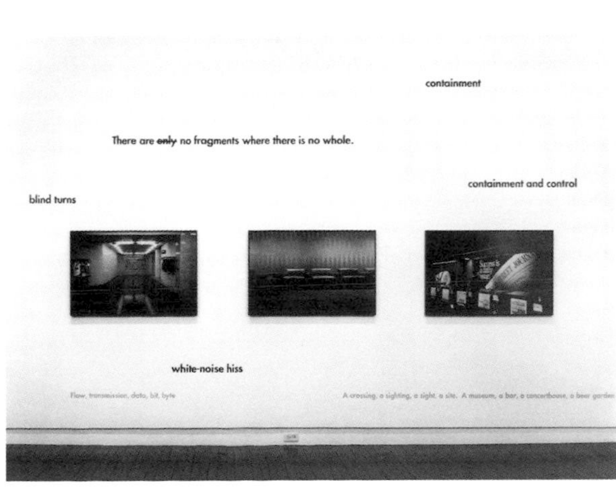

Martha Rosler

In the Place of the Public

1993

Detail from installation of texts and photographs, Jay Gorney Modern Art

PHOTOGRAPHER: Oren Slor

Christina Rupp

Synthetic Water

1990

Steel and plastic, 36 x 24 x 24"

PHOTOGRAPHER: Adam Reich

Allen Ruppersberg

Untitled Logs from Commercial Art (Installation view)

1985

Sandblasted logs, various dimensions

PHOTOGRAPHER: Bill Jacobson Studio

Alison Saar

Small Pox Demon

1995

Wood, plaster, tin, 35 x 11 1/2 x 9 1/2"

Courtesy Phyllis Kind Gallery, New York

Jim Sanborn

Implied Geometries (Triangle), Cainville, Utah

1995

Projected light, 100' triangle

PHOTOGRAPHER: J. Sanborn

Fred Sandback

Untitled

1988

Six-part vertical construction, acrylic yarn, 14 x 38 x 60'. Installed at the Dia Center for the Arts, New York

Courtesy Lawrence Markey, New York

PHOTOGRAPHER: Mary Bachmann

Hope Sandrow
Memories, Untitled XIII (Skinned)
1993

Silver print fragments, 11 x 14"

Collection of Tom Coyne

Miriam Schapiro
Medusa
1981

Acrylic, fabric, glitter painting in six parts, 84 x 168"

Collection of Carolyn Schneebeck, Courtesy Steinbaum Krauss Gallery, New York

PHOTOGRAPHER: D. James Dee

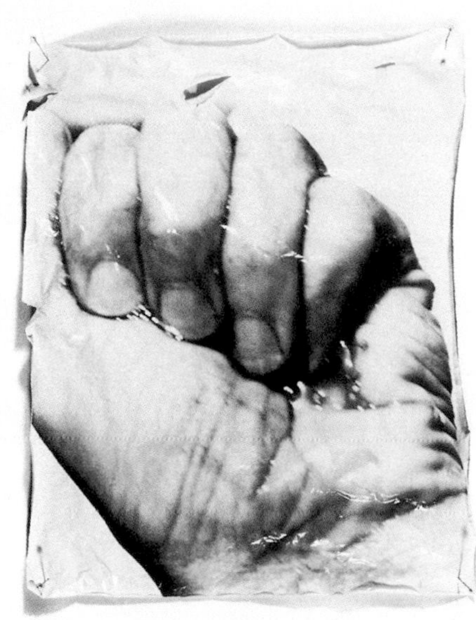

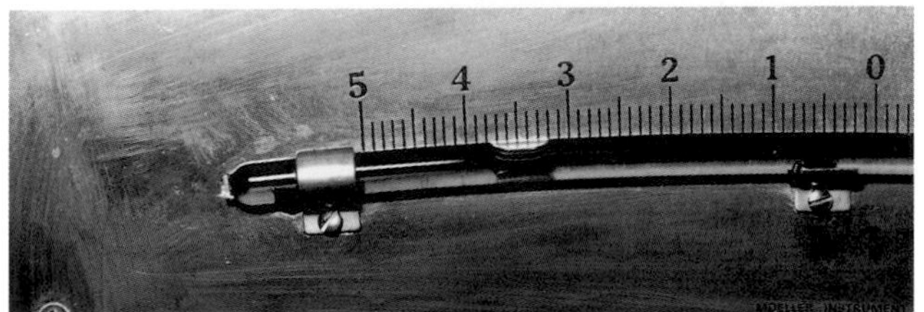

Sean Scully
Wall of Light Pink
1998

Oil on linen, 108 x 120"

PHOTOGRAPHER: Zindman/Fremont

Allan Sekula
Detail (Inclinometer), mid-Atlantic and *Panorama, mid-Atlantic* (both from *Fish Story*)
1995

Chromogenic development (cibachrome) prints, 12 x 32" and 16 x 32"

Collection Museum Boymans-Van Beuningen, Rotterdam

Beverly Semmes
Black Gowns
1994

Velvet, 12 x 9 x 12'

Collection Joel and Sherri Mallin

PHOTOGRAPHER: Charles DuPrat, Paris

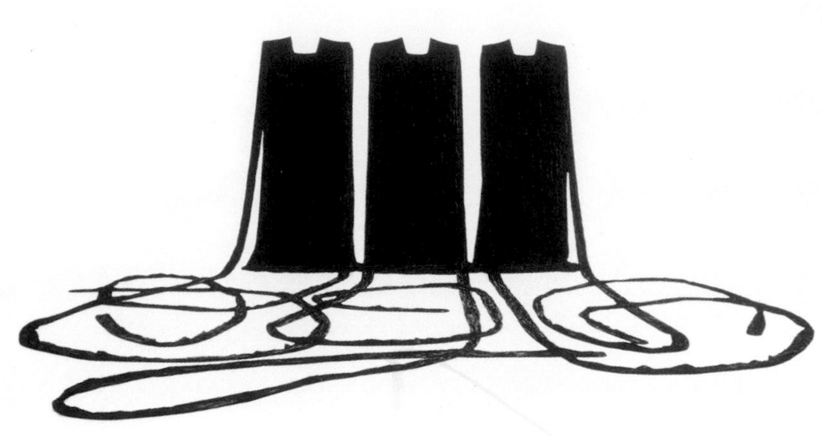

Andres Serrano
Nomads (Rene)
1990

Cibachrome, silicone, Plexiglas, wood frame, 60 x 50"

Courtesy Paula Cooper Gallery

Judith Shea
Artist
1992

Cast steel, 89 1/2 x 18 1/2 x 18 1/2"

Peter Shelton
churchsnakebedbone
1993

Bronze, water, copper, and pumps, 80 x 77 x 38"

Collection of the artist, Courtesy L.A. Louver, Venice, California

Buster Simpson
Brush with Illumination (www.brushdelux.com)
1998

Calligraphy brush with illuminated elements,
40 x 25 x 28' (-1+ tidal influences)

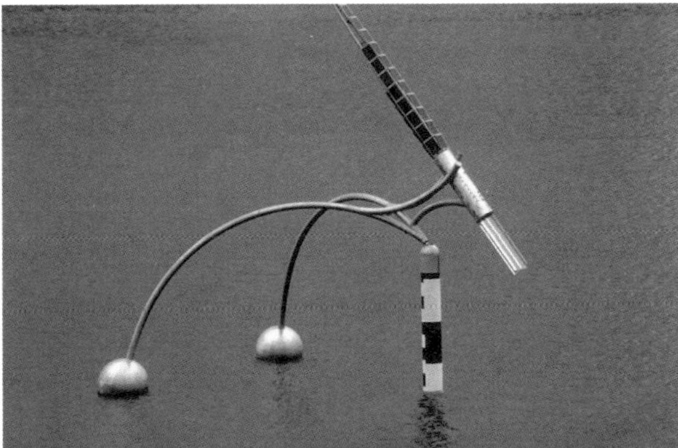

Michael Singer
Grand Rapids Riverwalk Floodwall,
(detail), Grand Rapids, Michigan
1996

Granite, 300 x 20 x 18'

PHOTOGRAPHER: Sterling McMurrin

Sandy Skoglund
Squirrels at the Drive-In
1996

Photolithograph, 20 x 25 1/2"

PHOTOGRAPHER: Sandy Skoglund

Clarissa Sligh
Mr. Taylor
1998

Gelatin silver print, 50 x 40"

Kit-Yin Snyder
Cosí È—It Is So! (detail)
1996

Wire mesh, fabric, light, sound, installation in 2-story space, 36 x 108 x 96"

Buzz Spector
Authors (Man with Cigarette)
1999

Torn printed papers on wood lectern, 19 x 19 x 8"

PHOTOGRAPHER: Wilmer D. Zehr

Robert Stackhouse
Drifter
1993

Watercolor on paper, 119 1/2 x 80 1/2"

Courtesy Morgan Gallery, Kansas City

PHOTOGRAPHER: Dan Wayne

Earl Staley
Powwow 80: Women's Northern Buckskin Dancers
1998

Acrylic on canvas, 24 x 36"

Collection of the artist

Richard Stankiewicz
Untitled 1981-1
1981

Steel. 20 3/8 x 21 3/4 x 15 1/4"

Collection, Richard Stankiewicz,
Courtesy Zabriskie Gallery Inc., New York

PHOTOGRAPHER: John A. Ferrari

Jessica Stockholder
1995

Acrylic and oil paints, acrylic fiber, glass, wood, plastic, cloth, resin, wood, 71 1/2 x 64 x 52"

Collection of the Whitney Museum of American Art, New York
Photograph courtesy of Gorney Bravin + Lee, New York

PHOTOGRAPHER: Oren Slor

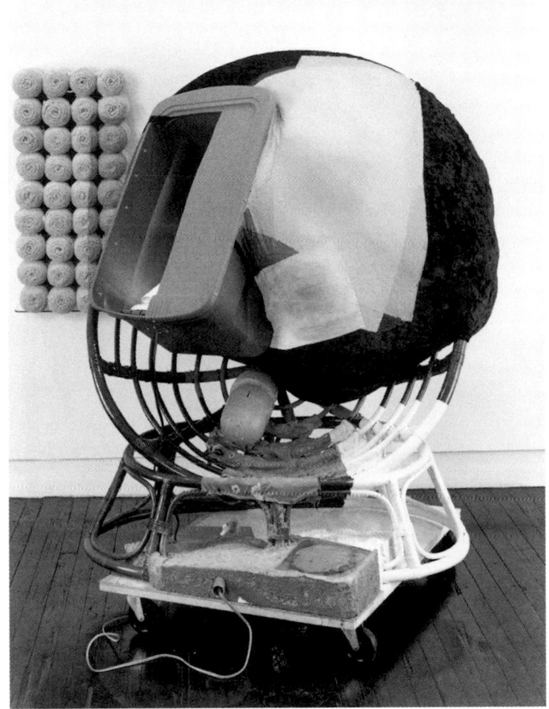

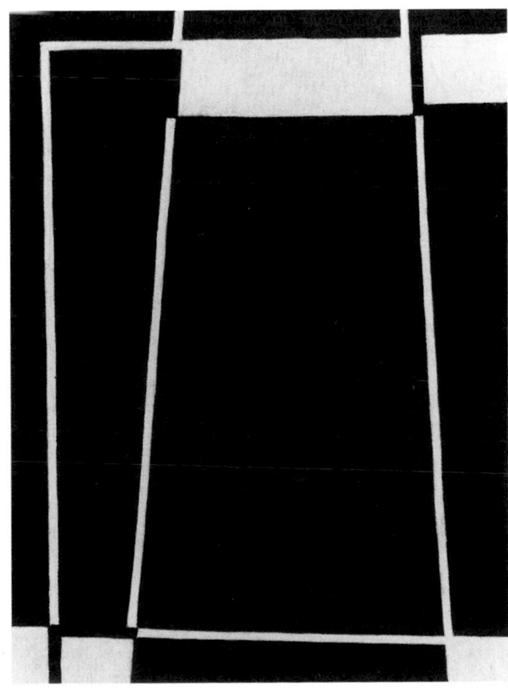

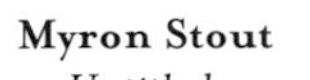

Myron Stout
Untitled
1950

Charcoal on paper, 25 x 19"

Courtesy Joan T. Washburn Gallery, New York, and
Miles Bellamy/Oil & Steel Gallery, New York

Michelle Stuart
Seed Containers: #3
1993

Seeds, beeswax, pine, 38 1/2 x 25 3/4 x 26 3/4"

Courtesy of the artist and John Weber Gallery, New York

PHOTOGRAPHER: Karen Bell

Larry Sultan

The Directors

1998

Color coupler print, 30 x 40"

Courtesy Janet Borden Inc.

James Surls

Turning Around

1998

Pinc, 80 1/2 x 57 1/2 x 50"

Courtesy Marlborough Gallery, New York, Gerald Peters Gallery, Dallas

Lenore Tawney

Wind of Autumn

1998

Linen, 96 x 48 x 24"

PHOTOGRAPHER: George Erml

Masami Teraoka

Tree of Life Series/Eve with Eggplants

1993

Watercolor and gold leaf
on paper mounted
as a scroll, 76 1/4 x 29 1/8"

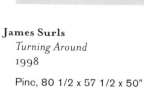

Courtesy Pamela Auchincloss Arts Management

Paul Thek
The Personal Effects of the Pied Piper
1975-76

Bronze, dimensions variable

Courtesy Alexander and Bonin, New York

PHOTOGRAPHER: D. James Dee

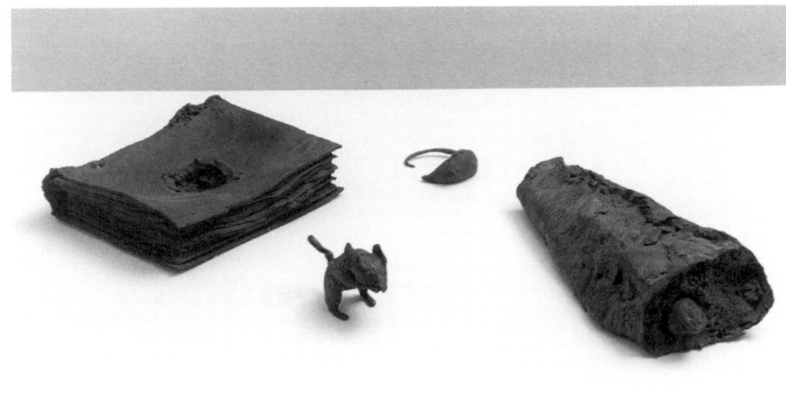

Diana Thater
The best animals are the flat animals (version #1)
1998

LCD video projector, three-lens video projectors, video monitor, laser disc players, laser discs, acetate film, 8' x 10' 6"

Courtesy David Zwirner, New York
Photograph courtesy MAK Center for Art and Architecture, Los Angeles

PHOTOGRAPHER: Fredrik Nilsen

William Tucker
Rider
1994

Bronze, 31 x 42 1/2 x 37"

Courtesy McKee Gallery, New York

Mierle Ukeles
The Social Mirror
1983

Mirror covered garbage truck with the NYC Department of Sanitation

Courtesy Ronald Feldman Fine Arts, New York

Steina Vasulka
Pyroglyphs
1995
Video, dimensions variable
Graphic realization by Woody Vasulka

Woody Vasulka
Scan Processor Studies
1982
Video, dimensions variable

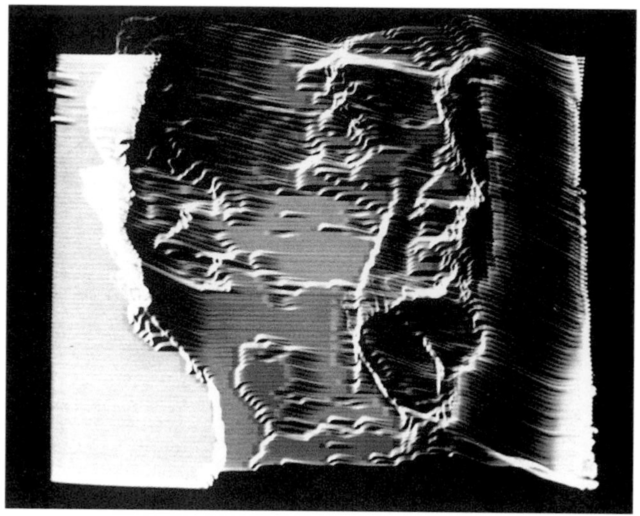

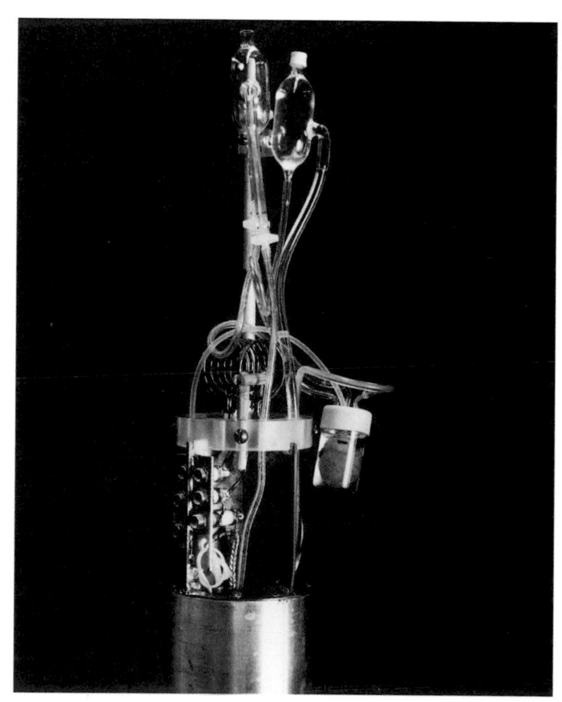

Edin Vélez
Dance of Darkness
1988
Video
Photograph courtesy of the artist

Catherine Wagner
Beating Heart—Heart Chamber
1994
Gelatin silver prints, diptych, 20 x 24" each
Courtesy Jack Shainman Gallery, New York

Nari Ward
Iron Heavens
1995

Mixed-media, 136 x 145 x 36"

PHOTOGRAPHER: Lawrence Gomez

Margaret Wharton
Eve
1998

Small wooden chair, shovel, epoxy, 48 x 33 x 7"

Courtesy Jean Albano Gallery, Chicago

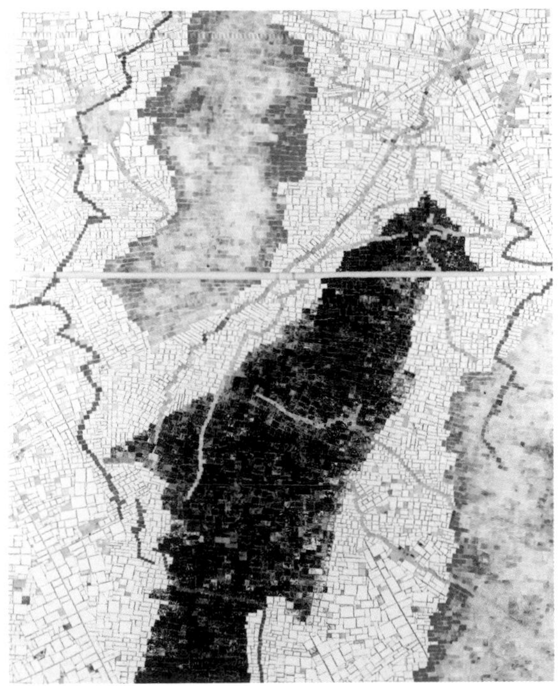

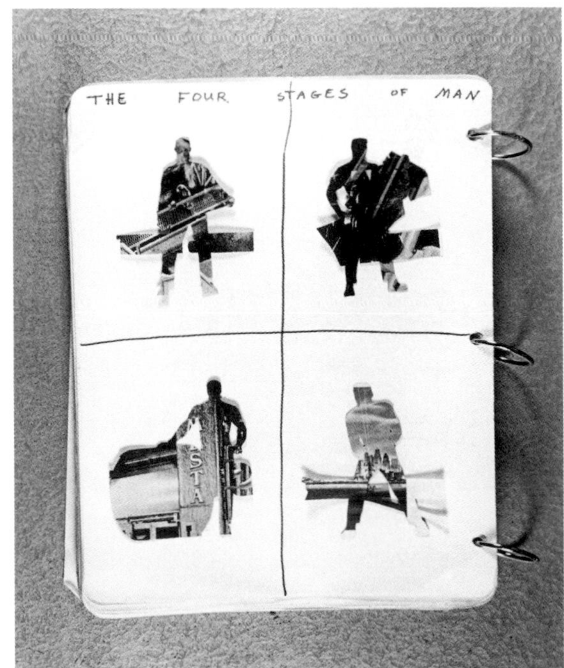

Jack Whitten
Flying High: Homage to Betty Carter
1998

Acrylic on canvas, 106 1/2 x 84 1/4"

Collection of the artist

PHOTOGRAPHER: John Berens

Gwen Widmer
From the series *Cloud Reading for Pilots*
1981

Hand-colored black-and-white photograph, 24 x 20"

Pat Williams
What You Lookn At
1993

Halftone dot mural print, color photos, spray paint and text, 9 x 20'

Courtesy P.P.O.W., New York

Christopher Wilmarth
Gift of the Bridge
1975-76

Steel and etched tempered glass, 72 x 72 x 48"

Wadsworth Atheneum Collection, Hartford, Connecticut

PHOTOGRAPHER: Jerry L. Thompson

Garry Winogrand
John Huston, "Annie" set, Burbank, California
1981

Gelatin silver print from "15 Big Shots"

Courtesy Fraenkel Gallery, San Francisco

Joel-Peter Witkin
Harvest
1984

Silver chlorobromide print, 12 x 12"

Courtesy Pace Wildenstein MacGill, New York, Frankel Gallery, San Fransisco

Christopher Wool
Untitled
1990

Alkyd on paper, 48 x 32 1/2"

Courtesy the artist and Luhring Augustine, New York

THESHOWISOV
ER THEAUDIE
NCEGETUPTOL
EAVETHEIRSE
ATS TIMETOC
OLLECTTHEIR
COATSANDGOH
OME THEYTUR
NAROUND NOM
ORECOATS AN
DNOMOREHOME

Jack Youngerman
Billow
1983

Steel, 81 x 96 x 25"

Courtesy Washburn Gallery, New York

PHOTOGRAPHER: J. Youngerman

Kate Ericson and Mel Ziegler
Camouflaged History
1991

House painted with 72 commercial paints in authentic colors of historic Charleston, South Carolina

PHOTOGRAPHER: John McWilliams

Edward Zucca
Mystery Robots Rip Off the Rain Forest
1989

Mahogany, yellow poplar, maple, acrylic paint, gesso, polyethylene ink, 31 x 30 1/2 x 132"

Collection of Charles Carpenter, New Caanan, Connecticut
Courtesy Leo Kaplan Modern, New York

NATIONAL RECIPIENTS

National Endowment for the Arts

Visual Artists' Fellowships 1967–1995

A

Jesse Aaron, Gainesville, FL. 1975 Artist $4,000
Pacita Abad, Washington, DC. 1989 Painting $5,000
Jon Abbott, Venice, CA. 1976 Artist $2,000
John Abduljaami, Oakland, CA. 1986 Crafts $5,000
Richard Aber, Santa Barbara, CA. 1980 Artist $3,000
Cecile Abish, North Bergen, NJ. 1975 Artist $4,000; 1977 Artist $7,500; 1980 Artist $10,000
Jane Abrams, Albuquerque, NM. 1983 Printmaking/Drawing/Artists' Books $15,000; 1993 Painting $20,000
Charles Abramson, Brooklyn, NY. 1984 Sculpture $5,000; 1985 Printmaking/Drawing/Artists' Books $5,000
Michael Abramson, Chicago, IL. 1979 Photo $3,000
Vito Acconci, Brooklyn, NY. 1976 Video $5,000; 1978 Video $7,500; 1983 Conceptual/Performance/New Genres $15,000; 1993 New Genres $20,000
Robert Ackerman, New York, NY. 1987 Painting $15,000
James Acord/Susan Shie, Wooster, OH. 1994 Crafts $20,000
Alice Adams, New York, NY. 1978 Artist $7,500; 1984 Sculpture $15,000
Allan Adams, San Francisco, CA. 1980 Artist $3,000
Dennis Adams, New York, NY. 1984 Sculpture $5,000; 1988 Sculpture $15,000; 1995 New Genres $20,000
Hank Adams, Albany, NY. 1986 Crafts $5,000; 1988 Crafts $5,000; 1990 Crafts $5,000
Mac Adams, New York, NY. 1976 Conceptual/Performance/New Genres $2,000; 1980 Conceptual/Performance/New Genres $3,000; 1982 Sculpture $25,000
Pat Adams, Bennington, VT. 1969 Artist $5,000; 1976 Artist $5,000; 1987 Painting $15,000
Peter Adams, Penland, NC. 1984 Crafts $5,000
Phoebe Adams, Philadelphia, PA. 1986 Sculpture $15,000
Robert Adams, Longmont, CO. 1973 Photo $5,000; 1978 Photo $7,500
Shelby Adams, Salem, MA. 1992 Photo $20,000
Yura Adams, New York, NY. 1985 New Genres $5,000
Terry Adkins, New York, NY. 1986 Sculpture $5,000
Billy Adler, Los Angeles, CA. 1971 Photo $2,000; 1974 Artist $3,000; 1976 Video $5,000
Jane F Aebersold, Aspers, PA. 1984 Crafts $15,000
Nicholas Africano, Normal, IL. 1978 Artist $7,500
Ann Agee, Sheboygan, WI. 1987 Painting $5,000; 1992 Crafts $20,000
Peter Agostini, New York, NY. 1969 Artist $5,000
Deborah Aguado, New York, NY. 1978 Crafts $7,500
John Ahearn, New York, NY. 1980 Artist $10,000
Mi Ahn, Skokie, IL. 1987 Painting $5,000; 1989 Works On Paper $5,000
Miran Ahn, Berkeley, CA. 1987 Painting $5,000
Hanno Ahrens, New York, NY. 1986 Sculpture $5,000; 1990 Sculpture $5,000
Robert Aielle, Amherst, MA. 1974 Artist $3,000
Lucien Aigner, Great Barrington, MA. 1975 Photo $5,000
Adela Akers, Guerneville, CA. 1974 Crafts $3,000; 1980 Crafts $10,000
Gwendolyn Akin/Allan Ludwig, New York, NY. 1990 Photo $5,000
Neda Al-Hilali, Santa Monica, CA. 1974 Crafts $3,000; 1979 Crafts $10,000
Ed Albers, New York, NY. 1987 Painting $5,000
John Albers, New York, NY. 1982 Sculpture $5,000
James Albertson, Oakland, CA. 1980 Artist $3,000; 1982 Painting $25,000
John Alberty, Norman, OK. 1978 Conceptual/Performance/New Genres $3,000
Lita Alburquerque, Malibu, CA. 1975 Printmaking/Drawing/Artists' Books $3,000
Bob Alderette, Sunset Beach, CA. 1983 Painting $5,000
Peter Aldridge, Bath, NY. 1982 Crafts $25,000
John Alexander, New York, NY. 1981 Painting $12,500
Peter Alexander, Topango, CA. 1980 Artist $10,000
Wick Alexander, San Diego, CA. 1989 Painting $5,000
Martha Alf, San Diego, CA. 1979 Printmaking/Drawing/Artists' Books $10,000; 1989 Works On Paper $15,000
Joey Alfieris, Savannah, GA. 1980 Artist $3,000
Carlos Alfonzo, Miami Beach, FL. 1983 Painting $5,000
Mario Algaze, Coral Gables, FL. 1991 Photo $5,000; 1992 Photo $20,000
James Alinder, Pebble Beach, CA. 1973 Photo $3,500; 1980 Photo $10,000
Rene Allain, Brooklyn, NY. 1991 Painting $20,000
William Allan, San Rafael, CA. 1995 Painting $20,000
Catherine Allen, New York, NY. 1989 Painting $5,000
Edward Allen, Albany, CA. 1989 Painting $15,000
Jo Harvey Allen, Fresno, CA. 1979 Conceptual/Performance/New Genres $3,000; 1983 Conceptual/Performance/New Genres $5,000
Judith Allen, San Francisco, CA. 1990 Photo $5,000
Lisa Allen, Portland, ME. 1983 Printmaking/Drawing/Artists' Books $5,000
Philip Allen, New York, NY. 1982 Painting $5,000
Terry Allen, Santa Fe, NM. 1973 Artist $7,500; 1979 Conceptual/Performance/New Genres $10,000; 1989 Works On Paper $15,000
William Allen, State University, AR. 1973 Artist $7,500
Janet Alling, New York, NY. 1989 Painting $15,000
Jerri Allyn, New York, NY. 1981 Conceptual/Performance/New Genres $4,000; 1985 New Genres $5,000; 1989 New Genres $5,000
Michael Almaguer, Berkeley, CA. 1983 Painting $5,000
Max Almy, Oakland, CA. 1982 Video $5,000
Natalie Alper, Brookline, MA. 1976 Printmaking/Drawing/Artists' Books $3,000
Merry Alpern, New York, NY. 1990 Photo $5,000
Richard Alpert, San Francisco, CA. 1979 Artist $10,000
Julio Alpuy, New York, NY. 1983 Painting $15,000
Lewis Alquist, Tempe, AZ. 1986 Sculpture $15,000
Mauro Altamura, Jersey City, NJ. 1988 Photo $5,000
Edith Altman, Chicago, IL. 1990 Sculpture $20,000
Harold Altman, Lemont, PA. 1977 Printmaking/Drawing/Artists' Books $5,000
Francisco Alvarado-Juarez, New York, NY. 1985 Painting $5,000; 1989 Painting $5,000
Gloria Alvarez, Carpinteria, CA. 1989 Works On Paper $5,000
Emma Alvarez-Pineiro, New York, NY. 1980 Artist $10,000
Jesse Amado, San Antonio, TX. 1990 Sculpture $5,000
Jane Aman, Sepulveda, CA. 1974 Printmaking/Drawing/Artists' Books $3,000
Taka Amano, New York, NY. 1989 Works On Paper $15,000
Michele Amateau, Dripping Springs, TX. 1987 Painting $15,000
Peter Ambrose, Brooklyn, NY. 1978 Artist $3,000; 1981 Painting $12,500
Gregory Amenoff, New York, NY. 1980 Artist $3,000; 1981 Painting $12,500; 1989 Painting $15,000
Grimanesa Amoros, New York, NY. 1993 Painting $20,000
Claudia Amory, Baltimore, MD. 1987 Painting $5,000
Emma Amos, New York, NY. 1983 Printmaking/Drawing/Artists' Books $15,000
Patricia Ancona, San Francisco, CA. 1979 Artist $3,000
Nancy Andell, Chatham, NY. 1987 Printmaking/Drawing/Artists' Books $5,000
Stanley Andersen, Penland, CA. 1982 Crafts $5,000
Chris Anderson, New York, NY. 1985 Painting $15,000
Daniel Anderson, Edwardsville, IL. 1990 Crafts $20,000
David Anderson, Columbus, OH. 1974 Artist $7,500; 1981 Sculpture $12,500; 1988 Sculpture $15,000
Doug Anderson, Newtonville, MA. 1987 Painting $5,000; 1989 Painting $5,000
Harry Anderson, Philadelphia, PA. 1975 Artist $4,000; 1984 Sculpture $15,000
Janet Anderson, Los Angeles, CA. 1980 Crafts $3,000
Jerome Anderson, Santa Monica, CA. 1975 Artist $4,000
Laurie Anderson, New York, NY. 1974 Artist $3,000; 1977 Conceptual/Performance/New Genres $7,500; 1980 Conceptual/Performance/New Genres $10,000
Lennart Anderson, Brooklyn, NY. 1967 Artist $5,000
Lois Anderson, Mill Valley, CA. 1978 Artist $7,500
Marilyn Anderson, Los Angeles, CA. 1977 Crafts $5,000
Marilyn Anderson, Rochester, NY. 1982 Photo $5,000
Robert Anderson, Bloomfield, NJ. 1985 Painting $15,000
Sally Anderson, Albuquerque, NM. 1977 Crafts $5,000

Bruno Andrade, Corpus Christi, TX. 1980 Artist $3,000; 1989 Painting $5,000
Carl Andre, New York, NY. 1969 Artist $5,000
Milet Andrejevic, New York, NY. 1976 Artist $5,000
Jo Andres, Brooklyn, NY. 1989 New Genres $5,000; 1991 New Genres $20,000
Benny Andrews, New York, NY. 1974 Artist $7,500; 1987 Painting $15,000
Dana Andrews, Chevy Chase, MD. 1986 Crafts $15,000
Ed Andrews, St. Louis, MO. 1990 Sculpture $5,000
Lawrence Andrews, Oakland, CA. 1989 New Genres $5,000; 1993 New Genres $20,000
Mari Andrews, Venice, CA. 1989 Works On Paper $5,000
Mel Andringa, Iowa City, IA. 1985 New Genres $15,000
Robert Andriulli, Millersville, PA. 1987 Painting $5,000
Damian Andrus, Pasadena, CA. 1982 Painting $5,000
Roswell Angier, Cambridge, MA. 1982 Photo $5,000
Matthew Antezzo, Brooklyn, NY. 1995 Painting $20,000
Peter Anthony, New York, NY. 1986 Sculpture $3,000
Eleanor Antin, Del Mar, CA. 1979 Conceptual/Performance/New Genres $10,000
Gale Antokal, Berkeley, CA. 1991 Works On Paper $20,000
Stephen Antonakos, New York, NY. 1974 Artist $7,500
Garo Antreasian, Albuquerque, NM. 1982 Printmaking/Drawing/Artists' Books $25,000
Carole Aoki, New York, NY. 1990 Crafts $5,000
Keith Aoki, New York, NY. 1980 Artist $3,000
Timothy App, Baltimore, MD. 1987 Painting $15,000
Jacki Apple, New York, NY. 1979 Conceptual/Performance/New Genres $3,000; 1981 Conceptual/Performance/New Genres $12,500
Ida Applebroog, New York, NY. 1980 Conceptual/Performance/New Genres $10,000; 1985 Painting $15,000; 1991 Painting $20,000
Daniel Appleby, Minneapolis, MN. 1985 New Genres $5,000; 1987 New Genres $5,000
Ken Aptekar, New York, NY. 1995 Painting $20,000
Tomie Arai, New York, NY. 1993 Works On Paper $20,000
Yoshiki Araki, Brooklyn, NY. 1989 Painting $5,000
Michele Araujo, Hoboken, NJ. 1989 Painting $5,000
Linda Arbuckle, Micanopy, FL. 1994 Crafts $20,000
Vincent Arcilesi, New York, NY. 1982 Painting $5,000
Stuart Arends, Roswell, NM. 1989 Painting $5,000; 1991 Painting $20,000
Douglas Argue, St. Paul, MN. 1987 Painting $5,000
Susana Arias, Aptos, CA. 1988 Sculpture $5,000
Akira Arita, New York, NY. 1985 Painting $15,000
Nancy Arlen, New York, NY. 1980 Artist $3,000
Siah Armajani, Minneapolis, MN. 1978 Artist $7,500
Tom Armbruster, Hudson, OH. 1981 Crafts $4,000
Frederico Armijo, Albuquerque, NM. 1980 Crafts $10,000
Richard Armijo, New York, NY. 1985 New Genres $5,000
John Arndt, Cleveland, OH. 1989 Painting $5,000
Robert Arneson, Benicia, CA. 1973 Artist $7,500; 1981 Sculpture $12,500; 1988 Sculpture $15,000
Rick Arnitz, Oakland, CA. 1991 Painting $20,000
David Arnold, Roosevelt, NJ. 1985 Printmaking/Drawing/Artists' Books $5,000
Skip Arnold, Los Angeles, CA. 1993 New Genres $20,000
William Arnold, Florence, MA. 1975 Photo $5,000
Charles Arnoldi, Venice, CA. 1974 Artist $7,500; 1982 Sculpture $25,000
Mark Aronson, New York, NY. 1976 Artist $2,000
Alfredo Arreguin, Seattle, WA. 1980 Artist $3,000; 1985 Painting $15,000
Maria Artemis, Atlanta, GA. 1988 Sculpture $5,000
Richard Artschwager, New York, NY. 1973 Artist $7,500
John Arvanites, Los Angeles, CA. 1981 Video $4,000; 1985 New Genres $15,000
Michael Aschenbrenner, New York, NY. 1992 Crafts $20,000
Eve Aschheim, New York, NY. 1989 Works On Paper $5,000
Eve Ashcraft, New York, NY. 1989 Painting $5,000
Michael Asher, Los Angeles, CA. 1975 Artist $8,000
Mary Ashley, San Francisco, CA. 1976 Video $2,000
Marc Asnin, New York, NY. 1988 Photo $5,000
Mary Lee Ataie, Coral Gables, FL. 1990 Sculpture $5,000
Dana Atchley, Crested Butte, CO. 1979 Video $10,000
John Atlas, Houston, TX. 1989 Painting $5,000
Dotty Attie, New York, NY. 1975 Printmaking/Drawing/Artists' Books $3,000; 1983 Printmaking/Drawing/Artists' Books $25,000
Shimon Attie, San Francisco, CA. 1993 New Genres $20,000
Tina Aufiero, Brooklyn, NY. 1988 Sculpture $5,000
Ellsworth Ausby, Brooklyn, NY. 1983 Painting $15,000
Rudy Autio, Missoula, MT. 1980 Crafts $10,000
Lynne Avadenka, Birmingham, MI. 1983 Printmaking/Drawing/Artists' Books $5,000
David Avalos, National City, CA. 1986 Sculpture $5,000; 1988 Sculpture $5,000
Edward Avedesian, New York, NY. 1969 Artist $5,000
David Avison, Evanston, IL. 1977 Photo $7,500
Elizabeth Awalt, Millis, MA. 1987 Painting $5,000
Jan Axel, New York, NY. 1981 Crafts $12,500
Dee Axelrod, New York, NY. 1980 Artist $3,000
Alice Aycock, New York, NY. 1976 Artist $5,000; 1980 Artist $10,000; 1986 Sculpture $15,000; 1994 Sculpture $20,000
Larry Ayers, New Brunswick, NJ. 1980 Artist $3,000; 1982 Painting $25,000; 1987 Painting $15,000
Helene Aylon, New York, NY. 1981 Conceptual/Performance/New Genres $12,500
Luis Azaceta, Ridgewood, NY. 1980 Artist $3,000; 1985 Painting $15,000; 1991 Painting $20,000

B

Jo Babcock, San Francisco, CA. 1990 Photo $20,000
Daniel Babior, Vallejo, CA. 1990 Photo $20,000
Laurence Babis, Manhasset, NY. 1977 Photo $7,500
Mary Ann Babula, Allston, MA. 1984 Crafts $5,000
Carolyn Bach, Newport, RI. 1984 Crafts $5,000
Laurence Bach, Philadelphia, PA. 1980 Photo $3,000
Elizabeth Bachhuber, West Germany, 1990 Sculpture $5,000
Shelley Bachman, Collegeville, PA. 1986 Photo $5,000
Jay Backstrand, Portland, OR. 1982 Painting $5,000
Jules Backus, San Francisco, CA. 1980 Video $3,000
Mowry Baden, Canada, 1977 Artist $7,500; 1984 Sculpture $15,000; 1990 Sculpture $20,000
Pat Badt, Allentown, PA. 1989 Painting $5,000
Donald Baechler, New York, NY. 1989 Painting $15,000
Fred Baehr, Morgantown, WV. 1989 Works On Paper $5,000
Jo Baer, New York, NY. 1969 Artist $5,000
Myrna Baez, Hato Ray, PR. 1980 Artist $3,000
Joel Bagnal, Boston, MA. 1976 Crafts $5,000
Mo Bahc, Brooklyn, NY. 1991 Painting $20,000
Cay Bahnmiller, Detroit, MI. 1989 Painting $5,000
Clayton Bailey, Port Costa, CA. 1979 Crafts $10,000; 1990 Crafts $20,000
Oscar Bailey, Lutz, FL. 1977 Photo $7,500
David Bailin, N. Little Rock, AR. 1989 Painting $3,000; 1988 Painting $5,000
John Baird, East Orland, ME. 1989 Works On Paper $15,000
Brenda Baker, Madison, WI. 1991 Sculpture $5,000; 1994 Sculpture $20,000
Jack Balas, Berthoud, CO. 1995 Painting $20,000
John Baldessari, Los Angeles, CA. 1974 Artist $7,500; 1982 Photo $25,000
Douglas Baldwin, Baltimore, MD. 1976 Crafts $5,000; 1979 Crafts $10,000
Mildred Baldwin, Washington, DC. 1987 Painting $5,000; 1989 Painting $5,000
Becherman Balken, Alexandria, VA. 1982 Sculpture $5,000
Meila Balkus, Alexandria, VA. 1984 Sculpture $5,000
Lillian Ball, New York, NY. 1986 Sculpture $5,000
Michael Ballou, Brooklyn, NY. 1989 Painting $5,000
Michael Balog, New York, NY. 1976 Artist $2,000
John Balsely, Milwaukee, WI. 1973 Artist $7,500; 1980 Artist $10,000
Lewis Baltz, Sausalito, CA. 1973 Photo $4,800; 1976 Photo $7,500
Thomas Bamberger, Milwaukee, WI. 1984 Photo $5,000
Gary Bandy, New York, NY. 1983 Painting $15,000
Thomas Bang, Rochester, NY. 1980 Artist $10,000
Diane Banks, Syracuse, NY. 1984 Sculpture $5,000
Ellen Banks, Boston, MA. 1987 Painting $15,000
Walter Bannard, Princeton, NJ. 1969 Artist $5,000
Yee Bao, New York, NY. 1980 Artist $3,000
Sarah Bapst, Cambridge, MA. 1991 Works On Paper $20,000
Donald Barasch, Miami, FL. 1982 Painting $5,000
Ross Barbera, Commack, NY. 1985 Painting $5,000
Anthony Barboza, New York, NY. 1980 Photo $10,000
Gayle Bard, Bainbridge Island, WA. 1987 Painting $5,000
Katherine Bard, San Francisco, CA. 1983 Printmaking/Drawing/Artists' Books $5,000
Robert Baribeau, Bangall, NY. 1983 Printmaking/Drawing/Artists' Books $5,000
Rande Barke, Syracuse, NY. 1982 Painting $5,000
Robert Barnard, Timberville, VA. 1978 Crafts $7,500; 1990 Crafts $20,000

Christopher Barnes, Chelsea, MA. 1988 Photo $5,000
Curt Barnes, New York, NY. 1993 Painting $20,000
Robert Barnes, Bloomington, IN. 1982 Painting $25,000
Sanford Barnett, Santa Cruz, CA. 1978 Crafts $7,500
Jill Baroff, Brooklyn, NY. 1988 Works On Paper $3,000; 1993 Painting $20,000
Burt Barr, New York, NY. 1985 New Genres $5,000; 1989 New Genres $5,000; 1993 New Genres $20,000
Paula Barr, New York, NY. 1974 Artist $3,000
Ros Barron, Brookline, MA. 1975 Video $4,000
Susan Barron, Brooklyn, NY. 1993 Works On Paper $20,000
Thomas Barrow, Albuquerque, NM. 1973 Photo $ 1,500; 1978 Photo $7,500
Judith Barry, New York, NY. 1989 New Genres $5,000
Robert Barry, Teaneck, NJ. 1976 Conceptual/Performance/New Genres $10,000
Steve Barry, Corrales, NM. 1986 Sculpture $5,000; 1988 Sculpture $5,000; 1990 Sculpture $20,000
Frances Barth, New York, NY. 1974 Artist $3,000; 1982 Painting $25,000
Jack Barth, New York, NY. 1983 Painting $15,000
Uta Barth, Venice, CA. 1990 Photo $5,000; 1994 Photo $20,000
Barry Bartlett, New York, NY. 1982 Crafts $5,000; 1990 Crafts $5,000
Jennifer Bartlett, New York, NY. 1976 Artist $2,000
Joseph Bartscherer, Seattle, WA. 1984 Photo $5,000; 1988 Photo $5,000
Dickens Bascom, San Anselmo, CA. 1977 Artist $3,000
Joel Bass, New York, NY. 1978 Artist $7,500; 1987 Painting $15,000
James Bassler, San Pedro, CA. 1977 Crafts $5,000; 1984 Crafts $15,000
Gary Bates, Manhattan, MT. 1984 Sculpture $5,000
Laura Battle, Tivoli, NY. 1989 Painting $5,000
Patti Bauer, Seattle, WA. 1975 Crafts $5,000
Don Baum, Chicago, IL. 1984 Sculpture $25,000
James Baumann, San Diego, CA. 1975 Artist $2,000
Matt Baumgardner, New York, NY. 1993 Painting $20,000
Douglas Baz, Annadale, NY. 1980 Photo $3,000
Dede Bazyk, Los Angeles, CA. 1988 Sculpture $5,000
Jack Beal, New York, NY. 1973 Artist $7,500
Nina Beall, Houston, TX. 1985 Painting $5,000
Bennett Bean, Blairstown, NJ. 1980 Crafts $10,000
Liza Bear, New York, NY. 1983 Video $15,000
Donald Beason, Nocadoches, TX. 1982 Sculpture $5,000
Robert Beauchamp, New York, NY. 1967 Artist $5,000; 1985 Painting $15,000
Betty Beaumont, New York, NY. 1973 Crafts $3,000; 1980 Artist $3,000; 1985 New Genres $5,000
Antonio Bechara, New York, NY. 1980 Artist $3,000
Robert Bechtle, San Francisco, CA. 1976 Artist $5,000; 1982 Painting $25,000; 1989 Painting $15,000
Jerry Beck, Boston, MA. 1988 Sculpture $5,000
Joel Beck, New York, NY. 1987 Painting $5,000
Rosemarie Beck, New York, NY. 1985 Painting $15,000
Theresa Beck, Tampa, FL. 1987 Painting $5,000
David Becker, Mt. Horeb, WI. 1993 Works On Paper $20,000
Fred Becker, Amherst, MA. 1974 Printmaking/Drawing/Artists' Books $3,000
Richard Beckett, New York, NY. 1979 Artist $3,000; 1982 Painting $5,000; 1983 Printmaking/Drawing/Artists' Books $5,000
Bill Beckley, New York, NY. 1978 Conceptual/Performance/New Genres $7,500
Connie Beckley, New York, NY. 1978 Conceptual/Performance/New Genres $3,000
Erica Beckman, New York, NY. 1980 Conceptual/Performance/New Genres $3,000
Michael Becotte, Horsham, PA. 1975 Photo $5,000; 1981 Photo $12,500
Bruce Beeken, Burlington, VT. 1980 Crafts $10,000
Malinda Beeman, Snowmass Village, CO. 1987 Painting $15,000; 1995 Works On Paper $20,000
Richard Beenen, New York, NY. 1988 Photo $5,000
Richard Beerhorst, Grand Rapids, MI. 1989 Painting $5,000
Gene Beery, Sutter Creek, CA. 1983 Printmaking/Drawing/Artists' Books $15,000
David Behrman, New York, NY. 1982 Video $5,000
Bill Beirne, New York, NY. 1980 Video $10,000
Andrea Belag, New York, NY. 1987 Painting $5,000
Raymond Belcher, Redondo Beach, CA. 1976 Photo $7,500
Nancy Belfer, Buffalo, NY. 1981 Crafts $12,500
Meg Belichick, Brooklyn, NY. 1995 Works On Paper $20,000
Deanne Belinoff, Los Angeles, CA. 1991 Painting $20,000
Dozier Bell, Richmond, ME. 1987 Painting $5,000
Larry Bell, Talpa, NM. 1975 Artist $8,000
Scott Bell, Oakland, CA. 1982 Painting $5,000; 1983 Painting $5,000
Gerald Bellas, Wausau, WI. 1976 Crafts $5,000
Leslie Bellavance, Milwaukee, WI. 1989 Works On Paper $5,000
Angelo Bellfatto, Danbury, CT. 1988 Sculpture $5,000
Sinibaldo Belmonte, Detroit, MI. 1984 Sculpture $5,000
Scott Belville, Spartanburg, SC. 1983 Painting $5,000
Howard Ben Tre', Providence, RI. 1980 Crafts $3,000; 1984 Crafts $15,000; 1990 Crafts $20,000
Zigi Ben-Haim, New York, NY. 1984 Sculpture $15,000
Gretchen Bender, New York, NY. 1985 New Genres $5,000
Lynda Benglis, New York, NY. 1979 Artist $10,000; 1990 Sculpture $20,000
William Bengston, Venice, CA. 1967 Artist $5,000
Carl Benjamin, Claremont, CA. 1983 Painting $15,000; 1989 Painting $15,000
Ernst Benkert, Burlington, VT. 1978 Artist $7,500; 1985 Printmaking/Drawing/Artists' Books $15,000
Garry Bennett, Alameda, CA. 1984 Crafts $15,000
Jamie Bennett, New Paltz, NY. 1974 Crafts $3,000; 1979 Crafts $10,000; 1988 Crafts $15,000
Larry Bennett, New York, NY. 1982 Painting $5,000
William Bennett, Manilus, NY. 1978 Artist $7,500
Joseph Bennion, Spring City, UT. 1990 Crafts $5,000
James Benson, Baltimore, MD. 1984 Sculpture $15,000
Curtis Benzle, Hilton Head, SC. 1980 Crafts $3,000
Thomas Berding, Bloomington, IN. 1990 Painting $5,000; 1993 Painting $20,000
Paulus Berensohn, Uniondale, PA. 1973 Crafts $3,000
Michael Beresford, Barrington, RI. 1986 Sculpture $15,000
Peter Berg, New York, NY. 1980 Artist $3,000; 1983 Printmaking/Drawing/Artists' Books $15,000
Eileen Berger, New York, NY. 1980 Photo $3,000; 1982 Photo $5,000
Paul Berger, Seattle, WA. 1979 Photo $10,000; 1986 Photo $15,000
Richard Berger, Oakland, CA. 1979 Artist $10,000
Benjamin Bergery, Cambridge, MA. 1980 Video $3,000
Allen Berke, Ferndale, MI. 1982 Painting $5,000
Pamela Berkeley, New York, NY. 1980 Artist $3,000
Ellen Berkenblit, New York, NY. 1993 Painting $20,000
Leon Berkowitz, Washington, DC. 1971 Artist $7,500
Michael Berkowitz, E. Rockaway, NY. 1982 Sculpture $5,000
Steven Berkowitz, Philadelphia, PA. 1980 Photo $3,000
Terry Berkowitz, River Edge, NJ. 1975 Video $4,000
Robert Berlind, New York, NY. 1993 Painting $20,000
Judith Berman, Somerville, MA. 1985 Printmaking/Drawing/Artists' Books $5,000
Phyllis Berman, Brookline, MA. 1985 Painting $5,000
Wallace Berman, Topanga, CA. 1967 Artist $5,000
Zeke Berman, New York, NY. 1988 Photo $15,000
Debra Bermingham, Romulus, NY. 1985 Painting $5,000; 1987 Painting $5,000
Luis Bermudez, Los Angeles, CA. 1988 Crafts $5,000
Louis Bernal, Tucson, AZ. 1980 Photo $10,000
Rosemarie Bernardi, Huntsville, AL. 1980 Printmaking/Drawing/Artists' Books $3,000
Jerry Berndt, Cambridge, MA. 1987 Printmaking/Drawing/Artists' Books $15,000
Judith Bernstein, New York, NY. 1974 Artist $7,500; 1985 Printmaking/Drawing/Artists' Books $15,000
Larry Bernstein, Carbondale, IL. 1985 Painting $15,000
William Bernstein, Burnsville, NC. 1974 Crafts $3,000
Mary Bero, Madison, WI. 1986 Crafts $15,000; 1992 Crafts $20,000
Jake Berthot, New York, NY. 1976 Artist $2,000; 1983 Painting $25,000
Alan Bertoldi, Fresno, CA. 1973 Artist $7,500
Diane Bertolo, Brooklyn, NY. 1985 Painting $5,000
Christina Bertoni, Pascoag, RI. 1979 Crafts $10,000; 1986 Crafts $15,000
Betsey Bess, Philadelphia, PA. 1973 Crafts $3,000
James Bettison, Houston, TX. 1989 Painting $5,000
Gary Beydler, Los Angeles, CA. 1975 Artist $8,000
Steven Beyer, Elkins Park, PA. 1981 Sculpture $4,000; 1988 Sculpture $5,000
Thomas Bezanson, Westwood, MA. 1982 Crafts $5,000
Anna Bialobroda, New York, NY. 1975 Artist $4,000
Michael Bidlo, New York, NY. 1989 Painting $5,000
Charles Biederman, Redwing, MN. 1967 Artist $5,000
James Biederman, New York, NY. 1979 Printmaking/Drawing/Artists' Books $10,000; 1982 Sculpture $25,000

Natalie Bieser, Venice, CA. 1976 Artist $2,000
Kathryn Bigelow, New York, NY. 1976 Conceptual/Performance/New Genres $2,000
Janet Biggs, New York, NY. 1989 Painting $5,000
Cathey Billian, Peekskill, NY. 1984 Sculpture $15,000
Linda Bills, Baltimore, MD. 1988 Crafts $5,000; 1990 Crafts $5,000; 1992 Crafts $20,000
Thomas Bills, New York, NY. 1980 Artist $3,000
Bob Bingham, Pittsburgh, PA. 1988 Sculpture $5,000
McArthur Binion, New York, NY. 1976 Artist $2,000
Willie Birch, Brooklyn, NY. 1984 Sculpture $5,000; 1989 Works On Paper $15,000
George Bireline, Raleigh, NC. 1968 Artist $5,000
Robert Birmelin, Leonia, NJ. 1976 Artist $2,000; 1982 Painting $25,000; 1989 Painting $15,000
Dara Birnbaum, New York, NY. 1991 New Genres $20,000
James Bishop, New York, NY. 1976 Artist $5,000
Michael Bishop, Rochester, NY. 1975 Photo $5,000; 1978 Photo $7,500
Helen Bitar, Portland, OR. 1974 Crafts $3,000
David Black, Columbus, OH. 1967 Artist $5,000
Ed Blackburn, Ft. Worth, TX. 1977 Artist $7,500; 1989 Painting $15,000
Edmund Blackburn, Walnut Creek, CA. 1979 Crafts $10,000
Linda Blackburn, Ft. Worth, TX. 1989 Painting $15,000
Benjamin Blackwell, Oakland, CA. 1979 Artist $10,000
Ronald Bladen, New York, NY. 1967 Artist $5,000; 1978 Artist $10,000; 1986 Sculpture $25,000
Nell Blaine, New York, NY. 1975 Artist $8,000
Nicholas Blair, New York, NY. 1984 Photo $5,000
John Blake, East Greenwich, RI. 1976 Conceptual/Performance/New Genres $2,000
George Blakely, Tallahassee, FL. 1981 Photo $12,500; 1988 Photo $15,000
Nancy Blanchard, Berkeley, CA. 1978 Conceptual/Performance/New Genres $3,000
Marc Blane, New York, NY. 1980 Artist $3,000
Jeffrey Blankfort, Studio City, CA. 1971 Photo $750
Ross Bleckner, New York, NY. 1975 Artist $4,000
Dianne Blell, New York, NY. 1980 Conceptual/Performance/New Genres $3,000
Weltzin Blix, Eugene, OR. 1984 Sculpture $15,000
Ricardo Bloch, St. Paul, MN. 1982 Photo $5,000; 1993 Works On Paper $20,000
Gay Block, Houston, TX. 1978 Photo $7,500
Richard Bloes, Ridgewood, NY. 1987 New Genres $5,000
Sonja Blomdahl, Seattle, WA. 1986 Crafts $5,000
Barbara Bloom, New York, NY. 1988 Photo $5,000
John Bloom, Albuquerque, NM. 1980 Photo $3,000
Miriam Bloom, New York, NY. 1993 Crafts $5,000; 1978 Artist $7,500; 1994 Crafts $20,000
Suzanne Bloom, Houston, TX. 1976 Video $2,000; 1979 Photo $3,000
Lisa Bloomfield, Los Angeles, CA. 1986 Photo $5,000
Nicholas Blosser, Johnson City, TN. 1987 Painting $5,000; 1991 Painting $20,000
Patt Blue, New York, NY. 1988 Photo $15,000
Andrea Blum, Chicago, IL. 1976 Artist $2,000; 1978 Artist $7,500
Skip Blumberg, Linesville, NY. 1977 Video $7,500; 1980 Video $3,000
Lyn Blumenthal, New York, NY. 1978 Artist $3,000; 1985 New Genres $15,000
Michael Board, Brooklyn, NY. 1989 Painting $5,000
Gina Bobrowski, Corrales, NM. 1988 Crafts $5,000; 1994 Crafts $20,000
Suzanne Bocanegra, New York, NY. 1991 Sculpture $5,000; 1993 Works On Paper $20,000
Mel Bochner, New York, NY. 1974 Artist $7,500; 1983 Painting $15,000
Peer Bode, Owego, NY. 1982 Video $5,000
Peter Bodnar, Urbana, IL. 1975 Artist $4,000
Caryl Boeder, East Glacier Park, MT. 1980 Crafts $3,000
Eric Bogosian, New York, NY. 1983 Conceptual/Performance/New Genres $5,000; 1985 New Genres $15,000
James Bohary, New York, NY. 1983 Painting $15,000
Blythe Bohnen, New York, NY. 1978 Printmaking/Drawing/Artists' Books $7,500
Leslie Bohnenkamp, New York, NY. 1973 Crafts $3,000; 1980 Artist $3,000
Thomas Bohnert, Flint, MI. 1978 Crafts $7,500
Bruce Boice, New York, NY. 1976 Artist $5,000; 1980 Artist $10,000
William Bollinger, New York, NY. 1969 Artist $5,000
Randy Bolton, Landenberg, PA. 1989 Works On Paper $5,000
Richard Bolton, Somerville, MA. 1989 New Genres $5,000; 1991 New Genres $20,000
Brian Bomeisler, New York, NY. 1985 Printmaking/Drawing/Artists' Books $5,000
Albert Bonai, Austin, TX. 1980 Artist $3,000; 1989 Painting $5,000
Stephen Bondi, San Anselmo, CA. 1980 Crafts $3,000
Jonathan G. Bonner, Providence, RI. 1974 Crafts $3,000; 1988 Crafts $15,000
Power Boothe, New York, NY. 1975 Artist $4,000
Antoine Bootz, Brooklyn, NY. 1986 Photo $5,000
Nina Borgia-Aberle, Johnstown, OH. 1988 Crafts $5,000; 1990 Crafts $5,000
Jonathan Borofsky, Santa Monica, CA. 1978 Artist $7,500
Elena Borstein, New York, NY. 1980 Artist $3,000
Derek Boshier, Houston, TX. 1987 Painting $15,000
Jack Bosson, New York, NY. 1980 Artist $10,000
Lynn Bostick, Berkeley, CA. 1980 Artist $3,000
Mark Boulding, Boulder, CO. 1979 Conceptual/Performance/New Genres $3,000
Robert Bourdon, Houston, TX. 1979 Crafts $10,000; 1986 Sculpture $15,000
Dana Boussard, Arlee, MT. 1980 Crafts $10,000
Thomas Boutis, New York, NY. 1976 Artist $5,000
Gaza Bowen, Santa Cruz, CA. 1994 Crafts $20,000
Nancy Bowen, Brooklyn, NY. 1994 Sculpture $20,000
Gary Bower, Charlottesville, NY. 1982 Painting $25,000
Vivian Bower, New York, NY. 1983 Printmaking/Drawing/Artists' Books $5,000
Harry Bowers, Berkeley, CA. 1978 Photo $7,500; 1980 Photo $10,000
Larry Bowers, Masontown, PA. 1982 Crafts $5,000
Edward Bowes, New York, NY. 1985 New Genres $15,000
Katherine Bowling, New York, NY. 1988 Crafts $3,000
Jozef Bowser, Long Beach, CA. 1981 Crafts $4,000
Stanley Boxer, New York, NY. 1989 Painting $15,000
Christopher Boyce, Chicago, IL. 1985 Painting $5,000
Mable Boyd, Compton, MA. 1982 Photo $5,000
Harold Boyde, Hudson, IL. 1978 Printmaking/Drawing/Artists' Books $7,500
Frank Boyden, Otis, OR. 1981 Crafts $12,500
Alice Boyle, McClellanville, SC. 1984 Photo $5,000
Keith Boyle, Palo Alto, CA. 1981 Painting $12,500
Kevin Boyle, Los Angeles, CA. 1980 Conceptual/Performance/New Genres $3,000
Peter Boyle, Port Chester, NY. 1981 Printmaking/Drawing/Artists' Books $4,000
Ante Bozanich, Los Angeles, CA. 1979 Video $3,000
Eli Bozickovich, Chicago, IL. 1974 Artist $3,000
Julie Bozzi, Fort Worth, TX. 1989 Works On Paper $15,000
Hilary Brace, Santa Barbara, CA. 1993 Works On Paper $20,000
Katherine Bradshaw, New York, NY. 1975 Crafts $5,000
Robert Brady, Berkeley, CA. 1981 Crafts $12,500; 1988 Crafts $15,000
Michael Brakke, Knoxville, TN. 1985 Painting $15,000
Frank Bramblett, Philadelphia, PA. 1978 Artist $7,500
Phyllis Bramson, Glenview, IL. 1976 Crafts $5,000; 1983 Painting $15,000; 1993 Works On Paper $20,000
Fred Brandes, New York, NY. 1982 Painting $5,000
Alice Brandon, Philadelphia, PA. 1981 Crafts $4,000
Wayne Branum, Stillwater, MN. 1978 Crafts $7,500
Christopher Bratton, New York, NY. 1988 Sculpture $5,000
Marna Brauner, Shorewood, WI. 1986 Crafts $5,000
Terry Braunstein, Washington, DC. 1985 Printmaking/Drawing/Artists' Books $15,000
Troy Brauntuch, Jersey City, NJ. 1979 Conceptual/Performance/New Genres $3,000; 1983 Printmaking/Drawing/Artists' Books $15,000; 1989 Works On Paper $15,000
Olga Bravo, Baltimore, MD. 1984 Crafts $5,000
Diane Brawarsky, Rochester, NY. 1978 Crafts $7,500
Thomas Breeden, Breckenridge, CO. 1980 Photo $3,000
Elaine Breiger, New York, NY. 1974 Printmaking/Drawing/Artists' Books $3,000
Cornelia Breitenbach, Los Angeles, CA. 1978 Crafts $7,500
Vernon Brejcha, Lawrence, KS. 1984 Crafts $15,000
Nancy Brett, New York, NY. 1991 Works On Paper $20,000
Jane Brettschneider, New York, NY. 1980 Video $3,000
Harvey Breverman, Buffalo, NY. 1974 Printmaking/Drawing/Artists' Books $3,000; 1980 Printmaking/Drawing/Artists' Books $3,000
Andrea Brewster, Oakland, CA. 1993 Works On Paper $20,000
Michael Brewster, Venice, CA. 1976 Artist $2,000; 1978 Artist $7,500; 1984 Sculpture $15,000; 1990 Sculpture $20,000
Farrell Brickhouse, New York, NY. 1980 Artist $3,000; 1983 Painting $15,000
Marilyn Bridges, Warwick, NY. 1984 Photo $15,000
Stephen Brigidi, Providence, RI. 1979 Photo $3,000
Glenn Brill, Oakland, CA. 1982 Crafts $5,000; 1986 Crafts $5,000
Rolando Briseno, Brooklyn, NY. 1985 Painting $5,000
Maria Brito, Miami, FL. 1984 Sculpture $5,000; 1988 Sculpture $5,000
Harry Brock, Charlestown, MA. 1982 Painting $5,000; 1983 Painting $5,000

Mitchell Brock, Brooklyn, NY. 1989 Works On Paper $5,000
Timothy Broderick, Del Mar, CA. 1980 Video $3,000
Gandy Brodie, Wenatchi, WA. 1969 Artist $5,000
Eugene Brodsky, New York, NY. 1976 Artist $2,000; 1983 Painting $15,000
Mary Brogger, Chicago, IL. 1988 Sculpture $5,000
Karin Broker, Houston, TX. 1985 Printmaking/Drawing/Artists' Books $5,000; 1987 Printmaking/Drawing/Artists' Books $5,000
Faith Bromberg, New York, NY. 1980 Artist $3,000
Corinne Bronfman, New York, NY. 1982 Photo $5,000
Anne Brooke, Putney, VT. 1980 Crafts $10,000
Drex Brooks, Ogden, UT. 1988 Photo $5,000; 1992 Photo $20,000
Ellen Brooks, New York, NY. 1976 Photo $7,500; 1980 Photo $10,000; 1990 Photo $20,000
James Brooks, New York, NY. 1973 Artist $7,500
Linda Brooks, Minneapolis, MN. 1982 Photo $5,000
Carol Brown, New York, NY. 1993 Painting $20,000
Carol Brown, Miami Beach, FL. 1984 Sculpture $5,000; 1986 Sculpture $15,000
Charlotte Brown, Woodbury, NY. 1977 Printmaking/Drawing/Artists' Books $5,000
Christopher Brown, Oakland, CA. 1987 Painting $15,000
Joan Brown, San Francisco, CA. 1976 Artist $2,000; 1980 Artist $10,000
Gillian Brown, Takoma Park, MD. 1990 Photo $20,000
Kathan Brown, Berkeley, CA. 1977 Printmaking/Drawing/Artists' Books $5,000
Larry Brown, New York, NY. 1979 Artist $10,000
Laurie Brown, Corona del Mar, CA. 1979 Photo $3,000
Pam Brown, Babylon, NY. 1988 Sculpture $5,000
Paul Brown, New York, NY. 1974 Artist $3,000; 1983 Painting $15,000
Peter Brown, Houston, TX. 1990 Photo $20,000
Polly Brown, Marblehead, MA. 1988 Photo $5,000
Robert Brown, San Francisco, CA. 1975 Photo $5,000
Tom Browne, Richmond, CA. 1973 Crafts $3,000
Sandra Brownlee-Ramsdale, Philadelphia, PA. 1988 Crafts $5,000
James Brozek, Milwaukee, WI. 1988 Photo $5,000
Harold J. Bruder, New York, NY. 1985 Painting $15,000
John Brumfield, Frazier Park, CA. 1980 Photo $10,000
Helen Brunner, Washington, DC. 1984 Photo $5,000
Gloria D. Brush, Duluth, MN. 1993 Photo $5,000; 1982 Photo $5,000
Leif Brush, Duluth, MN. 1983 Conceptual/Performance/New Genres $15,000
Lori Bryan, Valley Center, CA. 1982 Painting $5,000
Sukey Bryan, Baltimore, MD. 1993 Painting $20,000
Laura Bryant, St. Petersberg, FL. 1990 Crafts $5,000
Kevin Bubriski, Bennington, VT. 1988 Photo $5,000
Virginia Buchan, New York, NY. 1989 Works On Paper $5,000
Beverly Buchanan, Athens, GA. 1980 Artist $3,000; 1994 Sculpture $20,000
Jerry Buchanan, New York, NY. 1989 Painting $15,000
Nancy Buchanan, Los Angeles, CA. 1978 Conceptual/Performance/New Genres $3,000; 1980 Video $3,000; 1983 Video $15,000; 1989 New Genres $15,000
Sydney Buchanan, Omaha, NE. 1974 Artist $3,000
Bill/Mary Buchen, New York, NY. 1985 New Genres $15,000
James Buchman, New York, NY. 1980 Artist $3,000
Howard Buchwald, New York, NY. 1980 Artist $10,000; 1989 Painting $15,000
John Buck, Bozeman, MT. 1980 Artist $10,000
Jan Buckman, Hager City, WI. 1994 Crafts $20,000
Malcolm R Bucknall, Austin, TX. 1985 Painting $15,000
Barbara Buckner, New York, NY. 1978 Video $3,000; 1980 Video $3,000; 1981 Video $12,500
David Budd, New York, NY. 1974 Artist $7,500
Dan Budnick, New York, NY. 1973 Photo $3,500
John Buhler, Oxford, OH. 1975 Printmaking/Drawing/Artists' Books $3,000
Ken Buhler, New York, NY. 1987 Painting $5,000
Robert Buitron, Tempe, AZ. 1982 Photo $5,000
Richard Bunkall, Pasadena, CA. 1981 Painting $4,000; 1985 Painting $5,000
John Bunkley, Jamestown, RI. 1980 Artist $3,000
David Bunn, Los Angeles, CA. 1988 Photo $5,000; 1989 New Genres $5,000
Carol Burch-Brown, Blacksburg, VA. 1983 Printmaking/Drawing/Artists' Books $5,000
Jerry Burchard, San Francisco, CA. 1976 Photo $7,500; 1979 Photo $10,000
Jerry Burchfield, Laguna Beach, CA. 1981 Photo $12,500
Monika Burczyk, Brooklyn, NY. 1989 Works On Paper $5,000
Chris Burden, Los Angeles, CA. 1974 Artist $7,500; 1976 Conceptual/Performance/New Genres $5,000; 1980 Video $10,000; 1983 Conceptual/Performance/New Genres $15,000
James Burgess, Ithaca, NY. 1975 Printmaking/Drawing/Artists' Books $3,000
Lowry Burgess, Cambridge, MA. 1977 Conceptual/Performance/New Genres $7,500
Donald Burgy, Milton, MA. 1977 Conceptual/Performance/New Genres $7,500
Bill Burke, Dorchester, MA. 1976 Photo $7,500; 1982 Photo $25,000; 1988 Photo $15,000; 1994 Photo $20,000
Diane Burko, Philadelphia, PA. 1985 Painting $15,000; 1991 Painting $20,000
Kimberly Burleigh, Athens, OH. 1987 Painting $5,000
Paul Burlin, New York, NY. 1969 Artist $5,000
Ian Burn, New York, NY. 1975 Artist $4,000
Grace Burney, Brooklyn, NY. 1983 Printmaking/Drawing/Artists' Books $5,000
Gary Burnley, Staten Island, NY. 1984 Sculpture $15,000
James Burns, Seattle, WA. 1979 Photo $3,000
Mark Burns, Philadelphia, PA. 1976 Crafts $5,000; 1988 Crafts $15,000
Marsha Burns, Seattle, WA. 1979 Photo $3,000; 1988 Photo $15,000
Michael Burns, Seattle, WA. 1980 Photo $3,000
Nancy Burson, New York, NY. 1990 Photo $20,000
Scott Burton, New York, NY. 1975 Artist $8,000; 1986 Sculpture $15,000
Robert Bush, Stanford, CA. 1974 Artist $1,000
Alfredo Bustinza, Brownsville, TX. 1983 Printmaking/Drawing/Artists' Books $5,000
Ana Busto, Brooklyn, NY. 1990 Photo $5,000
Jose Bustos, San Francisco, CA. 1981 Conceptual/Performance/New Genres $4,000
Frances Butler, Berkeley, CA. 1973 Crafts $3,000; 1981 Printmaking/Drawing/Artists' Books $12,500
Jack Butler, Pasadena, CA. 1981 Photo $12,500
James Butler, Bloomington, IL. 1979 Printmaking/Drawing/Artists' Books $10,000; 1985 Printmaking/Drawing/Artists' Books $15,000
Kenneth Butler, Portland, OR. 1983 Conceptual/Performance/New Genres $5,000
Harlan Butt, Denton, TX. 1979 Crafts $10,000
Thomas Butter, New York, NY. 1980 Artist $3,000; 1982 Sculpture $5,000; 1986 Sculpture $5,000
Deborah Butterfield, San Diego, CA. 1977 Artist $3,000; 1980 Artist $10,000
Harvey Butts, Brooklyn, NY. 1986 Photo $5,000
Carole Byard, New York, NY. 1985 Printmaking/Drawing/Artists' Books $15,000; 1994 Sculpture $20,000
James Lee Byars, Los Angeles, CA. 1981 Conceptual/Performance/New Genres $12,500
Jerry Byrd, Venice, CA. 1975 Artist $4,000
James Byrne, Minneapolis, MN. 1976 Video $2,000; 1979 Video $3,000; 1982 Video $25,000
Michael Byron, New York, NY. 1989 Painting $5,000

C

Diana Cabouli, Forest Hills, NY. 1983 Painting $5,000
Yvette Cabrera-Vega, New York, NY. 1984 Sculpture $5,000
Jean Cacicedo, Centennial, WY. 1976 Crafts $5,000
Steve Cagan, Cleveland Heights, OH. 1982 Photo $5,000
Charlotte Cain, Fairfield, IA. 1980 Crafts $10,000
Nancy Cain, Lanesville, NY. 1977 Video $7,500
Michael Cajero, Tucson, AZ. 1993 New Genres $20,000
Charles Cajori, Watertown, CT. 1981 Painting $12,500
Marion Cajori, New York, NY. 1976 Conceptual/Performance/New Genres $5,000
Richard Calabro, Wakefield, RI. 1976 Artist $2,000
Gloria Calamar, Summerland, CA. 1980 Artist $3,000
Loren Calaway, New York, NY. 1982 Sculpture $5,000
Larry Calcagno, New York, NY. 1989 Painting $15,000
Eduardo Calderon, Kirkland, WA. 1992 Photo $20,000
John Caldwell, Long Beach, CA. 1979 Video $3,000; 1985 New Genres $5,000
Harry Callahan, Providence, RI. 1976 Photo $7,500
Andrea Callard, New York, NY. 1977 Printmaking/Drawing/Artists' Books $5,000
Jo Ann Callis, Culver City, CA. 1980 Photo $10,000; 1984 Photo $15,000; 1990 Photo $20,000
Jane Calvin, Chicago, IL. 1984 Photo $5,000
Robert Calvo, Portland, OR. 1984 Sculpture $5,000; 1990 Sculpture $5,000
Donald Camp, Philadelphia, PA. 1995 Works On Paper $20,000
Graham Campbell, New York, NY. 1993 Painting $20,000
Patricia Campbell, Chalfont, PA. 1979 Crafts $10,000
Wayne Campbell, San Francisco, CA. 1973 Artist $7,500
Remo Campopiano, New York, NY. 1990 Sculpture $5,000
Peter Campus, New York, NY. 1976 Video $10,000
Kevin Cannon, New York, NY. 1986 Sculpture $5,000

Canole, Rochester, NY. 1976 Artist $2,000
Sarah Canright, New York, NY. 1975 Artist $4,000; 1978 Artist $7,500; 1985 Painting $15,000
Paul Caponigro, ME. 1971 Photo $4,000; 1975 Photo $5,000; 1982 Photo $25,000
Suzanne Caporael, Los Angeles, CA. 1985 Painting $5,000
Kenneth Capps, Carlsbad, CA. 1983 Printmaking/Drawing/Artists' Books $5,000; 1986 Sculpture $15,000
Greg Card, Venice, CA. 1975 Artist $4,000
Ellen Carey, New York, NY. 1984 Photo $5,000
Cynthia Carlson, New York, NY. 1975 Artist $4,000; 1978 Artist $7,500; 1987 Printmaking/Drawing/Artists' Books $15,000
Deborah Carlson, Cleveland, OH. 1986 Crafts $5,000
Lance Carlson, Los Angeles, CA. 1982 Photo $5,000; 1988 Photo $5,000
Mary Carlson, New York, NY. 1988 Sculpture $5,000
Robert Carlson, Bainbridge Island, WA. 1990 Crafts $5,000
William Carlson, Champaign, IL. 1981 Crafts $12,500
Nancy Carman, San Francisco, CA. 1979 Crafts $10,000
Jack Carnell, Jenkintown, PA. 1980 Photo $3,000
Squeak Carnwath, Oakland, CA. 1980 Artist $3,000; 1985 Painting $15,000
Carole Caroompas, Los Angeles, CA. 1987 Painting $15,000; 1993 Painting $20,000
Art Carpenter, Bolinas, CA. 1976 Crafts $5,000
Dennis Carpenter, Lexington, KY. 1982 Photo $5,000
Edward Carpenter, Portland, OR. 1984 Crafts $15,000
James Carpenter, New York, NY. 1978 Crafts $7,500; 1988 Crafts $15,000
Miles Carpenter, Waverly, VA. 1982 Sculpture $5,000
Simon Carr, New York, NY. 1985 Painting $5,000
Eduardo Carrillo, Santa Cruz, CA. 1978 Artist $7,500
Graciela Carrillo, San Gabriel, CA. 1979 Artist $10,000
David Carrino, New York, NY. 1989 Painting $5,000
Candice Carson, Berkeley, CA. 1982 Sculpture $5,000; 1986 Sculpture $5,000
Jo Ann Carson, Chicago, IL. 1982 Painting $5,000
Karen Carson, Venice, CA. 1985 Painting $15,000
Rodney Carswell, Oak Park, IL. 1991 Painting $20,000
Carol A. Carter, University Park, PA. 1988 Crafts $5,000
Jack Carter, New York, NY. 1990 Sculpture $5,000
Nanette Carter, New York, NY. 1981 Printmaking/Drawing/Artists' Books $4,000
Roy Cartwright, Cincinnati, OH. 1990 Crafts $20,000
Josely Carvalho, New York, NY. 1995 New Genres $20,000
Craig Carver, Detroit, MI. 1982 Painting $5,000
James Casebere, New York, NY. 1982 Photo $5,000; 1986 Photo $5,000; 1990 Photo $20,000
Sydney Cash, Marlboro, NY. 1984 Crafts $15,000
Bill Cass, Chicago, IL. 1987 Painting $5,000
Wendell Castle, Scottsville, NY. 1973 Crafts $3,000; 1988 Crafts $25,000
Rosemarie Castoro, New York, NY. 1974 Artist $3,000; 1984 Sculpture $15,000
James Caswell, Santa Monica, CA. 1982 Crafts $5,000
David Caton, Houston, TX. 1985 Painting $5,000; 1987 Painting $5,000
Patrick Cauley, New York, NY. 1981 Painting $4,000
Gary Cawood, Ruston, LA. 1982 Photo $5,000
John Cederquist, Capistrano Beach, CA. 1975 Crafts $5,000; 1986 Crafts $15,000
Donald Celender, St. Paul, MN. 1975 Artist $2,000
Vija Celmins, Venice, CA. 1971 Artist $7,500; 1976 Artist $5,000
Paloma Cernuda, New York, NY. 1989 Works On Paper $5,000
Susan Cervantes, San Francisco, CA. 1979 Artist $10,000
Barbara Cesery, Jacksonville, FL. 1981 Printmaking/Drawing/Artists' Books $4,000
Theresa Cha, San Francisco, CA. 1979 Video $3,000
Aurore Chabot, Wilton, NH. 1982 Crafts $5,000
Enrique Chagoya, Oakland, CA. 1993 Works On Paper $20,000; 1992 Works On Paper $5,000
Ann Chamberlain, San Francisco, CA. 1994 Photo $20,000
John Chamberlain, New York, NY. 1974 Artist $7,500
Scott Chamberlin, Denver, CO. 1986 Crafts $5,000; 1990 Crafts $20,000
Park Chambers, Chicago, IL. 1976 Crafts $5,000
Judy Chan, Long Beach, CA. 1995 Works On Paper $20,000
Phillip Chan, Rootstown, OH. 1979 Artist $10,000
Bruce Chandler, Boston, MA. 1989 Works On Paper $15,000
Dana Chandler, Boston, MA. 1974 Artist $7,500
Bruce Chao, Rehoboth, MA. 1976 Artist $2,000; 1981 Sculpture $12,500; 1990 Sculpture $20,000
Karen Chapnick, Greatneck, NY. 1979 Crafts $10,000
Walter Chappell, El Rito, NM. 1977 Photo $7,500; 1980 Photo $10,000; 1984 Photo $15,000
William Charland, Berkeley, CA. 1985 Printmaking/Drawing/Artists' Books $5,000
Peter Charles, Washington, DC. 1982 Sculpture $5,000
Bruce Charlesworth, Minneapolis, MN. 1984 Photo $15,000
Sarah Charlesworth, New York, NY. 1976 Conceptual/Performance/New Genres $5,000; 1980 Conceptual/Performance/New Genres $3,000; 1983 Conceptual/Performance/New Genres $15,000
Jean Charlot, Honolulu, HI. 1968 Artist $5,000
Benjamin Chase, Los Angeles, CA. 1983 Video $5,000
Louisa Chase, New York, NY. 1978 Artist $7,500; 1982 Painting $25,000; 1989 Painting $15,000
Cedric Chatterley, Durham, NC. 1988 Photo $5,000
Humberto Chavez, New York, NY. 1982 Sculpture $5,000
Shu Lea Cheang, New York, NY. 1993 New Genres $20,000
Philip Chen, Chicago, IL. 1982 Printmaking/Drawing/Artists' Books $5,000
Carl Cheng, Santa Monica, CA. 1982 Sculpture $5,000; 1986 Sculpture $25,000
Emily Cheng, New York, NY. 1982 Painting $5,000
Myrel Chernick, New York, NY. 1989 New Genres $5,000
Carl Chew, Seattle, WA. 1988 Crafts $5,000
Carl Chiarenza, Rochester, NY. 1977 Photo $7,500; 1990 Photo $20,000
Judy Chicago, Santa Monica, CA. 1976 Artist $5,000
Dale Chihuly, Providence, RI. 1975 Crafts $5,000; 1979 Crafts $10,000
William Childress, New York, NY. 1980 Artist $3,000; 1983 Printmaking/Drawing/Artists' Books $15,000
Thomas Chimes, Philadelphia, PA. 1987 Painting $15,000
Mel Chin, New York, NY. 1988 Sculpture $5,000
Joseph Chirchirillo, Jersey City, NJ. 1984 Sculpture $5,000
Richard Chiriani, Middleburg, NY. 1983 Painting $15,000
Jim Chiros, Cambridge, MA. 1989 Works On Paper $5,000
Younghee Choi, New York, NY. 1982 Painting $5,000
Albert Chong, Boulder, CO. 1991 Photo $5,000; 1992 Photo $20,000
Ping Chong, New York, NY. 1980 Conceptual/Performance/New Genres $3,000; 1983 Conceptual/Performance/New Genres $25,000; 1989 New Genres $15,000
Chunghi Choo, Iowa City, IA. 1981 Crafts $12,500
William Christenberry, Washington, DC. 1976 Photo $7,500
Dan Christensen, New York, NY. 1969 Artist $5,000
Don Christensen, New York, NY. 1991 Painting $20,000
Wes Christensen, Los Angeles, CA. 1985 Painting $5,000
Linda Christianson, Lindstrom, MN. 1992 Crafts $20,000
Yoshiko Chuma, New York, NY. 1982 Conceptual/Performance/New Genres $5,000
Y. David Chung, Washington, DC. 1993 New Genres $20,000
Nancy Chunn, New York, NY. 1985 Painting $15,000; 1995 Painting $20,000
Sharon Church, Greenville, DE. 1977 Crafts $5,000
S. E. Ciriclio, Oakland, CA. 1979 Photo $10,000
George Cisneros, San Antonio, TX. 1981 Conceptual/Performance/New Genres $4,000
Bruno Civitico, Portsmouth, NH. 1981 Painting $12,500
Corwin Clairmont, Los Angeles, CA. 1978 Printmaking/Drawing/Artists' Books $3,000
Patrick Clancy, Kansas City, MO. 1994 Photo $20,000
Thomas Clancy, New York, NY. 1974 Artist $7,500
Jerry Clapsaddle, Riverdale, MD. 1980 Artist $10,000
Edward Clark, New York, NY. 1973 Artist $7,500; 1982 Painting $25,000
James Clark, Brooklyn, NY. 1982 Sculpture $5,000; 1983 Printmaking/Drawing/Artists' Books $5,000
Jon Clark, Elkins Park, PA. 1981 Crafts $12,500; 1986 Crafts $15,000
Kathryn Clark, West Lafayette, IN. 1974 Crafts $3,000
Kathryn Clark, New York, NY. 1992 Photo $20,000
Larry Clark, New York, NY. 1973 Photo $5,000
Robert Clark, Chicago, IL. 1978 Conceptual/Performance/New Genres $3,000
Marian Clayden, Los Gatos, CA. 1973 Crafts $3,000
Richard Cleaver, Baltimore, MD. 1994 Crafts $20,000
Alain Clement, Houston, TX. 1988 Photo $5,000
Morgan Clifford, St. Paul, MN. 1991 Crafts $5,000; 1992 Crafts $20,000
William Clift, Santa Fe, NM. 1973 Photo $4,000; 1980 Photo $10,000
John Cloonan, Atlanta, GA. 1974 Artist $3,000
Chuck Close, New York, NY. 1973 Artist $7,500
Charles Clough, New York, NY. 1982 Painting $25,000; 1989 Painting $15,000
Eleanor Clough, Chicago, IL. 1988 Sculpture $5,000

James Clover, Atlanta, GA. 1974 Artist $7,500
Brenda Coates, Zirconia, NC. 1990 Sculpture $5,000
Marvin Coats, Winston-Salem, NC. 1982 Sculpture $25,000
James Cobb, New York, NY. 1974 Artist $3,000; 1989 Painting $5,000
Malcolm Cochran, Bradford, NH. 1982 Sculpture $25,000
Sue Coe, New York, NY. 1989 Works On Paper $15,000
Susanna Coffey, Chicago, IL. 1993 Painting $20,000
Arthur M. Cohen, New York, NY. 1982 Printmaking/Drawing/Artists' Books $5,000
Cora Cohen, New York, NY. 1987 Painting $15,000
George Cohen, Evanston, IL. 1967 Artist $5,000
Helen Cohen, Groveland, CA. 1986 Sculpture $5,000
Mardi-jo Cohen, Philadelphia, PA. 1988 Crafts $5,000
Mark Cohen, Wilkes-Barre, PA. 1975 Photo $5,000
Maxi Cohen, New York, NY. 1977 Video $7,500; 1980 Video $3,000; 1983 Video $15,000
Michael Cohen, Amherst, MA. 1974 Crafts $3,000
Ronald Cohen, Iowa City, IA. 1980 Artist $3,000; 1984 Sculpture $15,000; 1993 Painting $20,000
Michael Cohn, Emeryville, CA. 1977 Crafts $5,000; 1984 Crafts $15,000
Anthony Cokes, New York, NY. 1991 New Genres $20,000
Corrine Colarusso, Atlanta, GA. 1982 Painting $5,000
Jon Colburn, New York, NY. 1980 Artist $3,000
Jeff Colby, Chicago, IL. 1987 Painting $5,000
Donald Cole, Sierra Madre, CA. 1978 Artist $7,500
Max Cole, New York, NY. 1983 Printmaking/Drawing/Artists' Books $15,000
Brian Coleman, Watsonville, CA. 1976 Crafts $5,000
Judy Coleman, Marina Del Rey, CA. 1984 Photo $5,000; 1988 Photo $15,000
Thelma Coles, Austin, TX. 1981 Crafts $4,000; 1984 Crafts $5,000; 1986 Crafts $5,000
Robert Colescott, Oakland, CA. 1976 Artist $5,000; 1980 Artist $10,000; 1983 Painting $15,000
Warrington Colescott, Hollandale, WI. 1975 Printmaking/Drawing/Artists' Books $3,000; 1979 Printmaking/Drawing/Artists' Books $10,000; 1983 Printmaking/Drawing/Artists' Books $25,000; 1993 Works On Paper $20,000
Colette, New York, NY. 1977 Conceptual/Performance/New Genres $3,000; 1984 Sculpture $15,000
Lois Colette, New York, NY. 1987 Painting $5,000
James Collins, New York, NY. 1977 Conceptual/Performance/New Genres $7,500
Jess Collins, San Francisco, CA. 1973 Artist $7,500
Kathy Collins, Rochester, NY. 1979 Photo $10,000
Stephen Collins, San Francisco, CA. 1980 Photo $3,000
Papo Colo, New York, NY. 1981 Painting $4,000; 1983 Painting $15,000
William Colon, New York, NY. 1978 Artist $7,500
Clair Colquitt, Seattle, WA. 1977 Crafts $5,000
Patricia Colville, Austin, TX. 1975 Artist $4,000
Ben Compton, New York, NY. 1976 Crafts $5,000
Robbie Conal, Venice, CA. 1989 Painting $5,000
Howard Conant, Tucson, AZ. 1985 Painting $15,000
Cecelia Condit, Milwaukee, WI. 1985 New Genres $5,000; 1989 New Genres $15,000; 1995 New Genres $20,000
Joseph Coninck, New York, NY. 1982 Painting $5,000; 1987 Painting $5,000
Brian Conley, Brooklyn, NY. 1989 Painting $5,000
Stone Conley, Newton, MA. 1980 Artist $3,000
William Conlon, New York, NY. 1989 Painting $15,000
David Conn, Fort Worth, TX. 1985 Printmaking/Drawing/Artists' Books $15,000
Danny Connally, Sacramento, CA. 1983 Painting $5,000
Julie Connell, San Francisco, CA. 1984 Crafts $15,000
Michael Connelly, Normal, IL. 1985 Painting $5,000
L. Conner, New York, NY. 1980 Photo $3,000
Gregory Conniff, Madison, WI. 1981 Photo $12,500; 1992 Photo $20,000
Bruce Conner, San Francisco, CA. 1973 Artist $7,500
Linda Connor, San Anselmo, CA. 1976 Photo $7,500; 1988 Photo $15,000
Maureen Connor, New York, NY. 1995 New Genres $20,000
Tony Conrad, Buffalo, NY. 1982 Video $25,000
Pierluigi Consagra, New York, NY. 1989 Painting $5,000
Thomas Consilvio, Boston, MA. 1977 Photo $7,500
Marika Contompasis, Piedmont, CA. 1975 Crafts $5,000
Houston Conwill, New York, NY. 1982 Sculpture $25,000; 1988 Sculpture $15,000
Jay Coogan, New York, NY. 1982 Sculpture $25,000
Gordon Cook, San Francisco, CA. 1981 Painting $12,500
Lia Cook, Berkeley, CA. 1974 Crafts $3,000; 1977 Crafts $5,000; 1986 Crafts $15,000; 1992 Crafts $20,000
Michael Cook, Kensington, CA. 1985 Painting $5,000
Shelley Cook, San Francisco, CA. 1993 New Genres $20,000
Judy Cooke, Portland, OR. 1989 Painting $15,000
Robert Cooke, Chatham, NJ. 1974 Artist $3,000
Michael Cooper, Santa Clara, CA. 1978 Crafts $7,500
Ron Cooper, Venice, CA. 1971 Artist $7,500; 1980 Photo $10,000
Thomas Cooper, Arcata, CA. 1978 Photo $7,500
John Coplans, New York, NY. 1986 Photo $5,000; 1992 Photo $20,000
Lisa Corinne Davis, New York, NY. 1995 Works On Paper $20,000
Philip Cornelius, Pasadena, CA. 1980 Crafts $10,000; 1984 Crafts $15,000
Michael Corris, New York, NY. 1975 Artist $4,000
Mary Corse, Los Angeles, CA. 1973 Artist $7,500
Steven Cortright, Santa Barbara, CA. 1980 Printmaking/Drawing/Artists' Books $10,000; 1987 Printmaking/Drawing/Artists' Books $15,000
Sam Costa, Los Angeles, CA. 1981 Sculpture $4,000; 1982 Sculpture $5,000
Chris Costan, New York, NY. 1989 Works On Paper $5,000
Tony Costanzo, Oakland, CA. 1978 Crafts $7,500
Alan Cote, Kingston, NY. 1989 Painting $15,000
Robert Cottingham, Brooklyn, NY. 1974 Artist $7,500
Paul Cotton, Oakland, CA. 1978 Conceptual/Performance/New Genres $7,500; 1984 Sculpture $15,000
Jane Couch, New York, NY. 1980 Artist $10,000
Catherine Courtenaye, Emeryville, CA. 1989 Works On Paper $5,000
Patricia Courtney, Atlanta, GA. 1989 Painting $5,000
Molly Cowgill, Richmond, VA. 1976 Crafts $5,000
Eileen Cowin, Culver City, CA. 1979 Photo $10,000; 1982 Photo $25,000; 1990 Photo $20,000
David Cox, Ogden, UT. 1975 Crafts $5,000
Kris Cox, Laguna Beach, CA. 1980 Crafts $3,000
Petah Coyne, New York, NY. 1990 Sculpture $20,000
John Craig, Pensacola, FL. 1976 Photo $7,500
John Craig, Chester, NJ. 1976 Photo $7,500
Joyce Crain, New York, NY. 1982 Crafts $5,000
Rollin Crampton, Woodstock, NY. 1967 Artist $5,000
Barbara Crane, Chicago, IL. 1975 Photo $5,000; 1988 Photo $15,000
Dena Crane, Windham, NY. 1980 Video $10,000
Richard Craven, Winston-Salem, NC. 1985 Printmaking/Drawing/Artists' Books $15,000
Garie Crawford, Cleveland Heights, OH. 1982 Photo $5,000
James Crawford, Claremont, CA. 1979 Photo $3,000
Mark Crawford, New York, NY. 1989 Painting $5,000
Thom Crawford, Long Island City, NY. 1985 Painting $15,000
Gregory Crewdson, Brooklyn, NY. 1992 Photo $20,000
Susan Crile, New York, NY. 1982 Painting $25,000; 1989 Works On Paper $15,000
Gerald Crimmins, Glenside, PA. 1983 Printmaking/Drawing/Artists' Books $5,000
Alan Crockett, Columbus, OH. 1983 Painting $5,000
Lawrence Crombez, Brooklyn, NY. 1988 Photo $5,000
William Crotty, Malibu, CA. 1991 Works On Paper $20,000
Nancy Crow, Baltimore, OH. 1980 Crafts $10,000
Christy Crowhurst, Brooklyn, NY. 1985 Painting $5,000
Charles Crowley, Bedford, MA. 1992 Crafts $20,000
William Crozier, New York, NY. 1986 Sculpture $15,000
Iris Crump, New York, NY. 1982 Sculpture $5,000
Dewey Crumpler, Berkeley, CA. 1995 Works On Paper $20,000
Dirck Cruser, Asheville, NC. 1984 Sculpture $5,000
Emilio Cruz, Newark, NJ. 1971 Artist $7,500; 1987 Painting $15,000
Donigan Cumming, Montreal, FO. 1980 Photo $10,000
Robert Cumming, West Suffield, CT. 1973 Photo $ 4,500; 1974 Artist $3,000; 1983 Printmaking/Drawing/Artists' Books $15,000
Bruce Cunningham, Ithaca, NY. 1975 Artist $4,000; 1989 Works On Paper $15,000
Darryl Curran, Los Angeles, CA. 1980 Photo $10,000
William Current, Pasadena, CA. 1971 Photo $2,000
Steven Currie, Brooklyn, NY. 1988 Sculpture $5,000
Anne Currier, Alfred, NY. 1986 Crafts $15,000
Merry Curtis, Astoria, OR. 1974 Crafts $3,000
Barbara Cushing, New York, NY. 1985 Painting $15,000
Val Cushing, Alfred, NY. 1982 Crafts $25,000
Steven Cushner, Washington, DC. 1993 Painting $20,000
Mario Cutajar, Pasadena, CA. 1991 Painting $20,000

Roger Cutforth, New York, NY. 1984 Photo $15,000

Peggy Cyphers, New York, NY. 1989 Painting $5,000

Dorit Cypis, Minneapolis, MN. 1979 Conceptual/Performance/New Genres $3,000; 1983 Conceptual/Performance/New Genres $5,000; 1989 New Genres $15,000

Daniel Cytron, Los Angeles, CA. 1978 Artist $7,500

Tom Czarnopys, Chicago, IL. 1990 Sculpture $5,000

D

Peter D'Agostino, Elkins Park, PA. 1974 Artist $3,000; 1977 Video $7,500; 1979 Video $10,000; 1989 New Genres $15,000

Robert D'Alessandro, Brooklyn, NY. 1975 Photo $5,000

Edward D'Arms, Seattle, WA. 1973 Photo $ 2,500

Bernard D'Onofrio, Somerville, MA. 1990 Crafts $5,000

Stephen Dahl, Minneapolis, MN. 1990 Photo $5,000

Joseph Dahm, New York, NY. 1974 Artist $1,000

Dan Dailey, Amesbury, MA. 1978 Crafts $7,500

Shirley Dailey, Columbia, MO. 1975 Crafts $5,000

Michael Dal Cerro, Brooklyn, NY. 1987 Painting $5,000

Willaim Daley, Elkins Park, PA. 1977 Crafts $5,000

Susan Dallas, Northbrook, IL. 1976 Artist $2,000

Norman Daly, Ithaca, NY. 1974 Artist $7,500

Jack Damer, Madison, WI. 1981 Printmaking/Drawing/Artists' Books $12,500

William Dane, Pt. Richmond, CA. 1976 Photo $7,500; 1978 Photo $7,500

Paul Daniel, Baltimore, MD. 1976 Artist $2,000

Linda Daniels, Brooklyn, NY. 1991 Painting $20,000

Peter Danko, Washington, DC. 1975 Crafts $5,000

Stephen Danko, Venice, CA. 1980 Photo $3,000

Joseph Dankowski, New York, NY. 1971 Photo $3,000

Jerry Dantzic, Brooklyn, NY. 1976 Photo $7,500

Avery Danziger, Chapel Hill, NC. 1980 Photo $3,000

Nallos Daphnis, New York, NY. 1967 Artist $5,000

Lowell Darling, Berkeley, CA. 1976 Video $2,000; 1980 Video $10,000; 1982 Video $25,000

Andrew Dasburg, Taos, NM. 1968 Artist $5,000

Craig Dascanio, West Springfield, MA. 1982 Crafts $5,000

Judy Dater, New York, NY. 1977 Photo $7,500; 1988 Photo $15,000

Ward Davenny, Carlisle, PA. 1985 Printmaking/Drawing/Artists' Books $5,000; 1993 Works On Paper $20,000

Rebecca Davenport, Washington, DC. 1979 Artist $10,000

Cyril David, Sag Harbor, NY. 1980 Printmaking/Drawing/Artists' Books $3,000

Michael David, New York, NY. 1983 Painting $5,000

Gregory Davidek, Brooklyn, NY. 1985 Painting $5,000

Jaime Davidovich, Kingston, NY. 1978 Video $7,500; 1983 Video $15,000; 1989 New Genres $15,000

Donald R. Davidson, Ann Arbor, MI. 1975 Artist $4,000

Nancy Davidson, Champaign, IL. 1978 Printmaking/Drawing/Artists' Books $3,000

Bevan Davies, New York, NY. 1978 Photo $7,500

Hanlyn Davies, Hadley, MA. 1975 Printmaking/Drawing/Artists' Books $3,000; 1981 Printmaking/Drawing/Artists' Books $12,500

Jordan Davies, New York, NY. 1971 Artist $7,500

Margaret Davies, Vernal, VT. 1974 Printmaking/Drawing/Artists' Books $3,000

Nelsie Davies, White Salmon, WA. 1980 Crafts $10,000

Bradley Davis, Carbondale, CO. 1987 Painting $15,000

Doug Davis, New York, NY. 1975 Video $4,000

Gene Davis, Washington, DC. 1967 Artist $5,000

Malcolm Davis, Oakland, CA. 1992 Photo $20,000

Michael Davis, San Pedro, CA. 1980 Artist $3,000; 1986 Sculpture $15,000

Phil Davis, Venice, CA. 1974 Artist $3,000; 1975 Artist $2,000

Ron Davis, Los Angeles, CA. 1968 Artist $5,000

Stephen Davis, New York, NY. 1975 Artist $4,000; 1978 Artist $7,500; 1987 Painting $15,000

Virginia Davis, New York, NY. 1982 Crafts $5,000; 1992 Crafts $20,000

David Davison, Dunstable, MA. 1984 Crafts $15,000

William Davison, Burlington, VT. 1974 Printmaking/Drawing/Artists' Books $3,000

Deirdre Daw, Cleveland, OH. 1982 Crafts $5,000; 1994 Crafts $20,000

Robert Dawson, San Francisco, CA. 1988 Photo $15,000

Gary Day, Omaha, NE. 1987 Printmaking/Drawing/Artists' Books $15,000

Linda Day, New York, NY. 1989 Painting $5,000

Dirk De Bruycker, Santa Fe, NM. 1989 Painting $5,000

Guy De Cointet, Los Angeles, CA. 1979 Conceptual/Performance/New Genres $10,000

John De Fazio, New York, NY. 1986 Crafts $5,000

Jay De Feo, Oakland, CA. 1973 Artist $7,500; 1985 Painting $15,000

Roy De Forest, San Francisco, CA. 1973 Artist $7,500

Constance De Jong, New York, NY. 1985 New Genres $15,000

Constance A. De Jong, Albuquerque, NM. 1982 Crafts $5,000

William De Lappa, Berea, OH. 1979 Photo $10,000

Peter De Lory, Sun Valley, ID. 1979 Photo $10,000

Helen De Mott, New York, NY. 1978 Artist $7,500

Linda De Palma, Baltimore, MD. 1984 Sculpture $5,000

W. Brett De Palma, New York, NY. 1987 Painting $5,000

Charles De Villier, Baton Rouge, LA. 1979 Crafts $10,000

Joseph Deal, Riverside, CA. 1977 Photo $7,500; 1980 Photo $10,000

Mark Dean, Philadelphia, PA. 1983 Painting $5,000

Peter Dean, New York, NY. 1981 Painting $4,000; 1987 Painting $15,000

John DeAndrea, Denver, CO. 1974 Artist $7,500

David Dear, San Juan Pueblo, NM. 1980 Crafts $3,000

Gloria DeArcangelis, Oberlin, OH. 1984 Sculpture $5,000

Miles DeCoster, Chicago, IL. 1989 Works On Paper $5,000

Patricia Degener, St. Louis, MO. 1988 Crafts $5,000

Barbara DeGenevieve, St. Joseph, IL. 1988 Photo $15,000

John deHeras, Long Beach, CA. 1987 Printmaking/Drawing/Artists' Books $15,000

Lee Dejasu, Providence, RI. 1985 Printmaking/Drawing/Artists' Books $15,000

Eduardo Del Valle/Mirta Gomez, Sunrise, FL. 1977 Photo $7,500; 1990 Photo $20,000

Beauford Delaney, Paris, France. 1969 Artist $5,000

Janet Delaney, San Francisco, CA. 1982 Photo $5,000; 1986 Photo $5,000

Tony DeLap, Corona del Mar, CA. 1983 Painting $25,000

Sidney Delevante, New York, NY. 1974 Artist $7,500

William DeLottie, Eastford, CT. 1983 Printmaking/Drawing/Artists' Books $15,000

Ella Delyanis, Grafton, MA. 1985 Printmaking/Drawing/Artists' Books $5,000

Paul DeMarinis, New York, NY. 1978 Conceptual/Performance/New Genres $3,000; 1983 Conceptual/Performance/New Genres $15,000; 1991 New Genres $20,000

Paul DeMarinis, New York, NY. 1978 Conceptual/Performance/New Genres $3,000; 1983 Conceptual/Performance/New Genres $15,000; 1991 New Genres $20,000

Donald DeMauro, Freindsville, PA. 1982 Printmaking/Drawing/Artists' Books $5,000

Jillian Denby, Greenwich, CT. 1976 Artist $5,000; 1980 Artist $3,000; 1985 Painting $15,000

Royce Dendler, Bristol, VT. 1975 Video $4,000

Agnes Denes, New York, NY. 1974 Artist $3,000; 1975 Printmaking/Drawing/Artists' Books $3,000; 1981 Printmaking/Drawing/Artists' Books $12,500; 1989 Works On Paper $15,000

John Dennehy, Brookline, MA. 1979 Video $3,000

James Denney, Pittsburgh, PA. 1987 Painting $5,000

Donna Dennis, New York, NY. 1977 Artist $7,500; 1980 Artist $10,000; 1986 Sculpture $15,000; 1994 Sculpture $20,000

Steven Dennis, Nordman, ID. 1977 Crafts $5,000

Roger Denson, Buffalo, NY. 1982 Painting $5,000

Robert Dente, West Hartford, CT. 1989 Works On Paper $15,000; 1995 Works On Paper $20,000

Mark Derby, Eugene, OR. 1990 Crafts $5,000

Stephen Derrickson, Brooklyn, NY. 1987 Printmaking/Drawing/Artists' Books $5,000

Francois Deschamps, New Paltz, NY. 1982 Photo $5,000; 1986 Photo $15,000

Vincent Desiderio, New York, NY. 1987 Painting $5,000; 1991 Painting $20,000

Lewis DeSoto, San Francisco, CA. 1995 New Genres $20,000

Nick Despota, Chicago, IL. 1980 Video $3,000

Steven DeStaebler, Berkeley, CA. 1979 Crafts $3,000; 1981 Sculpture $12,500

J. W. Dettman, Palm Beach Gardens, FL. 1982 Photo $5,000

Richard Deutsch, Santa Cruz, CA. 1984 Crafts $5,000

Mary Ann DeVine, Tarzana, CA. 1984 Sculpture $5,000

Cara DeVito, New York, NY. 1977 Video $7,500; 1980 Video $3,000

Lucinda Devlin, New Paltz, NY. 1992 Photo $20,000

Richard E. DeVore, Fort Collins, CO. 1976 Crafts $5,000; 1980 Crafts $10,000; 1986 Crafts $15,000

Dimitri Devyatkin, New York, NY. 1981 Video $4,000

Rita DeWitt, Hattiesburg, MS. 1984 Photo $5,000

Kristine Dey, Los Angeles, CA. 1978 Crafts $7,500

Dominic Di Mare, Tiburon, CA. 1977 Crafts $5,000; 1981 Crafts $12,500

Mark Di Suvero, New York, NY. 1967 Artist $5,000

Jessica Diamond, Brooklyn, NY. 1989 New Genres $5,000

Martha Diamond, New York, NY. 1980 Artist $10,000; 1983 Painting $15,000

Paul Diamond, Brooklyn, NY. 1978 Photo $7,500
Stuart Diamond, New York, NY. 1980 Artist $10,000; 1987 Painting $15,000
David Diao, New York, NY. 1980 Artist $10,000; 1987 Painting $15,000; 1993 Painting $20,000
Jane Dickson, New York, NY. 1985 Printmaking/Drawing/Artists' Books $5,000
John Dickson, Alexandria, VA. 1979 Artist $10,000; 1984 Sculpture $15,000
Philip-Lorca DiCorcia, New York, NY. 1981 Photo $4,000; 1986 Photo $5,000; 1990 Photo $20,000
Porfirio DiDonna, Brooklyn, NY. 1975 Artist $4,000
Sari Dienes, Pomona, NY. 1980 Artist $3,000
Marlys Dietrick, San Antonio, TX. 1985 Painting $5,000
David DiFrancesco, San Francisco, CA. 1974 Artist $3,000
John Dilg, Chicago, IL. 1981 Painting $12,500
Guy Dill, Venice, CA. 1974 Artist $7,500; 1981 Sculpture $12,500
Laddie Dill, Venice, CA. 1975 Artist $4,000; 1982 Painting $25,000
Lesley Dill, New York, NY. 1990 Sculpture $5,000
Rick Dillingham, Santa Fe, NM. 1977 Crafts $5,000; 1982 Crafts $25,000
Dominick Dimeo, New York, NY. 1982 Sculpture $5,000
Lisa Dinhofer, New York, NY. 1982 Painting $5,000
David DiSalvo, Long Island City, NY. 1983 Painting $5,000
John Divola, Venice, CA. 1990 Photo $20,000
Ervin Dixon, Beatrice, NE. 1978 Crafts $7,500
Willard Dixon, Jon Rafael, CA. 1989 Painting $15,000
Gary Dodson, New York, NY. 1987 Printmaking/Drawing/Artists' Books $5,000
Bill Doherty, Jersey City, NJ. 1987 Painting $5,000
Eileen Doktorski, East Brunswick, NJ. 1986 Sculpture $5,000
Garrick Dolberg, Brooklyn, NY. 1979 Artist $3,000; 1981 Sculpture $12,500
Stanley Dolega, Laramie, WY. 1975 Artist $4,000; 1980 Artist $3,000
Eddie Dominguez, Tucumcari, NM. 1986 Crafts $5,000; 1988 Crafts $5,000
Gerald Donato, Richmond, VA. 1981 Painting $12,500; 1987 Printmaking/Drawing/Artists' Books $15,000
Paul Donhawser, Oshkosh, WI. 1984 Crafts $15,000
Robert Donley, Oak Park, IL. 1980 Artist $10,000
Geralyn Donohue, New York, NY. 1991 Painting $20,000
Terence Donovan, Garrison, NJ. 1993 Painting $20,000
James Doolin, Los Angeles, CA. 1980 Artist $10,000; 1985 Painting $15,000; 1991 Painting $20,000
Susanne Doremus, DeKalb, IL. 1983 Painting $15,000
Jonas dos Santos, Philadelphia, PA. 1981 Conceptual/Performance/New Genres $4,000; 1991 New Genres $20,000
Edward Dougherty, Manhattan Beach, CA. 1980 Artist $3,000
Patrick Dougherty, Chapel Hill, NC. 1990 Sculpture $5,000
Mary Douglas, Long Island City, NY. 1994 Crafts $20,000
Anita Douthat, Boston, MA. 1992 Photo $20,000; 1991 Photo $5,000
Toni Dove, New York, NY. 1995 New Genres $20,000
Jim Dow, Belmont, MA. 1973 Photo $ 3300; 1980 Photo $10,000; 1990 Photo $20,000
John Dowell, Philadelphia, PA. 1974 Artist $7,500; 1985 Printmaking/Drawing/Artists' Books $15,000
Rackstraw Downes, New York, NY. 1980 Artist $10,000
Juan Downey, New York, NY. 1974 Artist $3,000; 1976 Video $5,000; 1980 Video $10,000; 1985 New Genres $15,000
Holly Downing, Santa Cruz, CA. 1975 Printmaking/Drawing/Artists' Books $3,000
Thomas Downing, Washington, DC. 1975 Artist $4,000
Tom Doyle, New York, NY. 1990 Sculpture $20,000
James Drake, El Paso, TX. 1989 Works On Paper $15,000
Peter Drake, New York, NY. 1985 Printmaking/Drawing/Artists' Books $5,000
Katherine Drasher, New York, NY. 1991 Painting $20,000
Gregory Drasler, New York, NY. 1993 Painting $20,000
Paul Dresang, Edwardsville, IL. 1988 Crafts $15,000
Rosalyn Drexler, New York, NY. 1989 Painting $5,000
Clarice Dreyer, Bozeman, MT. 1982 Sculpture $5,000; 1984 Sculpture $5,000; 1990 Sculpture $5,000
Russell Drisch, Buffalo, NY. 1976 Photo $7,500
Ellen Driscoll, Cambridge, MA. 1984 Sculpture $5,000; 1986 Sculpture $15,000
Carol Drobek, San Francisco, CA. 1977 Photo $7,500
Grant Drumheller, Brookline, MA. 1983 Painting $3,000
Sarah Drury, Brooklyn, NY. 1989 New Genres $5,000
Hildegarde Duane, Los Angeles, CA. 1980 Video $3,000
Eleanor Dube, New York, NY. 1978 Conceptual/Performance/New Genres $7,500
Anda Dubinskis, Philadelphia, PA. 1989 Painting $5,000; 1991 Painting $20,000
Douglas DuBois, Las Cruces, NM. 1990 Photo $5,000
Emily DuBois, Benicia, CA. 1984 Crafts $5,000
Donald Dubroff, Chicago, IL. 1982 Photo $5,000
Ruth Duckworth, Chicago, IL. 1980 Crafts $10,000
Joellyn Duesberry, New York, NY. 1985 Painting $15,000
Edward Dugmore, New York, NY. 1976 Artist $10,000; 1985 Painting $15,000
Carroll Dunham, Old Lyme, CT. 1976 Artist $2,000
Breon Dunigan, New York, NY. 1990 Sculpture $5,000
Loretta Dunkelman, New York, NY. 1975 Artist $4,000; 1982 Painting $5,000; 1993 Painting $20,000
David Dunlap, Iowa City, IA. 1989 New Genres $15,000
Catherine Dunn, Montevallo, AL. 1980 Artist $3,000
Fontaine Dunn, New York, NY. 1987 Printmaking/Drawing/Artists' Books $15,000
Brad Dunning, Los Angeles, CA. 1987 Painting $5,000
Robert Duran, New York, NY. 1979 Artist $10,000
Mark Durant, San Francisco, CA. 1988 Photo $5,000
Walter Dusenbery, New York, NY. 1980 Artist $10,000
William Dutterer, New York, NY. 1980 Artist $3,000
Jeanne Duval, Jaffrey, NH. 1983 Painting $5,000
Michael Dvortcsak, Santa Barbara, CA. 1981 Painting $12,500
Charles Dwyer, Newport, RI. 1981 Painting $12,500
Nancy Dwyer, New York, NY. 1982 Painting $5,000
Friedel Dzubas, New York, NY. 1969 Artist $5,000

E

Jack Earl, Lakeview, OH. 1974 Crafts $3,000; 1988 Crafts $25,000
East Los Streetscapers, Los Angeles, CA. 1980 Artist $3,000; 1981 Painting $12,500
Lois Ebel, Northampton, MA. 1975 Artist $2,000
Robert Ebendorf, Highland, NY. 1973 Crafts $3,000
Edward Eberle, Pittsburgh, PA. 1986 Crafts $15,000
Robert Ecker, Boulder, CO. 1981 Printmaking/Drawing/Artists' Books $12,500
Barbara Eckhardt, New Bedford, MA. 1984 Crafts $5,000
Michael Economos, Baltimore, MD. 1989 Painting $15,000
Don Eddy, New York, NY. 1977 Artist $7,500
Mary Beth Edelson, Washington, DC. 1981 Printmaking/Drawing/Artists' Books $12,500
Susan Eder, Williamstown, MA. 1979 Artist $3,000
Daniel Edge, New York, NY. 1975 Artist $2,000
Douglas Edge, Santa Barbara, CA. 1982 Sculpture $25,000
Perky Edgerton, Brooklyn, NY. 1981 Painting $4,000
Thomas Edinger, Nebraska City, NE. 1980 Printmaking/Drawing/Artists' Books $10,000
Allan Edmunds, Philadelphia, PA. 1991 Works On Paper $20,000
Katherine Edson, New York, NY. 1976 Crafts $5,000
Garth Edwards, Portland, OR. 1981 Crafts $12,500
James Edwards, Columbia , SC. 1974 Artist $3,000
Melvin Edwards, Plainfield, NJ. 1971 Artist $7,500; 1984 Sculpture $15,000; 1994 Sculpture $20,000
Stephen Edwards, Green Mountain, NC. 1982 Crafts $5,000; 1984 Crafts $5,000
William Eggleston, Memphis, TN. 1976 Photo $7,500
John Egner, New York, NY. 1980 Artist $10,000
Alma Eikerman, Bloomington, IN. 1975 Crafts $5,000
Stefan Eins, New York, NY. 1980 Conceptual/Performance/New Genres $3,000; 1987 Painting $15,000
Susan Eisler, Saint Louis, MO. 1979 Artist $10,000
Constance Elder, Chatsworth, CA. 1974 Artist $7,500
Lyman Elder, San Francisco, CA. 1976 Crafts $5,000
Dale Eldred, Kansas City, MO. 1967 Artist $5,000
Shirley Elgot, Westborough, MA. 1984 Crafts $5,000
Lillian Elliott, Berkeley, CA. 1975 Crafts $5,000
Lillian Elliott/Patricia Hickman, Berkeley, CA. 1986 Crafts $15,000
Andra Ellis, Charlotte, NC. 1990 Crafts $5,000
Stephen Ellis, New York, NY. 1991 Painting $20,000
John David Ellsworth, Quakertown, PA. 1984 Crafts $15,000
James Elniski, Provincetown, MA. 1981 Sculpture $4,000
Raymon Elozua, New York, NY. 1980 Artist $3,000; 1981 Sculpture $4,000; 1987 Painting $15,000
Albinas Elskus, New York, NY. 1980 Crafts $10,000
Stephen Elston, Brookline, MA. 1979 Photo $3,000
Timothy Ely, Snohomish, WA. 1981 Printmaking/Drawing/Artists' Books $12,500

Martin Emanuel, Atlanta, GA. 1981 Sculpture $4,000
Ed Emshwiller, Wantagh, NY. 1979 Video $10,000
Bill Enck, New York, NY. 1980 Artist $3,000
Heidi Endemann, Gualala, CA. 1989 Painting $5,000
Steve Engle, Seattle, WA. 1990 Sculpture $5,000
Chris Enos, Boston, MA. 1981 Photo $12,500
Susan Ensley, New York, NY. 1977 Conceptual/Performance/New Genres $3,000
Sandra Enterline, Cambridge, MA. 1988 Crafts $5,000; 1992 Crafts $20,000
Mitchell Epstein, Holyoke, MA. 1978 Photo $7,500
Albert Erdosy, Allentown, PA. 1989 Works On Paper $5,000
Eric Erickson, New York, NY. 1981 Painting $12,500
Gary Erickson, St. Paul, MN. 1986 Crafts $5,000
Gregory Erickson, Solvang, CA. 1974 Artist $1,000
Mark Erickson, Oakland, CA. 1988 Crafts $5,000
Melvin Ericson and Kate Ziegler, New York, NY. 1987 New Genres $5,000; 1993 New Genres $20,000
Martha Erlebacher, Elkins Park, PA. 1982 Painting $25,000
Geraldine Erman, Brooklyn, NY. 1986 Sculpture $5,000
Kathey Ervin, St. Joseph, IL. 1986 Crafts $5,000
Fred Escher, Janesville, WI. 1981 Painting $12,500
Clyde Espenschied, Spotswood, NJ. 1985 Painting $15,000
Barbara Ess, New York, NY. 1991 Photo $5,000; 1994 Photo $20,000
Dan Estabrook, Champaign, IL. 1991 Photo $5,000; 1994 Photo $20,000
Reed Estabrook, Cedar Falls, IA. 1976 Photo $7,500
Richard Estes, New York , NY. 1971 Artist $7,500
Susan Ettenheim, New York, NY. 1987 Painting $5,000
Dennis Evans, Seattle, WA. 1980 Artist $3,000
John Evans, New York, NY. 1985 Printmaking/Drawing/Artists' Books $15,000
Fred Eversely, Venice, CA. 1973 Artist $7,500
Wendy Ewald, Rhinebeck, NY. 1988 Photo $15,000
Gretchen Ewert, Arroyo Hondo, NM. 1988 Crafts $5,000
Lauren Ewing, New York, NY. 1982 Sculpture $25,000
Mary Ewing, New York, NY. 1980 Artist $3,000

F

Martin Facey, Albuquerque, NM. 1991 Painting $20,000
Barbara Factor, Galesburg, IL. 1973 Crafts $3,000
Steve Fagin, La Jolla, CA. 1989 New Genres $5,000
Charles Fahlen, Philadelphia, PA. 1980 Artist $3,000; 1988 Sculpture $15,000
Deb Fanelli, Dayton, OH. 1984 Sculpture $5,000; 1988 Sculpture $5,000
Thomas Farbanish, Strafford, VT. 1988 Crafts $5,000; 1994 Crafts $20,000
Amanda Farber, San Diego, CA. 1989 Painting $5,000
Dennis Farber, Albuquerque, NM. 1994 Photo $20,000
Manny Farber, New York, NY. 1969 Artist $5,000
William Fares, New York, NY. 1979 Artist $10,000
Ralston Farina, New York, NY. 1977 Conceptual/Performance/New Genres $7,500
William Farley, Oakland, CA. 1979 Conceptual/Performance/New Genres $3,000; 1983 Conceptual/Performance/New Genres $15,000
Bill Farrell, Chicago, IL. 1981 Crafts $12,500
Heide Fasnacht, New York, NY. 1990 Sculpture $5,000; 1994 Sculpture $20,000
Francis Faulkner, Winston-Salem, NC. 1974 Artist $7,500
Louis Faurer, New York, NY. 1978 Photo $7,500
Victoria Faust, San Francisco, CA. 1989 Works On Paper $15,000
Thomas Fawkes, Portland, OR. 1977 Artist $7,500
Christine Federighi, Miami, FL. 1988 Crafts $5,000
Thomas Feelings, New York, NY. 1982 Printmaking/Drawing/Artists' Books $5,000
Sandra Feeney, Providence, RI. 1986 Photo $5,000
Harriet Feigenbaum, New York, NY. 1984 Sculpture $15,000
Marsha Feigin, New York, NY. 1975 Printmaking/Drawing/Artists' Books $3,000
Elen Feinberg, St. Louis, MO. 1987 Painting $5,000
Jean Feinberg, New York, NY. 1979 Artist $3,000; 1983 Painting $5,000; 1989 Painting $5,000
Ken Feingold, Minneapolis, MN. 1979 Conceptual/Performance/New Genres $3,000; 1981 Video $4,000
Robert Feintuch, New Haven, CT. 1976 Artist $2,000
Brian Fekete, Detroit, MI. 1987 Painting $5,000
John Fekner, Jackson Heights, NY. 1978 Printmaking/Drawing/Artists' Books $3,000
Bella Feldman, Berkeley, CA. 1986 Crafts $15,000
Joel Feldman, Murphysboro, IL. 1993 Works On Paper $20,000; 1992 Works On Paper $5,000
Roger Feldman, Fullerton, CA. 1986 Sculpture $5,000
Peter Feldstein, Oxford, IA. 1988 Photo $15,000
David Felker, Anchorage, AK. 1988 Sculpture $5,000; 1990 Sculpture $5,000
Alice Fellows, Santa Monica, CA. 1991 Painting $20,000; 1990 Painting $5,000
Alan Feltus, Hughesville, MD. 1981 Painting $12,500
Lukas Felzmann, San Francisco, CA. 1994 Photo $20,000; 1993 Photo $5,000
Laurie Fendrich, Durham, NC. 1983 Painting $5,000
Concetta Fenicchia, Brooklyn, NY. 1984 Crafts $5,000
Maureen Fennelli, New York, NY. 1982 Photo $5,000
Fred Fenster, Sun Prarie, WI. 1977 Crafts $5,000
Samuel Fentress, Nashville, TN. 1979 Photo $3,000
Kenneth Ferguson, Shawnee Mission, KS. 1973 Crafts $3,000; 1980 Crafts $10,000
Teresita Fernandez, Miami, FL. 1994 Sculpture $20,000
Jackie Ferrara, New York, NY. 1975 Artist $8,000
Rafael Ferrer, Philadelphia, PA. 1973 Artist $7,500; 1983 Painting $15,000; 1989 Painting $15,000
Ann Fessler, Baltimore, MD. 1989 Works On Paper $5,000
Robert Fichter, Tallahassee, FL. 1980 Photo $10,000; 1984 Photo $15,000
John Fick, Oakland, CA. 1980 Artist $3,000
William Fick, High Point, NC. 1993 Works On Paper $20,000
Joyce Fillip, Philadelphia, PA. 1985 Printmaking/Drawing/Artists' Books $5,000
Richard Finch, Bloomington, IL. 1983 Printmaking/Drawing/Artists' Books $5,000
Jane Fine, Brooklyn, NY. 1989 Painting $5,000
Jud Fine, Los Angeles, CA. 1982 Sculpture $25,000
Perle Fine, The Springs, NY. 1979 Artist $10,000
Aaron Fink, East Boston, MA. 1982 Painting $5,000; 1987 Painting $5,000
Larry Fink, Martins Creek, PA. 1979 Photo $10,000; 1986 Photo $15,000
Alan Finkel, New York, NY. 1979 Artist $3,000
Louis Finkelstein, Stillwater, NJ. 1983 Painting $25,000
Jeanne Finley, San Francisco, CA. 1985 New Genres $5,000; 1987 New Genres $5,000; 1991 New Genres $20,000
Karen Finley, Nyack, NY. 1983 Conceptual/Performance/New Genres $5,000; 1987 New Genres $5,000
David Finn, Winston-Salem, NC. 1990 Sculpture $5,000
Howard Finster, Summerville, GA. 1981 Sculpture $4,000
Arline Fisch, San Diego, CA. 1974 Crafts $3,000
Gail Fischer, Austin, TX. 1988 Crafts $5,000
R. M. Fischer, New York, NY. 1981 Sculpture $12,500; 1986 Sculpture $15,000; 1994 Sculpture $20,000
Alida Fish, Wilmington, DE. 1994 Photo $20,000
Julia Fish, Chicago, IL. 1993 Painting $20,000; 1986 Painting $5,000
Mary Fish, Sundance, UT. 1981 Printmaking/Drawing/Artists' Books $12,500; 1994 Sculpture $20,000
Andrea Fisher, Chatham, NY. 1989 New Genres $5,000
Curtis Fisher, Chicago, IL. 1976 Conceptual/Performance/New Genres $2,000
Elaine Fisher, Charlottesville, VA. 1973 Photo $2,500
Hal Fisher, San Francisco, CA. 1980 Photo $3,000
Joel Fisher, Brooklyn, NY. 1984 Sculpture $15,000
Vernon Fisher, Sherman, TX. 1974 Artist $7,500; 1980 Artist $3,000; 1982 Painting $25,000
Beverly Fishman, Stratford, CT. 1989 Works On Paper $5,000
Louise Fishman, Worcester, NY. 1975 Artist $4,000; 1983 Painting $15,000; 1993 Painting $20,000
Judith Fiskin, Valencia, CA. 1990 Photo $20,000
Claudia Fitch, New York, NY. 1984 Sculpture $5,000
Stephen Fitch, Berkeley, CA. 1973 Photo $2,000; 1975 Photo $5,000
Cate Fitt, Richmond, VA. 1979 Crafts $10,000
Kit Fitzgerald/John Sanborn, New York, NY. 1977 Video $7,500; 1979 Video $10,000; 1985 New Genres $5,000
Colen Fitzgibbon, New York, NY. 1977 Video $7,500
Michael Flanagan, New York, NY. 1987 Painting $5,000; 1991 Painting $20,000
Dan Flavin, Cold Springs, NY. 1967 Artist $5,000
Richard Fleischner, Providence, RI. 1975 Artist $8,000; 1980 Artist $10,000; 1990 Sculpture $20,000
Stephen Fleming, Roswell, NM. 1987 Painting $15,000
Robert Flick, Inglewood, CA. 1982 Photo $5,000; 1984 Photo $15,000
Kent Floeter, New York, NY. 1980 Artist $3,000; 1983

Printmaking/Drawing/Artists' Books $15,000
Edward Flood, New York, NY. 1978 Artist $7,500
Pat Flynn, Accokeek, MD. 1984 Crafts $5,000; 1988 Crafts $15,000; 1994 Crafts $20,000
Jean Follett, St. Paul, MN. 1967 Artist $5,000
Fred Folsom, Wheaton, MD. 1985 Painting $15,000
Ron Fondaw, Miami, FL. 1988 Crafts $15,000
Betty Fong, Los Angeles, CA. 1986 Sculpture $5,000
Ignacio Font, Cora Gables, FL. 1989 Painting $5,000
Bill Fontana, New Orleans, LA. 1990 Sculpture $20,000
Luke Fontana, New Orleans, LA. 1973 Photo $5,000
Fol Fontes, Cranston, IL. 1981 Sculpture $4,000
Jean Foos, New York, NY. 1989 Works On Paper $5,000
Peter Forakis, Lexington, KY. 1981 Sculpture $12,500
Robert Forbes, Philadelphia, PA. 1982 Crafts $5,000
James Ford, New York, NY. 1980 Artist $3,000
John Ford, New York, NY. 1982 Painting $5,000
Margaret Ford, Seattle, WA. 1975 Crafts $5,000
Walton Ford, New York, NY. 1991 Painting $20,000
Edward Forde, Los Angeles, CA. 1973 Crafts $3,000
Robert Forman, Providence, RI. 1979 Crafts $10,000; 1978 Artist $7,500
Nathan Fors, Kansas City, MO. 1989 Painting $5,000
Chuck Forsman, Boulder, CO. 1979 Artist $3,000; 1985 Painting $15,000; 1995 Painting $20,000
Paul Forte, Elkhart, IN. 1978 Conceptual/Performance/New Genres $3,000
Carl Fosselius, San Francisco, CA. 1974 Artist $3,000
Llyn Foulkes, Topanga, CA. 1985 Painting $15,000
Stephen Foust, Detroit, MI. 1976 Artist $5,000
Judith Fox, New York, NY. 1988 Sculpture $5,000; 1994 Sculpture $20,000
Sheila Fox, East Setauket, NY. 1978 Crafts $7,500
Terry Fox, San Francisco, CA. 1974 Artist $7,500; 1976 Video $5,000; 1984 Sculpture $15,000; 1989 New Genres $15,000
Stephen Frailey, New York, NY. 1988 Photo $5,000
John Frame, Los Angeles, CA. 1982 Sculpture $5,000; 1986 Sculpture $5,000
Edgar Franceschi, New York, NY. 1980 Artist $3,000; 1982 Sculpture $5,000
Luciano Franchi De Alfaro, Chicago, IL. 1980 Photo $3,000
Linda Francis, New York, NY. 1980 Artist $10,000
Donald Francisco, Kalamazoo, MI. 1975 Crafts $5,000
Angel Franco, New York, NY. 1986 Photo $15,000
Mary Frank, New York, NY. 1969 Artist $5,000
Stephanie Frank, New York, NY. 1983 Painting $5,000
Sara Frankel, Honolulu, HI. 1991 Painting $20,000
Andrea Fraser, New York, NY. 1991 New Genres $20,000
Robinson Fredenthal, Berwyn, PA. 1979 Artist $10,000
Arthur Freed, New York, NY. 1973 Photo $2,500
Hermine Freed, New York, NY. 1974 Artist $3,000
Leonard Freed, New York, NY. 1981 Photo $12,500
Jill Freedman, New York, NY. 1973 Photo $5,000
Matthew Freedman, Brooklyn, NY. 1990 Sculpture $5,000
David Freelander, New York, NY. 1976 Artist $2,000
Daniel Freeman, New York, NY. 1978 Artist $7,500; 1989 Painting $15,000
Jeff Freeman, Vermillion, SD. 1990 Painting $5,000; 1991 Painting $20,000
John Freeman, San Diego, CA. 1992 Photo $20,000
Roland Freeman, Washington, DC. 1982 Photo $25,000; 1990 Photo $20,000
Vida Freeman, Northridge, CA. 1981 Photo $12,500
Jane Freilicher, New York, NY. 1976 Artist $5,000
Christopher French, Washington, DC. 1993 Works On Paper $20,000
David Freund, Brooklyn, NY. 1978 Photo $7,500
Mary Frey, Springfield, MA. 1981 Photo $12,500; 1992 Photo $20,000
Viola Frey, Oakland, CA. 1978 Crafts $7,500; 1986 Sculpture $15,000
Jem Freyaldenhoven, Atlanta, GA. 1977 Crafts $5,000
Tage Frid, North Kingstown, RI. 1990 Crafts $20,000
Howard Fried, San Francisco, CA. 1975 Artist $4,000; 1980 Video $10,000; 1983 Video $15,000
Nancy Fried, New York, NY. 1994 Sculpture $20,000
Robert Fried, Fairfax, CA. 1974 Printmaking/Drawing/Artists' Books $3,000
Richard Friedberg, New York, NY. 1974 Artist $3,000
Anthony Friedkin, Los Angeles, CA. 1977 Photo $7,500
Lee Friedlander, New City, NY. 1973 Photo $5,000; 1978 Photo $7,500; 1984 Photo $25,000
Alan Friedman, Terre Haute, IN. 1976 Crafts $5,000
Barton Friedman, Woodstock, NY. 1980 Video $10,000
Stan Friedman, New York, NY. 1985 Painting $15,000
Susan Friedman, Sunderland, MA. 1980 Artist $3,000
Nancy Marlene Friese, Cranston, RI. 1987 Painting $5,000; 1991 Painting $20,000
Ismael Frigerio, New York, NY. 1989 Painting $5,000
Michael Frimkess, Venice, CA. 1977 Crafts $5,000
Brian Frink, Mankato, MN. 1993 Painting $20,000
Dieter Froese, New York, NY. 1979 Video $3,000; 1981 Video $12,500; 1987 New Genres $15,000
George Fry, Atherton, CA. 1971 Photo $2,000
Sekio Fuapopo, San Francisco, CA. 1981 Painting $4,000
Douglas Fuchs, New York, NY. 1981 Crafts $12,500
John Fudge, Denver, CO. 1985 Painting $15,000
Larry Fuente, Mendocino, CA. 1979 Artist $10,000; 1988 Sculpture $15,000; 1994 Sculpture $20,000
Terry Fugate-Wilcox, New York, NY. 1976 Artist $2,000
Kenji Fujita, Brooklyn, NY. 1984 Sculpture $5,000; 1988 Sculpture $5,000; 1991 Works On Paper $20,000
Ellen Fullman, Austin, TX. 1989 New Genres $5,000
Jack Fulton, San Rafael, CA. 1981 Photo $12,500; 1990 Photo $20,000
Mark Fuoco, Sacramento, CA. 1987 New Genres $5,000
David Furman, Claremont, CA. 1975 Crafts $5,000
James Furr, Opelika, AL. 1981 Printmaking/Drawing/Artists' Books $12,500

G

Oliver Gagliani, San Francisco, CA. 1976 Photo $7,500
Charles Gaines, Fresno, CA. 1978 Printmaking/Drawing/Artists' Books $7,500
Pio Galbis, Brooklyn, NY. 1993 Painting $20,000
Philip Galgiani, New York, NY. 1978 Photo $7,500; 1981 Photo $12,500; 1986 Photo $15,000
Sally Gall, Houston, TX. 1982 Photo $5,000
Cynthia Gallagher, New York, NY. 1983 Painting $5,000; 1989 Works On Paper $5,000
Ron Gallas, University Park, PA. 1977 Crafts $5,000
Steve Galloway, Santa Monica, CA. 1987 Printmaking/Drawing/Artists' Books $15,000
Harry Gamboa, Los Angeles, CA. 1980 Conceptual/Performance/New Genres $10,000; 1987 New Genres $15,000
Lanie Gannon, Nashville, TN. 1988 Crafts $5,000
Robert Ganong, Boston, MA. 1983 Painting $5,000
James Ganzer, Venice, CA. 1976 Artist $5,000
Marjorie Gapp, Philadelphia, PA. 1979 Printmaking/Drawing/Artists' Books $3,000
Charles Garabedian, Santa Monica, CA. 1977 Artist $7,500
Domingo Garcia, New York, NY. 1981 Printmaking/Drawing/Artists' Books $12,500
Rupert Garcia, Oakland, CA. 1989 Painting $5,000
Nereyda Garcia-Ferraz, Chicago, IL. 1985 Painting $5,000; 1989 Painting $5,000
Lyn Gardiner, Cambridge, MA. 1977 Photo $7,500
Michael Gardiner, Seattle, WA. 1989 Painting $5,000
Ann Gardner, Seattle, WA. 1986 Crafts $5,000; 1994 Crafts $20,000
Christopher Gardner, Falls Church, VA. 1979 Artist $3,000
Jedd Garet, New York, NY. 1985 Painting $5,000; 1989 Painting $15,000
Peter Garfield, Brooklyn, NY. 1993 Painting $20,000
Dana Garrett, New York, NY. 1983 Painting $5,000
John Garrett, El Prado, NM. 1982 Crafts $5,000; 1994 Crafts $20,000
Elizabeth Garrison, Ithaca, NY. 1981 Crafts $4,000; 1988 Crafts $5,000
Cliff Garten, St. Paul, MN. 1986 Crafts $5,000
Ellen Garvens, Brooklyn, NY. 1986 Photo $5,000
Carmen Garza, San Francisco, CA. 1981 Printmaking/Drawing/Artists' Books $4,000; 1987 Painting $15,000
Gail Gash, Santa Fe, NM. 1983 Printmaking/Drawing/Artists' Books $5,000
Jeffrey Gates, Baltimore, MD. 1984 Photo $5,000; 1990 Photo $5,000
Grover Gatewood, Sag Harbor, NY. 1984 Photo $5,000
Cheri Gaulke, Los Angeles, CA. 1983 Conceptual/Performance/New Genres $15,000
William Gedney, Brooklyn, NY. 1975 Photo $5,000
Harry Geffert, Crowley, TX. 1990 Sculpture $20,000
Judith Geichman, Chicago, IL. 1983 Painting $5,000; 1989 Painting $5,000
William Geis, San Francisco, CA. 1967 Artist $5,000; 1980 Artist $10,000
Michael Gellatly, West Cornwall, CT. 1987 Painting $5,000
Matthew Geller, New York, NY. 1987 New Genres $5,000; 1989 New Genres $15,000

Vance Gellert, San Francisco, CA. 1988 Photo $5,000
Sandy Gellis, New York, NY. 1979 Artist $3,000; 1981 Sculpture $4,000; 1987 Printmaking/Drawing/Artists' Books $15,000
Jonathan Genkin, Brooklyn, NY. 1987 Painting $5,000
Raymond E. George, Bloomington, IL. 1985 Printmaking/Drawing/Artists' Books $15,000
Wallace George, Santa Rosa, CA. 1980 Photo $3,000
Tyrone Georgiou, Buffalo, NY. 1979 Photo $3,000
Ingeborg Gerdes, San Francisco, CA. 1975 Photo $5,000; 1977 Photo $7,500
George Geyer, Huntington Beach, CA. 1980 Artist $3,000
Raymond Ghirardo/Megan Roberts, Ithaca, NY. 1983 Video $5,000
Anne Ghory-Goodman, Cincinnati, OH. 1982 Photo $5,000
Gerald Giamportone, Los Angeles, CA. 1989 Painting $5,000
Cristos Gianakos, New York, NY. 1980 Artist $10,000
Steve Gianakos , New York, NY. 1979 Artist $10,000
Jennifer Gibbar, Gardengrove, CA. 1976 Printmaking/Drawing/Artists' Books $3,000
Edward Gibson, Billings, MT. 1988 Sculpture $5,000
Ralph Gibson, New York, NY. 1973 Photo $4,000; 1976 Photo $7,500; 1986 Photo $15,000
Jill Giegerich, Culver City, CA. 1984 Sculpture $5,000
Davidson Gigliotti, Lanesville, NY. 1974 Artist $3,000; 1976 Video $2,000
Jeremy Gilbert-Rolfe, Santa Monica, CA. 1980 Artist $3,000; 1989 Painting $15,000
Bruce Gilden, New York, NY. 1980 Photo $3,000; 1984 Photo $15,000; 1992 Photo $20,000
Andrea Gill, Kent, OH. 1978 Crafts $7,500; 1984 Crafts $15,000
John Gill, Alfred, NY. 1979 Crafts $10,000; 1992 Crafts $20,000
John Gillen, Pittsburgh, PA. 1980 Artist $3,000; 1984 Sculpture $5,000; 1986 Sculpture $15,000
Jo Ann Gillerman, Oakland, CA. 1980 Video $3,000
Frances Gillespie, Northampton, MA. 1983 Painting $15,000
Frank Gillette, New York, NY. 1976 Video $10,000; 1980 Video $10,000
Sam Gilliam, Washington, DC. 1967 Artist $5,000; 1989 Painting $15,000
Scott Gilliam, Atlanta, GA. 1980 Artist $3,000
Jan Gilligan, Madison, WI. 1975 Video $2,000
Denis Gillingwater, Scottsdale, AZ. 1982 Sculpture $5,000
Stanley Gilula, Northampton, MA. 1975 Artist $2,000
Maxwell Gimblett, New York, NY. 1989 Painting $15,000
Charles Ginnever, Putney, VT. 1974 Artist $7,500
Joe Giordano, New York, NY. 1985 Painting $15,000
Lawrence Gipe, New York, NY. 1989 Painting $5,000; 1995 Works On Paper $20,000
Terry Gips, Takoma Park, MD. 1986 Photo $5,000
Tina Girouard, New York, NY. 1976 Conceptual/Performance/New Genres $5,000; 1982 Conceptual/Performance/New Genres $25,000
Michael Gitlin, New York, NY. 1984 Sculpture $5,000
Gilles Giuntini, Ambler, PA. 1979 Artist $3,000
Deanna Glad, Santa Monica, CA. 1976 Crafts $5,000
Michael Glancy, Rehoboth, MA. 1986 Crafts $5,000
Lukman Glasgow, Los Angeles, CA. 1975 Crafts $5,000
Joel Glassman, San Francisco, CA. 1975 Video $4,000; 1977 Video $7,500
Linnea Glatt, Dallas, TX. 1986 Sculpture $15,000
Conrad Gleber, New York, NY. 1979 Photo $3,000
William Gledhill, Santa Barbara, CA. 1975 Photo $5,000
John Glick, Farmington Hills, MI. 1974 Crafts $3,000; 1977 Crafts $5,000; 1988 Crafts $15,000
Michael Glier, New York, NY. 1981 Printmaking/Drawing/Artists' Books $4,000
Alan Glovsky, New York, NY. 1982 Printmaking/Drawing/Artists' Books $5,000; 1984 Sculpture $5,000
Martha Glowacki, Madison, WI. 1982 Crafts $5,000
Aharon Gluska, New York, NY. 1989 Painting $5,000
Dewitt Godfrey, Houston, TX. 1985 Printmaking/Drawing/Artists' Books $5,000
Wilhelmina Godfrey, Buffalo, NY. 1974 Crafts $3,000
Frank Gohlke, Minneapolis, MN. 1978 Photo $7,500; 1986 Photo $15,000
Peter Goin, Reno, NV. 1982 Photo $5,000; 1990 Photo $20,000
Jo Going, La Jolla, CA. 1989 Painting $5,000
Joel Gold, New York, NY. 1975 Video $4,000; 1980 Video $3,000
Sharon Gold, New York, NY. 1981 Painting $12,500
Glenn Goldberg, New York, NY. 1989 Painting $5,000
Jim Goldberg, San Francisco, CA. 1980 Photo $3,000; 1988 Photo $5,000; 1990 Photo $20,000
Michael Goldberg, New York, NY. 1985 Painting $15,000; 1993 Painting $20,000
Pamela Goldblum, Los Angeles, CA. 1989 Works On Paper $5,000
Judith Golden, Inglewood, CA. 1979 Photo $10,000
Stuart Golder, Stout, OH. 1980 Crafts $10,000
David Goldes, Minneapolis, MN. 1984 Photo $15,000
Leon Goldin, New York, NY. 1980 Artist $10,000
Nan Goldin, New York, NY. 1990 Photo $5,000
Harvey Goldman, N. Dartmouth, MA. 1980 Crafts $3,000
Lester Goldman, Kansas City, MO. 1989 Painting $15,000; 1986 Painting $5,000
Robert Goldman, New York, NY. 1975 Video $4,000; 1985 Painting $5,000
Cheryl Goldsleger, Athens, GA. 1982 Printmaking/Drawing/Artists' Books $25,000; 1991 Works On Paper $20,000
Layne Goldsmith, Seattle, WA. 1984 Crafts $5,000
Lloyd Goldsmith, New York, NY. 1980 Printmaking/Drawing/Artists' Books $3,000
Jack Goldstein, Brooklyn, NY. 1979 Conceptual/Performance/New Genres $3,000; 1982 Painting $25,000
Juan Gomez, New York, NY. 1974 Printmaking/Drawing/Artists' Books $3,000
Guillermo Gomez-Pena, Imperial Beach, CA. 1987 Printmaking/Drawing/Artists' Books $5,000
Jeff Gompertz, New York, NY. 1983 Painting $5,000; 1985 Painting $5,000
Arthur Gonzalez, Oakland, CA. 1982 Sculpture $5,000; 1984 Crafts $5,000; 1986 Crafts $5,000; 1990 Crafts $5,000
Juan Gonzalez, New York, NY. 1979 Printmaking/Drawing/Artists' Books $10,000; 1985 Printmaking/Drawing/Artists' Books $15,000; 1991 Works On Paper $20,000
Maria Gonzalez, New Orleans, LA. 1982 Photo $5,000; 1988 Photo $5,000
Patricia Gonzalez, Houston, TX. 1987 Painting $5,000
Felix Gonzalez-Torres, New York, NY. 1989 New Genres $5,000; 1993 New Genres $20,000
Joe Goode, Los Angeles, CA. 1968 Artist $5,000; 1976 Artist $5,000
Kathy Goodell, San Francisco, CA. 1979 Artist $3,000; 1982 Sculpture $25,000
Larry Goodell, Placitas, NM. 1983 Conceptual/Performance/New Genres $5,000
Brenda Goodman, New York, NY. 1991 Painting $20,000
Mark Goodman, Millerton, NY. 1973 Photo $5,000
Sidney Goodman, Elkins Park, PA. 1974 Artist $7,500
Robert Goodnough, Thornwood, NY. 1967 Artist $5,000
Lawrence Goodridge, Florence, KY. 1976 Artist $2,000
Guy Goodwin, New York, NY. 1974 Artist $3,000; 1980 Artist $3,000
Ron Gorchov, New York, NY. 1975 Artist $8,000
Misha Gordin, Troy, MI. 1986 Photo $15,000
Bonnie Gordon, Buffalo, NY. 1975 Printmaking/Drawing/Artists' Books $3,000
David Gordon, Los Angeles, CA. 1987 Painting $5,000
John Gordon, Venice, CA. 1976 Artist $2,000
Richard Gordon, San Francisco, CA. 1982 Photo $5,000
Robert Gordon, New York, NY. 1969 Artist $5,000
Russell Gordon, Montreal, ON. 1980 Artist $10,000
Robert Gordy, New Orleans, LA. 1968 Artist $5,000; 1978 Artist $7,500; 1985 Printmaking/Drawing/Artists' Books $15,000
Shalom Gorewitz, New York, NY. 1979 Video $3,000; 1980 Video $3,000; 1983 Video $15,000; 1993 New Genres $20,000
Anthony Gorny, Philadelphia, PA. 1989 Works On Paper $15,000
Jennie Gorton, Greenville, MS. 1983 Painting $5,000
Carol Goss, Boston, MA. 1978 Crafts $7,500
John Goss, Los Angeles, CA. 1989 New Genres $5,000
John Gossage, Washington, DC. 1975 Photo $5,000; 1978 Photo $7,500
Joe Goto, Providence, RI. 1967 Artist $5,000
Jacqueline Gourevitch, Middletown, CT. 1976 Artist $2,000
Peter Gourfain, Brooklyn, NY. 1975 Artist $4,000
Philip Govedare, Seattle, WA. 1993 Works On Paper $20,000
Emmet Gowin, Newtown, PA. 1977 Photo $7,500; 1980 Photo $10,000
Sharon Grace, San Francisco, CA. 1980 Video $3,000
Barbara Grad, Chicago, IL. 1975 Artist $2,000
Dennis Grady, West Greenwich, RI. 1981 Photo $12,500
Allan Graham, Albuquerque, NM. 1985 Painting $15,000
Dan Graham, New York, NY. 1978 Conceptual/Performance/New Genres $7,500; 1985 New Genres $5,000; 1987 New Genres $25,000
David M. Graham, Richboro, PA. 1984 Photo $5,000
Gloria Graham, Albuquerque, NM. 1977 Crafts $5,000
Lisa Gralnick, Rosendale, NY. 1988 Crafts $5,000; 1992 Crafts $20,000
Timothy Grannis, Underhill, VT. 1981 Crafts $12,500
Peter Grass, New York, NY. 1978 Conceptual/Performance/New Genres $3,000
Anton Grassl, Cambridge, MA. 1992 Photo $20,000

Grace Graupe-Pillard, Freehold, NJ. 1985 Printmaking/Drawing/Artists' Books $5,000
Bradford Graves, New York, NY. 1980 Artist $10,000
Kenneth Graves, State College, PA. 1975 Photo $5,000; 1986 Photo $15,000
Nancy Graves, New York, NY. 1973 Artist $7,500
Nancy Gray, Brooklyn, NY. 1975 Printmaking/Drawing/Artists' Books $3,000
Edward Grazda, New York, NY. 1980 Photo $3,000; 1986 Photo $5,000
John Grazier, Washington, DC. 1975 Printmaking/Drawing/Artists' Books $3,000
George Green, Dallas, TX. 1977 Artist $7,500
Jonathan Green, Westerville, OH. 1978 Photo $7,500
Phyllis Green, Los Angeles, CA. 1984 Sculpture $5,000
Tom Green, Cabin John, MD. 1978 Artist $3,000; 1980 Artist $10,000
Vanalyne Green, New York, NY. 1983 Conceptual/Performance/New Genres $15,000
Marty Greenbaum, New York, NY. 1974 Artist $3,000
Stephen Greene, Valley Cottage, NY. 1967 Artist $5,000
Colin Greenly, McLean, VA. 1968 Artist $5,000
Caroline Greenwald, Madison, WI. 1982 Crafts $5,000
Mark Greenwold, Albany, NY. 1985 Painting $15,000
Jackie Greeves, Silver Spring, MD. 1982 Crafts $25,000
Mathieu Gregoire, San Diego, CA. 1988 Sculpture $5,000; 1990 Sculpture $5,000
Harold Gregor, Bloomington, IL. 1993 Painting $20,000
Barbara Grenell, Burnsville, NC. 1974 Crafts $3,000
Gregory Grenon, Portland, OR. 1991 Painting $20,000
Scott Grieger, Venice, CA. 1983 Painting $15,000
Eileen Griffin, San Diego, CA. 1976 Video $2,000
Gary Griffin, Rochester, NY. 1977 Crafts $5,000
Robert Griffin, New York, NY. 1987 Painting $15,000
Thomasin Grim, Berkeley, CA. 1986 Crafts $5,000
Nancy Grimes, Astoria, NY. 1985 Painting $5,000
Mineko Grimmer, Los Angeles, CA. 1986 Sculpture $5,000; 1993 New Genres $20,000
Erik Gronborg, Las Vegas, NC. 1973 Crafts $3,000
Deborah Groover, Athens, GA. 1992 Crafts $20,000
Jan Groover, New York, NY. 1978 Photo $7,500; 1990 Photo $20,000
Julie Gross, New York, NY. 1991 Painting $20,000
Mimi Gross, New York, NY. 1985 Painting $15,000
Francoise Grossen, New York, NY. 1977 Crafts $5,000
Maurice Grossman, Tucson, AZ. 1984 Crafts $15,000
Nancy Grossman, New York, NY. 1984 Sculpture $15,000
Robert Grosvenor, East Patchogue, NY. 1969 Artist $5,000; 1976 Artist $5,000; 1984 Sculpture $15,000
Ronald Grow, Albuquerque, NM. 1973 Artist $7,500
Vicky Grube, Kalona, IA. 1987 Painting $5,000
Leo Grucza, Champaign, IL. 1982 Painting $5,000; 1983 Painting $15,000
Slawomir Grunberg, University Park, IL. 1985 New Genres $5,000
Barbara Grygutis, Tucson, AZ. 1975 Crafts $5,000
Sidney Guberman, Atlanta, GA. 1980 Artist $3,000
Spence Guerin, Anchorage, AK. 1980 Artist $10,000
Dawn Guernsey, St. Louis, MO. 1985 Printmaking/Drawing/Artists' Books $5,000
Teresina Guerra, Austin, TX. 1982 Photo $5,000
Raul Guerrero, Santa Monica, CA. 1979 Photo $10,000
Melody Guichet, Baton Rouge, LA. 1985 Painting $15,000
Robert Guillot, Brooklyn, NY. 1981 Sculpture $4,000
Sam Gummelt, Dallas, TX. 1982 Painting $5,000; 1985 Painting $15,000
Donald Gummer, New York, NY. 1976 Artist $5,000
Karen Gunderman, Milwaukee, WI. 1988 Crafts $5,000
Anthony Gunn, Suitland, MD. 1984 Sculpture $5,000
Ernest Gussella, New York, NY. 1980 Video $3,000
Pier Gustafson, Boston, MA. 1986 Sculpture $5,000
Christopher Gustin, South Dartmouth, MA. 1978 Crafts $7,500; 1986 Crafts $5,000
Elizabeth Gutierrez, Los Angeles, CA. 1990 Sculpture $5,000
Peter Gutkin, San Francisco, CA. 1980 Artist $3,000; 1984 Sculpture $15,000
Steven Gwon, New York, NY. 1979 Conceptual/Performance/New Genres $3,000
Woody Gwyn, Galisteo, NM. 1978 Artist $7,500

H

Hans Haacke, New York, NY. 1978 Conceptual/Performance/New Genres $7,500
Richard Haas, New York, NY. 1978 Printmaking/Drawing/Artists' Books $7,500
Ira Joel Haber, New York, NY. 1974 Artist $3,000; 1977 Artist $7,500; 1983 Printmaking/Drawing/Artists' Books $15,000
Allan Hacklin, Houston, TX. 1976 Printmaking/Drawing/Artists' Books $3,000; 1980 Artist $3,000; 1984 Sculpture $15,000
Carol Haerer, Hoosick Falls, NY. 1985 Painting $15,000
Marcia Hafif, New York, NY. 1980 Artist $10,000; 1989 Painting $15,000
Kristi Hager, Butte, MT. 1989 Painting $5,000
Nancy Hagin, New York, NY. 1982 Painting $5,000; 1991 Painting $20,000
Betty Hahn, Albuquerque, NM. 1979 Photo $10,000; 1982 Photo $25,000
Jana Haimsohn, New York, NY. 1981 Conceptual/Performance/New Genres $12,500
James Hajicek, Mesa, AZ. 1979 Photo $10,000
Stephen Hale, New York, NY. 1985 Printmaking/Drawing/Artists' Books $5,000
Marcus Halevi, Cambridge, MA. 1992 Photo $20,000
Nade Haley, Washington, DC. 1980 Artist $3,000; 1982 Sculpture $5,000
Debra Hall, Venice, CA. 1977 Artist $3,000
Doug Hall, San Francisco, CA. 1978 Video $3,000; 1985 New Genres $15,000; 1995 New Genres $20,000
Jon Hall, Barrington, RI. 1980 Crafts $3,000
Michael Hall, Salt Lake City, UT. 1974 Artist $7,500; 1991 Painting $20,000
Susan Hall, New York, NY. 1979 Artist $10,000; 1987 Printmaking/Drawing/Artists' Books $15,000
Gary Hallman, Minneapolis, MN. 1975 Photo $5,000
Andre Haluska, Roebling, NJ. 1979 Photo $3,000
Diana Hamar, Juneau, AK. 1991 Painting $20,000
Lynn Hambrick-Lukas, Minneapolis, MN. 1991 Photo $5,000; 1992 Photo $20,000
Ann Hamilton, Columbus, OH. 1993 New Genres $20,000
Susan Hamlet, Stillwater, OK. 1979 Crafts $3,000; 1988 Crafts $5,000
Wayne Hammer, Philadelphia, PA. 1975 Crafts $5,000
Wanda Hammerbeck, Oakland, CA. 1980 Photo $3,000; 1981 Photo $12,500
Fred Hammersley, Albuquerque, NM. 1975 Artist $8,000; 1977 Artist $7,500
William Hammersly, Richmond, VA. 1980 Crafts $3,000
Harmony Hammond, New York, NY. 1979 Artist $10,000; 1983 Printmaking/Drawing/Artists' Books $15,000
Jane Hammond, New York, NY. 1989 Painting $5,000
Mary Hammond, Athens, GA. 1982 Photo $5,000
Red Hammond, New York, NY. 1981 Painting $4,000; 1987 Painting $5,000
David Hammons, New York, NY. 1982 Printmaking/Drawing/Artists' Books $25,000
Lloyd Hamrol, Los Angeles, CA. 1974 Artist $7,500; 1980 Artist $10,000; 1990 Sculpture $20,000
Xin Han, Los Angeles, CA. 1985 Painting $5,000
Vanessa Haney, New York, NY. 1993 Painting $20,000
Jack Hanley, Austin, TX. 1987 Painting $5,000
David Hannah, San Francisco, CA. 1975 Artist $4,000
Freya Hansell, New York, NY. 1989 Painting $5,000
James Lee Hansen, Boston, MA. 1987 Painting $5,000
David Hanson, Billings, MT. 1986 Photo $5,000; 1994 Photo $20,000
Jo Hanson, San Francisco, CA. 1977 Artist $7,500
Lawrence Hanson, Bellington, WA. 1980 Artist $10,000
Philip Hanson, Chicago, IL. 1978 Artist $7,500; 1983 Painting $15,000
Marvin Harden, Los Angeles, CA. 1973 Artist $7,500
Rodney Harder, New York, NY. 1990 Painting $5,000
John Harding, San Francisco, CA. 1977 Photo $7,500
Tim Harding, St. Paul, MN. 1986 Crafts $15,000
Richard Hardner, Brooklyn, NY. 1975 Artist $3,000
Patricia Hardy, North Berwick, ME. 1976 Printmaking/Drawing/Artists' Books $3,000
Chauncey Hare, Point Richmond, CA. 1975 Photo $5,000; 1978 Photo $7,500; 1982 Photo $25,000
James Harmon, Castille, NY. 1978 Crafts $7,500
Richard Harned, Columbus, OH. 1986 Sculpture $5,000
Karen Harper, Bay Village, OH. 1974 Artist $1,000
Mark Harper, Philadelphia, PA. 1980 Photo $3,000; 1984 Photo $5,000
William Harper, Tallahassee, FL. 1974 Crafts $3,000; 1978 Crafts $7,500; 1990 Crafts $20,000
Anne Harris, South Portland, ME. 1993 Works On Paper $20,000
Bob Harris, New York, NY. 1980 Video $3,000
Tracy Harris, DeSoto, TX. 1987 Printmaking/Drawing/Artists' Books $5,000; 1989 Works On Paper $5,000
Anthony Harrison, New York, NY. 1975 Printmaking/Drawing/Artists' Books $3,000
Newton Harrison, La Jolla, CA. 1975 Artist $8,000
Claudia Hart, New York, NY. 1989 Works On Paper $5,000
Gordon Hart, New York, NY. 1975 Artist $2,000
Willis Hartshorn, Brooklyn, NY. 1981 Photo $12,500; 1986 Photo $15,000

Martha Haslanger, Cambridge, MA. 1976 Video $2,000
Maren Hassinger, Los Angeles, CA. 1980 Artist $3,000; 1984 Sculpture $15,000
Connie Hatch, Los Angeles, CA. 1982 Photo $5,000; 1991 New Genres $20,000
Thomas Hatch, New York, NY. 1977 Conceptual/Performance/New Genres $3,000; 1984 Sculpture $5,000
Brower Hatcher, Diamond Point, NY. 1974 Artist $3,000; 1980 Artist $10,000; 1990 Sculpture $20,000
Walter Hatke, State College, PA. 1985 Painting $5,000
Julius Hatofsky, San Francisco, CA. 1967 Artist $5,000; 1977 Artist $7,500
Julian Hatton, Wayland, MA. 1993 Painting $20,000
Susan Hauptman, Venice, CA. 1985 Printmaking/Drawing/Artists' Books $15,000; 1991 Works On Paper $20,000
Joseph Havel, Houston, TX. 1986 Sculpture $5,000
John Hawthorne, Richmond, VA. 1982 Crafts $5,000
David Haxton, New York, NY. 1978 Video $7,500; 1980 Photo $3,000
Jacqueline Hayden, Goshen, MA. 1994 Photo $20,000; 1993 Photo $5,000
David Hayes, Salt Lake City, UT. 1983 Video $5,000
Nancy Haynes, Brooklyn, NY. 1987 Painting $5,000; 1989 Painting $5,000
Ronald Hays, Brookline, MA. 1975 Video $8,000
James Hayward, Moorpark, CA. 1993 Painting $20,000
Sherry Healy, Chicago, IL. 1986 Crafts $5,000; 1988 Sculpture $5,000
David Heany, Atlanta, GA. 1974 Artist $7,500
Michael Hearn, Cleveland, OH. 1987 Painting $5,000
Dennis Hearne, San Francisco, CA. 1975 Photo $5,000
Charles Heasley, Cortland, NY. 1983 Printmaking/Drawing/Artists' Books $5,000
Jane Heaven, Berkeley, CA. 1982 Crafts $5,000
Rachel Hecker, Greenville, SC. 1989 Painting $5,000
Wally Hedrick, Bodega, CA. 1968 Artist $5,000; 1982 Painting $5,000; 1993 Painting $20,000
Ana Lisa Hedstrom, Emeryville, CA. 1982 Crafts $5,000; 1988 Crafts $15,000
Willy Heeks, New York, NY. 1978 Conceptual/Performance/New Genres $3,000; 1987 Painting $5,000; 1989 Painting $15,000
Julie Heffernan, Julian, PA. 1995 Works On Paper $20,000
Philip Hefferton, Felton, CA. 1978 Artist $7,500
Mary Heilmann, New York, NY. 1979 Artist $10,000; 1987 Painting $15,000
John Hein, Trenton, NJ. 1990 Crafts $5,000
Robert Heinecken, Los Angeles, CA. 1977 Photo $7,500; 1981 Photo $12,500; 1986 Photo $25,000
Peter Heineman, New York, NY. 1983 Painting $15,000
Al Held, New York, NY. 1969 Artist $5,000
Nancy Hellebrand, Philadelphia, PA. 1984 Photo $15,000
Pamela Heller, Brooklyn, NY. 1986 Sculpture $5,000
Preston Heller, Englishtown, NJ. 1975 Artist $4,000
Susanna Heller, Brooklyn, NY. 1991 Painting $20,000
Suzanne Hellmuth/Jock Reynolds, Washington, DC. 1978 Conceptual/Performance/New Genres $7,500; 1986 Photo $15,000
Robert Helm, Pullman, WA. 1985 Painting $15,000
Phoebe Helman, New York, NY. 1983 Printmaking/Drawing/Artists' Books $25,000
Harold Helwig, Buffalo, NY. 1974 Crafts $3,000
Richard Helzer, Bozeman, MT. 1976 Crafts $5,000
Adele Henderson, Buffalo, NY. 1995 Works On Paper $20,000
Carl Henderson, Atlanta, GA. 1981 Sculpture $4,000
Edward Henderson, Stony Point, NY. 1989 Works On Paper $15,000
Mike Henderson, Oakland, CA. 1978 Artist $7,500; 1989 Painting $15,000
Victor Henderson, Venice, CA. 1983 Painting $15,000
Maxwell Hendler, Santa Monica, CA. 1975 Artist $4,000
David Hendricks, Chicago, IL. 1977 Artist $7,500; 1980 Printmaking/Drawing/Artists' Books $10,000
Geoffrey Hendricks, New York, NY. 1976 Conceptual/Performance/New Genres $10,000
Kenneth Hendry, Ft. Collins, CO. 1980 Crafts $10,000
Donna Henes, Brooklyn, NY. 1982 Conceptual/Performance/New Genres $5,000
James Henkel, Minneapolis, MN. 1980 Photo $10,000
Jan Henle, St. Croix, VI. 1989 New Genres $5,000
Lois Hennessey, Baltimore, MD. 1978 Crafts $7,500
Biff Henrich, Buffalo, NY. 1980 Photo $3,000; 1984 Photo $5,000
Dale Henry, Bullville, NY. 1982 Painting $25,000
Diane Henry, Chicago, IL. 1974 Printmaking/Drawing/Artists' Books $3,000
John Henry, Chicago, IL. 1975 Artist $4,000
Patti Henry, San Jose, CA. 1975 Crafts $5,000
Caspar Henselmann, New York, NY. 1979 Artist $10,000; 1984 Sculpture $15,000
Richard Hensley, Floyd, VA. 1986 Crafts $15,000
Tony Hepburn, Alfred Station, NY. 1984 Crafts $15,000
Carol Hepper, New York, NY. 1990 Sculpture $5,000
James Herbert, Athens, GA. 1982 Painting $25,000
Pinkney Herbert, Brooklyn, NY. 1987 Painting $5,000
Susan Hereford, Portland, OR. 1980 Photo $3,000
Alan Herman, New York, NY. 1982 Sculpture $5,000
Roger Herman, Los Angeles, CA. 1982 Painting $5,000; 1989 Painting $5,000
Joel Hermann, Hobart, IN. 1976 Video $5,000
Marcy Hermansader, Brattleboro, VT. 1977 Artist $3,000
George Herms, Venice, CA. 1968 Artist $5,000; 1977 Artist $7,500; 1984 Sculpture $15,000
Anthony Hernandez, Los Angeles, CA. 1975 Photo $5,000; 1978 Photo $7,500; 1980 Photo $10,000
John Hernandez, Dallas, TX. 1989 Painting $5,000
Sam Hernandez, San Jose, CA. 1984 Sculpture $15,000
Frank Herrera, Shenandoah Junction, WV. 1982 Photo $5,000
Linda Herritt, Boulder, CO. 1990 Sculpture $5,000
Lynn Hershman, 1991 Conceptual/Performance/New Genres $20,000
Paul Herzoff, Pleasant Hill, CA. 1971 Photo $2,500; 1973 Photo $3,500
Allen Hess, Boston, MA. 1981 Photo $12,500; 1990 Photo $20,000
Scott Hess, Los Angeles, CA. 1991 Painting $20,000
Marc Hessel, Center Hall, PA. 1975 Photo $5,000
Paul Hester, Houston, TX. 1973 Photo $ 1500; 1980 Photo $3,000
Sue Hettmansperger, Alburquerque, NM. 1983 Printmaking/Drawing/Artists' Books $5,000
Steven Heyman, Chicago, IL. 1987 Painting $5,000
Julia Heyward, New York, NY. 1974 Artist $1,000; 1976 Video $2,000; 1979 Conceptual/Performance/New Genres $3,000; 1981 Video $12,500
Patricia Hickman, Honolulu, HI. 1994 Crafts $20,000
Wayne Higby, Alfred Station, NY. 1973 Crafts $3,000; 1977 Crafts $5,000; 1988 Crafts $15,000
Kathryn High, Brooklyn, NY. 1995 New Genres $20,000
Timothy High, Austin, TX. 1989 Works On Paper $5,000
Jene Highstein, Salem, NY. 1976 Artist $2,000; 1977 Printmaking/Drawing/Artists' Books $5,000; 1978 Artist $7,500; 1994 Sculpture $20,000
John Hilgert, St. Louis, MO. 1988 Photo $5,000
Charles Hill, Venice, CA. 1976 Artist $2,000; 1991 Painting $20,000
Clinton Hill, New York, NY. 1976 Printmaking/Drawing/Artists' Books $3,000; 1980 Artist $10,000
Daniel G. Hill, New York, NY. 1993 Painting $2,000
Daniel A. Hill, Brooklyn, NY. 1975 Artist $2,000
Edward Hill, Houston, TX. 1973 Photo $1,500
Gary Hill, Seattle, WA. 1979 Video $3,000; 1985 New Genres $5,000; 1987 New Genres $15,000, 1990 New Genres $20,000
James Hill, New York, NY. 1982 Sculpture $25,000
Robin Hill, Brooklyn, NY. 1986 Sculpture $5,000
Candace Hill-Montgomery, New York, NY. 1981 Conceptual/Performance/New Genres $4,000; 1983 Conceptual/Performance/New Genres $5,000
Ed/Suzanne Hill/Bloom, Houston, TX. 1992 Photo $20,000
Susan Hiller, Coral Gables, FL. 1981 Conceptual/Performance/New Genres $12,500
Eric Hilton, Odessa, NY. 1981 Crafts $12,500
John Himmelfarb, Oak Park, IL. 1982 Painting $5,000; 1985 Printmaking/Drawing/Artists' Books $15,000
Charles Hindes, Iowa City, IA. 1976 Crafts $5,000
Kay Hines, New York, NY. 1981 Printmaking/Drawing/Artists' Books $12,500
Charles Hinman, New York, NY. 1980 Artist $10,000
Herbert Hintze, Cambridge, WI. 1990 Crafts $5,000
Anne Hirondelle, Port Townsend, WA. 1988 Crafts $5,000
Gilah Hirsch, Venice, CA. 1985 Painting $15,000
Jim Hirschfield, Chapel Hill, NC. 1990 Sculpture $5,000
Stewart Hitch, New York, NY. 1987 Painting $15,000; 1993 Painting $20,000
Lin Hixson, Chicago, IL. 1985 New Genres $5,000; 1987 New Genres $5,000; 1989 New Genres $15,000
Thomas Hoadley, Lansborough, MA. 1990 Crafts $5,000; 1992 Crafts $20,000
Joe Hobbs, Norman, OK. 1978 Conceptual/Performance/New Genres $3,000; 1980 Artist $10,000
Perry Hoberman, Brooklyn, NY. 1984 Sculpture $5,000
Louis Hock, Cardiff, CA. 1974 Artist $1,000; 1981 Conceptual/Performance/New Genres

$12,500; 1985 New Genres $15,000
Rick Hock, Rochester, NY. 1980 Photo $3,000; 1988 Photo $5,000
Ralph Hocking, Newark Valley, NY. 1982 Video $25,000
Christopher Hodge, Trumansburg, NY. 1981 Crafts $12,500
Arnold Hoffman, East Hampton, NY. 1975 Printmaking/Drawing/Artists' Books $3,000
George Hofmann, Worcester, NY. 1976 Printmaking/Drawing/Artists' Books $3,000
Patrick Hogan, Los Angeles, CA. 1976 Artist $2,000; 1980 Artist $10,000; 1985 Painting $25,000
Eileen Hohmuth-Lemonick, Princeton, NJ. 1992 Photo $20,000
Jan Holcomb, Pascoag, RI. 1979 Crafts $10,000; 1988 Crafts $15,000
Barry Holden, New York, NY. 1980 Artist $3,000
Kenneth Holder, Bloomington, IL. 1981 Painting $12,500
Fred Holland, New York, NY. 1987 New Genres $5,000; 1989 New Genres $5,000
Tom Holland, Berkeley, CA. 1975 Artist $8,000
Frank Holliday, New York, NY. 1989 Painting $5,000
Douglas Hollis, San Francisco, CA. 1980 Artist $10,000; 1984 Sculpture $15,000
David Holmes, Milwaukee, WI. 1976 Crafts $5,000
Jacqui Holmes, New York, NY. 1981 Printmaking/Drawing/Artists' Books $4,000
Robert Holmgren, San Francisco, CA. 1984 Photo $5,000
Thomas Holste, Orange, CA. 1980 Artist $3,000
Nancy Holt, New York, NY. 1975 Video $8,000; 1978 Video $7,500; 1988 Sculpture $15,000
Chuck Holtzman, Boston, MA. 1984 Sculpture $5,000
David Holzman, Dayton, OH. 1985 Printmaking/Drawing/Artists' Books $5,000
Eric Holzman, New York, NY. 1989 Painting $5,000
Mei-Ling Hom, Philadelphia, PA. 1994 Sculpture $20,000
Coille Hooven, Berkeley, CA. 1975 Crafts $5,000
Budd Hopkins, New York, NY. 1979 Artist $10,000
William Hoppe, Seattle, WA. 1981 Printmaking/Drawing/Artists' Books $12,500
Andrew Horn, New York, NY. 1987 New Genres $5,000
Roni Horn, Brooklyn, NY. 1984 Sculpture $5,000; 1986 Sculpture $5,000; 1990 Sculpture $20,000
George Horner, Brooklyn, NY. 1987 Painting $5,000
Beth Horowitz, New York, NY. 1976 Video $2,000
Kate Horsfield, New York, NY. 1985 Printmaking/Drawing/Artists' Books $5,000
Patrick Horsley, Portland, OR. 1980 Crafts $10,000
David Horton, Warwick, NY. 1985 Printmaking/Drawing/Artists' Books $5,000
Channa Horwitz, Hidden Hill, CA. 1978 Conceptual/Performance/New Genres $3,000
Jane Hosticka, Chicago, IL. 1985 Painting $5,000
Klindt Houlberg, Chicago, IL. 1980 Crafts $10,000
Suda House, Los Angeles, CA. 1980 Photo $3,000
Robert Hout, New York, NY. 1967 Artist $5,000
Mildred Howard, Berkeley, CA. 1994 Sculpture $20,000
Robert Howard, Chapel Hill, NC. 1973 Artist $7,500
Graham Howe, Pasadena, CA. 1982 Photo $5,000
Robert Hower, Louisville, KY. 1990 Photo $20,000
Rebecca Howland, New York, NY. 1981 Sculpture $12,500; 1995 Painting $20,000
Sharron Howlett, Norman, OK. 1975 Crafts $5,000
Tishan Hsu, Brooklyn, NY. 1990 Sculpture $5,000
Mary Lee Hu, Seattle, WA. 1976 Crafts $5,000; 1984 Crafts $15,000; 1992 Crafts $20,000
Sandria Hu, Stanford, CA. 1974 Printmaking/Drawing/Artists' Books $3,000
David Huchthousen, Smithville, TN. 1982 Crafts $5,000
Thomas Hucker, Charlestown, MA. 1982 Crafts $5,000; 1988 Crafts $15,000
Hudson, Chicago, IL. 1983 Conceptual/Performance/New Genres $5,000
Judith Hudson, New York, NY. 1981 Painting $4,000
Robert Hudson, San Francisco, CA. 1973 Artist $7,500
Douglas Huebler, Newhall, CA. 1978 Conceptual/Performance/New Genres $3,000; 1980 Conceptual/Performance/New Genres $3,000; 1983 Conceptual/Performance/New Genres $15,000
Dorothy Hughes, Winnetka, IL. 1976 Crafts $5,000
Helene Hui, New York, NY. 1977 Artist $7,500
Ka Kwong Hui, Jamesburg, NJ. 1976 Crafts $5,000
Crystal Huie, New York, NY. 1973 Photo $5,000
Peter Hujar, New York, NY. 1977 Photo $7,500; 1980 Photo $10,000
John Hull, Baltimore, MD. 1982 Painting $5,000; 1983 Painting $5,000; 1985 Painting $5,000; 1987 Painting $5,000
Shelly Hull, Baltimore, MD. 1983 Painting $5,000
John Hultberg, New York, NY. 1981 Painting $12,500
Richard Hume, Boulder, CO. 1976 Photo $7,500; 1978 Photo $7,500
David Humphrey, New York, NY. 1987 Painting $5,000; 1995 Painting $20,000
Margo Humphrey, Oakland, CA. 1983 Printmaking/Drawing/Artists' Books $5,000; 1985 Printmaking/Drawing/Artists' Books $15,000
Nene Humphrey, New York, NY. 1983 Printmaking/Drawing/Artists' Books $5,000
Su-Chen Hung, San Francisco, CA. 1987 New Genres $5,000
Jerry Hunt, Canton, TX. 1985 New Genres $15,000
Jim Huntington, Brooklyn, NY. 1980 Artist $10,000; 1984 Sculpture $15,000
Abby Huntoon, South Portland, ME. 1988 Crafts $5,000
Denzil Hurley, Amherst, MA. 1989 Painting $5,000; 1993 Painting $20,000
Michael Hurson, Chicago, IL. 1974 Artist $7,500; 1980 Artist $10,000
Lynn Hurst, Houston, TX. 1989 Painting $5,000
Michael Hurwitz, Philadelphia, PA. 1988 Crafts $5,000; 1990 Crafts $5,000; 1992 Crafts $20,000
Terry Husebye, Santa Fe, NM. 1981 Photo $4,000
Peter Hutchinson, New York, NY. 1975 Artist $4,000
William Hutson, San Antonio, TX. 1974 Artist $7,500
Frances Hynes, Bayside, NY. 1980 Artist $3,000

I

Mildred Iatrou, New York, NY. 1980 Video $3,000
Miyoko Ichiyasu, Chicago, IL. 1973 Artist $7,500
Takahiko Iimura, New York, NY. 1980 Video $3,000
Shiro Ikegawa, Altadena, CA. 1974 Printmaking/Drawing/Artists' Books $3,000; 1981 Conceptual/Performance/New Genres $12,500
Jonathan Imber, Somerville, MA. 1987 Painting $5,000
Birney Imes, Columbus, MS. 1984 Photo $5,000; 1988 Photo $15,000
Kim Ingraham, Binghamton, NY. 1983 Video $5,000
William Insley, Oberlin, OH. 1967 Artist $5,000
Kent Ipsen, Richmond, VA. 1975 Crafts $5,000
David Ireland, San Francisco, CA. 1978 Artist $7,500; 1983 Conceptual/Performance/New Genres $25,000
Jane Irish, Flushing, NY. 1981 Painting $4,000
Robert Irwin, Los Angeles, CA. 1973 Artist $7,500
Doug Ischar, Chicago, IL. 1992 Photo $20,000
Jim Isermann, Hollywood, CA. 1984 Sculpture $5,000; 1987 Painting $5,000
Michi Itami, Berkeley, CA. 1981 Printmaking/Drawing/Artists' Books $12,500
Michiko Itatani, Chicago, IL. 1980 Artist $3,000
The Estate of Diane Itter, Baltimore, MD. 1977 Crafts $5,000; 1979 Crafts $10,000; 1984 Crafts $15,000
Peter Ivers, Los Angeles, CA. 1980 Conceptual/Performance/New Genres $3,000
Susan Iverson, Richmond, VA. 1979 Crafts $10,000
Ron Ives, Norfolk, VA. 1982 Printmaking/Drawing/Artists' Books $5,000
Bill Ivey, Seattle, WA. 1967 Artist $5,000
Kiyomi Iwata, Upper Grand View, NY. 1986 Crafts $15,000
Kenro Izu, New York, NY. 1984 Photo $15,000

J

Alfredo Jaar, New York, NY. 1987 New Genres $5,000; 1992 Photo $20,000
Joseph Jachna, Oak Lawn, IL. 1976 Photo $7,500
Oliver Jackson, Sacramento, CA. 1980 Artist $10,000
William Jackson, Richmond, VA. 1975 Artist $4,000
Martha Jackson-Jarvis, Washington, DC. 1986 Sculpture $5,000
Lotte Jacobi, Deering, NH. 1977 Photo $7,500
Ferne Jacobs, Los Angeles, CA. 1973 Crafts $3,000; 1977 Crafts $5,000; 1990 Crafts $20,000
Carl Jacobson, New York, NY. 1987 Painting $15,000
Jeff Jacobson, Staten Island, NY. 1990 Photo $5,000
Susana Jacobson, New Haven, CT. 1983 Painting $5,000
Jerald Jacquard, Bloomington, IN. 1980 Artist $10,000
Susan Jahoda, Berkeley Heights, NJ. 1980 Photo $3,000
Michael James, Somerset Village, MA. 1978 Crafts $7,500; 1988 Crafts $15,000
Alex Jamison, Washington, DC. 1980 Photo $3,000
Judith Jampel, New York, NY. 1980 Crafts $10,000
Glenn Jampol, Oakland, CA. 1982 Painting $5,000
Jan Janeiro, Oakland, CA. 1984 Crafts $5,000
Ronald Janowich, New York, NY. 1976 Artist $2,000; 1989 Painting $15,000
Joel Janowitz, Watertown, MA. 1976 Artist $2,000; 1982 Painting $5,000
Angela Jansen, New York, NY. 1974 Printmaking/Drawing/Artists' Books $3,000
Catherine Jansen, Wyncote, PA. 1982 Photo $5,000

Virginia Jaramillo, 1973 Artist $7,500
Valerie Jaudon, New York, NY. 1987 Painting $15,000
Douglas Jeck, Chicago, IL. 1990 Crafts $5,000; 1992 Crafts $20,000
Thomas Jenkins, Santa Monica, CA. 1980 Artist $3,000
Ulysses Jenkins, Los Angeles, CA. 1980 Conceptual/Performance/New Genres $3,000; 1982 Video $25,000
William Jenkins, Rochester, NY. 1979 Photo $10,000
Ulysses Jenkins, Jr., Inglewood, CA. 1995 New Genres $20,000
Bill Jensen, New York, NY. 1985 Painting $15,000; 1993 Works On Paper $20,000
Judy Jensen, Austin, TX. 1986 Crafts $5,000
Len Jenshel, Little Neck, NY. 1978 Photo $7,500
Miles Jermanovich, San Francisco, CA. 1977 Photo $7,500
Marjorie Jervis/Susie Krasnican, Falls Church, VA. 1980 Crafts $10,000
John Jesurun, New York, NY. 1987 New Genres $5,000
Luis Jimenez, Hondo, NM. 1977 Artist $7,500; 1988 Sculpture $25,000
Juanita Jimenez-Mizuno, Los Angeles, CA. 1980 Crafts $10,000
Suzanne Joelson, New York, NY. 1987 Painting $5,000
Patricia Johanson, Buskirk, NY. 1975 Artist $4,000
Lawrence John, Pacific Palisades, CA. 1976 Photo $7,500
Marian John, Elton, LA. 1974 Crafts $3,000
Clifford Johnson, Stoughton, WI. 1974 Crafts $3,000
David Johnson, Minneapolis, MN. 1974 Printmaking/Drawing/Artists' Books $3,000
Dean Johnson, Cheyenne, WY. 1988 Sculpture $5,000
Don Johnson, New City, NY. 1982 Sculpture $5,000
Jerome Johnson, Carmichael, CA. 1974 Artist $7,500
Ralph Johnson, Sacramento, CA. 1977 Artist $7,500
Raymond Johnson, Locust Valley, NY. 1977 Conceptual/Performance/New Genres $10,000; 1985 Painting $15,000
Virginia Johnson, New York, NY. 1973 Artist $7,500
Robyn Johnson-Ross, Washington, DC. 1987 Painting $15,000
Randy Johnston, River Falls, WI. 1978 Crafts $7,500; 1990 Crafts $20,000
Ynez Johnston, Los Angeles, CA. 1976 Artist $2,000; 1985 Painting $15,000
Joan Jonas, New York, NY. 1975 Video $4,000; 1978 Video $7,500; 1980 Video $10,000; 1983 Conceptual/Performance/New Genres $15,000; 1991 New Genres $20,000
Benjamin Jones, Newark, NJ. 1974 Artist $7,500
Christopher Jones, New York, NY. 1974 Artist $3,000
David Jones, San Francisco, CA. 1974 Artist $3,000
Fay Jones, Seattle, WA. 1983 Painting $15,000; 1989 Painting $15,000
Harold Jones, Tucson, AZ. 1978 Photo $7,500
Howard Jones, St. Louis, MO. 1976 Conceptual/Performance/New Genres $5,000
Jerry Jones, New York, NY. 1980 Artist $10,000
Kim Jones, Boston, MA. 1986 Sculpture $15,000; 1993 New Genres $20,000
Otis Jones, Dallas, TX. 1982 Painting $5,000
Pirkle Jones, Mill Valley, CA. 1977 Photo $7,500
Robert Jones, Emeryville, CA. 1984 Sculpture $5,000
Ronald Jones, Sewanee, TN. 1983 Conceptual/Performance/New Genres $5,000
Kristin/Andrew Jones/Ginzel, New York, NY. 1986 Sculpture $5,000; 1994 Sculpture $20,000
Raymond Jonson, Albuquerque, NM. 1973 Artist $7,500
Kenneth Josephson, Chicago, IL. 1975 Photo $5,000; 1979 Photo $10,000
Donald Judd, New York, NY. 1967 Artist $5,000; 1976 Artist $10,000
Susan Julien, Chicago, IL. 1983 Painting $5,000
Brandt Junceau, Brooklyn, NY. 1988 Sculpture $5,000
Julio Juristo, Temple Terrace, FL. 1974 Printmaking/Drawing/Artists' Books $3,000
Nancy Jurs, Scottsville, NY. 1973 Crafts $3,000; 1977 Crafts $5,000
Gary Justis, Chicago, IL. 1984 Sculpture $5,000; 1990 Sculpture $5,000

K

Roderick Kagan, Ketchum, ID. 1984 Sculpture $5,000
Paul Kagawa, San Francisco, CA. 1977 Conceptual/Performance/New Genres $3,000
Barry Kahn, Minneapolis, MN. 1975 Artist $4,000
Ellen/Lynda Kahn, New York, NY. 1980 Conceptual/Performance/New Genres $3,000
Katie Kahn, Houston, TX. 1993 Painting $20,000
Ned Kahn, San Francisco, CA. 1990 Sculpture $5,000, 1994 Sculpture $20,000
Robin Kahn, New York, NY. 1989 Painting $5,000
Stephen Kahn, Malibu, CA. 1980 Photo $10,000
Tamarra Kaida, Mesa, AZ. 1986 Photo $5,000
Richard Kalina, New York, NY. 1991 Works On Paper $20,000
Howard Kalish, New York, NY. 1984 Sculpture $5,000
Kreg Kallenberger, Tulsa, OK. 1984 Crafts $5,000
Steve Kaltenbach, Woodland, CA. 1978 Artist $7,500
Ben Kamihira, Philadelphia, PA. 1974 Artist $7,500
Richard Kamler, San Anselmo, CA. 1983 Conceptual/Performance/New Genres $5,000
Deborah Kamy, Boston, MA. 1981 Painting $4,000
Bill Kane, San Francisco, CA. 1981 Photo $12,500; 1991 Painting $20,000
Jun Kaneko, Bloomfield Hills, MI. 1979 Crafts $10,000; 1984 Crafts $25,000
Lisa Kanemoto, San Francisco, CA. 1982 Photo $5,000
Robin Kaneshiro, Berkeley, CA. 1981 Printmaking/Drawing/Artists' Books $4,000
Tim Kanton, Sarasota, FL. 1973 Photo $2,000
Morris Kantor, New City, NY. 1969 Artist $5,000
Ruth Kao, Cedar Falls, IA. 1973 Crafts $3,000
Annette Kaplan, Oakland, CA. 1975 Crafts $5,000
Ileen Kaplan, Ithaca, NY. 1987 Printmaking/Drawing/Artists' Books $5,000
R. L. Kaplan, New York, NY. 1987 Painting $5,000
Allan Kaprow, Pasadena, CA. 1974 Artist $7,500; 1979 Conceptual/Performance/New Genres $10,000
Karen Karnes, Morgan, VT. 1976 Crafts $5,000; 1988 Crafts $25,000
Mark Karnes, Baltimore, MD. 1983 Painting $15,000
Diane Karol, New York, NY. 1979 Artist $3,000
Frederick Karoly, New York, NY. 1969 Artist $5,000
Terrance Karpowicz, Chicago, IL. 1980 Artist $3,000; 1982 Sculpture $5,000
Donald Karwelis, Santa Ana, CA. 1976 Artist $2,000
Kenneth Kashian, Normal, IL. 1978 Conceptual/Performance/New Genres $3,000
Chester Kasnowski, New Orleans, LA. 1974 Artist $3,000
Deborah Kass, New York, NY. 1987 Painting $15,000
Jacob Kass, Key Largo, FL. 1981 Painting $4,000
Ray Kass, Christiansburg, VA. 1981 Painting $12,500
Barbara Kasten, Inglewood, CA. 1978 Photo $7,500
Aleksandra Kasuba, New York, NY. 1982 Crafts $25,000
Joel Katz, Brooklyn, NY. 1995 New Genres $20,000
Leandro Katz, New York, NY. 1979 Conceptual/Performance/New Genres $3,000
Mel Katz, Portland, OR. 1975 Artist $4,000
Michael Katz, Miami, FL. 1979 Printmaking/Drawing/Artists' Books $10,000
Craig Kaufman, Venice, CA. 1968 Artist $5,000
Glen Kaufman, Athens, GA. 1976 Crafts $5,000; 1990 Crafts $20,000
Jane Kaufman, New York, NY. 1979 Artist $10,000; 1989 Painting $15,000
Kenneth Kaufman, Van Nuys, CA. 1989 Works On Paper $5,000
Reed Kay, Brookline, MA. 1981 Painting $12,500
Toshi Kazama, New York, NY. 1988 Photo $5,000
Brian Kazlov, New York, NY. 1983 Painting $15,000
Kazuko, New York, NY. 1979 Artist $10,000
Hilja Keading, Los Angeles, CA. 1989 New Genres $5,000
Jerry Kearnes, New York, NY. 1974 Artist $3,000
David Keating, Albuquerque, NM. 1994 Photo $20,000
Mary Keck, Providence, RI. 1974 Artist $3,000
Pamela Keech, Elyria, OH. 1982 Sculpture $5,000
David Keene, Arlington, TX. 1976 Crafts $5,000
Bayat Keerl, New York, NY. 1981 Painting $4,000; 1987 Painting $15,000
Robert Kehlmann, Berkeley, CA. 1977 Crafts $5,000
Patrice Kehoe, Hyattsville, MD. 1987 Painting $5,000
Stephen Keister, New York, NY. 1988 Sculpture $15,000
Germaine Keller, New York, NY. 1984 Sculpture $15,000
Kathryn Keller, Sacramento, CA. 1975 Printmaking/Drawing/Artists' Books $3,000
Martha Keller, New York, NY. 1989 Painting $5,000
Deborah Kelley, San Antonio, TX. 1987 Painting $5,000
Mike Kelley, Los Angeles, CA. 1985 New Genres $15,000
James Kelly, New York, NY. 1977 Artist $7,500
Mary Kelly, Snyder, NY. 1980 Artist $3,000; 1982 Sculpture $5,000; 1987 New Genres $15,000
Maureen Kelman, Providence, RI. 1990 Crafts $5,000
Authur Kemble, Washington Crossing, PA. 1974 Printmaking/Drawing/Artists' Books $3,000
Susan Kemenyffy, Albion, PA. 1973 Crafts $3,000; 1977 Crafts $5,000
Marilyn Kemppainen, Los Angeles, CA. 1979 Video $3,000
Melvin S. Kendrick, New York, NY. 1976 Artist $2,000; 1978 Artist $7,500, 1981 Sculpture $12,500; 1994 Sculpture $20,000
Mary Kenealy, Hartford, CT. 1989 Works On Paper $5,000
Brigid Kennedy, New York, NY. 1979 Artist $3,000; 1980 Artist $3,000; 1982 Sculpture $5,000

Gene Kennedy, Oakland, CA. 1984 Photo $5,000
Thomas Kenny, New York, NY. 1981 Painting $4,000
Jane Kent, New York, NY. 1989 Works On Paper $5,000
Hugh Kepets, New York, NY. 1976 Artist $2,000
Deans Keppel, New York, NY. 1983 Video $5,000
Gwenael Kerlidou, Brooklyn, NY. 1993 Painting $20,000
Robert Kerns, New York, NY. 1977 Artist $7,500
Charles Kessler, Venice, CA. 1983 Painting $5,000
Jon Kessler, Brooklyn, NY. 1984 Sculpture $5,000; 1990 Sculpture $5,000
Cavalliere Ketchum, Madison, WI. 1977 Photo $7,500
Richard Kevorkian, Richmond, VA. 1973 Artist $7,500
William Keyser, Rush, NY. 1974 Crafts $3,000
Constance Kheel, Tenant's Harbor, ME. 1992 Painting $5,000; 1987 Painting $15,000
Alan Kikuchi-Yngojo, New York, NY. 1981 Photo $12,500
Lance Kiland, Minneapolis, MN. 1985 Painting $15,000
Timothy Kilby, Sperryville, VA. 1981 Photo $4,000
Byron Kim, Brooklyn, NY. 1995 Painting $20,000
Cheonae Kim, Murphysboro, IL. 1993 Painting $20,000
Jin Soo Kim, Evanston, IL. 1984 Sculpture $5,000
Elizabeth King, Richmond, VA. 1988 Sculpture $15,000
John King, New York, NY. 1985 Printmaking/Drawing/Artists' Books $5,000
Ray King, Philadelphia, PA. 1982 Crafts $5,000; 1984 Crafts $15,000
Anne Kingsbury, Milwaukee, WI. 1976 Crafts $5,000
Brent Kington, Makanda, IL. 1974 Crafts $3,000; 1981 Crafts $12,500
Patricia Kinsella, San Rafael, CA. 1982 Crafts $5,000
Louis Kirchner, Long Island City, NY. 1987 Painting $5,000
Chris Kirk, New York, NY. 1979 Artist $3,000
Lawrence Kirkland, Portland, OR. 1981 Crafts $12,500
Bernard Kirschenbaum, New York, NY. 1976 Artist $5,000; 1981 Sculpture $12,500
Nancy Kitchel, New York, NY. 1975 Artist $4,000
Roger Kizik, Boston, MA. 1982 Painting $5,000
Elizabeth Klavun, New York, NY. 1974 Artist $7,500
Daniel Kleeman, Brooklyn, NY. 1974 Artist $3,000
Alan Kleiman, New York, NY. 1989 Painting $15,000
Jody Klein, Waban, MA. 1984 Crafts $15,000
Rodger Klein, Venice, CA. 1976 Video $2,000
Ron Klein, Glenside, PA. 1981 Sculpture $4,000
Alexandra Kleinbard, Havana, FL. 1979 Artist $3,000; 1982 Sculpture $5,000
Vera Klement, Chicago, IL. 1987 Painting $15,000
Mark Klett, Tempe, AZ. 1980 Photo $3,000; 1982 Photo $5,000; 1984 Photo $15,000
Stuart Klipper, Minneapolis, MN. 1979 Photo $10,000
Carole Ann Klonarides, Brooklyn, NY. 1987 New Genres $5,000
Carole Ann Klonarides/Michael Owen, New York, NY. 1991 New Genres $20,000
Suzanne Klotz-Reilly, Phoenix, AZ. 1976 Crafts $5,000; 1979 Crafts $10,000
Richard Knapp, Albuquerque, NM. 1979 Photo $3,000
Lewis Knauss, Macungie, PA. 1977 Crafts $5,000
Jonathan Knight, Venice, CA. 1987 New Genres $15,000
Gerhardt Knodel, Bloomfield Hills, MI. 1975 Crafts $5,000
Karen Knorr, London, England, . 1986 Photo $5,000
Christopher Knowles, New York, NY. 1978 Printmaking/Drawing/Artists' Books $3,000
Charlene Knowlton, Los Angeles, CA. 1987 Painting $5,000
Michael Knutson, Seattle, WA. 1982 Painting $5,000
John Koch, Albuquerque, NM. 1982 Sculpture $5,000
Mia Kodani, Oakland, CA. 1980 Crafts $10,000
Mary Koga, Chicago, IL. 1982 Photo $5,000
Paul Kohl, San Francisco, CA. 1976 Photo $7,500
Misch Kohn, Castro Valley, CA. 1980 Printmaking/Drawing/Artists' Books $10,000
John Kohring, Concord, MA. 1989 Painting $5,000
Silvia Kolbowski, New York, NY. 1989 New Genres $5,000
Vitaly Komar/Alexander Melamid, New York, NY. 1982 Conceptual/Performance/New Genres $25,000
Milton Komisar, Boston, MA. 1982 Sculpture $5,000
Richard Kooyman, Frankfort, MI. 1988 Crafts $5,000
Silas Kopf, Northampton, MA. 1988 Crafts $15,000
Steve Koplan, High Fall, NY. 1978 Video $3,000
Harriet Korman, Richmond, VA. 1974 Artist $3,000; 1987 Painting $15,000; 1993 Painting $20,000
Beryl Korot, New York, NY. 1975 Video $2,000; 1977 Video $7,500; 1979 Video $10,000
Paul Kos, Soda Springs, CA. 1974 Artist $3,000; 1976 Video $10,000; 1982 Video $25,000; 1993 New Genres $20,000
Hirokazu Kosaka, Los Angeles, CA. 1987 New Genres $5,000
Leonard Koscianski, Annapolis, MD. 1985 Painting $5,000; 1989 Painting $5,000
Elliot Kosloff, New York, NY. 1980 Artist $3,000
Jim Koss, Westchester, IL. 1983 Printmaking/Drawing/Artists' Books $5,000
Richard Kostelanetz, New York, NY. 1985 Printmaking/Drawing/Artists' Books $15,000
Michihiro Kosuge, Portland, OR. 1982 Sculpture $5,000
Jennifer Kotter, La Jolla, CA. 1979 Video $3,000
Howard Kottler, Seattle, WA. 1975 Crafts $5,000
Paul Kotula, Huntington Woods, MI. 1990 Crafts $5,000; 1992 Crafts $20,000
Josef Koudelka, New York, NY. 1980 Photo $10,000
Aris Koutroulis, New York, NY. 1976 Artist $2,000
Ronald Kovatch, Urbana, IL. 1990 Crafts $5,000
Dennis Kowalski, Chicago, IL. 1975 Artist $4,000
Solange Kowert, Sherwood, OR. 1975 Crafts $5,000
Joyce Kozloff, New York, NY. 1977 Artist $7,500; 1985 Printmaking/Drawing/Artists' Books $15,000
George Kozmon, Cleveland Heights, OH. 1987 Painting $5,000
Melanie Kozol, Cohasset, MA. 1983 Painting $5,000
Arnold Kramer, Washington, DC. 1975 Photo $5,000; 1979 Photo $10,000
Harry Kramer, New York, NY. 1982 Painting $25,000
Louise Kramer, Massapequa, NY. 1977 Printmaking/Drawing/Artists' Books $5,000
Margia Kramer, New York, NY. 1975 Printmaking/Drawing/Artists' Books $3,000; 1982 Conceptual/Performance/New Genres $5,000; 1989 Works On Paper $15,000
Peter Krasnow, Los Angeles, CA. 1977 Artist $7,500
George Krause, Houston, TX. 1973 Photo $5,000; 1979 Photo $10,000
Jerome Krause, Quebec, ON. 1981 Photo $12,500
Rockne Krebs, Washington, DC. 1971 Artist $7,500
Margo Kren, Manhattan, KS. 1982 Printmaking/Drawing/Artists' Books $5,000
Salem Krieger, Hoboken, NJ. 1987 Printmaking/Drawing/Artists' Books $5,000
Mitchell Kriegman, New York, NY. 1979 Video $3,000; 1980 Video $3,000; 1983 Video $15,000
Irving Kriesberg, New York, NY. 1981 Painting $12,500
Les Krims, Buffalo, NY. 1971 Photo $2,000; 1973 Photo $2,500; 1977 Photo $7,500
Harry Krizan, Fleetwood, PA. 1982 Painting $5,000; 1985 Painting $5,000
Jill Kroesen, New York, NY. 1983 Conceptual/Performance/New Genres $15,000
Linda Kroff, Charlotte, NC. 1994 Photo $20,000
Marilyn Kroplick, New York, NY. 1973 Photo $2,500
Jonathan Krout, Taos, NM. 1981 Crafts $12,500
Barbara Kruger, Los Angeles, CA. 1983 Conceptual/Performance/New Genres $15,000
Fred Krughoff, Webster Groves, MO. 1975 Video $2,000
Michael Krugman, Morristown, NJ. 1976 Conceptual/Performance/New Genres $2,000
Shigeko Kubota, New York, NY. 1976 Video $2,000; 1978 Video $7,500; 1980 Video $10,000; 1987 New Genres $15,000
Francis Kuehn, New York, NY. 1982 Painting $5,000
Gary Kuehn, Glen Gardner, NJ. 1967 Artist $5,000; 1977 Artist $7,500
Claudia Kuehnl, New Paltz, NY. 1975 Crafts $5,000
Suzanne Kuffler, Newton, MA. 1978 Video $7,500
Ronald Kuivila, Middletown, CT. 1985 New Genres $5,000
Heidi Kumao, Syracuse, NY. 1992 Photo $20,000
Carol Kumata, Pittsburgh, PA. 1981 Crafts $4,000; 1984 Crafts $15,000
Ted Kurahara, New York, NY. 1985 Painting $15,000
Tetsuo Kusana, Logan, UT. 1976 Crafts $5,000
Jane Kutzer, Oakland, CA. 1987 Painting $5,000
Takaaki Kuwayama, New York, NY. 1969 Artist $5,000
Jerry Kwan, New York, NY. 1995 Painting $20,000
Paul Kwilecki, Bainbridge, GA. 1980 Photo $10,000
Eva Kwong, Kent, OH. 1988 Crafts $5,000

L

Joan La Barbara, New York, NY. 1979 Conceptual/Performance/New Genres $10,000
Tony Labat, San Francisco, CA. 1983 Video $5,000; 1987 New Genres $15,000
Leslie Labowitz, Venice, CA. 1982 Conceptual/Performance/New Genres $5,000
Thomas Lacagnina, Alfred, NY. 1980 Crafts $10,000
Johannes Lacher, Los Angeles, CA. 1983 Painting $15,000
Stephen Lack, New York, NY. 1987 Painting $15,000; 1993 Painting $20,000
David Lackey, Columbia, SC. 1979 Conceptual/Performance/New Genres $3,000
Jane Lackey, Kansas City, MO. 1984 Crafts $5,000; 1988 Crafts $15,000
Suzanne Lacy, Oakland, CA. 1979 Conceptual/Performance/New Genres $3,000; 1981

Conceptual/Performance/New Genres $12,500; 1985 New Genres $15,000; 1993 New Genres $20,000
Gabriel Laderman, New York, NY. 1982 Painting $25,000; 1987 Painting $15,000
Cheryl Laemmle, New York, NY. 1985 Painting $5,000; 1987 Painting $5,000
Gyongy Laky, Berkeley, CA. 1976 Crafts $5,000
Gina Lamb, Inglewood, CA. 1991 New Genres $20,000
Ellen Land-Weber, Arcata, CA. 1975 Photo $5,000; 1980 Photo $10,000; 1982 Photo $25,000
Alan Lande, Seattle, WA. 1979 Video $3,000; 1985 New Genres $5,000
Mary Landi, Kalmazoo, MI. 1975 Printmaking/Drawing/Artists' Books $3,000
Richard Landis, Globe, AZ. 1977 Crafts $5,000
Richard Landry, New York, NY. 1976 Video $5,000
Lois Lane, New York, NY. 1978 Artist $7,500
William Lane, Long Beach, CA. 1987 Painting $15,000
Randolph Langenbach, Cambridge, MA. 1971 Photo $2,000
Bernard Langlais, Thomaston, ME. 1977 Artist $7,500
Ragnhild Langlet, Sausalito, CA. 1980 Crafts $10,000
Edna Langley, Elton, LA. 1976 Crafts $5,000
Dean Langworthy, Chicago, IL. 1988 Sculpture $5,000
Terence LaNoue, New York, NY. 1973 Artist $7,500; 1983 Painting $15,000
Ellen Lanyon, New York, NY. 1974 Artist $7,500; 1987 Painting $15,000
Louis Lanzano, New York, NY. 1979 Photo $10,000
Beth Lapides, New York, NY. 1982 Printmaking/Drawing/Artists' Books $5,000, 1985 New Genres $5,000
Benje LaRico, New York, NY. 1989 Painting $15,000
Lynda LaRoche, Bloomington, IN. 1988 Crafts $5,000
Edward Larson, Libertyville, IL. 1981 Crafts $12,500
Philip Larson, Minneapolis, MN. 1979 Artist $3,000; 1981 Sculpture $12,500
William Larson, Collegeville, PA. 1971 Photo $ 1500; 1980 Photo $10,000; 1986 Photo $15,000; 1992 Photo $20,000
Pat Lasch, New York, NY. 1980 Sculpture $10,000
Jonathan Lasker, New York, NY. 1987 Painting $5,000; 1989 Painting $15,000
Geoffrey Lasko, Manitou Springs, CO. 1985 Printmaking/Drawing/Artists' Books $5,000
David Lasry, New York, NY. 1993 Painting $20,000
Paul Laster, New York, NY. 1985 Printmaking/Drawing/Artists' Books $5,000; 1989 New Genres $5,000
Dennis Laszuk, Chicago, IL. 1984 Sculpture $5,000
Barbara Latham, Chicago, IL. 1980 Video $3,000
Barbara Lattanzi, Buffalo, NY. 1984 Photo $5,000
Stephen Laub, New York, NY. 1978 Conceptual/Performance/New Genres $3,000
Susan Laufer, New York, NY. 1983 Painting $5,000; 1991 Painting $20,000
Ruth Laug, Santa Monica, CA. 1977 Crafts $5,000
Clarence Laughlin, New Orleans, LA. 1973 Photo $5,000; 1976 Photo $7,500
Bruno LaVerdiere, Hadley, NY. 1976 Crafts $5,000; 1990 Crafts $20,000
Jenny Lavin, Brooklyn, NY. 1995 Works On Paper $20,000
Louise Lawler, New York, NY. 1984 Photo $15,000
Matthew Lawrence, Lancaster, PA. 1995 Works On Paper $20,000
Thomas Lawson, Brooklyn, NY. 1982 Painting $5,000; 1985 Painting $5,000; 1989 Painting $15,000
Carol Lawton, Fremont, CA. 1982 Photo $5,000
James Lawton, Penland, NC. 1984 Crafts $5,000; 1986 Crafts $5,000
Arthur Lazar, Albuquerque, NM. 1973 Photo $4,000
Dexter Lazenby, Boston, MA. 1986 Sculpture $5,000
Wayne Lazorik, Albuquerque, NM. 1976 Photo $7,500; 1980 Photo $10,000
Margaret Lazzari, Los Angeles, CA. 1995 Works On Paper $20,000
Dinh Le, Somerville, MA. 1994 Photo $20,000
Christine Le Page, Belleville, WI. 1980 Crafts $10,000
Barry Le Va, New York, NY. 1976 Artist $10,000
James Leach, New York, NY. 1984 Photo $5,000
June Leaf, New York, NY. 1989 Painting $15,000
Daniel Leary, Hudson Falls, NY. 1989 Works On Paper $15,000
Marcus Leatherdale, New York, NY. 1984 Photo $5,000
Ruth Leavitt, Minneapolis, MN. 1974 Printmaking/Drawing/Artists' Books $3,000
William Leavitt, Los Angeles, CA. 1976 Video $2,000; 1991 New Genres $20,000
Kenneth Leback, Seattle, WA. 1978 Video $3,000
Richard Lebowitz, Ballouville, CT. 1988 Photo $15,000
Michael Lebron, New York, NY. 1989 New Genres $5,000
Stanley Lechtzin, Melrose Park, PA. 1973 Crafts $3,000; 1976 Crafts $5,000; 1984 Crafts $15,000
Judy Ledgerwood, Oak Park, IL. 1993 Painting $20,000
Barry Ledoux, New York, NY. 1984 Sculpture $15,000; 1989 Works On Paper $15,000
Baldwin Lee, Oak Ridge, TN. 1984 Photo $5,000; 1990 Photo $20,000
Bing Lee, New York, NY. 1991 Works On Paper $20,000
Catherine Lee, New York, NY. 1989 Painting $5,000
Kermit Lee, Phoenix, AZ. 1979 Photo $3,000
James Leedy, Lake Lotawana, MO. 1990 Crafts $20,000
Doris Leeper, New Smyrna Beach, FL. 1973 Artist $7,500
John Lees, West New York, NJ. 1989 Works On Paper $15,000
Channing Lefebvre, Selkirk, NY. 1974 Artist $3,000
George Legrady, San Francisco, CA. 1994 Photo $20,000
Kathryn Lehar, Chicago, IL. 1988 Sculpture $5,000
Minette Lehmann, San Francisco, CA. 1976 Photo $7,500
Warren Lehrer, New Fairfield, CT. 1985 Printmaking/Drawing/Artists' Books $5,000
Andrew Leicester, Minneapolis, MN. 1974 Artist $1,000; 1976 Artist $5,000; 1981 Sculpture $12,500
Martha Leinroth, Somerville, MA. 1982 Photo $5,000
Mel Leipzig, Trenton, NJ. 1995 Painting $20,000
Elizabeth Leitner, Philadelphia, PA. 1979 Crafts $3,000
Malcolm Leland, Portero, CA. 1976 Crafts $5,000
Annette Lemieux, Brookline, MA. 1983 Printmaking/Drawing/Artists' Books $5,000; 1987 Painting $5,000; 1991 Painting $20,000
Marilyn Lenkowsky, New York, NY. 1975 Artist $4,000
Elizabeth Lennard, New York, NY. 1979 Photo $10,000
Erica Lennard, Sausalito, CA. 1976 Photo $7,500
Dennis Leon, Berkeley, CA. 1978 Artist $7,500
Mark Leong, Somerville, MA. 1992 Photo $20,000
Mark Lere, Los Angeles, CA. 1984 Sculpture $5,000; 1988 Sculpture $15,000
Richard Lerman, Boston, MA. 1989 New Genres $15,000
Arthur Lerner, Chicago, IL. 1980 Printmaking/Drawing/Artists' Books $3,000
Howard Lerner, Silver Spring, MD. 1979 Artist $3,000
Marilyn Lerner, Patchogue, NY. 1987 Painting $15,000
Marion Lerner-Levine, Brooklyn, NY. 1985 Painting $15,000
Alfred Leslie, New York, NY. 1967 Artist $5,000
Kenneth Leslie, Granville, NY. 1983 Painting $5,000
John Leuders-Booth, Cambridge, MA. 1981 Photo $4,000
Leslie Leupp, Lubbock, TX. 1984 Crafts $5,000
Robert Levers, Austin, TX. 1980 Artist $10,000
David Levi/Dimitri Michaelides, St. Louis, MO. 1988 Crafts $5,000
Robert Levin, Brooklyn, NY. 1976 Photo $7,500
Wayne Levin, Honaunau, HI. 1984 Photo $5,000
Arthur Levine, Brooklyn, NY. 1993 Painting $20,000
Edward Levine, Greenville, NC. 1986 Sculpture $15,000
Erik Levine, New York, NY. 1988 Sculpture $5,000; 1990 Sculpture $5,000
Les Levine, New York, NY. 1974 Artist $7,500; 1980 Conceptual/Performance/New Genres $3,000
Marilyn Levine, Oakland, CA. 1976 Artist $2,000; 1980 Artist $10,000
Martin Levine, Oakland, CA. 1977 Printmaking/Drawing/Artists' Books $5,000
Michael Levine, Los Angeles, CA. 1979 Photo $3,000; 1981 Photo $12,500
Sherrie Levine, New York, NY. 1985 New Genres $15,000
Mon Levinson, New York, NY. 1976 Artist $2,000
Peter Levinson, Brooklyn, NY. 1988 Sculpture $5,000
David Levinthal, New York, NY. 1990 Photo $20,000
Helen Levitt, New York, NY. 1976 Photo $7,500
Builder Levy, New York, NY. 1982 Photo $5,000
Jeffrey Lew, New York, NY. 1976 Artist $2,000
Donald Lewallen, New York, NY. 1989 Painting $15,000
Margrit Lewczuk, New York, NY. 1989 Painting $5,000
Lisa Lewenz, Baltimore, MD. 1984 Photo $5,000; 1990 Photo $20,000
Albert Lewis, Lafayette, CA. 1978 Crafts $7,500
Cynthia Lewis, New Haven, VT. 1984 Photo $5,000
John Lewis, Oakland, CA. 1980 Crafts $10,000
Joseph Lewis, New York, NY. 1982 Conceptual/Performance/New Genres $5,000
Marcia Lewis, San Jose, CA. 1976 Crafts $5,000
Norman Lewis, New York, NY. 1973 Artist $7,500
Roy Lewis, Hyattsville, MD. 1984 Photo $5,000
Russel Lewis, New York, NY. 1977 Printmaking/Drawing/Artists' Books $5,000
Sol LeWitt, New York, NY. 1971 Artist $7,500
Thomas Lieber, Tuscola, IL. 1975 Artist $2,000

Al Lieberman, Westport, CA. 1971 Photo $2,000; 1973 Photo $2,000
Louis Lieberman, New York, NY. 1979 Crafts $3,000
Jerome Liebling, Amherst, MA. 1973 Photo $2,500; 1980 Photo $10,000
Ben Lifson, Los Angeles, CA. 1971 Photo $2,000; 1977 Photo $7,500
Alvin Light, San Francisco, CA. 1967 Artist $5,000
Ken Light, Vallejo, CA. 1982 Photo $5,000; 1986 Photo $5,000
Joyce Lightbody, Malibu, CA. 1980 Conceptual/Performance/New Genres $3,000
Glenn Ligon, Brooklyn, NY. 1989 Works On Paper $5,000; 1991 Painting $20,000
Abra Ligorano/Marshall Reese, Brooklyn, NY. 1989 New Genres $5,000
Robert Limone, Des Moines, IA. 1981 Sculpture $12,500
Maya Lin, New York, NY. 1988 Sculpture $5,000
Zhi Lin, Springfield, MO. 1995 Painting $20,000
Ron Linden, Pasadena, CA. 1978 Artist $7,500
Carol Lindsley, New York, NY. 1977 Artist $7,500
Judith Linhares, New York, NY. 1979 Artist $10,000; 1987 Painting $15,000; 1993 Painting $20,000
Joan Lintault, San Bernadino, CA. 1973 Crafts $3,000
Kathryn Lipke, Farmington, CT. 1977 Crafts $5,000
Marvin Lipofsky, Berkeley, CA. 1974 Crafts $3,000; 1976 Crafts $5,000
Larry Lippold, San Francisco, CA. 1986 Crafts $5,000
Donald Lipski, Sag Harbor, NY. 1978 Artist $7,500; 1984 Sculpture $15,000; 1990 Sculpture $20,000
Ken Little, San Antonio, TX. 1982 Crafts $25,000; 1988 Sculpture $15,000
Harold Littlebird, Santa Fe, NM. 1980 Crafts $10,000
Harvey Littleton, Spruce Pine, NC. 1978 Crafts $7,500
Hung Liu, Oakland, CA. 1989 Painting $5,000; 1991 Painting $20,000
Joan Livingstone, Chicago, IL. 1979 Crafts $10,000; 1986 Crafts $15,000; 1992 Crafts $20,000
Gary Lloyd, Los Angeles, CA. 1980 Conceptual/Performance/New Genres $3,000
Marcia Lloyd, Boston, MA. 1981 Painting $12,500
Beth Lo, Missoula, MT. 1994 Crafts $20,000
Robert Lobe, New York, NY. 1979 Artist $10,000; 1984 Sculpture $15,000
Robert Loberg, Berkeley, CA. 1982 Painting $5,000
Mitchell Loch, San Francisco, CA. 1989 New Genres $5,000
Inverna Lockpez, New York, NY. 1976 Artist $2,000
Seymour Locks, San Francisco, CA. 1984 Sculpture $15,000
Peter Lodato, Pasadena, CA. 1976 Artist $2,000; 1978 Artist $7,500
Alan Loehle, Brooklyn, NY. 1985 Painting $5,000
Thomas Loeser, Albany, CA. 1984 Crafts $5,000; 1988 Crafts $5,000; 1990 Crafts $5,000; 1994 Crafts $20,000
Michael Loew, New York, NY. 1976 Artist $10,000
Christine LoFaso, Providence, RI. 1993 Crafts $5,000
Janet Lofquist, Minneapolis, MN. 1981 Sculpture $4,000
Susan Loftin, Atlanta, GA. 1981 Crafts $12,500
Joan Logue, New York, NY. 1978 Video $7,500; 1980 Video $3,000; 1981 Video $12,500; 1985 New Genres $15,000
William Lombardo, New York, NY. 1983 Painting $5,000
Antony Long, Paris, FO. 1979 Artist $10,000
Bert Long, Shepherd, TX. 1987 Painting $5,000
Charles Long, New York, NY. 1994 Sculpture $20,000
Randy Long, Bloomington, IN. 1982 Crafts $5,000; 1984 Crafts $5,000
Brian Longe, Oakland, CA. 1983 Painting $15,000
Robert Longo, New York, NY. 1978 Conceptual/Performance/New Genres $3,000; 1982 Conceptual/Performance/New Genres $25,000
Vincent Longo, New York, NY. 1974 Printmaking/Drawing/Artists' Books $3,000
Fred Lonidier, La Jolla, CA. 1980 Conceptual/Performance/New Genres $3,000; 1982 Photo $5,000
Dona Look, Algoma, WI. 1988 Crafts $5,000
Felix Lopez, Espanola, NM. 1984 Crafts $5,000
Martina Lopez, Chicago, IL. 1992 Photo $20,000; 1991 Photo $5,000
Stephen Lorber, New York, NY. 1976 Artist $5,000
Charles Lord, Santa Cruz, CA. 1977 Video $7,500; 1980 Video $10,000; 1985 New Genres $15,000
Sam Losavio, Baton Rouge, LA. 1987 Printmaking/Drawing/Artists' Books $5,000; 1989 Works On Paper $5,000
Robert Lostutter, Chicago, IL. 1985 Painting $15,000
Reagan Louie, Sacramento, CA. 1978 Photo $7,500
Al Loving, New York, NY. 1971 Artist $7,500; 1982 Painting $25,000
Richard Loving, Chicago, IL. 1983 Painting $25,000
David Lowe, New York, NY. 1983 Painting $5,000
Marvin Lowe, Bloomington, IL. 1974 Printmaking/Drawing/Artists' Books $3,000
Truman Lowe, Madison, WI. 1994 Sculpture $20,000
Bruce Lowny, Placitas, NM. 1974 Printmaking/Drawing/Artists' Books $3,000
Cynthia Luber, New York, NY. 1980 Conceptual/Performance/New Genres $3,000
Christopher Lucas, Brooklyn, NY. 1987 Painting $5,000
Manuel Lucero, San Francisco, CA. 1993 New Genres $20,000
Michael Lucero, New York, NY. 1979 Artist $3,000; 1982 Crafts $5,000; 1984 Crafts $15,000
Susan Lucey, Wakefield, MA. 1977 Artist $3,000
Gayle Luchessa, San Anselmo, CA. 1981 Crafts $12,500
Michael Luchs, Ann Arbor, MI. 1979 Artist $10,000; 1989 Painting $15,000
Mary Lucier, New York, NY. 1978 Video $7,500; 1980 Video $3,000; 1981 Video $12,500
Pedro Lujan, San Elozario, TX. 1974 Artist $3,000; 1977 Artist $7,500
Mary Lum, Hornell, NY. 1987 Printmaking/Drawing/Artists' Books $5,000
Jane Lund, Ashfield, MA. 1987 Painting $15,000
Norman Lundin, Seattle, WA. 1983 Printmaking/Drawing/Artists' Books $5,000
David Lurie, Torrance, CA. 1979 Conceptual/Performance/New Genres $3,000
James Lutes, Chicago, IL. 1993 Painting $20,000
Bix Lye, New York, NY. 1974 Printmaking/Drawing/Artists' Books $3,000
Mela Lyman, Cambridge, MA. 1985 Printmaking/Drawing/Artists' Books $5,000
Susan Lyman, Birmingham, MI. 1981 Crafts $12,500
Danny Lyon, Clintondale, NY. 1971 Photo $3,000; 1973 Photo $5,000; 1984 Photo $15,000
Robert Lyon, Baton Rouge, LA. 1984 Sculpture $5,000
Nathan Lyons, Rochester, NY. 1973 Photo $4,200; 1984 Photo $25,000

M

Mila Macek, New York, NY. 1993 Painting $20,000
Wendy Macgaw, Lathrup Village, MI. 1982 Crafts $5,000; 1986 Sculpture $5,000
Margo Machida, New York, NY. 1983 Painting $15,000
Roger Machin, Chicago, IL. 1986 Sculpture $5,000; 1988 Sculpture $5,000
George Maciunas, Great Barrington, MA. 1977 Conceptual/Performance/New Genres $7,500
Roger Mack, Little Rock, AR. 1968 Artist $5,000
Theresa Mack, New York, NY. 1980 Video $3,000
David MacKenzie, San Francisco, CA. 1975 Artist $2,000
David MaClay, San Francisco, CA. 1980 Photo $3,000
Frank Macmurtrie, San Francisco, CA. 1995 New Genres $20,000
Linda MacNeil, Amesbury, MA. 1984 Crafts $5,000
Wendy MacNeil, Lincoln, MA. 1975 Photo $5,000; 1978 Photo $7,500
Medrie MacPhee, New York, NY. 1985 Painting $5,000
Martha Madigan, Philadelphia, PA. 1995 Photo $5,000
Kristina Madsen, Northampton, MA. 1980 Crafts $3,000
Loren Madsen, New York, NY. 1975 Artist $8,000; 1980 Artist $10,000
Steven Madsen, Albuquerque, NM. 1981 Crafts $12,500
Richard Mafong, Atlanta, GA. 1974 Crafts $3,000
Andrew Magdanz, Cambridge, MA. 1979 Crafts $10,000; 1988 Crafts $15,000
Catharine Magel, Glendale, MI. 1986 Crafts $5,000
Mark Magill, New York, NY. 1983 Video $5,000
William Maguire, Homestead, FL. 1977 Photo $7,500; 1980 Photo $10,000
William Mahan, Venice, CA. 1974 Artist $3,000
Susan Mahlstedt, Deerfield, IL. 1980 Crafts $3,000
Ben Mahmoud, Genoa, IL. 1975 Artist $2,000
Tim Main, New York, NY. 1989 Painting $5,000
David Maisel, New York, NY. 1990 Photo $5,000
Christa Maiwald, New York, NY. 1977 Video $7,500; 1980 Video $3,000
Philip Makanna, San Francisco, CA. 1979 Video $3,000
Robert Maki, Seattle, WA. 1968 Artist $5,000; 1985 Printmaking/Drawing/Artists' Books $25,000
James Makins, New York, NY. 1976 Crafts $5,000; 1980 Crafts $10,000
Virginia Maksymowicz, Brooklyn, NY. 1984 Sculpture $5,000
Adal Maldonado, Staten Island, NY. 1975 Photo $5,000
Conrad Malicoat, Provincetown, MA. 1980 Artist $3,000
Constance Mallinson, Paramus, NJ. 1985 Painting $15,000
Samuel Maloof, Alta Loma, CA. 1984 Crafts $25,000
John Malpede, Los Angeles, CA. 1987 New Genres $15,000
Aida Mancillas, Solana Beach, CA. 1991 Works On Paper $20,000
Wesley Mancini, Charlotte, NC. 1980 Crafts $3,000
Mike Mandel, Santa Cruz, CA. 1988 Photo $15,000

Mike Mandel/Larry Sultan, Northridge, CA. 1973 Photo $ 1500; 1976 Photo $7,500
Louise Maney, Cherokee, NC. 1975 Crafts $5,000
Inigo Manglano-Ovalle, Chicago, IL. 1995 New Genres $20,000
Robert Mangold, New York, NY. 1967 Artist $5,000
Sylvia Mangold, Calliccon Center, NY. 1974 Artist $3,000
Kirk Mangus, Mercer, PA. 1982 Crafts $25,000
Roger Manley, Durham, NC. 1984 Photo $5,000
Andrew Mann, Houston, TX. 1975 Video $8,000; 1978 Video $7,500
Sally Mann, Lexington, VA. 1982 Photo $5,000; 1988 Photo $5,000; 1992 Photo $20,000
Story Mann, Durham, NC. 1980 Artist $3,000
Lee Manuel, Cambridge, MA. 1988 Crafts $5,000
Elsie Manville, New York, NY. 1981 Painting $12,500; 1985 Painting $15,000
Robert Mapplethorpe, New York, NY. 1984 Photo $15,000
Louis Marak, Eureka, CA. 1975 Crafts $5,000
Lizbeth Marano, New York, NY. 1978 Artist $7,500; 1984 Sculpture $5,000; 1988 Sculpture $15,000
Cork Marcheski, Minneapolis, MN. 1982 Sculpture $25,000
Christian Marclay, New York, NY. 1985 New Genres $5,000
John Marcoux, Providence, RI. 1990 Crafts $20,000
Marcia Marcus, New York, NY. 1991 Painting $20,000
Peter Marcus, St. Louis, MO. 1984 Works On Paper $3,000; 1985 Printmaking/Drawing/Artists' Books $15,000
Zella Marggraf, Los Angeles, CA. 1974 Crafts $3,000
Boris Margo, New York, NY. 1974 Printmaking/Drawing/Artists' Books $3,000
John Margolies, Santa Monica, CA. 1974 Artist $3,000
Margo Margolis, New York, NY. 1980 Artist $3,000; 1987 Painting $15,000
Louis Marinaro, Ann Arbor, MI. 1984 Sculpture $5,000
Paul Marioni, Seattle, WA. 1975 Crafts $5,000; 1988 Crafts $15,000
Tom Marioni, Berkeley, CA. 1976 Conceptual/Performance/New Genres $5,000; 1980 Conceptual/Performance/New Genres $3,000; 1984 Sculpture $25,000
Mary Ellen Mark, New York, NY. 1977 Photo $7,500; 1980 Photo $10,000; 1990 Photo $20,000
Graham Marks, Scottsville, NY. 1978 Crafts $7,500; 1984 Crafts $15,000
Thomas Markusen, Kendall, NY. 1975 Crafts $5,000
Megan Marlatt, Orange, VA. 1995 Painting $20,000
Jeffrey Maron, New York, NY. 1974 Artist $1,000; 1978 Artist $7,500; 1986 Sculpture $15,000
Dalton Maroney, Arlington, TX. 1986 Sculpture $5,000
William Marpet, New York, NY. 1975 Video $2,000; 1980 Video $3,000
Richard Marquis, Freeland, WA. 1974 Crafts $3,000; 1978 Crafts $7,500; 1990 Crafts $20,000
Gerald Marranca, New York, NY. 1975 Artist $4,000
Diane Marsh, New York, NY. 1985 Painting $5,000
Georgia Marsh, New York, NY. 1987 Painting $5,000; 1989 Works On Paper $15,000
Kerry James Marshall, Chicago, IL. 1991 Painting $20,000
Michael Marston, Brooklyn, NY. 1984 Photo $5,000
Agnes Martin, New York, NY. 1967 Artist $5,000
Andrew Martin, Denver, CO. 1986 Crafts $5,000
Bernard Martin, Richmond, VA. 1995 Painting $20,000
Christopher Martin, Brooklyn, NY. 1989 Painting $5,000; 1993 Painting $20,000
Fred Martin, San Francisco, CA. 1971 Artist $7,500
Katy Martin, New York, NY. 1989 Painting $5,000
Knox Martin, New York, NY. 1973 Artist $7,500
Ray Martin, Oak Park, IL. 1981 Printmaking/Drawing/Artists' Books $12,500; 1985 Printmaking/Drawing/Artists' Books $15,000
Daniel Martinez, Los Angeles, CA. 1989 New Genres $5,000; 1995 New Genres $20,000
Maria Martinez-Canas, Miami, FL. 1988 Photo $5,000
Babette Martino, Blue Bell, PA. 1985 Painting $5,000
Michael Martone, New York, NY. 1975 Photo $5,000
Patricia Martori, Brooklyn, NY. 1986 Sculpture $5,000
Wendy Maruyama, San Diego, CA. 1982 Crafts $5,000; 1984 Crafts $5,000; 1986 Crafts $5,000; 1990 Crafts $20,000
Vaea Marx, Berkeley, CA. 1980 Crafts $10,000
Dennis Masback, New York, NY. 1991 Painting $20,000
George Mason, Portland, ME. 1982 Crafts $5,000; 1986 Crafts $15,000
Karen Massaro, Mazomanie, WI. 1976 Crafts $5,000
Charles Massey, Columbus, OH. 1982 Printmaking/Drawing/Artists' Books $5,000
Julio Mateo, Brooklyn, NY. 1989 Painting $5,000
Grayson Mathews, San Francisco, CA. 1971 Photo $1,000
Gordon Matta-Clark, New York, NY. 1975 Artist $8,000
Alphonse Mattia, Boston, MA. 1984 Crafts $15,000
Charles Mattox, Albuquerque, NM. 1976 Artist $5,000
Cynthia Maughan, Pasadena, CA. 1975 Video $2,000
Richard Mawdsley, Normal, IL. 1977 Crafts $5,000; 1994 Crafts $20,000
William Maxwell, Sacramento, CA. 1983 Conceptual/Performance/New Genres $5,000; 1988 Sculpture $5,000; 1989 New Genres $5,000
Edward Mayer, Delmar, NY. 1979 Artist $10,000; 1986 Sculpture $15,000
Rosemary Mayer, New York, NY. 1979 Artist $10,000
Beverly Mayeri, Mill Valley, CA. 1982 Crafts $5,000; 1988 Crafts $15,000
Laurence Mayers, San Francisco, CA. 1976 Crafts $5,000
Elaine Mayes, San Francisco, CA. 1971 Photo $1,000; 1978 Photo $7,500
Edward Mayo, Washington, DC. 1980 Artist $10,000
Judith Mazur, Los Angeles, CA. 1975 Printmaking/Drawing/Artists' Books $3,000
Jill McArthur, New York, NY. 1989 Works On Paper $5,000
Skeet McAuley, Dallas, TX. 1984 Photo $5,000; 1986 Photo $5,000
Jay McCafferty, San Pedro, CA. 1976 Video $2,000
Anthony McCall, New York, NY. 1974 Artist $3,000
Barbara McCarren, Culver City, CA. 1988 Sculpture $5,000
Kathleen McCarthy, New York, NY. 1988 Sculpture $5,000; 1990 Sculpture $5,000
Paul McCarthy, Altadena, CA. 1976 Conceptual/Performance/New Genres $5,000; 1982 Conceptual/Performance/New Genres $5,000; 1985 New Genres $15,000
William McCartin, New York, NY. 1977 Artist $7,500
Robert McCauley, Rockford, IL. 1982 Printmaking/Drawing/Artists' Books $25,000
Michael McClard, New York, NY. 1977 Conceptual/Performance/New Genres $3,000; 1980 Video $3,000
Mark McCloud, San Francisco, CA. 1981 Sculpture $4,000; 1984 Sculpture $15,000
Allan McCollum, New York, NY. 1987 New Genres $15,000
Mike McCollum, Blue Diamond, NV. 1980 Artist $3,000
Sharon McConnell, Chicago, IL. 1994 Crafts $20,000
Patrick McCormick, Bellingham, WA. 1975 Crafts $5,000
Rod McCormick, Philadelphia, PA. 1990 Crafts $5,000
Sarah McCoubrey, Takoma Park, MD. 1989 Painting $5,000
Ann McCoy, New York, NY. 1975 Artist $4,000; 1977 Artist $7,500; 1989 Works On Paper $15,000
John McCracken, Venice, CA. 1968 Artist $5,000
Melvin McCray, New York, NY. 1980 Video $3,000
John McCuistion, Tacoma, WA. 1979 Crafts $10,000
Joyce McDaniel, Newton, MA. 1984 Sculpture $5,000
Laurie McDonald, Houston, TX. 1983 Video $15,000
Paul McDonough, New York, NY. 1977 Photo $7,500
James McElhinney, Philadelphia, PA. 1987 Painting $15,000
Mark McFadden, Herndon, VA. 1981 Photo $4,000
Lawrence McFarland, Austin, TX. 1979 Photo $10,000; 1984 Photo $15,000; 1990 Photo $20,000
James McGarrell, St. Louis, MO. 1985 Painting $25,000
Phyllis McGibbon, Wellesley, MA. 1995 Works On Paper $20,000
Ed McGowin, New York, NY. 1968 Artist $5,000; 1980 Artist $10,000
Edward McIlvaane, Riverside, RI. 1982 Crafts $5,000
Martha McKay, Chevy Chase, MD. 1980 Artist $3,000
Judy McKie, Boston, MA. 1979 Crafts $10,000; 1982 Crafts $25,000
Trish McKinney, Astoria, NY. 1989 Painting $5,000
John McLaughlin, Los Angeles, CA. 1967 Artist $5,000
Richard McLean, Oakland, CA. 1985 Painting $15,000
James McLendon, Dearborn, MI. 1985 Printmaking/Drawing/Artists' Books $5,000
Paul McMahon, Brooklyn, NY. 1989 New Genres $5,000
David McManaway, Dallas, TX. 1977 Artist $7,500
Jerry McMillan, Los Angeles, CA. 1984 Photo $15,000
Michael McMillen, Santa Monica, CA. 1978 Artist $7,500; 1986 Sculpture $15,000
Thomas McMillin, Los Angeles, CA. 1976 Artist $5,000
Cameron McNall, New York, NY. 1988 Sculpture $5,000
John McNamara, Brookline, MA. 1981 Painting $12,500
John McNaughton, Evansville, IN. 1976 Crafts $5,000; 1992 Crafts $20,000
Dean McNeil, New York, NY. 1988 Sculpture $5,000
George McNeil, Brooklyn, NY. 1967 Artist $5,000
Craig McPherson, New York, NY. 1983 Painting $15,000
Larry McPherson, Chicago, IL. 1975 Photo $5,000; 1979 Photo $10,000
John McQueen, Trumansburg, NY. 1977 Crafts $5,000; 1979 Crafts $10,000; 1986 Crafts $15,000; 1992 Crafts $20,000

Cornelia McSheehy, Boston, MA. 1974 Printmaking/Drawing/Artists' Books $3,000
John McWilliams, Atlanta, GA. 1976 Photo $7,500
Jon Meader, Washington, DC. 1974 Printmaking/Drawing/Artists' Books $3,000
Charles Meaker, Bozeman, MT. 1980 Crafts $3,000
Elizabeth Mechling, Richmond, VA. 1980 Artist $3,000
Rebecca Medel, Smithville, TN. 1986 Crafts $5,000; 1988 Crafts $15,000
Ada Medina, Pittsburgh, PA. 1987 Printmaking/Drawing/Artists' Books $15,000
Susan Meiselas, New York, NY. 1984 Photo $15,000
Neil Meitzler, Seattle, WA. 1967 Artist $5,000
David Mekelburg, Los Angeles, CA. 1974 Crafts $3,000
James Melchert, San Francisco, CA. 1973 Artist $7,500
Margery Mellman, New York, NY. 1993 Painting $20,000
Myron Melnick, Denver, CO. 1990 Crafts $20,000
Andrew Menard, Brooklyn, NY. 1974 Artist $3,000; 1976 Conceptual/Performance/New Genres $5,000
John Mendelsohn, New York, NY. 1987 Painting $15,000
Ana Mendieta, Iowa City, IA. 1977 Conceptual/Performance/New Genres $3,000; 1980 Artist $3,000; 1982 Sculpture $25,000
Tony Mendoza, Columbus, OH. 1981 Photo $4,000; 1986 Photo $5,000; 1990 Photo $20,000
James Merrell, Chicago, IL. 1974 Artist $3,000
Roger Mertin, Rochester, NY. 1976 Photo $7,500
Arnold Mesches, Los Angeles, CA. 1982 Painting $5,000
Ann Messner, New York, NY. 1986 Sculpture $15,000
Bruce Metcalf, Philadelphia, PA. 1977 Crafts $5,000; 1992 Crafts $20,000
Gary Metz, New York, NY. 1973 Photo $3,000; 1980 Photo $10,000
Matthew Metz, Helena, MT. 1990 Crafts $5,000
Ray K. Metzker, Philadelphia, PA. 1975 Photo $5,000; 1988 Photo $15,000
Brian Meunier, Swarthmore, PA. 1984 Sculpture $5,000
Raymond Meuse, Seattle, WA. 1975 Photo $5,000
Melissa Meyer, New York, NY. 1983 Painting $5,000; 1993 Painting $20,000
Joel Meyerowitz, New York, NY. 1978 Photo $7,500
Michael Meyers, Chicago, IL. 1979 Conceptual/Performance/New Genres $3,000; 1987 New Genres $15,000
Chester Michalik, Northampton, MA. 1982 Photo $5,000
Duane Michals, New York, NY. 1976 Photo $7,500
Cathleen Michel, Venice, CA. 1988 Crafts $5,000
Douglas Michels, San Francisco, CA. 1977 Conceptual/Performance/New Genres $7,500
Alan Michelson, Cambridge, MA. 1987 Painting $5,000
David Middlebrook, Los Gatos, CA. 1977 Crafts $5,000
Willie Middlebrook, Compton, CA. 1982 Photo $5,000; 1992 Photo $20,000
Edwin Mieczkowski, Cleveland, OH. 1967 Artist $5,000
Richard Milani, New York, NY. 1983 Painting $5,000
Susan Milano, New York, NY. 1980 Video $10,000
Jay Milder, New York, NY. 1989 Painting $15,000
John Milisenda, Brooklyn, NY. 1988 Photo $5,000
John Millei, Los Angeles, CA. 1989 Works On Paper $5,000
Bradley Miller, Woody Creek, CO. 1994 Crafts $20,000
Branda Miller, Troy, NY. 1985 New Genres $5,000; 1989 New Genres $5,000
Brenda Miller, Greenport, NY. 1976 Printmaking/Drawing/Artists' Books $3,000; 1979 Artist $10,000; 1987 Printmaking/Drawing/Artists' Books $15,000
David Miller, Gansevoort, NY. 1983 Painting $15,000
James Miller, Richmond, VA. 1975 Artist $2,000
John E. Miller, New York, NY. 1989 New Genres $5,000
John M. Miller, Los Angeles, CA. 1987 Painting $15,000; 1993 Painting $20,000
Kay Miller, Iowa City, IA. 1985 Painting $5,000
Larry Miller, New York, NY. 1979 Video $3,000; 1989 New Genres $15,000
Melissa Miller, Austin, TX. 1979 Artist $3,000; 1982 Painting $5,000; 1985 Painting $5,000
Michael Miller, Weyanoke, LA. 1978 Printmaking/Drawing/Artists' Books $7,500; 1990 Crafts $5,000
Sandi Miller, Pittsburgh, PA. 1974 Crafts $3,000
Steve Miller, New York, NY. 1987 Painting $5,000
Mark Milloff, Stockbridge, MA. 1984 Sculpture $5,000
Myra Mimlitsch Gray, East Kingston, NY. 1994 Crafts $20,000
Yong Min, Brooklyn, NY. 1989 New Genres $5,000
Norma Minkowitz, Westport, CT. 1986 Crafts $15,000
Gary Minnix, Cedar Falls, IA. 1981 Photo $4,000
Richard Minsky, New York, NY. 1977 Crafts $5,000
Marilyn Minter, New York, NY. 1989 Painting $5,000
Peter Miraglia, Philadelphia, PA. 1988 Photo $5,000
Richard Misrach, Emeryville, CA. 1973 Photo $3,000; 1977 Photo $7,500; 1984 Photo $15,000; 1992 Photo $20,000
Mary Miss, New York, NY. 1974 Artist $3,000; 1975 Artist $8,000; 1984 Sculpture $15,000
Julio Mitchel, Brooklyn, NY. 1982 Photo $25,000; 1992 Photo $20,000
Dennis Mitchell, Evanston, IL. 1975 Crafts $5,000
James Mitchell, San Francisco, CA. 1973 Photo $3,500
Robin Mitchell, Santa Monica, CA. 1987 Painting $15,000
Nancy Mitchnick, Lancaster, CA. 1987 Painting $15,000
George Miyasaki, San Francisco, CA. 1980 Printmaking/Drawing/Artists' Books $3,000; 1985 Painting $15,000
Mineo Mizuno, Los Angeles, CA. 1981 Crafts $12,500
David Mocarski, Irvine, CA. 1982 Printmaking/Drawing/Artists' Books $5,000
Stanley Mock, Santa Monica, CA. 1982 Photo $5,000
Paul Mogensen, New York, NY. 1980 Artist $10,000
Susan Mogul, Los Angeles, CA. 1989 New Genres $5,000
Gary Molitor, San Francisco, CA. 1967 Artist $5,000
Lynette Molnar, San Francisco, CA. 1992 Photo $20,000
Patrica Monaco, Oakland, CA. 1984 Photo $5,000
Janet Monafo, Lexington, MA. 1982 Painting $5,000
Carol Mondt, Los Angeles, CA. 1976 Crafts $5,000
Meredith Monk, New York, NY. 1987 New Genres $15,000
Nancy Monk, Pasadena, CA. 1986 Crafts $5,000; 1990 Crafts $5,000
Linda Montano, Kingston, NY. 1977 Video $7,500; 1985 New Genres $5,000
Clifton Monteith, Lake Ann, MI. 1992 Crafts $20,000
James Montford, Norwich, CT. 1993 New Genres $20,000
John Monti, Brooklyn, NY. 1986 Sculpture $15,000
Kenneth Montieth, Jamaica Plain, MA. 1976 Artist $2,000
Judith Moonelis, New York, NY. 1980 Crafts $3,000; 1986 Crafts $5,000
Benjamin Moore, Seattle, WA. 1990 Crafts $20,000
Frank Moore, Berkeley, CA. 1985 New Genres $5,000
Gordon Moore, New York, NY. 1982 Painting $5,000
John L. Moore, New York, NY. 1987 Painting $5,000
John P. Moore, Boston, MA. 1982 Painting $25,000; 1991 Painting $20,000
Shelley Moore, Seattle, WA. 1985 Painting $5,000
Stefan Moore, New York, NY. 1978 Video $7,500
Susan Moore, Philadelphia, PA. 1989 Works On Paper $5,000
Charlotte Moorman, New York, NY. 1978 Conceptual/Performance/New Genres $7,500
Ruth Mordy, 1981 Crafts $12,500
Joey Morgan, Brooklyn, NY. 1989 New Genres $5,000; 1995 New Genres $20,000
Kenneth Morgan, Coventry, CT. 1983 Painting $5,000
Jerry Moriarty, New York, NY. 1977 Artist $7,500
Hiromitsu Morimoto, New York, NY. 1980 Photo $10,000
Dennis Morinaka, 1982 Crafts $5,000; 1984 Crafts $15,000
John Morita, Honolulu, HI. 1985 Printmaking/Drawing/Artists' Books $5,000
Joan Morocco, Saratoga, CA. 1973 Photo $4,000
Bruce Morosko, N. Olmstead, OH. 1979 Crafts $3,000
Owen Morrel, New York, NY. 1981 Sculpture $12,500
Gregg Morris, Elkton, MD. 1987 Painting $5,000
Robert Morris, New York, NY. 1967 Artist $5,000
William Morris, Arlington, WA. 1994 Crafts $20,000
Art Morrison, Marion, IA. 1978 Crafts $7,500
Robert Morrison, Reno, NV. 1990 Sculpture $20,000
William Morrison, Fresno, CA. 1977 Conceptual/Performance/New Genres $7,500
Marcia Morse, Honolulu, HI. 1981 Crafts $12,500
Margaret Morton, New York, NY. 1992 Photo $20,000
Ree Morton, New York, NY. 1975 Artist $8,000
Edward Moses, Venice, CA. 1976 Painting $5,000
Robert Moskowitz, New York, NY. 1975 Artist $4,000
Sonia Moskowitz, New York, NY. 1980 Photo $3,000
Kim Mosley, Florissant, MO. 1981 Photo $12,500
Charles Moss, W. Brockport, ME. 1980 Crafts $10,000
Joe Moss, Newark, DE. 1980 Sculpture $10,000
Andrew Moszynski, New York, NY. 1985 Printmaking/Drawing/Artists' Books $5,000
Eleanor Moty, Madison, WI. 1975 Crafts $5,000; 1988 Crafts $15,000
Joyce Moty, Seattle, WA. 1978 Crafts $7,500
Grant Mudford, Los Angeles, CA. 1980 Photo $10,000
Kathy Muehlemann, New York, NY. 1987 Painting $5,000
Stephen Mueller, New York, NY. 1993 Painting $20,000

Phyllis Mufson, San Francisco, CA. 1980 Crafts $3,000
Kathlene Mulcahy, Pittsburgh, PA. 1979 Crafts $10,000
Michael Mulhern, New York, NY. 1987 Painting $15,000
Matt Mullican, New York, NY. 1978 Conceptual/Performance/New Genres $3,000; 1980 Conceptual/Performance/New Genres $3,000; 1983 Conceptual/Performance/New Genres $15,000
Barbara Munger, Los Angeles, CA. 1973 Artist $7,500
Celia Munoz, Arlington, TX. 1988 Photo $5,000; 1991 New Genres $20,000
Paul Munson, Radford, VA. 1979 Artist $10,000
Antonio Muntadas, New York, NY. 1985 New Genres $15,000
Steve Murakishi, Bloomfield Hills, MI. 1989 Works On Paper $5,000
Hiroshi Murata, New York, NY. 1975 Printmaking/Drawing/Artists' Books $3,000
Catherine Murphy, Poughkeepsie, NY. 1979 Artist $10,000; 1989 Painting $15,000
Mary Murphy, Elkins Park, PA. 1993 Painting $20,000
Clark Murray, Los Angeles, CA. 1967 Artist $5,000
Frances Murray, Tucson, AZ. 1986 Photo $5,000
Judith Murray, New York, NY. 1983 Painting $15,000
Robert Murray, Los Angeles, CA. 1969 Artist $5,000
Gwynn Murrill, Agoura, CA. 1984 Sculpture $15,000
Jay Musler, San Francisco, CA. 1982 Crafts $25,000
Forrest Myers, New York, NY. 1980 Artist $10,000
Frances Myers, Hollandale, WI. 1974 Printmaking/Drawing/Artists' Books $3,000; 1985 Printmaking/Drawing/Artists' Books $15,000
Gifford Myers, Altedena, CA. 1979 Crafts $10,000
Joel Myers, Bloomington, IL. 1976 Crafts $5,000; 1984 Crafts $15,000
Rita Myers, New York, NY. 1976 Video $2,000; 1980 Video $10,000; 1987 New Genres $15,000

N

Deborah Nadoolman, Los Angeles, CA. 1974 Crafts $3,000
Patrick Nagatani, Albuquerque, NM. 1984 Photo $15,000; 1992 Photo $20,000
Fred Nagelbach, Evanston, IL. 1986 Sculpture $5,000
Ron Nagle, San Francisco, CA. 1975 Crafts $5,000; 1979 Crafts $10,000; 1986 Crafts $15,000
Nabil Nahas, New York, NY. 1980 Artist $3,000
Jiro Naito, New York, NY. 1990 Sculpture $5,000
Kenjilo Nanao, Berkeley, CA. 1980 Printmaking/Drawing/Artists' Books $3,000
Anthony Naponic, Kansas City, MO. 1983 Painting $5,000
Dann Nardi, Bloomington, IL. 1986 Sculpture $5,000; 1988 Sculpture $5,000
Paul Narkiewicz, New York, NY. 1981 Painting $12,500
Bruce Nauman, Mill Valley, CA. 1968 Artist $5,000
Mario Naves, Brooklyn, NY. 1989 Works On Paper $5,000
Geoffrey Naylor, Gainsville, FL. 1968 Artist $5,000
Louise Neaderland, New York, NY. 1985 Printmaking/Drawing/Artists' Books $15,000
Mo Neal, Lincoln, NE. 1994 Sculpture $20,000
Joseph Nechvatal, New York, NY. 1985 Printmaking/Drawing/Artists' Books $5,000
Alice Neel, New York, NY. 1973 Artist $7,500; 1983 Painting $25,000
Eileen Neff, Philadelphia, PA. 1988 Photo $5,000
Thomas Neff, Lafayette, CO. 1982 Photo $5,000
Ross Neher, New York, NY. 1989 Painting $5,000
Roberta Neiman, New York, NY. 1978 Photo $7,500
Joyce Neimanas, Chicago, IL. 1979 Photo $10,000; 1982 Photo $25,000; 1990 Photo $20,000
Dona Nelson, New York, NY. 1979 Artist $10,000; 1987 Painting $15,000
James Nelson, Pittsburgh, PA. 1989 Painting $5,000
Joan Nelson, Brooklyn, NY. 1985 Painting $5,000
Lisa Nelson, Northampton, MA. 1980 Video $3,000
Manuel Neri, Benicia, CA. 1967 Artist $5,000; 1980 Artist $10,000
Beatrice Nettles, Urbana, IL. 1979 Photo $10,000; 1988 Photo $15,000
Jim Neu, Brooklyn, NY. 1985 New Genres $5,000
George Neubert, Oakland, CA. 1980 Artist $3,000
Max Neuhaus, New York, NY. 1977 Artist $7,500; 1981 Sculpture $12,500; 1988 Sculpture $15,000
Michael Newhall, Milwaukee, WI. 1985 Painting $5,000
Alan Newman, Brooklyn, NY. 1973 Photo $5,000
Elizabeth Newman, Chicago, IL. 1988 Sculpture $5,000
John Newman, Kansas City, KS. 1985 Printmaking/Drawing/Artists' Books $5,000
John Avery Newman, Fayetteville, AR. 1986 Sculpture $15,000
Carlton Newton, San Francisco, CA. 1980 Artist $10,000
Gordon Newton, Mason, MI. 1979 Artist $3,000; 1983 Printmaking/Drawing/Artists' Books $15,000
Lee Newton, Boston, MA. 1980 Artist $10,000
Long Nguyen, Oakland or Upland, CA. 1989 Works On Paper $5,000
Glugio Nicandro, Los Angeles, CA. 1983 Conceptual/Performance/New Genres $15,000
Daphne Nichols, Philadelphia, PA. 1983 Conceptual/Performance/New Genres $5,000
Laura Nicholson, Houston, TX. 1986 Crafts $5,000
Natasha Nicholson, Irvine, CA. 1979 Artist $3,000
George Nick, Georgetown, MA. 1976 Artist $5,000
John Nickerson, Louisville, CO. 1981 Crafts $12,500
Terry Niedzialek, Flicksville, PA. 1988 Sculpture $5,000
Margaret Nielsen, Los Angeles, CA. 1987 Painting $15,000
Gladys Nilsson, Wilmette, IL. 1974 Artist $7,500; 1989 Works On Paper $15,000
Susan Nininger, Seattle, WA. 1979 Crafts $3,000
Linda Nishio, San Carlos, CA. 1987 New Genres $5,000
Nicholas Nixon, Cambridge, MA. 1976 Photo $7,500; 1980 Photo $10,000; 1986 Photo $15,000
Kevin Noble, New York, NY. 1979 Artist $3,000; 1987 Painting $5,000
Jerry Noe, Chapel Hill, NC. 1976 Artist $5,000
Francis Noel, Bozeman, MT. 1982 Printmaking/Drawing/Artists' Books $5,000
Gary Noffke, Farmington, GA. 1990 Crafts $20,000
Anne Noggle, Albuquerque, NM. 1975 Photo $5,000; 1978 Photo $7,500; 1988 Photo $15,000
William Noland, New York, NY. 1986 Sculpture $15,000
Richard Nonas, New York, NY. 1976 Artist $2,000; 1986 Sculpture $15,000
Carol Nordgren, Washington, DC. 1980 Artist $3,000
Maria Nordman, Santa Monica, CA. 1974 Artist $7,500; 1982 Conceptual/Performance/New Genres $25,000
Barbara Norfleet, Cambridge, MA. 1982 Photo $5,000; 1984 Photo $15,000
Kenda North, Chicago, IL. 1978 Photo $7,500
Will Northerner, Chicago, IL. 1983 Painting $5,000
Ann Norton, Bristol, RI. 1981 Sculpture $12,500
Patsy Norvell, New York, NY. 1976 Artist $2,000
Richard Notkin, Myrtle Point, OR. 1979 Artist $3,000; 1981 Sculpture $12,500; 1988 Crafts $15,000
Walter Nottingham, River Falls, WI. 1974 Crafts $3,000
Lorie Novak, New York, NY. 1990 Photo $20,000
Barbara Novello, Malvern, PA. 1977 Crafts $5,000
Wayne Nowack, Cedar Falls, IA. 1973 Artist $7,500
Ira Nowinski, San Francisco, CA. 1973 Photo $4,000
Thomas Nozkowski, New York, NY. 1981 Painting $4,000
Robert Nugent, Mt. Shasta, CA. 1979 Crafts $10,000
James Nutt, Wilmette, IL. 1974 Artist $7,500; 1989 Painting $15,000
Obaji Nyambi, Chicago, IL. 1993 Works On Paper $20,000

O

Nance O'Banion, Oakland, CA. 1982 Crafts $5,000; 1988 Crafts $15,000
John O'Connor, Bergen, NY. 1974 Crafts $3,000
Thomas O'Connor, Albany, NY. 1974 Printmaking/Drawing/Artists' Books $3,000
Terrell O'Donnell, Redondo Beach, CA. 1974 Artist $3,000
Lorraine O'Grady, New York, NY. 1983 Conceptual/Performance/New Genres $5,000
Brigid O'Hanrahan, Bloomington, IN. 1980 Crafts $3,000
Carol O'Hara, Sacramento, CA. 1984 Sculpture $5,000
Alex O'Neal, Los Angeles, CA. 1987 Painting $5,000
Elaine O'Neil, Dorchester, MA. 1990 Photo $20,000
Matt O'Neill, Denver, CO. 1989 Painting $5,000
Jacqueline O'Regan, Baltimore, MD. 1987 Painting $5,000
John O'Reilly, Worcester, MA. 1988 Photo $5,000
Michael O'Reilly, Philadelphia, PA. 1995 New Genres $20,000
Arthur Oakes, Tuscaloosa, AL. 1974 Artist $3,000
John Obuck, New York, NY. 1979 Artist $3,000; 1980 Artist $10,000; 1987 Painting $15,000
Manuel Ocampo, Los Angeles, CA. 1995 Painting $20,000
Starr Ockenga, Boston, MA. 1981 Photo $12,500
Masayuki Oda, Los Angeles, CA. 1988 Sculpture $5,000
Jeffrey Oestreich, Taylors Falls, MN. 1986 Crafts $15,000
Jack Ogden, Sacramento, CA. 1973 Artist $7,500
David Ohannesian, Seattle, WA. 1980 Crafts $10,000
Douglas Ohlson, New York, NY. 1976 Artist $5,000

Tetsu Okuhara, New York, NY. 1988 Photo $15,000
Pat Oleszko, New York, NY. 1978 Conceptual/Performance/New Genres $3,000; 1985 New Genres $5,000; 1987 New Genres $15,000; 1993 New Genres $20,000
Nathan Oliveira, Stanford, CA. 1974 Artist $7,500
Marvin Oliver, Seattle, WA. 1988 Crafts $15,000
Arthur Ollman, San Francisco, CA. 1979 Photo $10,000
James Olson, Chicago, IL. 1988 Sculpture $5,000
Michael Olszewski, Philadelphia, PA. 1979 Crafts $10,000
Margit Omar, Venice, CA. 1980 Artist $3,000
John Opie, Pleasant Valley Station, PA. 1968 Artist $5,000; 1989 Painting $15,000
James Opinsky, Washington, DC. 1980 Artist $3,000
Dennis Oppenheim, New York, NY. 1974 Artist $7,500; 1981 Sculpture $12,500
Edmund Oppenheim, Santa Fe, NM. 1980 Crafts $10,000
John Opper, Amagansett, NY. 1974 Artist $7,500
John Orentlicher, Ann Arbor, MI. 1976 Video $2,000
Judith Ornstein, Brooklyn, NY. 1978 Printmaking/Drawing/Artists' Books $3,000; 1983 Painting $5,000
Deborah Oropallo, Berkeley, CA. 1991 Painting $20,000
Eric Orr, Venice, CA. 1978 Artist $7,500; 1982 Sculpture $25,000
Oliver Ortiz, Arroyo Seco, NM. 1981 Painting $4,000
Kevin Osborn, Arlington, VA. 1983 Printmaking/Drawing/Artists' Books $5,000; 1985 Printmaking/Drawing/Artists' Books $5,000
Jere Osgood, Wilton, NH. 1980 Crafts $10,000; 1988 Crafts $25,000
Mari Oshima, Brooklyn, NY. 1990 Sculpture $5,000
Kazuma Oshita, New York, NY. 1986 Sculpture $5,000
Pepon Osorio, Bronx, NY. 1988 Sculpture $5,000
Michael Osterhout, New York, NY. 1984 Sculpture $5,000; 1987 New Genres $5,000
Danuta Otfinowski, San Francisco, CA. 1979 Photo $10,000
Greg Ott, Baltimore, MD. 1976 Printmaking/Drawing/Artists' Books $3,000
Jacqueline Ott, Providence, RI. 1988 Crafts $5,000
Sabina Ott, Los Angeles, CA. 1989 Painting $5,000
Thomas Otterness, Brooklyn, NY. 1994 Sculpture $20,000
Tony Oursler, Jamaica Plains, MA. 1981 Video $4,000; 1983 Video $15,000; 1989 New Genres $5,000
John Outterbridge, Los Angeles, CA. 1994 Sculpture $20,000
Frank Owen, Keene Valley, NY. 1978 Artist $7,500; 1989 Painting $15,000
Gene Owens, Fort Worth, TX. 1968 Artist $5,000
William Owens, Livermore, CA. 1975 Photo $5,000
Winifred Owens, Alexandria, VA. 1976 Crafts $5,000
Michele Owings, New York, NY. 1983 Painting $5,000
Frank Ozereko, Auburn, AL. 1980 Crafts $10,000

P

Ann Pachner, New York, NY. 1984 Sculpture $15,000
Ann Page, Los Angeles, CA. 1984 Sculpture $15,000
John Page, Cedar Falls, IA. 1974 Printmaking/Drawing/Artists' Books $3,000
Karen Page, Beaver Falls, PA. 1992 Crafts $20,000
Geoffrey Pagen, Portland, OR. 1982 Crafts $5,000
Patti Paige, New York, NY. 1980 Artist $3,000
Nam June Paik, New York, NY. 1977 Video $10,000
Timo Pajunen, Point Richmond Station, CA. 1977 Photo $7,500; 1980 Photo $10,000
Carl Palazzolo, Robinhood, ME. 1987 Painting $15,000
Charlemagne Palestine, New York, NY. 1980 Video $10,000
Albert Paley, Rochester, NY. 1976 Crafts $5,000; 1979 Crafts $10,000; 1984 Crafts $25,000
Marion Palfi, Los Angeles, CA. 1975 Photo $5,000
Cynthia Pannucci, New York, NY. 1982 Crafts $5,000
Tod Papageorge, Cambridge, MA. 1973 Photo $4,000; 1976 Photo $7,500
Harriet Pappas, Nashville, TN. 1984 Sculpture $5,000
Marilyn Pappas, Miami, FL. 1973 Crafts $3,000
Will Pappenheimer, Somerville, MA. 1990 Crafts $5,000
John Paquette, Sacramento, CA. 1975 Printmaking/Drawing/Artists' Books $3,000
Esther Parada, Oak Park, IL. 1982 Photo $5,000; 1988 Photo $15,000
Joan Parcher, Providence, RI. 1990 Crafts $5,000
Bart Parker, Providence, RI. 1973 Photo $5,000; 1981 Photo $12,500
Ray Parker, New York, NY. 1967 Artist $5,000
William Parker, Eastford, CT. 1980 Photo $10,000; 1982 Photo $25,000
John Parks, New York, NY. 1987 Painting $5,000
Charles Parriott, Seattle, WA. 1990 Crafts $5,000
Ivy Parsons, Baltimore, MD. 1982 Sculpture $5,000
Helen Pashgian, Pasadena, CA. 1986 Sculpture $15,000
Phil Pasquini, Sacremento, CA. 1980 Artist $10,000
Peter Passuntino, New York, NY. 1983 Painting $15,000
Stephen Paternite, Akron, OH. 1974 Artist $3,000
Rosa Patino, Ann Arbor, MI. 1979 Conceptual/Performance/New Genres $3,000
Izhar Patkin, New York, NY. 1987 Painting $5,000
Mary Patten, Chicago, IL. 1993 New Genres $20,000
Curtis Patterson, Atlanta, GA. 1994 Sculpture $20,000
David Patterson, Somerville, MA. 1987 Painting $5,000
Raymond Patterson, Pacific Palisades, CA. 1980 Artist $3,000
Robert Patterson, Alpharetta, GA. 1985 Printmaking/Drawing/Artists' Books $5,000
Thomas Patti, Savoy, MA. 1978 Crafts $7,500
Tom Patton, Normandy, MO. 1990 Photo $5,000
Kathryn Paul, Murphysboro, IL. 1982 Photo $5,000
Rick Paul, Lafayette, IN. 1990 Sculpture $20,000
Brian Paulsen, Grand Forks, ND. 1981 Painting $4,000
Michael Paulson, Greenbush, MI. 1991 Works On Paper $20,000
Robert Paulson, 1989 Works On Paper $5,000
James Pavlicovic, New York, NY. 1976 Conceptual/Performance/New Genres $2,000
Michael Pavlik, Delhi, NY. 1984 Crafts $15,000
Mitchell Payne, San Francisco, CA. 1973 Photo $3,900
Cliffton Peacock, Boston, MA. 1981 Painting $4,000; 1983 Painting $5,000; 1987 Painting $5,000
Alix Pearlstein, New York, NY. 1988 Sculpture $5,000
Philip Pearlstein, New York, NY. 1969 Artist $5,000
J. Pearson, Albuquerque, NM. 1976 Crafts $5,000
John Pearson, Oberlin, OH. 1975 Artist $2,000
Nicholas Pearson, N. Bennington, VT. 1982 Sculpture $5,000
Ronald Pearson, Deer Isle, ME. 1973 Crafts $3,000; 1978 Crafts $7,500
Donalee Peden, Syracuse, NY. 1987 Printmaking/Drawing/Artists' Books $5,000
Michael Peed, Bozeman, MT. 1978 Crafts $7,500; 1984 Sculpture $5,000
Linda Peer, Brooklyn, NY. 1984 Sculpture $5,000
Jane Peiser, Penland, NC. 1975 Crafts $5,000
Mark Peiser, Penland, NC. 1974 Crafts $3,000
Rina Peleg, New York, NY. 1981 Crafts $12,500
Sally Pennington, Berkeley, CA. 1987 Painting $5,000
Blaylock Peppard, New York, NY. 1989 Painting $5,000
Gilles Peress, New York, NY. 1980 Photo $3,000; 1984 Photo $15,000; 1992 Photo $20,000
Gary Perkins, Highland Park, IL. 1974 Artist $3,000
Philip Perkis, Warwick, NY. 1978 Photo $7,500
Hirsch Perlman, Chicago, IL. 1989 New Genres $5,000; 1991 New Genres $20,000
Joan Perlman, San Francisco, CA. 1980 Printmaking/Drawing/Artists' Books $3,000
Joel Perlman, New York, NY. 1979 Artist $10,000
Abigail Perlmutter, Coral Gables, FL. 1976 Photo $7,500
Lincoln Perry, Moody, ME. 1983 Painting $5,000
Michael Pestel, Los Angeles, CA. 1988 Sculpture $5,000
Robert Peters, Lake Forest, IL. 1983 Conceptual/Performance/New Genres $5,000
Jon Peterson, Los Angeles, CA. 1980 Artist $10,000
Kristin Peterson, Emeryville, CA. 1986 Sculpture $5,000
Mario Petrirena, Decatur, GA. 1988 Crafts $5,000
Richard Petry, Elkins Park, PA. 1981 Photo $4,000
Richard Pettibone, Charlotteville, NY. 1988 Sculpture $15,000
Shirley Pettibone, Los Angeles, CA. 1976 Artist $2,000
Judy Pfaff, New York, NY. 1979 Artist $10,000; 1986 Sculpture $15,000
John Pfahl, Buffalo, NY. 1977 Photo $7,500; 1990 Photo $20,000
Mark Pharis, Houston, MN. 1977 Crafts $5,000; 1980 Crafts $10,000; 1986 Crafts $15,000
Ellen Phelen, New York, NY. 1978 Artist $7,500
Brent Phelps, Denton, TX. 1981 Photo $12,500
Timothy Philbrick, Narragansett, RI. 1988 Crafts $5,000
Donna-Lee Phillips, San Francisco, CA. 1980 Photo $10,000
John Phillips, Chicago, IL. 1983 Painting $5,000
Liz Phillips, Astoria, NY. 1983 Conceptual/Performance/New Genres $5,000; 1985 New Genres $15,000
Mary Phillips, New York, NY. 1984 Crafts $15,000
Matt Phillips, Annandale, NY. 1975 Printmaking/Drawing/Artists' Books $3,000
Michael Phillips, Goshen, MA. 1980 Artist $10,000

Tony Phillips, Chicago, IL. 1978 Video $7,500; 1985 Printmaking/Drawing/Artists' Books $15,000
Frank Piatek, Chicago, IL. 1985 Painting $15,000
Lil Picard, New York, NY. 1980 Conceptual/Performance/New Genres $3,000
Joseph Piccillo, Buffalo, NY. 1979 Artist $10,000
Richard Piccolo, Rome, Italy, 1989 Painting $15,000
Barbara Pickett, Newberg, OR. 1974 Crafts $3,000
Keri Pickett, Minneapolis, MN. 1990 Photo $5,000
Victor Pickett, Norfolk, VA. 1968 Artist $5,000
Pierre Picot, Los Angeles, CA. 1987 Painting $5,000
Robert Piepenburg, Dearborn, MI. 1980 Crafts $10,000
Peter Pierobon, Philadelphia, PA. 1988 Crafts $5,000
Conway Pierson, Santa Barbara, CA. 1975 Crafts $5,000
Hiroki/Eugene Pijanowski, Lafayette, IN. 1978 Crafts $7,500
Irene Pijoan, Roswell, NM. 1982 Painting $5,000
Donald Pilcher, Champaign, IL. 1981 Crafts $12,500
James Pile, Tempe, AZ. 1987 Painting $15,000
Peter Pinchbeck, New York, NY. 1981 Painting $12,500
Howardena Pindell, New York, NY. 1973 Artist $7,500; 1983 Painting $15,000
Sheila Pinkel, Santa Monica, CA. 1979 Photo $3,000; 1982 Photo $5,000
Jody Pinto, Philadelphia, PA. 1979 Artist $10,000
Adrian Piper, Cambridge, MA. 1979 Conceptual/Performance/New Genres $10,000; 1982 Conceptual/Performance/New Genres $25,000
Wenzel Pitelka, Pelham, MA. 1988 Crafts $5,000
Lari Pittman, Los Angeles, CA. 1987 Painting $5,000; 1989 Painting $5,000; 1993 Painting $20,000
Gregory Pitts, Bloomington, IN. 1990 Crafts $5,000
Peter Plagens, Los Angeles, CA. 1977 Artist $7,500; 1985 Painting $15,000
Nancy Pletos, Detroit, MI. 1980 Artist $3,000
Patti Podesta, Los Angeles, CA. 1985 New Genres $5,000; 1993 New Genres $20,000
Marilyn Poeppelmeyer, Tallahassee, FL. 1984 Sculpture $5,000
Lois Polansky, Roslyn, NY. 1983 Printmaking/Drawing/Artists' Books $5,000
Prentice Polk, Tuskegee Institute, AL. 1981 Photo $12,500
Charles Pollock, East Lansing, MI. 1967 Artist $5,000
Donna Polseno, Floyd, VA. 1978 Crafts $7,500; 1986 Crafts $15,000
James Pomeroy, San Francisco, CA. 1975 Artist $3,000; 1979 Conceptual/Performance/New Genres $10,000; 1983 Conceptual/Performance/New Genres $15,000
Carl Pope, Indianapolis, IN. 1993 New Genres $20,000
William L. Pope, Lewiston, ME. 1995 New Genres $20,000
Cynthia Porter, Philadelphia, PA. 1988 Crafts $5,000
Katherine Porter, Boston, MA. 1971 Artist $7,500
Brian Portman, Houston, TX. 1989 Works On Paper $5,000
Marjorie Portnow, Santa Cruz, CA. 1980 Artist $10,000; 1993 Painting $20,000
Richard Posner, Culver City, CA. 1977 Crafts $5,000
Reeva Potoff, Waterbury, CT. 1977 Artist $7,500; 1980 Artist $10,000
Christina Potoski, Fort Worth, TX. 1977 Video $7,500
Donn Potts, Berkeley, CA. 1971 Artist $7,500
Joanna Pousette-Dart, New York, NY. 1989 Painting $15,000
Richard Pousette-Dart, Suffern, NY. 1967 Artist $5,000
Alan Powell, Providence, RI. 1974 Artist $3,000
Carl Powell, Austin, TX. 1981 Crafts $4,000
Dan Powell, Champaign, IL. 1981 Photo $4,000
Gordon Powell, Oak Park, IL. 1986 Sculpture $15,000
Donald Powley, Brooklyn, NY. 1987 Painting $5,000
Judith Poxson-Fawkes, Portland, OR. 1980 Crafts $10,000
Lucio Pozzi, New York, NY. 1983 Painting $15,000
Martin Prekop, Chicago, IL. 1987 Painting $15,000
Conrad Pressma, Louisville, KY. 1979 Photo $10,000
Ann Preston, Valencia, CA. 1988 Sculpture $5,000
Astrid Preston, Santa Monica, CA. 1987 Painting $15,000
Kenneth Price, Los Angeles, CA. 1967 Artist $5,000; 1979 Artist $10,000
James Pridgeon, Seattle, WA. 1983 Conceptual/Performance/New Genres $5,000
Zigmonds Priede, Minneapolis, MN. 1974 Printmaking/Drawing/Artists' Books $3,000
David Prifti, Brighton, MA. 1986 Photo $5,000
Stephen Prina, Los Angeles, CA. 1987 New Genres $5,000; 1989 New Genres $5,000
Douglas Prince, Providence, RI. 1977 Photo $7,500; 1980 Photo $10,000
Richard Prince, New York, NY. 1984 Photo $15,000
Scott Prior, Northampton, MA. 1985 Painting $15,000
Janet Prip, Cranston, RI. 1986 Crafts $15,000
John Prip, Rehoboth, MA. 1986 Crafts $15,000
Joseph Procter, San Francisco, CA. 1978 Conceptual/Performance/New Genres $3,000
Jean Promutico, Sante Fe, NM. 1974 Artist $7,500
Janis Provisor, New York, NY. 1980 Artist $3,000; 1985 Painting $15,000; 1991 Works On Paper $20,000
Max Pruneda, Houston, TX. 1988 Sculpture $5,000
Gerald Pryor, New York, NY. 1976 Artist $2,000; 1978 Artist $7,500
Garnett Puett, Brooklyn, NY. 1988 Sculpture $5,000
Guillermo Pulido, Houston, TX. 1980 Video $3,000
Martin Puryear, Washington, DC. 1977 Artist $7,500
Florence Putterman, Sellingsgrove, PA. 1979 Printmaking/Drawing/Artists' Books $3,000

Q

Narcissus Quagliata, San Francisco, CA. 1977 Crafts $5,000; 1986 Crafts $15,000
Timothy Quay, Philadelphia, PA. 1977 Artist $3,000
Harvey Quaytman, New York, NY. 1983 Painting $15,000
Holt Quentel, Chicago, IL. 1989 Painting $5,000
Robin Quigley, Providence, RI. 1979 Crafts $10,000; 1986 Crafts $15,000
Langdon Quin, Cambridge, MA. 1983 Painting $5,000
Timothy Quinn, Los Angeles, CA. 1988 Sculpture $5,000

R

Raquel Rabinovich, Rhinebeck, NY. 1991 Painting $5,000
David Rabinowitch, New York, NY. 1986 Sculpture $15,000
Elsa Rady, Venice, CA. 1981 Crafts $12,500
Kaare Rafoss, New York, NY. 1975 Artist $2,000
Paul Rahilly, Lexington, MA. 1985 Painting $15,000
Yvonne Rainer, New York, NY. 1974 Artist $3,000
Christina Ramberg, Chicago, IL. 1978 Artist $7,500; 1983 Painting $15,000
Merrill Rambin, Okolona, AR. 1976 Crafts $5,000
Anthony Ramos, New York, NY. 1981 Video $12,500
Joe Ramos, Salinos, CA. 1971 Photo $1,250
Melvin Ramos, Oakland, CA. 1985 Painting $15,000
Mol Ramsden, New York, NY. 1976 Conceptual/Performance/New Genres $10,000
Daniel Ranalli, Newton, MA. 1981 Photo $4,000
Richard Randell, Sacramento, CA. 1967 Artist $5,000
Susan Rankaitis, Inglewood, CA. 1980 Photo $3,000; 1988 Photo $15,000
Scott Rankin, Chicago, IL. 1989 New Genres $5,000; 1993 New Genres $20,000
Edward Ranney, Santa Fe, NM. 1975 Photo $5,000
Brian Ransom, Claremont, CA. 1986 Sculpture $5,000
Armando Rascon, San Francisco, CA. 1987 Painting $5,000
Robert Rasmussen, Fairfax, CA. 1981 Sculpture $12,500
Alan Rath, Oakland, CA. 1988 Sculpture $5,000
William Ravanesi, Boston, MA. 1982 Photo $5,000
Charles Ray, Inglewood, CA. 1985 New Genres $5,000; 1988 Sculpture $5,000
James Raymo, Grosse Point Park, MI. 1980 Photo $3,000
Harold Reddicliffe, Newtonville, MA. 1981 Painting $12,500; 1985 Painting $15,000
David Reed, New York, NY. 1991 Painting $20,000
Robert Reed, New Haven, CT. 1980 Artist $3,000
Scott Reeds, Los Angeles, CA. 1983 Printmaking/Drawing/Artists' Books $5,000
Richard Reep, Memphis, TN. 1980 Photo $3,000
Richard Reese, McFarland, WI. 1975 Artist $4,000
Daniel Reeves, New York, NY. 1980 Video $10,000; 1987 New Genres $15,000; 1995 New Genres $20,000
Jane Regan, Chicago, IL. 1981 Photo $4,000
Peter Reginato, New York, NY. 1984 Sculpture $15,000
Murray Reich, New York, NY. 1980 Artist $10,000
Dorothy Reid, San Francisco, CA. 1982 Sculpture $5,000; 1985 Printmaking/Drawing/Artists' Books $15,000
David Reif, Laramie, WY. 1979 Artist $3,000
Stanley Reifel, Santa Barbara, CA. 1976 Crafts $5,000
Peter Reiquam, Seattle, WA. 1986 Sculpture $5,000
Peter Reiss, Los Angeles, CA. 1981 Photo $4,000; 1984 Photo $5,000
Roland Reiss, Claremont, CA. 1971 Artist $7,500; 1976 Artist $2,000; 1980 Artist $10,000; 1986 Sculpture $15,000
Don Reitz, Spring Green, WI. 1976 Crafts $5,000
Deborah Remington, New York, NY. 1979 Artist $10,000
Eric Renner, San Lorenzo, NM. 1980 Photo $10,000

Edda Renouf, New York, NY. 1978 Printmaking/Drawing/Artists' Books $3,000
Philip Renteria, Houston, TX. 1982 Painting $5,000
Dorothy Replinger, Urbana, IL. 1976 Crafts $5,000
Marcia Resnick, New York, NY. 1975 Photo $5,000; 1978 Photo $7,500
Minna Resnick, Fort Collins, CO. 1980 Printmaking/Drawing/Artists' Books $3,000
Florence Resnikoff, Oakland, CA. 1973 Crafts $3,000
Susan Ressler, W. Lafayette, IN. 1982 Photo $5,000
Barbara Revelle, Chicago, IL. 1979 Photo $10,000
Nancy Rexroth, Yellow Springs, OH. 1973 Photo $3,000
Jane Reynolds, Fullerton, CA. 1980 Conceptual/Performance/New Genres $3,000
Stephen Reynolds, Chicago, IL. 1987 Painting $5,000
Susan Reynolds, Columbus, OH. 1985 New Genres $5,000
Richard Rezac, Chicago, IL. 1976 Artist $2,000; 1986 Sculpture $15,000
Suzan Rezac, New York, NY. 1984 Crafts $5,000
Curtis Rhodes, Kalamazoo, MI. 1974 Printmaking/Drawing/Artists' Books $3,000
Barbara Riboud, Paris, FO. 1973 Artist $7,500
Anthony Rice, Macon, GA. 1985 Painting $15,000
Dan Rice, Deposit, NY. 1983 Painting $5,000
Jacquelyn Rice, Ann Arbor, MI. 1973 Crafts $3,000; 1977 Crafts $5,000
Leland Rice, Inglewood, CA. 1978 Photo $7,500
Garry Rich, New York, NY. 1974 Artist $3,000
Eugene Richards, Brooklyn, NY. 1975 Photo $5,000; 1982 Photo $25,000; 1990 Photo $20,000
William Richards, Los Angeles, CA. 1976 Artist $2,000
William Richards, Ossining, NY. 1977 Artist $7,500
Sam Richardson, Oakland, CA. 1975 Artist $8,000
Clark Richert, Boulder, CO. 1981 Painting $12,500
Scott Richter, New York, NY. 1984 Sculpture $5,000; 1986 Sculpture $15,000
Gary Rickson, Roxbury, MA. 1971 Artist $7,500
John Rigsby, Evergreen, CO. 1980 Artist $10,000
Faith Ringgold, New York, NY. 1978 Artist $7,500; 1989 Painting $15,000
Yande Rios, Fullerton, CA. 1980 Printmaking/Drawing/Artists' Books $3,000
Curtis Ripley, Richmond, VA. 1979 Crafts $10,000
Cynthia Ripley, Richmond, VA. 1982 Crafts $5,000
Earl Ripling, New York, NY. 1983 Conceptual/Performance/New Genres $5,000; 1985 New Genres $5,000
Thomas Rippon, Chicago, IL. 1974 Artist $1,000; 1981 Crafts $12,500
Rodney Ripps, Lenox, MA. 1980 Artist $10,000; 1989 Painting $15,000
Murray Riss, Memphis, TN. 1979 Photo $10,000
William Ritche, Seattle, WA. 1974 Printmaking/Drawing/Artists' Books $3,000
Richard Ritter, Bakersville, NC. 1984 Crafts $15,000
Victoria Rivers, Sacramento, CA. 1984 Crafts $15,000
Tony Robbin, New York, NY. 1975 Artist $2,000
Allan Robbins, New York, NY. 1981 Video $12,500
Michael Robbins, New York, NY. 1985 Painting $15,000
Sang Roberson, Ormond Beach, FL. 1994 Crafts $20,000
Amy Roberts, Seattle, WA. 1986 Crafts $5,000
Holly Roberts, Corrales, NM. 1986 Photo $5,000; 1988 Photo $15,000
James Roberts, Santa Rosa, CA. 1973 Photo $2,500
Kent Roberts, San Francisco, CA. 1980 Artist $3,000
Kirk Roberts, San Francisco, CA. 1979 Conceptual/Performance/New Genres $3,000
Sue Robinson, Boulder, CO. 1979 Photo $3,000
Walter Robinson, New York, NY. 1982 Painting $5,000
James Roche, Tallahassee, FL. 1975 Artist $8,000; 1982 Sculpture $25,000
Anne Rochette, Brooklyn, NY. 1990 Sculpture $5,000
Dorothea Rockburne, New York, NY. 1974 Artist $7,500
Don Rodan, New York, NY. 1984 Photo $15,000
Mike Roddy, New York, NY. 1980 Artist $3,000
Jose Rodeiro, Cumberland, MD. 1985 Painting $15,000
Geno Rodriguez, New York, NY. 1980 Photo $10,000
Jorge Rodriguez, New York, NY. 1980 Artist $3,000
Joseph Rodriguez, Los Angeles, CA. 1994 Photo $20,000
Patricia Rodriguez, San Francisco, CA. 1988 Sculpture $5,000
Richard Roehl, Venice, CA. 1981 Sculpture $12,500
Mary Roehm, Detroit, MI. 1988 Crafts $5,000
Art Rogers, Point Reyes, CA. 1990 Photo $20,000
Bryan Rogers, San Francisco, CA. 1982 Sculpture $5,000
Steve Rogers, Los Angeles, CA. 1988 Sculpture $5,000
Howard Rogovin, Kansas City, MO. 1969 Artist $5,000
Janice Rogovin, Jamaica Plain, MA. 1982 Photo $5,000
Robert Rohm, Wakefield, RI. 1974 Artist $7,500; 1986 Sculpture $15,000
David Rohn, Putney, VT. 1989 Works On Paper $15,000
Warren Rohrer, Christiana, PA. 1981 Painting $12,500
Charles Roitz, Boulder, CO. 1979 Photo $10,000
Christine Rojek, Chicago, IL. 1986 Sculpture $5,000
Tim Rollins, New York, NY. 1985 New Genres $5,000; 1987 Printmaking/Drawing/Artists' Books $15,000
John Roloff, Oakland, CA. 1977 Crafts $5,000; 1980 Artist $10,000; 1986 Crafts $15,000
Salvatore M. Romano, New York, NY. 1979 Artist $10,000
Mia Roosen, New York, NY. 1988 Sculpture $15,000
Garrison Roots, Boulder, CO. 1981 Sculpture $4,000; 1984 Sculpture $5,000
Mel Rosas, Royal Oak, MI. 1993 Painting $20,000
Lyle Rosbotham, Arlington, VA. 1983 Printmaking/Drawing/Artists' Books $5,000
Herman Rose, New York, NY. 1976 Artist $5,000; 1980 Artist $10,000
Iris Rose, New York, NY. 1989 New Genres $15,000
Leatrice Rose, New York, NY. 1977 Artist $7,500
Peter Rose, Philadelphia, PA. 1983 Conceptual/Performance/New Genres $5,000
Thomas Rose, Minneapolis, MN. 1976 Crafts $5,000; 1981 Sculpture $12,500
Annabeth Rosen, New York, NY. 1979 Crafts $3,000; 1986 Crafts $5,000
Jane Rosen, New York, NY. 1980 Artist $10,000
Kay Rosen, Gary, IN. 1987 Painting $5,000; 1989 Painting $5,000; 1995 Painting $20,000
Ralph Rosenberg, New York, NY. 1967 Artist $5,000
Elizabeth Rosenblum, Boston, MA. 1987 Painting $5,000
Walter Rosenblum, Long Island City, NY. 1977 Photo $7,500
Marc Rosenquist, Trenton, NJ. 1990 Sculpture $5,000
Howard Rosenthal, New York, NY. 1990 Sculpture $5,000
Mel Rosenthal, New York, NY. 1982 Photo $5,000
Rachel Rosenthal, Los Angeles, CA. 1983 Conceptual/Performance/New Genres $15,000
Stephen Rosenthal, New York, NY. 1981 Painting $12,500
Martha Rosler, Brooklyn, NY. 1975 Artist $4,000; 1980 Video $3,000; 1983 Video $15,000; 1994 Photo $20,000
Bobby Ross, Venice, CA. 1985 Painting $15,000
Charles Ross, New York, NY. 1976 Artist $2,000
Ivy Ross, New York, NY. 1982 Crafts $5,000
Judith Ross, Bethlehem, PA. 1986 Photo $5,000
Barbara Rossi, Chicago, IL. 1973 Artist $7,500; 1985 Painting $15,000
Michael Rossman, Philadelphia, PA. 1991 Works On Paper $20,000
Stephen Roszell, Chicago, IL. 1987 New Genres $5,000
Frank Roth, New York, NY. 1977 Artist $7,500
Richard Roth, Columbus, OH. 1991 Painting $20,000
Susan Rothenberg, New York, NY. 1979 Artist $10,000
Jerry Rothman, Laguna Beach, CA. 1984 Crafts $15,000
John Roush, Ranchos de Taos, NM. 1977 Crafts $5,000
Ann Rousseau, New York, NY. 1982 Photo $5,000
Brian Routh, Venice, CA. 1980 Conceptual/Performance/New Genres $3,000
David Row, New York, NY. 1987 Painting $15,000
Anne Rowland, Cambridge, MA. 1986 Photo $5,000
Susan Rowland, Sante Fe, NM. 1977 Artist $7,500
Richard Royal, Seattle, WA. 1988 Crafts $5,000
Richards Ruben, New York, NY. 1980 Artist $10,000
Meridel Rubenstein, Santa Fe, NM. 1982 Photo $5,000; 1992 Photo $20,000
Allan Rubin, New York, NY. 1977 Artist $7,500
Sandra Rubin, Boonville, CA. 1981 Artist ; 1991 Painting $20,000
Gail Rubini, New York, NY. 1982 Printmaking/Drawing/Artists' Books $5,000
Nancy Rubins, New York, NY. 1977 Artist $3,000; 1980 Artist $3,000; 1981 Sculpture $4,000
Edwin Ruda, New York, NY. 1980 Artist $3,000
Eriks Rudans, Tucson, AZ. 1984 Sculpture $5,000
Eric Rudd, Potomac, MD. 1979 Artist $3,000
Ginny Ruffner, Seattle, WA. 1986 Crafts $15,000
Gilberto Ruiz, Miami, FL. 1985 Painting $15,000
Christina Rupp, New York, NY. 1981 Sculpture $4,000; 1984 Sculpture $15,000
Sheron Rupp, Florence, MA. 1986 Photo $5,000; 1994 Photo $20,000
Allen Ruppersberg, Los Angeles, CA. 1976 Artist $5,000; 1982 Printmaking/Drawing/Artists' Books $25,000
Edward Ruscha, Los Angeles, CA. 1967 Artist $5,000; 1978 Artist $7,500
Cynthia Rush, New York, NY. 1980 Video $3,000

Jeffrey Russell, New York, NY. 1986 Sculpture $15,000
Laura Russell, Greenbrae, CA. 1981 Sculpture $4,000
Paul Rutkousky, New Haven, CT. 1979 Video $3,000
Lance Rutledge, Brooklyn, NY. 1989 Works On Paper $5,000
Richard Ryan, New Haven, CT. 1993 Painting $20,000
Bonnie Rychlak, Northampton, MA. 1976 Artist $2,000
Mitch Ryerson, Cambridge, MA. 1988 Crafts $5,000

S

Alison Saar, New York, NY. 1984 Sculpture $5,000; 1988 Sculpture $5,000
Betye Saar, Los Angeles, CA. 1974 Artist $7,500; 1984 Sculpture $25,000
Shuli Sade, New York, NY. 1991 Painting $20,000
Livio Saganic, North Bergin, NJ. 1980 Artist $3,000
Yoshitomo Saito, Oakland, CA. 1994 Sculpture $20,000; 1993 Sculpture $5,000
Ben Sakoguchi, Pasadena, CA. 1980 Artist $3,000; 1995 Painting $20,000
Jorge Salazar, New York, NY. 1980 Artist $10,000
Judith Salomon, Cleveland Heights, OH. 1981 Crafts $12,500
Mary Saltos, San Francisco, CA. 1978 Printmaking/Drawing/Artists' Books $3,000
Jerry Saltz, New York, NY. 1980 Artist $3,000
Mark Saltz, New York, NY. 1983 Painting $5,000
Joe Sam, San Francisco, CA. 1985 Painting $15,000
Samuel Samore, San Anselmo, CA. 1976 Conceptual/Performance/New Genres $2,000; 1979 Photo $3,000
Jim Sanborn, Washington, DC. 1982 Sculpture $5,000; 1986 Sculpture $15,000
John Sanborn, New York, NY. 1978 Video $3,000
Juan Sanchez, Brooklyn, NY. 1983 Painting $5,000
Pauline Sanchez, Inglewood, CA. 1989 Painting $5,000
James Sandall, Whitmore Lake, MI. 1985 Printmaking/Drawing/Artists' Books $5,000
Fred Sandback, New York, NY. 1975 Artist $2,000
Ludwig Sander, New York, NY. 1967 Artist $5,000
Rhea Sanders, New York, NY. 1985 Painting $15,000
Douglas Sanderson, New York, NY. 1981 Painting $12,500
Douglas Sandhage, New York, NY. 1975 Photo $5,000
Daniel Sandin, Chicago, IL. 1980 Video $3,000
Arturo Sandoval, Lexington, KY. 1973 Crafts $3,000; 1992 Crafts $20,000
Hope Sandrow, New York, NY. 1994 Photo $20,000
Jonathan Santlofer, New York, NY. 1983 Painting $15,000; 1989 Painting $15,000
Joseph Santore, New York, NY. 1993 Painting $20,000
Darryl Sapien, San Francisco, CA. 1975 Artist $3,000; 1979 Conceptual/Performance/New Genres $3,000; 1991 Painting $20,000
Alan Saret, Brooklyn, NY. 1975 Artist $4,000; 1986 Sculpture $15,000
Tomiyo Sasaki, New York, NY. 1982 Video $5,000
Toshio Sasaki, Brooklyn, NY. 1986 Sculpture $15,000
Norie Sato, Seattle, WA. 1978 Video $3,000; 1981 Video $12,500
Jane Sauer, St. Louis, MO. 1984 Crafts $5,000; 1990 Crafts $20,000
Richard Sauer, Worcester, MA. 1974 Crafts $3,000
Peter Saul, Austin, TX. 1979 Artist $10,000; 1985 Painting $25,000
Harold Saulson, New York, NY. 1987 Painting $5,000
Gayle Saunders, High Falls, NY. 1977 Crafts $5,000; 1988 Crafts $5,000
Raymond Saunders, Oakland, CA. 1977 Artist $7,500; 1983 Printmaking/Drawing/Artists' Books $15,000
Wade Saunders, Brooklyn, NY. 1988 Sculpture $15,000
E. L. Sauselen, Bucyrus, OH. 1985 Printmaking/Drawing/Artists' Books $5,000
Naomi Savage, Princeton, NJ. 1971 Photo $2,000
Tad Savinar, Portland, OR. 1984 Sculpture $5,000; 1995 Painting $20,000
Richard Savini, Washington, DC. 1982 Painting $5,000
Andrew Savulich, Long Island City, NY. 1986 Photo $5,000
Margo Sawyer, Austin, TX. 1986 Sculpture $5,000
Arthur Sawyers, Richmond, VA. 1973 Photo $5,000
Billy Sax, South Hadley, MA. 1974 Crafts $3,000
Adrian Saxe, Los Angeles, CA. 1986 Crafts $15,000
Italo Scanga, La Jolla, CA. 1973 Artist $7,500; 1980 Artist $10,000
Steven Scarff, Michigan City, IN. 1974 Artist $3,000
Thomas Scarff, Chicago, IL. 1974 Artist $7,500
Alan Scarritt, San Francisco, CA. 1979 Artist $3,000
Pamela Scarvie, Menlo Park, CA. 1974 Artist $3,000
Arthur Schade, New York, NY. 1984 Sculpture $5,000
William Schade, Albany, NY. 1982 Printmaking/Drawing/Artists' Books $5,000
Judith Schaechter, Philadelphia, PA. 1986 Crafts $5,000; 1988 Crafts $5,000
David Schafer, Brooklyn, NY. 1988 Sculpture $5,000
Miriam Schapiro, New York, NY. 1976 Artist $5,000
Lisa Scheer, Washington, DC. 1984 Sculpture $5,000; 1990 Sculpture $5,000
Stephen Scheer, New York, NY. 1981 Photo $4,000
Michael Scheiner, Central Falls, RI. 1986 Crafts $5,000; 1994 Crafts $20,000
Jeffrey Schiff, Boston, MA. 1976 Artist $2,000; 1984 Sculpture $5,000
Alfons Schilling, Brooklyn, NY. 1983 Conceptual/Performance/New Genres $15,000
Cynthia Schira, Lawrence, KS. 1974 Crafts $3,000; 1982 Crafts $25,000
Jeff Schlanger, New Rochelle, NY. 1973 Crafts $3,000
Gary Schlappal, Frederick, MD. 1981 Crafts $12,500
John Schlesinger, Brooklyn, NY. 1986 Photo $5,000; 1988 Photo $5,000
Edward Schmidt, Brooklyn, NY. 1985 Painting $5,000
Jack Schmidt, Toledo, OH. 1984 Crafts $5,000
Bruce Schnabel, New York, NY. 1980 Crafts $3,000; 1983 Printmaking/Drawing/Artists' Books $5,000
Julian Schnabel, New York, NY. 1977 Artist $3,000
Roy Schnackenberg, Chicago, IL. 1975 Artist $4,000
George Schneeman, New York, NY. 1980 Artist $3,000
Carolee Schneemann, New Paltz, NY. 1974 Artist $3,000; 1977 Conceptual/Performance/New Genres $7,500; 1983 Conceptual/Performance/New Genres $25,000
Ira Schneider, New York, NY. 1975 Video $4,000; 1979 Video $10,000
Ursula Schneider, New York, NY. 1985 Printmaking/Drawing/Artists' Books $15,000
Klaus Schnitzer/Charles Sennhauser, Upper Montclair, NJ. 1980 Photo $10,000
Diana Schoenfeld, Eureka, CA. 1980 Photo $3,000
Laure Schoenfeld, Great Neck, NY. 1974 Crafts $3,000
Carole Scholder, Dallas, TX. 1989 Painting $5,000
Laurence Scholder, Dallas, TX. 1975 Printmaking/Drawing/Artists' Books $3,000
Terry Schoonhoven, Los Angeles, CA. 1980 Artist $10,000
Charles Schoore, Houston, TX. 1980 Photo $10,000
Mira Schor, New York, NY. 1985 Painting $15,000
John Schott, New York, NY. 1978 Photo $7,500
Victor Schrager, New York, NY. 1980 Photo $3,000
Jon Schueler, New York, NY. 1980 Artist $10,000
Lee Schuette, Durham, NH. 1976 Crafts $5,000
Norman Schulman, Penland, NC. 1978 Crafts $7,500
Cornelia Schulz, Fairfax, CA. 1981 Painting $12,500
Buky Schwartz, New York, NY. 1988 Sculpture $15,000
Dina Schwartz, Brooklyn, NY. 1976 Crafts $5,000
Elliott Schwartz, New York, NY. 1978 Photo $7,500; 1988 Photo $15,000
Yuri Schwebler, Easton, MD. 1975 Artist $8,000; 1982 Sculpture $25,000
Robert Schwieger, Minot, ND. 1975 Printmaking/Drawing/Artists' Books $3,000
Bill Scott, Sun Valley, CA. 1975 Crafts $5,000
John Scott, Mill Valley, CA. 1981 Printmaking/Drawing/Artists' Books $4,000
Joyce Scott, Baltimore, MD. 1988 Crafts $5,000
Marlene Scott, Rochester, NY. 1974 Artist $3,000
Sean Scully, New York, NY. 1983 Painting $5,000
Steve Seaberg, Atlanta, GA. 1978 Artist $7,500
William Seaman, Cambridge, MA. 1987 New Genres $15,000
Charles Searles, Norristown, PA. 1978 Artist $7,500
Jill Sebastian, Milwaukee, WI. 1985 Printmaking/Drawing/Artists' Books $5,000
Carole Seborovski, Ojai, CA. 1991 Works On Paper $20,000
David Seccombe, New York, NY. 1984 Sculpture $15,000
Vickie Sedman, Jenkintown, PA. 1984 Crafts $5,000
Warren Seelig, Elkins Park, PA. 1975 Crafts $5,000; 1984 Crafts $15,000
Ilene Segalove, Venice, CA. 1976 Video $2,000; 1979 Video $10,000; 1983 Video $15,000
Allan Sekula, Cardiff, CA. 1977 Conceptual/Performance/New Genres $7,500
Johan Selleraad, New York, NY. 1975 Artist $4,000
Nancy Selvin, Berkeley, CA. 1980 Crafts $10,000; 1988 Crafts $15,000
Joan Semmel, New York, NY. 1980 Artist $10,000; 1985 Painting $15,000
Beverly Semmes, New York, NY. 1991 Sculpture $5,000; 1994 Sculpture $20,000
Jake Seniuk, Seattle, WA. 1984 Photo $5,000
Eileen Senner, Los Angeles , CA. 1982 Sculpture $5,000; 1986 Sculpture $5,000
Joseph Senungetuk, Anchorage, AK. 1980 Artist $3,000
Heikki Seppa, St. Louis, MO. 1975 Crafts $5,000
Richard Serra, New York, NY. 1974 Artist $7,500
Rudolph Serra, New York, NY. 1976 Artist $2,000; 1978 Artist $7,500; 1984 Sculpture $15,000

Andres Serrano, New York, NY. 1986 Photo $5,000
Luis Serrano, Los Angeles, CA. 1985 Painting $5,000
Raul Serrano, Brooklyn, NY. 1983 Painting $5,000
Robert Sestok, Detroit, MI. 1984 Sculpture $15,000
Alice Shaddle, Chicago, IL. 1979 Artist $10,000
Mary Shaffer, Silver Spring, MD. 1994 Crafts $20,000
Richard Shaffer, Arlington, TX. 1981 Painting $4,000
Barbara Shamblin, Tuscaloosa, AL. 1979 Photo $10,000
Isaac Shamsud-Din, Portland, OR. 1982 Printmaking/Drawing/Artists' Books $5,000
David Shaner, Bigfork, MT. 1973 Crafts $3,000; 1978 Crafts $7,500; 1990 Crafts $20,000
Ellen Shankin, Floyd, VA. 1990 Crafts $20,000
Joseph Shannon, Washington, DC. 1974 Artist $7,500
Howard Shapiro, Manchester, NH. 1973 Crafts $3,000
Joel Shapiro, New York, NY. 1975 Artist $8,000
Nancy Shapiro, Manchester, NH. 1973 Crafts $3,000
Kathryn Sharbaugh, Holly, MI. 1980 Crafts $10,000; 1992 Crafts $20,000
Susan Shatter, New York, NY. 1980 Artist $10,000; 1987 Painting $15,000
Jacqueline Shatz, Piermont, NY. 1989 Works On Paper $5,000
Jim Shaw, Los Angeles, CA. 1987 New Genres $5,000
Karen Shaw, Baldwin, NY. 1978 Conceptual/Performance/New Genres $3,000
Richard Shaw, Stinson Beach, CA. 1971 Artist $7,500; 1974 Crafts $3,000
Carol Shaw-Sutton, Long Beach, CA. 1981 Crafts $12,500; 1988 Crafts $15,000
Barbara Shawcroft, Berkeley, CA. 1975 Crafts $5,000
Edward Shay, Chicago, IL. 1975 Printmaking/Drawing/Artists' Books $3,000; 1982 Painting $5,000; 1985 Printmaking/Drawing/Artists' Books $15,000
Judith Shea, New York, NY. 1984 Sculpture $5,000; 1986 Sculpture $15,000
Hartley Shearer, New York, NY. 1976 Video $2,000
Arlene Shechet, New York, NY. 1986 Crafts $5,000
Stuart Shedletsky, New York, NY. 1975 Artist $4,000
Diane Sheehan, Madison, WI. 1988 Crafts $3,000; 1992 Crafts $20,000
Maura Sheehan, New York, NY. 1987 Painting $5,000
Fazal Sheikh, New York, NY. 1994 Photo $20,000
Peter Shelton, Los Angeles, CA. 1980 Artist $3,000; 1982 Sculpture $5,000; 1984 Sculpture $15,000; 1994 Sculpture $20,000
Alan Shepp, Berkeley, CA. 1979 Artist $10,000
Morris Sheppard, Big Sur, CA. 1977 Crafts $5,000
Sonia Sheridan, Evanston, IL. 1981 Printmaking/Drawing/Artists' Books $12,500
Bonnie Sherk, San Francisco, CA. 1975 Artist $3,000; 1980 Conceptual/Performance/New Genres $3,000
Cynthia Sherman, Buffalo, NY. 1977 Conceptual/Performance/New Genres $3,000; 1979 Conceptual/Performance/New Genres $3,000
Stuart Sherman, New York, NY. 1980 Conceptual/Performance/New Genres $3,000; 1981 Conceptual/Performance/New Genres $12,500
Philip Sherrod, New York, NY. 1982 Painting $5,000
Katherine Sherwood, Oakland, CA. 1989 Painting $5,000
Mary Sherwood, Boston, MA. 1985 Printmaking/Drawing/Artists' Books $5,000
Susan Shie, Wooster, OH. 1990 Crafts $5,000
Roy Shigley, San Francisco, CA. 1971 Photo $2,000
Roger Shimomura, Lawrence, KS. 1977 Artist $7,500; 1989 New Genres $5,000; 1991 Painting $20,000
Vincent Shine, Chicago, IL. 1990 Sculpture $5,000
Helen Shirk, La Mesa, CA. 1978 Crafts $7,500; 1988 Crafts $15,000
Melissa Shook, Brookline, MA. 1984 Photo $15,000
Stephen Shore, Berkeley, CA. 1975 Photo $5,000; 1980 Photo $10,000
Harriet Shorr, New York, NY. 1980 Artist $10,000
Kenneth Shorr, Chicago, IL. 1980 Photo $3,000; 1982 Photo $5,000; 1984 Photo $15,000; 1994 Photo $20,000
Richard Showalter, McKenzie Bridge, OR. 1974 Crafts $3,000
Irene Shwachman, Needham Heights, MA. 1985 Printmaking/Drawing/Artists' Books $15,000
Carol Shymanski, New York, NY. 1988 Sculpture $5,000
Robert Sibbison, Dayton, OH. 1976 Artist $5,000
Thomas Siefke, Richmond, VA. 1975 Crafts $5,000
Jane Siegel, New York, NY. 1981 Painting $4,000
Hollis Sigler, Prairie View, IL. 1987 Painting $15,000
Oli Sihvonen, Taos, NM. 1968 Artist $5,000; 1976 Artist $5,000
Brent Sikkema, Rochester, NY. 1975 Photo $5,000
Patrick Siler, Pullman, WA. 1990 Crafts $20,000
Christopher Silliman, Richmond, VA. 1993 Crafts $5,000; 1981 Crafts $12,500
Amy Sillman, Brooklyn, NY. 1995 Painting $20,000
Ernest Silva, La Jolla, CA. 1989 Painting $15,000
Ronna Silver, Philadelphia, PA. 1980 Crafts $3,000
Shelly Silver, New York, NY. 1989 New Genres $5,000; 1991 New Genres $20,000
Jeffrey Silverthorne, Central Falls, RI. 1986 Photo $15,000
Phillips Simkin, Philadelphia, PA. 1975 Artist $8,000; 1991 New Genres $20,000
Laurie Simmons, New York, NY. 1984 Photo $5,000
Frederick Simon, Lexington, MA. 1977 Video $7,500
Michael Simon, Watkinsville, GA. 1990 Crafts $20,000
Sandy Simon, Berkeley, CA. 1988 Crafts $5,000
Karen Simon-Peterson, Lexington, MA. 1979 Video $3,000
Charles Simonds, New York, NY. 1974 Artist $3,000; 1976 Artist $2,000; 1980 Artist $10,000
Robert Simone, Atlanta, GA. 1982 Photo $5,000
Judith Simonian, New York, NY. 1987 Painting $5,000
Sheryl Simons, Oakland, CA. 1986 Crafts $5,000
Buster Simpson, Seattle, WA. 1981 Sculpture $12,500; 1990 Sculpture $20,000
David Simpson, Berkeley, CA. 1989 Painting $15,000
Gail Simpson, Bloomington, IL. 1988 Sculpture $5,000
Thomas Simpson, Dobbs Ferry, NY. 1974 Crafts $3,000
M. K. Simqu, Cedar Hill, TX. 1984 Photo $5,000
Michael Singer, Wilmington, VT. 1974 Artist $3,000; 1990 Sculpture $20,000
Jean Singerman, Berkeley, CA. 1973 Crafts $3,000
Art Sinsabaugh, Champaign, IL. 1977 Photo $7,500
Jonathan Sires, Charlotte, NC. 1988 Crafts $5,000
Elizabeth Sisco, San Diego, CA. 1984 Photo $5,000; 1989 New Genres $5,000
Aaron Siskind, Providence, RI. 1976 Photo $7,500
Elena Sisto, New York, NY. 1983 Painting $5,000; 1989 Painting $5,000
Vincent Siville, Baltimore, MD. 1974 Artist $3,000
Theodora Skipitares, New York, NY. 1983 Conceptual/Performance/New Genres $15,000; 1989 New Genres $15,000
Gail Skoff, Berkeley, CA. 1976 Photo $7,500
Sandy Skoglund, New York, NY. 1981 Photo $4,000
Gail Skudera, Des Plaines, IL. 1990 Crafts $5,000
Blue Sky, Columbia, SC. 1980 Artist $3,000
Nancy Slagle, Bloomington, IN. 1988 Crafts $5,000
Susanne Slavick, Pittsburgh, PA. 1987 Painting $5,000
Arlene Slavin, New York, NY. 1977 Printmaking/Drawing/Artists' Books $5,000
Neal Slavin, New York, NY. 1973 Photo $4,500
Sylvia Sleigh, New York, NY. 1982 Painting $25,000
Clarissa Sligh, New York, NY. 1988 Photo $5,000
Ronald Sloan, Winsted, CT. 1987 Painting $5,000
Joan Slocum, Baldwin, WI. 1982 Crafts $5,000
Steven Sloman, New York, NY. 1974 Artist $3,000
Hunt Slonem, New York, NY. 1991 Painting $20,000
Jill Slosburg, Cambridge, MA. 1974 Crafts $3,000; 1986 Crafts $5,000
Howard Smagula, San Francisco, CA. 1979 Conceptual/Performance/New Genres $3,000
Deborah Small, La Jolla, CA. 1987 Painting $5,000; 1989 Painting $5,000
Alexis Smith, Venice, CA. 1976 Conceptual/Performance/New Genres $5,000; 1987 New Genres $15,000
Alfred Smith, Washington , DC. 1975 Crafts $5,000
Anne Smith, Somerville, MA. 1988 Crafts $5,000
Barbara Smith, Venice, CA. 1974 Artist $3,000; 1979 Conceptual/Performance/New Genres $3,000; 1985 New Genres $5,000
Cary Smith, Farmington, CT. 1991 Painting $20,000
Tony Smith, South Orange, NJ. 1967 Artist $5,000
Eugene Smith, New York, NY. 1975 Photo $5,000
Gail Smith, Berkeley, CA. 1988 Crafts $5,000
George Smith, Buffalo, NY. 1977 Artist $7,500
Hassel Smith, Sebastopol, CA. 1968 Artist $5,000
James Smith, Fair Oaks, CA. 1974 Artist $3,000
Keith Smith, Rochester, NY. 1979 Photo $10,000
Lee Smith, Dallas, TX. 1987 Painting $5,000
Leon Smith, New York, NY. 1967 Artist $5,000
Michael Smith, New York, NY. 1978 Conceptual/Performance/New Genres $3,000; 1982 Conceptual/Performance/New Genres $5,000; 1983 Conceptual/Performance/New Genres $15,000; 1991 New Genres $20,000
Michael Smith, New Orleans, LA. 1976 Photo $7,500
Michael Smith, Frenchtown, NJ. 1977 Photo $7,500

Mimi Smith, New York, NY. 1978 Conceptual/Performance/New Genres $3,000
Ming Smith, New York, NY. 1981 Photo $4,000
Philip Smith, Miami Beach, FL. 1987 Painting $5,000
Phyllis Smith, Berkeley, CA. 1973 Crafts $3,000
Steve Smith, Avon, CT. 1984 Photo $15,000
Susan Smith, New York, NY. 1981 Painting $12,500
Elaine Smollin, New York, NY. 1985 Printmaking/Drawing/Artists' Books $5,000
Ned Smyth, New York, NY. 1980 Artist $10,000
Jenny Snider, New York, NY. 1979 Artist $10,000; 1987 Painting $15,000
James Snitzer, New York, NY. 1981 Photo $4,000
Cindy Snodgrass, Pittsburgh, PA. 1981 Crafts $12,500
Charles Snyder, Bloomington, IN. 1980 Artist $10,000
Joan Snyder, New York, NY. 1974 Artist $7,500
Kit-Yin Snyder, New York, NY. 1974 Crafts $3,000; 1980 Artist $3,000; 1982 Sculpture $5,000; 1986 Sculpture $5,000
Robert Snyder, Chicago, IL. 1979 Video $10,000
June Sobel, Oceanside, NY. 1976 Artist $2,000
Nina Sobol, Venice, CA. 1975 Video $4,000
Ellen Soderquist, Dallas, TX. 1982 Printmaking/Drawing/Artists' Books $5,000
Sage Sohier, Boston, MA. 1981 Photo $12,500
Paul Soldner, Aspen, CO. 1976 Crafts $5,000
Cynthia Soloman, Chicago, IL. 1974 Artist $3,000
Elke Solomon, New York, NY. 1982 Printmaking/Drawing/Artists' Books $5,000; 1985 Printmaking/Drawing/Artists' Books $15,000
Jack Solomon, Richmond, VA. 1971 Artist $7,500
Rosalind Solomon, New York, NY. 1988 Photo $15,000
Rosanne Somerson, West Port, MA. 1984 Crafts $5,000; 1988 Crafts $15,000
Frederick Sommer, Prescott, AZ. 1973 Photo $ 4500
Jack Sonenberg, New York, NY. 1984 Sculpture $15,000
Alan Sonfist, New York, NY. 1991 New Genres
Alan Sonneman, Santa Monica, CA. 1985 Painting $5,000
Eve Sonneman, New York, NY. 1971 Photo $2,000; 1978 Photo $7,500
Keith Sonnier, New York, NY. 1976 Video $5,000; 1981 Sculpture $12,500; 1986 Sculpture $15,000
George Soppelsa, East Hartford, CT. 1987 Painting $15,000
Donald Sorenson, Pasadena, CA. 1980 Artist $3,000
Steven Sorli, Carlisle, MA. 1981 Crafts $12,500
Al Souza, Amherst, MA. 1979 Photo $10,000; 1987 Painting $15,000
Suzanne Spater, San Francisco, CA. 1979 Artist $3,000
Shigeko Spear, Lawrence, KS. 1980 Crafts $10,000
Buzz Spector, Los Angeles, CA. 1982 Printmaking/Drawing/Artists' Books $5,000; 1985 Printmaking/Drawing/Artists' Books $5,000; 1991 Works On Paper $20,000
Andrew Spence, New York, NY. 1987 Painting $15,000
Jeffrey Spencer, Omaha, NE. 1991 Painting $20,000
Nancy Spero, New York, NY. 1977 Artist $7,500
Robert Sperry, Seattle, WA. 1984 Crafts $15,000
Mamie Spiegel, Lake Hill, NY. 1982 Crafts $5,000
Victor Spinski, Newark, DE. 1974 Crafts $3,000
Harry Spitz, New York, NY. 1978 Artist $7,500
Neal Spitzer, New York, NY. 1974 Artist $3,000
Thomas Spleth, Alfred, NY. 1980 Crafts $3,000
Diane Spoderek, Detroit, MI. 1978 Video $3,000
John Spofforth, Cleveland, OH. 1980 Artist $3,000; 1981 Sculpture $12,500
Christopher Sproat, New York, NY. 1975 Artist $4,000; 1980 Artist $3,000; 1984 Sculpture $15,000
Joseph Squier, Alameda, CA. 1986 Photo $5,000
Jean St. Pierre, Newport Beach, CA. 1980 Artist $3,000
Gael Stack, Houston, TX. 1982 Painting $5,000; 1989 Painting $15,000
Robert Stackhouse, New York, NY. 1977 Artist $7,500; 1983 Printmaking/Drawing/Artists' Books $15,000; 1991 Works On Paper $20,000
Rudolf Staffel, Philadelphia, PA. 1977 Crafts $5,000; 1990 Crafts $20,000
Karen Stahlecker, Poulsbo, WA. 1984 Crafts $5,000; 1988 Crafts $5,000
Christopher Staley, State College, PA. 1986 Crafts $5,000; 1988 Crafts $5,000
Earl Staley, Houston, TX. 1975 Artist $2,000; 1977 Artist $7,500; 1986 Painting $15,000
Eric Staller, New York, NY. 1978 Photo $7,500
Jan Staller, New York, NY. 1980 Photo $3,000
Sven Stalman, Huntington, WV. 1976 Crafts $5,000
Budd Stalnaker, Bloomington, IN. 1977 Crafts $5,000
Ted Stamm, New York, NY. 1981 Painting $12,500
Theodoros Stamos, New York, NY. 1967 Artist $5,000
Jean Stamsta, Hartland, WI. 1974 Crafts $3,000
Nettie Standing, Gracemont, OK. 1976 Crafts $5,000
Deborah Stanitz, Philadelphia, PA. 1984 Crafts $5,000
Richard Stankiewicz, Huntington, MA. 1967 Artist $5,000
Louise Stanley, Emeryville, CA. 1982 Painting $5,000; 1989 Painting $15,000
Linda Stark, Los Angeles, CA. 1995 Painting $20,000; 1992 Painting $5,000
Douglas and Michael Starn, Boston, MA. 1986 Photo $5,000; 1994 Photo $20,000
Leslie Starobin, Watertown, MA. 1984 Photo $5,000
Jeff Starr, Denver, CO. 1987 Painting $5,000
Nicholas Starr, Syracuse, NY. 1982 Crafts $5,000
Jim Starrett, Raleigh, NC. 1985 Painting $25,000
Therman Statom, Washington, DC. 1980 Artist $3,000; 1982 Crafts $25,000
Wendy Stayman, Haydenville, MA. 1988 Crafts $5,000
Anita Steckel, New York, NY. 1983 Painting $15,000
Lewis Stein, New York, NY. 1980 Conceptual/Performance/New Genres $3,000
Joan Steiner, Greenville, NY. 1980 Crafts $10,000
Judith Steinhauser, Philadelphia, PA. 1973 Photo $1,200
Phel Steinmetz, San Diego, CA. 1982 Photo $5,000
Pat Steir, Venice, CA. 1974 Artist $7,500
Bradley Stensberg, La Jolla, CA. 1974 Artist $1,000; 1980 Video $3,000
Gary Stephan, New York, NY. 1985 Painting $15,000; 1991 Painting $20,000
William Stephens, New York, NY. 1985 New Genres $15,000
David Stephenson, Albuquerque, NM. 1981 Photo $4,000
James Stephenson, State College, PA. 1975 Crafts $5,000
John Stephenson, Ann Arbor, MI. 1986 Crafts $15,000
Joel Sternfeld, New York, NY. 1980 Photo $10,000
Joan Sterrenburg, Nashville, TN. 1979 Crafts $10,000
Coleen Sterritt, Los Angeles, CA. 1986 Sculpture $5,000
Louis Stettner, New York, NY. 1975 Photo $5,000
May Stevens, New York, NY. 1983 Painting $15,000
Robert Stevenson, Los Angeles, CA. 1973 Crafts $3,000
Frank Stewart, New York, NY. 1982 Photo $5,000; 1984 Photo $15,000
Leora Stewart, New York, NY. 1973 Crafts $3,000; 1977 Crafts $5,000
Lizbeth Stewart, Philadelphia, PA. 1976 Crafts $5,000
William Stewart, Hamlin, NY. 1976 Crafts $5,000
Robert Stiegler, Chicago, IL. 1980 Photo $10,000
Susan Stinsmuehlen-Amend, Hollywood, CA. 1982 Crafts $5,000; 1988 Crafts $15,000
Elizabeth Stirratt, Bloomington, IL. 1989 Crafts $5,000
Douglas Stock, Chicago, IL. 1988 Crafts $5,000
Jessica Stockholder, Brooklyn, NY. 1988 Sculpture $5,000
Kay Stocksdale, Berkeley, CA. 1974 Crafts $3,000
David Stoltz, New York, NY. 1980 Artist $3,000; 1981 Sculpture $12,500
Donald Stone, New York, NY. 1976 Artist $2,000
George Stone, Los Angeles, CA. 1986 Sculpture $15,000; 1993 New Genres $20,000
Sylvia Stone, New York, NY. 1974 Artist $7,500
Mary Stoppert, Chicago, IL. 1986 Sculpture $5,000
David Storey, New York, NY. 1991 Painting $5,000
Myron Stout, Provincetown, MA. 1967 Artist $5,000
Lou Stovall, Washington, DC. 1973 Artist $7,500
Barbara Strasen, San Diego, CA. 1975 Artist $4,000
Margaret Stratton, Iowa City, IA. 1990 Photo $5,000; 1987 Photo $5,000; 1995 New Genres $20,000
Martha Strawn, Charlotte, NC. 1980 Photo $3,000
Evon Streetman, Gainesville, FL. 1982 Photo $25,000
Marjorie Strider, New York, NY. 1974 Artist $3,000; 1980 Artist $10,000
Robert Strini, Santa Cruz, CA. 1975 Crafts $5,000; 1977 Crafts $5,000
Amy Stromsten, Rocky Hill, NJ. 1982 Photo $5,000
Charles Strong, Berkeley, CA. 1982 Painting $5,000
Patrick Strzelec, Hopewell, NJ. 1988 Sculpture $5,000
Michelle Stuart, New York, NY. 1974 Artist $3,000; 1977 Printmaking/Drawing/Artists' Books $5,000; 1980 Artist $10,000; 1989 Painting $15,000
Signe Stuart-Nelson, Brookings, SD. 1976 Artist $5,000
Romey Stuckart, Hope, ID. 1993 Painting $20,000
Pamela Studstill, Pipe Creek, TX. 1982 Crafts $5,000; 1988 Crafts $15,000
John Sturgeon, Herber City, UT. 1975 Video $4,000; 1977 Video $7,500; 1980 Video $10,000
Eugene Sturman, Venice, CA. 1975 Artist $2,000; 1986 Sculpture $15,000
George Sugarman, New York, NY. 1967 Artist $5,000

Don Suggs, Los Angeles, CA. 1991 Painting $20,000
Hiroshi Sugimoto, New York, NY. 1982 Photo $5,000
Bill Sullivan, New York, NY. 1989 Painting $15,000
Billy Sullivan, New York, NY. 1987 Painting $15,000
Janet Sullivan, Chicago, IL. 1975 Artist $8,000; 1982 Sculpture $5,000
Jim Sullivan, New York, NY. 1982 Painting $25,000
Altoon Sultan, New York, NY. 1983 Painting $15,000; 1989 Painting $15,000
Donald Sultan, New York, NY. 1980 Artist $3,000
Larry Sultan, Greenbrae, CA. 1980 Photo $10,000; 1986 Photo $5,000; 1992 Photo $20,000
Philip Sultz, Webster Groves, MO. 1975 Artist $4,000
May Sun, Los Angeles, CA. 1989 New Genres $5,000; 1993 New Genres $20,000
Mara Superior, Williamsburg, MA. 1990 Crafts $5,000
James Surls, Splendora, TX. 1979 Artist $10,000
Wendy Sussman, Berkeley, CA. 1989 Painting $5,000
William Suttle, New York, NY. 1971 Photo $2,000; 1975 Photo $5,000
William Sutton, Oakbrook, IL. 1981 Photo $12,500
Didi Suydam, Providence, RI. 1988 Crafts $5,000
Taro Suzuki, New York, NY. 1982 Sculpture $5,000
Robert Swain, New York, NY. 1976 Artist $5,000; 1989 Painting $15,000
Charles Swanson, New Bedford, MA. 1994 Crafts $20,000; 1993 Crafts $5,000
Janet Swanson, New York, NY. 1981 Crafts $12,500
Joel Swartz, Rochester, NY. 1981 Photo $12,500
Linda Swartz, Cambridge, MA. 1986 Photo $5,000
Andy Sweet, Miami Beach, FL. 1980 Photo $3,000
Roger Sweet, Jemez Spring, NM. 1988 Sculpture $5,000
Steven Sweet, New Orleans, LA. 1981 Conceptual/Performance/New Genres $4,000
Mitchell Syrop, Los Angeles, CA. 1987 New Genres $5,000
Joseph Szabo, Amityville, NY. 1984 Photo $15,000
Stephen Szabo, Washington, DC. 1986 Photo $5,000

T

Anne Tabachnick, New York, NY. 1989 Painting $15,000
Martha Tabor, Washington, DC. 1982 Photo $5,000
Athena Tacha, Oberlin, OH. 1975 Artist $4,000
Rea Tajiri, Brooklyn, NY. 1989 New Genres $5,000; 1993 New Genres $20,000
Toshiko Takaezu, Quakertown, NJ. 1980 Crafts $10,000
Akio Takamori, Vashon, WA. 1986 Crafts $5,000; 1988 Crafts $5,000; 1992 Crafts $20,000
Stephen Talasnik, Philadelphia, PA. 1985 Printmaking/Drawing/Artists' Books $5,000
Jude Tallichet, Philadelphia, PA. 1990 Sculpture $5,000
Richard Tannen, Rochester, NY. 1988 Crafts $5,000
Edward Tannenbaum, San Francisco, CA. 1982 Video $5,000
James Tanner, Janesville, MN. 1984 Crafts $15,000; 1990 Crafts $20,000
Reesa Tansey, Oakland, CA. 1982 Photo $5,000
Robert Taplin, West Haven, CT. 1988 Sculpture $5,000
Philip Tarlow, New York, NY. 1981 Painting $12,500
Arthur Taussig, Costa Mesa, CA. 1982 Photo $5,000
Andrew Tavarelli, Boston, MA. 1975 Artist $4,000; 1981 Painting $12,500
Jane Tavarelli/Jery Hudson Boston, MA. 1974 Artist $1,000; 1975 Video $2,000; 1978 Video $7,500
Lenore Tawney, New York, NY. 1979 Crafts $10,000
Al Taylor, New York, NY. 1988 Sculpture $5,000
Michael Taylor Rochester, NY. 1984 Crafts $5,000
Sam Tchakalian, San Francisco, CA. 1975 Artist $4,000; 1981 Painting $12,500; 1989 Painting $15,000
Kevin Teare, New York, NY. 1978 Artist $3,000
Jack Teemer, Baltimore, MD. 1981 Photo $12,500
Byron Temple, Louisville, KY. 1974 Crafts $3,000; 1990 Crafts $20,000
Fiona Templeton, New York, NY. 1983 Conceptual/Performance/New Genres $5,000
Peter Teneau, McMinnville, OR. 1968 Artist $5,000
Irvin Tepper, Petaluma, CA. 1992 Crafts $20,000
Masami Teraoka, Waimanalo, HI. 1980 Artist $10,000; 1989 Painting $15,000
Robert Terry, Long Island City, NY. 1987 Painting $15,000
Edmund Teske, Los Angeles, CA. 1975 Photo $5,000
Michael Tetherow, New York, NY. 1979 Artist $10,000; 1987 Painting $15,000
Diana Thater, Los Angeles, CA. 1993 New Genres $20,000
Carolee Thea, New York, NY. 1989 Works On Paper $5,000
Billie Jean Theide, Des Moines, IA. 1984 Crafts $5,000
Paul Thek, New York, NY. 1975 Artist $8,000
William Thielen, Carbondale, IL. 1982 Crafts $5,000
George Thiewes, South Woodstock, VT. 1986 Crafts $15,000
Rachelle Thiewes, El Paso, TX. 1988 Crafts $5,000
Janet Tholen, Los Angeles, CA. 1985 Painting $5,000
Jayne Thomas, Mount Desert, ME. 1982 Crafts $5,000
Larry Thomas, San Francisco, CA. 1980 Printmaking/Drawing/Artists' Books $3,000; 1987 Printmaking/Drawing/Artists' Books $15,000
Lew Thomas, Houston, TX. 1975 Photo $5,000; 1979 Conceptual/Performance/New Genres $3,000; 1980 Photo $10,000; 1986 Photo $15,000
Alan Thompson, New Bedford, MA. 1990 Crafts $5,000
Catherine Thompson, Seattle, WA. 1990 Crafts $5,000
Jerry Thompson, New Haven, CT. 1977 Photo $7,500
Mark Thompson, Oakland, CA. 1980 Conceptual/Performance/New Genres $3,000; 1989 New Genres $15,000
Rena Thompson, Chalfont, PA. 1980 Crafts $3,000; 1986 Crafts $5,000
Richard Thompson, Albuquerque, NM. 1978 Artist $7,500
Colin Thomson, New York, NY. 1991 Painting $20,000
Joan Thorne, New York, NY. 1979 Artist $10,000; 1983 Painting $15,000
Ruth Thorne-Thomsen, Denver, CO. 1982 Photo $5,000; 1988 Photo $15,000
Ann Thornycroft, Santa Monica, CA. 1982 Painting $5,000
Marc Thorpe, St. Augustine, FL. 1975 Artist $3,000
Bart Thrall, Brooklyn, NY. 1987 Painting $5,000
Linda Threadgill, East Troy, WI. 1984 Crafts $5,000
Rolling Thunder, Thunder Mountain, NV. 1984 Sculpture $5,000
Jacqueline Thurston, Menlo Park, CA. 1976 Photo $7,500; 1978 Photo $7,500
Roger Tibbetts, Danielson, CT. 1980 Artist $3,000; 1989 Painting $5,000
George Tice, Colonia, NJ. 1973 Photo $4,000
Robert Tiemann, San Antonio, TX. 1968 Artist $5,000
Sidney Tillim, New York, NY. 1974 Artist $7,500
Patricia Tillman, Waco, TX. 1986 Sculpture $5,000
George Timock, Shawnee Mission, KS. 1974 Crafts $3,000; 1981 Crafts $12,500
Rirkrit Tiravanija, New York, NY. 1994 Sculpture $20,000
Danny Tisdale, New York, NY. 1991 Sculpture $5,000; 1995 Works On Paper $20,000
Leonard Titzer, Evansville, IN. 1981 Sculpture $4,000
Harold Tivey, New York, NY. 1976 Artist $5,000
Julius Tobias, New York, NY. 1975 Artist $8,000; 1981 Sculpture $12,500
Richard Tobias, New York, NY. 1987 Painting $5,000
Dennis Tobin, Bloomington, IL. 1986 Crafts $5,000
Farley Tobin, Bostic, NC. 1978 Crafts $7,500
Michael Todd, Encinitas, CA. 1974 Artist $7,500
Deborah Toland, Seattle, WA. 1986 Crafts $5,000
Edgar Tolson, N. Middleton, KY. 1981 Sculpture $12,500
Lowell Tolstedt, Columbus, OH. 1982 Printmaking/Drawing/Artists' Books $5,000
Carter Tomassi, Atlanta, GA. 1977 Photo $7,500
Merrily Tompkins, Seattle, WA. 1979 Crafts $10,000
Michael Tompkins, Crockett, CA. 1987 Painting $5,000; 1989 Painting $5,000
Marvin Torffield, Branford, CT. 1971 Artist $7,500
Marilyn Torre-Whitesell, Charlestown, IN. 1977 Printmaking/Drawing/Artists' Books $5,000
John Torreano, New York, NY. 1978 Artist $7,500; 1982 Painting $25,000; 1989 Painting $15,000
Francesc Torres, New York, NY. 1980 Conceptual/Performance/New Genres $3,000; 1982 Conceptual/Performance/New Genres $25,000; 1993 New Genres $20,000
Carl Toth, Bloomfield Hills, MI. 1975 Photo $5,000; 1980 Photo $10,000; 1986 Photo $15,000
Xavier Toubes, Chapel Hill, NC. 1986 Crafts $5,000
George Trakas, New York, NY. 1979 Artist $10,000; 1988 Sculpture $15,000
Cesar Trasobares, Coral Gables, FL. 1979 Artist $3,000
Alex Traube, Espanola, NM. 1977 Photo $7,500
Donald Traver, New York, NY. 1987 Painting $5,000
Joyce Treiman, Pacific Palisades, CA. 1989 Painting $15,000
Gary Trentham, Opelika, AL. 1978 Crafts $7,500
Arthur Tress, New York, NY. 1973 Photo $3,500
Karla Trinkley, Boyertown, PA. 1986 Crafts $5,000
Robert Trotman, Casar, NC. 1984 Crafts $5,000; 1988 Crafts $15,000
David True, New York, NY. 1982 Painting $5,000; 1991 Painting $20,000
Anne Truitt, Washington, DC. 1973 Artist $7,500; 1977 Artist $7,500
Ida Trusch, Ashland, VA. 1974 Artist $7,500
Wen-Ying Tsai, New York, NY. 1976 Artist $2,000

Bernard Tschumi, New York, NY. 1979 Conceptual/Performance/New Genres $3,000
Philip Tsiaras, New York, NY. 1984 Photo $5,000
Toba Tucker, New York, NY. 1981 Photo $12,500
William Tucker, Pennington, NJ. 1986 Sculpture $15,000
Jane Tuckerman, Boston, MA. 1982 Photo $5,000
Nitza Tufino, New York, NY. 1980 Artist $3,000
Alan Turner, New York, NY. 1977 Artist $7,500; 1981 Painting $12,500; 1987 Painting $15,000
Alwyn Turner, New Orleans, LA. 1971 Photo $4,000; 1973 Photo $5,000
Tom Turner, Liberty, SC. 1974 Crafts $3,000
James Turrell, Santa Monica, CA. 1968 Artist $5,000
Elizabeth Tuttle, Eagle River, WI. 1982 Crafts $5,000
Richard Tuttle, New York, NY. 1969 Artist $5,000
Randy Twaddle, Dallas, TX. 1987 Printmaking/Drawing/Artists' Books $5,000
John Tweddle, San Antonio, TX. 1968 Artist $5,000; 1985 Painting $15,000
Douglas Tyler, Harrisonburg, VA. 1974 Artist $3,000
Lilian Tyrrell, Ravenna, OH. 1994 Crafts $20,000

U

Jerry Uelsmann, Gainesville, FL. 1973 Photo $3,300
Alan Uglow, New York, NY. 1989 Painting $15,000
Erica Uhlenbeck, New York, NY. 1994 Photo $20,000
Mierle Ukeles, Bronx, NY. 1977 Conceptual/Performance/New Genres $3,000; 1983 Conceptual/Performance/New Genres $15,000
Linn Underhill, Syracuse, NY. 1984 Photo $15,000; 1990 Photo $5,000
William Underhill, Alfred, NY. 1986 Crafts $15,000
Chris Unterseher, Reno, NV. 1981 Sculpture $12,500
Andrea Uravitch, Arlington, VA. 1976 Crafts $5,000
Steven Urry, Chicago, IL. 1967 Artist $5,000
Richard Usrey, Syracuse, NY. 1988 Crafts $5,000
Thomas Uttech, Saukville, WI. 1987 Painting $15,000
Connie Utterback, Los Angeles, CA. 1986 Crafts $5,000; 1988 Crafts $5,000
Burk Uzzle, Stone Ridge, NY. 1975 Photo $5,000

V

Boaz Vaadia, Brooklyn, NY. 1988 Sculpture $5,000
Robin Vaccarino, Studio City, CA. 1980 Printmaking/Drawing/Artists' Books $3,000
John Vachon, New York, NY. 1973 Photo $5,000
Patssi Valdez, Los Angeles, CA. 1989 Painting $5,000
Rogelio Valdovin, Tuscon, AZ. 1979 Crafts $3,000
Luis Valdovino, Pittsburgh, PA. 1993 New Genres $20,000
Barbara Valenta, Montclair, NJ. 1984 Sculpture $5,000
Dewain Valentine, Venice, CA. 1980 Artist $10,000
James Valerio, Ithaca, NY 1985 Painting $15,000
Leo Valledor, San Francisco, CA. 1979 Artist $10,000; 1985 Painting $15,000
John Van Alstine, Jersey City, NJ. 1986 Sculpture $15,000
Gerald Van De Weile, New York, NY. 1969 Artist $5,000
James Van Der Zee, New York, NY. 1976 Photo $7,500
George Van Duinwik, Newport, RI. 1977 Crafts $5,000
Erica Van Horn, Chicago, IL. 1982 Printmaking/Drawing/Artists' Books $5,000
Richard Van Pelt, Broomfield, CO. 1980 Photo $3,000
Lester Van Winkle, Richmond, VA. 1975 Artist $2,000; 1979 Artist $10,000
Richard VanBuren, New York, NY. 1969 Artist $5,000
Peter Vandenberge, Sacramento, CA. 1981 Crafts $12,500
Anton Vanderperk, New York, NY. 1981 Painting $12,500
Judy Varga, Elmont, NY. 1981 Sculpture $4,000
Kazys Varnelis, New York, NY. 1975 Artist $8,000
Steina Vasulka, Santa Fe, NM. 1981 Video $12,500; 1985 New Genres $15,000
Woody Vasulka, Santa Fe, NM. 1982 Video $25,000; 1989 New Genres $15,000
Kenneth Vavrek, Philadelphia, PA. 1977 Crafts $5,000
Edin Velez, New York, NY. 1980 Video $3,000; 1981 Video $12,500; 1987 New Genres $15,000
Tony Velez, Brooklyn, NY. 1984 Photo $5,000
Bernar Venet, New York, NY. 1979 Artist $3,000
Michael Venezia, New York, NY. 1981 Painting $12,500
Rene Verdugo, Tucson, AZ. 1980 Photo $3,000
David Vereano, Boston, MA. 1983 Painting $5,000
Tony Vevers, Lafayette, IN. 1967 Artist $5,000
Ted Victoria, New York, NY. 1975 Artist $2,000
Bonnie Vierthaler, Seattle, WA. 1977 Crafts $5,000
Frederico Vigil, Santa Fe, NM. 1987 Painting $5,000
Carlos Villa, San Francisco, CA. 1973 Artist $7,500
Armando Villasenor, Milwaukee, WI. 1978 Printmaking/Drawing/Artists' Books $3,000
Paul Villinski, Long Island City, NY. 1987 Painting $5,000
Frank Viner, Valley Cottage, NY. 1979 Artist $10,000; 1991 Painting $20,000
Bill Viola, Long Beach, CA. 1976 Video $5,000; 1978 Video $10,000; 1983 Video $15,000; 1989 New Genres $15,000
Jantje Visscher, Minneapolis, MN. 1989 Works On Paper $3,000
Anthony Vitale, San Diego, CA. 1975 Artist $2,000
Ann Volkes, New York, NY. 1979 Video $3,000
Michael Volonakis, New York, NY. 1982 Painting $5,000
Cynthia Von Der Embse, Playa del Rey, CA. 1977 Crafts $5,000
Martin Von Haselberg, Venice, CA. 1980 Conceptual/Performance/New Genres $3,000
Stephen Von Huene, Valencia, CA. 1974 Artist $3,000
Ursula Von Rydingsvard, New York, NY. 1979 Artist $3,000; 1986 Sculpture $15,000
David Von Schlegell, New York, NY. 1969 Artist $5,000
Eric Von Schmidt, Westport, CT. 1987 Painting $15,000
Peter Voulkos, Oakland, CA. 1976 Artist $10,000; 1978 Crafts $7,500; 1986 Crafts $15,000

W

Yoshi Wada, New York, NY. 1993 New Genres $20,000
Robert Wade, Dallas, TX. 1974 Artist $7,500; 1984 Sculpture $15,000
Catherine Wagner, San Francisco, CA. 1981 Photo $4,000; 1990 Photo $20,000
Gale Wagner, Raytown, MO. 1975 Artist $2,000
Merrill Wagner, New York, NY. 1989 Works On Paper $15,000
Jim Waid, Tucson, AZ. 1985 Painting $15,000
Peter Waite, Hartford, CT. 1983 Printmaking/Drawing/Artists' Books $15,000
Robert Walch, Brooklyn, NY. 1973 Photo $2,000
Max Waldman, New York, NY. 1973 Photo $5,000
Christian Walker, Atlanta, GA. 1990 Photo $5,000
Harold Walker, Gainsville, FL. 1971 Photo $2,000
Melanie Walker, Louisville, CO. 1994 Photo $20,000
Todd Walker, Tucson, AZ. 1982 Photo $25,000
William Walker, Chicago, IL. 1978 Artist $7,500
William Walker, Oakland, CA. 1975 Video $2,000; 1979 Video $10,000
Kay Walkingstick, Inglewood, NJ. 1983 Painting $15,000
Patricia Wall, Venice, CA. 1981 Painting $4,000
James Wallace, Memphis, TN. 1980 Crafts $3,000
John Wallace, Boston, MA. 1974 Printmaking/Drawing/Artists' Books $3,000
Niles Wallace, Memphis, TN. 1978 Crafts $7,500
Michael Walling, Kansas City, MO. 1983 Painting $15,000
Robert Wallis, San Francisco, CA. 1980 Photo $3,000
Susan Walp, Denver, CO. 1977 Artist $3,000
Peter Walsh, Baltimore, MD. 1995 New Genres $20,000
Gar Wang, Warwick, NY. 1987 Painting $5,000
Grace Wapner, Woodstock, NY. 1978 Artist $7,500
Patricia Warashina, Seattle, WA. 1986 Crafts $15,000
Cheryl Ward, Philadelphia, PA. 1980 Crafts $3,000
Nari Ward, New York, NY. 1994 Sculpture $20,000
William Wareham, Berkeley, CA. 1974 Artist $3,000
Deborah Warner, Philadelphia, PA. 1979 Crafts $10,000
Mary Warner, Norman, OK. 1985 Printmaking/Drawing/Artists' Books $5,000
Phillip Warner, New York, NY. 1979 Crafts $10,000
Donald Warnock, Wilton, NH. 1977 Crafts $5,000
Robert Warrens, Baton Rouge, LA. 1979 Artist $10,000; 1985 Painting $15,000
Jeffery Wasserman, New York, NY. 1987 Painting $15,000
James Watkins, Providence, RI. 1986 Crafts $5,000
Ron Watson, Grand Rapids, MI. 1975 Artist $4,000
Lynda Watson-Abbott, Santa Cruz, CA. 1977 Crafts $5,000; 1984 Crafts $15,000
Robert Watts, Bangor, PA. 1976 Conceptual/Performance/New Genres $10,000
Jack Wax, Jenkintown, PA. 1986 Crafts $5,000; 1988 Crafts $5,000
Jeffrey Way, New York, NY. 1989 Painting $15,000
Wayne, Chicago, IL. 1976 Photo $7,500; 1978 Photo $7,500
June Wayne, Los Angeles, CA. 1980 Artist $10,000
Alexander Webb, Brooklyn, NY. 1990 Photo $20,000
Patrick Webb, Brooklyn, NY. 1983 Painting $5,000; 1985 Painting $5,000; 1987 Painting $5,000

Todd Webb, Portland, ME. 1979 Photo $10,000
James Weeks, Bedford, MA. 1977 Artist $7,500
Carrie Mae Weems, Oakland, CA. 1991 Photo $5,000; 1994 Photo $20,000
William Wegman, New York, NY. 1975 Video $8,000; 1982 Photo $25,000
Ryan Weideman, New York, NY. 1984 Photo $15,000
Brian Weil, New York, NY. 1984 Photo $5,000
Sibyl Weil, New York, NY. 1974 Artist $3,000
Susan Weil, New York, NY. 1976 Artist $2,000
Steven Weinberg, Pawtucket, RI. 1980 Crafts $10,000; 1984 Crafts $15,000
Lawrence Weiner, New York, NY. 1977 Conceptual/Performance/New Genres $7,500; 1985 Printmaking/Drawing/Artists' Books $15,000
David Weinrib, Garnerville, NY. 1967 Artist $5,000; 1985 Printmaking/Drawing/Artists' Books $15,000
David Weinstein, Brooklyn, NY. 1985 New Genres $5,000
John Weir, Oakland, CA. 1979 Photo $10,000
Kurt Weiser, Tempe, AZ. 1988 Crafts $5,000; 1992 Crafts $20,000
Jeff Weiss, Los Angeles, CA. 1981 Photo $12,500; 1988 Photo $15,000
Jessica Weiss, New York, NY. 1989 Painting $5,000
Richard Weiss, Seattle, WA. 1981 Crafts $12,500; 1986 Crafts $15,000
Roger Welch, New York, NY. 1974 Artist $3,000; 1980 Artist $10,000
Theodore Weller, Providence, RI. 1985 Painting $15,000
James Welling, New York, NY. 1987 Painting $5,000
Alice Wells, Taos, NM. 1973 Photo $3,500
Lynton Wells, New York, NY. 1975 Artist $4,000
Jack Welpott, San Francisco, CA. 1979 Photo $10,000
Stanton Welsh, Oakland, CA. 1986 Crafts $5,000
Johanna Went, Los Angeles, CA. 1985 New Genres $5,000
Howard Werner, Mount Tremper, NY. 1988 Crafts $15,000
John Wesley, New York, NY. 1989 Painting $15,000
Katarina Weslien, Portland, ME. 1986 Crafts $5,000
Henry Wessel, Point Richmond, CA. 1975 Photo $5,000; 1977 Photo $7,500
Annie West, New York, NY. 1995 Works On Paper $20,000
Bruce West, Mount Angel, OR. 1967 Artist $5,000
H. C. Westermann, Brookfield Center, CT. 1967 Artist $5,000
Stephen Westfall, New York, NY. 1987 Painting $5,000; 1989 Painting $5,000; 1993 Painting $20,000
Brett Weston, Carmel, CA. 1973 Photo $5,000
Katherine Westphal, Berkeley, CA. 1977 Crafts $5,000
Mark Wethli, Brunswick, ME. 1974 Artist $3,000; 1995 Painting $20,000
Jo Whaley, Oakland, CA. 1994 Photo $20,000
Margaret Wharton, Glenview, IL. 1980 Artist $10,000; 1988 Sculpture $15,000; 1993 Works On Paper $20,000
Douglas Wheeler, Santa Monica, CA. 1968 Artist $5,000; 1977 Conceptual/Performance/New Genres $7,500
Stephen Whisler, New York, NY. 1984 Sculpture $5,000
Bill White, Baltimore, MD. 1979 Printmaking/Drawing/Artists' Books $3,000
John White, Venice, CA. 1976 Artist $5,000; 1979 Conceptual/Performance/New Genres $3,000; 1983 Conceptual/Performance/New Genres $25,000
John Wilson White, San Francisco, CA. 1994 Photo $20,000
Susan White, Brooklyn, NY. 1989 Works On Paper $5,000
Frances Whitehead, Chicago, IL. 1986 Sculpture $5,000
Robert Whitley, Solebury, PA. 1980 Crafts $10,000
Robert Whitman, New York, NY. 1975 Artist $8,000
Mac Whitney, Dallas, TX. 1979 Artist $10,000
Jack Whitten, New York, NY. 1973 Artist $7,500
Stephen Whittlesey, West Barnstable, MA. 1992 Crafts $20,000
Jay Wholley, Cliffside Park, NJ. 1981 Sculpture $12,500
Susan Whyne, Austin, TX. 1980 Artist $10,000; 1989 Painting $15,000
Edward Wicklander, Seattle, WA. 1988 Sculpture $5,000
Robert Widdicombe, Austin, TX. 1980 Photo $3,000
Gwen Widmer, Cedar Falls, IA. 1975 Photo $5,000; 1980 Photo $10,000
Paul Wiesenfeld, New York, NY. 1976 Artist $5,000
Phil Wilbern, Detroit, MI. 1967 Artist $5,000
Robert Wilbert, Detroit, MI. 1977 Artist $7,500
Frans Wildenhain, Pittsford, NY. 1974 Crafts $3,000
Robert Wilhite, Los Angeles, CA. 1979 Conceptual/Performance/New Genres $3,000; 1981 Sculpture $12,500; 1986 Sculpture $15,000
Hannah Wilke, New York, NY. 1976 Artist $2,000; 1979 Conceptual/Performance/New Genres $3,000
Larew Wilks, Chicago, IL. 1975 Printmaking/Drawing/Artists' Books $3,000
Dennis Will, Philadelphia, PA. 1976 Artist $2,000
John Willenbecher, New York, NY. 1977 Artist $7,500
Danny Williams, Dallas, TX. 1980 Artist $3,000
Emmett Williams, Cambridge, MA. 1979 Conceptual/Performance/New Genres $10,000
Franklin Williams, San Francisco, CA. 1968 Artist $5,000
Gerald Williams, Goffstown, NH. 1975 Crafts $5,000
Guy Williams, Santa Monica, CA. 1975 Artist $8,000
Larry Williams, New York, NY. 1979 Photo $10,000
Mark Williams, New York, NY. 1980 Artist $3,000; 1989 Works On Paper $5,000
Neil Williams, New York, NY. 1967 Artist $5,000
Pat Ward Williams, Valencia, CA. 1988 Works On Paper $3,000; 1990 Photo $5,000; 1994 Photo $20,000
Rachel Williams, San Francisco, CA. 1985 Painting $5,000
Reese Williams, New York, NY. 1978 Conceptual/Performance/New Genres $3,000; 1980 Conceptual/Performance/New Genres $3,000
William T. Williams, New York, NY. 1971 Artist $7,500
Philemona Williamson, New York, NY. 1987 Painting $5,000
Thornton Willis, New York, NY. 1980 Artist $10,000
William Willis, Adelphi, MD. 1980 Artist $10,000
Christopher Wilmarth, New York, NY. 1969 Artist $5,000; 1977 Artist $7,500; 1980 Artist $10,000
Ann Wilson, New York, NY. 1980 Conceptual/Performance/New Genres $3,000
Anne Wilson, Chicago, IL. 1982 Crafts $5,000; 1988 Crafts $15,000
Brett Wilson, Woodbridge, MA. 1980 Artist $3,000
Charles Wilson, Evanston, IL. 1988 Sculpture $15,000
Fred Wilson, New York, NY. 1993 Sculpture $5,000; 1993 New Genres $20,000
Helen-Miranda Wilson, Wellfleet, MA. 1983 Painting $15,000
Mark Wilson, West Cornwall, CT. 1982 Printmaking/Drawing/Artists' Books $5,000
Martha Wilson, Brooklyn, NY. 1978 Conceptual/Performance/New Genres $3,000; 1983 Conceptual/Performance/New Genres $15,000
Millie Wilson, Los Angeles, CA. 1993 New Genres $20,000
Stanley Wilson, Los Angeles, CA. 1986 Sculpture $5,000
Wes Wilson, San Anselmo, CA. 1968 Artist $5,000
Gayle Wimmer, Philadelphia, PA. 1973 Crafts $3,000
Fran Winant, New York, NY. 1989 Painting $5,000
James Wines, New York, NY. 1976 Artist $5,000
David Wing, San Diego, CA. 1977 Photo $7,500
Michael Wingo, Los Angeles, CA. 1989 Painting $15,000
Michael Winkler, Swarthmore, PA. 1985 Printmaking/Drawing/Artists' Books $5,000
Geoff Winningham, Houston, TX. 1975 Photo $5,000; 1977 Photo $7,500
Garry Winogrand, Los Angeles, CA. 1975 Photo $5,000
Neil Winokur, New York, NY. 1984 Photo $15,000
Paula Winokur, Horsham, PA. 1976 Crafts $5,000; 1988 Crafts $15,000
Robert Winokur, Horsham, PA. 1979 Crafts $10,000
Jackie Winsor, New York, NY. 1974 Artist $7,500; 1977 Artist $7,500; 1984 Sculpture $25,000
David Winter, Brooklyn, NY. 1988 Sculpture $5,000
Milo Winter, Providence, RI. 1975 Artist $2,000
Suzanne Winterberger, Vestal, NY. 1984 Photo $5,000
Robin Winters, New York, NY. 1980 Conceptual/Performance/New Genres $10,000
Karl Wirsum, Chicago, IL. 1971 Artist $7,500; 1977 Artist $7,500; 1983 Painting $15,000
Nina Wise, San Anselmo, CA. 1985 New Genres $5,000
Joel Peter Witkin, Albuquerque, NM. 1980 Photo $3,000; 1981 Photo $12,500; 1986 Photo $15,000; 1992 Photo $20,000
Randall Witlicki, Bristol, CT. 1980 Artist $3,000
Daniel Witz, New York, NY. 1982 Printmaking/Drawing/Artists' Books $5,000
Emerson Woelffer, Los Angeles, CA. 1974 Artist $7,500
Fred Woell, New Paltz, NY. 1977 Crafts $5,000; 1992 Crafts $20,000
Philip Wofford, Hoosick Falls, NY. 1974 Artist $7,500; 1980 Artist $10,000; 1989 Painting $15,000
Gary Wojcik, Trumansburg, NY. 1980 Artist $3,000
Eva Wolfe, Cherokee, NC. 1977 Crafts $5,000
James Wolfe, Bennington, VT. 1974 Artist $3,000
Dee Wolff, Houston, TX. 1989 Painting $5,000
Jeffrey Wolin, Bloomington, IN. 1988 Photo $5,000; 1992 Photo $20,000
Claudia Wolz, Oakland, CA. 1980 Photo $3,000
Robert Womack, Richmond, VA. 1994 Crafts $20,000
Al Wong, San Francisco, CA. 1983 Conceptual/Performance/New Genres $5,000

Tony Wong, New York, NY. 1983 Painting $5,000
Beatrice Wood, Ojai, CA. 1977 Crafts $5,000
Brian Wood, New York, NY. 1984 Photo $15,000
Joseph Wood, Cambridge, MA. 1990 Crafts $5,000
Nicholas Wood, Arlington, TX. 1981 Sculpture $4,000
John Woodall, San Francisco, CA. 1989 New Genres $15,000
Betty Woodman, Boulder, CO. 1980 Crafts $10,000; 1986 Crafts $25,000
George Woodman, Boulder, CO. 1968 Artist $5,000
Robin Woodsome, Chicago, IL. 1987 Painting $5,000
Steven Woodward, Minneapolis, MN. 1988 Sculpture $5,000
Christopher Wool, New York, NY. 1987 Painting $5,000
Ellamarie Wooley, San Diego, CA. 1974 Crafts $3,000
William Woolston, Genessee, ID. 1976 Photo $7,500
Don Worth, Mill Valley, CA. 1980 Photo $10,000
Dick Wray, Houston, TX. 1978 Artist $7,500
Boyd Wright, Moscow, ID. 1982 Sculpture $25,000
Kevin Wrigley, Linden, NJ. 1977 Photo $7,500
Tom Wudl, Venice, CA. 1976 Artist $5,000
Theo Wujcik, Temple Terrance, FL. 1977 Printmaking/Drawing/Artists' Books $5,000
Len Wujick, Lexington, KY. 1980 Crafts $3,000
Ann Wulff, Sacramento, CA. 1986 Photo $5,000
Sanford Wurmfeld, New York, NY. 1987 Painting $15,000
Ronald Wyffels, San Antonio, TX. 1982 Sculpture $5,000
Richard Wyman, Layton, NJ. 1976 Crafts $5,000
William Wyman, Scituate, MA. 1977 Crafts $5,000

Y

Jan Yager, Philadelphia, PA. 1984 Crafts $5,000
Mihoko Yamagata, San Juan Capistrano, CA. 1982 Photo $5,000
Nina Yankowitz, New York, NY. 1979 Artist $10,000
Robert Yarber, New York, NY. 1983 Painting $5,000; 1985 Painting $5,000
Bert Yarborough, Provincetown, MA. 1980 Artist $3,000
Richard Yarde, Brookline, MA. 1976 Artist $5,000
Kim Yasuda, Los Angeles, CA. 1990 Sculpture $5,000
Robert Yasuda, New York, NY. 1981 Painting $12,500
Steven Yates, Albuquerque, NM. 1980 Photo $3,000
Max Yavno, Los Angeles, CA. 1980 Photo $10,000
Peter Yelda, San Luis Obispo, CA. 1980 Crafts $3,000
Phyllis Yes, Portland, OR. 1987 Painting $5,000
Rita Yokoi, Los Angeles, CA. 1981 Sculpture $12,500
Bruce Yonemoto, Los Angeles, CA. 1983 Video $15,000
Bruce and Norman Yonemoto, Los Angeles, CA. 1989 New Genres $15,000
Norman Yonemoto, Venice, CA. 1985 New Genres $5,000
Ray Yoshida, Chicago, IL. 1989 Painting $15,000
Ann Young, Bolinas, CA. 1988 Crafts $5,000
Michael Young, New York, NY. 1987 Painting $15,000
Peter Young, New York, NY. 1969 Artist $5,000
Purvis Young, Miami, FL. 1979 Printmaking/Drawing/Artists' Books $3,000
Sara Young, Cranston, RI. 1988 Crafts $5,000; 1992 Crafts $20,000
Robert Younger, New York, NY. 1982 Sculpture $5,000; 1990 Sculpture $20,000
Jack Youngerman, New York, NY. 1967 Artist $5,000; 1984 Sculpture $15,000

Z

Dorian Zachai, Richmond, NH. 1975 Crafts $5,000
Michele Zackheim, Tesuque, NM. 1989 Works On Paper $3,000
Isaiah Zagar, Philadelphia, PA. 1979 Artist $10,000
Tino Zago, New York, NY. 1982 Painting $5,000; 1985 Painting $15,000
Stephen Zaima, Iowa City, IA. 1974 Artist $3,000
Mikhail Zakin, Closter, NJ. 1976 Crafts $5,000
Duane Zaloudek, New York, NY. 1987 Painting $15,000
Kes Zapkus, New York, NY. 1979 Artist $10,000
Leo Zarogoza, New York, NY. 1975 Crafts $5,000
Marian Zazeela, New York, NY. 1978 Conceptual/Performance/New Genres $3,000
Aggie Zed, Richmond, VA. 1986 Sculpture $15,000
Harold Zegart, Berkeley, CA. 1971 Photo $1,000
Connie Zehr, Fullerton, CA. 1986 Sculpture $15,000
Dorothy Zeidman, Norman, OK. 1976 Artist $2,000
Armando Zelada, Rochester, NY. 1973 Photo $5,000
Paul Zelevansky, New York, NY. 1982 Printmaking/Drawing/Artists' Books $5,000
Marci Zelmanoff, New York, NY. 1974 Crafts $3,000
Jerilea Zemple, New York, NY. 1981 Sculpture $4,000
Jerry Zeniuk, New York, NY. 1981 Painting $12,500
Patrick Zentz, Laurel, MT. 1990 Sculpture $5,000
Amy Zerner, East Hampton, NY. 1985 Painting $15,000
Hongtu Zhang, New York, NY. 1995 Works On Paper $20,000
Mel Ziegler/Kate Ericson, New York, NY. 1987 New Genres $5,000; 1993 New Genres $20,000
Arnold Zimmerman, New York, NY. 1982 Crafts $5,000; 1986 Crafts $5,000; 1990 Crafts $5,000
Elyn Zimmerman, Venice, CA. 1976 Artist $5,000; 1980 Artist $3,000; 1982 Sculpture $25,000
Thomas Zimmerman, San Francisco, CA. 1973 Photo $2,500
Philip Zimmermann, Barrytown, NY. 1995 Works On Paper $20,000
Georgette Zirbes, Ann Arbor, MI. 1975 Crafts $5,000
Peter Zokosky, Los Angeles, CA. 1987 Painting $5,000
Larry Zox, New York, NY. 1969 Artist $5,000
Edward Zucca, Putnam, CT. 1981 Crafts $12,500
Barbara Zucker, New York, NY. 1975 Artist $4,000
Michael Zwack, New York, NY. 1979 Artist $3,000
Janet Zweig, Cambridge, MA. 1985 Printmaking/Drawing/Artists' Books $5,000; 1994 Sculpture $20,000
Rhonda Zwillinger, Brooklyn, NY. 1984 Sculpture $5,000
Mary Ann Zynsky, Lynnfield, MA. 1982 Crafts $5,000; 1986 Crafts $15,000

REGIONAL RECIPIENTS

Mid-America Arts Alliance

Visual Artists' Fellowships

A

Byron K. Addison, Ballwin, MO. 1988 Works on Paper $3,000
Joseph H. Allen, Bellaire, TX. 1994 Painting/Works on Paper $5,000
Helen Altman, Fort Worth, TX. 1993 Sculpture $5,000
Ed Andrews, St. Louis, MO. 1989 Sculpture $3,000
Tre' Arenz, Austin, TX. 1993 Crafts $5,000
Kathryn Arnold, Lenexa, KS. 1996 Painting $5,000
Jeri Au, Pacific, MO. 1985 Crafts $3,000

B

Barry Badgett, Wichita, KS. 1995 Sculpture $5,000
David Bailin, N. Little Rock, AR. 1988 Painting $5,000
Karen Baldner, Fayetteville, AR. 1996 Painting $5,000
Alex Barde, Pittsburg, KS. 1991 Photography $5,000
Peter Beasecker, Dallas, TX. 1995 Crafts $5,000
Jill Bedgood, Austin, TX. 1989 Sculpture $3,000
Margaret Elizabeth Belcher, Dallas, TX. 1988 Painting $3,000
Kent Bellows, Omaha, NE. 1988 Works on Paper $3,000
Andrew Bennett, Dallas, TX. 1996 Painting $5,000
Thomas Berding, Bloomington, IN. 1990 Painting $5,000
Ellen Berman, Houston, TX. 1988 Painting $3,000
Edward Bernstein, Fayetteville, AR. 1984 Works on Paper $3,000
Pamela J. Berry, Omaha, NE. 1991 Photography $5,000
William A. Berry, Columbia, MO. 1994 Works on Paper $5,000
Linda Blackburn, Ft. Worth, TX. 1988 Painting $3,000
Sharon Bock, Bonner Springs, KS. 1989 Crafts $3,000
Alexandra Bowes, San Francisco, CA. 1990 Works on Paper $5,000
Ruth Bowman, Lawrence, KS. 1985 Sculpture $3,000
Marna Brauner, Shorewood, WI. 1985 Crafts $3,000
James Brewer, Heartwell, NE. 1986 Works on Paper $3,000
Curtiss Brock, Smithville, TN. 1989 Crafts $3,000
Larry D. Buechel, Kansas City, MO. 1989 Sculpture $3,000
Lisa Bulawsky, St. Louis, MO. 1996 Painting $5,000
James M. Butkus, Omaha, NE. 1987 Photography $3,000

C

Carla C. Cain, Oklahoma City, OK. 1987 Photography $3,000
Carol Carter, St. Louis, MO. 1994 Painting $5,000
Keith Carter, Beaumont, TX. 1991 Photography $5,000
Gary Cawood, Ruston, LA. 1995 Photography $5,000
Lynn Cazabon, Lewisburg, PA. 1993 Photography $5,000
Tom Chaffee, State University, AR. 1996 Painting $5,000
Ann Chamberlin, Los Angeles, CA. 1992 Painting $5,000
Isabelle Chapman, Houston, TX. 1996 Painting $5,000
Michael R. Charles, Cedar Park, TX. 1994 Painting $5,000
Martin Fan Cheng, Lawrence, KS. 1988 Works on Paper $3,000
Judith Child, St. Louis, MO. 1996 Painting $5,000
Les Christensen, State University, AR. 1995 Sculpture $5,000
Lisa Cole-Kronenburg, Lenexa, KS. 1994 Painting $5,000
Michael Collins, Houston, TX. 1994 Painting $5,000
Jennifer Colten Schmidt, St. Louis, MO. 1993 Photography $5,000
Eduardo Conde, Fayetteville, AR. 1990 Crafts $5,000
Diane Covert, Belmont, MA. 1983 Photography $3,000
Reece Crawford, Omaha, NE. 1993 Sculpture $5,000
Warren Criswell, Benton, AR. 1996 Painting $5,000
Alison Crocetta, St. Louis, MO. 1995 Sculpture $5,000
Steven John Cromwell, Kansas City, MO. 1983 Photography $3,000
Kevin Cunningham, Houston, TX. 1988 Works on Paper $3,000

D

Susan Davidoff, El Paso, TX. 1994 Works on Paper $5,000
Leila Daw, Somerville, MA. 1990 Works on Paper $5,000
Blane De St. Croix, Omaha, NE. 1993 Sculpture $5,000
Meredith Dean, St. Louis, MO. 1984 Works on Paper $3,000
Phillip Rick Dingus, Lubbock, TX. 1987 Photography $3,000
Kenneth R. Dixon, Lubbock, TX. 1986 Works on Paper $3,000
Michael Doga, Houston, TX. 1990 Painting $5,000
Deborah Donoghue, St. Louis, MO. 1986 Works on Paper $3,000
James Drake, El Paso, TX. 1988 Works on Paper $3,000

E

Celia Eberle, Longview, TX. 1994 Painting $5,000
G. Noah Edmundson, Houston, TX. 1989 Sculpture $3,000
Peggy Eng, St. Louis, MO. 1995 Crafts $5,000
Sharon Engelstein, Houston, TX. 1993 Sculpture $5,000
Ken Engquist, Wichita, KS. 1991 Photography $5,000
Gaspar Enriquez, El Paso, TX. 1994 Painting $5,000
Eleanor Herren Erskine, Kansas City, MO. 1984 Works on Paper $3,000
Terry Thompson Evans, Sylvia, KS. 1983 Photography $3,000

F

Vincent Falsetta, Denton, TX. 1996 Painting $5,000
Catherine Ferguson, Omaha, NE. 1985 Sculpture $3,000
Larry Ferguson, Omaha, NE. 1983 Photography $3,000
Russell Ferguson, Kansas City, MO. 1992 Printmaking/Drawing/Artists' Books $5,000
Sandra Fiedorek, Austin, TX. 1992 Painting $5,000
Elisa Forgelman, St. Louis, MO. 1992 Works on Paper $5,000
Bill Frazier, Houston, TX. 1987 Photography/Experimental $3,000
Barbara Frets, Shawnee Mission, KS. 1986 Painting $3,000
Hirokazu Fukawa, Kansas City, MO. 1995 Sculpture $5,000
Janna Fulbright, Beaumont, TX. 1995 Photography $5,000

G

Michael Galbreth,, TX. 1995 Sculpture $5,000
William G. Ganzel, Lincoln, NE. 1983 Photography $3,000
Lilian Garcia-Roig, Austin, TX. 1994 Painting $5,000
Sid Garrison, Houston, TX. 1985 Crafts $3,000
Cathy Lynn Gasser, Lawrence, KS. 1993 Sculpture $5,000
Robin Dru Germany, Slaton, TX. 1991 Photography $5,000
Richard Gillespie, Lawrence, KS. 1985 Sculpture $3,000
Jake Gilson, Fort Worth, TX. 1996 Painting $5,000
Robly Glover, Lubbock, TX. 1993 Crafts $5,000
Steven Goff, Odessa, TX. 1987 Photography $3,000
Gary Goldberg, Wichita Falls, TX. 1983 Photography $3,000
Lester Goldman, Kansas City, MO. 1986 Painting $5,000
Jessica Gondek, Grand Rapids, MI. 1994 Painting $5,000
Shea Gordon, Kansas City, MO. 1986 Works on Paper $3,000
Thomas Gormally, Wichita, KS. 1985 Sculpture $3,000
Thomas S. Gregg, Kansas City, MO. 1994 Painting $5,000
Marcia Miller Gross, Kansas City, MO. 1993 Crafts $5,000
Dawn Guernsey, St. Louis, MO. 1996 Painting $5,000
John Gutowski, Kansas City, MO. 1987 Photography $3,000
Joe Guy, Fort Worth, TX. 1990 Painting $5,000

H

John Hadley, Norman, OK. 1985 $3,000
Kenneth J. Hale, Manchaca, TX. 1990 Works on Paper $5,000
Joan Hall, St. Louis, MO. 1984 Works on Paper $3,000
Leah Hardy, Huntsville, TX. 1993 Crafts $5,000
Cynthia Harper, Omaha, NE. 1994 Works on Paper $5,000
Susan Harrington, Fort Worth, TX. 1990 Painting $5,000
Lynn Havel, El Dorado, KS. 1984 Works on Paper $3,000
Jon Havener, Lawrence, KS. 1985 Sculpture $3,000
Edgar Heap of Birds, Geary, OK. 1988 Crafts $3,000

Frank Herbert, Longview, TX. 1990 Painting $5,000
John Hernandez, Dallas, TX. 1988 Painting $3,000
T. Paul Hernandez, Austin, TX. 1989 Sculpture $3,000
Richard Hinson, Houston, TX. 1993 Photography $5,000
Mark Hogensen, San Antonio, TX. 1994 Works on Paper $5,000
Kathleen Holder, Little Rock, AR. 1984 Works on Paper $3,000
Susan Horn, Lincoln, NE. 1983 Photography $3,000
Mary Jo Horning, Omaha, NE. 1992 Painting $5,000
Martha Horvay, Lincoln, NE. 1992 Painting $5,000
Perry House, Houston, TX. 1990 Painting $5,000
Randolph B. Howard, Austin, TX. 1990 Painting $5,000
Sandria Hu, Stanford, CA. 1986 Painting $3,000
Gerard D. Huber, Dallas, TX. 1994 Painting $5,000
Benito Huerta, Houston, TX. 1990 Painting $5,000
Debora Hunter, Dallas, TX. 1987 Photography $3,000
Gretchen Hupfel, Kansas City, MO. 1996 Painting $5,000

I

Earl Iversen, Lawrence, KS. 1983 Photography $3,000

J

Keith Jacobshagen, Lincoln, NE. 1983 Photography $3,000
Emily Jennings, Abilene, TX. 1989 Sculpture $3,000
Marilyn K. Jolly, Dallas, TX. 1986 Painting/Works on Paper $3,000
Mary Anne Jordan, KS. 1989 Crafts $3,000

K

Janet E. Kastner, Austin, TX. 1989 Crafts $5,000
Cima N. Katz, Baldwin, KS. 1984 Works on Paper $3,000
John Keech, State University, AR. 1992 Painting $5,000
Pat Kelly, Arlington, MA. 1988 Painting $3,000
Barbara F. Kendrick, Lincoln, NE. 1985 Sculpture $3,000
Bill Kennedy, Austin, TX. 1987 Photography $3,000
Christopher Ketchie, New Haven, CT. 1993 Sculpture $5,000
Christopher J. Kilmer, Shawnee, KS. 1983 Photography $3,000
Paul Kittelson, Houston, TX. 1989 Sculpture $3,000
Doug Koch, Kansas City, MO. 1983 Photography $3,000
Howard C. Koerth, Rutherford, OK. 1993 Crafts $5,000
Sharon Kopriva,. 1993 Sculpture $5,000
Kevin Kresse, Little Rock, AR. 1996 Painting $5,000
Bethany L. Kriegsman, Denver, CO. 1984 Works on Paper $3,000
Kathleen Kuchar, Hays, KS. 1986 Painting $3,000
Karen Kunc, Lincoln, NE. 1996 Painting $5,000
Randall J. Kust, Wichita, KS. 1984 Works on Paper $3,000

L

Pok-Chi Lau, Lawrence, KS. 1983 Photography $3,000
Thana Lauhakaikul, Austin, TX. 1989 Sculpture $3,000
Sherry Leedy, Lake Lotawana, MO. 1984 Crafts $3,000
Joan Levinson, St. Louis, MO. 1990 Painting $5,000
Anne Lindberg, Kansas City, MO. 1993 Crafts $5,000
Eric Lindveit, Chicago, IL. 1993 Sculpture $5,000
Harry Littell, Omaha, NE. 1989 Sculpture $3,000
Ken Little, Norman, OK. 1985 Sculpture $3,000
Kathy Lovas, Dallas, TX. 1995 Photography $5,000
Mark Lyman, St. Louis, MO. 1985 Crafts $3,000
Giles Lyon, Houston, TX. 1994 Painting $5,000

M

Margaret MacKichan, Lincoln, NE. 1983 Photography $3,000
David Mackie, Cypress, TX. 1990 Painting $5,000
Joe Mancuso, Houston, TX. 1994 Painting/Works on Paper $5,000
Peter Marcus, St. Louis, MO. 1984 Works on Paper $3,000
Neil Maurer, San Antonio, TX. 1995 Photography $5,000
Mary F. McCleary, Nacogdoches, TX. 1988 Painting $3,000
Sharon McConnell, Chicago, IL. 1989 Crafts $5,000
Judith B. McCrea, Lawrence, KS. 1988 Painting $3,000
Patrick Mcfarlin, Benton, AR. 1986 Painting $3,000
David McGee, Houston, TX. 1996 Painting $5,000
Elizabeth McGrath, San Antonio, TX. 1995 Sculpture $5,000
David Melby, Leavenworth, KS. 1986 Painting $3,000
C. Meng, San Marcos, TX. 1992 Painting $5,000
Sunni Mercer, Yukon, OK. 1995 Crafts $5,000
Hugh J. Merrill, Kansas City, MO. 1992 Works on Paper $5,000
Neva Mikulicz, Houston, TX. 1994 Works on Paper $5,000
Michael C. Miller, Commerce, TX. 1992 Painting $5,000
John Moler, New Braunfels, TX. 1995 Photography $5,000
Bernice Montgomery, Dallas, TX. 1996 Painting $5,000
Anthony Montoya, Lincoln, NE. 1983 Photography $3,000
Pamela Moore, Dallas, TX. 1994 Works on Paper $5,000
Diane Morley, West Memphis, AR. 1990 Painting $5,000
Rosalind-Kimball Moulton, Columbia, MO. 1987 Photography $3,000
James Munce, Manhattan, KS. 1984 Works on Paper $3,000
Deborah J. Murphy, Omaha, NE. 1994 Painting $5,000

N

David Najjab, Garland, TX. 1993 Photography $5,000
Christina Narwicz, Omaha, NE. 1996 Painting $5,000
Edward Navone, Topeka, KS. 1986 Painting $3,000
Fredrick J. Nelson, St. Louis, MO. 1990 Painting $5,000
Nic Nicosia, Dallas, TX. 1991 Photography $5,000
Leon Niehues, Huntsville, AR. 1995 Crafts $5,000
Garry Noland, Independence, MO. 1994 Painting/Works on Paper $5,000
Michael Nye, San Antonio, TX. 1991 Photography $5,000

O

Raymond Olivero, Ft. Lauderdale, FL. 1992 Painting $5,000
Lisa Orr, Austin, TX. 1995 Crafts $5,000

P

James R. Pace, Tyler, TX. 1992 Works on Paper $5,000
Suzanne Paquette, San Antonio, TX. 1990 Painting $5,000
Aaron Parazette, Houston, TX. 1994 Painting $5,000
Jorge J. Pardo, Austin, TX. 1988 Painting $3,000
Gregory Parker, Topeka, KS. 1986 Painting $3,000
Gary Passanise, St. Louis, MO. 1994 Painting/Works on Paper $5,000
Gloria Osuna Perez, El Paso, TX. 1994 Painting $5,000
Mario Perez, Houston, TX. 1992 Works on Paper $5,000
Sarah Perkins, Springfield, MO. 1995 Crafts $5,000
Sammy Peters, Little Rock, AR. 1992 Painting $5,000
Bradley R. Petersen, Austin, TX. 1994 Painting $5,000
Michael Peven, Fayetteville, AR. 1983 Works on Paper $3,000
David Phelps, Norman, OK. 1985 Sculpture $3,000
E. Barry Phillips, Odessa, TX. 1988 Works on Paper $3,000
Donna Pinckley, Little Rock, AR. 1995 Photography $5,000
James B. Pink, Norman, OK. 1984 Works on Paper $3,000
Jason Pollen, Kansas City, MO. 1989 Crafts $3,000
John Pomara, Dallas, TX. 1990 Painting $5,000
J. Alex Potter, Hutchinson, KS. 1994 Painting/Works on Paper $5,000
Carolyn Prescott, Austin, TX. 1992 Painting $5,000
Susan Puelz, Lincoln, NE. 1986 Painting $3,000

Q

William Quinn, St. Louis, MO. 1986 Painting $3,000

R

Roxanne Rackerby, Fayetteville, AR. 1983 Photography $3,000
Chris Ramsay, Stillwater, OK. 1993 Crafts $5,000
Kathleen A. Raymond, Richardson, TX. 1994 Painting/Works on Paper $5,000
Dave Read, Lincoln, NE. 1983 Photography $3,000
Dianne L. Reeves, Austin, TX. 1986 Works on Paper $3,000
Joseph M. Renard, St. Louis, MO. 1986 Painting $3,000
Nancy Newman Rice, St. Louis, MO. 1986 Painting $3,000
Patricia D. Richards, Plano, TX. 1991 Photography $5,000
Linda Murphy Robbennolt, Oklahoma City, OK. 1983 Photography $3,000
Riley B. Robinson, Helotes, TX. 1995 Sculpture $5,000
Dana Romeis, St. Louis, MO. 1989 Crafts $3,000
Craig Roper, Lincoln, NE. 1991 Photography $5,000
Gloria Ross, Plano, TX. 1992 Works on Paper $5,000
Dean Ruck, Houston, TX. 1989 Sculpture $3,000
Robert Ruello, Houston, TX. 1992 Painting $5,000
Ricardo Ruiz, Corpus Christi, TX. 1992 Painting $5,000
Kent T. Rush, San Antonio, TX. 1991 Photography $5,000

S

Jim Sajovic, Kansas City, MO. 1986 Painting $3,000
John Salvest, State University, AR. 1993 Sculpture $5,000
Arturo Sanchez, Houston, TX. 1986 Painting $3,000
William Sapp, Little Rock, AR. 1985 Sculpture $3,000

Majorie Schick, Pittsburg, KS. 1985 Crafts $3,000
Shirley Luke Schnell, Lee's Summit, MO. 1996 Painting $5,000
Patrick Schuchard, St. Louis, MO. 1993 Sculpture $5,000
Larry W. Schwarm, Emporia, KS. 1991 Photography $5,000
Beth Secor, Houston, TX. 1994 Painting $5,000
Cindy Sims, Arlington, TX. 1987 Photography $3,000
Luther Smith, Fort Worth, TX. 1993 Photography $5,000
Sharon E. Smith, Austin, TX. 1995 Crafts $5,000
Hills Snyder, Helotes, TX. 1995 Sculpture $5,000
John Sparagana, Houston, TX. 1988 Painting $3,000
F. L. Doc Spellmon, San Antonio, TX. 1990 Painting $5,000
John Spence, Lincoln, NE. 1983 Photography $3,000
Laurie Spencer, Tulsa, OK. 1985 Crafts $3,000
Mary Sprague, St. Louis, MO. 1984 Painting $3,000
Lin Stanionis, Amarillo, TX. 1993 Crafts $5,000
Robert Starck, Roca, NE. 1983 Photography $3,000
Henry Stein, San Antonio, TX. 1995 Sculpture $5,000
Sharon Stewart, Chaconn, NM. 1991 Photography $5,000
Donna Phipps Stout, Winslow, AR. 1996 Painting $5,000
Ken Stout, Winslow, AR. 1990 Painting $5,000
Stan Strembicki, St. Louis, MO. 1993 Photography $5,000
Beryl Striewski, Houston, TX. 1987 Photography $3,000
Charles Stroh, Manhattan, KS. 1996 Painting $5,000
Kim Strommen, St. Louis, MO. 1985 Sculpture $3,000
Corky Stuckenbruck, Weston, TX. 1989 Crafts $3,000
Edward Sturr, Manhattan, KS. 1995 Photography $5,000
Gary Sutton, Independence, MO. 1991 Photography $5,000
Jon Keith Swindell, Lawrence, KS. 1989 Sculpture $3,000
David Szafranski, Irving, TX. 1994 Painting/Works on Paper $5,000

T

Tom Tarnowski, Overland Park, KS. 1991 Photography $5,000
Ronald W. Thomas, St. Louis, MO. 1984 Works on Paper $3,000
Sally Thomas, Manhattan, KS. 1996 Painting $5,000
William R. Thomas, Houston, TX. 1995 Photography $5,000
Donald Thompson, Tulsa, OK. 1993 Photography $5,000
Richard Thompson, San Antonio, TX. 1986 Painting $3,000
Jackie Tileston, Houston, TX. 1994 Painting $5,000
James Tisdale, Austin, TX. 1995 Painting/Works on Paper $5,000
Mark Todd, San Marcos, TX. 1986 Works on Paper $3,000
Lana Turner, Kansas City, MO. 1996 Painting $5,000

U

Munya Avighil Upin, San Antonio, TX. 1989 Crafts $3,000

V

Kathy Vargas, San Antonio, TX. 1995 Photography $5,000
David Vertacnik, Lawrence, KS. 1985 Sculpture $3,000
Joseph Vitone, Austin, TX. 1993 Photography $5,000

W

Susan Elaine Wallace, Houston, TX. 1992 Painting $5,000
Lloyd Walsh, San Antonio, TX. 1996 Painting $5,000
Kenny Walton, Avoca, NE. 1995 Crafts $5,000
Liz Ward, Houston, TX. 1992 Photography $5,000
Mary Warner, Norman, OK. 1984 Works on Paper $3,000
Jacqueline Warren, Springfield, MO. 1986 Painting $3,000
Linda Warren, Oklahoma City, OK. 1986 Painting $3,000
Wendy Watriss, Houston, TX. 1987 Photography $3,000
Steven D. Watson, Fort Worth, TX. 1995 Photography $5,000
Sam Wayne, St. Louis, MO. 1986 Painting $3,000
Bruce West, Mount Angel, OR. 1987 Photography $3,000
Barbara Westerfield, Indianapolis, IN. 1986 Works on Paper $3,000
Gina Westergard, Lawrence, KS. 1995 Crafts $5,000
David Wharton, Austin, TX. 1987 Photography $3,000
Michael Whitehead, Dallas, TX. 1996 Painting $5,000
Lea Whittington, Houston, TX. 1995 Sculpture $5,000
Marjorie Williams-Smith, Little Rock, AR. 1984 Works on Paper $3,000
Geoff Winningham, Houston, TX. 1993 Photography $5,000
Roger Winter, Dallas, TX. 1988 Painting $3,000
William Wolfram, Seward, NE. 1984 Works on Paper $3,000
Alexis E. Wreden, St. Louis, MO. 1985 Sculpture $3,000

Y

Sydney P. Yeager, Austin, TX. 1996 Painting $5,000
Hugh Charles Yorty, Springfield, MO. 1988 Painting $3,000

Z

Gregory Zeorlin, Tyler, TX. 1993 Crafts $5,000
Robert Ziebell, Port Bolibar, TX. 1987 Photography $3,000

Mid-Atlantic Arts Foundation

Visual Artists' Fellowships

A

Elizabeth Albert, Brooklyn, NY. 1996 Painting $5,000
Mike Alewitz, New Brunswick, NJ. 1992 Painting $5,000
Pat Alexander, Baltimore, MD. 1989 Crafts $3,000
Candida Alvarez, New Haven, CT. 1988 Works on Paper $3,000
Suzanne Amendolara, Edinboro, PA. 1995 Crafts $5,000
Barbara E. Ames, Richmond, VA. 1995 Photography $5,000
Humberto Aquino, New York, NY. 1988 Works on Paper $3,000
Ilan Averbuch, Long Island City, NY. 1991 Sculpture $5,000

B

Pat Bacon, Lyons, NY. 1992 Works on Paper $5,000
Eugene Baguskas, Philadelphia, PA. 1990 Painting $5,000
Xenobia Bailey, New York, NY. 1993 Crafts $5,000
V. Bambini, Brooklyn, NY. 1994 Works on Paper $5,000
William Baran-Mickle, Rochester, NY. 1989 Crafts $3,000
Jill Baroff, Brooklyn, NY. 1988 Works on Paper $3,000
Ronald Baron, Brooklyn, NY. 1991 Sculpture $5,000
Barron Burke, Erie, PA. 1988 Works on Paper $3,000
Catherine Batza, Washington, DC. 1988 Works on Paper $3,000
Miriam Beerman, Montclair, NJ. 1996 Works on Paper $5,000
Catherine Behrent, Baltimore, MD. 1994 Painting $5,000
Dawoud Bey, New Haven, CT. 1991 Photography $5,000
Michael K. Bisbee, New York, NY. 1988 Works on Paper $3,000
Dike Blair, New York, NY. 1988 Works on Paper $3,000
Miriam Bloom, New York, NY. 1993 Crafts $5,000
Suzanne Bocanegra, New York, NY. 1991 Sculpture $5,000
Katherine Bowling, New York, NY. 1988 Crafts $3,000
Roger Boyce, New York, NY. 1990 Painting $5,000
Daniel R. Brewer, Philadelphia, PA. 1996 Works on Paper $5,000
Lucinda Brogden, Rochester, NY. 1989 Crafts $3,000
Jane Bruce, New York, NY. 1989 Crafts $3,000
Wayne Edson Bryan, Alexandria, VA. 1990 Painting $5,000
Charlie Buck, Philadelphia, PA. 1989 Crafts $3,000
Kendall Buster, Washington, DC. 1995 Sculpture $5,000
John Eric Byers, Philadelphia, PA. 1993 Crafts $5,000
Judy Byron, Washington, DC. 1992 Works on Paper $5,000

C

Syd Carpenter, Philadelphia, PA. 1989 Crafts $3,000
Paul Chaleff, Pine Plains, NY. 1989 Crafts $3,000
Nancy Chalker-Tennant, Rochester, NY. 1994 Works on Paper $5,000
Catherine Chalmers, New York, NY. 1995 Photography $5,000
John Cleary, Salisbury, MD. 1994 Painting $5,000
M. J. Connors, Brooklyn, NY. 1991 Photography $5,000
Douglas Cooper, Pittsburgh, PA. 1994 Works on Paper $5,000
Teri Cotruzzola, New Paltz, NY. 1993 Crafts $5,000
Annette Cyr, New York, NY. 1996 Painting $5,000

D

Ardyth Davis, Reston, VA. 1989 Crafts $3,000
Lisa Corinne Davis, New York, NY. 1992 Works on Paper $5,000
Nancy Diamond, New York, NY. 1996 Painting $5,000
Judite Dos Santos, New York, NY. 1988 Works on Paper $3,000
Leonardo Drew, New York, NY. 1993 Sculpture $5,000

E

Jean Edelstein, New York, NY. 1996 Works on Paper $5,000
Barbara Ess, New York, NY. 1991 Photography $5,000
Roger Essley, Alexandria, VA. 1988 Works on Paper $3,000

F

Rochelle Feinstein, New York, NY. 1990 Painting $5,000
Robert Flynt, New York, NY. 1995 Photography $5,000
Walton Ford, New York, NY. 1990 Painting $5,000
Claire Freeman, Edgewater, MD. 1990 Painting $5,000

G

Sonia Gechtoff, New York, NY. 1988 Works on Paper $3,000
Michele Godwin, New York, NY. 1994 Works on Paper $5,000
Kenneth P. Goldsmith, New York, NY. 1991 Sculpture $5,000
Mark Goodwin, Philadelphia, PA. 1996 Works on Paper $5,000
Don Green, Delhi, NY. 1995 Crafts $5,000
Joseph Grigely, Jersey City, NJ. 1995 Sculpture $5,000
Kenneth Groves, Nettie, WV. 1989 Sculpture $3,000
Will Guy, New York, NY. 1994 Painting $5,000

H

Matthew Haberstroh, New York, NY. 1990 Painting $5,000
Beth Haggart, Gillette, NJ. 1993 Sculpture $5,000
Rodney Harder, New York, NY. 1990 Painting $5,000
Mark D. Harrell, Baltimore, MD. 1991 Photography $5,000
Bryan Hillstrom, New York, NY. 1990 Painting $5,000
Alyssa Hinton, Fleetwood, PA. 1990 Painting $5,000
Richard A. Hirsch, Churchville, NY. 1995 Crafts $5,000
Miriam Hitchcock, Ithaca, NY. 1990 Painting $5,000
Frank I. Hobbs, Staunton, VA. 1996 Works on Paper $5,000
Jim Hodges, New York, NY. 1992 Works on Paper $5,000
Ricardo Hoegg, Baltimore, MD. 1992 Painting $5,000
Marilyn Holsing, Merion Station, PA. 1996 Painting $5,000
Sharon Horvath, Brooklyn, NY. 1994 Painting $5,000
Richard Hricko, Philadelphia, PA. 1994 Works on Paper $5,000
Thomas Hubert, Fairview, PA. 1995 Crafts $5,000
Woody Hughes, Wading River, NY. 1989 Crafts $3,000
Jenny Humphreys, Brooklyn, NY. 1990 Painting $5,000
Frank Hyder, Philadelphia, PA. 1993 Crafts $5,000

J

Jeanne Jaffe, Philadelphia, PA. 1993 Crafts $5,000
Sungjoon Joh, New York, NY. 1994 Painting $5,000
Sue Johnson, Hollywood, MD. 1994 Painting $5,000
Mablen Jones, New York, NY. 1988 Works on Paper $3,000
Sally Jones, Worcester, NY. 1989 Crafts $3,000
Mary Judge, New York, NY. 1996 Works on Paper $5,000

K

Shirley Kaneda, New York, NY. 1996 Painting $5,000
Enid Kaplan, New York, NY. 1989 Crafts $3,000
Taka Kawachi, Brooklyn, NY. 1990 Painting $5,000
Shirley Keys, Potomac, MD. 1989 Crafts $3,000
Barbara Klein, Lawrenceville, NJ. 1992 Works on Paper $5,000
Peter W. Krashes, Brooklyn, NY. 1996 Painting $5,000
Alyssa Dee Krauss, Newton, NJ. 1995 Crafts $5,000
David Krueger, Hyattsville, MD. 1996 Painting $5,000

L

Eve Andree Laramee, Brooklyn, NY. 1995 Sculpture $5,000
Jenny Lavin, Brooklyn, NY. 1994 Works on Paper $5,000
Ora Lerman, New York, NY. 1992 Painting $5,000
David Lewin, Millville, NJ. 1995 Crafts $5,000
Susan Lipper, New York, NY. 1995 Photography $5,000
Hilary S. Lorenz, New York, NY. 1996 Works on Paper $5,000
Patrick Loughran, New York, NY. 1989 Crafts $3,000
Whitfield Lovell, New York, NY. 1992 Works on Paper $5,000
Kate Loye, Brooklyn, NY. 1993 Sculpture $5,000
Mark Lueders, Strafford, PA. 1995 Crafts $5,000
Marlen Lugo, New York, NY. 1993 Sculpture $5,000
Marcia Lyons, New York, NY. 1994 Works on Paper $5,000

M

Daniel Mack, Warwick, NY. 1989 Crafts $3,000
Martha Madigan, Philadelphia, PA. 80 Photography $3,000
Henrietta Mantooth, New York, NY. 1996 Painting $5,000
Sherwin Mark, Baltimore, MD. 1991 Sculpture $5,000
Jenny Marketou, New York, NY. 1991 Photography $5,000
China Marks, New York, NY. 1994 Works on Paper $5,000
Fidel Marquez, New York, NY. 1990 Painting $5,000
Frederick Marshall, Paterson, NJ. 1989 Crafts $3,000
Claudia Matzko, Brooklyn, NY. 1993 Sculpture $5,000
Scott L. Mccarney, Rochester, NY. 1996 Works on Paper $5,000
Jan Mehn, Newark, DE. 1988 Works on Paper $3,000
Geanna Merola, Ocean Grove, NJ. 1995 Photography $5,000
Marianne Mitchell, Lafayette Hills, PA. 1992 Painting $5,000
Chevelle Makeba Moore, Baltimore, MD. 1996 Painting $5,000
Susan Moore, Philadelphia, PA.1988 Works on Paper $3,000
Jim Morris, Buffalo, NY. 1991 Sculpture $5,000
Annette Morriss, Pawling, NY. 1992 Works on Paper $5,000

N

Tom Nakashima, Washington, DC. 1992 Painting $5,000
Shirin Neshat, New York, NY. 1995 Photography $5,000

O

Matt Nolen, New York, NY. 1995 Crafts $5,000
Aric Obrosey, New York, NY. 1996 Works on Paper $5,000
Trisha Orr, Charlottesville, VA. 1994 Painting $5,000

P

Lawley Paisley-Jones, Arlington, VA. 1992 Painting $5,000
Joyce Pensato, Brooklyn, NY. 1992 Works on Paper $5,000
Phyllis Plattner, Bethesda, MD. 1988 Painting $3,000
Rona Pondick, New York, NY. 1991 Sculpture $5,000
Liliana Porter, New York, NY. 1994 Works on Paper $5,000
Nadezda Prvulovic, Columbia, MD. 1990 Works on Paper $5,000
Ernesto Pujol, Brooklyn, NY. 1994 Painting $5,000

Q

Laurel Quarberg, Norfolk, VA. 1995 Sculpture $5,000

R

Ann Reeves, Hackettstown, NJ. 1994 Painting $5,000
David Riffle, Charleston, WV. 1994 Painting $5,000
Supratman Rikin, Baltimore, MD. 1995 Crafts $5,000
Nancy Ring, New York, NY. 1988 Works on Paper $3,000
Jack Risley, Brooklyn, NY. 1995 Sculpture $5,000
Douglas Ritter, Baltimore, MD. 1990 Painting $5,000
Jose M. Riveros, New York, NY. 1994 Works on Paper $5,000
Angel Rodriguez-Diaz, Brooklyn, NY. 1994 Painting $5,000
Ruth Root, New York, NY. 1996 Painting $5,000
Michael Ross, Brooklyn, NY. 1995 Sculpture $5,000
Stephanie Rowden, Brooklyn, NY. 1993 Sculpture $5,000
Eleanor Rufty, Richmond, VA. 1994 Works on Paper $5,000
Barnaby Ruhe, Emmaus, PA. 1994 Painting $5,000

S

Debra M. Sachs, Gloucester City, NJ. 1995 Crafts $5,000
Glen Sacks, New York, NY. 1994 Works on Paper $5,000
Robert Allen Salazar, Baltimore, MD. 1995 Photography $5,000
Meg Fish Saligman, Philadelphia, PA. 1996 Painting $5,000
Rodney Sappington, Garden Grove, CA. 1988 Works on Paper $3,000
Jeffrey Henson Scales, New York, NY. 1991 Photography $5,000
Bill Scanga, New York, NY. 1995 Sculpture $5,000
Ruth Scheuer, New York, NY. 1989 Crafts $3,000
Julie Schneider, Arlington, VA. 1988 Works on Paper $3,000
Elinore Schnurr, Long Island City, NY. 1994 Works on Paper $5,000
Beverly Semmes, New York, NY. 1991 Sculpture $5,000
Paul Sherman, Le Roy, NY. 1989 Crafts $3,000
Sandra Sherman, Philadelphia, PA. 1989 Crafts $3,000
James Sherwood, Silver Spring, MD. 1991 Photography $5,000
David T. Shevlino, Swedesboro, NJ. 1996 Painting $5,000
Drew Ellen Shiflett, New York, NY. 1993 Sculpture $5,000
Stuart Shils, Philadelphia, PA. 1996 Painting $5,000
Beth Shively, Roanoke, VA. 1992 Painting $5,000
Robert Sholties, New Kensington, PA. 1990 Painting $5,000
Ann Shostrom, New York, NY. 1990 Painting $5,000
Christopher Silliman, Richmond, VA. 1993 Crafts $5,000
Sara Sosnowy, Brooklyn, NY. 1996 Works on Paper $5,000
Taylor Spence, Jersey City, NJ. [illegible] Works on Paper $5,000
Carla Starkey, Easton, MD. 1989 Crafts $3,000
Elizabeth Stephens, Jersey City, NJ. 1993 Sculpture $5,000
Alan Stone, Washington, DC. 1991 Sculpture $5,000

Lawre Stone, Brooklyn, NY. 1990 Painting $5,000
Karen Stool, Pittsburgh, PA. 1993 Crafts $5,000
Laura Stout, Brooklyn, NY. 1994 Works on Paper $5,000
Renee Stout, Washington, DC. 1993 Sculpture $5,000
Helen Stummer, Metuchen, NJ. 1991 Photography $5,000

T

Denyse Thomasos, New York, NY. 1994 Painting $5,000
Michael Tighe, Trenton, NJ. 1990 Works on Paper $5,000
Danny Tisdale, New York, NY. 1991 Sculpture $5,000
Andrew L. Topolski, Brooklyn, NY. 1995 Sculpture $5,000
Richard Torchia, Philadelphia, PA. 1995 Photography $5,000
Anne Turyn, New York, NY. 1991 Photography $5,000
Scott Tyler, Brooklyn, NY. 1995 Photography $5,000

U

Shari Urquhart, Brooklyn, NY. 1993 Crafts $5,000
Josette Urso, New York, NY. 1994 Painting $5,000

V

Pamela Vanderzwan, Brooklyn, NY. 1991 Crafts $5,000
Francisco Vidal, Flushing, NY. 1992 Painting $5,000
Kurt Von Voetsch, Niagara Falls, NY. 1995 Sculpture $5,000

W

Ronald Lee Washington, Philadelphia, PA. 1992 Painting $5,000
Steven S. Waterman, Jersey City, NJ. 1993 Crafts $5,000
William T. Williams, New York, NY 1994 Painting $5,000
Fred Wilson, New York, NY. 1993 Sculpture $5,000

Y

Yuriko Yamaguchi, Vienna, VA. 1995 Sculpture $5,000

Z

Philip Zimmermann, Rhinecliff, NY. 1994 Works on Paper $5,000

Arts Midwest

Visual Artists' Fellowships

A

Hilary Abuhove, Chicago, IL. 1994 Works on Paper $5,000
Iris Adler, Highland Park, IL. 1989 Sculpture $3,000
Harold Allen, Highland Park, MI. 1988 Painting $3,000
Arthur Amiotte, Custer, SD. 1996 Painting $5,000
John Andrews, Oxford, IA. 1992 Works on Paper $5,000
Marilyn Annin, Ames, IA. 1993 Sculpture $5,000

B

Brenda Baker, Madison, WI. 1991 Sculpture $5,000
Pamela Bannos, Chicago, IL. 1995 Photography $5,000
Brenda Barnum, Chicago, IL. 1986 Painting $3,000
Frank Barsotti, Chicago, IL. 1985 Photography $3,000
Harriet Bart, Minneapolis, MN. 1993 Sculpture $5,000
Sonya Baysinger, Chicago, IL. 1995 Crafts $5,000
Leslie Bell, Davenport, IA. 1994 Painting $5,000
Sara Belleau, Plymouth, WI. 1995 Photography $5,000
Paul S. Benson, Minneapolis, MN. 1994 Painting $5,000
Steve Benson, Ferndale, MI. 1985 Photography $3,000
Mary Bero, Madison, WI. 1985 Crafts $3,000
Jerry Bleem, Cicero, IL. 1993 Crafts $5,000
Janet Bloch, Chicago, IL. 1996 Painting $5,000
Monica Bock, Chicago, IL. 1993 Sculpture $5,000
J. Karl Bogartte, Milwaukee, WI. 1990 Works on Paper $5,000
Lowell Boileau, Highland Park, MI. 1990 Painting $5,000
Andrew Borowiec, Akron, OH. 1985 Photography $3,000
George Bowes, Cleveland, OH. 1993 Crafts $5,000
K. Johnson Bowles, Webster, TX. 1990 Works on Paper $5,000
Steve P. Bradford, Cleveland, OH. 1989 Crafts $5,000
Virginia Bradley, Minneapolis, MN. 1990 Painting $5,000
Werner Brause, Paterson, NJ. 1986 Painting $3,000
Deborah Brod, Cincinnati, OH. 1995 Crafts $5,000
Queen E. Brooks, Columbus, OH. 1994 Painting $5,000
Matt Brown, Minneapolis, MN. 1986 Painting $3,000
Wendy Brown, Riverside, CA. 1989 Photography $3,000
Daniel Bruggeman, Saint Paul, MN. 1994 Painting $5,000
Fred L. Bruney, Arlington Heights, IL. 1993 Sculpture $5,000
Gloria D. Brush, Duluth, MN. 82 Photography $5,000
James Bruss, Columbus, OH. 1986 Works on Paper $3,000
Jan Buckman, Hager City, WI. 1985 Crafts $3,000
Joel Bujnowski, Downers Grove, IL. 1990 Works on Paper $5,000
Douglas Bulka, Detroit, MI. 1996 Painting $5,000
Byron Burford, Iowa City, IA. 1988 Painting $3,000

C

Steve Cagan, Cleveland Heights, OH. 1995 Photography $5,000
Michael Peter Cain, Fairfield, IA. 1989 Photography $3,000
Jane Calvin, Chicago, IL. 1995 Photography $5,000
Cole Carothers, Milford, OH. 1986 Painting $3,000
Rodney Carswell, Oak Park, IL. 1988 Painting $3,000
Bill Cass, Chicago, IL. 1986 Painting $3,000
Nick Cave, Chicago, IL. 1993 Crafts $5,000
Victoria Christen, Minneapolis, MN. 1987 Crafts $3,000
Diane T. Christiansen, Chicago, IL. 1992 Painting $5,000
Laurie Beth Clark, Madison, WI. 1989 Sculpture $3,000
Morgan Clifford, St. Paul, MN. 1991 Crafts $5,000
Jay Constantine, Grand Rapids, MI. 1994 Painting $5,000
Jon Cook, Chicago, IL. 1989 Sculpture $3,000
Barbara Cooper, Chicago, IL. 1993 Sculpture $5,000
Amy Cordova, St. Paul, MN. 1987 Crafts $3,000
Frances A. Cox, Evanston, IL. 1996 Painting $5,000

D

Ioana Datcu, Saint Paul, MN. 1994 Works on Paper $5,000
Robin Davis, New Harmony, IN. 1986 Painting $3,000
Pamela De Marris, Muncie, IN. 1993 Photography $5,000
Miles DeCoster, Chicago, IL. 1988 Works on Paper $3,000
Harris Deller, Carbondale, IL. 1991 Crafts $5,000
Carl Demeulenaere, Detroit, MI. 1994 Works on Paper $5,000
William Depalma, Cleveland, OH. 1991 Photography $5,000
Daniel J. Devening, Chicago, IL. 1994 Painting $5,000
John Di Stefano, Chicago, IL. 1996 Works on Paper $5,000
David Dick, Minneapolis, MN. 1995 Sculpture $5,000
Rose Divita, Chicago, IL. 1996 Painting $5,000
John Dunn, Iowa City, IA. 1988 Painting $3,000

E

Fred Easker, Cedar Rapids, IA. 1996 Painting $5,000
Kathleen Eaton, Sleepy Hollow, IL. 1994 Painting $5,000
David Eckard, Chicago, IL. 1991 Sculpture $5,000
Jil Evans, Northfield, MN. 1986 Painting $3,000
Kevin Jerome Everson, Cleveland, OH. 1995 Photography $5,000

F

Brian Fekete, Detroit, MI. 1986 Painting $3,000
Joel Feldman, Murphysboro, IL. 1992 Works on Paper $5,000
Julia Fish, Chicago, IL. 1986 Painting $5,000
Claude Fixler, Waterville, OH. 1986 Painting $3,000
John William Ford, Lomira, WI. 1991 Sculpture $5,000
Ed Fraga, Detroit, MI. 1992 Painting $5,000
John Fraser, St. Charles, IL. 1992 Works on Paper $5,000
Jeff Freeman, Vermillion, SD. 1990 Painting $5,000
Clare Frigo, St. Paul, MN. 1993 Photography $5,000

G

Linda Gammell, St. Paul, MN. 1989 Photography $3,000
Cliff Garten, St. Paul, MN. 1985 Crafts $3,000
Rebecca Gee, Chicago, IL. 1995 Sculpture $5,000
Lynn Geesaman, Minneapolis, MN. 1993 Photography $5,000
Ronald Geibert, Dayton, OH. 1985 Photography $3,000
Richard George, Hamilton, OH. 1986 Painting $3,000
Gaylen Gerber, Chicago, IL. 1994 Painting $5,000
Meg Gerken, Chicago, IL. 1991 Photography $5,000
Jane Gilmor, Cedar Rapids, IA. 1985 Crafts $3,000
Nancy Gipple, Afton, MN. 1985 Crafts $3,000
Karen Glaser, Chicago, IL. 1991 Photography $5,000
Robert Gniewek, Dearborn, MI. 1988 Painting $3,000
Gadi Gofbarg, Albuquerque, NM. 1991 Photography $5,000

David Goldes, Minneapolis, MN. 1995 Photography $5,000
Mark Gordon, Des Moines, IA. 1989 Sculpture $3,000
Michael Goss, Chicago, IL. 1985 Photography $3,000
Michelle A. Grabner, Milwaukee, WI. 1996 Painting $5,000
Vicki Grafentin, Madison, WI. 1992 Works on Paper $5,000
Myra Mimlitsch Gray, Kingston, NY. 1991 Crafts $5,000
Richard L. Gray, South Bend, IN. 1985 Photography $3,000
Harold Gregor, Bloomington, IL. 1986 Painting $5,000
Dennison W. Griffith, Columbus, OH. 1990 Painting $5,000
Vicky Grube, Kalona, IA. 1986 Painting $3,000
Olivia Gude, Chicago, IL. 1996 Painting $5,000
Sheridan Dan Gustin, Chicago, IL. 1992 Painting $5,000
Terry Gydesen, Minneapolis, MN. 1989 Photography $3,000

H

David Hall, Bloomington, MN. 1989 Sculpture $3,000
Lynn Hambrick-Lukas, Minneapolis, MN. 1991 Photography $5,000
Tim Harding, St. Paul, MN. 1985 Crafts $3,000
William Harroff, Edwardsville, IL. 1994 Works on Paper $5,000
Don Harvey, Cleveland, OH. 1992 Painting $5,000
Masumi Hayashi, Cleveland, OH. 1989 Photography $3,000
Lillian Heard, Chicago, IL. 1992 Painting $5,000
Steven Heilmer, Greenville,. 1995 Sculpture $5,000
Paula Henderson, Evanston, IL. 1996 Painting $5,000
Frank Herrmann, Cincinnati, OH. 1990 Painting $5,000
Nancy Hild, Lisle, IL. 1990 Works on Paper $5,000
Craig Hinshaw, Davison, MI. 1993 Crafts $5,000
Stephen Hodder, Princeton, MN. 1985 Crafts $3,000
David Hodges, Chicago, IL. 1994 Painting $5,000
Angelika Hofmann, Berkeley, CA. 1995 Sculpture $5,000
Steven B. Hudson, Chicago, IL. 1994 Painting $5,000
Doug Huston, Chicago, IL. 1994 Works on Paper $5,000

I

Clary Illian, Ely, IA. 1987 Crafts $3,000

J

Jed Jackson, Murphysboro, IL. 1992 Painting $5,000
Carol Jacobsen, Ann Arbor, MI. 1989 Sculpture $3,000
Barbara Jaffee, Chicago, IL. 1986 Painting $3,000
Valerie Jenkins, Minneapolis, MN. 1996 Painting $5,000
Indira Johnson, Evanston, IL. 1989 Crafts $3,000
Janel Johnson, Des Moines, IA. 1993 Sculpture $5,000
Geary A. Jones, Grand Rapids, MI. 1991 Crafts $5,000
Kathy Hemingway Jones, Minneapolis, MN. 1987 Photography $3,000
Richard Judd, Paoli, WI. 1991 Crafts $5,000
Anita Jung, Normal, IL. 1992 Works on Paper $5,000

K

Shana Kaplow, Hastings, MN. 1994 Painting $5,000
Michael Kareken, Minneapolis, MN. 1994 Works on Paper $5,000
Anne Karsten, Chicago, IL. 1994 Works on Paper $5,000
Dina Kawer, Huntington Woods, MI. 1993 Photography $5,000
Ann B. Keister, Bloomington, IL. 1987 Crafts $3,000
Richard E. Kelley, Des Moines, IA. 1988 Painting $3,000
Angela Kelly, Oak Park, IL. 1987 Photography $3,000
Gail Kendall, Lincoln, NE. 1985 Crafts $3,000
Peggy Kendellen, Portland, OR. 1989 Crafts $3,000
Kate Kern, Cincinnati, OH. 1990 Works on Paper $5,000
Gregory King, Chicago, IL. 1996 Painting $5,000
Joseph Kress, Minneapolis, MN. 1989 Crafts $3,000
Charles Krider, Columbus, OH. 1985 Photography $3,000
Kristy Krivitsky, Savannah, OH/Milwaukee, WI. 1996 Painting $5,000
David Kroll, Elgin, IL. 1996 Painting $5,000
Ron Kroutel, Athens, OH. 1992 Works on Paper $5,000
Jeff Krueger, Chicago, IL. 1995 Sculpture $5,000
Eva Kwong, Kent, OH. 1987 Crafts $3,000 1988 Crafts $5,000

L

Richard C. Lange, Chicago, IL. 1990 Painting $5,000
Anthony M. Lauro, Columbus, OH. 1985 Photography $3,000
Maryann Golden Lee, Galesburg, IL. 1988 Works on Paper $3,000
David Lefkowitz, Minneapolis, MN. 1994 Painting $5,000
Riva Lehrer, Chicago, IL. 1996 Painting $5,000
Erika Leppmann, Beverly Shores, IN. 1989 Photography $3,000
Janice Lessman-Moss, Kent, OH. 1987 Crafts $3,000
Eleftheria Lialios, Chicago, IL. 1989 Photography $3,000
Jeff Lipschutz, Oshkosh, WI. 1992 Painting $5,000
Denise Lisiecki, Kalamazoo, MI. 1988 Works on Paper $3,000
Stephen Litchfield, Ravenna, OH. 1995 Crafts $5,000
Ken Loeber, Algoma, WI. 1987 Crafts $3,000
Martina Lopez, Chicago, IL. 1991 Photography $5,000
Mark Lorenzi, Mc Farland, WI. 1993 Sculpture $5,000
Constance Lowe, Minneapolis, MN. 1988 Works on Paper $3,000
Lynn Lukkas, Minneapolis, MN. 1991 Photography $5,000

M

Susan Maakestad, Northfield, MN. 1988 Painting $3,000
Thomas Macaulay, New Carlisle, OH. 1991 Sculpture $5,000
Paul Madalinski, Chicago, IL. 1990 Works on Paper $5,000
Michaela Mahady, Stillwater, MN. 1991 Crafts $5,000
Silvia Malagrino, Chicago, IL. 1993 Photography $5,000
Stephen Marc, Chicago, IL. 1991 Photography $5,000
Charlene Marsh, Nashville, IN. 1993 Crafts $5,000
Frederik Marsh, Columbus, OH. 1985 Photography $3,000
Donald Mcfadyen, Chicago, IL. 1988 Painting $5,000
Rhondal Mckinney, Normal, IL. 1991 Photography $5,000
Margo Mensing, Stevensville, MI. 1995 Crafts $5,000
Adelheid Mers, Chicago, IL. 1995 Sculpture $5,000
Tim Miller, Columbus, OH. 1989 Sculpture $3,000
Kathleen Mitchell, Hartland, WI. 1987 Photography $3,000
Deirdre Monk, Bowling Green, OH. 1989 Photography $5,000
Gregg B. Montgomery, Winnetka, IL. 1993 painting $5,000
Laura V. Montgomery, Winnetka, IL. 1996 Painting $5,000
David H. Moose, Oak Park, IL. 1996 Painting $5,000
Aldo Moroni, Minneapolis, MN. 1991 Sculpture $5,000
David Morrison, Plainfield, IN. 1994 Works on Paper $5,000
Deborah Morrissey-McGoff, Cincinnati, OH. 1990 Painting $5,000
Thomas P. Muir, Perrysburg, OH. 1987 Crafts $3,000
Steve Murakishi, Bloomfield Hills, MI. 1988 Works on Paper $3,000

N

Michael Nakoneczny, Evanston, IL. 1994 Painting $5,000
Eric D. Nation, San Diego, CA. 1993 Crafts $5,000
Dennis Nechvatal, Madison, WI. 1988 Painting $3,000
Calvin Niemeyer, Grand Rapids, MI. 1986 Painting $3,000
Mike Noland, Woodstock, IL. 1990 Painting $5,000
Lisa Norton, Chicago, IL. 1995 Crafts $5,000

O

Bill O'Donnell, Chicago, IL. 1987 Photography $3,000
Paul O'Keeffe, Kent, OH. 1991 Sculpture $5,000
Diane Olivier, Long Island City, NY. 1988 Works on Paper $3,000
Charles Olson, Fort Atkinson, WI. 1985 Crafts $3,000
Judy Onofrio, Rochester, MN. 1993 Sculpture $5,000

P

Xan Palay, Columbus, OH. 1995 Sculpture $5,000
Giulio Pallone, Clawson, MI. 1993 Photography $5,000
Laurie Palmer, Chicago, IL. 1989 Sculpture $3,000
Gail Panske, Oshkosh, WI. 1996 Works on Paper $5,000
Carrie Anne Parks, Riverdale, MI. 1993 Crafts $5,000
Mary Patten, Chicago, IL. 1992 Works on Paper $5,000
George C. Peer, Minneapolis, MN. 1993 Photography $5,000
James Pernotto, Youngstown, OH. 1994 Painting $5,000
Melissa Ann Pinney, Evanston, IL. 1987 Photography $5,000
John Ploof, Chicago, IL. 1989 Sculpture $3,000
Joanna Poehlmann, Milwaukee, WI. 1994 Works on Paper $5,000
Herb Potzus, Chicago, IL. 1992 Painting $5,000
Angelica Pozo, Cleveland, OH. 1989 Crafts $3,000
Melba Price, St. Paul, MN. 1990 Works on Paper $5,000
Carol Pyland, Madison, WI. 1988 Painting $3,000

R

Judith Raphael, Chicago, IL. 1992 Painting $5,000
Lynne Resch, Brooklyn, NY. 1990 Painting $5,000
Bruce Riley, Cincinnati, OH. 1992 Painting $5,000
Rebecca Ripple, Chicago, IL. 1991 Sculpture $5,000

Christina Root, Lakeside, MI. 1995 Crafts $5,000
Ann-Marie Rose, St. Paul, MN. 1995 Photography $5,000
Adolph Rosenblatt, Shorewood, WI. 1995 Sculpture $5,000
Katherine Ross, Chesterton, IN. 1995 Crafts $5,000
Kay Ruane, Minneapolis, MN. 1996 Works on Paper $5,000
Jeanine Coupe Ryding, Chicago, IL. 1990 Works on Paper $5,000

S

Amy Sabrina, Minneapolis, MN. 1991 Crafts $5,000
Lyle Salmi, Normal, IL. 1994 Painting $5,000
Elise M. Sanford, Athens, OH. 1991 Photography $5,000
Lisa Schare, Cincinnati, OH. 1996 Painting $5,000
Diane Schmidt, Chicago, IL. 1987 Photography $3,000
Rosalyn Schwartz, Champaign, IL. 1994 Painting $5,000
Scott Seekins, Minneapolis, MN. 1990 Painting $5,000
Joseph Seigenthaler, Chicago, IL. 1991 Sculpture $5,000
Risa Sekiguchi, Chicago, IL. 1988 Painting $3,000
Gail Sellers, Riverside, IL. 1989 Crafts $3,000
Richard Sennott, Medina, MN. 1995 Photography $5,000
Rik Sferra, Minneapolis, MN. 1991 Photography $5,000
Peggy Shaw, Tolono, IL. 1988 Painting $3,000
Diane Sheehan, Madison, WI.87 Crafts $5,000
Doug Shelton, Tucson, AZ. 1992 Painting $5,000
Rebecca Shore, Chicago, IL. 1991 Crafts $5,000
James Shrosbree, Fairfield, IA. 1993 Crafts $5,000
Brian Sikes, Chicago, IL. 1990 Painting $5,000
Diane Simpson, Wilmette, IL. 1993 Sculpture $5,000
Todd Slaughter, Columbus, OH. 1991 Sculpture $5,000
Jerry Smith, Chicago, IL. 1994 Painting $5,000
Leo R. Smith III, Fountain City, WI. 1989 Crafts $3,000
Gilda Snowden, Detroit, MI. 1990 Works on Paper $5,000
Daniel Socha, Urbana, IL. 1990 Painting $5,000
Eleanor Spiess-Ferris, Chicago, IL. 1990 Painting $5,000
Thomas Stancliffe, New Hartford, IA. 1991 Sculpture $5,000
James L. Stephens, Detroit, MI. 1986 Painting $3,000
Susanne G. Stephenson, Ann Arbor, MI. 1987 Crafts $3,000
Elizabeth Stirratt, Bloomington, IL. 1989 Crafts $5,000
Fred Stonehouse, Milwaukee, WI. 1988 Painting $3,000
Mary Ann Strandell, Vermillion, SC. 1996 Painting $5,000
Mary Strasevicius, Hinsdale, IL. 1990 Painting $5,000
Margaret Stratton, Iowa City, IA. 1987 Photography $5,000
Bibiana Suarez, Chicago, IL. 1992 Works on Paper $5,000
Alan Sue, Evanston, IL. 1995 Photography $5,000
Kazuaki Sugi, Collegeville, MN. 1993 Sculpture $5,000
Connie Sullivan, Cincinnati, OH. 1989 Photography $3,000

T

Jason Tannen, San Diego, CA. 1987 Photography $3,000
Bruce Thayer, Mason, MI. 1990 Works on Paper $5,000
Karen Thompson, Fort Wayne, IN. 1989 Photography $5,000
Steven Thurston, Bexley, OH. 1995 Crafts $5,000
Charles Timm-Ballard, Appleton, WI. 1995 Crafts $5,000
James Tittle, Saint Paul, MN. 1987 Photography $3,000
Lewis Toby, Chicago, IL. 1989 Photography $3,000
Stephanie Torbert, Minneapolis, MN. 1993 Photography $5,000
Julie W. Tourtillotte, South Bend, IN. 1995 Crafts $5,000
Andree Tracey, St. Louis Park, MN. 1994 Painting $5,000
Lilian Tyrrell, Ravenna, OH. Crafts $5,000

U

Douglas L. Unger, Peninsula, OH. 1993 Crafts $5,000
Thomas Uttech, Saukville, WI. 1986 Painting $3,000

V

Fern Valfer, Chicago, IL. 1986 Painting $3,000
Jantje Visscher, Minneapolis, MN. 1988 Works on Paper $5,000

W

Kate Wagle, Milwaukee, WI. 1993 Crafts $5,000
Marilyn Waligore, Wooster, OH. 1987 Photography $3,000
Carolyn Warfield, Indianapolis, IN. 1992 Works on Paper $5,000
Kathryn Waters, Evansville, IN. 1996 Painting $5,000
Lynn Whitford, Madison, WI. 1989 Crafts $3,000
Linda Whitney, Valley City, ND. 1994 Works on Paper $5,000
Barbara Wiesen, Chicago, IL. 1995 Sculpture $5,000
Elaine S. Wilson, Ann Arbor, MI. 1996 Painting $5,000
Karen Wirth, Minneapolis, MN. 1992 Works on Paper $5,000
Jay Wolke, Chicago, IL. 1995 Photography $5,000
Ann L. Wood, St. Paul, MN. 1995 Sculpture $5,000
Tilly Woodward, Pella, IA. 1984 Painting $3,000

Y

Judith Yourman, St. Paul, MN. 1993 Photography $5,000

Z

Mary Lou Zelazny, Chicago, IL. 1992 Painting $5,000
Harold Zisla, South Bend, IN. 1986 Painting $3,000
Terri Zupanc, Chicago, IL. 1990 Painting $5,000

New England Foundation for the Arts

Visual Artists' Fellowships

A

Aparna Agrawal, Cambridge, MA. 1997 Crafts $5,000
Nancy Aleo, Roslindale, MA. 1994 Painting $5,000
Mary M. Anderson, Columbia Falls, ME. 1996 Sculpture $5,000
Peter Anthony, New York, NY. 1986 Sculpture $3,000
Miroslav Antic, Cambridge, MA. 1997 Painting $5,000
McCrady Axon, Madison, CT. 1994 Painting $5,000

B

Karl Baden, Cambridge, MA. 1991 Photography $5,000
Richard Baker, Provincetown, MA. 1992 Painting $5,000
Mary Barringer, Shelburne Falls, MA. 1993 Crafts $5,000
Harry Bartnick, Beverly, MA. 1992 Printmaking/Drawing/Artists' Books $5,000
W. Perry Barton, Boston, MA. 1994 Printmaking/Drawing/Artists' Books $5,000
Robert Bauer, Watertown, MA. 1997 Painting $5,000
Derrill Bazzy, Boston, MA. 1991 Photography $5,000
Linda L. Behar, Lexington, MA. 1996 Crafts $5,000
Gerry Bergstein, Cambridge, MA. 1992 Painting $5,000
Nancy Berlin, Cambridge, MA. 1996 Works on Paper $5,000
Rachel Berwick, New Haven, CT. 1993 Sculpture $5,000
David Binder, Cambridge, MA. 1993 Crafts $5,000
Laura Blacklow, Cambridge, MA. 1990 Photography $5,000
Lorey Bonante, Arlington, MA. 1997 Crafts $5,000
Barbara Bosworth, Beltmont, MA. 1993 Crafts $5,000
Paul Bowen, Provincetown, MA. 1993 Sculpture $5,000
Gail C. Boyajian, Cambridge, MA. 1997 Painting $5,000
Ann Brauer, Shelburne Falls, MA. 1991 Crafts $5,000
Jessyca M. Broekman, Falmouth, ME. 1994 Printmaking/Drawing/Artists' Books $5,000
Maggi Brown, Cambridge, MA. 1990 Painting $5,000
Bill Burk, West Hartford, CT. 1996 Sculpture $5,000
Polly Burnell, Provincetown, MA. 1997 Painting $5,000
Lawrence A. Bush, Providence, RI. 1993 Crafts $5,000

C

Maria Magdelena Campos-Pons, Jamaica Plain, MA. 1993 Sculpture $5,000
Geoffrey Chadsey, Cambridge, MA. 1993 Photography $5,000
Daniel G. Clayman, Rumford, RI. 1996 Crafts $5,000
Laura Cloud, Mansfield, CT. 1993 Sculpture $5,000
Erika Marquardt Cohen, Jackson, NH. 1994 Painting $5,000
Alan Colby, Quincy, MA. 1994 Painting $5,000
Mark F. Cooper, Somerville, MA. 1993 Sculpture $5,000
Allan Rohan Crite, Boston, MA. 1990 Works on Paper $5,000
Maryjean Viano Crowe, North Easton, MA. 1996 Photography $5,000

D

Paul D'Amato, South Portland, ME. 1996 Photography $5,000
Tomas Vu Daniel, Boston, MA. 1997 Painting $5,000
Michael V. David, Boston, MA. 1990 Painting $5,000
Laura Davidson, Boston, MA. 1994 Works on Paper $5,000
Ruth Frisch Dealy, Providence, RI. 1994 Painting $5,000
John Devaney, Cambridge, MA. 1992 Painting $5,000
Peggy Diggs, Williamstown, MA. 1993 Sculpture $5,000
Stephen DiRado, Worcester, MA. 1991 Photography $5,000

Ron DiRito, Swampscott, MA. 1996 Photography $5,000
Anita Douthat, Boston, MA. 1991 Photography $5,000
Grant Drumheller, Brookline, MA. 1983 Painting $3,000

E

Diane Edstrom, Jamaica Plain, MA. 1994 Painting $5,000
Vicki P. Eisenfeld, West Hartford, CT. 1991 Crafts $5,000
Danette English, Somerville, MA. 1992 Painting $5,000
Dan Estabrook, Champaign, IL. 1991 Photography $5,000
Tom Evans Jr, Holliston, MA. 1993 Sculpture $5,000
Emily Eveleth, Sherborn, MA. 1994 Painting $5,000
Joel Evett, Newton, MA. 1991 Crafts $5,000

F

Joseph Fekieta, New Haven, CT. 1992 Works on Paper $5,000
Sally S. Fine, Brighton, MA. 1996 Sculpture $5,000
Stephen E. Fisher, Pawtucket, RI. 1994 Works on Paper $5,000
Eck Follen, New Bedford, MA. 1993 Crafts $5,000
Gayle J. Fraas, North Edgecomb, ME. 1996 Crafts $5,000
Janet Fredericks, Burlington, VT. 1994 Works on Paper $5,000
Donald Friedlich, Providence, RI. 1991 Crafts $5,000
Alexandra S. Friedman, Hartford, CT. 1991 Crafts $5,000

G

Jessica Gandolf, Portland, ME. 1994 Painting $5,000
Dore Gardner, Marblehead, MA. 1993 Photography $5,000
Wendy Gedanken, Newton, MA. 1996 Sculpture $5,000
Karen Gilg, Hallowell, ME. 1994 Works on Paper $5,000
Stephen Golding, Newtonville, MA. 1993 Photography $5,000
Jennifer L. Gordon, Brookline, MA. 1997 Painting $5,000
Barbara Grad, Chicago, IL. 1997 Painting $5,000
Robin Grebe, Newtonville, MA. 1993 Crafts $5,000

H

Michael Hachey, Cherry Valley, MA. 1994 Painting $5,000
Susan W. Halter, Boston, MA. 1993 Sculpture $5,000
Jacqueline Hayden, Goshen, MA. 1993 Photography $5,000
Ralph Helmick, Newton, MA. 1996 Sculpture $5,000
Kathleen Henderson, Boston, MA. 1992 Works on Paper $5,000
Chuck Holtzman, Boston, MA. 1994 Works on Paper $5,000
Wayne Hopkins, Merrimac, MA. 1990 Works on Paper $5,000
Pamela Hoss, Brookline, MA. 1994 Works on Paper $5,000
Lillian Hsu-Flanders, Cambridge, MA. 1996 Sculpture $5,000

J

Melinda James, Milford, CT. 1994 Painting $5,000
Mark D. Johnson, South Portland, ME. 1991 Crafts $5,000

K

Kofi Kayiga, Cambridge, MA. 1994 Works on Paper $5,000
David Kelley, Boston, MA. 1992 Painting $5,000
Constance Kheel, Tenant's Harbor, ME. 1992 Painting $5,000
Constance Kiermaier, Tenant's Harbor, ME. 1992 Painting $5,000
Ron Wontae Kim, Florence, MA. 1994 Painting $5,000
Vladimira Klumpar, Shelburne Falls, MA. 1991 Crafts $5,000

L

Pat Lasch, New York, NY. 1996 Sculpture $5,000
Nicholas Lawrence, Provincetown, MA. 1997 Crafts $5,000
Bruce Lenore, Providence, RI. 1991 Crafts $5,000
Michael H. Lewis, Orono, ME. 1990 Painting $5,000
Marja Lianko, Cambridge, MA. 1994 Works on Paper $5,000
Erica Licea-Kane, Arlington, MA. 1993 Crafts $5,000
Linda Lindroth, New Haven, CT. 1996 Photography $5,000
Christine LoFaso, Providence, RI. 1993 Crafts $5,000

M

J. Paul MacDonald, Plymouth, MA. 1996 Photography $5,000
Donna Rhae Marder, Winchester, MA. 1991 Crafts $5,000
Kristina E. Mast, Bennington, VT. 1993 Photography $5,000
Daniel J. McLaughlin, Jamaica Plain, MA. 1994 Painting $5,000
Laura McPhee, Brookline, MA. 1996 Photography $5,000
Arno Rafael Minkkinen, Andover, MA. 1991 Photography $5,000
Janet Monafo, Lexington, MA. 1994 Works on Paper $5,000
Marjorie Moore, Brunswick, ME. 1992 Works on Paper $5,000
Abelardo Morell, Brookline, MA. 1996 Photography $5,000
Steven Muller, Boston, MA. 1994 Works on Paper $5,000

N

Hiroshi Nakayama, Sunderland, MA. 1993 Crafts $5,000
Lynn Newcomb, Worcester, VT. 1997 Works on Paper $5,000
Dean Nimmer, Hyde Park, MA. 1997 Works on Paper $5,000

O

Alice Ogden, Henniker, MA. 1996 Crafts $5,000

P

Linda S. Perry, Lexington, MA. 1996 Crafts $5,000

R

Anne Rearick, Somerville, MA. 1996 Photography $5,000
Jeanee Redmond, Cambridge, MA. 1996 Crafts $5,000
Wellington Reiter, Newton, MA. 1992 Works on Paper $5,000
Naomi Ribner, Brookline, MA. 1990 Works on Paper $5,000
Ronald Rizzi, Jamaica Plain, MA. 1994 Painting $5,000
Ellen Rothenberg, Chicago, IL. 1993 Sculpture $5,000
Bradley J. Rubenstein, New Haven, CT. 1994 Painting $5,000

S

Katherine Schneider, Northampton, MA. 1997 Painting $5,000
Barbara Seidenath, Providence, RI. 1996 Crafts $5,000
Jonathan Sharlin, Providence, RI. 1996 Photography $5,000
Michael Shaughnessy, Gorham, ME. 1996 Sculpture $5,000
Cort Sierpinski, Higganum, CT. 1991 Crafts $5,000
Dean Snyder, Bennington, VT. 1996 Sculpture $5,000
Elizabeth Solomon, Northampton, MA. 1997 Crafts $5,000
Esther Solondz, Providence, RI. 1992 Painting $5,000
Dawn Southworth, Gloucester, MA. 1993 Sculpture $5,000
Peggy Steinway, Canton, CT. 1996 Crafts $5,000
Michael Donne Stevens, Fiskdale, MA. 1992 Works on Paper $5,000
Randy Stevens, Providence, RI. 1992 Works on Paper $5,000
Jim Stone, Dorchester, MA. 1993 Photography $5,000
James Stroud, Boston, MA. 1997 Works on Paper $5,000
Martin Stupich, Dorchester, MA. 1993 Photography $5,000
Margaret Swan, Melrose, MA. 1996 Sculpture $5,000
Charles Swanson, New Bedford, MA. 1993 Crafts $5,000

T

Bill Thompson, Boston, MA. 1997 Painting $5,000
Randal G. Thurston, Somerville, MA. 1990 Works on Paper $5,000
Nan Tull, Boston, MA. 1994 Works on Paper $5,000
Peter Tytla, East Lyme, CT. 1994 Works on Paper $5,000

W

Frank Ward, Williamsburg, MA. 1991 Photography $5,000
Mark Warren, South Boston, MA. 1990 Works on Paper $5,000
Carrie Mae Weems, Oakland, CA. 1991 Photography $5,000
Thomas Wiggins, St. Louis, MO. 1996 Crafts $5,000
Janine Wong, North Dartmouth, MA. 1994 Works on Paper $5,000
Richard Wrigley, Holyoke, MA. 1996 Crafts $5,000

Y

Lisa Young, Brooklyn, NY. 1992 Works on Paper $5,000
Tom Young, Charlemont, MA. 1996 Photography $5,000

Southern Arts Federation

Visual Artists' Fellowships

A

R. S. Ackiss, Atlanta, GA. 1991 Photography $5,000
Mario Algaze, Coral Gables, FL. 1991 Photography $5,000
Heather J. Allen, Asheville, NC. 1995 Crafts $5,000
Amalia K. Amaki, Atlanta, GA. 1995 Photography $5,000
Robert Amberg, Durham, NC. 1987 Photography $3,000
Donald R. Anderson, Louisville, KY. 1991 Photography $5,000
Linda Anderson, Clarkesville, GA. 1994 Painting/Works on Paper $5,000
Gordon Andrus, Hardin, KY. 1993 Crafts $5,000
Don Gregorio Anton, Arcata, CA. 1993 Photography $5,000
Julio Antonio, Miami Beach, FL. 1992 Painting $5,000
Cecelia Arboleda, Miami, FL. 1995 Photography $5,000
Linda Armstrong, Atlanta, GA. 1992 Painting $5,000

Steve Armstrong, Lexington, KY. 1995 Crafts $5,000
Michael Aurbach, Nashville, TN. 1987 Sculpture $3,000

B

Barry Bailey, New Orleans, LA. 1987 Sculpture $3,000
Marty Baird, Raleigh, NC. 1994 Painting/Works on Paper $5,000
Nancy S. Baker, Cary, NC. 1994 Painting/Works on Paper $5,000
Robbie Barber, Williamston, NC. 1993 Sculpture $5,000
Mark Barone, Paducah, KY. 1994 Painting/Works on Paper $5,000
Elizabeth Barton, Athens, GA. 1995 Crafts $5,000
Luisa Basnuevo, Miami, FL. 1996 Painting/Works on Paper $5,000
Pinky M. Bass, Fairhope, AL. 1995 Photography $5,000
Rick Beck, Spruce Pine, NC. 1995 Crafts $5,000
Richard Beckman, Temple Terrace, FL. 1995 Sculpture $5,000
Scott Bellville, Athens, GA. 1996 Painting/Works on Paper $5,000
Helene Berkowitz, North Miami Beach, FL. 1992 Painting $5,000
Garry Bibbs, Lexington, KY. 1994 Painting/Works on Paper $5,000
Kell Black, Clarksville, TN. 1994 Painting/Works on Paper $5,000
Tarleton Blackwell, Manning, SC. 1994 Painting/Works on Paper $5,000
Steve J. Bliss, Savannah, GA. 1993 Photography $5,000
Brian Borrello, New Orleans, LA. 1990 Painting/Works on Paper $5,000
Joe Bova, Baton Rouge, LA. 1985 Crafts $3,000
Pamela Bowens, Miami, FL. 1986 Works on Paper $3,000
Loy Bowlin, McComb, MS. 1992 Painting $5,000
Susan Brenner, Charlotte, NC. 1992 Painting $5,000
Douglas Brewster, Covington, LA. 1994 Painting/Works on Paper $5,000
Hasmig Brewster-Vartanian, Covington, LA. 1986 Painting/Drawing $3,000
Barbara Bullock, Nashville, TN. 1994 Painting/Works on Paper $5,000
Arlene Burke-Morgan, Greenville, NC. 1990 Painting/Works on Paper $5,000
Bruce Burris, Lexington, KY. 1994 Painting/Works on Paper $5,000

C

Susan Callaway, Atlanta, GA. 1992 Painting $5,000
Jill Cannady, Miami, FL. 1991 Sculpture $5,000
Gerald L. Cannon, New Orleans, LA. 1992 Painting $5,000
Jim Cantrell, Bardstown, KY. 1994 Painting/Works on Paper $5,000
Stephen C. Cappelli, Montgomery, AL. 1986 Painting/Drawing $3,000
Kenneth W. Carder, Penland, NC. 1985 Crafts $3,000
Philip Carpenter, Atlanta, GA. 1988 Painting $3,000
Edouard Carrie, Miami Beach, FL. 1996 Painting/Works on Paper $5,000
Nancy F. Cassell, Union, KY. 1988 Works on Paper $3,000
Juan Carlos Castellanos, Miami, FL. 1990 Painting/Works on Paper $5,000
Kim Chalmers, Hartsville, SC. 1994 Painting $5,000
Ying K. Chan, Louisville, KY. 1992 Painting $5,000
Gary H. Chapman, Birmingham, AL. 1996 Painting/Works on Paper $5,000
Stephen Chesley, Columbia, SC. 1996 Painting/Works on Paper $5,000
Paul Chojnowski, East Point, GA. 1996 Painting/Works on Paper $5,000
Routh Cline, Rocky Face, GA. 1990 Painting/Works on Paper $5,000
Jane Burch Cochran, Burlington, KY. 1993 Crafts $5,000
Marie Cochran, Statesboro, GA. 1995 Sculpture $5,000
Marcia R. Cohen, Atlanta, GA. 1988 Painting $3,000
Donald B. Cooper, Atlanta, GA. 1992 Painting $5,000
Michael Crespo, Baton Rouge, LA. 1994 Painting/Works on Paper $5,000
Patricia Cunfer, Griffin, GA. 1989 Crafts $3,000
Jerry Cutler, Gainesville, FL. 1986 Painting $3,000

D

Dean Dablow, Ruston, LA. 1987 Photography $3,000
Ron Dale, Oxford, MS. 1985 Crafts $3,000
Lynn Davison, Naples, FL. 1992 Painting $5,000
Fernando Long De La Rosa, Atlanta, GA. 1987 Photography $3,000
Francis Long De La Rosa, New Orleans, LA. 1990 Painting/Works on Paper $5,000
Joseph Delappe, Reno, NV. 1993 Photography $5,000
Warren Cameron Dennis, Winston-Salem, NC. 1993 Photography $5,000
Edward F. Deren, Pacific Grove, CA. 1985 Crafts $3,000
George Dombek, Tallahassee, FL/Goshen, AR. 1994 Painting/Works on Paper $5,000
Patrick Dougherty, Chapel Hill, NC. 1989 Sculpture $5,000

E

Diane Edison, Atlanta, GA. 1994 Painting/Works on Paper $5,000

F

Warren Farr, Paducah, KY. 1990 Painting/Works on Paper $5,000
Frank Fleming, Birmingham, AL. 1987 Sculpture $3,000
Debbie Fleming Caffery, Franklin, LA. 1987 Photography $3,000
Robert Flynn, Miami Beach, FL. 1996 Painting/Works on Paper $5,000
Ke Francis, Tupelo, MS. 1987 Sculpture $3,000
Candace Freeland, Charlotte, NC. 1991 Photography $5,000

G

Paula B. Garrett, Charlotte, NC. 1985 Crafts $3,000
Janie Geiser, New York, NY. 1986 Painting/Drawing $3,000
Doyle Gertjejansen, New Orleans, LA. 1996 Painting/Works on Paper $5,000
Michael Gibson, Atlanta, GA. 1996 Painting/Works on Paper $5,000
Jan Gilbert, New Orleans, LA. 1990 Painting/Works on Paper $5,000
Scott Gilliam, Atlanta, GA. 1993 Sculpture $5,000
Richard Gladson, Atlanta, GA. 1996 Painting/Works on Paper $5,000
Karekin Goekjian, Athens, GA. 1987 Photography $3,000
Scott Goldsmith, Greenville, SC. 1990 Painting/Works on Paper $5,000
Linda Adele Goodine, New Orleans, LA. 1991 Photography $5,000
Denzil Goodpaster, North Middleton, KY. 1987 Sculpture $3,000
Lida G. Gordon, Louisville, KY. 1992 Painting $5,000
Henry Gorham, McRae, GA. 1996 Painting/Works on Paper $5,000
Gabrielle Gould, St. Augustine, FL. 1993 Crafts $5,000
Eddie Granderson, Atlanta, GA. 1992 Painting $5,000
Anthony Greco, Atlanta, GA. 1988 Painting $3,000
Anne Gregory-Bepler, Efland, NC. 1995 Sculpture $5,000
Matthew Groshek, Chapel Hill, NC. 1991 Sculpture $5,000
Tom Grubb, Fayetteville, NC. 1989 Sculpture $3,000
John Gurbacs, Tampa, FL. 1986 Painting $3,000

H

James Hall, Sadieville, KY. 1993 Photography $5,000
Douglas Harling, Greensboro, NC. 1995 Crafts $5,000
Ken Hassell, Raleigh, NC. 1995 Photography $5,000
Pattie Hastings, Atlanta, GA. 1992 Painting $5,000
Saul Haymond, Tchula, MS. 1994 Painting/Works on Paper $5,000
Richard Heipp, Gainesville, FL. 1996 Painting/Works on Paper $5,000
James Herring, Miami Beach, FL. 1993 Sculpture $5,000
Stephan C. Hillerbrand, Atlanta, GA. 1995 Photography $5,000
Jim Hirschfield, Chapel Hill, NC. 1989 Sculpture $5,000
Victoria Hirt, Tampa, FL. 1995 Photography $5,000
Ann Holcomb, Atlanta, GA. 1991 Photography $5,000
William Holton, Atlanta, GA. 1996 Painting/Works on Paper $5,000
Billy Howard, Atlanta, GA. 1991 Photography $5,000
Charles E. Humes, Jr., Miami, FL. 1990 Painting/Works on Paper $5,000

I

Marcia Isaacson, Gainesville, FL. 1990 Painting/Works on Paper $5,000
David Ivie, Atlanta, GA. 1994 Painting/Works on Paper $5,000

J

Herb Jackson, Davidson, NC. 1986 Painting $3,000
Stefanie Jackson, Athens, GA. 1986 Works on Paper $3,000
Carol Jacque, Miami, FL. 1995 Sculpture $5,000
John Jensen, Savannah, GA. 1987 Sculpture $3,000
James W. Jipson, Pensacola, FL. 1993 Photography $5,000
Christopher K. Johns, Baton Rouge, LA. 1988 Painting $3,000
Robert Johnson, Burnsville, NC. 1994 Painting/Works on Paper $5,000
W. Medford Johnston, Atlanta, GA. 1990 Painting/Works on Paper $5,000
Benjamin Jones, Riverdale, GA. 1994 Painting/Works on Paper $5,000
Terri Jones, Memphis, TN. 1992 Painting $5,000
Tom Jones, Asheville, NC. 1990 Painting/Works on Paper $5,000
Cary E. Jordan, Athens, GA. 1995 Crafts $5,000
Mark Jordan, Athens, GA. 1991 Sculpture $5,000

K

Eunice Kambara, Tampa, FL. 1995 Sculpture $5,000
Bart Kasten, Penland, NC. 1991 Photography $5,000
Clive King, Miami Beach, FL. 1996 Painting/Works on Paper $5,000
Martha King, Jackson, MS. 1987 Sculpture $3,000
Thomas Koole, Orlando, FL. 1991 Sculpture $5,000
Linda Kroff, Charlotte, NC. 1993 Photography $5,000
Pete Kuentzel, Homestead, FL. 1985 Crafts $3,000

L

Mernet Larsen, Tampa, FL. 1988 Painting $3,000
Patti Lechman, Memphis, TN. 1993 Crafts $5,000
Susan W. Lee, Weddington, NC. 1989 Crafts $3,000

Jack Leigh, Savannah, GA. 1987 Photography $3,000
Nicolas Leiva, Bay Harbor Islan, FL. 1996 Painting/Works on Paper $5,000
Kathleen Lemoine, Baton Rouge, LA. 1986 Painting/Drawing $3,000
Robert Levin, Burnsville, NC. 1995 Crafts $5,000
Elizabeth Leyh, New Orleans, LA. 1993 Sculpture $5,000
Mark Lindquist, Quincy, FL. 1989 Crafts $3,000
Philip Livingston, Knoxville, TN. 1989 Sculpture $3,000
Silvia Lizama, Hollywood, FL. 1993 Photography $5,000
Pam Longobardi, Knoxville, TN. 1994 Painting/Works on Paper $5,000
E. George Lorio, Greensboro, NC. 1991 Sculpture $5,000
Steve Loucks, Anniston, AL. 1995 Crafts $5,000
Beauvais Lyons, Knoxville, TN. 1988 Works on Paper $3,000

M

Joni Mabe, Athens, GA. 1991 Sculpture $5,000
Lee A. Malerich, Orangeburg, SC. 1989 Crafts $3,000
Thomas Mann, New Orleans, LA. 1989 Crafts $3,000
Lou Marcus, Tampa, FL. 1987 Photography $3,000
Janet Markarian, Tallahassee, FL. 1985 Crafts $3,000
Rosario Marquardt, Miami Beach, FL. 1994 Painting/Works on Paper $5,000
Nancy Marshall, Atlanta, GA. 1987 Photography $3,000
Lynn Marshall-Linnem, Atlanta, GA. 1993 Photography $5,000
Zephra May-Miller, Louisville, KY. 1989 Crafts $3,000
John D. Mcdonald, Bay St. Louis, MS. 1990 Painting/Works on Paper $5,000
Carrie McGee, Nashville, TN. 1996 Painting/Works on Paper $5,000
Joseph L. McGee, Louisville, KY. 1988 Printmaking/Drawing/Artists' Books$3,000
Carl McKenzie, North Middleton, KY. 1987 Sculpture $3,000
Maggie McMahon, Signal Mountain, SC. 1985 Crafts $3,000
John McNaughton, Evansville, IN. 76 Crafts $5,000
Judith McWillie, Athens, GA. 1986 Works on Paper $3,000
Rebecca Medel, Smithville, TN. 1985 Crafts $3,000
A. J. Meek, Baton Rouge, LA. 1987 Photography $3,000
Larry Merriman, Darlington, SC. 1989 Sculpture $3,000
Mark Messersmith, Tallahassee, FL. 1988 Painting $3,000
James Michaels, Palm Harbor, FL. 1994 Painting/Works on Paper $5,000
Chris Mills, Atlanta, GA. 1989 Sculpture $3,000
Katherine Mitchell, Atlanta, GA. 1992 Painting $5,000
Suzanne Mitchell, Louisville, KY. 1993 Photography $5,000
Judith Mogul, Chattanooga, TN. 1988 Painting $3,000
Clarence Morgan, Greenville, NC. 1988 Painting $3,000
Kevin M. Mullins, Hamilton, NY. 1988 Painting $3,000
Marilyn Murphy, Nashville, TN. 1990 Painting/Works on Paper $5,000

N

Nina Neily, Raleigh, NC. 1993 Crafts $5,000
Craig Nutt, Northport, Al. 1989 Crafts $3,000

O

John O'Connor, Bergen, NY. Painting $5,000
Susan O'Connor, Elberta, AL. 1991 Photography $5,000
Jeanette Oliver, Winston-Salem, NC. 1989 Sculpture $3,000
Richard Olsen, Athens, GA. 1988 Painting $3,000

P

Roger Palmer, Tampa, FL. 1994 Painting/Works on Paper $5,000
Herb Parker, New Orleans, LA. 1989 Sculpture $3,000
Mary Jane Parker, New Orleans, LA. 1990 Painting/Drawing $5,000
Daniel Piersol, New Orleans, LA. 1986 Painting/Drawing $3,000
Cynthia W. Pimental, Raleigh, NC. 1988 Painting $3,000
Mary Porter, Athens, GA. 1990 Painting/Works on Paper $5,000 q

Q

Ciro Quintana, Coral Gables, FL. 1996 Painting/Works on Paper $5,000

R

Richard Ramsdell, Sarasota, FL. 1991 Photography $5,000
Hystercine Rankin, Port Gibson, MS. 1993 Crafts $5,000
Bob Ray, Greenville, NC. 1986 Painting/Drawing $3,000
Edward T. Rice, N. Augusta, SC. 1988 Painting $3,000
Francie Rich, Covington, LA. 1988 Painting $3,000
Patricia Rieger, Chapel Hill, NC. 1987 Sculpture $3,000
Rocio A. Rodriguez, Atlanta, GA. 1990 Painting/Works on Paper $5,000
Ann Ropp, Germany, GR. 1994 Painting/Works on Paper $5,000
Arthur Rosenbaum, Athens, GA. 1986 Painting $3,000
W. Steve Rucker, New Orleans, LA. 1991 Sculpture $5,000
Ginny Ruffner, Seattle, WA. 1985 Crafts $3,000

S

Blandine Saint-Oyant, Durham, NC. 1994 Painting/Works on Paper $5,000
Richard E. Santiago, Tampa, FL. 1995 Sculpture $5,000
Debrah Santini, Carrollton, GA. 1996 Painting/Works on Paper $5,000
William Sapp, Athens, GA. 1993 Sculpture $5,000
Michael Sastre, Miami, FL. 1996 Painting/Works on Paper $5,000
Claire Satin, Dania, FL. 1996 Painting/Works on Paper $5,000
Ted Saupe, Athens, GA. 1995 Crafts $5,000
Cort Savage, Davidson, NC. 1993 Sculpture $5,000
Thomas H. Sayre, Raleigh, NC. 1995 Sculpture $5,000
Mary Segal, Roseland, FL. 1992 Painting $5,000
Xuhong Shang, Savannah, GA. 1995 Sculpture $5,000
Ward M. Shelley, Miami, FL. 1991 Sculpture $5,000
Steve Shepard, Gautier, MS. 1996 Painting/Works on Paper $5,000
Randy Shull, Asheville, NC. 1993 Crafts $5,000
David J. Sibbitt, Tampa, FL. 1990 Painting/Works on Paper $5,000
Bobby Silverman, Baton Rouge, LA. 1995 Crafts $5,000
Peggy Simmons, Tallahassee, FL. 1989 Crafts $3,000
Victoria Skinner, Lake Worth, FL. 1994 Painting/Works on Paper $5,000
Nan Smith, Gainesville, FL. 1993 Sculpture $5,000
Tanja Softic, Orlando, FL. 1996 Painting/Works on Paper $5,000
Andrew Speer, Louisville, KY. 1986 Painting/Drawing $3,000
Cooper Spivey, Birmingham, AL. 1995 Photography $5,000
Richard Stenhouse, Charlotte, NC. 1986 Painting/Drawing $3,000
Scott Stephens, Calera, AL. 1986 Works on Paper $3,000
Adam Straus, Tallahassee, FL. 1989 Sculpture $3,000
Tom Sullivan, Asheville, NC. 1992 Painting $5,000

T

Maxwell Taylor, Orangeburg, SC. 1990 Painting/Works on Paper $5,000
Patricia Telesco, Huntsville, AL. 1993 Crafts $5,000
Larry Thomas, Atlanta, GA. 1994 Painting/Works on Paper $5,000
Roxie Thomas, Sarasota, FL. 1995 Sculpture $5,000
Lisa Tuttle, Atlanta, GA. 1991 Sculpture $5,000 1995 Photography $5,000

V

Dee Van Dyke, Bluewater Bay, FL. 1988 Works on Paper $3,000
Michael Venezia, Atlanta, GA. 1996 Painting/Works on Paper $5,000
Chad Voorhees, Beaufort, NC. 1989 Crafts $3,000

W

Ralph H. Waldrop, Columbia, SC. 1990 Painting/Works on Paper $5,000
Melanie Walker, Lexington, KY. 1991 Sculpture $5,000
Sarah A. Walker, Chapel Hill, NC. 1992 Painting $5,000
Joe Walters, Charleston, SC. 1995 Sculpture $5,000
Sam Wang, Clemson, SC. 1987 Photography $3,000
Kurt Warnke, Charlotte, NC. 1986 Works on Paper $3,000
Steve Welch, Knoxville, TN. 1993 Crafts $5,000
Elizabeth Whitfield-Cargile, Aiken, SC. 1989 Sculpture $3,000

Y

Kathy M. Yancey, Atlanta, GA. 1988 Painting $3,000

Z

Dennis Zaborowski, Chapel Hill, NC. 1986 Works on Paper $3,000
Therese Zemlin, Blowing Rock, NC. 1993 Crafts $5,000
Miriam S. Karp, Atlanta, GA. 1988 Painting $3,000
Paul Harcharik, Sequim, WA. 1986 Works on Paper $3,000
Amy Landesberg, Decatur, GA. 1986 Painting/Drawing $3,000
Art Werger, Macon, GA. 1988 Works on Paper $5,000
Sandra Winters, Miami Shores, FL. 1987 Sculpture $3,000

Western States Arts Federation

Visual Artists' Fellowships

A

James L. Acord, Richland, WA. 1994 works on paper $5,000
Seyed Alavi, Oakland, CA. 1993 Sculpture $5,000
Danae Anderson, Truckee, CA. 1989 Crafts $3,000
Dennis L. Angel, Henderson, NV. 1994 Painting $5,000

Kim Anno, Oakland, CA. 1996 Painting $5,000
Anne Appleby, Jefferson City, MT. 1996 Painting $5,000
Chester Arnold, Sonoma, CA. 1996 Painting $5,000
Jaime Arredondo, Long Island City, NY. 1996 Painting $5,000
Anthony J. Aziz, San Francisco, CA. 1991 Photography $5,000

B

Zhao Baiwei, Seattle, WA. 1992 Works on Paper $5,000
Julia M. Barello, Mesilla, NM. 1995 Crafts $5,000
Maura Bendett, Los Angeles, CA. 1994 Painting $5,000
Sandow Birk, Los Angeles, CA. 1994 Painting $5,000
Vivian Bower, New York, NY. 1995 Sculpture $5,000
Mala Breuer, Abiquiu, NM. 1996 Painting $5,000
Leslee Broersma, Boulder, CO. 1996 Works on Paper $5,000
Carl Bronson, Los Angeles, CA. 1995 Sculpture $5,000
Kaucyila Brooke, Wilsonville, OR. 1991 Photography $5,000
Joy Broom, Martinez, CA. 1992 Works on Paper $5,000
Michael F. Brophy, Portland, OR. 1990 Painting $5,000
Beliz Brother, Seattle, WA. 1993 Sculpture $5,000
Brad Brown, San Francisco, CA. 1996 Works on Paper $5,000
Elizabeth R. Bryant, Los Angeles, CA. 1996 New Genres $5,000
Chad Buck, 1988 Works on Paper $3,000

C

Mark A. Calderon, Seattle, WA. 1993 Sculpture $5,000
Cristina Cardenas, Tucson, AZ. 1994 Painting $5,000
Stuart J. Caswell, Rosemead, CA. 1988 Works on Paper $3,000
Francis M. Celentano, Seattle, WA. 1990 Painting $5,000
Susan Cervantes, San Francisco, CA. 1994 Painting $5,000
Aurore Chabot, Wilton, NH. 1995 Crafts $5,000 82
Enrique Chagoya, Oakland, CA. 1992 Works on Paper $5,000
Lauri Chambers, Seattle, WA. 1992 Painting $5,000
Frances Charteris, Boulder, CO. 1993 Photography $5,000
Monica Chau, Los Angeles, CA. 1995 Photography $5,000
Susan Cheal, Salt Lake City, UT. 1992 Painting $5,000
Tina Chinn, El Cerrito, CA. 1993 Crafts $5,000
Albert Chong, Boulder, CO. 1991 Photography $5,000
Charles B. Cobb, Santa Rosa, CA. 1989 Crafts $3,000
Robert D. Cocke, Phoenix, AZ. 1988 Works on Paper $3,000
Tony Cockrell, Boulder Creek, CA. 1992 Painting $5,000
Andrew S. Cooperman, Seattle, WA. 1989 Crafts $3,000
Keith Cottingham, San Francisco, CA. 1995 Photography $5,000
Dennis L. Cunningham, Portland, OR. 1988 Works on Paper $3,000

D

Erik D'Azevedo, Berkeley, CA. 1992 Painting $5,000
Joyce Dallal, Los Angeles, CA. 1995 Photography $5,000
Caryl Davis, Venice, CA. 1991 Sculpture $5,000
Paul H. Davis, Salt Lake City, UT. 1988 Works on Paper $3,000
Roseline Delisle, Santa Monica, CA. 1989 Crafts $3,000
Bailey Doogan, Tucson, AZ. 1996 Painting $5,000
Tim Doud, Chicago, IL. 1994 Painting $5,000
Susan Dunshee, Santa Fe, NM. 1989 Crafts $3,000

E

Tom Eckert, Tempe, AZ. 1989 Crafts $3,000
C. C. Elian, Sedro-Wooley, WA. 1992 Works on Paper $5,000
Dick Elliott, Ellensburg, WA. 1993 Sculpture $5,000
Timothy Ely, Snohomish, WA. 1994 Works on Paper $5,000
Jennifer R. Empey, San Francisco, CA. 1995 Photography $5,000
John O. Erickson, Salt Lake City, UT. 1990 Painting $5,000

F

Dorothy A. Faison-Meder, Kailua, HI. 1994 Painting $5,000
Judith Poxson Fawkes, Portland, OR. 1993 Crafts $5,000
Alice Fellows, Santa Monica, CA. 1990 Painting $5,000
Lukas Felzmann, San Francisco, CA. 1993 Photography $5,000
Mary Fish, Sundance, UT. 1993 Sculpture $5,000
Cinthea Fiss, New York, NY. 1994 New Genres $5,000
Claudia Fitch, New York, NY. 1995 Sculpture $5,000
Susanne Forestieri, Las Vegas, NV. 1996 Painting $5,000
David French, Seattle, WA. 1995 Sculpture $5,000
Kay French, Portland, OR. 1994 Painting $5,000
Dan Fuller, Albuquerque, NM. 1990 Painting $5,000

G

Ann Gale, Seattle, WA. 1996 Painting $5,000
Jeff Gambill, Los Angeles, CA. 1990 Painting $5,000
Terri Garland, Soquel, CA. 1991 Photography $5,000
Beth Lindsey Gellar, Los Angeles, CA. 1991 Sculpture $5,000
Debra Goldman, Denver, CO. 1995 Photography $5,000
Ken Gonzales-Day, W. Hollywood, CA. 1996 New Genres $5,000
Ricardo Gouveia (Rigo 97), San Francisco, CA. 1994 Painting $5,000
David Green, Seattle, WA. 1994 Works on Paper $5,000
Paul Green, Portland, OR. 1994 Painting $5,000
Cameron Gregg, Santa Fe, NM. 1991 Sculpture $5,000

H

James Hajicek, Mesa, AZ. 1995 Photography $5,000
Diane Andrews Hall, San Francisco, CA. 1994 Painting $5,000
Alfred Harris, Buffalo, NY. 1992 Works on Paper $5,000
Lyle Ashton Harris, Los Angeles, CA. 1991 Photography $5,000
Thomas Harris, Seattle, WA. 1991 Photography $5,000
Randy Hayes, Seattle, WA. 1988 Works on Paper $3,000
Stephen P. Hayes, Portland, OR. 1994 Works on Paper $5,000
Matt Heckert, San Francisco, CA. 1991 Sculpture $5,000
F. Scott Hess, Los Angeles, CA. 1990 Painting $5,000
Judy Hill, Portland, OR. 1995 Crafts $5,000
Caroline Hinkley, Boulder, CO. 1993 Photography $5,000
Anthony Holdsworth, Oakland, CA. 1990 Painting $5,000
David Hollowell, Woodland, CA. 1988 Works on Paper $3,000
Margaret Honda, Santa Monica, CA. 1991 Sculpture $5,000
Deborah Horrell, Portland, OR. 1995 Crafts $5,000

I

Jody Isaacson, Bernalillo, NM. 1988 Works on Paper $3,000

J

Gendron Jensen, Vadito, NM. 1996 Works on Paper $5,000
Anne Griffin Johnson, Portland, OR. 1990 Painting $5,000
Robert C. Jones, Mt. Vernon, WA. 1990 Painting $5,000

K

Kim Lee Kahn, Los Angeles, CA. 1991 Sculpture $5,000
Beanie Kaman, Santa Fe, NM. 1992 Works on Paper $5,000
Annetta Kapon, Los Angeles, CA. 1995 Sculpture $5,000
Ed Kashi, San Francisco, CA. 1991 Photography $5,000
Jeffrey C. Keith, Denver, CO. 1990 Painting $5,000
Kimberly Kelzer, Freeland, WA. 1993 Crafts $5,000
Suzy Kerr, Los Angeles, CA. 1991 Photography $5,000
Young Kim, San Francisco, CA. 1993 Photography $5,000
Don C. King, Challis, ID. 1989 Crafts $3,000
Susan Kingsley, Carmel, CA. 1995 Crafts $5,000
Janine Klees, DeKalb, IL. 1993 Sculpture $5,000
Lisa Kokin, Richmond, CA. 1995 Crafts $5,000
Cindy Kolodziejski, Venice, CA. 1993 Crafts $5,000
Chris Komater, San Francisco, CA. 1995 Sculpture $5,000
Jeff Kotun, Oakland, CA. 1996 Painting $5,000
Scott Kuykendall, Albuquerque, NM. 1990 Painting $5,000

L

Ann Lacy, Santa Fe, NM. 1988 Works on Paper $3,000
Deborah F. Lawrence, Seattle, WA. 1994 Works on Paper $5,000
Gavin Lee, Alhambra, CA. 1993 Photography $5,000
George Legrady, San Francisco, CA. 1993 Photography $5,000
Xavier Leonard, San Diego, CA. 1996 New Genres $5,000
Leslie Lerner, Sarasota, FL. 1990 Painting $5,000
Lauren Lesko, New York, NY. 1993 Sculpture $5,000
Saiman Li, San Francisco, CA. 1995 Photography $5,000
Jean Lowe, Encinitas, CA. 1991 Sculpture $5,000
James Luna, Valley Center, CA. 1991 Sculpture $5,000
Tom Lundberg, Fort Collins, CO. 1995 Crafts $5,000
Marilyn Lysohir, Moscow, ID. 1989 Crafts $3,000

M

Ming-Yuen S. Ma, Los Angeles, CA. 1996 New Genres $5,000
Susan Magnus, Berkeley, CA. 1994 Works on Paper $5,000
Dianne Malley, Venice, CA. 1991 Photography $5,000
Michael Robert Marlowe, Phoenix, AZ. 1994 Painting $5,000
Alden Mason, Seattle, WA. 1992 Painting $5,000

Phyllis McGibbon, Wellesley, MA. 1992 Works on Paper $5,000
David McMurray, Seattle, WA. 1996 Works on Paper $5,000
Myron Melnick, Denver, CO. 1989 Crafts $5,000
Kevin Miller, Los Angeles, CA. 1994 Painting $5,000
Kenna Moser, Seattle, WA. 1994 Painting $5,000

N

John Neely, Logan, UT. 1989 Crafts $3,000
Ronna Neuenschwander, Mill Valley, CA. 1989 Crafts $3,000
Domingo Nuno, Oakland, CA. 1995 Photography $5,000

O

Brian O'Connor, Veguita, NM. 1990 Painting $5,000
Heidi Oberheide, Palouse, WA. 1990 Painting $5,000
Frank Okada, Eugene, OR. 1990 Painting $5,000
Mark C. Olsen, Pullman, WA. 1991 Photography $5,000
Ellen Oppenheimer, Oakland, CA. 1995 Crafts $5,000
Susan Otto, Los Angeles, CA. 1995 Photography $5,000
Jeff T. Overlie, Cass Lake, MN. 1995 Sculpture $5,000

P

Carolanne Patterson, New York, NY. 1995 Crafts $5,000
Ernie Pepion, Bozeman, MT. 1992 Painting $5,000
Mark Perlman, Sebastobol, CA. 1996 Works on Paper $5,000
Pipo, Albuquerque, NM. 1996 Works on Paper $5,000
Thomas Prochaska, Portland, OR. 1996 Painting $5,000

R

Jean Rasenberger, Los Angeles, CA. 1994 New Genres $5,000
Fran Reed, Anchorage, AK. 1993 Crafts $5,000
David Regan, Los Angeles, CA. 1993 Crafts $5,000
Greg Reser, San Diego, CA. 1992 Painting $5,000
Nanilee S. Robarge, San Francisco, CA. 1995 Crafts $5,000
Sara Roberts, Frazier Park, CA. 1994 New Genres $5,000
Jose Luis Rodriguez, Albuquerque, NM. 1994 Works on Paper $5,000
Hanneline Rogeberg, Seattle, WA. 1996 Painting $5,000
Garrison Roots, Boulder, CO. 1995 Sculpture $5,000
Glen Walter Rubsamen, 1988 Works on Paper $3,000
Ross Rudel, Santa Monica, CA. 1993 Sculpture $5,000

S

Yoshitomo Saito, Oakland, CA. 1993 Sculpture $5,000
Cristina Salvador, Long Beach, CA. 1993 Photography $5,000
Gregory Schulte, Logan, UT. 1994 Works on Paper $5,000
Stephen Schultz, Hope, ID. 1990 Painting $5,000
June Schwarcz, Sausalito, CA. 1993 Crafts $5,000
Robert Schwartz, San Francisco, CA. 1992 Works on Paper $5,000
Vicki Scuri, Seattle, WA. 1988 Works on Paper $3,000
David Secrest, Somers, MT. 1989 Crafts $3,000
Martina M. Shenal, Tempe, AZ. 1996 New Genres $5,000
Patricia W. Sherwood, Los Altos, CA. 1994 Painting $5,000
Kathy Shiroki, Buffalo, NY. 1991 Sculpture $5,000
Collin Shutz, Seattle, WA. 1996 Works on Paper $5,000
Timothy Siciliano, Seattle, WA. 1992 Works on Paper $5,000
Suzanne Simpson, 1996 Works on Paper $5,000
Paul Singdahlsen, Santa Fe, NM. 1988 Works on Paper $3,000
Christina Y. Smith, Fullerton, CA. 1989 Crafts $3,000
Jaune Quick-To-See Smith, Corrales, NM. 1988 Works on Paper $3,000
Michael K. Speaker, Portland, OR. 1989 Crafts $3,000
Linda Stark, Los Angeles, CA. 1992 Painting $5,000
Tom Stephenson, Tempe, AZ. 1996 Painting $5,000
George Stillman, Ellensburg, WA. 1990 Painting $5,000
Thaddeus Strode, Los Angeles, CA. 1992 Painting $5,000

T

Lynn Taber-Borcherdt, Tucson, AZ. 1990 Painting $5,000
Brian D. Taylor, Monte Sereno, CA. 1991 Photography $5,000
Christopher T. Terry, Logan, UT. 1994 Painting $5,000
Ev Thomas, Bolinas, CA. 1994 Painting $5,000
C. S. Tlefa, Albuquerque, NM. 1988 Works on Paper $3,000
Sarah M. Timberlake, Denver, CO. 1991 Sculpture $5,000
Canan Tolon, Berkeley, CA. 1994 Painting $5,000
Trimpin, Seattle, WA. 1994 New Genres $5,000
Hulleah J. Tsinhnahjinnie, Phoenix, AZ. 1995 Photography $5,000
Mary Tsiongas, Oakland, CA. 1995 Sculpture $5,000
Carmalita Little Turtle, Flagstaff, AZ. 1993 Photography $5,000

V

Eric Van Eimeren, Helena, MT. 1993 Crafts $5,000
Rudi Verhoeven, Albuquerque, NM. 1992 Painting $5,000
Barbara Vos, San Francisco, CA. 1996 Painting $5,000

W

Christopher Warner, Los Angeles, CA. 1990 Painting $5,000
Fan Warren, Oakland, CA. 1994 Works on Paper $5,000
Gail Weissberg, 1989 Crafts $3,000
Albert J. Winn, Santa Monica, CA. 1993 Photography $5,000
Kurt Wold, Napa, CA. 1995 Sculpture $5,000

Z

Michele Zackheim, Tesuque, NM. 1988 Works on Paper $5,000

INDEX

Page references in italics refer to illustrations